Queens of the Conquest

By the same author

Non-Fiction

BRITAIN'S ROYAL FAMILIES:
The Complete Genealogy

THE SIX WIVES OF HENRY VIII

THE PRINCES IN THE TOWER

LANCASTER AND YORK:
The Wars of the Roses

CHILDREN OF ENGLAND:
The Heirs of King Henry VIII
1547–1558

ELIZABETH THE QUEEN

ELEANOR OF AQUITAINE

HENRY VIII:
King and Court

MARY QUEEN OF SCOTS
AND THE MURDER OF LORD DARNLEY

ISABELLA:
She-Wolf of France, Queen of England

KATHERINE SWYNFORD:
The Story of John of Gaunt and
His Scandalous Duchess

THE LADY IN THE TOWER:
The Fall of Anne Boleyn

MARY BOLEYN:
'The Great and Infamous Whore'

ELIZABETH OF YORK:
The First Tudor Queen

THE LOST TUDOR PRINCESS:
A Life of Margaret Douglas, Countess of Lennox

As co-author

THE RING AND THE CROWN:
A History of Royal Weddings,
1066–2011

Fiction

INNOCENT TRAITOR

THE LADY ELIZABETH

THE CAPTIVE QUEEN

A DANGEROUS INHERITANCE

THE MARRIAGE GAME

KATHERINE OF ARAGON: THE TRUE QUEEN

ANNE BOLEYN: A KING'S OBSESSION

Quick Reads

TRAITORS OF THE TOWER

Queens of the Conquest

England's Medieval Queens

1066–1167

Alison Weir

JONATHAN CAPE
LONDON

1 3 5 7 9 10 8 6 4 2

Jonathan Cape, an imprint of Vintage Publishing,
20 Vauxhall Bridge Road,
London SW1V 2SA

Jonathan Cape is part of the Penguin Random House group of companies whose
addresses can be found at global.penguinrandomhouse.com.

Copyright © Alison Weir 2017

Maps by John Gilkes

penguin.co.uk/vintage

A CIP catalogue record for this book is available from the British Library

Hardback ISBN 9781910702079
Trade paperback ISBN 9781910702086

Typeset in India by Integra Software Services Pvt. Ltd, Pondicherry

Printed and bound in Great Britain by Clays Ltd, St Ives PLC

Penguin Random House is committed to a sustainable future for our business, our
readers and our planet. This book is made from Forest Stewardship Council®
certified paper.

To Wendy and Brian,
and to Eileen Don and Eileen Latchford,
who are examples to us all,
with love.

Contents

List of Illustrations

Statue of William the Conqueror in his birthplace, Falaise. (Getty Images/Nicolas Thibaut)

The Norman Kings from a manuscript of 1250: (top) William I and William II, (bottom) Henry I and Stephen. ('Historia Anglorum', 1250 (vellum), Paris, Matthew (c.1200–59)/British Library, London, UK/© British Library Board. All Rights Reserved/Bridgeman Images)

The ill-fated Robert Curthose, Duke of Normandy. (Glenn Harper/Alamy Stock Photo)

The foundations of Malcolm's Tower, Dunfermline, where Matilda of Scotland was born. (Wikimedia Commons)

Anselm of Aosta, Archbishop of Canterbury. (Hulton Archive/Stringer)

Margaret, Queen of Scots. (Stained glass window in St Margaret's Chapel, Edinburgh Castle. Cindy Hopkins/Alamy Stock Photo)

Matilda as benefactress of St Alban's Abbey. (Cotton Nero D.VII, f.7 Matilda, queen of King Henry I, seated and holding a charter, illustration from the Golden Book of St Albans, 1380 (vellum), Strayler, Alan (fl.1380)/British Library, London, UK/© British Library Board. All Rights Reserved/Bridgeman Images)

Matilda's seal, the earliest one of an English queen to survive. (Empress Maud's seal/British Library, London, UK/Bridgeman Images)

Statue that may represent Matilda from the west door of Rochester Cathedral. (René & Peter van der Krogt, http://statues.vanderkrogt.net)

Matilda's brother, David I, King of Scots. (From the Kelso Abbey Charter, National Library of Scotland, Edinburgh; reproduced by kind permission of the Duke of Roxburghe)

The wedding feast of the Lady Maud and the Emperor Heinrich V. (Corpus Christi College, Cambridge MS. 373; with thanks to the Master and Fellows of Corpus Christi College, Cambridge)

Henry I mourning the loss of his son in the *White Ship* disaster (Royal 20 A. II, f.6v King Henry I on his throne, mourning, illustration from the 'Chronicle of England' by Peter de Langtoft, c.1307–27 (vellum), English School, (fourteenth century)/British Library, London, UK/Bridgeman Images)

Probably Adeliza of Louvain, Henry's second Queen. (The Shaftesbury Psalter, Lansdowne MS. 383, British Library; British Library, London, UK/© British Library Board. All Rights Reserved/Bridgeman Images)

Burial of King Henry I at Reading Abbey in January 1136 by Harry Morley, 1916; © Reading Museum; Reading Borough Council)

SECTION 2

The ruthless Geoffrey Plantagenet, Count of Anjou. (Getty Images/ullstein bild/Contributor)

Robert, Earl of Gloucester, loyal mainstay of the Empress Maud. (Wikimedia Commons)

The Norman keep of Arundel Castle, where the Empress Maud sought shelter with Queen Adeliza in 1139. (Motte and Keep at Arundel Castle, eleventh–twelfth century (photo)/Bridgeman Images)

Stone heads, probably of Adeliza and her second husband, William d'Albini, on either side of the east window, Boxgrove Priory, Sussex. (© Alison Gaudion; www.gaudions.co.uk)

Head said to represent Matilda of Boulogne, from Furness Abbey. (Photographer Roy P. Chatfield)

Victorian engraving of Matilda of Boulogne. (Getty Images/Hulton Archive/Stringer)

King Stephen's brother, the wily Henry of Blois, Bishop of Winchester. (The Henry of Blois plaques, England (c.1150) © The Trustees of the British Museum)

The Empress Maud: modern illustration showing the kind of dress she would have worn. (Getty Images/Print Collector/Contributor)

The great Norman cathedral at Winchester, where Maud was received as 'Lady of the English' in 1141. (North transept, built by Bishop Walkelin, 1079–98 (photo)/ Winchester Cathedral, Hampshire, UK/Photo © Paul Maeyaert/Bridgeman Images)

Seal of the Empress Maud (Seal of Empress Matilda. Engraving, English School, twelfth century (after)/Private Collection/Bridgeman Images)

Artist's impression of the Empress Maud, based on her seal. (Chronicle/Alamy Stock Photo)

Coin showing Stephen and Matilda of Boulogne, struck to mark the King's restoration in 1141. (Granger Historical Picture Archive/Alamy Stock Photo)

St George's Tower, Oxford Castle, from which Maud descended by ropes in 1142. (Lesley Pardoe/Alamy Stock Photo)

One of many popular images of Maud, camouflaged in white, making her miraculous escaping from Oxford. (Chronicle/Alamy Stock Photo)

Wallingford Castle, where Maud sought refuge with the devoted Brian FitzCount. (Graham Mulrooney/Alamy Stock Photo)

The wall encircling the mound and the gatehouse are all that remain of the mighty Devizes Castle, Maud's headquarters for several years. (© Steve King/flickr)

Hedingham Castle, Essex, where Matilda of Boulogne died (The Lindsay Family of Hedingham Castle; photography by Paul Highnam)

Golden, jewel-studded reliquary cross from the abbey of Valasse. (Musée Departmentale des Antiquités, Rouen, Normandie)

Interior of the keep, showing the largest surviving Romanesque arch in Britain. (The Lindsay Family of Hedingham Castle; photography by Paul Highnam)

Henry II and Eleanor of Aquitaine. Contemporary stained glass in Poitiers Cathedral commemorating their marriage in 1152. (Crucifixion; detail of the Henry II and Eleanor of Aquitaine panel; stained glass, c.1170; akg-images/Paul M.R. Maeyaert)

The marriage of Maud's granddaughter, Matilda, to Henry the Lion, Duke of Saxony in 1168. ('Evangeliar Heinrichs des Löwen' (Gospel of Henry the Lion); coronation of Duke Henry and Duchess Mathilda, King Henry of England's daughter, right. Fol. 171 v. Wolfenbüttel, Herzog August Library; akg-images)

Henry II quarrelling with Archbishop Thomas Becket. (Becket before Henry II/British Library, London, UK/© British Library Board. All Rights Reserved/Bridgeman Images)

The chapel of Saint-Julien at Petit-Quevilly, founded by Henry II in 1160, and adorned with frescoes that may have been commissioned by Maud. (© Bruno Maury)

Rouen Cathedral, where Maud's remains were reinterred in 1847. (Zoonar GmbH/ Alamy Stock Photo)

England and Wales in the
eleventh and twelfth centuries

Northern Europe in the
eleventh and twelfth centuries

ENGLAND

London

English Channel

Cal·
Wissant

Boulogne

Montre·

Saint-Valéry

Dieppe   Eu

Fécamp   Bures-en-Bray

Vallasse   Saint-Wandrille

Cherbourg   Barfleur   Montvilliers   Lillebonne   Jumièges   Gerb·
La Hougue

Cotentin   Rouen   L·
Peninsula   la

Saint-Grestain   Saint-Léger de Préaux

Dives   Boscherville

Bayeux   Bonneville-   Bec-Hellouin

Caen   sur-Touques

Val-ès-Dunes   Lisieux   Evreux

Coutances   Le Sap

Falaise   Saint-Evroult

N o r m a n d y   l'Aigle

Argentan

Mont Saint-Michel   Domfront   Silly-en-Gouffern

Carrouges   Sées   B l o i s

Alençon

M a i n e

B r i t t a n y

Vilaine   Le Mans

Anjou

Angers   Loire

Saumur   Touraine

Fontevrault

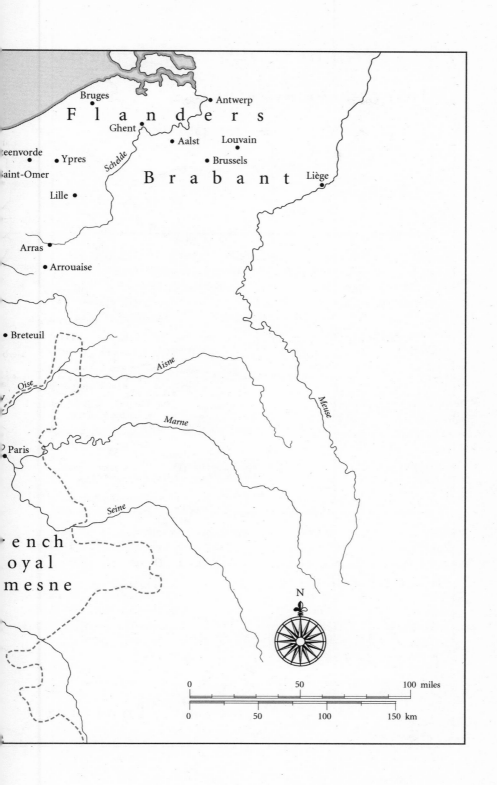

Bruges

● Antwerp

F l a n d e r s

Ghent

● Aalst   Louvain

eenvorde   ● Ypres   ● Brussels

aint-Omer   B r a b a n t   Liège

Lille ●

Schelde

Arras ●

● Arrouaise

● Breteuil

Aisne

Oise

Marne

Meuse

Paris

Seine

ench

oyal

mesne

N

0   50   100 miles

0   50   100   150 km

The Norman Kings and Queens of England

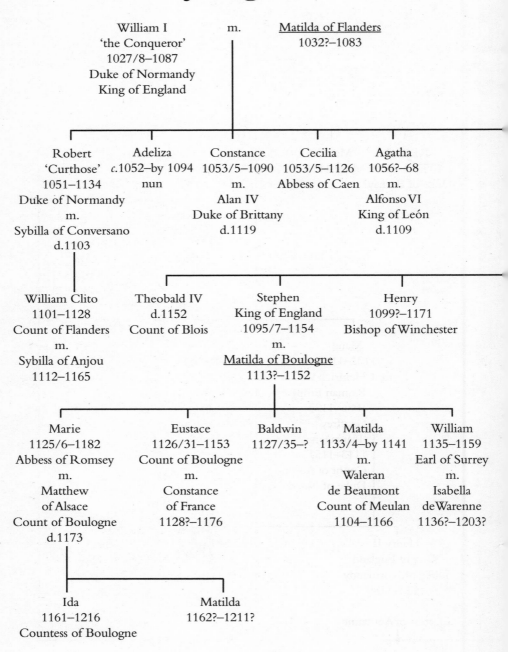

William I
'the Conqueror'
1027/8–1087
Duke of Normandy
King of England

m.

Matilda of Flanders
1032?–1083

Robert
'Curthose'
1051–1134
Duke of Normandy
m.
Sybilla of Conversano
d.1103

Adeliza
c.1052–by 1094
nun

Constance
1053/5–1090
m.
Alan IV
Duke of Brittany
d.1119

Cecilia
1053/5–1126
Abbess of Caen

Agatha
1056?–68
m.
Alfonso VI
King of León
d.1109

William Clito
1101–1128
Count of Flanders
m.
Sybilla of Anjou
1112–1165

Theobald IV
d.1152
Count of Blois

Stephen
King of England
1095/7–1154
m.
Matilda of Boulogne
1113?–1152

Henry
1099?–1171
Bishop of Winchester

Marie
1125/6–1182
Abbess of Romsey
m.
Matthew
of Alsace
Count of Boulogne
d.1173

Eustace
1126/31–1153
Count of Boulogne
m.
Constance
of France
1128?–1176

Baldwin
1127/35–?

Matilda
1133/4–by 1141
m.
Waleran
de Beaumont
Count of Meulan
1104–1166

William
1135–1159
Earl of Surrey
m.
Isabella
de Warenne
1136?–1203?

Ida
1161–1216
Countess of Boulogne

Matilda
1162?–1211?

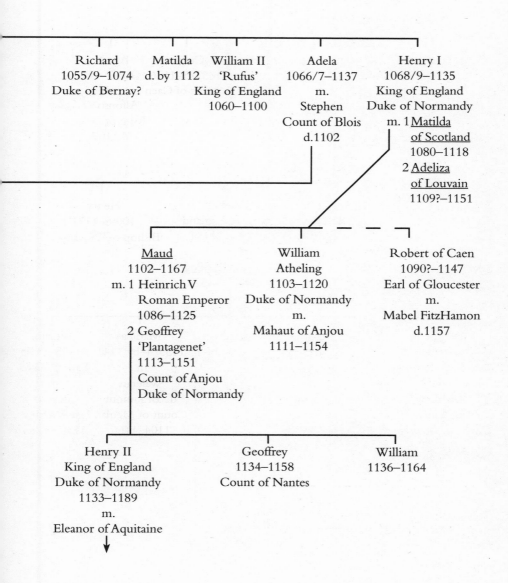

Richard
1055/9–1074
Duke of Bernay?

Matilda
d. by 1112

William II
'Rufus'
King of England
1060–1100

Adela
1066/7–1137
m.
Stephen
Count of Blois
d.1102

Henry I
1068/9–1135
King of England
Duke of Normandy
m. 1 Matilda
of Scotland
1080–1118
2 Adeliza
of Louvain
1109?–1151

Maud
1102–1167
m. 1 Heinrich V
Roman Emperor
1086–1125
2 Geoffrey
'Plantagenet'
1113–1151
Count of Anjou
Duke of Normandy

William
Atheling
1103–1120
Duke of Normandy
m.
Mahaut of Anjou
1111–1154

Robert of Caen
1090?–1147
Earl of Gloucester
m.
Mabel FitzHamon
d.1157

Henry II
King of England
Duke of Normandy
1133–1189
m.
Eleanor of Aquitaine

Geoffrey
1134–1158
Count of Nantes

William
1136–1164

The Saxon Royal Connections

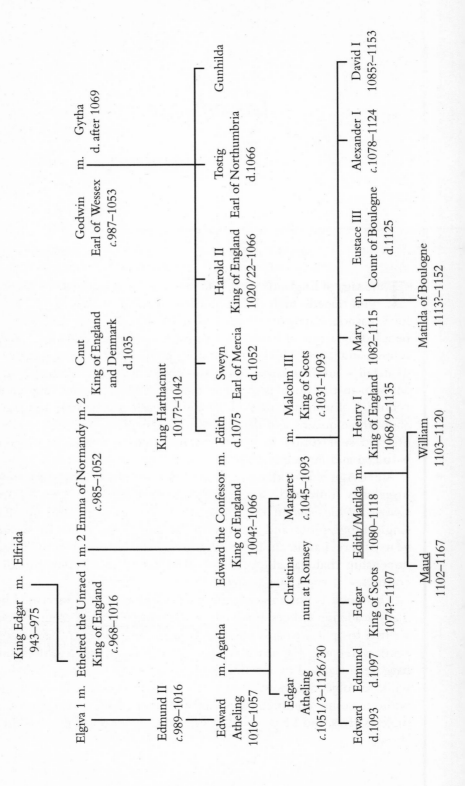

Introduction

The saga of England's medieval queens is vivid and stirring, packed with tragedy, high drama and even comedy. It is a chronicle of love, passion, intrigue, murder, war, treason, betrayal and sorrow, peopled by a cast of heroines, villains, Amazons, stateswomen, adulteresses and lovers. Much, of course, is obscured by time and a paucity of detail – and yet enough survives to reconstruct a dramatic tale. My aim in this book is to piece together the fragments, strip away centuries of romantic mythology and legends that obscure the truth about these queens, and delve beyond the medieval prejudice, credulity and superstition in contemporary sources to achieve a more balanced and authentic view.

Since Agnes Strickland published her groundbreaking, but now hopelessly outdated, subjective and romanticised *Lives of the Queens of England* in the 1840s, there have been some notable single biographies and some popular composite ones. In recent years, there has been increasing academic interest in medieval queenship that has allowed it to be assessed in a much broader context.

This book is not an academic history, although it is informed by many academic sources. It is a narrative account of a turbulent period, written to appeal to anyone who loves history, and based largely on primary records. Popular historians all the way back to Strickland have been accused of emotionalising history, but I strongly feel that, while an objective view is essential, no history would be complete without some comprehension of the emotional realities of the subjects' lives, and I have tried to offer that here, where the evidence allows.

Much of my research on England's medieval queens was undertaken over a number of years; it was based on a vast number of sources and covered twenty lives in depth, and for some time I have been keen to write up this huge mass of material. There is so much of it that this is actually the first of four volumes telling a story that spans the centuries from the Norman Conquest of 1066, when Matilda of Flanders presented her husband, Duke William, with his flagship, the *Mora*; to the mysterious death of Richard III's queen, Anne Neville, in 1485. My aim has been to offer intimate insights into how queens lived and how they exercised power and influence in what was very much a brutal man's world. Many of their lives overlap, and therefore, far from writing separate biographies of each, I have interwoven their stories to craft a seamless royal saga, which also offers an overarching view of the nature and development of English medieval queenship and a sweeping panorama of five hundred years of British history. Eleanor of Aquitaine and Isabella of France are not included: I have already published biographies of them, which will slot into sequence in this series.

This first book in the series focuses on the consorts of the Norman kings of England. Four of them were called Matilda (or Mathilde, Mahaut, Mald or Maud – the names were interchangeable, while Maud is an ancient German variant); therefore, in the interests of clarity, I have referred to them as follows: Matilda of Flanders, Matilda of Scotland, the Empress Maud and Matilda of Boulogne.

The domains of the Norman monarchs of England, who ruled from 1066 to 1154, straddled two lands: they were dukes of Normandy and kings of England. They had little concept of nationalism, ruling in a feudal world where every man had an overlord, the King was accountable only to God, and land tenure counted for everything. Thus they had a European perspective, and it would be from Continental kingdoms and principalities that they took their queens. All but one of England's medieval queens were of the high royal blood of Europe. It was not until 1464 that an English king married an English-born commoner.

The English had a Norman queen before the Norman Conquest. She was the wealthy, spendthrift Emma of Normandy (*c.*985–1052), twice queen of England as the wife of Ethelred II and King Cnut, and mother of King Edward the Confessor. However, her story is not included in this book because she was the wife of kings who ruled before the Norman Conquest of 1066, and not the consort of a Norman king.

How do we define the word 'queen'? A queen regnant is a female monarch who succeeds to the throne and reigns in her own right, exercising sovereign power, in contrast to a queen consort, who is the wife of a reigning king and shares her husband's majesty, rank and titles, but not his sovereignty. A queen dowager, or dowager queen, is the widow of a king. A queen mother is a queen dowager who is also the mother of a reigning sovereign.

Four of the five Norman queens were crowned queen consort. Between the Norman Conquest of 1066 and the coup that placed Lady Jane Grey on the throne in 1553, there were no queens regnant in England. In these centuries, English queenship was embodied by queens consort, with one exception, the Empress Maud, who claimed – with some justification – to be queen regnant of England in her own right, and fought a war to that end. I have included her here because she was her father's acknowledged heir to the throne and should, constitutionally, have succeeded him.

Many realms have forbidden succession by or through women, citing the ancient civil code of the Salian Franks, said to have been first drawn up around AD 500 by the legendary French King Clovis. In England the Salic Law never applied, and four kings, Stephen, Henry II, Edward IV and Henry VII, owed their titles entirely or in part to their female ancestors, while Edward III's claim to the French throne, which led to the Hundred Years War, derived from his mother. It is also worth noting that four of the five Norman queens were chosen as consorts for their maternal ancestry.

Yet while women were respected as the transmitters of dynastic lineage, they were universally regarded as inferior beings who were emotional and irrational, and it was generally seen as unnatural and undesirable for a woman to wield dominion over men. Few women enjoyed autonomy. Girls were subject to their fathers, wives to their husbands. 'A woman is completely in the power of her husband,' pronounced Ranulf Glanville, the Chief Justiciar of England, 'so it is not surprising that all her property is at his disposal.' Only widows escaped male supervision and had the freedom to act independently.

Generally, in the medieval period, queens consort did not rule as equal partners with kings. It was accepted that kings would not be overly influenced by them in political matters, and that queens wielded power only by the authority of their husbands, to whom, like all married women, they owed their status. They had permitted spheres of authority, and there was an expectation that they would offer wise counsel to their lords. In theory they were not supposed to have political ambitions, but in practice some certainly did.

The Norman queens, however, were recognised as equal sharers in the royal authority. Three ruled as regents while their husbands were abroad. Where necessary, they took up arms. Without the support of their wives, the Norman kings could not have ruled their disparate dominions as effectively. It has become accepted practice for academic scholars to refer to the three queens consort called Matilda as Matilda I, Matilda II and Matilda III, a useful means of avoiding confusion, but there is in this style a certain apprehension, not unfounded, of regnal power, bolstered by references to their years as consort as their 'reign'. Certainly Matilda of Scotland referred to herself as Matilda II on her seal,[1] probably to differentiate herself from her predecessor, Matilda of Flanders.

There have also been several cases of queens consort being shrewd or ambitious stateswomen and acting unofficially as trusted advisers to their husbands or sons. Some, like Matilda of Boulogne, were the driving power behind the throne. Consorts were uniquely placed to exert considerable influence on the monarch and rule at one remove. Although no medieval English queen save Isabella of France ever wielded sovereign power during the minority of a son who had ascended the throne, royal mothers often exercised influence over their children, even if it was only in a cultural or religious sphere. In this period we see the Empress Maud functioning as a respected elder stateswoman in her son's reign, while two Norman kings, William II and Henry I, grew up seeing their mother, Matilda of Flanders, ruling Normandy effectively as regent. Henry's Queen, Matilda of Scotland, was regent in England for several years. The Empress Maud was begged to rule the Roman Empire after the death of her husband, the Emperor Heinrich V. Matilda of Boulogne fought a war on her lord's behalf – and won it. Thus it could never be said that the Norman queens were mere ciphers.

It might be claimed that many medieval queens are unknowable. Their characters are elusive. We are looking at them from a perspective of hundreds of years – nearly a thousand in the case of Matilda of Flanders – and sadly, a lot of information has been lost over the centuries, if it was ever recorded in the first place. For example, we would probably know more about the Empress Maud if Arnulf of Lisieux's life of her had survived.[2] There are inevitably tantalising gaps, which are the bane of the medieval biographer, particularly when writing about women, because the deeds of women, unless they were notably pious, politically important or scandalous, were rarely thought worth recording. Enough remains, however, to tell a vivid and dramatic tale, and I have constructed the story of these queens from what I believe to be the most reliable contemporary sources.

Go back to the eleventh century and you are lucky if part of a building that Matilda of Flanders knew survives. Sometimes it's impossible to determine just where that building stood. Records even of royal castles are sparse before the reign of Henry II (1154–89). Much of what we do know has been determined by archaeology.

We have no real idea of what these early queens looked like. No tomb effigy of an English queen survives from the Norman period (the earliest, at Fontevrault Abbey, date from the beginning of the thirteenth century), and portraiture as an art did not exist – the first portrait of an English king, Richard II, was painted in the 1390s. The chief aim of representations of royalty was to show a crowned head, and the few images that survive are on seals, on coins or in manuscripts (often of a later date), or crude sculptures, none of which are true likenesses. Thus we must rely on contemporary descriptions, where they exist, yet all too often queens are merely described as 'fair', which means good-looking, not blonde-haired.

Much of our information about the Norman queens comes from monastic chronicles – some reliable, some credulous. There are occasional tantalising details of their daily lives, although most contemporary observers only wrote about women who did something of note or scandalous. Monkish writers vowed to celibacy – and distrustful of the female sex for having lured men into original sin – invariably saw women as saints or devils with all the frailties of Eve, so theirs can be a biased view. It was customary for even the most misogynistic to call queens fair and extol their beauty, so it's hard to assess how true such laudatory descriptions were. Quotes are few, and often we have no way of knowing if the words put into these women's mouths were what they actually said, an approximation of it, or what the chronicler made up. It was accepted practice to put speeches into the mouths of the public figures about whom the chroniclers wrote.

Few royal letters survive from this period. We have none from Matilda of Flanders, Adeliza of Louvain or Matilda of Boulogne. Before the fifteenth century, English queens dictated all their letters to their clerks or secretaries, who wrote them in Latin, the universal language of Christendom; therefore their own words may have been edited. Some of the letters sent by, or to, the Norman queens are very long. For this reason, they have been summarised in the text and given in full in Appendix 2 for those who wish to gain deeper insights into the characters of these women.

Telling insights might also come from dry records of expenditure such as charters or the Pipe Rolls, which can yield rich information. Charters were a means by which feudal kings and queens could ally themselves to their people by conferring gifts and liberties. They can tell us a lot about the patronage of medieval queens and where they preferred to bestow their bounty and privileges. They can place a queen in a certain time and place, which may help to date other evidence or build an itinerary. One advantage we do have is that these sources are all in Latin or Norman French, which translate well into modern English and add more freshness to the narrative than is possible in books on later periods for which the sources are in archaic English. When quoting from contemporary sources, I have sometimes substituted names or titles for pronouns, or vice versa, or added the occasional conjunction or verb to facilitate a smooth reading of the text. Where the Empress Maud is disparagingly referred to as 'the Countess of Anjou', I have substituted 'the Empress' for clarity.

For all the dearth of information about the Norman queens, enough survives to underpin the stories of their lives in some detail and show that they were all extraordinary women by the standards of their time, and cannot be viewed as mere corollaries of their husbands. Indeed, these women set the standard – and it was generally a high one – for later medieval queenship in England. Their successors, however, would rarely enjoy such authority and influence.

Among the numerous key original sources for the book, I have relied heavily on evidence from contemporary chronicles, of which there are many for the long period covered by the lives of the Norman queens; some, like those written by Orderic Vitalis and William of Malmesbury, are among the principal sources for the period. For readers who would like to know more, I have included short accounts of the chroniclers, in alphabetical order, in Appendix 1.

I am indebted to the myriad works of other historians who have trodden this path before me, and published their research in the years after I completed mine, and in particular to the brilliant scholarship of four historians who have written definitive works on the Norman queens: Dr Tracy Borman for her biography *Matilda, Queen of the Conqueror*; Professor Lois Huneycutt for *Matilda of Scotland: A Study in Medieval Queenship* and various related articles; Dr Patricia Dark for her thesis, 'The Career of Matilda of Boulogne as Countess and Queen in England', which I had the privilege of reading before it went into print; and the late Dr Marjorie Chibnall OBE for *The Empress Matilda* and related articles. I did not want my portrayal of the Norman queens to be a mirror image of theirs, so reading these works was the final phase of my research, by which time the book was in its penultimate draft and incorporated most of the contemporary sources.

No historical currency conversion tables exist for the Norman period. The earliest are for the thirteenth century. The silver penny (*denarius*) dated from Saxon times, and was the only coin in circulation, but by Norman times the shilling (*solidus*) (12d.) and the pound (*librum*) (20s. or 240d.) had been introduced as accounting units, a system that lasted until decimalisation of the coinage in 1971. There already existed another unit of accounting called the mark, which, after the Conquest, was worth 13s. 4d., or two thirds of a pound sterling.

In the two centuries after 1080, there were 22.5 grains of silver in a penny. Today, 22.5 grains (or 1.46 grams) of silver would be worth about 61p, although prices can fluctuate, and silver was worth more in Norman England.

I am deeply grateful to Tracy Borman for taking the time out of a busy schedule to read the draft text, and for her very kind response. As ever, I am indebted to my agent, Julian Alexander, and my commissioning editors, Dan Franklin at Jonathan Cape and Susanna Porter at Ballantine, for their help in bringing this project to fruition, and for supporting me in the conviction that a single volume could not do justice to the lives of England's medieval queens and giving me the scope to explore their stories in detail in four books. Huge thanks go to my editors, Anthony Whittome, for his sensitive and wonderfully creative approach to my work, and Bea Hemming at Jonathan Cape, for her support. I owe a big debt of gratitude to the fabulous production team at Jonathan Cape: to Neil Bradford for production; Clare Bullock and Madeleine Hartley for picture research; Rowena Skelton-Wallace and Jane Selley for copy-editing; Alison Rae for proofreading; and Alex Bell for the index. Thanks are also due to Stephen Parker for the marvellous jacket.

I could not write without the support of my husband, Rankin, and words cannot do justice to what he does for me. But from the heart I say this to him: thank you for everything.

Prologue

I magine a land centuries before industrialisation, a rural, green land
of vast royal forests and open fields, wild moorlands and undrained
marshlands, with scattered villages overshadowed by towering castles,
and small, bustling walled towns. A land inhabited by just two million
people, whose lives were dominated by the twin calendars imposed
by farming and the Church.

This was a realm torn by conflicts between Church and Crown,
and by centuries of strife between the indigenous Anglo-Saxon
population and the land-hungry Danes; a realm that bore the scars
of the savagery of the Viking invaders, who had colonised parts of
the island's north and east – yet nevertheless a realm in which trade
and learning flourished, and kings traced their lineage back through
the mists of time to Noah and the Norse god Woden. This was an
age of faith and superstition, and an age of bloody warfare.

Imagine, in place of today's modern traffic and electronic noise,
the sound of birdsong, animals, church bells, plainchant, human voices,
and the occasional hunting horn or strumming of a lyre. This pleasant
land, this rural landscape, was England in the time of the Norman
queens.

'We Are Come for Glory'

The news was stupendous.

The messenger from England arrived in Normandy soon after 14 October 1066. He found the Duchess, Matilda of Flanders, on her knees, praying for her lord's safety, in a chapel of the priory she had founded, Notre-Dame de Pré, near Rouen.

Her husband, William, Duke of Normandy, had launched his invasion of England the previous month, intent on seizing the throne he believed was rightfully his. He had endured a terrible crossing in stormy weather. Making land on 28 September at Pevensey, on England's south coast, he had stumbled and fallen on the beach. His followers had cried out, 'struck with fear at so evil an augury', but William turned the fall to his advantage, holding up handfuls of sand and announcing, 'I have taken seisin of this land with both my hands.' He was borne ashore to hearty acclaim.[1]

William soon learned that the English King, Harold, was away in the north, repelling an invasion by King Harold Hardrada of Norway. After defeating and killing Harold Hardrada at Stamford Bridge in Yorkshire, Harold marched south to deal with the Norman threat. On 14 October, the two armies met at Senlac Hill in Sussex, five miles inland from the coast at Hastings, and engaged in a battle that would last for six hours and later become known as the Battle of Hastings.

Before the fighting began, William addressed his men: 'I have no doubt of the victory; we are come for glory; the victory is in our hands, and we may make sure of obtaining it if we so please.' He fought tirelessly: 'to see him reining in his horse, shining with sword, helmet and shield, and brandishing his lance, was a pleasant yet terrible sight'. It was said that three horses were killed under him that day, but still he fought on.

Harold and his men had spread out along the ridge called Senlac Hill, which placed the Normans in the fields below at a disadvantage; but when, at length, on William's order, the Normans staged a retreat, the English made the fatal decision to abandon their strong position and chase after them, at which point the tide of battle turned in William's favour, for without warning the Normans swung around and engaged the English in a fight that quickly turned into a bloodbath. Harold fell, mortally wounded, beneath his standards depicting the Fighting Man and the Gold Dragon of Wessex. Traditionally, he was shot in the eye by an arrow, but that scene in the Bayeux Tapestry also shows a soldier, who may well be Harold, being cut down with axes. His mother and his mistress were able to identify his mutilated body only from secret marks on it.

The victory was William's, and, in fulfilment of a vow he had made before he sailed, 'on the very spot where God granted him the conquest of England, he caused a great abbey to be built; and settled monks in it and richly endowed it'.[2] Here Harold and many others had died, and in the abbey William provided for prayers to be offered in perpetuity for his own sins, for those of his wife Matilda, and for those of the fallen. Today, Battle Abbey stands on the site, although there is very little that remains of William's original foundation.

William had now to consolidate his victory and establish himself as king, but first he sent his messenger across the sea to Normandy to tell Matilda that she was now, by the grace of God, queen of England.

Part One

Matilda of Flanders
Queen of William I

1

'A Very Beautiful and
Noble Girl'

Count Baldwin V of Flanders was famed throughout Christendom as the wisest of men,[1] a firm ruler and a precursor of the knights of chivalry – the kind of prince whose friendship was much sought after. He was 'a man of great power who towered above the rest. Counts, marquises, dukes, even archbishops of the highest dignity were struck dumb with admiration whenever the duty of their office earned them the presence of this distinguished guest. Kings too revered and stood in awe of his greatness.'[2] He was descended from a powerful and noble family,[3] and from the Emperor Charlemagne and England's King Alfred (reigned 871–899); Alfred's daughter Elfrida had married his ancestor Baldwin II.

Baldwin ruled one of the greatest territories in northern Europe. He was strong of body, mighty in arms, wise in council, of 'well-tried integrity' and 'admirable alike for loyalty and wisdom, grey-haired yet with the vigour of youth'. Although not at heart a man of war, if he thought a cause was just he would support it whole-heartedly and keep faith with his allies.[4] His reputation was such that in 1060 his brother-in-law, Henry I, King of France, would name him regent for his young son Philip.

Baldwin's exalted position owed much to his being the husband of the French King's sister.[5] By the pious, strong-willed Adela, the daughter of Robert II, King of France, he had 'gifted sons and daughters': Baldwin, Robert and Matilda.[6] Through the 'wise and blessed' Countess Adela, the children inherited 'a lineage many times greater even' than their father's bloodline.[7]

There is no record of the order in which they were born. Matilda's date of birth is unknown. The earliest possible date – if she was the eldest child – was 1031, her parents having consummated their marriage that year in the face of opposition from her grandfather, Baldwin IV, which was one reason why Baldwin rose against his father soon afterwards[8] in a rebellion incited by his wife. More likely Matilda was born in 1032 or later. She was connected to most of the ruling houses of Europe: 'she sprang from the stock of the kings of Gaul and emperors of Germany, and was renowned equally for nobility of blood and character'.[9]

Matilda grew up at her father's court, which was established mainly in Bruges (or Bryghia, as it was originally known), in the ninth-century castle that served as the administrative centre of the counts of Flanders. Built around 850 by Count Baldwin I 'Iron Arm' on the bank of the River Reie, it occupied what is now Burgplatz (Castle Square), and stood next to the contemporary Romanesque church of St Donatian.[10] From Bruges, Baldwin 'Iron Arm' pursued an aggressive expansionist policy to establish the principality of Flanders. Under Matilda's brother, Count Robert the Frisian, Bruges would become its capital. By Matilda's time it was a prosperous centre of commerce, and enjoyed 'very great fame for the number of its inhabitants and for its affluence'.[11]

Matilda would also have spent time at her father's castle in the Flemish city of Lille. It stood on an island – l'Isle, hence the name Lille – in a rural setting on the left bank of the Basse Deule river, with a vineyard to the east. Dating from before 1039, it housed the Chapelle de la Treille, in which the Blessed Virgin was venerated.[12] Within the encircling wall and moat there was a donjon, or keep, and the Count's residence, which was called La Salle.[13]

Count Baldwin owned other residences in which Matilda would have stayed: a ninth-century wooden castle at Ghent, on the site of which the present Gravensteen – the Castle of the Counts – was built in 1180; a hilltop castle at Thérouanne, overlooking the cathedral; and the tenth-century 'bourg' at Saint-Omer, which was visited by the court for the observance of holy and feast days.[14]

The Flanders into which Matilda was born was a turbulent place. 'Daily homicides and the spilling of human blood troubled the peace and quiet of the entire area.' The nobles would urge the bishops to 'visit the places where this atrocious cruelty especially raged, and to instruct the docile and bloody spirit of the Flemings in the interest of peace and concord'.[15] But trade and commerce were expanding, ushering in a new era of prosperity.

Matilda may have been old enough to be present in 1037 when the exiled Queen of England, Emma of Normandy, widow of King Cnut, was 'honourably received' by Count Baldwin and Countess Adela in

Bruges,[16] having been driven out of England by her stepson, King Harold Harefoot.[17] Baldwin offered Emma a refuge for 'as long as she had need'.[18] Now aged about fifty-two, she was to stay at his court, paying her own way, until 1040, when Harold Harefoot died and her own son, Harthacnut, succeeded to the English throne. During this time, the young Matilda may have come to know her, and perhaps been impressed by some rudimentary apprehension of Emma's grandiose and forceful style of English queenship. Emma had wielded political influence and been respected for it; she had used her wealth to patronise scholars. In Bruges, she worked tirelessly for the right of Harthacnut to succeed his half-brother. She may also have told Matilda something of Normandy, where she had grown up.

When her son became king and Queen Emma finally returned to England, the people of Flanders 'wept, that she, whom during her whole exile they had regarded as a fellow citizen, was leaving them. Such was the lamentation on the whole shore, such was the wailing of all the people standing by', while 'a great abundance of tears' was shed by Baldwin, Adela and Emma as they said their farewells.[19]

The chronicler Orderic Vitalis would one day praise Matilda's intelligence and her learning. The early education of royal children, up to the age of seven, was the responsibility of their mother. Learning was respected at Baldwin's court, and, like her brothers, Matilda was probably taught to read in Latin, although, in common with most high-born children, she was not taught to write. There would always be clerks to do that for her. Much of her tuition would have focused on the Holy Scriptures and the lives of the saints. She may well have read the life of the tenth-century Roman Empress, the highly influential Adelaide of Burgundy, which her mother had commissioned.[20] She would have been grounded in needlework and the management of a great household, and had piety instilled into her. This, above all, was an age of faith. The chronicler William of Poitiers, Archdeacon of Lisieux, recorded that Matilda's most praiseworthy quality was 'a strong faith and fervent love of Christ'.

The daughters of kings and lords – who were referred to as princesses, but not so styled until the eighteenth century – were brought up to accept that marriages would be arranged for them, and that it was their duty to render obedience first to their parents and later to their husbands. Marriage was seen as a desirable estate for both sexes, and for many women it defined their role in life. The alternative was the cloister, but it was generally expected that most royal and aristocratic women would marry, and marry well; it was rare to find one who died unwed or unprofessed.

The upbringing of high-born girls was therefore geared towards finding a suitable husband, one of fitting rank and standing, and it was incumbent largely upon their mothers to see that their daughters grew up chaste, discreet, humble, pious and obedient, and were prepared for marriage.

Like most girls, princesses were reared to an awareness that they had been born of an inferior sex, and that consequently their freedoms were limited – although the example of their mothers might have demonstrated that women of rank could be enormously influential. The concept of female inferiority was older than Christianity, but centuries of Christian teaching had rigidly enforced it. Woman was an instrument of the devil, the author of original sin who would lure man away from the path to salvation – in short, the only imperfection in God's creation. Medieval women were regarded variously as weak and passive, or as domineering harridans, temptresses and whores. It was held that young girls needed to be protected from themselves so that they could be nurtured as chaste and submissive maidens and mothers. Marriage was essential to the medieval concept of the divine order of the world: the husband ruled his family, as the King ruled his realm, and as God ruled the universe, and – like subjects – wives were bound in obedience to their husbands and masters.

Matilda grew up to be fair, graceful, devout, learned and proud[21] – 'a very beautiful and noble girl of royal stock', enthused Duke William of Normandy's chaplain, William of Jumièges, who must have met her.

In the nineteenth century, it was claimed that, according to charters of Lewes Priory, Sussex, the young Matilda was married to Gherbod, advocate of St Bertin's Abbey in Flanders, and that she bore him a son, Gherbod the Fleming, Earl of Chester, but these charters have since been proved spurious.[22]

However, there may have been some truth in the later assertion that, 'when she was a maiden', Matilda 'loved a count [earl] of England' called Brihtric Meaw, whose wealth was said to be surpassed only by that of King Edward the Confessor.[23] Rarely in medieval times was royalty associated with romance; until comparatively recently, most royal marriages were the subject of treaties and alliances. In medieval times, marrying for love was regarded as an aberration and irresponsible – and shocking. As the great chronicler

William of Malmesbury observed, 'Kingship and love make sorry bedfellows and sort but ill together.'

Even if it was merely an accepted fiction, there was some apprehension that love and freedom of choice played their roles in courtship, although they were not allowed to override the more powerful factors at play.

Brihtric was lord of the extensive honour of Gloucester, an honour being a great feudal lordship comprising dozens or hundreds of manors, held by great magnates (tenants-in-chief) of the Crown. He was a handsome man with snowy white hair, 'meaw' meaning snow in Anglo-Saxon English. He may have been somewhat older than Matilda, as he had inherited Tewkesbury in 1020 and attested royal charters in the 1040s.[24] She met him when King Edward sent him as an envoy to her father's court at Bruges. Smitten, she resolved to obtain his love. It was not a wild or unrealistic fancy. In 1051, her aunt, Judith of Flanders, was to marry Tostig, a younger son of an English earl, Godwin of Wessex; Brihtric was a man of rank and far greater wealth than Tostig.

Boldly, Matilda sent a messenger to Brihtric, summoned him to see her, declared her feelings and proposed marriage. But he refused her.[25] Fortunately another suitor was in view.

2

'Great Courage and High Daring'

The formidable William the Bastard, sovereign Duke of Normandy and great-nephew of Emma of Normandy, was at that time being urged by his barons to marry.[1] Normandy was then a great independent duchy, the most powerful in western Christendom, and its Duke was the most dominant vassal of the King of France, his feudal overlord, to whom he owed homage and loyalty. Naturally his barons wanted to ensure the future security of Normandy and the continuance of stable government, so they 'urgently drew his attention to the problem of his offspring and succession'[2] and gave him 'divergent counsels about his marriage'.[3] William made up his own mind.

The desirability of a noble wife lay not so much in her looks or character as in her wealth and breeding. Marriage was essentially a contract, and princesses diplomatic assets. As King Henry III stated in the thirteenth century, 'Friendship between princes can be obtained in no more fitting manner than by the link of conjugal troth.'[4] Therefore royal marriages were almost always made to benefit kingdoms by ensuring the succession and forging alliances that averted war and brought prosperity. 'When love buds between great princes, it drives away bitter sobs from their subjects,' went a political song of the thirteenth century.

William wanted a wife of high lineage who would add to his growing prestige. 'Kings from far away would gladly have given him their very dearest daughters in marriage',[5] but he had learned that Count Baldwin had 'a daughter named Matilda of noble origins and character, and of delicate beauty', who was strong in body.[6] Contemporaries – and possibly the young lady herself – regarded Matilda as being of greater birth and ancestry than William was,[7] so securing such a prize would go far towards counteracting the slur of bastardy.

There were other sound political reasons for the marriage. Re-establishing an old alliance with Flanders, a rising power, and strengthening ties with the King of France, Matilda's uncle, could only increase Norman prestige and influence in western Europe, and could protect the Duke's eastern border, beyond which lay France and, to the north, Flanders, and quell the rebellious subjects of both Baldwin and William, who were making trouble on the fringes of their territories.

Haven taken counsel with his lords,[8] William sent envoys to Count Baldwin to ask for Matilda's hand.[9] This was in, or before, 1049,[10] when Matilda was eighteen at most; the marriage may have been mooted as early as May 1048, when William and Baldwin were together witnessing a charter of Henry I at Senlis, north of Paris.[11] Baldwin had long desired an alliance with William,[12] whom he had protected from the treasonable designs of William's enemies during the young Duke's troubled minority.[13] It was his aim to forge closer relations with his nearest neighbours, especially France, with whom he had been involved in a conflict with the Holy Roman Empire; the aim had been to secure disputed territory and ultimately undermine the Emperor's power. As France's vassal, Duke William was bound to support King Henry against the Empire. Thus Baldwin received the Norman envoys with much courtesy, expressed great satisfaction at the proposed marriage[14] and gladly consented to it, promising a large dowry.[15]

But, if we believe a tale related in four thirteenth-century chronicles, the headstrong Matilda had her own views on marrying Duke William. The story appears in Norman,[16] French[17] and Flemish[18] chronicles, which recount how, from the vantage point of having been reared in a conventional family, and untainted by the insecurity of illegitimacy, she loftily – and publicly – declared 'she would not have a bastard for her husband'.[19] Count Baldwin was exceedingly embarrassed by her rudeness. His daughter must have taken leave of her senses, he said. He would talk to her. But all the talk in the world would not move her, and in the end the Count had to send the envoys back to William with her answer. Baldwin had demonstrated remarkable indulgence towards his daughter in an age in which many high-born girls were forced into marriage, and now that her father had backed down, Matilda no doubt thought that that would be the end of the matter. It wasn't.

The tale goes that, one Sunday morning not long afterwards, Matilda was returning from Mass with her ladies when she was suddenly overtaken by a furious man on horseback – her rejected suitor, Duke William. He is said to have waylaid her either in the streets of Bruges[20] or in the courtyard of Baldwin's castle at Lille,[21] and even to have dragged her to her bedchamber. Accounts differ as to the location, but they are unanimous in reporting what William did. 'Infuriated by the scorn with which Matilda had treated him', he seized her by her long hair, 'beat her, rolled her in the mud, spoiled her rich array, and then rode off at full speed', leaving her in such a bad way that she had to take to her bed.[22] The Chronicle of Tours states that he used his 'fists, heels, and spurs', such was his rage. Given that William had such strength in his arm that no one else was able to draw his bow, and that he could bend it when his horse was galloping at speed,[23] it would have been a vicious beating.

Count Baldwin was outraged. He chose another husband for his daughter, said to have been Bernard II, Duke of Saxony, though as Bernard was already married, the chroniclers perhaps meant his son, Ordulf. Baldwin also armed for war. But no sooner had the skirmishing started than Matilda sprung her father another surprise. Most girls of royal blood would surely have felt grossly insulted by William's assault, but the Duke's rough wooing had prompted an astonishing change of heart in this spirited young lady, who suddenly announced from her sickbed that it would please her well to marry none but William.[24] When asked by the astonished Baldwin why she had reconsidered, she replied, 'Because I did not know the Duke as well then as I do now, for he must be a man of great courage and high daring who could venture to come and beat me in my own father's palace.'[25]

It may be that, lying in her sickbed, Matilda had been reflecting on Brihtric's rejection and concluding that her pride would be salvaged by the announcement of her marriage to the far higher-born William, who could offer her so much more. Or possibly Brihtric had only just turned her down, and she accepted William on the rebound.

Her father was delighted with her change of heart. He withdrew his soldiers and let it be known that his daughter was now amenable to the marriage. William renewed his proposal and negotiations were reopened. This time, Matilda readily assented.

'His request pleases me well,' she said,[26] and preparations for the wedding began in earnest.

Historians have questioned the truth of the story, asserting that it is a later tradition, and possibly French propaganda designed to discredit the Norman dukes after the duchy fell to the French in 1204. Certainly the Chronicle of Tours is a hostile source. But the tale appears in three other chronicles, one written in Normandy and two in Flanders. Baldwin of Avesnes, who wrote one of the latter, was drawing on older sources lost to us. There may be a grain of truth in the tale.

3

'William Bastard'

The taint of bastardy had haunted William all his life. His mother, Herleva of Falaise, had been a tanner's daughter. His father, Duke Robert the Magnificent, was said to have noticed her washing clothes in the river, and the result was William, born around 1027–8. Herleva nearly died giving birth, and while her attendants worked to save her, her newborn son was laid on the floor, where he grasped the rushes in such a strong little fist that those watching are said to have predicted he would grow into 'a mighty man, ready to acquire anything within his reach, and that which he acquired he would with a strong hand steadfastly maintain against all challengers'.[1]

'He is little, but he will grow,' the Duke his father said in 1035, when he went on a pilgrimage to Jerusalem and left seven- or eight-year-old William, his only son, to govern Normandy during his absence. But that year Robert died in Asia Minor on his way home. Since he left no legitimate heir, the child William succeeded him as duke.

Unlike Matilda's, William's early years were turbulent. 'I have been continually involved in numberless troubles,' he recalled on his deathbed. 'I was bred to arms from my childhood.'[2] Many Norman lords resented a bastard wearing the ducal crown. The boy's tutors and guardians were murdered, and there were attempts on his life, one in his own bedchamber. But the young Duke survived and grew into a man to be reckoned with, and with him grew his legend. 'He was mild to the men that loved God, and beyond all measure severe to the men that gainsaid him. He was very stern, and a wrathful man, so that none durst do anything against his will.'[3] At twenty, in 1047, at the battle of Val-ès-Dunes, William proved his skill as a soldier, and thereafter his reputation spread. Every battle he fought he won, and in Normandy and beyond he came to be greatly admired and respected – but never loved, although he possessed considerable powers of leadership and courage, and inspired loyalty in his followers.

In an age in which the average male height, based on a study of surviving armour, was about 5'5", William was tall at 5'10" – a height estimated from his thighbone, examination of which revealed that he was strong and muscular.[4] Contemporaries described him as thickset, with 'a fierce countenance', reddish hair that receded early in life, and a rasping, guttural voice. When his tomb was opened in 1522, his body – that of a large man with long arms and legs – was sufficiently well preserved for a portrait to be made, which was painted on wood and hung above the tomb.[5] It shows a man in early-sixteenth-century dress with red hair, a beard and a strong resemblance to the French King François I or even Henry VIII. If the face is that of the Duke as he looked in life, it is very different from traditional representations of him, such as the helmet-haired, clean-shaven images in the famous Bayeux Tapestry, which depicted the Norman Conquest of 1066 and still survives today.

William 'was majestic whether sitting or standing', although increasingly 'the protuberance of his belly deformed his royal person', despite his being moderate in eating and drinking.[6] He enjoyed excellent health, and frequently indulged his great passion for hunting.[7]

He was a hard, active and forceful man, with great presence and authority, resolute, iron-willed and avaricious. Despite his ruthlessness, he was known as a just and pious ruler, albeit one to be feared. Men quaked in the face of his righteous anger. He set great store by loyalty, abhorred drunkenness[8] and, especially in early youth, 'esteemed chastity to such an extent' that 'it was believed certain that he could do nothing in a woman',[9] which was a matter of concern to contemporaries who were concerned about the succession. Unlike his ducal forebears for four generations, he never sired a bastard.[10]

William's attitude to sexual morality was probably a reaction to his own bastardy, which he found deeply shameful, as his violent treatment of those who taunted him with it makes clear. While defiantly signing his letters 'William Bastard', the Duke would not suffer anyone to remind him of his base birth. After the besieged inhabitants of Alençon in Normandy hung tanned hides over the walls in mockery of his grandfather's trade, the town fell to William, and he meted out a grim revenge, ordering the hands and feet of thirty-two of those who had jeered to be chopped off, himself standing by to see it done.

For all the concerns of contemporaries, he would soon prove himself capable of siring children, although it is possible that he could only achieve sexual release within the hallowed security of the marriage bed.

This was the man – the stark, stern, upright man – whom Matilda had consented to wed.

4

'The Greatest Ceremony and Honour'

But wed, it seemed, they would not be. In 1049, Count Baldwin's ally Godfrey, Count of Upper Lorraine, was defeated in battle by his overlord, the 'Roman' Emperor Henry III. The Holy Roman Empire was a feudal state encompassing present-day Germany and the surrounding regions, parts of northern Europe and northern Italy. It had been established in 800, when the Pope crowned Charlemagne, King of the Franks, as emperor in Aachen Cathedral, an act that was seen as the restoration of the old Roman Empire. From 962, Charlemagne's German descendants had presided over the Empire, in an uneasy partnership with the Pope. However, the German emperors did not style themselves 'Holy' Roman Emperor until 1254.

Flanders was also a fief of the Holy Roman Empire, so Baldwin was obliged to go to Aachen with Godfrey to make formal submission to the Emperor, who was apparently determined on revenge. In October that year, at the Papal Council of Rheims, Henry III's protégé and ally, the reforming Pope Leo IX, asserted the authority of the Holy See as never before in imposing celibacy on the clergy and the enforcement of canon law on simony, marriage, consanguinity and incest. While he was about it, he forbade Count Baldwin to give his daughter in marriage to William, and prohibited William from receiving her. No reason was given for the sudden ban, apart from the assertion that such a marriage would be contrary to canon law, and even today it is hard to explain Leo's decision.

There is no evidence that Matilda had been precontracted to Brihtric Meaw or anyone else, which would have prevented her marrying William, a precontract then being as binding as a marriage. Orderic Vitalis called Matilda William's 'cousin', implying that the couple were related within the prohibited degrees of consanguinity, a view taken by several twelfth-century chroniclers. There has been much conjecture as to the nature of this relationship, and speculation that the affinity arose from Matilda's mother, Adela of France, having perhaps been the wife of William's uncle, Richard III, Duke of Normandy, prior to her marriage to Count Baldwin. Richard was certainly betrothed at one time to a lady named Adela (or Adelais), but her identity is uncertain, and if such a marriage took place, it was never consummated.

Other writers allege that Matilda, like William, was descended from Rollo, the Viking who gained Normandy from the French and became its first ruler in 911, but there is no evidence for this, and even if there were, the blood tie was too far back to constitute a bar to marriage. Yet another source states that William and Matilda were cousins in the fifth degree, but that relationship is hard to determine.

The consanguinity possibly arose from Matilda's grandfather, Baldwin IV, having married William's aunt, Eleanor of Normandy, after the death of his first wife, the mother of Baldwin V, creating consanguinity even though there was no blood tie. This connection made William and Matilda first cousins once removed − or cousins in the first degree. At that time, the Church prohibited marriages between cousins related up to the seventh degree,[1] yet it also frequently granted dispensations for such unions, although the more closely the couple were related, the more difficult it was to obtain one.

It was not unusual for feudal rulers to ignore such niceties, but William was a devout son of the Church who devoted himself wholeheartedly to the worship of God.[2] Already, thanks to his utmost zeal[3] in undertaking great ecclesiastical reforms in Normandy, he had gained favour with the clergy. He may already have been aware of a possible impediment to marrying Matilda, for he had sent a strong contingent of churchmen to Rheims with Lanfranc of Pavia, the respected Benedictine Abbot of Bec-Hellouin (and future archbishop of Canterbury), probably to persuade the Pope to sanction the union. It would not have done for a man with William's reforming reputa- tion to contract an uncanonical marriage, for any controversy over that marriage would have an adverse impact on the ducal succession and future standing of the Church in Normandy. Most Norman bishops were hostile to the union after the Pope's ban had been announced. This was probably why Norman chroniclers, most of whom were monks, were reticent about discussing the prohibition.

But underlying all the ecclesiastical histrionics, there were shrewd political reasons for Pope Leo's ban. Leo was an imperialist, and aware that an alliance between Flanders and Normandy would produce a strong coalition against the Empire. He knew that William 'was growing in power and influence, and surpassing all his neigh- bours in the magnificence and display of his new way of life'.[4] Furthermore, a Norman adventurer, Robert Guiscard, had just conquered southern Italy and made himself its ruler, which the Pope perceived as another threat. Possibly his ban was motivated purely by political revenge, or intended to block an alliance that boded ill for the Emperor and to curb the power of the Normans.

No doubt William was aware of the Pope's true motives. In 1050, he sent Lanfranc, Abbot of Bec-Hellouin, and Geoffrey, Bishop of Coutances, to Rome to seek the Pope's advice.[5] Lanfranc was one of the most admired and sincere churchmen in Normandy. William 'venerated him as a father, respected him as a teacher, and loved him like a brother or son'.[6] Lafranc was 'a man comparable with the Ancients for learning and religious fervour',[7] his reputation for 'admirable genius and erudition'[8] had already spread far beyond the duchy, and his name was spoken of with reverence in Rome itself. The outcome of this embassy is not known. It has been suggested that the matter was quickly resolved and the Pope was persuaded to issue a dispensation,[9] but other evidence conflicts with that theory, and it seems more likely that in the end William flouted the ban.

It has also been suggested that when Pope Leo engaged in a war to drive out the Normans who had conquered southern Italy, and was taken prisoner by them after the Battle of Civitate on 15 June 1053, William seized his chance and married Matilda.[10] Various chroniclers give dates for the marriage as far apart as 1050 and 1056, with most stating 1050, which was almost certainly the year it took place, when William was twenty-three and Matilda nineteen at most.

It was long claimed that the earliest references to Matilda as William's consort and Duchess of Normandy appear in two charters granted in 1053, one to the abbey of the Holy Trinity at Rouen,[11] and the other to the Benedictine abbey of Saint-Julien at Tours.[12] But Matilda appears with William as a witness to two original charters to the abbey of Saint-Wandrille dated 1051,[13] as does their eldest child Robert. It was not unusual for high-born infants to be witnesses to charters, and since William and Matilda must have been married after October 1049, and most likely in 1050, Robert was probably born in 1051. This fits with his being described as adolescent in 1066.[14]

From earliest times, royal weddings have been seen as a cause for great celebrations. Royal nuptials signify something momentous for society at large. Securing the royal succession has always been a matter of public concern, which is why the marriages of monarchs and lords have always been of crucial importance to the welfare and common weal of their people. They symbolise a ruler's dynastic responsibility to his subjects, and a promise that the ancient sanctified bloodline will be continued and its purity maintained.

The outward trappings of royal marriages were only half the story – the velvet glove, rather than the iron fist inside – and belied the fact that they could be the ceremonial cover for an unholy and sometimes brutal alliance. Age was not the most important consideration, and a king or lord might be much older than his bride. It was considered beneficial for a husband to be older than his wife, as she would be the more easily subject to his governance, whereas older wives might not take too kindly to it. Children could be betrothed or married in infancy, and the Church permitted conjugal cohabitation at fourteen for boys and twelve for girls, which was when they were considered capable of having intercourse. At least two of the queens in this book were twelve or younger when they married.

Many a young princess had to endure a difficult journey to her bridegroom, knowing she had to bid farewell, perhaps for ever, to her family and homeland, and that she would be joined in marriage to a stranger almost as soon as she arrived. Whatever she felt about him, and however he treated her, she was expected immediately to sleep with him and produce children to secure his succession. Arguably, she was as much a sacrificial victim as any chained virgin in classical mythology.

Matilda had to travel over 150 miles to reach the county of Eu on Normandy's eastern border, where her wedding was to take place. This was an age in which travelling could be challenging. There were no 'carriages'; journeys were made by horse, on foot, or by cart or wagon, a means largely favoured by ladies, although such conveyances were unsprung and uncomfortable. Women also rode on horseback, by which means one could cover twenty to thirty miles a day. Matilda's journey probably took about a week. She was escorted 'with all honour' by her father 'even as far as Eu', and attended by a magnificent train of nobles and ladies.[15]

William, an eager bridegroom, arrived at Eu first, attended by many knights and his mother, Herleva, and stepfather, Herluin, Viscount of Conteville.[16] He lodged at the chateau of Eu[17] as a guest of his cousin, Robert, Count of Eu. The chateau was surrounded by a hunting park and overlooked the River Bresle.[18] Here William received Matilda and Count Baldwin who had brought him rich gifts.[19] A few days later, the marriage was solemnised, either in the cathedral of Notre-Dame d'Eu or in the chapel of the chateau, which was dedicated to the Virgin and still survives today. The ceremony itself took place in strict privacy,[20] probably to pre-empt any objections. The Pope's ban had clearly stung William. 'He married her legally as his wife,' emphasised his chaplain, William of Jumièges, 'with great pomp and much joy and jubilation'.

In 1476, an inventory of all the jewels, ornaments and books preserved in the treasury of Bayeux Cathedral recorded two cloaks of 'incomparable richness', which were described as the wedding garments of William and his bride. Matilda went to her wedding decked out in a rich, cope-like mantle embroidered with jewels and precious stones. William's cloak was adorned with golden crosses, flowers, intaglios, gems and rich embroidery. He wore a helmet, also preserved at Bayeux.

Matilda brought with her a generous dowry: 'her father gave her joyfully to Duke William with a very large store of wealth and very rich apparelment'.[21] Upon marriage, however, William did not dower his bride lavishly: he gave her lands of only moderate value in the Pays-de-Caux, a vast plateau between the English Channel and the River Seine.

After the ceremony, William and Matilda presided over a wedding feast in the chateau. Feasting was the traditional way to celebrate not only weddings, but also the great feasts of the Church – Easter, Whitsun and Christmas – and various holy days. Honoured guests, including Count Baldwin and his wife, would have been seated with the ducal couple at the high table, which was set with a cloth. Servitors carried napkins over their arms and offered wine goblets to the Duke and Duchess. Bread for the table came as flat rolls, decorated with a cross. Fish was served in dishes and meat – kebab-style – on spits, and every dish was shared between two people. Everyone carried a knife that they brought to table for cutting and spearing food, which was then eaten with the fingers, which explains why hands were washed before and after meals; forks were unknown. The company would have been entertained by minstrels, troubadours, jongleurs or mummers. Fools and jesters made jokes, and there might have been dancing. Then the bride and groom would be ceremonially put to bed together by the guests, the priest would bless the bed, and everyone would depart, leaving the couple alone to do their dynastic duty. The public nature of the bedding ceremony reflected the accepted view that the getting of royal heirs was a matter of legitimate common interest.

When the celebrations were over and the guests had dispersed, William conducted his bride and her father 'with the greatest ceremony and honour'[22] to Rouen, his capital. It was 'a populous and wealthy city thronged with merchants, and a meeting place of trade routes – a fair city set among murmuring streams and smiling meadows, abounding in fruit and fish and all manner of produce. It stands surrounded by hills and woods, strongly encircled by walls and ramparts and battlements, and fair to behold with its mansions and houses and churches.'[23]

They made a ceremonial entry so that the new Duchess could be seen and received by William's subjects, who gave themselves over to 'such rejoicing as was beyond description at the entry of his spouse'.[24] The celebrations continued for a fortnight, with the bridal party staying in the tenth-century ducal chateau with its great stone tower, the Tower of Rouen, which appears in the Bayeux Tapestry and was demolished in 1204. From it the new Duchess could see 'the beauty of the country': to the south, 'a beautiful hunting region, wooded and well stocked with beasts of the chase', and the Seine, full of fish, lapping at the city walls, and daily conveying 'ships laden with merchandise of many lands'. On the other side was 'the fair and populous city with its ramparts and churches and town buildings, which has rightly dominated the whole of Normandy from the earliest days'.[25]

Soon afterwards, Matilda's parents and their retinue departed for Flanders, and William took his bride on a leisurely progress through the duchy. Everywhere she was greeted with enthusiasm and tokens of affection. She was the first Duchess of Normandy for fifty years (several earlier dukes having lived with their mistresses) and was warmly welcomed. A household was established for her, headed in turn by her chamberlains.[26] She did not lack for intellectual stimulation, for 'illustrious men excellently versed and learned in letters' were made welcome at the ducal court.[27]

Soon she was to give the people further cause for rejoicing, for it was not long before William was exacting oaths of fealty from his barons to himself and to his heir, as yet unborn.[28]

5

'Illustrious Progeny'

Matilda was at most nineteen when she married, 'a singular mirror of prudence' and 'the perfection of virtue'.[1] She was even 'more distinguished for the purity of her mind and manners than for her illustrious lineage'. Imbued with the piety of her saintly mother, 'she united beauty and gentle breeding with all the graces of Christian holiness'[2] and was 'very comely of person and generous of heart'.[3]

This kind of praise was bestowed on all royal ladies who led virtuous, blameless lives. Monkish chroniclers were usually scathing

about those who strayed or flouted the conventions, so there is
no reason to disbelieve what was written about Matilda, although
other evidence suggests that she had a forceful and spirited personality. Her beauty was extolled unanimously, which, again, was to
be expected, for she was royal. Above all else, her noble birth made
her the 'most beautiful' woman of her age.⁴ In regard to some
royal ladies, the flattery was not as effusive, a clear hint that they
were lacking in looks. But observers stress how fair and graceful
Matilda was,⁵ how 'very elegant of body', and how skilled in
'feminine arts'. She was 'endowed with fairness of face, noble birth,
learning, beauty of character and – what is and ever will be more
worthy of praise – strong faith and fervent love of Christ'.⁶ In
short, she was 'a model of wisdom and exemplar of modesty
without parallel in our time'.⁷

As so often in this period, there is no surviving description of
what she actually looked like – monastic chroniclers rarely gave
specific details. Misconceptions have arisen. It is said that Matilda
commissioned wall paintings of herself, William and their sons, Robert
and William Rufus, for Saint-Étienne's Chapel in the abbey of the
Holy Trinity, which she was to found in Caen. The chapel was
demolished in 1700, but not before a Benedictine monk, Bernard
de Montfaucon, had made drawings of the frescoes.⁸ They are usually
cited as authentic contemporary images, but they look very much
like thirteenth-century work, especially the crowns. The originals
would not have been true portraits anyway; the copy of Matilda's
depicts a crowned woman with dark, straggly shoulder-length hair,
parted in the middle, a long nose and an oval face. A Victorian
engraving based on this forms the frontispiece to Volume 1 of Agnes
Strickland's *Lives of the Queens of England*, but the artist, Henry
Colburn, has made Matilda (and most of the other medieval queens
in the series) look like Queen Victoria, to whom the books were
dedicated. We cannot deduce from these that Matilda was dark-haired
and slender.

A myth has arisen that she was tiny in stature. It was long claimed
that she was just 50" in height. This estimate rested on an examination of her bones in 1819 by Dr Dominel, a surgeon of Caen, before
they were sealed away in a lead box. But in 1959,⁹ a further study
of the remains was made, using more modern anthropological tests.
The skull and other bones were missing, but examination of the
tibia and femur showed that, if this was indeed Matilda, she had
been about 5' tall,¹⁰ not so diminutive when it is considered that

the average height of a man then was about 5'5". The identification cannot be made with certainty, given the desecration of her tomb and others nearby in the sixteenth century; the bones that were retrieved by Abbess Anne de Montmorency may not all have been Matilda's.[11] However, the reconstructed pelvis was wide, which would explain why Matilda managed to present William with ten children, which she probably could not have done had she been just over four feet tall.[12]

Contraception was not an option for Matilda. Like all nobly born ladies, her first duty was to bear male heirs to ensure the ducal (and later the royal) succession and lead her husband's armies in war, as well as daughters who could be given in advantageous alliances. Large families were not uncommon, and childbirth could be almost an annual event, as Matilda would find.

Infant mortality was high, and many mothers had to bear the grief of losing at least one child. Of the ninety-three royal children born to fifteen of England's twenty medieval queens, twenty-seven died in childhood – nearly thirty per cent. This bears sad testimony to the fatal lack of understanding of the process of childbirth, good hygiene and the proper care of infants in medieval times, and to the tragic consequences that could ensue when a child contracted an infection in an age before antibiotics.

There may have been more lost babies than we know of, for children who died in infancy, even royal ones, may not have been recorded. Often the dates of birth of royal offspring have to be estimated, as they were not written down, as is the case with three of the five queens in this book. Often historians have to make educated guesses based on circumstantial evidence, such as the date of the parents' marriage (if known), the seniority of siblings, and other factors.

In order for them to produce as many surviving children as possible, high-born ladies did not normally breastfeed their infants. It was thought worthy of notice that Ida of Lorraine, the grand-mother of Matilda of Boulogne, insisted on suckling her infants, 'fearing lest they be contaminated by perverse morals',[13] which were thought to be transmitted through breast milk.

Matilda 'bore her distinguished husband the offspring he desired, both sons and daughters'.[14] Probably all but one of their 'illustrious progeny'[15] were born in Normandy, but evidence for their dates of birth is sparse. Those born while the Papal ban was in place were illegitimate in the eyes of the Church, bastards like their father. The chroniclers are silent on this, but it may have been a taint that clung.[16]

The eldest son, the heir to whom William had insisted on his nobles swearing allegiance while the babe was still in the womb, was called Robert, after William's father and Matilda's grandfather, Robert II, King of France. In 1054 and 1063 he appears in documents as the heir to both William and Matilda – in the latter as 'Robert, their son, whom they had chosen to govern the realm after their deaths'.[17] The wording of this document reveals that Matilda was already very much a sharer in the ducal power.

William and Matilda's second son was Richard, named after three previous dukes of Normandy. His epitaph describes him as duke of Bernay in Normandy, but he is never called that in written sources or referred to as 'comitas' in contemporary documents.[18] He witnessed charters from 1067. William of Jumièges places his birth around 1055, but he could have been born as late as 1059.[19]

The third son, William, later nicknamed Rufus because of his ruddy face, red beard and equally flaming temper, was born shortly before August 1060; when he died in August 1100, he was above the age of forty.[20] He was the son most like his father and namesake and, accordingly, the Duke's favourite.

It appears that William chose the names of the couple's sons and Matilda the names of their daughters. Her choice reflects her pride in her royal French ancestry,[21] which is evident in her signing herself in charters as 'daughter of Baldwin, Duke [sic] of the Flemings, and niece of Henry, most illustrious King of the French'.[22] Constance was named for Matilda's grandmother, the French Queen, Constance of Arles;[23] Adela was named for Matilda's mother, a princess of France; and Matilda after herself. Adeliza (or Adelida or Adelaide – the names are interchangeable at this date) may have been called after Adelaide of Aquitaine, queen of Hugh Capet, King of France; Queen Adelaide's mother, Adela, had been the daughter of Rollo of Normandy.

There has been much debate about the number and names of the daughters. Orderic Vitalis gives two lists in different books of his *Historia Ecclesia*: Adeliza, Constance, Cecilia and Adela appear on both, but Agatha appears only on the later list. William of Malmesbury also lists five daughters: Cecilia, Constance, Adela and two others whose names had escaped him. William of Jumièges and a later chronicler, Robert of Torigni, both state that there were four daughters. In fact, there were probably six.

None of these chroniclers lists a daughter called Matilda. In 1086–7, at the order of William the Conqueror, the vast Domesday survey of England was carried out, and all the landholdings in the kingdom, and their values, were recorded in what became known as the Domesday Book. The King's daughter Matilda is mentioned in the Domesday Book[24] and in a mortuary roll written for her sister Cecilia in June 1112 by the nuns of Holy Trinity, Caen, in which prayers are requested for Queen Matilda, and Cecilia's sisters, 'Adilidis' (Adeliza), Constance and Matilda, who were all deceased.[25]

It has been suggested that the younger Matilda married a Norman magnate, Walter d'Aincourt,[26] whose wife *was* called Matilda and whose son, William, was described on an inscription on his tomb in Lincoln Cathedral as being 'born of royal stock' and a kinsman of Remigius de Fécamp, Bishop of Lincoln, who was also related to William the Conqueror.[27] William gave Walter d'Aincourt no fewer than fifty-five lordships in Lincolnshire, Yorkshire and other counties. Walter and Matilda were benefactors of St Mary's Abbey, York, and Walter was buried in York Minster. According to the epitaph at Lincoln, his son William died 'while living in fosterage' at the court of William II, in or after 1092, when Lincoln Cathedral was consecrated. These circumstances, and the fact that several of Walter and Matilda's descendants were called William or Matilda, have given rise to the theory that William d'Aincourt's mother was Matilda of Normandy.[28]

The chronological listing of the three sisters in the mortuary roll suggests that Adeliza was the eldest daughter of William and Matilda, born in 1052 or later, and named in honour of Matilda's mother. By all accounts, Constance was the second daughter, born in 1053–5. It is impossible to list the other daughters in any certain order. Cecilia and Agatha probably came after Constance. Cecilia was aged between ten and twelve in June 1066, so was born around 1054–6. Agatha was at least twelve in 1068, so was born in 1056 at the latest. Adela is the youngest in three sources, and was born in 1066–7. It is not known where Matilda fits into this sequence.

Adeliza was 'very beautiful. When she reached the age of marriage, she piously devoted herself to God, and made a holy end under the guardianship' of her father's trusty cousin and liegeman, Roger de Beaumont, a man famed for his wisdom.[29] Thus she must have died before his death in November 1094. The earliest canonical age for marriage or religious profession was twelve. If Adeliza was the eldest daughter, she was born in 1052 or later, and possibly entered religion as early as 1064.

She was probably placed under the guardianship of Roger de Beaumont because she took the veil at the abbey of Saint-Léger-de-Préaux, founded by his father in *c*.1050, and under his patronage. Possibly she was buried in the abbey,[30] although Holy Trinity, Caen, and – less credibly – Bayeux Cathedral have been suggested as her resting place.[31] Roger's own daughter, Aubrey, became abbess at Saint-Léger-de-Préaux, and Matilda, the first Abbess of Queen Matilda's future foundation, Holy Trinity at Caen, came from there. In 1112 the mortuary roll of Matilda, Abbess of Holy Trinity, mentions Adelina, Prioress of Saint-Léger, and Adeliza, a nun there; either could have been William and Matilda's daughter,[32] although she was long dead by then.

Adeliza was almost certainly the royal nun called Adelaide who, around 1071–2, wrote asking Anselm of Aosta, Abbot of Bec (Archbishop of Canterbury from 1093), to send for her use some verses from his work *Flowers of the Psalms* (which is now lost). He made some selections and sent them to her with prayers and a letter, in which he enjoined her: 'Despise with an elevated mind everything that must be given up even while you have it. Strive with a humble mind towards that which alone can blessedly be kept for ever as long as you do not have it.'[33]

Adeliza was clearly of an age to know her own mind, in keeping with her having been born in the early 1050s. The above passage hints that, for all her piety, she still enjoyed wealth and worldly treasures, and was finding difficulty in sacrificing them for a life of piety, which was why Anselm was exhorting her to seek the love of God. Yet taking religious vows was evidently her own choice, not a case of her parents making a decision to dedicate her to God, as they did her sister Cecilia. Adeliza evidently overcame worldly temptations, for 'after her death, the callus found on her knees bore witness to her constancy in prayer'.[34]

A few historians still assert that Matilda had another daughter. Southover (now Lewes) Priory in Sussex was founded by William de Warenne, 1st Earl of Surrey, and his Flemish wife, Gundrada (or Gundred), in 1078–82. A document purporting to be its foundation charter refers to Warenne establishing the priory for the health of 'Queen Matilda, mother of my wife'. Gundrada's tomb inscription, which dates from the twelfth century, records that she was the 'distinguished offspring of dukes and a noble shoot in her own time'. A late-medieval tradition, fostered by the monks of the priory before the Reformation, held that William and Matilda were Gundrada's parents, or that Matilda was her mother.[35] In 1846, the historian Thomas Stapleton argued that, prior to her marriage to William, Matilda had married Gherbod, advocate of the abbey of Saint-Bertin at Saint-Omer, and by him had Gundrada and two sons, Gherbod the Fleming, Earl of Chester, and Frederick of Oosterzele-Scheldewindeke. This, supposedly, was why the Pope had forbidden Matilda's marriage to William in 1049.[36]

Gundrada was indeed the sister of Gherbod,[37] who is described as 'the brother of the Countess Gundred',[38] but her kinship with Frederick is based only on speculation.[39] However, it has long been established that the so-called foundation charter said to have been granted by Warenne dates only from the fifteenth century, and is probably spurious. In the original charter, there is no reference to Gundrada being related to William or Matilda. It is not feasible that Matilda was married to Gherbod before she married William, for many sources refer to her as a maiden. She knew Gundrada, a fellow Fleming – she gave her the manor of Carlton, Cambridgeshire[40] – but there is no contemporary evidence that they were related.

The tradition that was born at Lewes in the fifteenth century probably arose out of a deliberate doctoring of the evidence.[41] If Gundrada had been William's daughter, her epitaph would surely have described her as the offspring of a king; if she had been Matilda's daughter, she could not have been 'the offspring of dukes'. Conclusive evidence that Gundrada was not the child of William and Matilda can be found in a letter from Anselm of Aosta, Archbishop of Canterbury, to their son, Henry I, in which Anselm refused to sanction the marriage of Gundrada's son, William de Warenne, 2nd Earl of Surrey, to a daughter of the King because there was consanguinity in the fourth degree on one side and the sixth degree on the other. Had Gundrada been Henry's half-sister, they would have been related in the first degree.[42]

This was an age of high infant mortality, yet we have no record of any of Matilda's children dying at birth or in infancy, which seems remarkable, unless the loss of any such infants went unrecorded. But each of her children, 'in their day, was subject to mischance'.[43]

As a mother, Matilda 'resembled Martha in her solicitous care'.[44] She was 'most tender towards her children'.[45] The evidence suggests that she had charge of them in their early years, and possibly for longer – Robert, for example, remained with her for most of his childhood and youth.

6

'The Tenderest Regard'

William was proud of his family, and of Matilda, whose 'obedience to her husband and fruitfulness in children excited in his mind the tenderest regard for her',[1] as well it might, for the Norman succession was soon firmly assured. Theirs was a true partnership. Throughout their marriage, emulating the queens of France,[2] Matilda would preside with William over his courts and witness his charters – she witnessed no fewer than a hundred charters issued up to 1066, far more than any other signatory[3] – and he would rely on her to exercise authority in his absence. She also presided with him when he heard lawsuits.

The relationship between the Duke and Duchess seems to have been harmonious from the first. When strangers wed, it was hoped that love would develop after marriage, and indeed it was the duty of a wife to love her husband. Some royal couples did come to love one another; others were hopelessly mismatched, with disastrous consequences; many simply made the best of it. In this case, love seems to have flourished.

Unusually in an age of arranged marriages, and given the promiscuity of his forebears, William 'conducted himself, during many years, in such wise as never to be suspected of any criminal intercourse'.[4] 'He had learnt that marriage vows were holy and respected their sanctity.'[5] Infidelity was tolerated in kings and nobles, but in 1079 he was openly to declare that he had been 'faithful and devoted in his affection', and referred to Matilda as 'she whom I have loved as my own soul'. Matilda, in turn, was devoted to her husband,[6] and faithful, in which William was fortunate, since infidelity on her part could have compromised not only her honour, but also her husband's

bloodline, which was why adultery was regarded as a serious trans-
gression in women. She remained – with one notable lapse – a loyal
and supportive wife and helpmeet throughout her married life.
Undoubtedly she was in William's confidence, and privy to his
counsels, and he grew to trust her and rely on her good sense and
wisdom. Her influence over him was known to be considerable.

There is good evidence that Matilda came to love William. When
he was at Cherbourg, shortly before 1066, when he was about thirty-
eight and she at least four years younger, he became so ill that 'his
life was wholly despaired of and he was laid on the ground, as at
the point of death, and gave the canons of the church the relics
of the saints which he carried in his own chapel'. Relics – body
parts, clothing or mementoes of saints – were objects of veneration
and important aids to devotion, conferring a special sanctity on holy
buildings. It was an act of penitence for a dying person to be laid
flat on the ground, sometimes on a bed of ashes. Lying there, William
vowed that, 'if God and St Mary would raise him from this sickness',
he would establish a house of canons at Coutances Cathedral.[7]

Matilda was distraught. She rode to Coutances, seventy-five miles
south of Cherbourg, and offered 100s. at the altar of the cathedral,
praying 'that God and St Mary might give her back her dearest
husband'. The clergy were astonished to see her with her hair loose
and dishevelled, which also symbolised penitence and even bereavement, and which may have been a measure of her distress. When
William recovered, 'she helped him in her joy to re-establish the
church', and to build another close by the chateau of Coutances.
The charters they granted were witnessed by their sons, Robert and
Richard.[8]

If there were spirited clashes between the couple – both were
proud and opinionated, with formidable personalities – they are not
recorded.[9] However, some monastic writers seem to have relished
recounting tales of William's violence towards Matilda. One
thirteenth-century account described him kicking her in the breast
with his spur, and claimed she had died from the wound,[10] which
was patently untrue, although wife-beating was common in the
Middle Ages, and not seen as incompatible with medieval notions
of conjugal love. It was even thought praiseworthy that a man correct
his erring wife, and the Church itself condoned such punishment,
although in the twelfth century it did take steps to limit the size of
the stick a husband might use for chastisement.

★

Matilda was to spend much of her married life in castles or palaces, where she enjoyed domestic living on a grand scale; at other times she would have resided in smaller places, such as manor houses or hunting lodges. Castles offered not only protection but also splendid royal apartments. The sparse, if precious, belongings listed by kings and queens in their wills testify to the fact that the Normans did not live in a consumer society. Life was often turbulent, and material comforts took second place to security. But the Norman queens did inhabit a world where beauty and luxury were appreciated, and furnishings were opulent and colourful. Such comforts not only made life more pleasant, they proclaimed their owner's wealth, power and status.[11]

There was, however, little privacy, even for the highest in rank. Castle life was largely communal, and focused on the hall, where the Queen presided alone or with the King over business, courts, meals or feasts. Trestle tables were set up and removed as required. The design of the Norman hall was simple – it was a large, lofty chamber. The earliest reference to a screens passage at the end of the hall opposite the dais dates only from the fourteenth century. The walls might have been adorned with embroidered woollen or cloth hangings, or tapestries, an ancient craft that was revived in Poitiers in the eleventh century and quickly gained popularity. Early examples portrayed – crudely, compared to later tapestries – kings, emperors, saints, biblical characters, animals and flowers.

Servants often slept on pallets in the chambers where they performed their duties, and many slept in the hall at night, near the fire on the central hearth, while hunting dogs scavenged for scraps among the rushes that were strewn on the floor. The rushes were sometimes sprinkled with herbs to mask the stench of rotting food and dog piss. Halls would have been smoky, stuffy places, the smoke from the fire rising to a louvre in the roof.

The Queen, like the King, had her own great chamber.[12] The chamber was where royalty lived, and it was the most comfortable and well-appointed room in the castle. If it was situated behind the hall, on the first floor, it was sometimes called a solar. In the chamber the royal family enjoyed a degree of privacy. It would have been quite dark, lit only by arrow slits or narrow windows, torches in wall brackets, oil lamps or candles set into chandeliers, sconces or candlesticks. No royal candlesticks survive from the period, but they would have been of ornate craftsmanship, such as the gold Gloucester Candlestick, dating from 1107–13.[13] Glass was rarely used in this period, even in royal residences. Instead, windows were covered by oiled linen, canvas, wooden shutters or grilles. The lack of light indoors – a great drawback to reading or doing embroidery – was one reason why window seats were built into castle walls.

In the chamber, where the Queen spent much of her time, the walls would have been whitewashed with plaster of Paris or gypsum, painted with murals or patterns, and perhaps hung with tapestries or painted cloths. Furniture was usually made of wood, and consisted of beds, chairs, stools, cupboards and tables.

Beyond the chamber there might have been one or more private rooms, each opening onto the next; the last, and most private, was the bedchamber. Its walls were hung with curtains, and the bed had a canopy 'for the avoiding of flies and spiders'. There are no records of royal beds before the reign of Henry III (1216–72), but the beds of the Norman queens would most likely have had a canopy and curtains to afford privacy and help keep out draughts.

The only other items of furniture in the bedchamber were usually a chair, stools and a bench, placed near the bed, a chest, and a perch for a hawk. Clothing hung from poles or wooden pegs, and body linen was stored in chests.[14] The bed would have been made up with a feather mattress with an attached bolster. A quilted pad of striped cloth would cover this, on which a cushion was placed. Queens probably slept in sheets of muslin or pure linen, beneath a coverlet of cloth or wool lined with fur – a necessity since most people slept naked. There are several manuscript illustrations of kings and queens naked in bed together wearing only their crowns.

We have a rare description of a royal bedchamber, dating from 1107. It belonged to Adela, the daughter of William and Matilda, and was a beautiful hall hung with tapestries of wool, silk, gold and silver. On one wall was the story of the Creation, the Fall of Man, the killing of Abel by Cain and the Flood. Another showed Old Testament history from Noah to Solomon. The hangings on the third wall portrayed the Greek gods and myths, and those on the fourth the ancient Roman kings. Above Adela's bed hung panels of the conquest of England.

The ceiling was colourfully painted as the sky with its constellations, the signs of the zodiac, the stars and the planets. The floor was inlaid with a map of the world as it was known then, showing Asia, Europe and Africa, with their seas, rivers, mountains and cities. Adela's bed was decorated with three groups of allegorical statues: at the head were Philosophy and the liberal arts, or the *quadrivium*:

music, arithmetic, astronomy, geometry; at the foot, the *trivium*: rhetoric, dialectic, and grammar. The third group represented Galen and Hippocrates, the fathers of medicine, with the four humours – blood, yellow bile, black bile and phlegm – that were linked to the four elements, the seasons of the year and various illnesses.[15]

The decoration of the room reflected Adela's intellectual and spiritual interests, fostered under the auspices of her parents, who probably enjoyed a similarly luxurious style of living in their residences. Today, with those that do survive reduced to ruins or bare stone walls, it is hard to imagine the rich colours of murals and hangings, or the quality of the furnishings.

The chapel was an essential part of a Norman royal household. Here, the royal chaplains would celebrate Mass for the King and Queen and their retinue, and perform the offices of the Church. Royal chapels, like St John the Evangelist in the Tower of London – a magnificent survival of Norman, or Romanesque, architecture – may have been furnished with a throne on a dais, facing the high altar, for the King or Queen.

Castles could be chilly, draughty places. Stokers were paid to maintain the fires and braziers, which were allowed only between Michaelmas and Easter. After Easter Sunday, whatever the weather, the hearths – then in the centre of the room – were arrayed with flowers and green rushes.[16]

Garderobes (the commonest contemporary term for latrines or privies) set into the thickness of the walls had wooden seats. The waste was evacuated down a chute to the moat or ditch below, or into a cesspit. Private chambers often boasted a garderobe. The Queen's would probably have been equipped with a niche in the wall for a candle, and a basin or a washstand, called a laver, for washing her hands.

Water came from wells – most castles had them – or from streams, rivers and ponds. When the Queen bathed, she did so in a wooden tub lined with sponges and cloth, prepared by her female attendants. When the King had a bath, the ewerer received 4d. except on the great feasts of the year, which suggests that royalty bathed regularly – although how often is not known. In the early twelfth century King John had eight baths a year. There was a washerwoman to care for the King's linen,[17] and perhaps the Queen's.

In Norman times, the day began early, around 5 a.m., and most people were in bed by nine o'clock. In the early twelfth century, at Henry I's court, the mornings were devoted to state affairs and settling disputes. After dinner there was a midday siesta, and the afternoons were passed in sports, recreation and 'hilarity'.[18] When not engaged on administrative or state business, the Queen probably spent most of her time sewing or doing embroidery with her ladies. She might have played chess, which had been introduced into England by the early eleventh century. Games of dice were also played in the royal chambers, as well as tables (backgammon). Very little music survives from the Norman period, but it was played in halls and castles, as manuscript illustrations testify. They portray a variety of instruments, including horns, pipes, harps, organs, vielles and cymbals. Most music, of course, was performed in church, forming part of the liturgy; some was polyphonic.

The Steward, the Master Dispensers of the Larder and Bread, the Master Butler and the pantler were responsible for providing the royal household with food and wine. Already the royal kitchens were divided into separate offices. There were cooks, scullions and ushers (including an usher of the roasting house), all with their subordinates, as well as slaughterers and serjeants of the kitchen, who received supplies including venison from the royal parks. One cook exclusively served the King's personal servants. In the pantry there were four bakers who prepared a vast supply of 'bakers' loaves', 'superior simnels' and 'salt simnels'. Simnels were buns made of very fine flour, boiled before they were baked. There were about twenty different kinds of bread in the twelfth century, but manchet, made with white flour, and wheaten loaves were eaten by the upper classes. Two meals a day were served at the Norman court – dinner was eaten as early as 9 or 10 a.m., and supper at 5 or 6 p.m. – but food was usually available for the peckish at other times. In Lent and on fast days meat was replaced with fish, which is why there were fishponds at many royal residences, and millers paid dues in eels.

The Normans enjoyed a varied diet, more sophisticated than the food eaten in Saxon England before the Conquest of 1066, which they found too plain. The chief cook in a Norman establishment would keep a pepper mill and a cupboard for aromatic spices – imported at great cost, which was why they were locked up. The Normans ate a lot of meat, game and fowl, and fish, often pickled, on fast days, as well as cheese. Meat might be served in pastry. Vegetables included cabbage, lentils, peas, shelled beans, millet and onions. Favoured drinks were cider, beer, pure wine, unfermented wine, mixed wine, red wine and 'clove-spiced wine for gluttons whose thirst is unquenchable'.[19]

7

'The Piety of Their Princes'

The wrath of God did not descend on the Duke and Duchess for having dared to defy the Pope. Indeed, it seemed that God had blessed the union by making it fruitful. And in 1051, as William later asserted, he learned that a crown was in his sights.

That year, England's King, the half-Norman pious albino Edward the Confessor, son of Ethelred II by Emma of Normandy, was forced to address the problem of the English succession. Until recently he had been in thrall to the powerful family of Godwin, Earl of Wessex, whose daughter Edith he had married. She had borne no children because the saintly Edward loved chastity too much to indulge in marital relations.[1] In 1051 there occurred a dramatic falling-out between Edward and Godwin, and the latter fled into exile with his family, seeking refuge with Matilda's father, Count Baldwin of Flanders. Baldwin was eager to discountenance Edward the Confessor, who was an ally of the Emperor. Earlier that year, Baldwin's half-sister, Matilda's aunt Judith, had married Tostig Godwinson, Godwin's third son, thereby strengthening his connection to the powerful Earl.

Godwin and his family spent the winter in exile at the court of Flanders. This was not the first time Baldwin had granted asylum to the Godwins. Matilda may have met the eldest son, the unsavoury Swein, in 1046, when he had fled to her father's court after seducing and abducting Edgiva, the Abbess of Leominster.

Edward's anger with the Godwins extended to his wife, Queen Edith, whom he banished to a nunnery. It looked as if she might remain there. With no prospect of an heir, there was no clear successor to the English throne. The only candidate of Anglo-Saxon royal blood was the King's nephew, Edward Atheling, 'Atheling' being the Saxon title for a prince or lord. Edward Atheling was the son of Edward's late half-brother, Edmund II 'Ironside', and was living far away in Hungary.

There was a legend – probably invented later with the benefit of hindsight – that, before Duke William's birth, his mother Herleva had had a dream in which she saw a tree growing out of her pregnant body, and the branches of the tree stretching out over Normandy and England. William was to claim that, in 1051, Edward promised him the crown of England on his death, knowing that he would be a strong ruler.

It may have been true. Edward had spent his childhood in Normandy, and later had almost certainly known William as a boy. His court was modelled on the civilised Norman model, and his sympathies were pro-Norman. Edward would have heard that William was 'well worthy' of a crown, 'being a young man of high spirit, who had reached his high dignity by energy and strength of character'.[2] He may have taken into account the fact that William's Duchess was a descendant of King Alfred. Possibly his promise was conveyed to William by his Norman Archbishop of Canterbury, Robert of Jumièges. To show that Edward was intent on keeping that promise, Godwin's son Wulfnoth and grandson Haakon were left with William as hostages.[3]

The law of primogeniture – whereby the eldest son succeeded – had not yet been established in regard to the English royal succession. The right to the crown had been disputed several times in the past century or so. It was often a case of the fittest man getting the prize. In 1016, King Cnut of Denmark had gained the English throne by right of conquest, wresting it from the old Saxon line. In the light of this, William's chances of succeeding looked promising, especially after Edward Atheling died in 1057, leaving a six-year-old boy, Edgar, as his heir. According to the *Anglo-Saxon Chronicle*, King Edward invited William to England in 1051, and confirmed his promise, giving him a ring and a ceremonial sword in token of his good faith.

By 1052, the political situation in Normandy was such as to prove that William's marriage to Matilda had been not only desirable but necessary. South-west of Normandy lay two small feudal counties: Maine, and further south still, Anjou, a strategically important state on the lower Loire, governed by aggressive expansionist rulers. That year, Geoffrey Martel, Count of Anjou, conquered Maine, from which vantage point it looked as if he might overrun Normandy too. France, William's most powerful neighbour, was no longer friendly, for its king, his feudal overlord Henry I, had allied himself with Anjou in a confederacy hostile to Norman interests. The only other strong power in the west was Flanders, so William's alliance with Count Baldwin now assumed a new importance.

England was hostile to Flanders because of the Godwins, but Baldwin's alliance with William counterbalanced that. Their friendship cemented by the bond of marriage, they were ready to deal together with the threats from Anjou and France. Naturally, those two powers had been against William's marriage. But William was not to be intimidated.

Yet still, in the eyes of the Church, he and Matilda were not lawfully wed. Norman chroniclers are silent on the Pope's reaction to their marriage. Leo, intent on crushing the Normans in Italy, was clearly not amenable to lifting the ban. Even so, there appears to have been no enduring rift between William and Rome. After Leo's defeat at Civitate in 1053, relations were cordial, and in 1055, a Papal legate attended a Norman synod at Lisieux. But there were rumblings of ecclesiastical disapproval from some Norman bishops, who reproved William for marrying his 'cousin'.[4]

Among them was Abbot Lanfranc. He had long been William's right-hand man in matters of church reform and ecclesiastical policy, therefore it shocked the Duke to hear, probably in 1053, that Lanfranc had publicly condemned his marriage to Matilda because it had been banned by the Pope, and personally rebuked William for his defiance.

William summoned Lanfranc to his court, where the Abbot made matters worse by administering another rebuke to his glowering Duke, who retaliated by stripping him of his abbacy, ordering him into exile and sending soldiers to sack the abbey of Bec-Hellouin. A saddened Lanfranc prepared to go on a pilgrimage, but no sooner was he on his way than he encountered William, who claimed to have met him by chance on the road. Whatever the circumstances, the meeting resulted in a reconciliation, with Lanfranc agreeing to persuade the Pope to withdraw the ban on the marriage.

Lanfranc may have been engaged in negotiations for the next six years, in which successive popes proved obdurate and refused to back down.[5] During this prolonged conflict, William and Matilda doubt-less suffered great anxiety, for in the eyes of Christendom they were living in mortal sin, and must have been concerned for the safety of their souls. Moreover, the legitimacy of their children, and the security of the Norman succession, remained in question.

Matters were made worse by the behaviour of William's uncle, Mauger, Archbishop of Rouen. He too was baseborn, and had always resented the fact that his illegitimate nephew was Duke of Normandy. 'He treated me with contempt as a bastard,' William remembered in later years.[6] That contempt extended to Matilda. 'In his zeal for the Christian faith, Mauger could not endure that they should riot in the bed of consanguinity.' An irritated William bore with his uncle's troublemaking until 1054 or 1055, when Mauger 'hurled the weapon of excommunication' at the Duke and Duchess.[7] The duchy appears to have been placed under an interdict.[8]

Thoroughly frightened at being cast out from the Church, and all that implied, Matilda complained of Mauger to William.[9] So incensed was the Duke that he appealed to the Pope to lift the sentence of excommunication and demanded that Mauger be removed from his see. The Pontiff agreed, on payment of a fine by William, and, in the presence of the Papal legate, Mauger was deposed at a council at Lisieux and banished to Guernsey, on the grounds that he had been 'devoting himself more often than was right to hunting and cockfighting and spending the treasures of his church on over-lavish hospitality'. But, according to William of Malmesbury, 'some say that there was a secret reason for his deposition. The young man was furious, his wife added her protests, and so (it was said) they had been looking for opportunities to drive from his see the man who had denounced their sin.' William never forgave his uncle, or recalled him.[10]

Leo IX died in 1054; his two successors did not reign for long. In 1058, when Nicholas II overthrew Benedict X and became pope, he recognised the Normans who had defeated Pope Leo as the rulers of southern Italy and Sicily. William now seized his chance. When he heard that Benedict was warring with Nicholas, he offered to dispatch an army to support the latter. He then sent Lanfranc and other envoys to Rome with an earnest plea that the Pope sanction his marriage. He expressed concern that Count Baldwin might make war on Normandy to avenge William's dishonouring of his daughter, instigating a conflict that might engulf their neighbours.

Lanfranc warned the Pope that William was resolved never to abandon Matilda, and that Count Baldwin's pride would not suffer his daughter to be returned to him, since she had children whose legitimacy might be in question. He urged the Pontiff to yield,[11] whereupon Nicholas capitulated, on condition that William and Matilda agreed to found two abbeys in penance for having married without Papal sanction.[12] It was probably at Easter 1059, at the second Lateran Council, that the Pope at last pronounced judgement in William's favour, and granted a retrospective dispensation formally recognising the marriage and the legitimacy of its issue, declaring that, 'if he were to order a divorce, this might cause a serious war between Flanders and Normandy'. A relieved William and Matilda willingly agreed to endow two monasteries, one for men and one for women, 'where monks and nuns should zealously pray for their salvation'.[13]

The Norman chroniclers, reticent as ever, recorded only that, having brought peace to the land, William 'was minded to found an abbey';[14] they were hardly likely to have written that this zealous reforming son of the Church did so as a penance. The foundation charters of the abbeys also omit to mention the penitential reason for their existence.

In fulfilment of their promise, the Duke and Duchess founded two Benedictine abbeys in Caen. William's was the abbey of Saint-Étienne, begun in 1060; by 1063, work on it was so far advanced that Lanfranc was summoned from Bec-Hellouin to become its first Abbot.

Matilda's abbey was dedicated to the Holy Trinity, but became known as the 'Abbaye aux Dames'. It was begun around 1059, under the auspices of an abbess called Matilda, who came from the abbey of Saint-Léger-de-Préaux, where the ducal princess, Adeliza, would become a nun. Duchess Matilda endowed and beautified Holy Trinity with 'earnest care' and a steady stream of lands and 'goodly gifts', among them liturgical vestments, wool and rich fabrics, golden lamp chains adorned with crosses, large candelabras crafted at Saint-Lo, a crown, a sceptre, a chalice, many jewels[15] and an impressive collection of holy relics: splinters of wood from the True Cross and the manger, a piece of bread touched by Christ, some of the Virgin's hair, a finger of St Cecilia, a hair of St Denis, the blood of St George and the preserved bodies of several saints. She assigned to the nuns tithes on wool to fund fuel, lighting and clothing, ploughlands and mills to supply them with flour and grain.[16] In later years, she sent a hooded robe of English work made in Winchester, and English 'animals, bacon and cheeses' to supplement the nuns' diet. Matilda also witnessed twenty of the twenty-one charters granted to both abbeys.[17] Her largesse to Holy Trinity has been estimated to equate to at least £650,000 in today's values.[18]

Architecturally, the two abbeys differ significantly: William's was built on severe, unadorned lines, while Matilda's was elaborately decorated. It has been noted that they may well reflect the contrasting characters and tastes of their founders.[19] They were also symbolic of the ecclesiastical revival in Normandy, and in founding them William and Matilda inspired others. The barons of Normandy were moved 'by the piety of their princes to do likewise, and encouraged each other to undertake similar enterprises for the salvation of their souls'.[20]

In addition to these two magnificent abbeys – which still dominate the skyline of modern Caen, having survived the intervening centuries and wartime bombing (although only the eastern part of Matilda's church now remains) – the Duke and Duchess also founded the church of Saint-Gilles in Caen[21] and four hospitals at Caen, Rouen, Bayeux and Cherbourg, all in penance for their unhallowed union, while in 1060–3 Matilda founded the church of Notre-Dame de Pré at Emandreville, near Rouen, which was soon afterwards recognised as a priory of Bec-Hellouin.[22] In 1076, moved by the plight of the congregation, Matilda gave money for the rebuilding of the church of Notre-Dame de Guibray, which was too small to accommodate them all.[23]

The generous religious benefactions of the Duke and Duchess were not confined to Normandy. They enriched the cathedrals of Chartres and Le Mans, the abbeys of Saint-Denis, near Paris, Saint-Florent de Saumur in Anjou – to which Matilda gave a gold chalice – and Cluny in Burgundy, which received from her a golden liturgical robe so stiff that it could not be folded.[24] The wealthy and influential Order of Cluny held that perpetual prayer was best offered up in an elaborate liturgy and surroundings of breathtaking splendour. At the height of its influence at this time, it boasted 1,200 houses and 10,000 monks, making it the most powerful Order in Europe. It had long enjoyed the patronage of royalty, and the Norman kings and queens would continue to extend favour and largesse.

From 1060, when visiting Caen, the Duke and Duchess would have stayed in the chateau, built of Caen stone by William around that time, but much altered in the centuries since. One of the twelve towers is called the Tour de la Reine Mathilde (Queen Matilda Tower), but it dates only from the thirteenth century. The keep was largely demolished in the French Revolution, and the walls, which trace roughly the circumference of William's outer wall, date from the twelfth to fifteenth centuries. William's ducal palace lay in the north of the chateau precinct, near the main entrance tower (and the present university of Caen). The chateau contained a hall measuring eighteen by six metres, a chamber and a chapel; it was a small royal residence compared with those that William would later build in England.[25]

8

'Without Honour'

In 1063, William conquered Maine and annexed it to Normandy. He betrothed Margaret, sister and designated heiress of the last Count of Maine, to his son Robert, and ordered that she be 'guarded with great honour in safe places'[1] until the pair were of marriageable age. The wedding was never to take place, as Margaret died later that year.

William was now the undisputed and respected lord of a duchy that was at peace and growing prosperous, and a ruler of impressive stature in the eyes of Christendom. Secure and contented in his marriage, with his family increasing steadily, he now had leisure to focus his energies on England. To this enterprise, Matilda was to lend her enthusiastic support.

In 1052, Earl Godwin had raised an army, enlisted English backing, and forced King Edward to receive him back into favour. But he had died suddenly at a royal banquet in 1053, whereupon his oldest son, Harold, had succeeded him as earl of Wessex. With Godwin dead, Harold, a warrior of great renown who was popular both at court and with the English people, had won Edward's favour, and now stood highest in his court. Before long, there was speculation that the King would name Harold his successor. But William had not forgotten Edward's promise that he should have the crown and riches of England.

Soon Matilda was to meet Harold, because – if the Bayeux Tapestry is to be believed, although no contemporary English source mentions the episode – in 1064 fate played into William's hands. On his way to see the Duke to ask for the return of his brother Wulfnoth and his nephew Haakon, who had been hostages at William's court for the past thirteen years,[2] Earl Harold was shipwrecked on the Norman coast, and taken prisoner by Guy, Count of Ponthieu, one of William's vassals.

The Duke commanded that Harold be brought to his court at Eu, where he 'received him with great respect, and fed and clothed him splendidly, according to the custom of his country'.[3] He treated Harold as an honoured guest, feasted with him, hunted with him and bestowed gifts upon him. He even took him skirmishing in Brittany, to demonstrate what a fearsome general he himself was, showing off his 'warlike preparations, so that Harold could see how far Norman swords were superior to English axes'.[4]

Harold soon found that he had exchanged his chains for silken bonds, for the Duke would not allow him to return to England until he had sworn on holy relics that he would do all in his power to help William gain the English throne when King Edward died. Harold had no choice but to agree. He swore the oath either at Bonneville-sur-Touques[5] or Rouen.[6] To cement their pact, William offered Harold the hand of an unnamed daughter of his, 'who was not yet of age', promising the couple 'half the kingdom of England'.[7]

An Icelandic saga, dating from 1230 but based on earlier histories and oral traditions, asserts that, at dinner, Harold was seated on the high seat on one side of William, with Matilda on the other side. William and Harold 'often talked together for amusement at the drinking-table', but the Duke usually went to bed early, leaving Harold and Matilda sitting 'long in the evenings talking together'.[8] It was incumbent upon great ladies to take an interest in the marriages of their children, so if this story is true, Matilda was perhaps discussing Harold's marriage to her daughter. Probably she charmed this 'very tall and handsome' man, who was 'remarkable for his physical strength, his courage and eloquence, his ready jests and acts of valour'.[9]

If we believe the later saga, it was Harold who was seeking the hand of one of William's daughters. According to this source, William was jealous of these late-night chats, and Matilda told Harold, 'The Duke has asked me what it is we have to talk about so much, for he is angry at it.'

Harold explained himself to William. 'I have to inform you, Duke, that there lies more in my visit here than I have let you know. I would ask your daughter in marriage, and have often spoken over this matter with her mother, and she has promised to support my suit with you.'[10] In reality, Harold probably had no choice but to consent to a betrothal.[11]

Confusion as to the princess's identity has arisen from conflicting evidence relating to the betrothals and marriages of the ducal princesses. One unnamed daughter was betrothed in turn to Herbert II, Count of Maine (before 9 March 1062), Harold of Wessex (1064) and a Spanish prince, one of two brothers who fought for her hand.[12] Three chroniclers claimed it was Adeliza who was betrothed to

Harold, and remained single after his death in 1066;[13] more recently, scholars have mistakenly identified Adeliza with a female figure called Aelfgyva, who appears in the Bayeux Tapestry immediately after the scene showing William and Harold in conversation at Rouen.[14] But Adeliza was dedicated to God, so the daughter promised to Harold was probably Agatha. It has been suggested that Orderic invented Agatha or confused her with Adeliza, but the omission of Agatha from his lists of the daughters is probably not significant, as Matilda doesn't appear in either,[15] and in a later book of his history he states that it was Agatha who was betrothed to Harold.

The girl was much taken with the English Earl.[16] She was 'very young' at the time – eight years or thereabouts – and therefore 'it was resolved that the wedding should be deferred for some years'.[17] After Harold jilted her early in 1066, when he married Edith of Mercia, widow of the Welsh King, Gruffydd ap Llewelyn,[18] this devout girl wanted to drown her sorrows in a nunnery.[19] Hearing of Harold's marriage to Edith, William demanded in vain that he honour his betrothal.[20]

Harold did not keep his oath to William either. For all his gifts, he was 'without honour, which is the root of all good'.[21] When the Confessor died on 5 January 1066, and was buried in the newly consecrated Westminster Abbey, which he himself had rebuilt, Harold claimed that he was the late King's chosen successor, appointed by him on his deathbed, and the Witan – the council that advised the Anglo-Saxon kings of England – elected him king. The very next day, he hastened to his coronation.

9
'A Prudent Wife'

When the news of Harold's perfidy was reported to William, he resolved to take England by force and win the throne by right of conquest. This led to a flurry of preparations throughout Normandy, with nobles, clergy, burghers and private citizens contributing ships, horses, men and provisions, each according to his means. On 24 April, Halley's Comet was seen trailing across the sky, 'remaining visible for fifteen days',[1] which was interpreted as a sign of divine approval. 'This portended the transfer of a kingdom,' declared Orderic. Divine approval also came via the Pope, who, angered at Harold's perjury, sent a banner he had blessed, with heartfelt prayers for William's victory; the Pontiff had been pleased to learn of the Duke's resolve to reform the degenerate English Church along Norman lines. Now William could claim that he was fighting a holy war.

On 18 June 1066, although still unfinished, Matilda's new abbey of Holy Trinity at Caen was consecrated by Maurilius, Mauger's successor as archbishop of Rouen, in a lavish ceremony graced by the Duke and Duchess and their three sons, in the presence of four bishops, eight abbots and the flower of Norman society. The abbey would not be completed until 1080,[2] but on that June day, Matilda ratified her generous endowment to her foundation, and she and William bestowed on it an even more precious gift, their daughter Cecilia, a 'girl child'[3] of between ten and twelve years, the latter being the earliest age for entry to the novitiate. She was presented at the altar by her father as an oblate, a child who would be raised in the religious life and in time, when she was of an age to make the choice for herself, enter the novitiate with a view to taking vows as a nun. In 656, a church council at Toledo had ruled that a child had to be at least ten years old before it could be accepted as an oblate. William declared to the congregation that Cecilia was to be dedicated to God, by whose grace he and Matilda had been blessed with so many offspring and other gifts.[4] They may have anticipated that she would one day become abbess of Caen.

Dedicating a daughter to God – the oblation – was then seen as a means of laying up treasure in Heaven, or as an act of thanksgiving. For any feudal lord it involved a degree of sacrifice, because daughters were valuable pawns in the making of advantageous political alliances. But William, of course, had a very pressing reason for giving this child to God. He wanted the crown of England, and needed all the divine help he could get. He and Matilda had already allowed their eldest daughter, Adeliza, to take religious vows, and William doubtless thought that dedicating another daughter would win even greater favour with God and bring the hoped-for blessings.

It has been suggested that it was in 1075, when Cecilia took her final vows, that the French poet Fulcoius of Beauvais wrote a satirical poem comparing the sacrifice of Jephthah's daughter Selia, in return for her father's victory in battle, to William's offering of his daughter

Cecilia – there is a parallel in the names alone – in the hope of taking England.[5] But Fulcoius is far more likely to have written his poem in 1066, because Cecilia was under no obligation to take the veil. When she reached twelve, the age of decision, she could choose to stay in the convent or leave it for the world – which is what she did choose. In the meantime she would be 'brought up and carefully educated' by Abbess Matilda, who was vigorous in enforcing the Rule of St Benedict.[6]

According to Fulcoius, Matilda was deeply unhappy about losing her child to the cloister. In the poem, he has Cecilia refer to herself as the daughter 'of my father and my wholly wretched mother'.[7]

Cecilia was one of about twenty well-born girls dedicated to God that day, for many barons were eager to follow the example of the Duke and Duchess and offer their daughters with rich dowries. Matilda not only gave land to Holy Trinity, she also purchased estates for it and persuaded others to offer gifts.[8] Thus her abbey quickly grew wealthy, and was able to fund watermills, saltworks and the purchase of estates, fishing rights and vineyards.[9]

By midsummer 1066, preparations for the invasion of England were well advanced. Planning for a long absence, William summoned a great assembly of barons and commanded them all to swear homage to his fifteen-year-old son Robert as his heir.[10] Robert, for whom Matilda had a special fondness, and who, for now, always did 'exactly as his father told him',[11] had grown into a stocky adolescent; he would never achieve a commanding stature, prompting his disappointed father to nickname him 'Curthose' in childhood, on account of his short legs. The name stuck. Nevertheless, he was 'already a young man of established prowess and proven courage'.[12] Not yet of an age to rule the duchy in his father's absence, he was to be regent in name only, for in August, at the chateau of Bonneville-sur-Touques, the Duke 'entrusted the duchy of Normandy to both his wife Matilda and his young son Robert, leaving God-fearing bishops and warlike lords to help them'.[13] In so doing William demonstrated the great confidence he had in Matilda, for it was effectively to her that 'the kingdom's wealth and authority' were delegated,[14] and it was she who would act as regent and rule in William's stead.

It was unusual for a woman of rank to have control of her older sons, but at the same time Matilda was made Robert's guardian. 'First in dignity' on the council of regency William appointed to assist her was the ageing Roger de Beaumont,[15] capably assisted (until he went

to England in 1067) by the wise, prudent and learned Roger of
Montgomery, Hugh, Viscount of Avranches, and Ralph of Tancarville,
William's chamberlain, who was to look after the duchy's finances.
All were loyal friends and advisers of the Duke.

By now William had assembled 'an immense army of Normans,
Flemish, French and Bretons'[16] with six thousand horses and his
mighty fleet. William of Jumièges claimed that he had three thousand
ships, but modern historians suggest that the number was between
500 and 750. They were anchored in the sheltered bay at the mouth
of the River Dives. Here, the Duke solemnly invested Matilda with
the regency. In response to Philip I of France, who expressed his
concern about the safety of the duchy, he wrote: 'By the grace of
God, we are blessed with a prudent wife and loving subjects, who
will keep our border securely during our absence.'[17]

Early in September, as William was preparing to depart, he sent
to Flanders to ask for military support in his enterprise. But Count
Baldwin was in France, acting as regent for his nephew, the young
French King. His eldest son, another Baldwin, was not of his
father's mettle, and refused the Duke's request. Angrily William
sent back the retort that Baldwin should expect to receive nothing
in spoils, and reminded him that 'the honour that the Duke seeks
will be for the advantage of your sister and her children, and their
greatness will be the advancement of yourself'. When that failed
to move the younger Baldwin, the messenger left, declaring, 'My
lord will conquer England without your help!' Although Baldwin
did agree to send a force of men, at a price, the hitherto close
bond that had existed between Normandy and Flanders was loos-
ened; and this unpleasant incident presaged a deeper rift to come.

Saddened and mortified though she may have been at the falling-
out, Matilda showed herself cheerful and optimistic. She had secretly
ordered a great longship to be built 'in honour of the Duke'[18] and
fitted out at her expense, and named it the *Mora*. The name may have
derived from the Greek word for a Spartan military force of six
hundred men – the number the ship was built to hold. Matilda's
vessel had striped scarlet sails, painted planking and a gold figurehead
of a carved boy, which was said to resemble her young son William;
she had directed that one hand should hold an ivory horn to its lips,
while the other was to grasp a bow pointing towards England.[19]
Matilda herself was standing at the prow of this fine vessel as it sailed
into the harbour of Dives, much to William's delighted astonishment.[20]
He was so impressed with the *Mora* that he announced she should

be his flagship, the one in which he would lead his great enterprise, and on which he would display the Pope's banner – a gold cross on a silver ground. The *Mora* is depicted in the Bayeux Tapestry, looking slightly different from contemporary descriptions of her, but it is unlikely that the embroiderers had seen the real ship. In gratitude, William promised Matilda the revenues from the county of Kent, when he was in a position to grant them.[21]

By 12 September, William had assembled his fleet at Saint-Valéry at the mouth of the Somme.[22] It was ready to sail, but bad weather delayed its departure. At last, on 27 September, the wind changed, and he gave orders for embarkation. He said farewell to Matilda, asking if he and his companions might have the benefit of her prayers and those of her ladies.[23] She gladly consented, and bade him adieu in good spirits. Then she watched him and his ships sail ever further into the distance, to England, and the hoped-for crown.

10

'The Splendour of the King'

Matilda returned to Rouen and got on with the business of governing Normandy. It was a challenging task, for the Normans, as William himself said, 'when under the rule of a kind but firm master, are a most valiant people. But in other circumstances they bring ruin on themselves by rending each other in pieces. They are eager for rebellion, ripe for tumults, and ready for any sort of crime. They must therefore be restrained by the strong hand of justice.'[1] Seemingly never satisfied, 'they envied their equals and sought to rival their superiors. They plunder their subjects though they defend them from others. They are faithful to their lords, though a slight offence renders them perfidious. They weigh treachery by its chance of success.'[2]

Matilda ruled the turbulent duchy and presided over her viceregal court with great prudence, wisdom, assurance and skill. William of Poitiers conceded that the government was 'carried on smoothly by our lady Matilda, a woman of masculine wisdom', but the fact that there had been no revolts 'must, we think, be attributed primarily to the king himself, whose return they feared'.[3] Yet Matilda's own wise statesmanship was undoubtedly responsible to a degree. She was 'liberal of mind' and gifted with great abilities that equipped her for the task.[4] A statue of her in the Luxembourg Gardens in Paris, by Jean-Jacques Elshoecht, dates only from 1850, but depicts her holding a sword, symbolic of the power she wielded in Normandy.

In the main she acted independently of Robert, confirming grants by herself in William's name.[5] Nevertheless, their association in the regency may well have strengthened the bond between mother and son.[6]

When, in October, she heard of William's victory at Hastings, a jubilant Matilda returned joyful thanks to God, and promptly renamed the priory of Notre-Dame de Pré 'Notre-Dame de Bonnes Nouvelles' – Our Lady of Good News.[7] Over the next weeks, she expressed her gratitude in lavish gifts to religious houses. 'The alms which this princess daily distributed with such zeal brought more succour than I can express to her husband, struggling on the field of battle.'[8] By December, she had begun styling herself 'Queen of England', even though she had not been crowned.[9]

William had left her pregnant. According to the contemporary humanist Godfrey, Archbishop of Rheims, God granted William the victory at Hastings so that the child, Adela, might have 'fully royal blood',[10] so she was probably born soon after 14 October 1066, when he became king of England, and before June 1067. Godfrey went on:

> The Duke's child would rise to become an excellent woman,
> The goddess did not think it sufficient for her to be of ducal status.
> The royal virgin obtained by fate that her father would be a king.
> In order for Adela to be the daughter of a king,
> The Fates allowed the father to establish himself as a king.
> Because the virgin was not allowed to leave the womb,
> Her father owed the kingdom of England to her.[11]

Adela was probably named for her grandmother, Adela, Countess of Flanders.

Hastings did not immediately make William a king. He had to fight for his crown. The Saxons did not give up without a fight: they were a proud people with their own customs and laws, the descendants of Germanic tribes who had crossed to England centuries before and subdued or driven westwards the indigenous Romano-British population. The invading Duke and his followers were the kinfolk of Viking marauders who had subjected England to centuries of raiding and destruction. One prayer of intercession read: 'Free us, oh God, by preserving our bodies and those in our keeping from the cruel Norse people who ravage our realms.' But the Vikings had settled and colonised vast swathes of northern and eastern England, which were known as the Danelaw. For fear of further incursions from Scandinavia, English kings would wield a tax known as Danegeld for the defence of the realm until 1162. Thus the Norman invasion was fiercely resisted.

William was determined to make England his. He seized England's capital, Winchester, and marched on London, leaving a trail of devastation in his wake as he crushed his opponents. In London, the Witan had chosen the child Edgar Atheling as their monarch, since he had a better claim than either William or Harold; but William, by a show of force, overcame their objections, and on Christmas Day 1066, they elected him king. Immediately afterwards, he went to his coronation in Edward the Confessor's newly built Westminster Abbey, then a fine Romanesque church occupying much the same position as the present abbey, which was rebuilt in the thirteenth and fourteenth centuries.[12]

The coronation ceremony has its roots in biblical times and remains one of the oldest institutions of government. The ritual of coronation sets a king or queen apart from the people. It is an investiture with crown and regalia, the symbols of office – and an ordination. The monks of Westminster wanted William to use Edward the Confessor's regalia, which they held in safe keeping. It consisted of a crown, sceptre, rod, chalice, paten, cross and royal robes,[13] and they claimed the Confessor had directed that it be used at all future coronations. But William had already commissioned a new crown for himself, of gold set with precious stones and a circle of pearls, supposedly like that of King Solomon.[14] Like Anglo-Saxon crowns, Norman ones were modelled on examples from antiquity.[15]

He had wanted to wait; he had said that, 'if God granted him the honour' of conquering England, 'he wished for his wife to be crowned with him', but his barons urged him to consolidate his position at once.[16] His coronation, which used the form of service drawn up in 973 by St Dunstan for King Edgar, set a precedent for his successors to be crowned in Westminster Abbey, thus linking them spiritually to the half-Norman Confessor. The singing of the triumphant hymn *Laudes Regiae*, with its Imperial acclamations, harked back to the coronation of the Emperor Charlemagne in 800. It had been sung at the coronations of French kings ever since, and William established a precedent that would be followed at English coronations until the Reformation.[17]

When William was crowned, he was acclaimed in both Norman French and English, so that his new subjects could understand what was happening. But his Norman lords shouted their acclamation so loudly that the soldiers keeping control over the crowds outside the abbey feared that a riot had broken out, and even that William was being assassinated. They set fire to nearby houses in order to make the people take fright and scatter, but several deaths ensued. As smoke filled the abbey and those inside poured out to see what was happening, the frightened bishops hastened to complete the consecration of the new King, who was trembling from head to foot with anger.[18] The English, it was said, never trusted the Normans again.

William returned to Normandy in February 1067, after an absence of five months, and in March was reunited with Matilda and their children, including, perhaps, the newborn Adela, at the abbey of Fécamp near the coast.[19] 'His ship had come home.'[20] It was the tradition of the Norman rulers to hold ceremonial courts at Easter, Christmas and other festivals of the Church, at which they wore their crowns, and at Easter that year, William and Matilda held a magnificent court for the first time together as king and queen, in the great hall of the chateau of Fécamp, and celebrated his victory with much magnificence and the singing of the *Laudes Regiae*.[21] The chateau had been built in the French Carolingian style by William's ancestor, Duke William 'Longsword', in 932, and rebuilt in stone by Dukes Richard I and Richard II.[22]

The King had brought with him Edgar Atheling and two prominent English earls, the brothers Edwin of Mercia and Morcar of Northumbria, who had been enemies of the Godwins. It was at this time that William betrothed one of his daughters to Edwin of Mercia, whose sister Edith had been married to King Harold. It was not Agatha,[23] but could have been Constance, Matilda or even the newly born Adela.

The Normans were surprised to see the English nobles, 'these sons of the north, wearing their hair long', as beautiful as girls. They marvelled at 'the finely woven, gold-encrusted garments of the King and his companions, the vessels of gold and silver. At a great banquet they drank only from such goblets, or from horns of wild oxen decorated with the same metal at both ends. They noted many such things fitting the magnificence of a king, but they recognised that, far more distinguished and memorable than these things, was the splendour of the King himself.'[24]

As William and Matilda made a triumphal progress to Rouen, the whole duchy celebrated, with even the bishops breaking the Lenten fast.[25] It was still 'a time of winter and of the austere Lenten penances. Nevertheless, everywhere celebrations were held as if it were a time of high festival. The sun seemed to shine with the clear brightness of summer. The inhabitants of humble or remote places flocked to the towns or anywhere else where there was a chance of seeing the King. When he entered his metropolitan city of Rouen, old men, boys, matrons and all the citizens came out to see him. They shouted out to welcome his return, so that you could have thought the whole city was cheering. Monks and clerks vied with each other to show the greatest deference at the arrival of their beloved protector.'[26]

On 1 July, William – and probably Matilda – attended the consecration of the Benedictine abbey of Jumièges,[27] one of the great bastions of Norman Church reform. Tradition has it that at this time the King and Queen also visited the abbey of Montvilliers, founded in 685, to see how progress was being made with the construction of a new church, begun in 1065.

A lurid legend, dating from no earlier than the fourteenth century, asserted that, as soon as he arrived in Normandy, William discovered that his finances were in disarray, and sent for his steward, Grimoult de Plessis, whom he had appointed to assist Matilda in the regency, demanding that he account for the shortfall. Grimoult had secretly fallen in love with the Queen, but she had rejected his advances. Now, to pre-empt her accusations, he had his revenge. He blamed her for squandering William's wealth; he also accused her of committing adultery. This gave rise to yet another tale of an enraged William ill-treating Matilda, for he is said to have ordered that she be divested of her robes, tied by her hair to a horse's tail, and dragged naked through the streets of Caen, as the terrified citizens hid themselves behind barred doors. As she suffered this violence, Matilda, chilled to the bone, cried out, 'My God, the cold street!' This is said to have been the origin of the name of the rue Froide – Cold Street. *Le Croix Pleureuse*

(the Crying Cross) in the rue de Falaise marked the spot where Matilda
was supposedly dragged along the street by an enraged William.[28]

After this ordeal, according to the tale, William had her thrown
into a dungeon in the chateau. But then he was plunged into doubts
about her guilt. Disguising himself as a priest, he heard her confession, in which she affirmed her innocence and revealed the truth
about her accuser, whereupon William threw back his hood and
flung himself weeping into her arms.

When Grimoult heard that his villainy was exposed, he fled to
Plessis, but William gathered a posse of horsemen and rode swiftly in
pursuit, seizing him, hanging him by the feet from a tree, and skinning
him alive with a wooden knife. Finding that he was still alive, the
King and his men tied his limbs to four wild horses, who tore him
apart. It was claimed that William made a saddle from Grimoult's skin
and rode on it back to Caen. Later, as penance, he is supposed to have
founded the Chapelle-au-Cornu (the *Corps Nu*, which refers to the
naked body of Grimoult) at Montchauvet. It is now a ruin.[29]

There is no basis to the tale. The real Grimoult de Plessis had
been among those who had defied William at Val-ès-Dunes in 1047.
Imprisoned at Rouen, he had probably been strangled in his dungeon
before being buried in chains as a traitor.

The legend is echoed in a tale from the eighteenth century,
recounted by J. R. Planché in 1874, of how Matilda discovered that
William was betraying her with two novices from the abbey of
Saint-Léger-de-Préaux (where, probably, their daughter Adeliza was
a nun). She sent soldiers to seize the girls, but William drove them
off, slaying or scattering them. When he learned that Matilda had
sent them, he had her dragged at the horse's tail through Caen.[30]

The autumn of 1067 brought tragic news for Matilda. Her father,
Count Baldwin, died on 1 September, and was succeeded by her
brother, now Baldwin VI. 'For all her powerful government and
her resources vast, she was plunged into the deepest affliction by the
death of her father and her mother's bereavement.'[31] Effectively, she
suffered a double loss, for soon after being widowed, the Countess
Adela departed for Rome to be veiled as a nun by Pope Alexander II,
then retired to the Benedictine abbey of Notre-Dame de Messines
near Ypres, which she had founded in 1057 for thirty noble maidens
and twelve canons.

Baldwin's death had serious implications for William. Since 1060
he had been in France acting as regent for the young King

Philip I, and protecting William's interests. Now that he was gone, France's ancient hostility towards Normandy surfaced again.

On 6 December, William sailed back to England from Dieppe. This time Robert Curthose was invested as regent by his father, having been assigned the lordship of the duchy.[32] He was now about sixteen, which was then considered man's estate, and was to be advised by the same counsellors who had supported his mother, while Matilda herself was there to be consulted – for the time being at least, for William intended to have her crowned queen of England as soon as possible. It was probably for this reason that she had not been appointed regent.

In England at this time there was malicious gossip that William had been unfaithful to Matilda. Adelise, the wife of Hugh de Grantmesnil, one of William's barons, had a grudge against the King, and aroused the jealousy of other lordly wives left behind in Normandy by putting about stories that their husbands were committing adultery in England. She even accused William of trying to seduce her.[33] The tale gained currency, with embellishments, and Gytha, the mother of King Harold, gleefully reported it to Sweyn II, King of Denmark, adding that the King had also laid siege to the virtue of a daughter of a canon of Canterbury Cathedral, which led to the girl's furious father, Merleswen, joining an ill-fated rebellion in Kent.[34] Of course, the Saxons had sufficient reason for rebellion without scandalous tales about royal adultery; there was great discontent, for which this story was obviously a gloss.

William of Malmesbury thought it 'folly to believe' those 'who prate about the King's having renounced his former chastity'. He reports a story going the rounds after 1066, which claimed that William had 'wallowed in the embraces of the daughter of a certain priest', and that, when Matilda found out, she was filled with jealous rage and took a bloody and brutal revenge, sending a servant to sever the young woman's hamstrings. 'The Conqueror was so enraged at the barbarous revenge taken by his consort that, on his return to Normandy, he beat her with his bridle so severely that she soon after died.' This was a blatant fabrication. Later versions of the tale have Matilda ordering the girl's jaw to be slit or having her secretly slain.[35] This story, and those others alleging that William was violent towards Matilda, may reflect perceptions that the Queen was something of a firebrand in character,[36] and that the marriage was known to be tempestuous.

According to William Dugdale, writing in the seventeenth century, William took as his mistress Maud, said to have been 'a Saxon princess', although she was in fact the daughter of one Ingelric, founder or benefactor of the collegiate church of St Martin le Grand in London, who was probably a foreign priest. Maud is said to have borne William a son, William Peverell, Lord of Nottingham and Derby, but, despite some wild claims made six or seven hundred years after his death, there is no good evidence that the Conqueror fathered any bastard children. Reliable sources show that he was a faithful husband who had embraced the Church's new teaching that marriage was an exclusive sacrament between man and woman.[37] He honoured his vows, as he honoured Matilda.

11

'Power and Virtue'

Easter 1168 fell on 23 March, and William kept it at Winchester, then the capital city of England; despite being more important commercially because of its advantageous situation on the Thames, London would not replace it as the capital until the late twelfth century. Having firmly – and brutally – established his rule, at least in the south, the King felt that it was safe for Matilda, now perhaps five months into another pregnancy, to be crowned queen of England.

There had been queens in ancient Britain, but English queenship had evolved in Anglo-Saxon times. In the centuries known as the 'Dark Ages' which succeeded the fall of the Roman Empire in the fifth century, Europe was a melting pot in which kingdoms and feudal principalities were forged, often by violence. Nevertheless, the role of kings was sanctified by a religious coronation liturgy that had its roots in biblical times and conferred on monarchs an almost priestly aura and function, setting them apart, through their hallowing with holy oil, from the rest of humankind, and investing them with a wisdom believed to be denied to ordinary mortals.

It is often claimed that, prior to 1066, the Anglo-Saxon kings of England did not have queens. Matilda of Flanders, the wife of

William the Conqueror, is usually credited with being the first queen of England. But that is a myth.

Anglo-Saxon England was comprised of various kingdoms. The most important were successively those of Northumbria, Mercia and Wessex. It wasn't until the tenth century that the country was finally united under one monarch, King Athelstan, of the House of Wessex.

By the middle of the eighth century, queens were being blessed when their husbands were crowned. A hundred years later, the duties of a queen were defined as running the royal household, keeping 'good order for the presentation of the king in dignified splendour' and giving 'annual gifts to the men of the household'.[1] Already the queen was seen as representing the epitome of virtue, and there was an expectation that she would act as a prudent counsellor to her husband and exercise her own authority.[2] She would also, by dressing magnificently and wearing gold and jewels, reflect his exalted status and his wealth.[3]

In the eighth century, a powerful king of Mercia called Offa had married a woman named Cynethryth and made her his Queen. He allowed her to witness charters and had coins struck with her name. She was described as the mistress of the royal household. Other wives of Mercian kings used the title *regina*.

But in the kingdom of Wessex it was a different story. King Alfred's biographer, Asser, Bishop of Sherborne, writing in the late ninth century, stated: 'The West Saxons did not allow the Queen to sit beside the King, nor indeed did they allow her to be called queen, but rather "king's wife". The elders of the land maintain that this disputed, and indeed infamous, custom originated on account of a certain grasping and wicked queen, who did everything she could against her lord and the whole people.'

That queen was Cynethryth's daughter, Eadburh, although her story was probably much embellished over the years. She dominated her husband, King Beorhtric of Wessex. Some called her a tyrant, and it was said that she poisoned men whom Beorhtric liked or trusted. But one day Beorhtric took the poison by mistake, and died. Exit Eadburh with a lot of treasure to France, where the Frankish Emperor Charlemagne gave her the rule of a convent of nuns. She was soon caught in a compromising situation with a lover and was thrown out of the nunnery to live out the rest of her days in poverty in Italy. It's an object lesson in how not to be a queen. 'Not only did she earn hatred for herself, leading to her expulsion from the Queen's throne, but she also brought the same foul stigma on all queens who came after her.'⁴ It was because of Eadburh that the consorts of the kings of Wessex were not called queen.

That changed in 856 when Ethelwulf, King of Wessex, married Judith, daughter of Charles the Bald, King of the Franks, at Verberie, France. Following French custom, Hincmar, Archbishop of Rheims, consecrated her and placed a diadem on her head, and Ethelwulf formally conferred on her the title of queen. Such a ceremony was not customary to him or his people,⁵ or indeed in Europe prior to the ninth century.

The wife of Ethelwulf's son, Ethelred I, was referred to in a charter as 'Wulfthryth Regina'. By then the Saxon word *cwen* meant not only the King's wife, but also a female ruler or queen. Wulfthryth and her successors – the title *regina* was still being used in the late tenth century – are shadowy figures who may not have been accorded the honour of coronation, but that changed in 973, when Elfrida, the wife of King Edgar, became the first woman known to have been crowned queen in England. Thereafter, with very few exceptions, the wife of the King of England automatically became queen.

Emma of Normandy's colourful career shows that English queens in the first half of the eleventh century could and did wield significant political power, which set a precedent for the future. There are similarities between Anglo-Saxon and Norman queenship, suggesting that Emma's example was remembered, as was the piety and erudition of the Confessor's Queen, Edith of Wessex, and that there was continuity in many aspects of it after the Conquest of 1066.⁶

William dispatched many high-ranking lords to escort Matilda to England. She 'quickly obeyed her husband's commands with a willing mind'.⁷ Leaving Robert Curthose as regent, she crossed the Channel⁸ in the company of her son Richard; her chaplain, Guy, Bishop of Amiens, the most distinguished of the clergy at her court, who – possibly at her request⁹ – had written 'Carmen de Hastingae Proelio' (or 'The Song of the Battle of Hastings'), a laudatory poem about the Conquest that compares William to Julius Caesar;¹⁰ and (probably) Hugh, Bishop of Lisieux, with a host of learned clerks and a great train of knights and noble ladies.¹¹ Soon after Easter,¹² she landed at Dover, where William was waiting to welcome her, with a great company of nobles. Together they rode to London.

As the royal procession passed, the Saxons came running to see 'the strange [i.e. foreign] woman' who was to be crowned their

Queen. It is understandable that they found Matilda strange. Their native kings had usually married English women from powerful families. From now on, they would have to accustom themselves to seeing their Norman invaders bring into England queens from European kingdoms and feudal states. Few may have realised that Matilda was descended from their own Alfred the Great, and that royal Saxon blood ran in her veins.

Matilda probably thought the Saxons strange too. 'They had their hair cropped, their beards shaven, their arms laden with gold bracelets, their skin adorned with punctured designs. They were accustomed to eat until they were surfeited, and to drink till they were sick.' They wore their moustaches 'formidably long and turned up at the ends'. This must have seemed alien to one now used to living among the Normans, who, 'being a race inured to war, were proudly apparelled, delicate in their food, but not at all gluttonous', and 'liked to live in large edifices, but with economy'.[13]

William brought Matilda to the palace of Westminster, which had been built by Edward the Confessor by the River Thames, facing the great Benedictine abbey dedicated to St Peter, which he had also rebuilt, and which had been consecrated in 1065. Here Matilda was to be crowned.[14] It was claimed in her day that it was on the shore at Westminster that King Cnut was said to have demonstrated to his courtiers that he could not command the tide, which has led some historians to suggest that there had been an earlier royal residence on the site, but there is no evidence for it.

Both palace and abbey stood on marshy ground known as Thorney Island. 'It was a delightful spot, surrounded with fertile lands and green fields, and near the main channel of the river, which bore abundant merchandise of every kind for sale from the whole world to the town on its banks.'[15] If the Bayeux Tapestry's depiction of the palace is accurate, which is by no means certain, it was a single large building with the royal apartments above the hall. It was fortified and surrounded by a moat. It soon became the chief royal residence, and William was to enlarge it.

He and Matilda kept a great court at Westminster that Whitsun, at which their son Richard and many leading Norman and English lords, both spiritual and temporal, were present. Among them were the King's half-brothers (his mother's sons by her second husband), Robert, Count of Mortain, and Odo, Bishop of Bayeux; Roger of Montgomery; Robert, Count of Eu; Geoffrey, Bishop of Coutances; and the foremost English earls, Edwin of Mercia and Morcar of

Northumbria.[16] It was William who established in England the custom of holding crown-wearings at Christmas, Easter and Whitsuntide, which, when he was not overseas, he usually kept at Gloucester, Winchester and Westminster respectively, hosting great gatherings of his magnates. 'All the great men of England were assembled about him: archbishops, bishops, abbots, earls, thanes, and knights.'[17] It was at one of these ceremonies that 'a silly cleric', seeing the King pass by majestically in his crown and royal robes, exclaimed, 'Behold, I see God!' – and earned himself a rebuke from Archbishop Lanfranc and a flogging.[18]

As with kings, the anointing of a queen consort with holy oil conferred on her an almost holy sanctity. From 973 there had been provision for queens consort to be crowned with their husbands, but Matilda was the first to have a separate coronation. William may have intended it as the first great state celebration of his reign, since his own coronation had been hurried and marred by the riot at Westminster.

He spared no expense on Matilda's crowning, which took place on Whitsunday, 11 May 1068, in Westminster Abbey. The abbey was packed with nobles and guests, who watched the Queen arrive, escorted by Norman lords. It was fitting that, in this, the foremost royal church of the Anglo-Saxons, William arrived wearing his own crown, which the Norman kings did only at great ceremonies or important feast days of the Church.

There is no detailed description of the coronation of an English queen prior to 1236.[19] The *ordo*, or form of service, used for Matilda's coronation had originally been devised by St Dunstan for that of King Edgar's Queen, Elfrida, in 973. It provided for a queen consort to be consecrated immediately after her husband and 'adorned with the ring for the integrity of her faith, and with a crown for the glory of eternity'. She was almost certainly given a sceptre too. Matilda is recorded as owning one and they appear on the seals of queens from 1118 onwards.[20]

When Cnut and Emma of Normandy were crowned in 1017, the *ordo* had been changed, making Emma a partner in her husband's rule, as Imperial consort and peace-weaver.[21] Between 1066 and 1200, the service was again altered to conform to the European model used for the crowning of the Roman Emperor. It is not known for certain whether Matilda entered the church to be blessed and greeted by a prayer asking that she might 'obtain the crown that is next unto virginity', or whether she and her crown were blessed as she knelt at the altar before the anointing and crowning,[22] but the hymn *Laudes Regiae* was sung in her honour, which suggests that the new form of service was already in use. If so, Matilda would have been hallowed by holy oil as a sharer in the royal dominion.

This revised service defined medieval queenship as a role in which a queen was the helpmeet of her husband, a model of virtue through her symbolic virginity, a guardian and fosterer of religious faith, and a benefactor of the Church.[23] In a departure from precedent, the words of the *Laudes Regiae* proclaimed that the Queen was 'placed by God among the people' and shared royal power; and that the English people were 'blessed to be ruled by the power and virtue of the Queen'.[24] Female saints were omitted from the *Laudes*, in favour of male patrons.[25] It was almost as if Matilda was a queen regnant, masculinised as an honorary man.[26] She shared the King's power in a very real sense, set apart − like him − from ordinary mortals by her hallowing, and exercising his authority both in concert with him and in his absence.

Ealdred, Archbishop of York, placed the consort's crown on her head.[27] It was probably made for her, as there was no medieval tradition in England of the consort's crown being handed down from queen to queen. Sadly, like the rest of the early English regalia, it was probably lost in 1216 with King John's baggage train, which was swept away by the tide in the Lincolnshire estuary known as the Wash.

When the long rite was over, English nobles − as was thought fitting − conducted the Queen out of the abbey to the palace. Here a lavish banquet was held, during which one of the King's knights, Robert de Marmion, rode his horse into the hall and cried three times: 'If any person denies that our most gracious sovereign, King William, and his spouse Matilda are king and queen of England, he is a false-hearted traitor and a liar; and here I, as champion, do challenge him to single combat.' Thus was established the custom of the King's Champion inviting all comers to challenge the right of the King at subsequent coronations. For his good service, Marmion was rewarded with the hereditary office of Champion and estates in England and Normandy.

He was not the only one to benefit from that day. The royal cook, Tezelin, had prepared such an excellent dish − there are various versions of the story, but it appears to have been a *dillegrout*, a white pottage or soup made with capons, almond milk, sugar and spices

– that the King gave him the manor of Addington, Surrey, declaring that henceforth the lords of Addington would prepare the dish for future coronation banquets, or once during the reign of each successive king.[28]

Matilda's coronation had enhanced not only her own prestige and influence, but also that of her children, and strengthened their right to the succession; it also marked the beginning of a new era of female influence. Not for centuries had a woman been so honoured in England. 'The Queen adorned the King, the King the Queen.'[29]

12

'In Queenly Purple'

The Queen of England occupied a powerful and socially desirable position. Her status was reflected in every aspect of the ritual and ceremonial that surrounded her and governed her life; and she would have been aware of the weight of responsibility that brought with it. A queen had to be the embodiment of piety, beyond reproach morally, the guardian of the royal bloodline, a gentle and moderate mediator in the conflicts of men and a helpmeet to her husband. Her virtue was exemplified by her chastity and humility, her charity and her acts of mercy. People looked to her as 'a kind mother, from whom no one goes away empty-handed'.[1]

A queen had to negotiate the political institution that was the court, which might mean subsuming her private loyalties to her duty to the King her husband. She was a fount of patronage to the Church and to scholars and artists. It was her duty to love her husband, and to play a subordinate role to him. She had to forge good relations with his relatives, his ministers and his household officers. Sometimes she had to be a regent, an administrator, a lawgiver and an intercessor.

Queens consort might find their loyalties torn in different ways. They served as political and cultural links between their blood family and the dynasty into which they had married. They were dynasts in their own right. In the field of family politics, in a world in which royalty and the nobility were closely interrelated, they were influential regardless of how much political power they actually exercised. The impact of this international networking should not be underestimated. However, as the administration of government became more insti-tutionalised in the early twelfth century, and power devolved away from family politics, the influence of queens began to decline.[2] This trend would not have a great impact on English queenship until after the Norman period. For all her towering reputation, Eleanor of Aquitaine, the first Plantagenet queen, who lived from 1122 to 1204, did not enjoy the power wielded by her predecessors.

Indeed, it could be said that, with dominions straddling the English Channel, the Norman kings could not have ruled as successfully as they did without the support of their queens, who helped to enforce their authority and administration in England and Normandy, disparate territories with their own racial and cultural differences. Naturally, this authority was reinforced by the Norman aristocracy, most of whom held, or would acquire, lands in England as well. It is worth pointing out that, for a long time to come, the English and the Normans were regarded – and regarded themselves – as two distinct peoples, and their territories were ruled and perceived as separate entities.

Queens were allocated their own income, paid from revenues from the estates they were assigned by the King as dower; the income from these estates, in which the Queen had a life interest, would support her and her children in the event of her widowhood. There are very few records of the financial affairs of the Norman queens. Their husbands had overall control of their finances, with the Queen's treasurer being accountable to the Exchequer, but queens consort were wealthy women in their own right, with greater landed estates than most magnates, and could choose how to bestow their patronage and which charitable ventures they pursued, which made them enormously influential. They promoted culture, art and learning. Queens were not just about family and dynasty – they were exem-plars of Christianity too, and the rituals of civilised living. The pres-ence of a queen at court generally called for higher standards in dress, manners and behaviour.

Few people in Norman times were ignorant of the story of Eve, who disobeyed God by tempting Adam, and so brought about the Fall of Man. Thanks to Eve, women were seen to be weak and foolish – but they also had power and might use it unwisely. The late eleventh and early twelfth centuries, however, saw a remarkable improvement in perceptions of women, with the spread of the cult of the Virgin

Mary from the East to western Europe. This was due to various factors: returning crusaders, the preaching of great theologians like St Bernard of Clairvaux, and the adoption of Mary by the new monastic Cistercian Order as their patron saint, although the dedication of many churches to Mary in eleventh-century Normandy shows that the mother of Jesus was already widely venerated there, as she had in fact been for centuries in the West. The cult was fostered by churchmen close to Henry I,[3] who reigned from 1100 to 1135. As Mary came to be worshipped more widely for her virginal, maternal and wifely purity, and as the Queen of Heaven, so women who personified the Marian virtues were revered by society generally, and queens themselves, her earthly counterparts, began to be seen as the idealised mirror of the Virgin Mary, and to be invested with symbolic virginity. It has been suggested that queens came to be regarded as the earthly personification of the Virgin, just as kings were seen as vicars of Christ.[4] Expectations of queenliness were therefore almost supernaturally high.

It was seen as incumbent on a wife – and still more on a queen – to encourage her husband to patronise religious institutions and be charitable. In this period, every queen was a benefactress of the Church in one way or another, and most laid up treasure in Heaven for themselves or their loved ones by founding or endowing religious houses. In so doing, they not only sought the protection of the saints to whom these houses were dedicated, but also placed themselves at the forefront of the new monastic movements that dominated the age. Some queens became involved in debates about the burning spiritual issues of the day. All were expected to be the epitome of holy virtue. Wealth was deemed a privilege, and those who had it were expected to share it as alms with those less fortunate than themselves, thereby obtaining some spiritual benefit, since charity was an act of contrition that freed one from sin. Thus queens set aside money for their charities. They aided the poor and the sick, made offerings at shrines, and endowed or founded churches, religious houses and hospitals.

Queens were the gentler face of monarchy, exercising a civilising influence on their husbands, protecting their joint interests, taking compassion on the poor, the sick, widows, orphans and those in prison. They were applauded when they used their feminine influence to intercede with the King in favour of those facing a harsh fate, thus enabling him to rescind a decision without losing face. Many instances of queens using their influence probably went largely unrecorded, for a queen enjoyed a unique advantage over other petitioners due to her intimate relationship with the King. If she interceded with her husband it was usually in private, so it can be hard to assess the extent of it. The medieval ideal of queenship constrained her to a role that was essentially decorous, symbolic and dynastic. She was to be beautiful – officially, even if not in actuality – devout, fertile and kind: the traditional good queen.

As queen, as she had been as duchess, Matilda was 'munificent and liberal of her gifts. She exceeded all commendations and won the love of all hearts.'[5] Many spoke of her great abilities. She heard Mass daily, was the 'true friend' of piety, and gave lavishly to many religious houses. There are numerous references to her charity to the poor and the sick. Frequently she relieved them with 'bounteous alms, in the name of her Redeemer'. 'While the victorious arms of her illustrious spouse subdued all things before him, she was indefatigable at alleviating distress in every shape, and redoubled her alms.'[6]

In England, as in Normandy, Matilda heard pleas with William and gave judgement jointly. He authorised her to hear lawsuits over land disputes in his stead. Domesday Book mentions several such cases, as when a dispossessed thane, Aeldred, proved his right to the manor of Compton 'before the Queen, after the King crossed the sea', or when Wulfstan, Bishop of Worcester, established his claim to a manor. In the early 1080s, Matilda confirmed that, at her request, the King's friend Osbern FitzOsbern, Bishop of Exeter, had given to Giso, Bishop of Wells, the church of Wedmore, Somerset, with all its appurtenances, to which he had often laid claim, for it had originally been granted to his diocese by Edward the Confessor.[7]

One unnamed English woman had such confidence in Matilda's power that she made over her estate in Surrey to the Queen in exchange for her protection.[8] Matilda witnessed numerous royal charters, mostly in Normandy, some jointly with William, in which she was designated '*regina Anglorum et comitissa Normannorum et Cenomannorum*' (Queen of England and Countess of Normandy and Maine); one attests to an agreement made before the Queen at Bayeux by the Abbot of Mont Saint-Michel in Normandy and William Paynel. In charters Matilda's name appears immediately below William's, taking precedence over their sons.[9] Neither she nor William could write. 'The King marked it, so did the Queen and their sons.' Matilda signed herself with a fine-calligraphy Jerusalem cross.

In 1079, Matilda and William were holding court at the palace of Sées when Earl Roger of Montgomery complained that Robert, Bishop of Sées, had excommunicated the priory of Bellême 'without cause'. The King and Queen both asked about the circumstances, and Earl Roger and the monks explained that 'no archbishop or bishop had possessed any rights in the priory or any power to excommunicate in it'. William and Matilda ordered John of Avranches, Archbishop of Rouen, to censure the Bishop.[10]

A thirteenth-century statue of Matilda survives on the west front of Croyland Abbey, Lincolnshire, of which she was a patron and benefactress. She appears (with Abbot Serlo) in modern stained glass in Gloucester Cathedral and in the south transept of Selby Abbey, Yorkshire, in a window made by the firm Ward and Hughes in 1909. It has been claimed that her likeness can be seen on a stone capital in Holy Trinity, Caen, but there is no evidence to substantiate this.[11]

Matilda brought Flemish artisans into England and encouraged them to teach their crafts and trades to the English. Her cultural interests were broad. She encouraged architects to come from the Continent, and gave them her patronage. She was also a great patron of painters, sculptors, poets, chroniclers and those skilled with the needle. She employed English seamstresses, among them 'Aelfgyth the Maid' and Leviet, the widow of Leofgyth, who 'made the gold fringe for the King and Queen'.[12] From bequests of clothing in her will, it is clear that Matilda admired the famed English art of embroidery – the *'opus Anglicanum'*.

At the Christmas, Easter and Whitsun courts, Matilda 'dressed in queenly purple, in a prosperous condition, with sceptre and crown'.[13] Female attendants – her damsels, or maidens of gentle birth – helped her to dress in the mornings or for special occasions. The duties of chamber maids were to knit or unknit silk thread, make knots of orphrys (gold lace), sew linen garments and woollen clothes, and do any mending. They were often given gloves with the fingertips removed, leather thimbles to protect their fingers, scissors, needles of various sizes and spools of thread. They were supposed to have faces that would 'charm and render tranquil the chamber'.[14]

From early Norman times, merchants brought to London examples of fashions and headwear from Paris, and rich silks from Italy, the Mediterranean or the Byzantine Empire.[15] Surviving depictions of dress in early Norman times are often crude. Many derive from the Bayeux Tapestry, in which few women appear. Both sexes dressed similarly, wearing long-sleeved tunics, or gowns, of silk, wool or linen, which in this period hung to the knee; later, the hemlines of women's tunics became floor-length. Tunics were sometimes adorned with bands of exquisite English embroidery, a fashion adopted early in his reign by William the Conqueror. Later, brooches called 'fermails' or 'agrafes' were worn to fasten the split neckline of the tunic. Throughout the Norman period, women wore girdles around the waist, knotted in front with the ends hanging down.

Beneath the tunic, a woman would wear a sleeveless undergown of rich fabric, and beneath that a floor-length, long-sleeved chemise, or undertunic, of fine wool, fine linen (chainsil) or silk. Sometimes a surcoat, or 'chlamys', with shorter sleeves, or a sleeveless pelisse lined with fur – ermine for royalty – was worn over the tunic; the surcoat too could be embroidered around the neckline and cuffs. Hair was usually styled in the Byzantine fashion, parted in the centre, then braided in one or two plaits.

Dress was generally modest: ladies were usually clothed from neck to feet, with long sleeves to the wrist. Married women covered their hair with a *couvrechef*, or veil, of soft, lightweight material, such as linen or cambric. One end was often draped over the opposite shoulder.

Outdoors, or on ceremonial occasions, queens wore semicircular mantles with rich borders, sometimes embroidered in gold and lined with a contrasting colour or fur. The mantle was fastened on the shoulder, or across the collarbone, with cords attached to large gold agrafes. Mantles kept out the cold or lent status.

Great ladies wore many jewels, including ropes of pearls, probably imported from Venice. Eleventh-century jewellery could be of highly intricate craftsmanship, as the Townley Jewel in the British Museum bears witness. The Norman queens, like their husbands, kept their jewellery in their bedchambers, not in the treasury at Winchester; it travelled with them, ready for when they wanted to wear it. Jewellery consisted mainly of brooches, agrafes, rings, girdles, circlets and crowns. They were made of gold and silver, and set with precious stones and enamels.

An inventory of the robes and jewels of Matilda of Flanders is preserved in the library of the abbey of the Holy Trinity at Caen. The Queen owned forty-two gowns or tunics, some richly embroidered in silk, wool or thread. She had fourteen pairs of shoes; six had heels, and five were embroidered with gold thread. Her five mantles were of various colours, some lavishly bordered, and probably lined, with ermine. Her cloak, beautifully embroidered, hung from her shoulders like a long train. She had ten warm undershirts, eighteen veils and several girdles decorated with gold and beads.

Matilda of Flanders did not own a large collection of jewellery, but the pieces she had were costly. She possessed just one crown.

13
'Sword and Fire'

After her coronation, Matilda stayed in England for some months. It was probably in 1068 that she had to say farewell to her daughter Agatha, who was sought in marriage at this time by two Spanish kings,[1] the brothers Alfonso VI, King of León, and Sancho II, King of Castile.[2] 'A bitter quarrel arose between them on her account for, far from being unworthy, she was in every way worthy of such a parent, and shone with such virtues and such zeal.'[3] Alfonso emerged victorious, and Agatha was 'delivered to his proxies to be conducted to him'. Spanish historians call her Agueda and date her proxy marriage to 1068.

Agatha was a reluctant bride. Her heart had been given to Harold. 'But she, she who had not enjoyed union with her first betrothed, shrank with loathing from a second marriage. The Englishman she had seen and loved, but the Spaniard she was more averse to because she had never set eyes on him. She therefore fervently prayed to the Almighty that she might never be carried into Spain, but that He would rather take her to Himself. Her prayers were heard, and she died a virgin while she was en route. Her corpse was brought back by her attendants to her native country, and interred in Bayeux Cathedral. Mercifully God released her from this odious contract.'[4] She must have died before 1069, when Alfonso married Agnes of Aquitaine, but she is not listed in Bayeux Cathedral's mortuary roll of 1113.[5] Possibly the account above is incorrect and she had been buried elsewhere.

Agatha's grieving mother and father may well have shared the sentiments of a contemporary Byzantine historian, Michael Psellus, whose oration on the death of his daughter proves that, even in an age of high infant mortality, the death of a child was mourned no less than it is now: 'O my child, formerly so beautiful and now a frightful sight to see! Go then on that good eternal journey and rest in those heavenly places. Reveal yourself in our dreams as you were prior to your illness, bringing solace to our hearts. You will thus bring joy to your parents, and they may recover a little from this heavy sorrow. Nothing is stronger than Nature; nor is there anything more calamitous than the loss of a child.'[6]

The turbulent year of 1068 saw William battling to consolidate his rule. The Saxon earls, Edwin and Morcar, and the people of the north were gathering, determined to make a stand against his governance. One of their grievances was William's failure to marry his daughter to Edwin, Earl of Mercia. Having heeded 'the dishonest counsels of his envious and greedy Norman followers', the King had 'withheld the maiden from the noble youth'[7] – who was in fact about forty. Not long after the coronation, Edwin rebelled against him. In the summer of 1068, the King rode north to Nottingham, where he built a castle, and then to York, where he built two.[8] Others followed. 'The King surveyed the less fortified places of his realm, and to meet the danger he had powerful strongholds built at strategic sites, which he entrusted to excellent military garrisons and large numbers of mercenaries.'[9]

Despite the risks to her safety, the pregnant Matilda is said by a late source to have travelled two hundred miles to the unsubdued and resistant north, 'to enjoy her husband's company'.[10] Tradition has it that their fourth son, probably their last child, was born at Selby, fourteen miles south of York, in September 1068,[11] although he was perhaps born in early December.[12] He was named after Matilda's uncle, Henry I, King of France, suggesting that the name was her choice, for she was proud of her royal Capetian blood, whereas William hated King Henry.[13]

There is no contemporary evidence for Henry being born in Selby, although it may be significant that his first wife gave gifts to the abbey. It seems strange that William permitted Matilda to venture into the unsettled north in an advanced state of pregnancy, although he may have felt that the birth of a prince there might inspire loyalty.[14] Probably he had kept Matilda in England so that their child could be born there, perhaps in York itself, but Matilda's labour may have begun too soon for that, and they had to divert.

It is highly unlikely that Henry was born in Selby Abbey, as is sometimes asserted, for the abbey's foundation charter was not granted

by William and Matilda until 1069.[15] The only monastery they
co-founded, it was built by a French monk, Benedict of Auxerre,
the founder of Battle Abbey, who had been inspired by a vision to
establish a monastery at Selby, on which work began in 1069. In the
eighteenth century, a painted chamber in the abbey, hitherto pointed
out to visitors as Henry's birthplace, was shown to be no older than
the sixteenth century. One local tradition has it that Henry was born
in a wooden church by the river at Church Hill, Selby. A modern
stained-glass window in Selby Abbey shows the infant Henry lying
in his cradle at the feet of Matilda; another depicts William, Matilda
and Abbot Benedict.

Certainly Matilda gave birth to Henry in England;[16] and he was
'the only one of William's sons born in royalty'.[17] Many considered
that Henry was the true heir to England by right of being born in
the kingdom. For all that, he was a younger son who would need
to be provided for, so Matilda made a settlement whereby all her
lands in England and Normandy would pass to him on her death.
Thus he had 'his father's blessing and his mother's inheritance'.[18]

After forcing the submission of Edwin and Morcar, William moved
south via Lincoln, Huntingdon and Cambridge, presumably with
Matilda.[19]

One of those who had witnessed a royal charter granted at the
Westminster court at Whitsun 1068 was Brihtric Meaw.[20] Hell, to
paraphrase the seventeenth-century playwright William Congreve,
hath no fury like a woman scorned. The story goes that Matilda had
not forgotten that long-ago rejection by Brihtric, and now she was
in a position to pay him back for insulting her.

It was customary for the King of England to make financial provision for his Queen, assigning her lands from which rents and dues
would provide her with an income. But the lands assigned to Queen
Edith were still in her hands,[21] and could not be given to Matilda.

Brihtric's extensive lands were in a region where King Harold's
mother, Gytha, wielded territorial influence, herself owning estates
in Devon, Somerset and Cornwall. Gytha and her followers were
now entrenched at Exeter,[22] and a focus for those who opposed
Norman rule, and William possibly feared that they would rise against
him in favour of Harold's dispossessed sons. In the autumn of 1068,
incensed because the citizens of Exeter, incited by Gytha's party,
refused to acknowledge him as king or pay taxes, William took the
city after a siege of eighteen days, forcing Gytha to flee.[23]

In the wake of the siege, members of the old royal house scattered. Gytha sailed to Flanders with Queen Edith, while Edgar Atheling fled abroad with his sisters, Margaret and Christina, and their mother, Agatha of Hungary, a kinswoman of the Roman Emperor, and were blown by a tempest to Scotland, where King Malcolm III married Margaret and made her his Queen.[24]

Given that his landholdings and interests were in the west, Brihtric Meaw may well have defected to Gytha after Matilda's coronation. It was later said that the Queen stirred up the King's wrath against him and persuaded William to confiscate his lands and grant them to her as her settlement, but probably William needed very little persuading, which suggests that he had evidence of Brihtric's treason. Certainly he granted her Brihtric's estates, making her very 'wealthy and powerful'[25] and enabling her to spread her patronage wide. Domesday Book confirms that Avening, Tewkesbury, Fairford, Thornbury, Whitenhurst and other possessions spread out between Cornwall and Winchester, formerly the property of Brihtric, son of Algar, had been granted to the Queen.[26]

William's vengeance did not end there. Brihtric's city of Gloucester was stripped of its charter and liberties, and he himself was 'seized by the King's order' at his manor of Hanley, Worcestershire, and conveyed to Winchester, where he died a prisoner. The loyal William FitzOsbern, a son of William's former guardian, Osbern the Steward (who had been murdered trying to protect the child William from assassins), was tasked with seizing and despoiling other property owned by Brihtric.[27] This sounds very much like a punishment for committing treason, rather than revenge on the part of a woman whom Brihtric had rejected twenty years before.

Matilda also owned lands in Buckinghamshire and Surrey. In all, her annual revenues amounted to at least £1,070.[28] 'Queen Matilda was now a powerful ruler with vast resources at her command,' Orderic observed. It was probably because she was now the wealthiest woman in England that William did not grant her Kent, as he had promised, but created his half-brother Odo, Bishop of Bayeux, who had fought for him at Hastings, earl of Kent instead.

Domesday Book records that nearly a quarter of those who inhabited the Queen's manors in Devon were slaves, and there must have been more elsewhere. Slavery had been common in England since before the Romans came; under the Normans the custom was gradually abolished, but that took time. Of course, serfs (or villeins) under the new feudal system imposed by William were little more than slaves, tied to their manors, and obliged, in return for the protection of their overlord, to work on his lands.

Matilda's lands are listed in Domesday Book mostly as *terra regis*, or Crown property, although those in Buckinghamshire were owned privately. The dues varied, and most were forwarded by the Queen's agents when she was in Normandy.[29] The city of Norwich was required to give her £5 and 'an ambling palfrey' each year, while the Sheriff of Worcester and the town of Warwick paid the same amount for the use of her property there.

Matilda also enjoyed financial privileges as queen of England. Agnes Strickland claimed that she was the first consort to be granted the right to claim 'queengold', a tenth of every voluntary fine (such as a pardon or licence) paid to the Crown, a right that was also reserved for her successors, although there is no record of when this right was established, and it may have been Matilda of Scotland, her successor as queen, who was the first to be granted it.

Matilda was granted a soke − an area of jurisdiction − in London that encompassed Aldgate, the ward of Ethelred's Hythe (meaning 'harbour') and the wharfs by the River Thames. Her dock lay on the Thames just south of St Paul's Cathedral, and she was entitled to the tolls levied on goods landed there.[30] The City of London provided money to buy oil for her lamps and wood for her hearth, and ensured that she ate exceedingly well − the food served at her table each day cost the civic authorities 40s.; by contrast, 12d. each was allowed for the hundred attendants who served her. Domesday Book records the names of two of them: Aubrey, her chamberlain, and Humphrey, who collected her wool from his holding in Kingston, Surrey, and to whom she granted lands. In England, three other chamberlains served her in turn: Reginald, Gerald and John.

From Saxon times the Queen's household had been separate from the King's. The Queen's personal household was headed by her chamberlain, and her steward was in charge of the servants who looked after her every need. In the reign of Henry I, there were about 150 household servants, and it has been estimated that between 70 and 80 people served the Queen, at court and on her estates.[31] Most were male. The greater part of a queen's income was used to support her household and administrative officers. They were an extension of the King's court, and very much a part of it, although they operated separately, enabling her to fulfil her duties in her husband's absence. Her household and estates were her legitimate sphere of influence, and it was through them that she could exercise patronage, but no queen could function without an army of officers and servants to support her, and all were answerable ultimately to the King.

The Queen had her own knights, esquires, chaplains and master of horse. She was attended daily by her ladies, unmarried damsels[32] and female attendants who would have undertaken menial tasks for her. Her treasurer, chancellor and attorneys were responsible for administering her estates, assisted by their clerks. Men–at–arms protected her; officers and geld-collectors wrote the letters she dictated, ran her estates and collected and processed her revenues; some, like Wulfweard White, who served Matilda of Flanders, had also served her predecessor, Queen Edith. The day-to-day running of her estates was undertaken by stewards and bailiffs. All reported to the Receiver General at the Exchequer.

The Queen's butler looked after her wine. Cooks and pastrycooks prepared her food; Matilda's cook, Albold, was given lands formerly owned by her in Mapledurham.[33] Huntsmen, serjeants, falconers, fewterers (who looked after greyhounds), archers and horn–blowers attended her during the chase; laundresses looked after her body linen, towels and sheets; blacksmiths and stable grooms cared for her horses, which played an integral part in her daily life. Goldsmiths, grooms, carpenters, smiths, falconers, swineherds, dog handlers, clerks and jesters were all at hand to do her service.[34] These servants were part of the fabric of an efficiently functioning household, and they were paid in cash, food and perquisites. Some ate at the King's expense, or received an allowance for their own servants.

The Norman queens lived a cosmopolitan existence. The Norman court was essentially a political and military institution, and an itinerant one, moving to one '*domus Regis*' (King's house) to another, its progress dictated by the requirements of state, the need to find fresh provisions and good hunting, or the necessity of having the vacated accommodation cleansed, sanitation being primitive. Moving about enabled the King to be seen by his subjects, and to enforce his authority and justice in all parts of his realm.

The royal household maintained teams of packhorses, bearers and carts for every department, including the King's bed, the chapel and the kitchen. Nearly all the royal furnishings, plate, clothes, jewels and chamber textiles were transported with the travelling household, with smaller items packed in lockable domed oaken chests banded with iron; others were carried in waxed canvas coffers covered in leather or saddle bags laden on sumpter horses. The court travelled around the kingdom in a lumbering procession of royalty, men-at-arms, officers, clerks, kitchen staff, laundresses, horses, falconers, laden carts, sumpter mules and dogs, with merchants, jongleurs, entertainers and prostitutes straggling in its wake. The tentkeeper and his man had charge of the tents that were needed when there was no overnight accommodation available at castles or abbey guest houses. The bearer of the King's bed got his keep and a daily allowance for his man and one packhorse. Many demands were made on local populations for food, drink and other necessities.

There were four great highways: the former Roman roads known as Ermine Street (London to York) and the Fosse Way (Exeter to Lincoln), and the more ancient Watling Street (Dover to Wroxeter in Shropshire) and the Icknield Way (Norfolk to Wiltshire). In Norman times, travellers on these highways enjoyed, by law, the protection of the King's peace, while Henry I decreed that these main routes should be wide enough for two wagons to pass.[35] Other roads, where they existed, were largely unpaved and could be muddy or poorly maintained. Some were not even proper roads, but merely rights of way. Possibly there were milestones, but in remote areas travellers had to hire local guides. Always there was the risk of being waylaid by robbers or outlaws, so a military escort would invariably accompany the Queen on her journeys.

Crossing the English Channel between England and Normandy was an occupational hazard that was very much a part of royal lives. Sea travel was fraught with dangers, as medieval ships were not always built to withstand violent storms, and their passage was always at the mercy of the weather, which could cause long delays. Ships could be lost en route, or blown way off course. We hear of travellers' hearts failing at the sight of a ship, and of journeys being a test of faith, while seasickness must have been a common problem. These factors may account for why Matilda visited England only five times. She spent fewer than four years in her husband's kingdom; the rest of the time she was based largely in Rouen, the Norman capital.

The King and Queen went to Normandy for the winter of 1168. Early the next year, William received news that Edgar Atheling had returned to England and was leading another rebellion in the still-festering north, so they returned to England with Richard, leaving Robert as regent once more.[36] William marched to deal with his rebels, sacking York, which they had occupied, defeating them and driving Edgar Atheling overseas. It may have been on this campaign that Matilda accompanied him, bearing her son at the safe distance of Selby, early in 1069.

William returned south before Easter, which fell on 13 April. Matilda and Richard kept the festival with him at Winchester Castle, a strong motte-and-bailey fortress that he had begun building two years previously as the official seat of government. Here Matilda was witness to a charter he granted to the abbey of Saint-Denis near Paris.[37] The castle, which occupied several acres to the south of the west gate of the city, was long to remain a favourite royal residence. 'The King's house' in the castle keep boasted halls, private chambers and chapels, but its plan cannot now be traced since the site has never been excavated. Only the later great hall survives, dating from the thirteenth century. Winchester Castle remained a popular residence with Norman royalty, and William kept Easter there five times.[38]

That spring Matilda was with William at Wells, Somerset, for the Whitsun council, and attested a charter to Wells Cathedral. It may have been during this visit to the West Country that she established thirteen burgesses and a market at Tewkesbury,[39] which had been laid waste during the Norman Conquest. This was the beginning of the town's prosperity.

Edgar Atheling returned with a Danish fleet in the autumn of 1069, raiding the north and retaking York. Again William marched against him, intent this time on crushing resistance once and for all. As the rebels fled before him, Edgar escaped to Scotland.

His patience at an end, William now ordered the widespread devastation that became known as the 'harrying of the north', a savage, merciless campaign that lasted well into 1070. 'By sword and fire' his soldiers 'massacred almost the entire population from the very young to the old and grey'.[40] A horrified Orderic recorded: 'The King stopped at nothing to hunt his enemies. He cut down many people and destroyed homes and land. Nowhere else had he shown such cruelty. To his shame, William made no effort to control his fury, punishing the innocent with the guilty. He ordered that crops and herds, tools and food be burned to ashes. More than a hundred thousand people perished of starvation. I have often praised William in this book, but I can say nothing good about this brutal slaughter. God will punish him.'[41]

Villages were burned, and the starving survivors ate dogs and cats or resorted to cannibalism.[42] 'It was horrible to observe, in houses, streets and roads, human corpses rotting. For no one survived to cover them with earth, all having perished by the sword and starvation, or left the land of their fathers because of hunger.'[43]

On his deathbed, William would confess, 'In mad fury I descended on the English of the north like a raging lion, and ordered that their homes and crops should be burnt at once, and their great flocks and herds of sheep and cattle slaughtered everywhere. So I chastised a great multitude of men and women with the lash of starvation and, alas! was the cruel murderer of many thousands, both young and old, of this fair people. I am stained with the rivers of blood that I have shed.'[44] Sixteen years later, many northern estates recorded in Domesday Book were described simply as 'Waste'. The north would not recover until the middle of the next century.

Matilda's reaction to its harrying is not recorded.

14
'Much Trouble'

William was tightening his grip on England. He retained the laws of Edward the Confessor and showed 'great wisdom' in government, and 'although stern beyond measure to those who opposed his will, he was kind to those good men who loved God'.[1]

He exemplified the Norman passion for building and encouraged the raising of castles all over the land, for they were essential in strengthening the power of the new ruling class and subduing the resentful Saxons. Five hundred were raised between 1066 and 1100. Built on the motte-and-bailey model, most were wooden towers, or keeps, towering on man-made mounds surrounded by palisades. They served as military bases, administrative centres and places of refuge in times of trouble. Above all, they were dominant symbols of the new order. In granting them lands and titles, and empowering them to build castles, William rewarded the Norman barons who had supported his conquest of England. They, in turn, would hold their land for him, and were required to swear fealty for it and provide military service and troops when required.

The situation in England was volatile, so William decided that it was safer for Matilda to leave. She was needed in Rouen. In the early summer of 1069, he 'sent his beloved wife back into Normandy, so that she might give up her time to religious devotions in peace, away from the English tumults, and, together with the boy Robert, could keep the duchy secure'. On parting, William asked her to pray 'for the speedy termination of the English troubles, to encourage the arts of peace in Normandy, and to take care of the interests of their youthful heir'.[2]

Matilda almost certainly took her infant son Henry to Normandy, and he probably spent his childhood there with her.[3] Back in the duchy, she was received with great honour. Henceforth, she would reside there for much of her time,[4] bringing up her children, attending councils of state with her sons, issuing charters and ruling during William's absences. They remained devoted, and their children all showed great promise.[5]

Again Matilda took up the reins as regent, ably supported by Robert Curthose, Roger de Beaumont and John of Avranches, Archbishop of Rouen. The trust William continued to repose in her is evident. One Gauslin, a monk of the abbey of Saint-Martin of Marmoutier, near Tours, of which William and Matilda were benefactors, had journeyed all the way to England to complain to the King that a Norman viscount, Robert Bertran, had plundered the abbey. A 'wrathful' William, too busy to deal with the matter, sent Gauslin with his own chaplain, Bernard, to Matilda, who was then at Cherbourg, 'directing her to do St Martin's justice and restore the plunder. The Queen, obeying him, compelled Bertran to restore all he had taken.'[6]

The only surviving letter written by William to Matilda relates to the problem with the abbey of Saint-Martin:

> William, by the grace of God King of the English, to Queen Matilda, his dear spouse, perpetual health. I want you to know that I grant to Saint-Martin at Marmoutier the church of Sainte-Marie des Pieux and the lands that depend on it, free of all rents, as priest Hugh held them on the day of his death. Furthermore, I charge you to render, as is just, all the land in Normandy belonging to Saint-Martin, free and secure from all those who would wish to burden it, as well as from the demands of the foresters; above all forbid Hugolin de Cherbourg to meddle further with the affairs of this house.[7]

Documents like these give insights into the working relationship between William and Matilda. Though often apart, they clearly worked in unison for the general benefit of their realms, and trusted each other.

Sometime between 1069 and 1078, at Bonneville-sur-Touques, a favoured ducal chateau commanding a magnificent view of the port of Touques and the sea beyond,[8] Matilda witnessed a trial by ordeal. The case was a sad one. The heir to a property in Bayeux had died in infancy, and, to secure the inheritance, his mother had 'rented' a changeling from a woman called Ulberga. When Ulberga tried in vain to reclaim her son, John of Avranches, Archbishop of Rouen, and Roger de Beaumont advised that she should undergo ordeal by hot iron, so that God could judge the case.

Ulberga had to walk nine steps carrying an iron bar weighing one pound that had been heated over a fire. If her hand healed within three days – and this had to be certified by a priest – it would be deemed that divine judgement had decided in her favour. She won her case, which suggests that the iron could not have been very hot.[9] This may have been an example of how a pragmatic approach could be taken to a barbaric means of seeing that justice was done, and it may be that the Queen had commanded it.

Matilda was responsible for the early education of her children, and although she and William appear to have made joint decisions about this with 'the greatest care', she would have exerted considerable influence over her brood. Like William, she was 'a pious parent', sharing his determination to teach their offspring Christian doctrine. Sadly, it sometimes had little effect. Robert grew up preferring pleasure to piety, and Rufus to display contempt for religion. This may have been William's fault for being a repressive parent, or Matilda's; evidence will emerge that she was overindulgent.

Tutors named Rahere and Hilgerius – who was attesting Robert's charters when his pupil was in his teens[10] – and a grammatician called Theobald were initially appointed to educate the heir, but Lanfranc himself later tutored the boys, while the girls were sent to Matilda's abbey of Holy Trinity at Caen. Here they were tutored by a Flemish monk, Arnold of Chocques, whose oratory was renowned, and who had been appointed by the Duke and Duchess to educate the nuns. He taught Cecilia the *trivium*, an essential part of the universal medieval academic curriculum that comprised grammar, rhetoric and logic, probably because she was going to be a nun.[11] The girls could read Latin, which Matilda herself may have taught them; Cecilia was known for her literary bent,[12] and

Constance and Adela were impressively learned,[13] while Cecilia and Adela won plaudits for their beauty. Of Adela, it was said: 'She surpasses her father in her appreciation of poetry and her knowledge of books. She rewards the merits of poets, she has critical judgement, and she has her own store of songs and poems to dictate.'[14]

Matilda's return to Normandy was clouded by troubles.[15] There was a rebellion in Maine, and the King of France and Hoël II, Duke of Brittany, mounted a joint invasion of the duchy. Matilda sent an urgent request for help to William, who immediately dispatched William FitzOsbern, 'the bravest of the Normans',[16] to defend her. Later in 1069, William himself came to Normandy, and invested Robert with the county of Maine.

This was an age in which the appointment of bishops had great political significance. Many of those appointed by William were Normans, and in 1070 Matilda and Robert joined him in persuading their friend Abbot Lanfranc to become archbishop of Canterbury. A reluctant Lanfranc appealed to his old friend and former spiritual father, Herluin, Abbot of Bec-Hellouin, for counsel, but the saintly old man only urged him to go to the Queen and her son Robert and seek their advice.[17] When he did, they both 'prayed that Lanfranc would accept' the primacy.[18] It was due to their influence, and that of Abbot Herluin and Pope Alexander II, that he did so. He was consecrated at Canterbury on 29 August.

As archbishop, Lanfranc would fulfil William's wishes and reform the English Church on the Norman model. Both William and Matilda disapproved of ecclesiastical abuses, and she supported his determination to rid the English Church of slack practices. With Lanfranc's staunch assistance, William vigorously revived 'the observances of religion, which were everywhere grown lifeless in England'. Senior ecclesiastical offices were often filled by Normans, who were zealous to implement the King's reforms. 'You might see churches rise in every village, and monasteries in the towns and cities, built after a style unknown before.'[19] William and his sons and their wives presided over the foundation and building of many churches, religious houses and magnificent Romanesque cathedrals, many of which still stand today as testimony to their religious fervour. Some, of course, look very different now, where they survive intact; when they were new, they would have been decorated throughout with vivid wall paintings, to instruct illiterate congregations in biblical teachings and stories. Lanfranc encouraged learning in the monastic schools, which would in time provide clerks to run the royal administration.

Matilda's bounty to the Church was lavish, yet the chronicler of Abingdon Abbey, a great Saxon foundation, struck a discordant note when he asserted that 'the ornaments of the sanctuary itself were stolen' by the Queen, who commanded that they be sent to her so that she could choose objects to enrich a monastery in Normandy. The Abbot sent her a selection that did not include the most valuable items, but Matilda guessed she was being duped and demanded 'more precious treasures'. The Abbot had no choice but to comply, and she despoiled his abbey of its richest possessions: 'a chasuble wonderfully embroidered throughout with gold; an alb with a stole, and a gospel book decorated with gold and precious gems'.[20]

The death of Matilda's brother, Baldwin VI, in July 1070 precipitated a dynastic crisis in Flanders. His son, Arnulf III, was a minor, therefore his widow, Richilde of Hainault, was appointed regent. Because Richilde, 'with a woman's ambition, was forming plans beyond her sex' and imposing punitive taxes on the people, Matilda's younger brother, Robert the Frisian, rose in rebellion,[21] and after just a few months Arnulf and Richilde were overthrown.

Robert the Frisian was no friend to William, and soon the King's enemies were seeking refuge at the court of Flanders. William had his hands full in England, dealing with a rebellion led by Hereward the Wake in the Fens and the subversive activities of earls Edwin and Morcar. Matilda's mother, the Countess Adela, disapproved of her son Robert depriving Arnulf of his rights, and she and Matilda raised money and troops in support of Arnulf, and sought the aid of King Philip of France, overlord of both Flanders and Normandy.[22] In December 1070, Matilda sent the trusty William FitzOsbern at the head of 'a large army' into Flanders[23] to support her in a joint enterprise with Philip against her brother Robert. He rode off 'gaily, as if to a tournament'.[24]

Soon after he arrived, Richilde proposed that FitzOsbern marry her, with a view to his wresting back Flanders from Robert.[25] But in February 1071, Robert emerged victorious at the Battle of Cassel, in which both Arnulf and FitzOsbern were killed. This left William in great grief at the loss of his friend and Robert indisputably Count of Flanders, which put an end to the alliance between Flanders and Normandy. There was 'mutual and lasting hostility between the Normans and Flemings, partly because of the slaying of the Queen's brother [nephew] and other kinsfolk, but chiefly because of the fate of William fitzOsbern'.[26] Count Robert made alliances with England's enemies and offered Edgar Atheling asylum in Flanders. Matilda was 'deeply afflicted', especially by 'the cruelty of one brother, which caused the loss of her beloved nephew and a number of her friends', for which she blamed Robert the Frisian. It had also, temporarily, disturbed the peace in Normandy.[27]

By 1072, after William had laid waste the north and subdued other parts of the kingdom that had resisted his rule, the Norman Conquest was complete. 'At last, for a while, the storm of wars and rebellions dying out, he now powerfully holds the reins of the entire English monarchy and even more prosperously reigns in glory.'[28] Feudalism – the system of land tenure and overlordship based on service and obligation, under which everyone owed fealty to an overlord, and the lowest ranks of society were bound in serfdom – was established in England, and the administration overhauled. From the castles that were springing up throughout the land, the new Norman aristocracy governed the conquered Saxons, or defended their lands and vassals from attack. But 'there was much trouble in these times and very great distress. The King oppressed the poor', inflicting heavy taxes on them, for 'he was given to avarice and greedily loved gain. The rich complained and the poor murmured, but he was so sturdy that he reckoned nought of them.'[29]

The indigenous Saxon population was oppressed by its conquerors and regarded as an inferior race. The old Saxon nobility was inexorably replaced by a land-hungry Norman military aristocracy. Inequality and corruption flourished, as ancient customs were swept away by the new order. The English language was abhorred by the Normans 'with such intensity, that the laws of the land and the statutes of the English kings were treated of in the Latin tongue. Even in the very schools, the rudiments of grammar were imparted to the children in French and not in English. The English mode of writing was also abandoned, and the French manner adopted in charters and in all books.'[30] The King did not long persevere in his short-lived attempt to learn English.[31] Norman French was now established as the official language of the court, and would remain so until the fourteenth century.

William's rule was harsh but effective. He abolished capital punishment but replaced it with castration and mutilation. Small wonder that, after his death, the *Anglo-Saxon Chronicle* applauded 'the good order he kept in the land, so that a man of any substance could travel unmolested throughout the country with his bosom full of gold. No man dared to slay another, no matter what evil the other might have done to him. If a man lay with a woman against her will, he was forthwith condemned to forfeit those members with which he had disported himself.' This was enlightened justice for women in an age that regarded them as chattels. Nevertheless, added the chronicler, 'a hard man was the King'.

15
'An Untimely Death'

Early in 1072, William visited Normandy. Matilda probably returned to England with him, for at Easter they held court together at Winchester. It was here, in the palace chapel, that a long-running battle for primacy between the archbishops of Canterbury and York was resolved, with William acknowledging the superior right of Canterbury. Matilda's mark is on the deed.[1]

At Whitsun the King and Queen stayed at Windsor, probably in the royal manor of Kingsbury, built by Edward the Confessor at Old Windsor. William favoured this 'palace of kingly splendour'[2] on account of it being 'suitable and convenient' due to its closeness to the River Thames and 'a forest fit for the chase'.[3] Set in twenty-two acres, it stood three miles from the site of the new castle that William had begun building around 1070 to the north-west on a steep hill at Clewer, a hundred feet above the Thames, as part of a ring of nine castles raised as strategic defences surrounding London.[4] Not only was this a prime key military location, but the new castle was surrounded by the old hunting forest of the Saxon kings, later to be enclosed as Windsor Great Park.[5]

The first Norman castle at Windsor consisted of a circular wooden keep on a high mound (or motte) on the crest of the hill, where the Round Tower now stands, and two large baileys covering thirteen acres, containing various timber buildings and surrounded by a great palisade.

The Chronicle of Abingdon records that, sometime after Adelelm of Jumièges became abbot in 1071, Matilda was residing at Windsor while the King was in Normandy, but since there is no record of her being in England without him, this was probably at a time when he was elsewhere in the kingdom. While there, she heard a complaint by one Alfsi, the King's bailiff in Sutton Courtenay, who had with impunity cut and carried off wood from Abingdon Abbey's estate in Cumnor for the King's use. The Abbot had come after him with a vengeance, beating him with a stick and forcing Alsi to jump in the River Ock, where he hid in water up to his neck. Understandably he was much aggrieved, but the Abbot got to the Queen before him, and offered her money to compensate for his treatment of Alfsi. She decreed that the bailiff must not exploit his position by taking the abbey's property.[6]

It may have been at this time that Matilda befriended Ingulph, a Norman clerk of the King and future abbot of Croyland, who later recalled that 'my most illustrious lady, Queen Matilda, always used her good offices for me with my lord the King, often relieved me by her alms-deeds, and very frequently aided me in all matters of business and cases of necessity'.[7]

Later in 1072, when the King of Scots threatened to invade England, Matilda returned to Normandy for her own safety, and again ruled as co-regent with Robert Curthose.[8] William had joined them by early 1073. By now he was 'so powerful that there was no one in all England, all Normandy, all the province of Maine, who dared lift a finger against his rule'.[9] With his authority in England well established, he was able to spend more time in Normandy, and would actually be there more often than he was in England in the years to come.[10]

Hunting was one of the absorbing passions of the medieval upper classes. Regarded as an aristocratic sport, it provided food for the royal or lordly table, exercise, recreation and of course the thrill of the chase. William loved hunting to the point of obsession. 'He delighted to follow the chase, I will not say for days, but even months together.'[11] He established twenty-two royal preserves, including Cranborne Chase and Poorstock, both in Dorset. The greatest of them was the vast New Forest, which was created solely to satisfy the needs of a king whose chief passion was hunting. To make this royal hunting ground, he commandeered great stretches of land in Hampshire, destroying churches and more than twenty villages, turning out the inhabitants so that 'he might there pursue his pleasures'.[12] He passed fierce forest laws to protect it: 'If anyone killed a stag or a wild boar, his eyes were put out. Beasts of chase he cherished as if they were his children.'[13] Many of his subjects resented what they perceived to be a wanton waste of good land, and it was prophesied that the New Forest would bring disaster to William and his descendants.

Matilda's second son, Richard, was said to be the one who most resembled William in appearance. 'He afforded his noble father hopes of his future greatness; he was a noble youth of an aspiring disposition, considering his age.'[14] There were rumours that the scholarly Richard was intended for the Church. But on 13 September 1074,[15] 'an untimely death quickly withered the bud of this promising flower'.

There are varying accounts of how Richard died. William of Malmesbury first stated that, 'while hunting deer in the New Forest, he contracted a disorder from a stream of foul air', but in a revised text he says Richard was 'hanged by the throat on the branch of a tree when his horse ran underneath'. Orderic stated that, galloping in pursuit of a wild beast, he was 'badly crushed between a strong hazel branch and the pommel of his saddle, and mortally injured'. Robert of Torigni asserts that he was riding so fast that he collided with the branch of a tree, which smacked him on the head and toppled him from his horse.[16] Richard did not die immediately, but lingered for a few days before making his confession, receiving the Last Sacrament and passing away, 'to the great sorrow of many of the English'.[17]

He was only of tender age and learning to hunt when he died.[18] He had not yet received the belt of knighthood,[19] which has led to speculation that he was between thirteen and twenty-two.[20] There was no set age for knighthood in this period, but most achieved the accolade at eighteen.[21] The Conqueror's other sons were knighted at the ages of sixteen or seventeen (Rufus) or eighteen (Henry). There is no record of Robert being dubbed a knight. Richard was born before Rufus, thus he was between fourteen and eighteen at most when he died.

His grieving parents made generous gifts in their son's memory.[22] Richard was buried in Winchester Cathedral, in the south choir aisle, in a stone sarcophagus that is still almost in its original position, on a low wall supporting the choir arcade piers. The inscription survives: INTVS EST CORPVS RICHARDI WILLHELMI CONQVESTORIS FILII ET BEORNÆ DUC (Within this wall is the body of Richard, son of William the Conqueror and Duke of Beornia). With his death, the prophecy about the New Forest appeared to be fulfilled.

16

'The Praise and Agreement of Queen Matilda'

Matilda was briefly regent of Normandy early in 1074, but William spent most of that year in the duchy with her and their children. With Richard gone, he 'blessed and favoured' Rufus and Henry above Robert, for they were 'always dutiful' to their father and for that 'received his hearty blessing'.[1] Rufus could do no wrong, 'always obedient, displaying himself in battle before his father's eyes, and walking by his side in peacetime',[2] although even Rufus may have found his father's high expectations daunting, for they may have been one cause of a stutter he developed, which grew worse when he was agitated.[3] It must have grieved Matilda to see her favourite son excluded. Certainly it angered Robert.

William had recently written to congratulate the new Pope, Gregory VII, on his election, and Gregory had responded warmly. In April 1074 he also wrote to his 'beloved daughter' Matilda, having heard praiseworthy reports from William's barons of her generosity, love and humility, which he regarded as 'certain hope' of her eternal salvation. 'Urge your husband, do not cease to suggest useful things to his soul,' he exhorted, 'for it is certain that, if the infidel husband is saved by a believing wife, a believing husband can be made better by a believing wife.'[4]

In May and November 1074, the ducal family were at Rouen, having stayed at Lillebonne – where nothing now remains of William's castle – and other places in the intervening months. Late in the year, William returned to England.

He was back in Normandy between April and the late autumn of 1075. At Easter, he and Matilda held court at Fécamp, where, on 5 April, with great state, William gave their daughter Cecilia to be consecrated as a nun before John of Avranches, Archbishop of Rouen.[5] It had been nine years since Cecilia had entered Holy Trinity as an oblate, which was a long time in an age in which the novitiate (the probationary period before a nun made her final vows) was in theory supposed to last for a year, but in practice often lasted months or even weeks.[6] A probationary year had to be served beforehand, so the earliest age at which a nun could take final vows was between thirteen and fourteen. In 1075 Cecilia was aged between nineteen and twenty-one, and had waited at least six years to be professed. Possibly she had wanted time to test her vocation.

That year, 1075, Matilda again visited Holy Trinity, where she witnessed a charter.[7] It was 'with the praise and agreement of Queen Matilda' that William granted a charter to Le Mans Cathedral, excusing all dues and customs fees while the building was repaired following damage caused during his subjugation of Maine.[8] In the autumn of 1075, he crossed to England to quell a rebellion, leaving Matilda as regent once more, assisted as usual by her son Robert, Roger de Beaumont and John of Avranches, Archbishop of Rouen.

Matilda's cousin on her mother's side was the highly respected Simon de Crépy, who would become count of Amiens, the Vexin and Valois in 1074. Until 1067, when he returned to his father's castle, he had been brought up at the court of William and Matilda,[9] probably at her invitation. Late in 1075, Matilda was present with Robert in Rouen to witness Simon restoring the fief of Gisors to the cathedral.[10] In time to come, Simon would prove himself a true friend to Matilda and repay her kindness.

That December, Queen Edith died at Winchester, and at Matilda's behest 'the King had her brought to Westminster with great honour and laid her near King Edward, her lord'.[11] It was his 'deep feeling' for his wife that had moved him to have the late Queen buried so honourably.[12]

17

'Ties of Blood'

When William returned once more to Normandy in spring 1076, trouble flared between him and his eldest son.

Matilda loved Robert above her other children. Some years earlier, William of Jumièges had described the heir as 'brilliantly shining in the blossoming flower of his handsome body and his advantageous age', and praised his 'noble virtue'. But despite Robert's undoubted cheerfulness, generosity and spirit of adventure, and his being very

courageous in battle and a powerful and sure archer, he had proved
a disappointment to his father. Short and 'pot-bellied', with fat legs,[1]
he was garrulous, licentious, extravagant, rash, imprudent, and hopeless with money – 'a proud and foolish fellow'[2] who was altogether
too sure of himself. Part of this may have been the bravado of a
young man in the face of a disapproving, critical father who made
hurtful jokes at his expense. Matilda may well have acted as an
intermediary between them, trying to smooth the troubled waters,
but Robert was ambitious and land-hungry.

The exact date when William invested his son with Normandy
is not recorded. Evidence in charters shows that Robert was recognised as duke, and ruled the duchy, from the mid-1070s, after Matilda
stepped down as regent.[3] But William would not allow him full
autonomy, and Robert resented his father's intermittent resumption
of power.

Around 1076–7, William, Matilda and their family were in residence at the Norman chateau of l'Aigle, so-called after an eagle's
nest was discovered during its construction at the turn of the eleventh century. Robert was lodging in a house in the town, where a
quarrel broke out between him and his brothers, Rufus and Henry,
who threw dirty water over him. In retaliation, Robert drew his
sword on them. Informed of the rumpus, King William stormed into
the house 'in a terrible rage' with his own sword unsheathed, and
prevented Robert from obtaining satisfaction for the insult, even
arresting his supporters. Furious, Robert retired from court with a
group of the young lords whom he had cozened by his prodigal
open-handedness, and tried ineffectually to take Rouen. But no one
offered him any serious support, and any money he received in
charity from friends was 'recklessly squandered' on 'jongleurs, parasites
and courtesans'.[4]

Lanfranc and other bishops were present with the King and Queen
on 14 July 1077 when Bayeux Cathedral, built by William's half-
brother, Odo, Bishop of Bayeux, was consecrated. There is no record
of the famous Bayeux Tapestry depicting the Norman Conquest of
1066 being on display in the new church for the worldly and
sensual Odo to show his royal guests. However, it may have been
made for the cathedral, since its dimensions match the length of
the nave.[5]

The Bayeux Tapestry is not a tapestry as such, but an embroidery
on a linen cloth seventy-seven yards long, dating from the 1060s–70s;

the last section is missing. We know nothing of its history prior to 1476, when it was certainly hanging in Bayeux Cathedral. Whether it had been there since Bishop Odo's time is debatable, for the chronicler Robert Wace, a canon of Bayeux in the twelfth century, does not mention it,[6] although he describes the fire that badly damaged the cathedral in 1106, and mentions that its treasures were carried to safety before the flames took hold.[7]

The Bayeux Tapestry is still sometimes called *La Tapisserie de la Reine Mathilde*, a name given to it before the nineteenth century in the belief that it was the work of Matilda and her ladies. That tradition was well established in Bayeux before 1729,[8] and still has some currency there today. However, the first recorded reference to the tapestry, in the 1476 inventory of Bayeux Cathedral, does not mention Matilda. Surprisingly, as William's Queen, she does not appear in the tapestry. There are several Romantic-era paintings of her at work on it, notably one by Alfred Guillard, painted in 1848 and now in the Baron-Gérard Museum in Bayeux. The modern stained-glass window in Selby Abbey also shows Matilda working with her ladies on the Bayeux Tapestry.

In 1107, Baudri, Abbot of Bourgeuil, described tapestry hangings depicting the Norman Conquest that adorned the bedchamber of Matilda's daughter, Adela, Countess of Blois. 'The walls are covered with tapestries, woven according to her design, and all seem alive. Around her bed the conquest of England, William's claims to the throne as Edward's chosen successor, the comet, the Norman council and preparations, the fleet, the battle of Hastings with the feigned flight of the Normans and the real one of the English, and the death of Harold.' There has been speculation that, when Adela became a nun at Marcigny Abbey in 1120, she donated her hangings to Bayeux Cathedral. However, Baudri describes only seven scenes, when there are about twice that number in the tapestry as we know it, and he speaks of Adela's hangings as being woven, not embroidered.

In 1430, an inventory of Philip the Good, Duke of Burgundy, listed 'A large tapestry of the type woven on a high warp [loom], without gold, of the history of Duke William of Normandy, telling of his conquest of England.'[9] It has been suggested that this was the Bayeux Tapestry, but again the latter was not woven on a loom.

After 1476, the Bayeux Tapestry disappears from the historical record until its rediscovery by Bernard de Montfaucon in 1729. In the early nineteenth century, Matilda's association with it was challenged, amid concerns that it was an insult to attribute a work with such explicit sexual details to a woman of renowned virtue.

In 1824, the theory that the tapestry was commissioned by Odo, Bishop of Bayeux, William's half-brother, was first put forward. Odo appears twice in it; he is shown playing an active role in the Battle of Hastings, wielding a mace or club and rallying William's troops. In 1025, the Council of Arras had decreed that churches should be hung with tapestries to enlighten unlettered congregations, so Odo would have been adhering to this new tradition in hanging it in his cathedral. The Bayeux Tapestry is almost certainly English work, perhaps made in St Augustine's Abbey in Canterbury, Kent, of which county Odo was earl. Some Latin words in the embroidery have a Saxon affinity, and some of the designs match manuscript decoration produced in Canterbury.[10] The attribution to Odo has been challenged, but so far not successfully.

The year in which William probably reached fifty, 1077, was a year of dedications. On 13 September, Matilda and William, accompanied by their sons Robert and Rufus, attended the consecration of his abbey dedicated to Saint-Étienne in Caen, in the presence of Archbishop Lanfranc, a host of bishops and barons, and 'an immense multitude of people', which made William 'puffed up with worldly pride'.[11]

He and the Queen also attended the dedication of the restored abbey of Saint-Evroult, of which Matilda was patron, and where Orderic Vitalis was a monk. Then, on 23 October, the new abbey church at Bec-Hellouin was consecrated by Lanfranc. Bec-Hellouin was a monastery long favoured by the dukes of Normandy, and regarded as being under their special protection. It gave England its first two post-Conquest archbishops of Canterbury, Lanfranc and Anselm of Aosta, who both enjoyed the friendship of William and Matilda. The King and Queen were unable to attend the dedication ceremony. 'Queen Matilda would willingly have been present had not other royal affairs detained her; she was, however, present through the generosity of her gifts.'[12]

In 1077, hearing that Simon de Crépy's betrothal to Judith of Auvergne had fallen through, William proposed to him a marriage with his daughter Adela. While they were discussing it, Simon realised that he and Adela were too nearly related, and told William, 'My lady the Queen, your wife, and I, as they say, are bound by ties of blood and close kinship in such a way that we have to ask wise men their advice if this marriage is at all possible and why.'

William's response was pragmatic. He said he would have his clergy 'look round and search whether a gift of alms or the building of a monastery or anything of that kind deals with this problem legally'. Simon preferred to travel to Rome to ask the Pope himself for a dispensation, but was apparently turned down, for soon afterwards he became betrothed to another 'young girl of high rank', and subsequently both of them renounced the world and entered the religious life, with Simon becoming a hermit renowned for his sanctity.[13]

Around 1077–8, William ordered the building of the Tower of London, the greatest of three fortresses that commanded the City's defences. The others, at its western end, were Baynard's Castle and Montfitchet Castle. He chose as his architect Gundulf, Bishop of Rochester. The great stone keep that Gundulf built, the largest of its kind in England after that of Colchester, arose in the south-eastern corner of the old Roman city wall, next to an existing 'little castle' that had been built by a Norman called Ravenger and was incorporated into the precincts of the new keep.[14] Completed around 1097–1100, the Norman Tower of London and the new wall or rampart that enclosed it on its north and west sides occupied a much smaller area than it does today.

Built of Caen stone as an impregnable defence, with walls between eleven and fifteen feet thick, the keep also contained royal apartments.[15] Informed guesses have been made about the interior, which is divided into two sections by a stout stone wall. Above the vaulted undercroft, which housed a well and was used as storerooms, the first storey was accessed by an external staircase and probably consisted of the constable's lodging, a refectory and dormitory for the garrison, and the crypt of the beautiful Romanesque chapel on the second floor, which was dedicated to St John the Evangelist. The royal apartments, galleried hall and great chamber were located on the upper floor.[16] The keep was equipped with garderobes and, in most of the rooms, probably the earliest fireplaces ever seen in England. Four of the original Norman arched windows remain today. Yet there is no record of any king or queen staying in these apartments until King Stephen held court there in 1140.

18

'A Mother's Tenderness'

When, late in 1077, Robert Curthose demanded autonomous rule in the duchy of Normandy, his father was furious. 'It is not my custom to strip until I go to bed!' he exploded. 'As long as I live, I will not relax my grip on it, neither will I divide it with another; for it is written: every kingdom that is divided against itself shall become desolate. It is not to be borne that he who owes his existence to me should aspire to be my rival in my own dominions.'[1]

It was unwise to argue with William when his mind was set, but Robert was stubborn. He was now twenty-four and still chafing bitterly at his father's refusal to delegate full power to him. This impasse led to a bitter conflict between them.[2] 'The cause of their disagreement was that King William did not allow his son to act according to his own free will in matters concerning the duchy, even though he had appointed him as his heir.'[3]

Towards the end of 1077,[4] Robert threatened to leave Normandy and seek justice from strangers. An angry William ordered him to go at once, and he 'ran from his father', sought refuge with his uncle, Count Robert the Frisian, in Flanders,[5] and allied himself to him, a move guaranteed to rile William further.[6] Philip I of France, ever ready to discountenance his Anglo-Norman rival, granted Robert Curthose the castle of Gerberoi, to use as a base of operations against his father, and towards the end of 1078, he himself prepared to join Robert in rebellion against William, although William managed to dissuade him early the next year. Robert, however, had the support of his friends, who were young lords 'of noble birth and knightly prowess, men of diabolical pride and ferocity terrible to their neighbours, always far too ready to plunge into acts of lawlessness'.[7] Backed by them, he again besieged Rouen, 'ravaged in Normandy far and often, burnt townships, killed people, and caused his father much trouble and worry'.[8]

At Christmas, hostilities broke out. By now William was becoming so fat that King Philip jeeringly likened him to a pregnant woman, but that did not deter him from mounting a three-week siege against Robert at Gerberoi. During a skirmish, Robert – who himself was overweight – 'became personally engaged with his father, wounded him and killed his horse'.[9] William, who was only hurt in the hand, would have been killed had not Robert recognised his voice. Chastened, Robert gave him his own mount and bade him ride away,[10] and a humiliated William was forced to retreat to Rouen.

The feud between William and Robert caused Matilda much distress, which must have been exacerbated by news from Messines of the death of her mother on 8 January 1079.[11] Distress moved her to deceit. 'Queen Matilda, compassionating her son's distress with a mother's tenderness, often sent him, without the knowledge of her husband, large sums of silver and gold, and other things of value. The King, discovering this, forbade her with terrible threats from continuing to do so.'[12] But she 'recklessly renewed her offence',[13] using her substantial revenues to provide Robert with an army, and pawning her jewels and rich garments in order to raise money for him, which the evidence suggests was smuggled to him by one of the Queen's messengers, a Breton called Samson, who was 'shrewd and eloquent and chaste'.[14] Matilda also sent Samson to William to plead Robert's case – in vain.[15]

Someone[16] found out what she was doing behind her husband's back, and informed the King that she was 'contumaciously repeating the offence'. It was nowhere near as heinous as that of Henry II's Queen, Eleanor of Aquitaine, who in 1173 incited her sons to rebel against their father and spent sixteen years in prison as punishment. All the same, William was 'in great wrath'. He confronted Matilda and berated her publicly, in front of his court.

'A wise man remarked truly, as I myself have reason to find, that a faithless woman is her husband's bane!'[17] he declared and, turning to his courtiers, asked, 'Who in the world can henceforth reckon on finding a companion who will be faithful and devoted to him? Behold my own wife, whom I love as my very soul, and who is entrusted by me with my treasures and jurisdictions through my whole dominions. She succours my enemies who are plotting against my life, enriches them with my wealth, carefully supplies them with arms to attack me, abets and strengthens them in every way.'

Matilda knelt humbly at his feet, but stood her ground. 'Do not wonder, I pray you, my lord, that I feel a mother's tenderness for my first-born son. By the power of the Most High, I protest that, if my son Robert was dead and buried seven feet in the earth, out of the sight of the living, and I could bring him to life at the expense of my own blood, I would freely shed it for him, and I would undergo sufferings greater than can be expected from female weakness. How can you suppose that I can take any delight in the abundance of wealth, while I suffer my son to be crushed by the extremity of want and distress? Far from me be such hardness of heart, nor should you, in the fullness of your power, lay such an injunction upon me.' She may have hoped that her defence of maternal devotion – which was held as sacred by contemporaries – would touch William deeply, but 'the stern prince turned pale with anger and, bursting with rage, he commanded Samson to be arrested and blinded'.[18]

Matilda had got off lightly, but she again risked William's wrath, for Samson learned of the King's animosity 'by intelligence from those the Queen trusted', who advised him to seek refuge at the abbey of Saint-Evroult, of which she was patron, 'to save at the same time his body and his soul'. At her request, he was received as a monk by Abbot Mainier, and so escaped the King's vengeance. It was he who related to Orderic what had happened.[19]

William forgave Matilda,[20] and we hear no more of her succouring Robert. William of Malmesbury dismisses this episode as 'a slight disagreement' between the couple, and says that William proved afterwards that 'his conjugal affection was not in the least diminished by this circumstance'. In the meantime, marital relations were probably a little fraught. As the chronicler observed, 'Kingship and love make sorry bedfellows and sort but ill together.'[21]

This sad episode probably left Matilda feeling drained. Between 1077 and 1081, when Adelelm of Loudun (later St Adelelm, Bishop of Burgos) was abbot of the abbey of La Chaise-Dieu in the Auvergne, an English queen sent to ask him for a cure for lethargy. It must have been Matilda. He sent her bread he had blessed, which reportedly cured her – or maybe it was the strength of her belief in it that did that. Adelelm refused to accept money as a reward, so she sent him 'a precious priestly vestment' and £100 to fund a new dorter for his monks.[22]

In January 1080, William, Matilda and their younger sons witnessed several Norman charters, and gave gifts to the abbey of Saint-Georges at Boscherville; after Matilda's death, it would be rebuilt in a style identical to her abbey church at Caen.

From around 1080 to 1086, her youngest son, Henry, appears to have lived in England in the care of the saintly Osmund, Bishop of Salisbury, a Norman nobleman who had taken holy orders and served as lord chancellor to the King, to whom he was related by marriage. It was probably under Osmund's auspices that Henry received the excellent education that would stand him in good stead in later life.

'The early years of instruction he passed in liberal arts, and thoroughly imbibed the sweets of learning.'[23] Possibly, since he was the youngest son, he was intended for a career in the Church, for which education was primarily regarded as a preparation. In an age in which kings were illiterate, Henry even learned to read and write Latin, and from the fourteenth century was nicknamed 'Beauclerc' because of his famed literary skills. As he grew up, he often quoted, 'in his father's hearing, the proverb, "An illiterate king is a crowned ass"'. William did not take offence. 'Observing his son's disposition, the King never omitted any means of cherishing his lively prudence; and once, when he had been ill-used by one of his brothers, and was in tears, he spirited him up by saying, "Weep not, my boy, you too will be a king."'[24]

It was probably early in 1080 that Matilda heard of a hermit in Germany who was reputed a great prophet. So troubled was she by the rift between William and Robert that she sent messengers with gifts for the hermit, craving his prayers for her husband and son, and asking him to 'send her a prediction of what would happen to them in time to come'. The hermit asked for three days in which to make his reply, during which he had a vision in which he saw a fierce horse in a grassy flower meadow, doing its best to drive off a herd of cows. But 'a wanton cow' let the rest into the field to eat the grass and defile it with their ordure. The hermit concluded that the meadow was Normandy, the grass its people, and the flowers its churches, while the horse was William, protecting them from their envious enemies, represented by the cattle. The wanton cow was Robert Curthose.

Chilled by the revelation, the hermit told the Queen's messengers, 'Return to your mistress, and tell her I have prayed to God in her behalf, and the Most High has made known to me in a dream the things she desires to learn.' He told them of his vision, and prophesied:

> When, since he is human, the King comes to die, Robert his son will succeed him in the duchy of Normandy. Whereupon his enemies from all sides will invade the honourable and wealthy land deprived of its guardian, strip it of its beauty and riches and, disregarding this foolish ruler, trample up Normandy contemptuously underfoot. He, like the wanton cow, will give himself up to lust and indolence, and will be the first to plunder the wealth

of the Church and give it to base panders and other lechers. Under their rule, vice and wretchedness will abound. Towns and villages will be burned, and many thousands of men will be destroyed by fire and sword. Normandy, who once so proudly lorded it over her conquered neighbours, will now, under a foolish and idle duke, be despised, and will long and wretchedly lie at the mercy of the swords of her neighbours. The weak Duke will enjoy no more than an empty title, and a swarm of nobodies will dominate both him and the captive duchy, bringing ruin to many.

He had a special message for Matilda: 'But you, venerable lady, will not witness the calamities with which Normandy is threatened, for, after a good confession, you will die in peace, and neither behold your husband's death, nor the misfortunes of your son, nor the desolation of your beloved country.' Orderic wrote this passage with hindsight – he knew what would befall Normandy after William's death – yet the hermit must have predicted some dread doom of this nature, for the impact on Matilda was profound. According to Orderic Vitalis, the prophecy – and no doubt the warning of her death – preyed on her mind for the rest of her life.[25]

William remained implacable in regard to Robert. 'Which of my ancestors from the time of Rollo ever had to endure such hostility from any child of his as I do?' he asked his barons. 'He would not hesitate, if he could, to stir up the whole human race against me and slay me, and you as well. According to divine law, given to us through Moses, he is deserving of death.' With anguished tears, Matilda interceded with William for their son. William's barons were also anxious to see an end to the conflict. They urged him, 'Correct your child when he errs, welcome him when he returns, mercifully spare him when he repents.'[26]

Others, including Pope Gregory, King Philip, Roger of Montgomery and many clergy also spoke up for Robert.[27] Pope Gregory himself wrote to William and Robert individually, trying to bring about a reconciliation. He exhorted Robert to 'wholly banish the counsels of wicked men and in all things agree to the will of your father'.[28] Matilda was indefatigable in seeking a resolution to the quarrel. 'The Queen and representatives of the King of France, with noble neighbours and friends, all combined to restore peace.'[29]

One who championed Robert was Matilda's cousin, the saintly Simon de Crépy. On the fourth Sunday in Lent 1079, he was present at the abbey of Saint-Corneille in Compiègne when a length of fabric venerated as the Holy Shroud of Christ[30] was translated into a gold reliquary ornamented with precious stones given by Queen Matilda, who may herself have been present, or had sent a representative. It was probably at this gathering of notables that Simon heard of what had happened at Gerberoi and resolved to help bring about a reconciliation between William and Robert, setting off the very next day. Matilda herself may have urged her cousin's intervention, for she was present at the 'sweet talks' between Simon and William.[31]

At Easter 1080 (12 April), after protracted intercessions, 'the stern King yielded to the pressure of these great persons and, surrendering to paternal duty, became reconciled with his son'. Robert came to Rouen and was forgiven, in a carefully orchestrated assembly attended by Papal nuncios and French envoys, and William again recognised him as the heir to Normandy. Robert had long been associated with the rule of the duchy, and William almost certainly had other plans for the succession of the throne of England, where Robert was barely known. Thus the 'fiendish dispute' was brought to an end.[32]

In the presence of his parents and brothers, Robert witnessed a charter to the abbey of La Trinité-du-Mont in Rouen.[33] Orderic asserts that William 'continually poured abuse and reproach on him in public for his failing', but other sources show that relations between the King and his eldest son were generally cordial from then on.

On 8 May 1080, not knowing that William and Robert had been reconciled, Pope Gregory wrote to his 'dearest daughter' the Queen, praising the love she had for God and her neighbour, urging, 'With these and similar weapons, arm your husband when God gives you the opportunity, and do not cease to do so.'[34]

On 14 July, attended by Robert and Rufus, William and Matilda held court at Holy Trinity, Caen, to hear lawsuits. Soon afterwards, they and their children gathered at Breteuil for the betrothal of Adela to Stephen, Count of Blois, which would seal a peace with a troublesome adversary. The date of the marriage is not recorded, but it perhaps took place between 1080 and 1083.[35] Adela had grown into a strong-minded, devout, intelligent girl with 'beauty, dignity, grace and the brilliance of a goddess';[36] two of her thirteen children were named for Matilda and William, and another was the future King Stephen, born around 1096–7. Adela took after her mother; like her, she would become 'a powerful woman with a reputation for her worldly influence'.[37]

19

'The Noblest Gem of a Royal Race'

In the late summer of 1080, William took Robert to England for the first time, and Matilda came too. That autumn the King even trusted Robert with leading an army to Scotland. King Malcolm III – Malcolm Canmore, or 'Greathead' – had recognised William as his overlord in 1072, but that had not precluded him from harrying Northumbria. William sent Robert north with a show of strength, and Malcolm made peace.

Afterwards, Robert visited the Scottish court and met the pious and influential Queen Margaret. Margaret, 'the very image of virtues',[1] was the daughter of Edward Atheling, nephew of Edward the Confessor, and sister of the troublesome Edgar Atheling. She had introduced many English customs at the Scottish court, and even given her first six children Anglo-Saxon royal names. Her family would eventually number six sons and two daughters, although the three oldest sons died in youth.

Around this time, Margaret presented Malcolm with their fifth child and first daughter, born probably in the autumn of 1080 at Malcolm's Tower,[2] the King's palace, where he and Margaret had married, and where all their children were born. Built around 1060, it stood on a seventy-foot-high hill at Dunfermline, which Malcolm had designated the Scottish capital. Nearby stood the abbey of Dunfermline, founded by Queen Margaret, who had asked Archbishop Lanfranc to send her monks from Canterbury. Not far off was the cave the devout Queen liked to use for her private devotions.[3]

The new princess was christened Edith,[4] probably after Edward the Confessor's Queen, or possibly after the tenth-century saint, Edith of Wilton, the bastard daughter of King Edgar. Royal Saxon, Imperial and Scots blood flowed in Edith's veins. Robert was probably invited to be her godfather,[5] and Queen Matilda consented to be godmother, and travelled north to Scotland for the baptism. At the christening the infant Edith took firm hold of the Queen's veil, pulling it towards her own head, which was later construed as a sign that she was destined for queenship.[6]

In time, Edith was indeed to prove a worthy successor to Matilda as queen consort. She grew up under the governance of an intelligent mother who was interested in fostering closer cultural and trading links between Scotland and Europe, and raised living standards in her adopted land. 'The Queen, herself the noblest gem of a royal race, made the splendour of her husband's royal magnificence much more splendid, and contributed much glory and honour to all the nobility of the kingdom.'[7] Malcolm's halls now sported hangings and gold and silver plate, while dress and manners at the Scottish court improved considerably.[8] And yet, while the Queen 'walked in state clad in splendid apparel, she in her heart trod all these trappings beneath her feet, and bore in mind that, under the gems and gold, there was nothing but dust and ashes'.[9] Hildebert of Lavardin, Bishop of Le Mans and a future correspondent of her daughter, remembered her thus: 'Chaste she was, modest, beautiful, elegant, prudent, cautious, generous, religious, pious. A rose from the root of a rose; from religion, piety flowed from piety, splendour from a star.'[10]

Edith and her older brothers, Edward, Edmund, Edgar and Ethelred, were soon joined in the nursery by Mary, Alexander and David. Their mother Margaret loved books and religion, and her charitable works embracing the poor and the sick, and her patronage of art and education, were an outstanding example to her children. They grew up seeing their illiterate father devotedly holding the book their mother was reading. Books were costly, precious objects, produced entirely by hand, with the script, illustrations, borders and illuminations carefully copied, using natural dyes, onto prepared animal skins, which were themselves expensive. Books took a long time to produce, and were high-status possessions; some were exquisite works of art. The children learned that they were to be greatly prized.

They also saw their mother take poor children on her knee and feed them mashed food.[11] Margaret's biographer, Turgot, Prior of Durham, has left a vivid account of the upbringing of the Scottish royal offspring, which was probably based on the reminiscences of Edith herself, who commissioned him to write her mother's life. He described how devoted a mother Queen Margaret had been.

> She poured out care to her children, seeing that they were nurtured with all diligence, and that they were introduced to honest matters as much as possible. And because she knew the Scripture, "Who spares the rod hates the child", she had ordered her household steward that, whenever the children committed some childish mischief, as young children will, they should be punished by him with threats and beatings. And because of the religious zeal of

their mother, the children's manners were far better than those of other children older than they. And they never fought amongst themselves, and the younger children always displayed respect to the elder ones. For this reason, during solemn Mass, when they followed their parents up to the altar, the younger never tried to outdo the elder, but went up by age, oldest first.

Margaret had her children brought to her often. 'She taught them about Christ and faith in Christ, using words suitable to their age and understanding. She admonished them diligently: "Fear the Lord," she said, "O my children, because those that fear Him will not be in need, and if you delight in Him, O my flesh, He returns goodness to you through prosperity in the present life, and by giving you a happy afterlife with all the saints." This was the desire of the mother, these were the admonishments, this was the prayer that she prayed day and night, with tears on behalf of her offspring, so that they might come to know their Creator in faith that works through love, and knowing that they might worship, worshipping, that they might love Him in everything and above all things, loving, that they might arrive at the glory of the heavenly kingdom.'[12]

20

'Twofold Light of November'

In the winter of 1080, William nominated William de Saint-Calais to the see of Durham. Wanting to build a new cathedral to house the relics of St Cuthbert, the Bishop consulted the King and Queen, who advised him to consult the Pope, which he did. Consent was obtained, and work began on the great Romanesque cathedral that can still be seen today. In 1082, Matilda would assist Bishop William in promulgating his plan to replace canons with monks in his cathedral.

The King and Queen kept Christmas at Gloucester.[1] In February 1081 they were at Salisbury with Robert, celebrating the Feast of the Purification. At this time, William granted a charter to Malmesbury Abbey 'at the request of Queen Matilda'.[2] Soon afterwards they

were together in Cambridgeshire when William took Ramsey
Abbey under his protection and confirmed all grants made by his
predecessors.³ At Easter and Whitsun (24 May), they wore their
crowns at Winchester.⁴

Sometime after May 1081, Matilda returned to Normandy. That
year, 'hearing a good report of the life of the monks, she came to
Saint-Evroult to pay her devotions; and being received by the brethren
with due honours, offered a mark of gold on the altar, and
commended herself with her daughter Constance to the prayers of
the brethren. She also ordered that a refectory of stone, for their
common use, should be built at her expense. She further gave to
Saint-Evroult a chasuble enriched with gold and jewels, and an
elegant cope for the chanter, with a promise to make further offerings if she lived; but she was prevented by death from fulfilling it.'
With her came Adelina of Meulan, the wife of Roger de Beaumont,
who donated an alb. Afterwards Matilda dined with the monks in
their existing refectory, displaying great humility.⁵ Constance may
have been unwell, hence her mother's intercession for her, but clearly
she recovered; she was said to be the most gifted of Matilda's daughters, and in 1086–7 would marry Alan IV 'Fergant', Duke of Brittany.

That year, Simon de Crépy undertook a pilgrimage to the Holy
Land and then to Rome, where he died in September, having been
given the last rites by Pope Gregory himself. When, in 1082, Matilda
heard of his death, she sent gold and silver to pay for a fine marble
tomb in St Peter's Basilica, and gifts to adorn it.⁶

William, Matilda and Robert were together in Normandy in the
summer and autumn of 1082.⁷ Matilda had always been lavish in her
gifts to religious houses, but at this time her benefactions increased,
probably because she was unwell and thinking of the salvation of her
soul. That year, for example, she granted manors formerly owned by
Brihtric Meaw in Essex, Gloucestershire and Dorset to Holy Trinity
at Caen, for wardrobes and firewood. Holy Trinity had also received
properties in Rouen and Barfleur, and some lands in England.⁸ She
gave the manor of Longbridge Deverill, Wiltshire, to Lanfranc's abbey
of Bec-Hellouin,⁹ and gifts to Cluny and Saint-Evroult.

In 1082, she travelled with William to Saint-Grestain to meet his
half-brother, Odo, Bishop of Bayeux. William bestowed endowments
and privileges on the abbey where their mother lay buried, but Odo,
a born intriguer with great wealth at his disposal, made it clear at
their meeting that he was intent on going to Rome to take advantage of a schism in the Church that had weakened the position of

Pope Gregory. Odo's aim was probably to secure the Papacy for himself. William forbade it absolutely. He was already angered by the ostentation on which Odo was squandering his riches.

But Odo was determined to go anyway. He crossed to England, aiming to reach Rome by a roundabout route, but just as he was about to set sail from the Isle of Wight, William and Matilda appeared from Normandy with their sons, and William personally arrested him, as the King's soldiers would not lay hands on a man of God. William had his brother tried for corruption, not in an ecclesiastical court, which would have dealt with him leniently, but in the royal court, which refused to convict him. Declaring that he was not trying the Bishop of Bayeux, but the Earl of Kent, the King grabbed Odo by the collar and ordered his guards to take him off to prison in Rouen. Odo would not be released until after William's death.[10]

Matilda was a witness to Odo's fall. Orderic says that, at this time, she fell sick with an illness that was 'prolonged and serious'. She had perhaps been ailing since 1081. Medical knowledge was rudimentary, and treatment often consisted of a mixture of herbal remedies and folklore. In Matilda's case, whatever was tried proved ineffective.

She returned to Normandy with William at Easter 1083, when they kept the festival at Fécamp. Robert was with them then, and at Caen on 18 July.[11]

The flow of Matilda's gifts continued. That year, she gave plough-land, three gardens and other estates to the abbey of Saint-Amand at Rouen. Her son Henry would later endow this abbey in her memory.[12] She even, 'in her last illness', granted the village of Northam, Devon, to Saint-Étienne in Caen,[13] and manors in Essex and Dorset to provide the nuns of Holy Trinity with clothing and firewood. She also endowed three churches in Falaise, her husband's birthplace – Saint-Laurent, Saint-Gervais and Holy Trinity.[14]

William's love for his wife, and the good influence she exerted over him over thirty years of marriage, were a constant blessing – a blessing that, sadly, he was not to enjoy for much longer.

The nature of Matilda's final illness is not known. All the Norman queens died of natural causes, but it is impossible to be specific as to what actually killed them. Descriptions of illness in the chronicles are often vague, with the terms 'fever' and 'dropsy' covering a multitude of ailments. Orderic believed that Matilda died of a broken heart,[15] said to have been brought about by worrying over the hermit's prophecy. There was plague in Caen in 1083, but that is unlikely to have killed her,[16] for she was ailing for at least a year. When her condition deteriorated in the autumn, William was summoned urgently from England to Rouen, in time to be with her in her last days. She may have been attended by Baldwin, Abbot of Bury St Edmunds, who acted as physician to the King and Queen both in England and in Normandy.

In her will, dated 1083,[17] and dictated in William's presence, Matilda named her youngest son, Henry, heir to her English estates, which had once belonged to Brihtric Meaw.[18] Her other bequests afford us a fascinating glimpse of the treasures of an early medieval queen:

> I give to the abbey of Holy Trinity my tunic, worked at Winchester by Alderet's wife, and the mantle embroidered with gold, which is in my chamber, to make a cope. Of my two golden girdles, I give that which is embroidered with emblems for the purpose of suspending the lamp before the great altar. I give my large candelabra, made at Saint-Lo, my crown, my sceptre, my cups in their cases, another cup made in England, with all my horse trappings and all my gold and silver vessels. And lastly I give the lands of Quettehou and Cotentin, except those which I may already have disposed of in my lifetime, with two dwellings in England. And I have made all these bequests with the consent of my husband.

Unless Matilda had already given some things away to her family, her personal possessions did not amount to much, given her exalted status. Her epitaph (see below) records that she was 'poor to herself and rich to the needy'. Probably, despite her great wealth, she was not materialistic.

In the small hours of Thursday 2 November 1083, 'on the day after All Saints',[19] Matilda's condition worsened. 'Growing apprehensive because her illness persisted, she confessed her sins with bitter tears, and after fully accomplishing all the offices that the Christian profession requires, and being fortified by the life-giving Sacrament', died peacefully in her bed,[20] after Prime (in the first hour of daylight). She was fifty-two at most. That was in fact a good span in an age in which average life expectancy was around thirty-five, men were old at fifty and many women died young in childbed. The average age at death of England's twenty medieval queens was just under fifty. The shortest-lived, Isabella of Valois, died at twenty, and the longest-lived, Eleanor of Aquitaine, at eighty-two. Compared with this, the average age at death of the five Norman queens was about forty-seven.

Cast into loneliness after thirty-three years of marriage, William was inconsolable. 'He showed by many days of the deepest mourning how much he missed the love of her whom he had lost. Indeed from that time forward, if we believe what we are told, he abandoned pleasure of every kind.'[21] The marriage had been a most successful partnership: he had been 'rich in empire, children, wife', according to his epitaph by Baudri de Bourgueil, and apart from when Matilda had aided Robert, there is no record of any discord between them. When she was no more, William never looked at another woman.

Hours after her death, Matilda's body 'was carried to the convent of the Holy Trinity' at Caen, her own foundation. The Queen's bier was attended by a 'great throng of poor people', many of whom she had befriended, and who greatly mourned her.[22] Her corpse was reverently received at the portal of Holy Trinity by a long procession of bishops and abbots, who conducted it into the choir and laid it before the high altar. William had her buried in Holy Trinity with great magnificence, ordering 'a most splendid funeral'[23] that lasted for two days. The obsequies were celebrated by monks, with great pomp, and the Queen's body was interred with deep respect by many bishops and abbots between the choir and the altar.[24]

The tomb raised by William to Matilda's memory in the middle of the choir was 'wonderfully' decorated with gold and precious stones.[25] The thirteen-verse Latin epitaph, still legible and carved in letters of gold along the edges and down the centre of the plain black Tournai marble ledger stone (which miraculously survives), attests to her faith and charity, and was recorded by Orderic:

> Here rests within this fair and stately tomb Matilda, scion of a regal line; the Flemish Duke [*sic*] her sire, and Adelais, her mother, to great Robert, King of France, daughter, and sister to his royal heir. In wedlock to our mighty William joined, she built this holy temple and endowed it with lands and goodly gifts. It was here her holiest work was seen, this shrine, this house, where cloistered sisters dwell, and with their notes of praise the anthem swell, endowed and beautified by her earnest care. She was the true friend of piety and soother of distress,

enriching others, indigent herself, reserving all her treasures for the poor; and by such deeds as these, she merited to be a partaker of eternal life, to which she passed November 2 1083.[26]

Two elegies to Matilda – '*Cere si fortes*' and '*Tempe qui nostra*' – were composed by the French poet Fulcoius of Beauvais.[27] They proclaim that she had proved her mettle to William's subjects, and that 'the common people, the rich, every gender and age, the whole clergy, every tongue, every class' had come to admire her 'just' and 'prudent' disposition. 'If she could be brought back from death through tears, money, fair or foul means, then rest assured there would be an abundance of these things.' Fulcoius wanted this inscription placed on her tomb: 'Matilda, Queen of the English, known for her twofold honour, ruled over the Normans, but here rests entombed in good state, blessed in title that Nature cannot revoke from her. O twofold light of November, it is a little plot, a small pile of ash, but nevertheless a source of glory and grace.'[28]

Orderic remembered Matilda as 'the most amiable, the most courteous, the most intelligent woman of her time; the most chaste, the most devoted to her husband, the most tender towards her children'.

The tomb was opened in 1512 in circumstances that are obscure. In 1562, the Calvinists who sacked Caen during the Reformation destroyed it and Matilda's coffin, broke her effigy, and stole a gold ring set with a sapphire from one of her fingers. The ring was given to Gaspard de Coligny, Admiral of France, who, moved by the grief and anger of Abbess Anne de Montmorency at the desecration, returned it to her. The following year she gave it to her father, Anne de Montmorency, Constable of France, in the presence of King Charles IX.[29] Abbess Anne had Matilda's bones collected and placed in a small lead casket and piously reinterred beneath the original black marble slab – all that was left of the desecrated tomb – in the middle of the choir.

In 1702, the nuns built a new tomb over the original grave site. It was a coffin-shaped sarcophagus of black and white marble, surrounded by iron spikes and hung with an ancient tapestry. This tomb was destroyed in 1793 during the French Revolution. The lead casket, however, was spared and placed in a chapel in the abbey of Saint-Étienne. In 1819 it was reburied in the middle of the choir of Holy Trinity, probably slightly east of Matilda's original resting place,[30] and the original black marble stone bearing her epitaph, and measuring six feet by three,[31] was restored and placed over her grave. In 1819 and 1959 the lead casket was opened and the bones in it examined in the hope of conclusively identifying them as the Queen's and discovering more about her.

Matilda was mourned throughout Normandy, where she was far better known than in England, and Masses were offered up in many churches for the repose of her soul. At Saint-Evroult, as in other places, acts of remembrance were performed.[32] As they had done while Matilda lived, William, many of her blood kin and the lords who had known her endowed abbeys and offered up treasure to Heaven so that perpetual intercessions could be made for the repose of her soul.

Matilda had spent between three and four years in total in England, the land of which she was queen, yet her influence in her husband's kingdom had been considerable. 'Her death represents tragedy for both the clergy and the common folk,' it was said. She would be 'wept for by the English and the Normans for many years'.[33] 'After the death of the glorious Queen Matilda, King William was deeply involved in severe troubles, which closed around him like stormy clouds.'[34]

According to a fifteenth-century chronicler (who had evidently not heard of the harrying of the north), he 'became a thorough tyrant', whereas, as long as she had lived, he had heeded her advice and 'treated the English kindly'.[35] This is perhaps borne out by a posthumous tribute paid to Matilda in a eulogy by the poet Godfrey of Cambrai, Prior of Winchester: 'The King dominated his enemies with arms, and you, Matilda, you dominated them with peace. And your peace turned out to be far more efficient than war.'[36]

Part Two

Matilda of Scotland
First Queen of Henry I

1

'Casting off the Veil of Religion'

William did not long survive his beloved wife. According to Orderic, the peace between him and Robert Curthose, 'which had taken so long to achieve, was soon clouded. The stubborn young man contemptuously refused to follow or obey his father, while the quick-tempered King continually poured abuse and reproach on him in public for his failings.' Other evidence suggests that Orderic exaggerated the rift between father and son, for it is clear that at times they did co-operate.

On 9 September 1087, while besieging the town of Mantes, west of Paris, William fell from his horse and was mortally wounded. He died abandoned, 'without a friend or kinsman near his bed',[1] and was buried in the abbey he had founded at Caen, leaving England securely established under Norman rule. The *Anglo-Saxon Chronicle* observed: 'He was a very wise and a great man, more honoured and more powerful than any before him. Amongst other things, the good peace that he made in the land must not be forgotten.' From the 1120s at the latest he was popularly known as William 'the Conqueror',[2] and William of Malmesbury also refers to him as 'William the Great'.

The usual method of succession in European monarchies in medieval times was through primogeniture – right of the firstborn – in the male line, passing to the sons of the monarch in order of seniority, followed by their children, and only then, failing any male line, to the daughters. But that principle had not fully evolved in Norman times. William left Normandy to his eldest son, Robert Curthose, and England to his next surviving son, the wily, able, but ruthless William Rufus, who now had a broad girth like his father. Because Rufus had been born after the Pope's ban on his parents' marriage had been lifted, his legitimacy was indisputable, and this may have been one reason why William left his kingdom to him – another being that Robert was barely known in England; he had been destined as the heir to Normandy since before his birth, and had long been associated with his mother in its government. Rufus, moreover, had always got on well with his father, unlike the rebellious Robert.

William had never given his youngest son, Henry, possession of the lands Matilda had left him, but had bequeathed him £5,000. Henry petitioned Rufus for his maternal inheritance, but in 1088 Rufus gave Matilda's lands to one of his courtiers, Robert FitzHamon, probably to spite Henry.[3] Understandably there was to be continual strife between the landless Henry and his brothers.

William II was a harsh and unpopular king. He never married and his court was seen as decadent, with churchmen frowning on the King's effeminate favourites, who wore long hair, beards and extravagant shoes. William Rufus fuelled the wrath of the Church by appropriating its income and resisting reform, thereby earning himself a bad monastic press. 'In his days righteousness declined and evil of every kind towards God and man put up its head. Everything that was hateful to God and to righteous men was the daily practice in this land during his reign. Therefore he was hated by almost all his people, and abhorrent to God.'[4]

William Rufus was unmarried, but a possible consort was near at hand. Queen Margaret of Scotland had always envisaged 'the elevation of sons and daughters of hers to the summit of earthly dignity'.[5] To that end, her daughters, Edith and Mary, were 'educated from infancy among the nuns of Wilton and Romsey, where letters were trained into the female heart'.[6] It was the best education they could have had anywhere in the British Isles.[7] These two great royal Saxon foundations lay in Wiltshire and Hampshire, in the heart of the ancient Anglo-Saxon kingdom of Wessex, and were renowned for their sanctity and their erudite traditions.

In 1086, the girls' aunt, Queen Margaret's sister, Christina, became a nun at Romsey Abbey, and Margaret sent Edith and Mary 'to be instructed by her in holy writ'. The great abbey of Romsey, which still stands in all its Romanesque glory, had been founded in 907, when King Edward the Elder established a community of nuns under the rule of his daughter Elfleda. It was refounded as a Benedictine house in 967 by King Edgar. After being sacked by Viking raiders, it was rebuilt in stone around the year 1000. Since then, Romsey had become famous for the education in letters and morals it afforded the daughters of kings and nobles.[8] Edith and Mary were to stay there for seven years. 'These princesses were a long time pupils among the nuns. They were instructed by them, not only in the art of reading, but in the observance of good manners.'[9]

The trouble was that, from the first, Christina did her best to force Edith to become a nun, or at least wear a nun's veil. Edith later recalled, in a statement made to the Archbishop of Canterbury: 'I do not deny having worn the veil in my father's court, for when I was a child, my Aunt Christina had put a piece of black cloth over my head.' At Romsey, 'I went in fear of the rod of my aunt', who 'used to put a little black hood on my head, and when I threw it off, she would often make me smart with a good slapping and a most horrible scolding, as well as treating me as being in disgrace. That hood I did indeed wear in her presence, chafing at it and fearful; but as soon as I was able to escape out of her sight, I tore it off and threw it on the ground and trampled on it; and in that way, although foolishly, I used to vent my rage and the hatred of it that boiled up in me.'[10]

When Edith approached puberty, Christina made her wear the veil 'to preserve me from the lust of the Normans, which was rampant and at that time ready to assault any woman's honour'.[11] It was wise advice, for Saxon women were especially vulnerable to the persistent advances of the conquering race, while 'noble maidens were exposed to the insults of low-born soldiers, and mourned their dishonour by filthy ruffians'.[12]

It may have been Edith's complaints about being forced to wear the veil that prompted her parents to send her and Mary to Wilton. Wilton Abbey, founded in the ninth century by King Alfred the Great, had long had Saxon royal connections, and housed a nail from the True Cross, relics of St Bede the Venerable,[13] and the golden shrine of St Edith, a bastard daughter of King Edgar, which attracted pilgrims and brought great prosperity to the abbey. The young Edith of Scotland, who was later to encourage the fine English art of needlework, may well have been impressed by an alb that adorned the shrine of her namesake, for it had been embroidered by the saint herself with gold thread, gems and pearls, and showed her as a supplicant kneeling at the feet of Christ.[14]

The abbey had been rebuilt in stone by Edward the Confessor's Queen, Edith of Wessex, who had herself benefited from the excellent education that Wilton afforded young girls of rank. She had become accomplished in languages, literacy and the arts, and in the special polish that an education at Wilton conferred on girls who were earmarked for great destinies. Queen Edith had died in retirement at Wilton in 1075.

The Scottish princesses received a similar grounding in literature and languages. They had escaped Christina's vigilance,[15] but as Edith grew older, she began to see the wisdom of pretending to be a nun. 'In order to have a colour for refusing an ignoble alliance, which was more than once offered by her father, she wore the garb of the holy profession.'[16] She later recounted: 'I made a pretence of wearing it to excuse myself from unsuitable marriages.'[17] One suitor whom she rejected, probably in 1093,[18] was William de Warenne, 2nd Earl of Surrey.

In the early years of his reign, William Rufus may have considered marrying Edith himself.[19] Her uncle, Edgar Atheling, was an adherent of his brother, Robert Curthose, and Rufus sought to counterbalance and neutralise his influence. The marriage would have pleased the English and helped to unite the two peoples.[20] But by 1093, it had become clear to King Malcolm that Rufus would not cede lands in Cumbria that Malcolm claimed were his, and he began seeking an alliance with a great northern magnate who could back his cause. The fabulously wealthy Alan the Red (or Alan Rufus), Lord of Richmond, Yorkshire, a son of Odo, Count of Brittany, was willing to fill that role and asked for Edith's hand.[21] She was not quite thirteen; he was fifty-three, and his heart lay elsewhere. Malcolm may not have been aware that, sometime since the spring, Alan had ridden to Wilton Abbey and carried off Gunhilda, the bastard daughter of Harold II of England, who was living there, perhaps as a postulant or novice, having not long since told the saintly and erudite Anselm of Aosta, Lanfranc's successor as archbishop of Canterbury, that she wanted to become a nun. Being in her thirties or forties, she may have given up hopes of a marriage, and willingly went with Lord Alan and lived with him out of wedlock.[22]

An alliance between Alan and King Malcolm, cemented by marriage, might have had ominous consequences for Rufus, as the King and his barons feared when they learned what was afoot. Malcolm was summoned to the court at Gloucester to do homage to Rufus for his lands in England, and perhaps to discuss a marriage alliance between the King and Edith.

In August 1093, on their way to Gloucester for the meeting with King Malcolm, William Rufus and a party of knights arrived unheralded at Wilton. They dismounted at the gates and demanded to be allowed into the church to pray. The Abbess was flustered at the presence of armed men in her house of women. She had heard of the King's reputation and that he often acted deter-minedly on impulse, and feared that, if he saw the pretty young Edith, he might behave inappropriately, even violently. Hurriedly she bade Edith don a nun's habit and go to Vespers. Then she admitted the King to the cloister, where he asked to see her rose garden before going into the church, but after he spied Edith, veiled, amid the other nuns, he made an abrupt departure from the abbey. The fact that Rufus recognised Edith suggests that he had visited her at Wilton before.[23] The Abbess concluded that he had come only to see the princess, and suspected that this boded no good to her.[24] But his purpose may have been to speak of marriage, and he was perhaps angered by the sight of her in nun's garb, especially if he thought that she was deliberately avoiding him.

Both kings were at Gloucester on 24 August, but their meeting never went ahead, as Malcolm refused to pay homage and Rufus refused to receive him.[25] The reason for this is not known. Malcolm may have heard of Rufus's visit to Wilton and concluded that its purpose was less than honourable. Possibly Rufus was angered that Malcolm had dedicated to God the daughter he himself wanted to wed, or he was angered at being snubbed by Malcolm's daughter – or that Malcolm had contemplated marrying her to Alan. He may have forbidden the match.

Within a week, King Malcolm turned up at Wilton, and 'when by chance he saw me veiled', Edith later recalled, 'my father snatched the veil off in rage, and, tearing it to pieces' and trampling on it,[26] 'invoked the hatred of God upon the person who had put it on me, observing[27] that it was his intention to give me in marriage, not to devote me to the Church'. He told Edith he would 'rather have chosen to marry me to Earl [*sic*] Alan than consign me to a house of nuns'.[28] He doubtless said this scathingly, having found out about Alan's abduction of Gunhilda.[29] Furious, Malcolm bore his daughters off to Scotland without further ado.

Any possibility of a marriage between Edith and Alan Rufus had been extinguished when Alan died on 4 August, before the meeting at Gloucester.[30] Afterwards, Archbishop Anselm wrote witheringly to Gunhilda, the lapsed nun: 'Go now to where Count Alan lies. Kiss the bare teeth from which his flesh has fallen.' He warned that she would be damned if she did not return to her convent. Instead, she sought refuge in the arms of Alan's brother, whom she soon married.[31]

Edith and Mary returned home to Scotland to find their mother ill. But Malcolm did not stay by his wife's side. Seething at having been unpardonably snubbed by Rufus, he raised an army and led a raid across the border – 'with greater folly than behoved him',[32] for on 13 November 1093, he was killed with his oldest son, Edward, by his kinsman and steward Archil Morel of Bamburgh, in an ambush near Alnwick, Northumberland.[33] Three days later, when the news reached Edinburgh Castle, his devoted wife Margaret, who was already 'wasted away with the fire of a long illness' and suffering agonies, died of grief, enjoining Turgot, Prior of Durham: 'To you I commit the charge of my children. Teach them, above all things, to love and fear God, and above all see that you expend them love.'[34] Edith and Mary were perhaps with their mother when she died.[35]

At a stroke, Malcolm and Margaret's surviving children were orphaned. Edith was then thirteen, Edmund, Ethelred, Edgar and Alexander all older, Mary was eleven and David nine. In Scotland, the eldest son of a monarch did not necessarily succeed to the throne. The custom of tanistry was observed, whereby a successor was elected by the nobles or clan chiefs. They chose Donald, the son of King Duncan I (d.1040), who was famously murdered by Macbeth in Shakespeare's play (in fact, he was killed in battle). Donald succeeded Malcolm as King Donald III.

By the end of 1093, King Donald had driven the children of Malcolm and Margaret out of Scotland. Turgot and perhaps their uncle, Edgar Atheling, may have assisted with the escape of Edith and Mary to England.[36] They took very little with them. Orphaned, and deprived of the support of their brothers, they looked to God to aid them.[37]

Anselm of Aosta, a worthy successor to Lanfranc as archbishop of Canterbury, had not approved of Edith leaving Wilton Abbey. His understanding was that she was a nun, and in February 1094, in some outrage, he wrote to Osmund, Bishop of Salisbury (the former tutor of Rufus's brother Henry), in whose diocese Wilton lay, reminding him of the importance of spiritual marriage, and informing him that the 'prodigal daughter of the King of Scots, whom the Devil made to cast off the veil of religion, and causes to persist shamelessly in wearing secular clothing', had returned to the world.

However, he had hesitated to condemn her sin openly, lest King William had been the cause of her fleeing north, or had condoned it. Fortunately he had since met with the King, who, to Anselm's relief, had said he would like to see Edith back in her cloister, 'as a good king should', and was only concerned about her having enough to eat. Anselm instructed Bishop Osmund to compel her to 'return to the Order which she arrogantly despised'.[38] It no doubt suited William Rufus to have Edith shut up in a cloister, out of reach of ambitious men who might scheme to marry her and claim the throne in her name.

Probably Edith and Mary returned to Wilton. They had nowhere else to go, and were possibly relieved to avail themselves of the good offices of Bishop Osmund, especially as King William had offered to pay for their keep. But they would have stayed there as lay boarders; certainly they did not resume wearing the veil. Edith's upbringing had made her 'a rival of her mother's piety',[39] but not to the point where she wanted to forsake marriage and motherhood.

For now, she 'learned and practised the literary art' and 'gave her attention to literature'.[40] She even mastered the reading of Latin, and perhaps French. The surviving letters she wrote reveal a good knowledge of the Scriptures, the Church Fathers and the Greek and Roman philosophers, which she probably acquired at Wilton. In an age in which even kings were illiterate, it was extraordinary for a woman to acquire such skills, which would stand Edith in good stead in the years to come. She never lost her love of learning. In later years, William of Malmesbury would write to her brother David: 'For certain your family is known to love the study of letters. Our lady, your sister, never ceased to support literature and to advance those who were devoted to it.'

'These devoted maidens, as they approached the age of womanhood, waited for the consolation of God. They were orphans, deprived of both their parents, separated from their brothers, and far from the protecting care of kindred and friends. They had no home or hope but the cloister, and yet, by the mercy of God, they were not professed as nuns. They were destined by the Disposer of all earthly events for better things. Edith was, by the grace of God, reserved for a higher destiny.'[41]

In 1097, with the support of William Rufus and Edgar Atheling, Edith's oldest surviving brother, another Edgar, overthrew Donald III and took the crown of Scotland himself. As the sister of a king, Edith's status in the world was restored.

2

'Her Whom he so Ardently Desired'

On 2 August 1100, while hunting in the New Forest, King
William Rufus was shot dead by a stray arrow from the bow
of one of his men, later named as Walter Tyrell. It could have been
an accident, and probably was, but the finger of suspicion has long
pointed at the childless King's heir, his brother Henry, who stood
to gain the throne. Henry was aware that Rufus and Robert Curthose
had long ago agreed that each would be the other's heir. But Robert
was away on the First Crusade, having ruled Normandy with an
inefficiency that exasperated his barons.

It is possible that the death, while hunting, of Robert's bastard
son in May, in that same New Forest, had suggested to Henry a
means of getting rid of the hated Rufus, whom few would mourn.
Rufus's reputation in battle was so formidable that any other
method of removing him would probably have been doomed to
failure. But this, and the fact that Henry did not punish Tyrell,
but was generous to him and his family, amounts only to circumstantial evidence, and there is no proof of a regicidal plot. The
chroniclers were in fact unanimous in declaring Rufus's death an
accident.

Henry had been among those hunting with the King on that
fateful day. As soon as he heard that his brother was dead, he raced
to Winchester to secure the royal treasury, then galloped the sixty
miles to London, where he was crowned just two days later. Then
he settled down to rule firmly and efficiently, enforcing law and
order and maintaining peace, as his oppressed subjects groaned under
the burden of the taxes he imposed and complained that they were
in misery and want.

The new King's friends, foremost among them the bishops, urged
him to marry.[1] In the interests of uniting Normans and Saxons,
boosting his hold on the throne and cementing an alliance with
Scotland established by William Rufus in 1097, Henry set his sights
on the 'high-born maiden'[2] Edith of Scotland, a princess of the royal
Saxon blood of the Confessor, illustriously descended on both sides
from the ancient kings of Scotland and the old royal House of
England.[3] She could trace her ancestry 'for many centuries through

fourteen kings', including Alfred, and – it was believed – from Adam, through a son of Noah born in the Ark and not recorded in the Bible.[4] Some still considered Edgar Atheling and the issue of his sister, Queen Margaret, to have a better right to the English throne than the Norman kings.

Many had spoken favourably of Edith, saying how good and fair she was. At twelve, she had been called beautiful, but that was a word indiscriminately used to describe royal and noble ladies. William of Malmesbury thought her 'by no means despicable in beauty', which sounds like a tactful way of saying that she wasn't anything special to look at. Nevertheless, other chroniclers remarked on her beauty, equanimity and chastity, her excellent manners and 'fluent, honeyed speech'. They thought her 'very fair and elegant in person, as well as learned, holy and wise'. She was skilled at music and loved literature.[5]

There is no certain contemporary image of Edith. Manuscript depictions of her date from after her lifetime and are in no sense portraits. Twelfth-century statues on either side of the Romanesque West Door of Rochester Cathedral, dating from *c.*1125–37 and therefore among the oldest sculpted figures in England, have been identified as Edith and Henry, although it has also been suggested that they represent Solomon and the Queen of Sheba. They bear a similarity to the elongated stone figures that adorn the slightly later Royal Portal of Chartres Cathedral in France, but at Rochester the faces are irretrievably weathered. The statue of the Queen is attired as Edith might have been. She has two plaits hanging to her knees and holds a scroll. She wears a crown and veil, a heavily pleated robe edged with bands of elaborate embroidery, and a mantle.

King Malcolm had decreed that Gaelic be replaced by Anglo-Saxon at his court, so English was probably Edith's first language, which would be an advantage. Marriage to Edith would, above all, help Henry to unite Normans and Saxons, and preserve good relations with Scotland. Thus the King, 'appreciating the high birth of the maiden whose perfection of character he had long adored, chose her as his bride'.[6] William of Malmesbury says Henry had 'long been greatly attached to her', and 'long after she discarded the veil, the King fell in love with her', which places the start of their courtship 'long after' 1094. The attraction was mutual.[7] Wace states that Henry was jealous of Edith's former suitor, William de Warenne, Earl of Surrey, and hated him 'to the death'.

We do not know when Henry had first seen Edith, or when these feelings were fostered. They could not have met at the English court, for Rufus had no queen, so it would not have been fitting for Edith to visit or stay at court; and her uncle, Edgar Atheling, was now abroad, also taking part in the First Crusade. Possibly Henry knew Edith through his old tutor, Bishop Osmund, and had visited her at Wilton.[8] He 'little regarded the marriage portion, provided he could possess her whom he so ardently desired, for though she was of noble descent, being great-niece of King Edward, yet she possessed but little fortune, being an orphan, destitute of either parent'.[9] There is evidence that her brother, King Edgar, had perhaps granted her rights in some northern lordships,[10] but that did not amount to much. Love aside, what was most important to Henry was Edith's lineage – and the fact that she was 'a truly incomparable woman'.[11]

Thus a 'special love' flowered between Henry and Edith, 'so that he willed her to wife', and asked her brother, King Edgar, for her hand. In this he was supported by his bishops and the barons.

Saxon chroniclers claim that Edith initially showed some reluctance to encourage Henry's proposal of marriage, which probably gave rise to the thirteenth-century chronicler Matthew Paris's unsubstantiated assertion that she would have preferred to remain in the cloister, but emerged only so that she could be a second Esther and mitigate the sufferings of the Saxons whose blood she shared. Her reluctance was evidently a matter of public knowledge, for there survives a heartfelt plea to her in the *Anglo-Saxon Chronicle*: 'O, most noble and most gracious of women! If thou wouldst, thou couldst raise up the ancient honour of England; thou wouldst be a sign of alliance, a pledge of reconciliation. But if thou persist in thy refusal, the enmity between the Saxon and Norman races will be eternal; human blood will never cease to flow.' That brought home to Edith, if she was not already aware, that marrying Henry was a sacred obligation, for through her it would restore the ancient royal blood of Wessex to the royal line. Their children would be the living embodiment of the union between the Saxon and Norman monarchies.

Edith consented to marry Henry on one condition: that he grant a new charter to his English subjects, promising to govern them according to the laws of Edward the Confessor – which he did that very year. An anonymous poet praised her for persuading him to change the law, and lauded him as a Caesar who listened to his wife, answered her prayers and abolished the unjust laws of the kingdom.[12] Thus the betrothal was sealed.

★

Henry was then thirty-two, of medium height and very like his father, the Conqueror. He was 'a young man of extreme beauty'.[13] 'His hair was black, but scanty near the forehead; his eyes were mildly bright, his chest brawny, his body well fleshed.' His 'thunderous' voice only added to his intimidating presence. 'He was inferior in wisdom to no king in modern time.' He enjoyed plain food, eaten in moderation, and was temperate, drinking only to allay thirst.[14]

In public he wore 'a supercilious look, darting his threatening eye on the bystander, and with assumed severity and ferocious voice, assailing such as conversed with him'. His temper was fearsome, and there is evidence to suggest that Edith found him intimidating, but she would also have seen more of the private Henry, the one who appeared amiable and was 'jocular in proper season'. When relaxing at table with his friends, he was a convivial and amusing companion, making facetious jests about his own failings in order to deflect criticism.[15]

Henry had the Norman love of order. As a ruler, 'he clearly surpassed all his predecessors in England, and preferred contending by counsel, rather than by the sword. If he could, he conquered without bloodshed.'[16] Astute and able, he had three brilliant advantages: great wisdom, success in war and wealth.[17] His counsels were profound, his foresight keen, his eloquence commanding. He was a wise ruler and an accomplished diplomat. 'His learning assisted him in the science of government.'[18]

He also had 'three gross vices': avarice, wantonness and cruelty.[19] He could be calculating, suspicious, devious, deceitful and faithless. He taxed his subjects mercilessly and had a heavy-handed approach to lawbreaking, for which he was widely feared. He had once violently pushed a rebel called Conan from the high Tower of Rouen, swearing on the soul of his mother Matilda that traitors must not be allowed to live.[20] On another occasion, he had put out the eyes of one of his kinsmen with his own hands. When his chamberlain tried unsuccessfully to assassinate him, Henry had him blinded and castrated – a lenient punishment, some thought, for a man who should have been hanged. He once had all the moneyers (or coiners) in the kingdom mutilated, just in case they were counterfeiting coin. Under his rule, men were chained in dungeons and left to starve. Certainly such rough justice acted as a deterrent, but it was Henry who established the practice of sending judges on circuit to ensure that justice was dispensed fairly, and later he replaced the penalty of mutilation with fines. By the end of his reign a Saxon chronicler had bestowed on him the nickname 'The Lion of Justice'.

His court was to be described as a 'Babylonish furnace'[21] and he 'constantly accustomed himself to concubinage',[22] for he was a man of voracious sexual appetite who was 'perpetually enslaved by female seductions'.[23] He fathered about twenty-five bastards, most of them before his marriage. Yet William of Malmesbury, far from condemning his 'chasing after whores', rather naïvely insisted that the King only gratified his lusts because he wanted children. He 'was free, during his whole life, from impure desires. He was led by feminine blandishments, not for the gratification of incontinency, but for the sake of issue. Nor did he condescend to casual intercourse, unless where it might produce that effect. In this respect he was the master of his natural inclinations, rather than the passive slave of lust.'[24] Henry apparently did feel that political strength lay in having many sons and daughters — certainly they played an important role in his life, for he married off several to his advantage and employed others effectively in his service — but it's hard to believe that lust didn't play a part in it, or in his feelings for Edith.

Now, however, he was resolved not to 'wallow in lasciviousness like any horse or mule which is without the use of reason';[25] he would stop using concubines and settle down with a wife.[26]

3
'A Matter of Controversy'

It seemed that there remained no obstacle to Edith's marriage going ahead. But now Christina spoke out. She protested that her niece was a veiled nun, and that it would be an act of sacrilege to remove her from her convent.[1] Because it was known that Edith had been brought up from early childhood in a convent and grown to womanhood there, many believed that she had been dedicated by her parents to God's service, as she had been seen walking around wearing a nun's veil. And when it became known that the King was about to 'advance her to his bed', this became 'a matter of controversy'.[2] When it was seen that Edith had discarded the veil, tongues began wagging. This proved an obstacle to the couple marrying and 'embracing one another, as they desired',[3] for the King realised that it would be unwise for him to join himself with a woman who was widely believed to be a nun. The matter must be settled, for the sake of the salvation of them both, and for the future security of the succession.

Immediately, Henry recalled Archbishop Anselm, whom Rufus had driven into exile. He asked the renowned Anselm to rule on whether or not Edith was free to marry. Anselm arrived in England in October 1100 and wasted no time in advising the King not to wed her because he had been reliably informed that she was in truth a nun. Henry protested that he had promised to marry her and had even sworn to do so on oath to her father.[4]

Henry must have informed Edith what the Archbishop had said. 'Accordingly, as all were looking for a sign from Anselm on this question', she took the initiative and herself travelled from Wilton to see him at Salisbury, where she humbly sought his advice and help.[5]

What transpired at their meeting was recorded by Eadmer, whose account was written to counter later criticisms of Anselm's handling of the case. The Archbishop made it clear to Edith at the outset that he had grave doubts that she was free to wed. He warned her 'that he was not to be induced by any pleading to take from God His bride and join her in marriage with an earthly husband'.

Edith protested that she had been sent to Wilton only to be educated, and that her parents had never intended her to be a nun. She denied 'absolutely that she had been so dedicated' or 'had ever at any time been veiled with her own consent, and declared that, if it was necessary to convince him, she would prove it at the judgement seat of the whole English Church'. She told Anselm how her aunt Christina, whom he knew quite well, had tried to make her wear the veil, and how she had rebelled. 'In that way, and only in that way, I was veiled, as my conscience bears witness,' she insisted. 'That is my answer to the slanders which are spread abroad about me. This I ask your wisdom to consider, and do for me as your fatherhood knows should be done.'[6]

Anselm would not give a ruling himself. He 'declared that the case ought to be determined by the judgement of the chief persons of religion in the kingdom. So, at his bidding, on the appointed day, the bishops, abbots and all the nobles and leading men of the religious profession assembled on the Surrey shore of the River Thames near London, in a manor house at Lambeth.[7] In due order, the case was brought up for discussion. From various sources, credible witnesses came forward, declaring that the simple truth supported the girl's story.'[8] They swore she had worn the veil to protect her from unwanted suitors, but had never made her vows.[9]

Just to be certain, Anselm had sent two archdeacons, William of Canterbury and Hambald of Salisbury, to Wilton Abbey. They declared before the whole assembly that they had made most careful inquiries of the sisters, and that they had not been able to gather from them anything at all which was inconsistent with the account given by Edith.[10]

Warning that 'the matter should be rightly decided' so that God was not defrauded of what was justly His, Anselm withdrew so that the bishops could consider without 'fear or favour' what judgement should be given. There was much discussion about Archbishop Lanfranc approving of women wearing the veil to avoid rape, from which it is clear that it had become a common practice. Lanfranc had ruled that those who had hidden in nunneries after the Normans invaded were not bound by any vows and could not be forced to become nuns against their will; they must be afforded 'unrestricted leave to depart'.[11]

The bishops took the view that Edith had worn the veil under compulsion, and when Anselm returned, they gave their opinion: 'Under the circumstances of the matter, it seemed to them established that the girl could not rightly be bound by any decision to prevent her being free to dispose of her person in whatever way she legally wished.'[12] Only now was Anselm 'induced to consent to her marriage'.[13] He accepted the judgement of the bishops, 'with all the more confidence as I am told that it is supported by the authority of so great a father' as Lanfranc, and Edith was summoned before the assembly. Calmly she listened to an account of the proceedings, then petitioned that she might make a brief statement. 'She offered to prove by oath that her story was in accordance with the real truth of the matter. This she declared that she would do, not as thinking that they did not believe her, but to cut away any opportunity for ill-affected persons to utter any scandal in the future.' They replied that there was no need for any such thing. The Archbishop ruled that she 'had proved that she had not embraced a religious life, either by her own choice, or the vow of her parents; and she was therefore free to contract marriage with the King'. Dismissing her, he said he regretted to see one who might have been God's bride placed in a carnal bed. Nevertheless, having obtained Anselm's blessing, Edith departed 'with a happy face',[14] and would always remain devoted to the man who had made her marriage possible.

Herman, Abbot of Tournai, later claimed that, as a young monk, he had discussed the case with Anselm, although he would have been nineteen at most when Anselm died. Nevertheless, he stated that the Archbishop had said that no good would come of the marriage. It was not in dispute that Edith had often worn the veil, and surely, he declared, the King could have found an unencumbered bride among the daughters of kings and counts. Anselm had said as much to Henry, begging him not to wed Edith. 'England will not long rejoice in the children she will bear,' he warned.[15]

4
'Godric and Godgifu'

The wedding took place 'a few days later'[1] at Martinmas, the feast of St Martin of Tours, which fell on Sunday 11 November 1100, when Edith was given to Henry 'with great honour' at Westminster Abbey,[2] with Archbishop Anselm officiating.[3] 'When this union was due to be made and established in accordance with the ritual of the Church, and all the nobility of the realm and the people of lesser degree were come together for this ceremony and were crowding around the King and the maid in front of the doors of the church, Father Anselm himself, standing raised up above the crowd, instructed them all how the girl's case, about which there had been so much talk, had been inquired into and determined by the bishops. He then, on divine authority, charged them that, if anyone was aware of anything contrary to the judgement, so that it could be shown that, according to Christian law, this union ought not to be made, he should, without any hesitation and without incurring the displeasure of anyone, openly declare it. At this they all cried out with one accord that the matter had been rightly decided, and that there was now no ground on which anyone, unless possibly led by malice, could properly raise any scandal. Thereupon the pair were joined together in lawful matrimony with the dignity befitting a king and queen', and Anselm gave them his blessing.[4]

Eadmer concluded his account with this sceptical observation: 'So there I have described the girl's story without asserting whether it was true or not.' Yet it is hardly likely that Anselm would have allowed the marriage to go ahead if there was any room for doubt. Even so, a germ of scepticism remained, as will become clear, and in the thirteenth century the chronicler Matthew Paris would lambast Edith as a professed nun who had brought a curse on her descendants.

At the door of the abbey, as the couple emerged, Henry paused and formally settled on Edith a dower that made her one of the richest magnates in England.[5] It comprised most of the lands held by Edith of Wessex. Although few details survive, we know that Henry gave his bride lands in the north, and extensive holdings in the City of London, the rights to dues and taxes from Exeter, Winchester, Rockingham and much of the county of Rutland, and several abbeys, including Malmesbury, Barking (which dated from the seventh century) and Waltham.[6] She also received at least one manor that had been owned by, or confiscated from, her father's killer, Archil Morel. That the dower was substantial is suggested by the fact that, soon after becoming queen, Edith was exercising extensive patronage.[7] Also on the wedding day, Henry issued a charter to Abingdon Abbey, which was to become one of the new Queen's favoured religious houses and would enjoy her bounty.[8]

It is often said that, to make his Queen more acceptable to the Norman barons, Henry insisted that she change her name to Matilda, in honour of his mother, her godmother. It has also been suggested that Edith was given Matilda as a baptismal name by Robert Curthose or Matilda of Flanders, but that she did not use it until she lived in England.[9] It would make sense that, in the interests of reconciling the Saxon and Norman peoples, a queen with Saxon blood would agree to adopt a Norman name; or that, having lived in evident fear of predatory Norman suitors, she had already chosen to abandon her Saxon name, hoping that they might approach a woman with a Norman name more respectfully. Chroniclers would call the new Queen 'the second Matilda'; like the first, she set an example of devout queenship that would be emulated by her successors.[10]

On 14 November, Edith – or Matilda, as she was now known – was consecrated queen and crowned by Archbishop Anselm.[11] She prostrated herself before the altar before her anointing, and a ring was placed on her finger. The prayers offered up made reference to

Old Testament heroines: Judith, who decapitated the fearsome Holofernes and saved her people from war; Sarah, who was fruitful in her old age; Rebecca, who was brave, resourceful and wise; Rachel, who was loved enduringly by Jacob; and Esther, who delivered the Jews from persecution – as the Saxons doubtless hoped Matilda would deliver them from Norman oppression. The message was clear: these were the virtues embodied by, and expected of, the new Queen.[12]

At the coronation of Matilda of Scotland, a verse was recited recalling a prophecy of Edward the Confessor that 'the green tree' of the old royal line would be re-grafted and England's ills would cease:[13]

> Now by the tree is set the root,
> And like to bear both flower and fruit.
> The tree, ye may well understand,
> To be the kingship of England;
> The root, ye trow, is King's seed,
> Whereof our kings should come indeed.
> Now gotten hath the tree the root,
> And like to bear both flower and fruit:
> Dame Matilda, our Queen and lady,
> That wedded is with King Henry.[14]

This theme is echoed in a later work, *Le Livere de Reis*: 'And the tree returned to its trunk, when she, who was of the lineage of Alfred, was made queen of England.'

Since before her marriage, Matilda of Scotland had corresponded with the venerable scholar and poet Hildebert of Lavardin, Bishop of Le Mans, whom she may have met when he visited England in 1099. To mark her nuptials, he composed Latin verses congratulating King Henry and England on the possession of a doubly royal bride. He extolled Matilda's virtues, and the way her modest and maidenly deportment enhanced her charms, as, 'with blushes redder than the crimson of her royal robe, she stood at the altar invested with her royal insignia, a virgin queen and bride, in whom England's hopes hailed the future mother of a mighty line of kings'.

This undated homily may have been a reminder not to let all the adulation blind her to the fact that she was mortal: 'Among the wealth and delights and favours of the people, let the spirit take this in: let your tongue sound this: Death equates the lord to the servant, the sceptre to the bonds, drawing the dissimilar to a similar condition.'[15]

Yet Hildebert himself contributed to the adulation in another panegyric written soon after Matilda's coronation:

Daughter of a past king, wife of a present, mother of a future king, this is special to you. Rarely if ever is a woman found who is at the same time the daughter, wife, and parent of kings. Your nobility did not begin with you, nor will it end with you, but live on after you as it was. You do not dishonour her, revered daughter of a mother who gave birth to you such as she was. Your father had one, you have two kingdoms. The English venerate you as queen, the Normans as countess [*sic*]: both people as their ruling lady. You do not come to the sceptre raw, birth gave you usage. It is yours to reign, a paternal thing for you. You rule by nature, others by fate; these give you rule, fate gives it to others. Nothing is more powerful than you in the kingdom; nothing as beautiful; everyone is less in religion. You so compose your customs, Queen, and your actions, that there is nothing in them more or less than just. Could you do harm? You do not wish to. Could you take offence? You condone voluntarily. Do you see sorrow? You condole. Do you wish to give? You do not hesitate. To live sparingly? You do not know how. If you speak, the speech has force. If you are silent, it is firm; if you laugh, it is honourable laughter. Do you pray? Mouths are moist with the tears of the praying. Do you fast? You rejoice. Do you eat? Never to satiety. Whatever you do, you have the rein of sobriety. Simplicity adorns your mind within, honesty your face without, graces individually and more together.[16]

The Christmas crown-wearing at Westminster following the royal wedding was attended by the future Louis VI of France, who sat between the King and Archbishop Anselm at the Yuletide feast. But while the marriage pleased the English, it now became clear that the Norman barons were contemptuous, and that Henry's plan to bring unity was not immediately successful. During the festivities, 'the malice of certain evil-minded men busied itself in inventing the most cutting railleries on King Henry and his wife of English blood'. Behind Henry's back[17] they made racial comments and 'openly branded their lord with sarcasms, calling him Godric and his consort Godgifu', despised names common among the conquered Saxons,[18] while Matilda was disparagingly referred to as 'the Saxon woman'.[19]

Initially, acceptance of Matilda by the Normans had more to do with her Scots royal connections than her English ones.[20]

But gradually, as time passed, some followed their King's example and took Saxon wives. 'By intermarriage, and by every means in his power, he bound the two peoples into a firm union.'[21] Within a few years,'English and Normans were living peacefully together in boroughs, towns, and cities, and were inter-marrying with each other. You could see many villages or town markets filled with displays of French wares and merchandise, and observe the English, who had previously seemed contemptible to the French in their native dress, completely transformed by foreign fashions.'[22] Integration was a slow process, though. Not until a century after the Conquest could it be said,'It can scarcely be decided who is of English birth and who of Norman.'[23]

The marriage of Henry and Matilda proved famously successful, one of partnership rather than passion. They 'either other loved withouten strife', which suggests that Matilda did not complain about her husband's infidelities. Pragmatically she accustomed herself to Henry's bastards, several of whom were being brought up and educated in his household. One of the eldest, Robert of Caen, born of an unknown Norman mother around 1090, was a special favourite of Henry's, who took the boy with him everywhere and had him styled 'Robert, the King's son'.

Matilda herself never committed 'any impropriety, and with the exception of the King's bed' remained 'completely chaste and uncontaminated, even by suspicion'.[24] But it was only by 'careful investigation' that she discovered the good will in the heart of her husband.[25]

5

'Another Esther in Our Own Time'

Queen Matilda became 'right well loved' throughout England,[1] and was often referred to as 'the good Queen'.[2] One bishop called her 'the common mother of all England'.[3] She set a sterling example of queenly conduct that would long be remembered. Following the example of her mother, she gladly undertook her traditional duties of helping the poor and sick, and interceding for prisoners. Traditionally she has been seen as something of a pious nonentity, but the recent scholarship of Lois L. Huneycutt and others has shown that this was far from the case. Matilda played a prominent political role, unique in the annals of English queens consort. In fact, when asked by her grandson, Henry II, to write about his ancestors, the saintly chronicler Aelred of Rievaulx felt unequal to addressing 'the magnitude of the matter' of doing justice to Matilda, who was 'another Esther in our own time'.[4] It was an image she herself was to cultivate.

Charter evidence shows that she was able to influence Henry,[5] and that he relied on her advice. A contemporary assessed her as 'not dissimilar to the King in competence'.[6] She attended meetings of the King's Council, although charters testify to her being present on fewer occasions than Matilda of Flanders when the King resolved legal disputes – only rarely does her mark appear on such charters. However, she attested more charters than most other signatories. She issued writs as well as thirty-three charters in her own name and under her own seal, while her signature, as witness, almost always appears immediately below the King's on sixty-five of the charters he issued during her lifetime; the only exception is a charter granted to the abbey of Saint-Étienne, Caen, where her brothers' signatures take precedence.[7] Her seal survives in the British Library, and shows a full-length figure of a crowned queen holding an orb and sceptre. It is the earliest extant example of an English queen's seal.

Matilda involved herself in ecclesiastical affairs, and her letters to Archbishop Anselm reveal that she had some say in the bestowal of benefices and abbacies. Like her mother, she supported reform of the Church, and she was at the forefront of religious innovation, encouraging the new monastic orders that were beginning to flourish at that time.

It was thanks to her influence that the King sought regular absolution for his sins.[8] She was 'a woman of exceptional holiness, in piety her mother's rival, and in her own character exempt from all evil influence',[9] 'the very mirror of piety, humility and princely bounty'.[10] She founded many religious houses and set up gilded crosses on highways throughout the land, at her own expense.[11]

She gave two jewelled brass candlesticks to Le Mans Cathedral, prompting Bishop Hildebert to write a letter to the 'venerable Queen of the English, most worthy in glory and honour', extolling her munificence and praising the carving: 'Its value is increased by the majesty of the sender; art and nature add less to it than that it comes from the Queen. It is manifest from this how devoted you are to the Lord's sacraments for which you provide the instruments since, as a woman, you cannot administer them, imitating as far as possible the holy women who first came to the Cross with tears and then to the tomb with spices.'[12]

On learning that the seventh-century church of St Mary at Southampton was falling into ruin, and that congregations had to be crammed into a side chapel dedicated to St Nicholas, Matilda founded 'the great church of Our Lady', which has since been rebuilt several times.[13] When Henry granted the nuns of Malling the right to hold a lucrative weekly market, it was 'for the love of, and at the request of, my wife, Queen Matilda'.[14]

In 1103, Matilda persuaded Henry to repeal the hated curfew law, introduced by his father in 1068 to prevent not only fires, but also confederacies of Saxons plotting against Norman rule under cover of darkness. Every night since then, the curfew bell had been rung at eight o'clock, obliging everyone to damp down their fires.

Matilda's marriage drew England and Scotland closer together, and she probably played no small role in helping to accomplish this. Her brothers sought brides at the English court. Around 1107, Alexander I, King of Scots, would marry Sybilla, one of Henry I's bastard daughters, and before Christmas 1113, 'the arguments and petitions of the Queen' persuaded the King to allow her younger brother, the future David I of Scots, who probably lived at Henry I's court as a dependant from around 1100, to wed Henry's cousin and ward, Maud, daughter and heiress of Waltheof, Earl of Huntingdon and Northumbria, and widow of Simon de St Liz (or Senlis), Earl of Huntingdon, through whom the earldom of Huntingdon became attached to the Scottish Crown.[15]

Matilda's innate qualities made her a queen contemporaries could respect. 'Successes did not make her happy, nor did troubles make her sad. Troubles brought a smile to her, successes fear. Beauty did not produce weakness in her, nor power pride; she alone was both powerful and humble, both beautiful and chaste.'[16]

Matilda resided often at Westminster. In her day it boasted a magnificent new hall − at 240 feet by 67 the largest then seen in England (if not Europe), with walls six feet thick − built by William Rufus probably around the shell of the Confessor's hall.[17] It soared to a height of forty feet, and halfway up, a clerestory gallery ran all the way around the walls; fragments of the Norman windows could still be seen in the nineteenth century. The original wooden roof[18] was supported by a row of posts along either side. At one end stood the King's marble throne, which would have resembled a classical-style stool, perhaps decorated with lions' heads or feet.[19]

Westminster Hall, which still stands today and continues to be used for important state occasions, such as the lying-in-state of monarchs, was a bold statement of the king's power and splendour, and its magnificence probably accounted for Westminster becoming the premier royal residence and – later in the twelfth century – the centre of the royal administration. The hall was often used for state ceremonies and feasting. Then as now, it played an important role in government; in 1102 Henry I held his first meeting of the Great Council there. To the south of it lay a yard that remained from the Confessor's palace, which is still called Old Palace Yard. Queen Matilda issued at least eight charters at Westminster.[20]

There was a chapel in the palace, possibly the one dedicated to St Stephen, which is first mentioned in 1184. It may have been founded by King Stephen,[21] or even by William the Conqueror, whose abbey in Caen was dedicated to St Étienne. The chapel was rebuilt in the thirteenth century by Henry III and Edward I to rival the Sainte-Chapelle in Paris.

Matilda loved Westminster Abbey, and would often lie for whole days and nights in prayer and penance before the shrine of Edward the Confessor, who had been revered as a saint since his death in 1066, but not yet been formally canonised. She gave to the abbey relics of the cell and garments of her favourite saint, St John the Evangelist, which were kept in the chapel specially dedicated in his honour, and Henry I's charter and other grants to the abbey were bestowed 'at the prayer of Queen Matilda'. She herself gave to Westminster land along the Thames shore in London.[22] A fifteenth-century inventory of the abbey lists the gifts she donated, among them a black woven girdle embroidered in gold with the words of the hymn '*Nesciens Mater*' and the prayer '*Deus qui salutis*'. She also gave a relic of St Mary Magdalene and a bone of St Christine, who was said to have been tortured to death for her faith in the third century.[23]

Waltham Abbey, Essex, part of the Queen's dower, yielded an annual income of £100. There had been a church on the site in the seventh century, and the abbey had been founded and rebuilt by King Harold, who was buried there after his defeat at Hastings.[24] In the last decade of the eleventh century, work had begun on a new

Norman church, although in Matilda's time this was as yet unfinished – it was not completed until 1150. A massive cruciform building, in appearance similar to Durham Cathedral, Waltham was famous for its miraculous black cross or rood; around 1016, instructed in a dream, a blacksmith at Montacute had climbed a hill and unearthed this cross. When it was placed on a cart, the oxen refused to go in any other direction than Waltham, and dragged it all the way there. Pilgrims from far and wide came to venerate it, making the abbey very rich.

The Queen employed servants from Waltham Abbey. She held court there, according to the King's charter granting her the property, gave gifts, and interested herself in the community's affairs. Geoffrey, one of her chaplains, was a canon of the abbey, and later its dean. Around 1108–15, Matilda authorised the canons to hold an annual fair, which would boost the abbey's revenue.[25]

Malmesbury Abbey was another of Matilda's dower properties, a 'place where she herself ruled', and which was 'closely associated with her household'.[26] The monks would later testify that she 'helped in almost all our affairs and gave solace for the most part in all things and endowed our church with a royal dowry. We were cherished richly by her mercy. Indeed, religion shone abundantly in that government, where the fullness of all charity excelled.'[27]

Other religious institutions that benefited from Matilda's largesse were Durham Cathedral and the abbeys of Abingdon, Barking, Wilton, St Albans, Selby, St Peter's in Gloucester, St Mary's in Tavistock, St Mary's in York, St Mary's in Northampton, St Mary's in Huntingdon, and Merton Priory. Outside England she issued many charters confirming gifts to monasteries, among them the abbeys of Troarn near Bayeux, Saint-Vincent at Le Mans, Bec-Hellouin and Cluny.[28] Her gift of a huge candelabrum prompted Bernard of Clairvaux to rant against the worldliness of Cluny, with its 'great trees of brass fashioned with wondrous skill, glittering with jewels'.[29]

It was important that kings and queens looked the part, dressing magnificently to proclaim their majesty. Fashions were slow to change in the Middle Ages, but by the 1090s, the sleeves of the tunic, or robe, had become wider and more flowing, and women's gowns were now 'as long behind as they were before', trailing all around them on the floor, while the bodice was closer-fitting. Sleeves grew so long that they had to be knotted to keep them from sweeping the ground. Yet Matilda seems not to have been interested in fashion or personal adornment. It has been said that her seal shows her in the costume of fifty years earlier,[30] but the seal may be based on that of Matilda of Flanders, which does not survive.[31] The second Matilda wears almost the same costume in which her daughter and her grandson's Queen, Eleanor of Aquitaine, would later be portrayed on their seals. Yet other evidence suggests that she did not make the most of her attributes, and spurned artifice, preferring to be her natural self, according to a poem dedicated to her by Marbodius, Bishop of Rennes:

> It is the value of this work to have seen a queen to
>   whom none
> can be compared in beauty of body and face.
> Though she alone hides it under a loose dress,
> desiring to disguise it with unusual modesty,
> she cannot hide it because it shines with its own light
> and the sun piercing the clouds sets the rays in motion.
> Outstanding customs and words flowing with honey:
> it is better to be silent than to speak too little of it.
> Other women affect what nature denied them,
> paint their purple cheeks with snowy milk.
> The embalmed face draws together painted colours,
> distinguishing signs by the adultery of art.
> In some, bands compress the projecting breasts
> and a draped dress suggests a long flank.
> They partly uncover their hair with an extended [shaved]
>   forehead
> and wish to please with iron-wrought curls.
> You, O Queen, fear to seem beautiful, because you are,
> having gifts freely which others purchase.
> It is better to have openly what nature blessed you with;
> you would be ungrateful to God if you denied His gifts.
> You wish to hide your lighted lantern under a bushel:
> it is not yours, but the gifts of a giving Lord that you have.
> A virgin, though modest, may yet look beautiful
> and a lovely form suit a chaste mind.
> O royal spouse born from royal forebears!
> Great things cannot be covered, small usually lie hidden.
> Your fame will live as long as my songs live,
> and he who reads my writings will sing of you.[32]

6

'Lust for Glory'

The English court was the seat of government and a major administrative centre, and the royal household that moved about with the King and Queen was the greatest establishment in the kingdom. We know something about how Henry I's court functioned from the 'Constitutio Domus Regis' ('The Establishment of the King's Household'), drawn up around 1136.[1]

Two officers of state shared responsibility for the court. The Master Chamberlain ruled over the King's house or hall, and was responsible for guarding the jewels and treasure he carried with him. From this office evolved another, that of Treasurer. The Seneschal, or Steward, with his white staff of office, was in charge of the domestic services that supported the King's house, including the kitchens. He enjoyed the status of a baron, and under him came the Master Butler – who took care of the wine, varieties of both red and white being imported and enjoyed in this period – and the Sewer, who arranged the seating at table. The royal household was also a military concern. The Constable was in command of the household knights and archers, and his subordinate, the Marshal, kept order in the royal residences and arranged tournaments.[2] Matilda of Scotland's household was headed by her chamberlain, who was called Alwin,[3] and she had her own chancellor and chaplains.

The court encompassed most of the government departments, which, apart from the Treasury at Winchester, travelled around with the King. It was only in the latter half of the twelfth century that these departments began to be established at Westminster.

They were run by officers of state. The Chancellor kept the King's Great Seal and was responsible for the clerks of the writing chamber, who scribed documents and writs and kept records. He presided over the Court of Exchequer – literally a table with a checked cloth – that administered the royal revenues. The role of his subordinate clerk was to evolve into that of Chancellor of the Exchequer. The Chancellor also had responsibility for the royal chapels, which he delegated to the King's chaplains.[4] The chief officers all received a wage of 5s. a day, and had the privilege of dining at the King's table. They also enjoyed lavish daily perquisites of fine and ordinary bread, a large wax candle, forty candle ends and eight gallons of wine.

The court was a hub of patronage and culture, in which Matilda was highly influential. Her literary and musical interests were famous. It was almost certainly she who asked a poet called Benedeit to translate his Latin poem 'The Voyage of St Brendan' into French:

> Lady Mahaut, who Queen
> By the grace of Heaven hath been
> Y-crowned, who this land hath blest
> With peace and wholesome laws and rest,
> Both by King Henry's stalwart might
> And by thy counsels, mild and bright.
> For this, their holy benisons,
> May the Apostles shed, each one,
> A thousand thousandfold on thee!
> And since thy mild command hath won me
> To turn this goodly history
> Into romance, and carefully
> To write it out and soothly [truthfully] tell
> What to St Brendan erst befell,
> At thy counsel I undertake the task right gladly.[5]

In the sixth century, the Irish saint had made missionary voyages to Iona and other parts of Scotland, which would have been of more interest to Matilda. The poetic cycle of St Brendan's voyage may have been recited at the Easter court of 1107 or 1108.[6]

Some thought Matilda extravagant in her patronage of singers and scholars. William of Malmesbury complained:

> She had a singular pleasure in hearing the service of God, and on this account was thoughtlessly prodigal towards clerks of melodious voice. She addressed them kindly, gave to them liberally, and promised still more abundantly. Her generosity becoming universally known, crowds of scholars, equally famed for verse and for singing, came over [to England], and happy did he account himself who could soothe the ears of the Queen by the novelty of his song. Nor on these only did she lavish money, but on all sorts of men, especially foreigners, that, through her presents, they might proclaim her celebrity abroad. For the

desire for fame is so rooted in the human mind that hardly anybody is satisfied with the reward of a good conscience, but is fondly anxious. Hence it was justly observed that the disposition crept upon the Queen to reward all the foreigners she could, while others were kept in suspense, sometimes with effectual, but oftener with empty promises. Hence too it arose that she fell into the error of prodigal givers: bringing many claims on her tenantry, exposing them to injuries, and taking away their property, by which, obtaining the credit of a liberal benefactress, she little regarded the sarcasms of her own people.

Naturally the scholars were not among the grumblers. 'The English poets of those days made full notable verse' lauding her 'courtesy, humility, silence and other good manners'.[7] William of Malmesbury, himself one of her tenants, frowned on Matilda's 'lust for glory' and lack of consideration for her people, yet defended her in part, asserting that her servants had designs of their own. 'Harpy-like, they conveyed everything they could gripe into their purses, or wasted it in riotous living. Her ears being infected with the base insinuations of these people induced this stain on her noble mind, holy and meritorious in every other respect.' Lingering concerns about Matilda's indiscriminate liberality would dog her to the end of her life,[8] and there is evidence that for a time she did impose harsh taxes on her tenants.

Yet it was at her request, expressed during a visit she made to Malmesbury shortly before her death,[9] that William of Malmesbury wrote his *Gesta Regum Anglorum*, a history of the deeds of the kings of England, which was dedicated to her, and is such a rich source for the period. She had earlier spoken to him and his fellow monks about the blessed St Aldhelm,[10] in whose kinship she took well-deserved pride, having investigated his genealogy and found that she was related to him. William recounted: 'She asked that we set forth his whole family in a little book, asserting that it was not unworthy to be honoured as in the old way with a volume of the deeds of the English kings. Nor could our humility deny what such royal authority willed. We therefore had the required document prepared with the list and names and years of the kings of the English. Then, indeed, allured by the desire for a larger narration with easy sweetness, she prevailed on us to do a full history of her ancestors.'[11] Matilda may also have helped to fund the journeys that William made in order to do his research.[12]

William of Malmesbury may have criticised Matilda's actions during her early years as queen, but his work – which was not finished in her lifetime – reveals great admiration for her. He patently admired her kindness, amiability, piety and literary patronage. Later he made it clear that he thought her a candidate for sainthood.[13]

7

'The Common Mother of All England'

For several years Matilda kept up a correspondence with Archbishop Anselm. Her learning is evident in her many quotations from the Bible and the Church Fathers – saints Paul, Jerome, Gregory and Augustine – and the Greek and Roman philosophers, notably Quintilian and Cicero's moving essay on old age, *Cato Maior de Senectute*.[1] Six of her letters to Anselm survive. Letters from queens are rare in this period, and while they are characterised by the sometimes startling stilted formal and rhetorical style of the age, Matilda's give insights into her emotional character and her piety. They would have been dictated to a clerk, not written in her own hand. No holograph letters of English queens survive from before the fifteenth century.

In the first of these letters to Anselm, written around 1102, she styled herself 'Matilda, by the grace of God Queen of the English, his most humble handmaid', and effusively expressed her indebtedness to him: 'I am under great obligation to your kindness. You are such a brave athlete of God, a vanquisher of human nature, a man by whose untiring vigour the peace of the kingdom and the dignity of the priesthood have been strengthened and defended; such a faithful and prudent steward of God, by whose blessing I was sanctified in legitimate matrimony, by whose consecration I was raised to the dignity of earthly royalty, and by whose prayers I shall be crowned, God granting, in heavenly glory.' She exhorted Anselm to relax his long fasts and not to be so zealous in his ascetic habits, lest they make him ill, and to follow St Paul's comfortable advice to Timothy to drink wine for the stomach's sake. 'May your Holiness thrive in the Lord,' she ended, 'and with your prayers do not give up helping

Harold Godwinson swears to make William of Normandy king of England.

Thirteenth-century wall paintings of William, Matilda of Flanders and their eldest son, Robert, from the abbey of Saint-Etienne, Caen.

Left: William sails to England in *The Mora*, the ship given to him by Matilda of Flanders

Below: The abbeys founded by Matilda and William at Caen in penance for their forbidden marriage (*left*) Matilda's, Holy Trinity (*right*) William's, Saint-Etienne

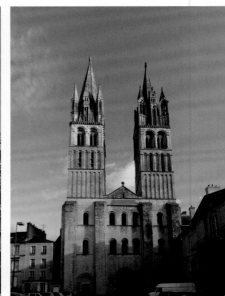

Charter to Holy Trinity bearing the crosses of William and Matilda.

Westminster Abbey, where Matilda was crowned queen in 1068.

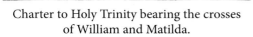

Copy of the portrait taken from
William's corpse 435 years
after his death.

William I granting a charter to
the City of London.

Matilda with her infant son Henry.

Matilda as patroness of Gloucester
Abbey.

This aerial view of Windsor shows the footprint of William I's castle. The Round Tower stands o the site of the wooden keep on its high mound (or motte) in the centre, with the two large baileys either side. The royal apartments have always been in the upper ward.

Above: William and Matilda as founde Selby Abbey, with Abbot Benedict of Aux

Left: Embroidering a n Queen Matilda at work on the Ba Tapestry, painting by Alfred Guillard, 1

Matilda's tomb in the abbey of Holy Trinity, Caen, with its original marble ledger stone.

Statue of William the Conqueror in his birthplace, Falaise.

The Norman Kings from a manuscript 1250: (*top*) William I and William II, (*bottom*) Henry I and Stephen.

The ill-fated Robert Curthose, Duke of Normandy.

The foundations of Malcolm's Tower, Dunfermline, where Matilda of Scotland was born.

Anselm of Aosta, Archbishop of Canterbury, whom Matilda revered.

Margaret, Queen of Scots, Matilda's saintly mother.

Above: Matilda of Scotland's seal, the earliest one of an English queen to survive.

Left: Matilda as benefactress of St Alban's Abbey.

...atue that may represent Matilda, from the west door of Rochester Cathedral.

Matilda's brother, David I, King of Scots. He was to champion the cause of her daughter, Maud.

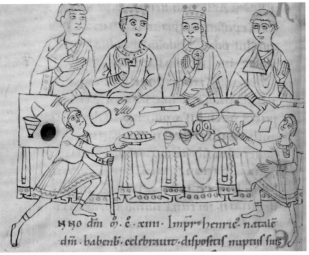

Above: The wedding feast of the future Empress Maud and the Roman Emperor Heinrich V.

Left: Probably Adeliza of Lou[...] Henry I's second Qu[...]

Above: Henry I mourning the loss o[...] son in the *White Ship* disa[...]

Below: The burial of Henry Reading Abbey, 1

me, your faithful handmaiden, who loves you with all the affection of her heart.'[2]

Anselm's replies to Matilda's letters were generally reserved in tone, in contrast to her extravagant outpourings. Addressing her as 'glorious Queen of the English, reverend lady, dearest daughter', he thanked her for her generosity, and urged her, if she wished to render thanks for her marriage 'in a proper, good and efficacious manner by your deeds, consider that Queen whom it pleased the Lord to choose for Himself as His bride from this world' – the Church. 'Therefore, exalt, honour and defend this spouse so that with her and in her you may be pleasing to her spouse, God, and live, reigning with her, in eternal beatitude. Amen. May it be so.'[3]

Between 1100 and 1107, Matilda commissioned Turgot, Prior of Durham, who had tutored her brothers and followed her to England, to write a life of her mother, Queen Margaret, who was already earning a reputation for saintliness. But it was not just the commemoration of her mother's virtues that motivated Matilda as much as the desire to profit from her example, as Turgot perceived. He dedicated his work:

> To the honourable and excellent Matilda, Queen of the English, Turgot. The manner of life of your mother of venerable memory that pleased God, which you have heard spoken of so often with the harmonious praise of many, you ordered me to offer you in writing. You said you believed me to be especially appropriate for this since you had heard that, because of my great intimacy, with her I was aware in great part of her secrets. I willingly embrace these orders and these desires; embracing, I venerate them; venerating, I rejoice with you that you wish not only to hear but to see in writing the life of your mother, who always longed for the kingdom of the English; so that you, who knew the face of your mother too little, might have a fuller knowledge of her virtues. For the grace of the Holy Spirit, which gave her the power of virtues, will furnish me, I hope, with help to narrate them.[4]

Matilda inspected the work when it was completed, and asked for it to be read to her.[5] Hildebert of Lavardin acknowledged that the Queen had in her 'all things of her mother', so that, even though Margaret was in her sepulchre, she continued to illuminate the English realm with her merits.[6] Certainly Matilda continued consciously to identify herself with, and emulate, her mother.

Matilda corresponded with the great canon lawyer Ivo, Bishop of Chartres, who, confident of her liberality, sent her two canons, 'who will tell you about the needs of our church and receive the favour God will inspire in your heart. I ask also that, in order to impress the memory of your excellence more sharply on my mind, you send a chausuble or some other priestly garment to my smallness, which is fitting for a queen to give and a bishop to wear in celebration of the divine sacraments.'[7]

Bishop Ivo was clearly keen to have an example of the renowned embroidery known as the *opus Anglicanum*, probably having heard that Matilda promoted English needlework. What he got were church bells, and the promise of money for a new roof for his church, for which he wrote a warm thank-you letter. Matilda's gift would not go unnoticed, he declared. He had placed the bells 'in a special place to be heard by the people who come together there. Whenever they are sounded to announce the hours, they touch the minds of the hearers renewing your memory in the hearts of individuals.'[8] We do not know whether he ever received the chasuble he asked for, but the Queen did give a golden cross to Chartres Cathedral, and money to help repair the roof.[9]

Matilda continued to correspond with Hildebert of Lavardin. After her marriage he sent a long letter full of extended homilies, in which he rejoiced in her honour and good reputation and reminded her that God had shown her much favour. 'You were placed over the heads of the sons of men. You implored no one for the glory of your form, and you were made beautiful to the delight of a king. The Lord God did these things.' He ended with the exhortation: 'Use your delights for the Queen, not for yourself.'[10]

In another letter, Bishop Hildebert expressed his concern for Matilda's health:

Humble minister of Le Mans, Hildebert, to Matilda, venerable Queen of the English, to stand at the right hand of one at whose right the Queen assists in gold and varied vestment. I heard from the bearer of the presents that you are well in health and deigned to greet me; I am joyful about the first, from the second my name and glory are full. For I am convicted of sin by law and the church unless my spirit can rejoice and exult in the health of one whose health preserves reverence of laws and the status of the church unimpaired. For nothing is more fitting to make a Christian soul rejoice than the health of those by whom the integrity of laws and the status of the church is preserved unimpaired. I rejoice therefore and I shall rejoice as long as the breeze announces to my ears that you are safe, as long as I hear that you live and thrive as queen, on whom the power to judge crime and the behaviour to be an exemplar of honesty is conferred.[11]

When Alexius I Comnenus, the Emperor of Byzantium, sent letters and gifts to Henry I, he did not omit to send them to Matilda too.[12] And when Herbert de Losinga's foundation at Norwich received cathedral status in 1101, Henry I, Matilda and Archbishop Anselm confirmed the charter under their seals. Now Bishop of Norwich, Herbert became Matilda's clerk of the closet, and it was at his request that 'Matilda the Good', by divine will, granted the royal manor of Thorpe to the cathedral.[13] A letter of high praise he wrote to her, likening her to the Virgin Mary, survives. In it she is once again compared to Queen Esther, 'who delighted more in piety than in the daintiness of the kingdom, the eastern Queen [of Sheba] who filled the earthly Jerusalem with gowns and stones, unguents and spices, whose excellence amazed Solomon, but did not have a spirit beyond yours. So you, most blessed Queen, have so enriched our west with wealth of faith and virtues, customs and acts, that we do not wish to adhere with similar love to any beyond what we have.'[14]

It was Herbert who wrote a prayer for Matilda, calling her 'the common mother of all England', and signing it, 'Herbert, her priest of Norwich'. He may also have composed for her his long prayer lauding the virtues of virginity and invoking the disciple John the Evangelist, to whom Matilda had a special devotion. It reads: 'Before all other saints I have chosen you alone. Indeed, I have chosen as my patron the one whom I hear to have been beloved above all others.'[15]

Matilda might have overspent on singers and versifiers, but she otherwise lived up to her reputation. She was 'an assiduous visitor of the sick, a continual reliever of the poor, a fellow sufferer with prisoners, a minister to women with child, and one who in everything showed herself to be a most humble servant of Christ'.[16] 'Clothes, meat and bedding, new and undefiled, and wine and ale she gave when she saw need', throughout the land.[17] The annalist of Westminster Abbey recorded: 'This Queen would, every day in

Lent, walk from her palace to this church, barefoot and bare-legged, and wearing a garment of hair.' William of Malmesbury says she wore 'hair cloth under her royal habit'. A chafing hair shirt worn next to the skin was a form of penance, its purpose being to mortify the flesh. Public penance had a newly special significance in Matilda's day. From the late eleventh century, absolution was given before penance was performed, rather than after, as hitherto, and the display of penance proclaimed to onlookers that the sinner was in a state of grace.[18]

It had been the Lenten custom of her parents, Malcolm and Margaret, to wash the feet of the poor in emulation of Christ,[19] and Matilda likewise 'would wash and kiss the feet of the poorest people, and give them alms. Nor was she disgusted at washing the feet of the diseased, handling their ulcers dripping with corruption, and finally pressing their hands, for a long time together, to her lips, and decking their table.'[20]

Matilda's brother David later recounted to Aelred of Rievaulx an episode that had occurred at the Easter court of 1105: 'When I was a youth, serving at the royal court, one night I was in my quarters with my companions. I went up to the Queen's apartments when I was summoned by the Queen herself, and behold – the place was full of lepers, and there was the Queen standing in the middle of them. And, taking off a linen cloth she had wrapped around her waist, she put it into a water basin and began to wash and dry their feet, and kissed them most devotedly when she was bathing them, and drying them with her hands.'

'My lady! What are you doing?' David cried. 'Surely if the King knew about this, he would never deign to kiss you with his lips after you had been polluted by the putrefied feet of lepers!'

Matilda smiled. 'Who does not know that the feet of the Eternal King are to be preferred over the lips of a king who is going to die? Surely for that reason I called you, dearest brother, so that you might learn such works from my example. Take some cloths and do in the same way what you see me doing.' David was 'greatly terrified', and 'unable to say anything in return to her'. Leprosy was then incurable, and it was one of the most feared contagious diseases of medieval times. Those who contracted it had the funeral rite said over them and were cast out of their communities to live as social pariahs; when approaching human habitations they had to wear prescribed attire and carry a clapper to warn of their coming. But, David recalled, Matilda 'began vehemently insisting, and I, to my

shame, laughingly returned to my companions'.[21] The Queen's courageous ministrations demonstrated her invincible faith in divine
protection, which must have been bolstered by the fact that she did
not become a leper herself. The episode gained wide currency and
persisted for centuries as evidence of Matilda's saintliness.

8

'Most Noble and Royal on Both Sides'

Queen Matilda's eldest child was a short-lived girl, born on
31 July 1101[1] in Winchester, and given the Scots name Euphemia.
But according to William of Malmesbury, writing in 1125, and better
informed, as he knew her personally, Matilda had just two children
with Henry I, and neither was called Euphemia.

The early weeks of her first pregnancy were overshadowed by
an invasion of England led by Robert Curthose, who had returned
from the crusade and was determined to secure the restitution of
the lands of his great ally, William de Warenne, Earl of Surrey,
which Henry I had confiscated as punishment for Warenne's
support of Robert. In the summer of 1101, Robert landed an
army at Portsmouth and marched north through Hampshire. His
god-daughter, Queen Matilda, was said to have been in confinement at Winchester, and when Robert was informed, he 'showed
her great kindness' in refraining from mounting an assault on the
city, declaring, 'it should never be said he commenced the war by
an assault on a woman in childbed, for that would be a base
action'.[2] In fact Matilda was not in confinement or childbed at
this time, as will become clear, although she was expecting a child.
Possibly she was suffering from morning sickness or a threatened
miscarriage.

Robert was aware that Henry had raised an army and was
lurking at Arundel, determined to be avenged on his brother for
coming to England uninvited if he did not return to Southampton
immediately and sail for home. Fortunately for him, Robert,
Count of Meulan, the son of Roger de Beaumont, came to
see him.

'Sire,' he advised, 'the Queen is apprised of the news, and you know that you showed her great kindness when you gave up the assault on Winchester because she lay in childbed there. Hasten to her and commit yourself and your people to her care, and I am sure she will guard you from all harm.'

Robert hastened to see Matilda, who received him in friendship and assured him of her protection. She and Anselm worked together to bring about a good accord between Henry and Robert, but still the brothers quarrelled, and Henry had Robert arraigned on various charges; it was Robert who backed down and asked for terms. That July, the two protagonists and their armies met at Alton and agreed a treaty, with Robert renouncing his claim to England, Henry renouncing his to Normandy and both undertaking to make the other his successor. At Matilda's behest, Henry agreed to pay Robert a substantial annual pension of 3,000 marks.

The Queen entertained Robert well afterwards, and when he was drunk, she brought her considerable diplomatic skills to bear on him, and asked if, in return for the restoration of Warenne's lands, he would assign to her the pension Henry had awarded him, implying that she needed the money to supplement her revenues. Henry had probably put her up to it.

Robert thought about her request, 'as if contending with Fortune whether she should give or he squander most', and, 'discovering the mere wish of the Queen, who silently desired it, kindly forgave the payment of this immense sum for ever, thinking it a very great matter that female pride should condescend to ask a favour, though he was her godfather'.[3] 'Cheerfully', without a word of protest, he granted an acquittance of the pension and 'surrendered to the Queen's pleasure an immense sum of money, because she desired it',[4] telling Henry afterwards, 'I have quitted to the Queen all you owe me for this kingdom. Enter we now together into perfect amity.'

Peace had been bought – for a time – but Robert had made the fatal mistake of trusting his brother.

In August, he was at Henry's court in London, and on 3 September, he was present at a meeting of the Great Council at Windsor, which was attended by the Queen, Archbishop Anselm and many nobles, including Matilda's former suitor, William de Warenne.[5] Soon afterwards, Robert returned to Normandy, where his first act was to visit the tomb of his mother, Queen Matilda, at Holy Trinity, Caen, and present gifts to his sister Cecilia.

★

Matilda's younger sister Mary had probably left Romsey and come to the English court. In 1102,[6] having tried unsuccessfully to wed the penniless Mary to his cousin, William, Count of Mortain, who had turned her down, Henry I arranged a marriage for her with one of the wealthiest landowners in England: Eustace III, Count of Boulogne, who was the son of Eustace II and Godgifu, daughter of King Cnut and Emma of Normandy, and 'renowned for his prudence and valour'.[7] It is likely that Mary was often at court in the early years of her marriage, for Eustace witnessed many of Henry I's charters up to 1108. After that, defending his patrimony against the French kept him largely in Boulogne,[8] where the couple resided in the comital castle, of which only the twelfth-century foundations of the keep – now the belfry, and the oldest building in the city – survive today. Mary was described as barren,[9] for the marriage produced only one surviving child, Matilda (or Maud), who was most likely named for her aunt, the Queen. A son, known only from a charter of Queen Matilda of Boulogne to Durham Cathedral, given for the soul of, among others, 'my brother', must have died young.[10] Mary was a staunch patroness of Bermondsey Priory, on the Surrey shore of the Thames opposite the Tower of London, near London Bridge.[11] Founded in 1082 on the site of an ancient Saxon monastery in Southwark, and built on land granted by William the Conqueror, Bermondsey had a 'new and handsome church' by the time of the Domesday survey, enjoyed the patronage of the Norman kings and the counts of Boulogne, and housed royal lodgings within its precincts.

Naturally, it was important to Henry that his Queen bear him an heir. Matilda may have suffered complications – or even a threatened miscarriage[12] – early in pregnancy, for in the summer of 1101, the King summoned Faricius, the Italian Abbot of Abingdon,[13] a Benedictine who was so renowned as a physician that he earned sufficient remuneration from his fees to rebuild the abbey's nave and conventual buildings and commission many books for its library.[14] 'Skilled in all laws which medicine teaches, he won favour from kings for his healing gifts.'[15] As Matilda's pregnancy advanced, Henry sent her to stay near Abingdon Abbey, then in Berkshire, so that Faricius could attend her regularly. The Abbot was assisted in his care of Matilda by another Italian doctor, Grimbald, an interpreter of dreams, who slept in the King's own bedchamber.[16]

In the autumn of 1101, Faricius and Grimbald received several royal gifts dated at London or Abingdon, probably rewards for their

services to the Queen.[17] Later it would become customary for queens
to be attended only by women during their confinements, setting a
trend that would see men banished from birthing chambers for
centuries, but in this period it was acceptable for male physicians to
be in attendance, although it was recommended that they avoided
looking the mother in the face, as women 'were accustomed to be
shamed by that during and after birth'.[18]

Matilda was probably lodging three miles from the abbey at the
Saxon royal palace at Sutton (known after *c.*1177 as Sutton Courtenay).
Between September 1101 and February 1102, Henry issued three royal
writs from there. Only a vaulted undercroft remains from this period,
beneath Norman Hall (which dates from 1192) and the manor house,
which was built on the site of the palace and dates from the thirteenth
to the sixteenth centuries. While the Queen was at Sutton, the Abbot
brought to her attention the state of disrepair into which a royal
residence at nearby Andersey had fallen, and she used her influence
with the King to have it demolished and the lead, stone and timber
conveyed to Abingdon for the building of the abbey.[19]

Matilda was twenty-one and Henry thirty-four when their first
child, a girl, was born, on 7 February 1102,[20] probably at Sutton.
The chronicler William FitzStephen, writing many years later, is
probably incorrect in stating that she was born in London, and there
is no evidence that she was born at Winchester, as some historians
have suggested. She was baptised Matilda – or Maud, as she will be
known here, to avoid confusion – after her mother, to please the
Norman barons,[21] although within the family she was called by
the Saxon name Aethelice,[22] which is probably the name her mother
had chosen. Possibly the child was given both Saxon and Norman
baptismal names.

The assertion by Robert Wace that Matilda was in childbed in
July 1101, and bore a daughter Euphemia soon afterwards, must be
incorrect. For Euphemia to have been born at the end of July or
early in August 1101, she must have been conceived on the wedding
night or soon after, but Maud would have had to be conceived in
May. The earliest a woman can ovulate after giving birth is twenty-
five days. Had Matilda borne a child in the summer of 1101, the
first possible date on which she could have got pregnant again was
around the end of August, in which case her child would have been
expected around 7 June. Thus it is unlikely that Matilda ever bore
a child called Euphemia. Probably she was suffering the discomforts
of early pregnancy when Robert saw her at Winchester.

Maud 'was born of ancient lineage, most noble and royal on both sides',[23] and in her mingled the royal blood of the Saxons and the Normans. For eighteen months, while she was Henry's sole issue, she was the heir to his dominions. She took after him greatly in character, apparently resembling her mother very little, although Matilda had great influence over her upbringing in childhood. There is no record of the child being placed in a convent to be educated, and it has been suggested that this was because of Matilda's own unhappy experiences in youth.[24] Maud almost certainly stayed with her mother until she was married, and it was under Matilda's auspices that she was taught to read Latin and imbued with a strong sense of piety.

9
'Daughter of Archbishop Anselm'

On 25 May 1102, Matilda presided alone over the Whitsun court at Westminster, for the King was away quelling a minor baronial rebellion. Later that year she became involved in a long-running dispute between the archbishops of Canterbury and York; Canterbury's primacy had been established under William I, but they were still wrangling over whether York owed obedience to Canterbury.

In September, Anselm convened an ecclesiastical council at Westminster. It began badly, as his seat was set higher than that of Archbishop Gerard of York, who threw a tantrum, kicking furniture over and refusing to sit down until his chair was level with Anselm's.[1] Ranulf Flambard, Bishop of Durham, was present. Henry had imprisoned him in the Tower of London for embezzlement, but he had escaped and later been pardoned. He now offered both the King and Queen bribes to rule in favour of Canterbury, but neither heeded him, because Henry knew 'full well which side could make the better offer'.[2] Later that year, the Pope censured Gerard and ordered him to swear an oath to Anselm.

On 13 January 1103, Matilda was present when Henry settled a dispute between William, Abbot of Fécamp, and Philip de Braose. By then, relations between Archbishop Anselm and King Henry were fraught. They had quarrelled over the burning issue of the day, that of who had the right to appoint and invest bishops and abbots – the Pope or the King. Kings had long enjoyed this right, and that of receiving homage from prelates for lands held by them, and some monarchs, having been hallowed by holy oil at their coronations, were reluctant to concede that they were not sufficiently sanctified to carry out investitures.

The great dispute had arisen in 1075 during the famous contest between the Roman Emperor Heinrich IV and the Papacy. Heinrich IV had famously presented himself as a penitent at the castle of Canossa in Italy in 1077 and submitted to Pope Gregory VII, and Gregory thereafter banned investiture by laymen, but the dispute had nevertheless dragged on and become a struggle for supremacy between the Church and the monarchs of Christendom.

Several bishops felt strongly about the issue. Matilda's own chancellor, Reynelm, had been nominated bishop of Hereford by the King at Christmas 1102, but Anselm, vigorously taking the Pope's part, refused to consecrate him, whereupon Reynelm dutifully returned his crozier and ring on the grounds that his appointment had been uncanonical.[3]

Anselm had spoken to Matilda of the growing tension between him and the King, and in the autumn of 1102 he wrote urging her to use her influence with Henry to put an end to it:

> I give thanks to God and to your Highness for the good will which you have for me and for the Church of God, and I pray Almighty God in His love to increase your devotion, and so make you persevere in it that you may receive an eternal reward from Him. I also pray that he may cause your good intention to progress in such a way that through you the heart of our lord the King may turn away from 'the counsel of princes', which the Lord rejects and be made to follow God's counsel 'which stands firm for ever'. I gratefully accept your counsel and exhortation as from a lady and friend in God, for I realise that they proceed from the love of God. If it pleases your love to send me information about anything, you can safely tell it by word of mouth to the bearer of this letter as if to myself. May Almighty God guide all your actions and protect you from all evil.[4]

Matilda made no secret of the fact that she sided with Anselm. In the spring of 1103, witnessing a charter at Rochester, she signed herself 'Queen Matilda, daughter of Archbishop Anselm'.[5] In defying her husband the King on this crucial issue, she showed that she was decidedly her own woman, capable of thinking for herself and adhering to her principles. This difference of opinion caused tensions in the marriage. In 1104, Matilda would confide to Anselm: 'My lack of moderation has disturbed the peace of mind of my lord the King and his nobles, and this has prevented the good, begun by your efforts, from being brought to an end.'[6]

Matilda was apparently unaware that the Archbishop was about to leave England. In April, with his position in the kingdom becoming untenable, he departed for Rome to seek advice from the Pope, with a view to restoring peace to the English Church. Matilda was greatly distressed. Five of her six surviving letters to Anselm date from the period 1103 to 1106. In them, she frequently expressed her longing for his return. Anselm's responses were guarded. It must have been clear that she was sincere in her concerns for him, but he knew that her first loyalty must be to Henry.

In June or July 1103, he wrote to Matilda urging her to 'strive for the peace and tranquillity of the churches in England'. He prayed 'that God Himself may repay you in my stead for what I am unable to do myself'.[7]

In August, Anselm wrote again, in response to an enquiry from Matilda about his well-being. He assured her that God had kept him 'in complete prosperity. Up to now I have been staying at Bec, waiting for a suitable time to resume my journey; but in the near future, before the Assumption of Saint Mary, I shall start out from here with the intention of completing, God willing, what I have begun.' Ever assiduous in urging the Queen to spiritual perfection, he reminded her of her priorities:

> Since it is my duty to encourage you to desire the heavenly kingdom, I exhort, beg and advise with as much affection as I can that you do not have more pleasure in rejoicing exceedingly in the passing glory of an earthly kingdom than in yearning for the eternal bliss of the celestial one. You could do this more sincerely and efficaciously if you arranged the matters subject to your authority according to the design of God rather than to the design of men. Reflect on these things, tell them to our lord the King in private and in public, and repeat them often, and as far as they concern you consider them carefully again.

He was clearly hoping that, through Matilda's good offices, the King might be brought to cede the investiture argument to his Archbishop.

He also told her he had 'recently learnt that God is pleased to exalt the dignity of the kingdom of my lord the King and yours, and to restore, according to your will, those things for your honour and use which were not to his liking or yours or that of your faithful servants'. As her faithful servant, Anselm rejoiced and gave thanks for this.[8] It has been suggested that he was referring to Robert's surrender of his pension,[9] but that had been two years before, and Anselm would have heard of it long since. Since nothing else happening at that time was of such moment, it may well refer to an event that had been long awaited by the royal couple, which would restore security to the realm by settling the succession.

10

'Reprove, Beseech, Rebuke'

Matilda's second child was a 'delicate'[1] boy whom Henry named William after his father, the Conqueror; he was born shortly before October 1103 at Winchester, and given the Saxon title 'Atheling'.[2] The prince thrived, and was hailed as the embodiment of the united royal bloodlines, the fulfilment of a vision believed to have been vouchsafed to Edward the Confessor on his deathbed: 'the hopes of England, like a tree cut down, would, through this youth, again blossom and bring forth fruit'.[3]

The contemporary *Anglo-Saxon Chronicle* asserted that there was a second son, Richard, who died young. Herman of Tournai says that this Richard drowned in 1120. Gervase of Canterbury, writing after 1180, and Robert of Gloucester, active in the late thirteenth century, both mention Queen Matilda's son Richard, while in the fifteenth century John Hardying says Henry begot on her William, Richard and Maud. But all probably mistakenly assumed that Henry I's bastard, Richard of Lincoln, Lord of Breteuil, who did drown in 1120, was actually his legitimate son by Matilda. William of Malmesbury states that Matilda had one son only, William. Three hundred years later, a Scots historian, Hector Boece, asserted that she had a daughter called Clarice, and sometimes one called Elizabeth, said to have been born around 1104, is listed as the youngest of Matilda's children, but there is no contemporary evidence for the existence of either.

At Matilda's request, Anselm's close friend, the elderly Gundulf, Bishop of Rochester, builder of the Tower of London, baptised the child in the Archbishop's absence. Gundulf had always stood in high favour with the Norman kings; Matilda enjoyed his conversation and admired his holiness and good work, and they had become friends. He was 'a kind intercessor' who always 'confidently approached the King or Queen and often obtained from them some work of mercy or alleviation for those coming to him for help'.[4] He was also an early exponent of the cults of the Virgin Mary and Mary Magdalene, and celebrated the Feast of the Immaculate Conception at a time when it was a relatively new concept in the West and hugely controversial, theologians being unable to agree as to whether Mary had been subject to original sin.

News of the birth of Henry's heir had reached Rome by 23 November, when Pope Paschal II himself wrote to congratulate the King: 'We have heard that you have had the male issue you so much desired by your noble and religious consort.' He tried in vain to persuade Henry not to oppose Anselm, and to submit on the investiture question, promising absolution for him and Matilda, and undertaking to cherish the son that that 'noble and exemplary lady had borne him'. It all fell on deaf ears.

Matilda would bear Henry no more children. 'Satisfied with a child of either sex, she ceased having issue or to desire them.'[5] The decision to cease having marital relations was apparently mutual. It may have coincided with Henry's affair with the beautiful Welsh Princess Nest, daughter of Rhys ap Twedwr, last King of Deheubarth (south Wales) and ancestor of the Tudor dynasty that ruled England from 1485 to 1603. Nest, whose fame was legendary, while her love affairs were notorious, bore the King a son, Henry FitzHenry, around 1103.

Possibly Henry ceased sleeping with his wife because he was put off by her close contact with the poor and diseased, which may be one reason why he left her in England when he made his frequent sojourns in Normandy; she is known to have accompanied him there only once. There may have been a physical problem that prevented her from conceiving again, such as an injury in childbirth, which might have rendered intercourse painful or out of the question. Maybe Matilda merely objected to Henry's 'frequent snoring'[6] and preferred not to share a bed with him. We have also to consider that taking opposing sides in the investiture dispute may have driven a rift between the couple.

The year 1104 was one of conflict. When Anselm got to Rome, the Pope excommunicated those English bishops who had been invested by the King, and Henry, in retaliation, forbade Anselm to return. When Matilda heard that Henry had written to Pope Paschal II offering to reinstate the Archbishop if Paschal would cede the investiture argument, she wrote a passionate letter to the Pope, pleading with him to settle the matter:

> I visit the threshold of the most holy Roman Apostolic seat and, as far as it is lawful and I am able, clasping your paternal knees with my whole heart, my whole soul, my whole mind, praying with importune and opportune petition, I cease not, nor will I cease, to entreat, till I know that my submissive humility, or rather the persevering importunity of my application, is heard by you.

She reminded him that England had once had a 'pious father', Anselm, but now the people had been deprived of that blessing.

> In such lugubrious mourning, in such opprobrious grief, in such deformity and loss of our kingdom, nothing remains to me, stunned as I am, but, shaking off my stupor, to fly to the blessed Apostle Peter and his vicar, the Apostolic man. Let your paternal bowels be moved towards us, that we may both rejoice at the return of our dearest father, Archbishop Anselm.[7]

In response, Paschal wrote to both Matilda and Henry. His letter to the King was uncompromising. He reminded him that he had twice before admonished him, but that the situation had since deteriorated. Henry had set himself up against God by assuming the right of investiture, which belonged only to Christ. Paschal warned that, unless the King rectified his errors, received Anselm back in his rightful place, and recognised the freedoms of the Church, he would have no choice but to excommunicate him.[8]

To Matilda, 'his dearest daughter', the Pope wrote in a gentler vein, saying he was greatly saddened about your husband because, although he started well at the beginning of his reign, he is now trying to spoil what follows. Now, having been placed in the fullness of power, he does not fear to provoke to fury the Almighty Lord. We do not believe that you are unaware of what this husband of yours promised the Almighty Lord in faithful devotion when he first accepted the royal crown. Now he has taken over the churches through investitures, and he has expelled the holy man, Bishop Anselm, from the kingdom because he opposed his wicked deeds. Therefore we fear greatly for his salvation.

Paschal laid upon Matilda an onerous duty:

Beloved daughter, we beg you to watch more carefully over his keeping and to turn his heart away from wrong counsel so that he will not continue provoking God's fury so greatly against himself. Remember what the Apostle says: 'The unbelieving husband will be saved by the believing wife.' Reprove, beseech, rebuke, so that he may reinstate the Archbishop in his See and permit him to act and preach as his office demands.

If Henry did not heed her, or the Pope, he would face 'perpetual anathema'.[9]

Anselm, aware of the influence Matilda enjoyed with Henry, also spurred her to 'beg, plead with and chide' her lord to make him back down. 'Counsel these things, intimate these things publicly and privately to our lord the King, and repeat them often.'[10] Matilda rose to the occasion, and succeeeded in retrieving for the archbishopric of Canterbury half the revenues of the see, which Henry had sequestered on Anselm's departure.[11]

Matilda's letters reveal her understanding of the complex investiture controversy, and her fears for the English Church. It was at this time that she wrote her second letter to Anselm, calling herself his 'lowliest handmaid'. When he wrote to her, she was ecstatic:

The clouds of sadness in which I was wrapped were driven away, the stream of your words broke through to me like a ray of new light. I embrace the parchment sent by you in place of a father, I press it to my breast, I move it as near to my heart as I can, I reread with my mouth the words flowing from the sweet fountain of your goodness, I go over them in my mind,

I ponder them again in my heart and when I have pondered over them I place them in the sanctuary of my heart.

She asked after Anselm's nephew and namesake, who had entered an Italian monastery at a young age; the Archbishop took a paternal interest in his career. In the lines that follow, it is clear that Matilda was using all her sweet tact and diplomatic skills to smooth the path for a reconciliation:

> The confidence which I have in the prayers of good men and the benevolence which, after careful investigation, I consider comes from the heart of my lord, gives me assurance. For he is more kindly disposed towards you than most people might think. With God's help and my suggestions, as far as I am able, he may become more welcoming and compromising towards you. What he now permits to be done concerning your revenues, he will permit to be done better and more abundantly in future when you ask for it in the right way and at the right time.[12]

Anselm sent Matilda 'boundless thanks' for 'trying to soften the heart of my lord the King towards me. If he has any bitterness of heart towards me, I am not aware of ever having deserved it in any way at all.' Yet in this letter Anselm betrayed his anger towards Henry, and his determination to stand on principle:

> You promise me that the King will in future grant me better and more abundant access to our revenues, of which at present he allows me a small amount. I should not be ungrateful to your benevolence because you are doing this, as far as you are able, through your goodwill. But it should not be necessary to make me such a promise because no confiscation or decrease of them should take place against my will. Whoever advised him to appropriate any of these revenues advised him to commit a sin which is no slight one, nor one that should ever be tolerated.

Nevertheless, Matilda's

> kindness prays me not to take my love away from my lord the King, but to intercede for him, for yourself, for your offspring and for your realm. I have always done this up to now. But as

to the future I commit myself to the providence of God, with whom the son does not bear the iniquity of the father nor the wife that of her husband. I hope in God that I may not harbour any rancour against anybody in my heart which could separate me from God. May almighty God guard you and your offspring forever in His grace.[13]

Later that year, probably in the summer, Matilda wrote her third surviving letter to Anselm, begging him to return to England. Once again, it is full of biblical quotations. She begged her 'tender father' to

> bend this severity a little and soften – let me say it, with your leave – your heart of iron. Come and visit your people, and among them your handmaid who yearns for you from the depths of her heart. Find a way by which neither you, the shepherd who leads the way, may give offence, nor the rights of royal majesty be diminished. If these cannot be reconciled, at least let the father come to his daughter, the lord to his handmaid, and let him teach her what she should do. Let him come to her before she departs from this world. Indeed, if I should die before being able to see you again – I speak shame-lessly – I fear that, even in the land of the living, every joyful occasion of exulting would be cut off. You are my joy, my hope, my refuge.[14]

The next surviving letter written by Anselm to the Queen was sent in August 1104 in response to one of hers, in which she gently complained that one of his missives had offended the King and his barons unnecessarily by its 'lack of moderation', and impeded hopes of the reconciliation for which she was working so diligently. It had driven King Henry himself to write to Anselm to express his indig-nation. She added that the King and his advisers had also accused her of a lack of moderation in her last letter to Anselm, but she was adamant that 'nothing indiscriminate, nothing unreasonable (although this was imputed to me in the King's letter) can be found in what is written there'.

In referring in his response to 'the bitterness, sadness and solicitude' that Matilda was suffering on account of his absence, Anselm felt bound to remind her that it had 'not been extended for so long through any fault of mine'. All he had done was tell Henry that I was not going to disobey the law of God. That distorted interpretation of my utterances, according to which I am said to have spoken unreasonably, I do not ascribe to the King's mind or yours. The King received our letter kindly at first, according to what I heard, but later someone with a spiteful and insincere intention, I know not who, incited him against me by a distorted interpretation through no fault of mine. Who that may be I do not know; but I do not doubt that either he does not love, or does not know how to love, his lord. May Almighty God so favour you and your children with prosperity in this life that he may lead you to the happiness of the life to come.[15]

11

'Incessant Greetings'

Henry had grown up seeing his mother, Matilda of Flanders, acting as regent in Normandy, and doubtless been impressed by her abilities. She had proved to him that a woman could rule effectively, and he had seen how his father relied on her. He recognised similar qualities in his wife, and was confident that she would exercise similar jurisdiction with the same kind of statesmanship and efficiency. On 4 August 1104, he departed for Normandy, leaving Matilda ruling as regent in England, presiding over the Great Council in his absence, as she was to do several times in the future, and wielding informal but wide-ranging authority in his name.[1] No chronicler thought it unusual that a woman should enjoy such autonomy in government.[2] In fact, it would be observed, 'Many were the good laws that were made in England through Matilda, the good Queen.'[3]

Henry had conferred on her 'the power to judge crime'.[4] Riding around the kingdom, the Queen issued charters, heard lawsuits and criminal cases, and in so doing became the patroness of many royal justices, with whom she developed good working relationships. She carried on exercising patronage in her own right, making gifts of land and granting – for example – liberties to the canons of St Mary of Huntingdon and a charter, sealed at Rockingham, to Lincoln Cathedral.[5] In her autonomous position, she was able to influence the King's patronage as well.[6]

In August, Matilda was at Abingdon, lodging with a local worthy, Robert FitzHervey. She persuaded him to grant to her the knight service he owed his friend Robert Gernon, with Gernon's consent, and gave it to Abingdon Abbey, along with valuable lead (used in construction, plumbing, pottery and food) from the royal hunting lodge on St Andrew's Isle on the Trent at Burton, Staffordshire.[7] Between 1101 and 1113, she gifted St Andrew's Isle itself and land at Colnbrook and the manor of Langley Marish, both then in Buckinghamshire, to Abingdon Abbey.[8] She was present in the abbey on 15 August when Abbot Faricius celebrated the feast of the Assumption.

Thus was established the future pattern of Matilda's life. Henry's frequent absences in Normandy left her much to her own devices. 'Enduring with complacency when the King was elsewhere employed the absence of the court, she continued many years at Westminster; yet was no part of royal magnificence wanting to her, but at all times crowds of visitors and news-bearers were, in endless multitudes, entering and departing from her superb dwelling. For this the King's liberality demanded, this her own kindness and affability attracted.'[9] She did not spend all her time at Westminster, but travelled widely around the country. We find her overseeing building works at the Tower of London and Windsor Castle. At the Tower, Henry I had probably begun the construction of the Wardrobe Tower, to house new royal lodgings.

Matilda's closest companions were perhaps the ladies and damsels who attended her daily. One of her maidens, Helisend, was widely celebrated for her skill in embroidery. Three others – Emma, Gunhilda and Christina - shared their mistress's piety, and later retired to a hermitage at Kilburn, north of London; when it became a Benedictine priory in 1128, they were received as its first nuns.

Henry returned to England in December 1104, kept Christmas at Kingsbury, Old Windsor, and spent the rest of the winter with Matilda at Northampton. Relations were fast deteriorating between the King and his brother Robert. In 1104, Robert, still clearly simmering about being tricked out of his annuity, had reproached Henry 'with having cheated and despoiled him by employing the Queen to beguile him with fair words out of his pension when he was under the influence of wine'.[10] The brothers were now on the brink of hostilities.

The Norman barons' patience with Robert's misgovernment was at an end; the duchy was descending into chaos. They erupted in a timely rebellion, and appealed to Henry for aid to address their Duke's incompetence. This gave him a pretext to invade Normandy in 1105. It has been suggested that Matilda went with him, although one source states that she stayed behind as regent in England.

Henry took western Normandy, and pushed eastwards. Fighting and negotiations between the brothers continued for months with no conclusive victory or peace.

During this campaign, Serlo, Bishop of Sées, preached before the King, thundering that men wearing long hair 'in women's fashion' was only for those 'bristling with sin', while men with long beards were like 'he-goats whose filthy vices are shamefully imitated by the degradation of fornicators and sodomites'. Henry, who himself had long hair and a beard, was suitably chastened, and allowed the Bishop personally to shear them off, whereupon his courtiers hurriedly followed his example.[11]

It was around this time that Anselm rebuked Matilda for her treatment of the churches she held in dower. He was probably refer-ring to the high rents of which William of Malmesbury complained. The Archbishop was not one to mince words, even when addressing the Queen:

Let me speak briefly, but from the heart, as to that person whom I desire to advance from an earthly kingdom to a heav-enly one. When I hear anything about you which is not pleasing to God or advantageous for you, and if I then neglected to admonish you, I would neither fear God nor would I love you as I should. After I left England I heard that you were dealing with the churches in your hands otherwise than is expedient for them or for your own soul. I do not wish to say here how you are acting – according to what I have been told – because to no one is it better known than to yourself. Therefore, I beseech you as my lady, advise you as my Queen and admonish you as my daughter – as I have done before – that the churches of God which are in your power should know you as mother, as nurse, as kind lady and queen. Again I beg, advise and admonish you, my dearest lady and daughter, not to consider these things heedlessly in your mind, but, if your conscience testifies that you have anything to correct in this matter, hasten to correct it so that in future you will not offend God, as far as this is possible for you through His grace. Concerning the past, if you see that you have failed in your duty, you should make Him favourable towards you. [12]

This stinging admonishment from the Archbishop she so revered prompted Matilda to relax her demands on her tenants. [13] Anselm was pleased to hear of it. He wrote:

Your Highness gave me great joy with your letter, insofar as you have given me good hope about yourself. For the humble accept-ance of disapproval and admonition is usually followed by hope of improvement. Therefore I give thanks to God who gives you the good will you indicated in your reply to me, and I give thanks to you that you maintain it with sweet affection.

He referred to the seeming impossibility of his being able to return to England, as Matilda hoped. In her letter she had

demonstrated sufficiently with holy and sweet affection that you desire my return to England. But I do not see that he in whose power my return chiefly rests – as far as it depends on a man – agrees in this matter with the will of God, and it would not be good for my soul to disagree with God's will. I fear that he may realise too late that he has gone astray from the right path, having despised God's counsel and having followed the advice of princes, which the Lord brings to nothing. I am certain, however, that he will realise this one day. [14]

★

In August, Henry was back in England, determined to take Normandy from Robert and rule it himself. To finance the continuance of the war, he imposed a crippling tax on married clergy. Anselm had imposed celibacy on the English clergy and excommunicated all who refused to relinquish their wives, and Henry was enforcing it rigorously. In 1105, during a royal procession held 'when the blast of this campaign of extortion was raging, two hundred priests, walking barefoot, went to the Queen and implored her to intervene' and ask the King to remit the taxes. But it is clear that Matilda stood in fear of her husband. 'She was so touched with sympathy that she dissolved

into tears, but was too frightened to intervene.'[15] Possibly her influence was waning. Matilda's support of Anselm may have undermined
it, while the cessation of sexual relations between the royal couple
may also have been a factor. Perhaps, too, Matilda did not support
Henry's offensive against her godfather Robert.[16]

Henry and Matilda celebrated the Easter of 1106 at Bath, and in
the early summer went on a progress that took them through Aylesbury
in Buckinghamshire, where the King owned a house, the King's
Burgh, next to the church.[17] He returned to Normandy in July,
leaving Matilda as regent once more, advised by Robert Bloet, Bishop
of Lincoln, and Roger, Bishop-elect of Salisbury, among others.

In August 1106, to Matilda's joy, Henry's quarrel with Anselm was
resolved. He had agreed to cede his authority over investitures in
return for an assurance that the clergy would do homage to him
for their temporal possessions, a solution suggested by the King's
sister, Adela, Countess of Blois.

But when illness prevented Anselm's return to England, Matilda
wrote expressing her consternation, in her fourth surviving letter
to him:

> To her dearest Lord and Father, Archbishop Anselm: Matilda,
> Queen of the English, wishing him the strength of good health.
>   The sweetness of expected joy recently promised me the
> arrival of your Holiness. As great as was the joy and consolation
> you were about to grant me, so much greater was the disap-
> pointment of lonely sadness brought to me when that arrival
> was prevented by sickness. Knowing the affection of your
> Paternity for me, I come with pitiable weeping, begging that
> if your care for me has not completely melted away, you should
> put an end to the anxiety of my concern about your health
> by some messenger as soon as possible. I shall immediately
> rejoice either over your health and mine, or − which God in
> His mercy forbid − I shall suffer the blow of our mutual fate
> with indifference. May the most holy omnipotence of God
> make you healthy. Amen.[18]

This was followed by another anxious letter:

> To her most beloved lord and father, Anselm, archbishop of
> Canterbury: Matilda, Queen of the English, sending incessant

greetings with love and faithful service. The consoling love of
your Holiness may not be unaware, dearly beloved father, that
my soul will be seriously disturbed by your very long and
wearisome absence. Indeed, the sooner and the closer the date
of your desired return is promised to me by many people, the
more it is desired by me, since I long to enjoy your presence
and conversation. My soul, most reverend father, will therefore
not be delighted by any perfect joy or brightened by any true
affection until I am able to rejoice at seeing again your presence for which I long with all the strength of my soul. In the
meantime, separated from you, I implore the mellifluous sweetness of your kindness to deign to console and gladden me by
the charm of your correction and the charm of your letter.
May the almighty and holy Lord protect you everywhere and
make me happy by your return into my presence. Amen.[19]

Matilda's last extant letter to Anselm was probably written in the
late summer of 1106, before his return, and refers to his kindness
in writing to her informing her that he was restored to health.
'You brighten the nebulous gloom of my soul through the light of
renewed happiness. Holding your letter and the pleasing, oft-repeated
reading of it, is, as it were, like seeing you again, although you are
absent.' She gushed with praise over his erudite style of writing
letters that were

> replete with meaning. They do not lack the seriousness of
> Fronto, the fluency of Cicero or the wit of Quintilian; the
> doctrine of Paul, the precision of Jerome, the learning of Gregory
> and the interpretation of Augustine are indeed overflowing in
> them. And what is even greater than all this: from them pours
> the sweetness of evangelical eloquence. Through this grace
> pouring over me from your lips, my heart, and my flesh thrill
> with joy at the affection of your love and the effect of your
> paternal admonition.

She informed him that, relying on his favour, she had

> committed the abbey of Malmesbury, in those things which
> are under my jurisdiction, to Dom Eadwulf, a monk and once
> sacristan of Winchester, who I believe is known to you. You
> retain completely whatever pertains to that monastery for

your own donation and disposition, so that the bestowal of the crozier and pastoral care is delivered wholly to the judgement of your discretion.[20]

In leaving the decision on the election of Eadwulf open for Anselm's approval, Matilda was effectively siding with the Archbishop on the issue of investiture.[21]

Anselm replied that he 'would gladly confirm your will if I could', but for the fact that Eadwulf had sent him a bribe.

> In what pertains to you, you have acted well and according to the will of God, in what you did there; but he himself did something very foolish in this matter which he should not have done. For, by the same messengers who brought me the letters from you and from others about this case, he sent me a goblet. This goblet I did not wish to keep under any circumstances, but I was very sorry because I do not see how he can be excused from guilt in this matter.[22]

Eadwulf was nevertheless elected abbot of Malmesbury in 1106. Possibly Matilda had interceded for him with Anselm.

Matilda was overjoyed to welcome the Archbishop back at Dover in September. At his arrival there was 'rejoicing of men of every age and rank'. As for the Queen, 'no earthly concerns, no pageantry of this world's glory, could keep her from going on before to the different places to which Anselm was coming. And as the monks and canons went out to meet the Archbishop, she went on ahead, and by her careful forethought saw to it that his various lodgings were richly supplied with suitable furnishings.'[23]

12

'Pious Devotion'

Henry's ambition came to fruition on 28 September 1106, when, aged thirty-eight, he defeated Robert at the Battle of Tinchebrai, took Normandy and the title of duke for himself, and imprisoned his brother in England, keeping him in comfortable captivity for twenty-eight years in the Tower of London and later in the castles of Devizes, Bristol and Cardiff – until Robert's death in 1134. Matilda's ageing uncle, Edgar Atheling, was also taken prisoner at Tinchebrai and brought to England, but, at her intercession, Henry pardoned him, for love of his Queen, who persuaded Henry to grant Edgar a pension.

Thereafter Henry was master of Normandy, although Robert's son, William Clito,[1] Count of Flanders, would in years to come ineffectually press his claim to be the rightful King of England and Duke of Normandy, and in so doing become a constant thorn in Henry's side.

After the victory, Matilda joined Henry in Normandy and stayed for some months. This may have been her only visit to the duchy.[2]

The last of Anselm's letters to the Queen, written around 1106–7, relates to a man whom she used as an intermediary between her and the Archbishop, but who was now in trouble of some kind. She wanted Anselm to intercede with the King on the man's behalf, but Anselm did not know enough about him to vouch for him. He wrote:

> The bearer of this letter brought me your seal with a letter from you. This indicated to me that you wish his disgrace to be driven from him by the testimony of my letter because of a certain act of expiation he had made, and that through my intercession he might regain from my lord the King what he had lost on the King's order.
>
> I ought not, nor do I wish to disregard your will, but I am certain about the benevolence of your Highness, that you do not wish me to act otherwise than is fitting for me. Your prudence knows that it is not for me to give testimony about matters I have neither seen nor heard, but that it is for those who have seen. Nor is it for me to intercede for someone whose life and character I know nothing about, so that he may recover what he had lost by royal command. Therefore I pray that the benevolence of your Highness may not be displeased that I hesitate to do anything which I perceive not mine to do.
>
> May almighty God always protect and guide you with his blessing. Amen.[3]

★

In January 1107, Matilda's brother Edgar, King of Scots, died, and was succeeded by another brother, Alexander the Fierce. Henry and Matilda were still in Normandy, and from there the Queen wrote to Ivo, Bishop of Chartres, soliciting his prayers for Edgar's soul. He responded:

> The reputation of your pious devotion has inspired the minds of many religious and sweetened them with a certain delight of holy love. Wherefore for the grace divinely conferred on us we give thanks to the Bestower of all goods who placed a man's strength in a woman's breast, not only to avoid shame and crime but also to give necessary aid to those in need. We pour out devoted prayers to God for the soul of your brother, the religious King, which, given our sins, are of little value though we are confident that his soul reposes in Abraham's bosom.[4]

In March, Matilda and Henry were together at Rouen.[5] It may have been during her visit that the philosopher and scientist Adelard of Bath, who had studied at the cathedral schools in France, played the cithara – an early form of guitar – for her and some French students.[6]

Henry returned to England during Lent, and spent Easter, which fell on 21 April, at Old Windsor.[7] But Matilda must have remained for a time in Normandy, for that same Easter she issued a charter at Lillebonne.[8] She probably returned to England in time to keep Whitsun with Henry at Westminster.[9]

In 1107, for the weal of her father's soul, Matilda gifted Old Bewick, Northumberland, the manor of his assassin, Archil Morel, to Tynemouth Priory, where Malcolm had been interred in 1093 after his death at Alnwick.[10] Soon his body would be returned to Scotland for reburial at Dunfermline Abbey.[11]

On 11 August, the King and Queen were at Canterbury to witness Anselm consecrating those bishops who had been elected during his absence, among them Reynelm, Matilda's former chancellor.[12]

Now that Normandy was his, Henry was to spend about two thirds of his time there, while Matilda invariably stayed in England. This was probably an arrangement that suited them both; the signs are that they were growing even further apart.

Henry left Anselm as regent when he crossed to Normandy in July 1108. However, the Archbishop's health was failing, and by 1109,

Matilda was again acting as regent in concert with the Chancellor, Roger 'the Great', Bishop of Salisbury, whose power was now 'second only to the King'. The Queen and the Bishop appear to have worked harmoniously together, and he was no doubt grateful for her gifts to his cathedral. Bishop Roger established the Exchequer and laid the foundations of an enduring centralised administrative system of government,[13] independent of the itinerant court, and as this evolved, Matilda's executive powers as regent gradually declined. Nevertheless, for the rest of her life she would attend council meetings and issue charters.

Around 1109, Herbert de Losinga, Bishop of Norwich, wrote to the Queen and Bishop Robert asking if they would restore an exemption from geld due from his manor of Thorpe. He was not sure if he was appealing to the right persons; should he approach the King on his return? In his letter to Matilda he wrote:

I have said little though I desire to say much; but I feared to add burdens to the royal business which you administer with praiseworthy solicitude. I seek high things, but the accustomed favours of your munificence have strengthened my presumption to seek high things. May your greatness greet the lord Bishop of Salisbury on my part, telling him not to find occasion to forsake my love, scornful of my poverty, nor to believe enemies about his friends. Further about my sickness, which your excellency deigned to ask about, your brother and our son Starnard, who bore the present letters to you, will answer.

To Bishop Roger he wrote: 'You will not find our lady the Queen to be difficult in this matter, for out of her kindness she has been a very mother to me. It is well known that she takes advantage of your advice in all matters.' In the end, it was the King who granted the exemption.[14]

As her political influence declined, Matilda had other projects to occupy her. Henry had granted her the same soke of Ethelred's Hythe in London that his mother had held. By 1152, it had been renamed Queenhithe after Matilda, who was entitled to duty on goods that were landed there. This was a privilege that would be enjoyed by succeeding queens of England. Matilda built a 'necessary house', or latrine, with piped water, near the shore to accommodate sailors and officials.[15]

Soon after 1106,[16] she built a leper hospital at St Giles in the Fields, outside the City of London, for the afflicted were not allowed inside its walls. In this she was following the example of her mother, Queen Margaret, who had founded a leper hospital in Edinburgh. Matilda funded this project with 60s. a year out of her revenues from Queenhithe.[17] She appointed her chaplain John as its head.[18] The thirteenth-century chronicler Matthew Paris called St Giles 'a memorial for Queen Matilda'.

Nearly five hundred years later, John Stow, the Elizabethan antiquarian, recorded that, when the hospital was dissolved at the Reformation and its chapel became a parish church, the guardians still cared for 'fourteen persons leprous, according to the foundation of Matilda the Queen, which was for leprous persons in the City of London and the shire of Middlesex'.[19]

Matilda was responsible for other beneficial building projects, which would have been regarded as 'practical works of mercy'.[20] Having been almost drowned – or at least 'well washed' – riding across the River Lea at Stratford, east of London, she erected a 'beautiful bridge' there, with stone arches and a chapel, 'for the benefit of travellers', and had the approach well paved with gravel. 'Before that time the like had never been seen in England.'[21] Thereafter the town was known as Stratford-le-Bow.[22] Her bridge was still standing in 1839. She built another bridge over the Channelsea brook, a tributary of the Lea, and linked the two by a causeway – now Stratford High Street. She built a third bridge, of timber, over the River Mole at Cobham, Surrey; in the thirteenth century, it was stated that she did so for the repose of the soul of one of her maidens, who had drowned when crossing the ford.[23] It lasted until 1782, when it was replaced by a stone bridge. Matilda bought Stratford Abbey's mill and land in West Ham, and assigned with them manors in Cobham and a mill called Wiggin Mill for the maintenance of both bridges, entrusting that task to the nuns of Barking, the nearest abbey, which already paid her rents and tithes.[24] She also had new highways laid and caused several old Roman roads to be repaired.

She was a patroness not only of the abbeys of Barking and Malmesbury, but also of Romsey, where she had received her early education. In 1105, the King granted the right to hold a fair to her and Romsey Abbey, to boost the convent's income.[25]

In 1107–8, the second Augustinian priory in England[26] was founded 'at the prayer of Queen Matilda', on the advice of Archbishop Anselm and Richard Belmeis, Bishop of London.[27] The Augustinian Order

provided for groups of canons to live together under the rule of St Augustine. In the eleventh century, groups of regular canons had formed communities and evolved into the first religious Order of ordained priests to join together in a common monastic life. From the early twelfth century, they followed the rule of St Augustine and wore white habits. Matilda supported this Order, and the King himself followed her lead in appointing an Augustinian canon as his chaplain, rather than a Benedictine. In founding a priory for Augustinian canons, the Queen was at the forefront of the monastic reforms that characterised the twelfth century, for this was a time when the Benedictine Order was perceived to have become lax, and new, stricter orders were coming into being. Others, including the King and the nobility, would follow the Queen's example and found Augustinian monasteries in England and Normandy.[28]

In order to make way for her new foundation, Matilda acquired the old church of St Mary Magdalene and the Holy Cross, which stood on land in Aldgate, London, from which the canons of Waltham received substantial revenues. She bought them out, purchasing a lucrative mill in compensation, demolished the church and built her new priory on a grand scale in the Romanesque style. On 5 April 1108, she appointed her austere French confessor, Norman, a native of Thanet, Kent, and a canon of Colchester, to be the first Prior of Holy Trinity, and granted him and the canons who came to London with him the plot of Aldgate with three churches and all its attached franchises, as well as a mill and a two-thirds share in her rents from the city of Exeter.[29]

In the foundation charter, she named the priory Christ Church, and enriched it with lands in the City[30] and holy relics, including a piece of the True Cross that Alexius I Comnenus, Emperor of Byzantium, had sent her. Almost certainly its dedication to the Holy Trinity was no accident, for her mother had also dedicated her foundation at Dunfermline to the Holy Trinity, and Matilda of Flanders had founded the abbey of Holy Trinity in Caen.[31] The canons' role was more social than spiritual, for they provided much-needed support for the needy.[32] Through these important foundations, Matilda's role in reconciling a resentful and not wholly subdued London to Norman rule should not be underestimated.[33] They may well have been brought into being in concert with a plan by Henry to win over the city that had supported Edgar Atheling.[34]

One of Matilda's first chaplains was Ersinius, who soon tired of court intrigues and 'their manifold false subtleties'. He joined an eremitical, or reclusive, community founded by Walter de Lacy, son of a Norman lord, in the Vale of Ewyas, north of Abergavenny, in the Black Mountains of Wales. Archbishop Anselm persuaded the founders to convert the priory into an Augustinian house, in which the influence of the King and Queen might be perceived, and in 1108, Llanthony Priory was consecrated. As its fame grew, the King and Queen offered to take the priory under their patronage and endow it richly, but Walter de Lacy refused, for he wanted his community to observe an ascetic life of prayer and study.[35] When Matilda met him, she noticed the mail shirt he had vowed always to wear next to his skin so that he would be armed to fight the Devil; being 'not sufficiently acquainted with the sanctity of this gentle man', she asked if she might touch the mail. He blushed as she reached inside his gown, but then he realised that she had placed a purse of gold in his bosom.[36]

13
'A Girl of Noble Character'

Henry remained in Normandy until shortly before Whitsuntide 1109. Earlier that year, or late in 1108, Heinrich V, King of Germany, had asked for the hand of his daughter, the Lady Maud.[1] Heinrich was the son of Heinrich IV, the Roman Emperor who had clashed with Pope Gregory VII over investitures. The younger Heinrich had forced his father to abdicate in 1105,[2] and bore the title 'King of the Romans', having been elected as his father's Imperial successor; although he had not yet been crowned emperor, he was sometimes styled as such. In accordance with a custom going back to the coronation in 800 of Charlemagne, the Pope himself placed the Imperial crown on the heads of the medieval Roman Emperors.

The Salian dynasty to which Heinrich belonged had established itself as a major European power, but it was impoverished, and the Emperor was looking for a bride who could bring a great dowry. Henry I saw the advantages of a prestigious alliance with Imperial Germany, which offered solidarity against French designs on Normandy. In the spring of 1109, the King, then in Rouen, wrote to inform Archbishop Anselm that, 'in the matter being discussed between me and the Emperor of the Romans, we brought it to a good end, by the grace of God'.[3]

On 21 April, during Lent, Anselm died. Matilda must have felt his loss keenly, for he had been her spiritual mentor, and she had adored him, but she busied herself by becoming involved in the marriage negotiations. King Heinrich, her future son-in-law, would write to commend her zeal on his behalf:

> Heinrich, by the grace of God King of the Romans, to Matilda, Queen of the English, greetings and every good.
>
> As we have learned from many, we owe great thanks to your goodness and great proof of friendship, because our honour and love is very precious in your mouth and heart, and you have spoken well of us often, publicly and privately, to your lord and to all who listen to you. For which, with God willing and granting life, we will not be unmindful. And we will respond worthily to your benevolence in all things, as our honour demands. If, therefore, there is anything in the kingdom or in our power that is worthy for you to desire, you may believe that we neither wish nor are we able to deny it to you. Wherefore, now persevere attentively in that benevolence which you have always had towards us, so that in all things with which we charge your lord, we may know by experience your zeal.[4]

Medieval queens were expected to interest themselves in the marriages of their children, especially their daughters, and this may be the first recorded instance of an English queen doing so, although it is possible that the custom had existed before, yet gone unrecorded. As has been noted, Matilda of Flanders may have pressed for the marriage of one of her daughters to the future King Harold. Henry passed on some of Heinrich's gifts to Matilda for Holy Trinity, Aldgate.[5]

On 24 May, the King 'received from the Emperor's legates the oaths he required concerning his daughter's marriage',[6] and the contracts were completed. Henry returned to England at the end of May, and on 13 June presided with Matilda over a great Whitsun court at Westminster, which was remembered as the most splendid court of his reign. There he welcomed an embassy sent by his son-in-law. The noble German envoys were 'remarkable for their massive physique, magnificent apparel'[7] and 'polished manners'.[8] The betrothal ceremony took place, with one of them standing proxy for the bridegroom.[9]

To raise the huge sum of 10,000 marks in silver for Maud's dowry, Henry imposed on his subjects a hefty 'aid for the King's daughter' of 3s. per hide (120 acres) of land, the usual rate being 2s. To do this, he had to reform the Exchequer. Predictably the marriage was not very popular in England. 'This was a disastrous year here in this country on account of the aid which the King levied for the marriage of his daughter.'[10]

On 17 October 1109, at Nottingham, in the presence of her parents, Maud undertook her first formal court duty, witnessing – as 'promised bride of the King of the Romans' – her father's charter establishing the see of Ely.[11] Growing up under the auspices of her mother, this child, who was to become one of the most important and controversial women of the twelfth century, had been imbued with the culture and learning of the English court.[12] 'She was a girl of noble character, distinguished and beautiful, and gave promise of abundant future virtue in everything she said and did.'[13]

It had been agreed that, for the time being, the child Maud – she was only eight – would remain with her mother. But not for long. The King of the Romans wanted his bride, and he wrote appealing to Matilda to ensure that the arrangements for her daughter's journey to Germany went well. 'We have from experience come to know of your zeal in all those things that we ask of your lord,' he told her. She would not fail him.

At the beginning of Lent 1110, Matilda had to say farewell to her eight-year-old daughter – as it turned out, for the last time – and Maud left England in the care of a German cleric, Burchard, later bishop of Cambrai, and was 'given to the Emperor in a manner that was fitting',[14] sailing to Boulogne handsomely provided with a magnificent train of German envoys, 'famous men, bishops, counts acting as envoys, laden with innumerable presents from both her parents', and lords, ladies and clergy.[15] The Norman barons who had the responsibility of conveying that fabulous dowry had ambitions to rise high in the Empire, but in the event the King of the Romans just gave them gifts and sent most of them home.[16] Henry, Archdeacon of Winchester, was perhaps allowed to remain, for he was made bishop of Verdun in 1117;[17] another who stayed with Maud was a knight, Sir Drogo.[18]

'In accordance with her father's wishes, she crossed the sea, passed over mountains, penetrated into unknown regions, to be married at her father's command.'[19] Towards the end of February, Heinrich received her at Liège. At twenty-three, he must have seemed old to a child of eight as he 'welcomed her to his realm'.[20]

Immediately Maud was thrust into the turbulent world of Imperial politics. Heinrich's dominions encompassed Germany, Burgundy, Austria, northern Italy, Bohemia, Hungary and part of Poland, stretching south across Europe from the Baltic to the Adriatic, and east to west from Lyons to Vienna. Through treachery, he had imprisoned and deposed his father. He was a ruthless man, often at violent odds with his subjects, or with Pope Paschal II over the thorny matter of investiture – and while Heinrich was wrangling with the Pope, his vassals had taken advantage. One, Godfrey of Louvain, Duke of Lower Lorraine, had recently led a serious uprising in Germany, and Maud, young as she was, and newly arrived, was asked to intercede for him with the King of the Romans;[21] it cannot have had much effect, as Godfrey and Heinrich did not make peace until 1118. Godfrey's daughter Adeliza would later become Maud's stepmother.

When Maud was formally betrothed to Heinrich[22] at Easter (10 April) at Utrecht,[23] he gave her costly gifts and dowered her with substantial estates, which apparently comprised lands around Utrecht, where in 1122 she gave land for the founding of a church by four eremitical knights at Oostbroek.[24]

They travelled on via Cologne, Speyer and Worms to Mainz, where, on St James's Day, 25 July, in the cathedral where the hand of the Apostle was venerated, Maud was crowned queen of Germany and queen of the Romans by Frederick of Schwarzenburg, Archbishop of Cologne, as Bruno, Archbishop of Trier, her husband's chief counsellor, held her 'reverently' in his arms.

Heinrich wanted his future bride to be 'nobly brought up and honourably served. She should learn the language and customs and laws of the country, and all that an empress ought to know, now, in the time of her youth.'[25] He established Maud in the ancient Roman city of Trier on the banks of the Moselle. He sent home most of her English attendants, appointed Germans to serve her, and placed her in the charge of his kinsman and wise adviser, Archbishop Bruno. She probably lived at the Aula Palatina, the great palace that had been built by the Emperor Constantine in the fourth century. Its massive hall, 67 feet long and 33 feet high, still stands, and the apse was used by the archbishops of Trier as their residence in the Middle Ages. Maud's seal survives in the British Museum; it shows her with a crown and sceptre and bears the legend MATHILDIS DEI GRATIA ROMANORUM REGINA.

Soon after Maud arrived in Germany, Pope Paschal drove a bargain: if Heinrich would cede the investiture question, Paschal would make the German clergy surrender to the King all lands and rights given to them by his predecessors.

The chronicler Robert of Torigni, writing at least forty years later, asserts that, on 12 February 1111, in 'the city of Romulus, the Imperial diadem was placed on Queen Maud's head by the Supreme Pontiff'. Torigni knew Maud, and had a good opinion of her, thanks to her generous patronage of the abbey of Bec-Hellouin,[26] of which he became prior in 1149. But it has been disputed that Heinrich took her with him when he marched to Rome that year at the head of an army – funded by Maud's dowry – and demanded that Pope Paschal II crown him Roman emperor.

Maud herself was to insist that she had been crowned empress; she enjoyed Imperial status as the wife of the Emperor,[27] called herself empress, and was widely acknowledged as such. Henry I was under the impression that she had twice been crowned in Rome by the Pope himself,[28] and Maud would later lead the Norman chroniclers to believe that she had indeed been crowned empress twice,[29] but it seems she was only ever crowned once, as queen of the Romans, the title by which she continued to style herself.

When the new treaty was announced from the steps of St Peter's, the German clergy erupted in furious protest, and it immediately became clear that Heinrich would be unable to keep his part of the bargain. Paschal refused to crown him, whereupon Heinrich refused to concede the right of investiture. Seizing the Supreme Pontiff and sixteen cardinals, he carried them out of Rome as his prisoners. Paschal had no choice but to admit defeat, so Heinrich escorted him back to Rome and was crowned emperor there on 13 April.

14
'The Peace of the King and Me'

Matilda was with Henry when, at Whitsun 1110, he held court for the first time in the new castle at Windsor,[1] staying in 'the King's house'. He had built a round stone shell keep[2] on the site of his father's wooden castle, and a great hall measuring 71 feet by 41, which stood in the lower bailey, or ward. Attached, or nearby, were chambers, offices and kitchens; kitchens were often housed in separate buildings because of the risk of fire.

At the top of the upper ward stood the King's house, built of wood, in which were to be found the fine range of apartments Henry had raised for himself and his Queen. Occupying a square quadrangular palace, with towers at its two northern corners, they comprised a smaller hall, chambers, chapels and the King's kitchen.[3] Henry had also raised new walls around the two baileys.

In 1110, we have the first record of Henry I visiting his newly built hunting lodge at Woodstock, Oxfordshire, which stood on the site of a Saxon royal residence. It lay amid the King's demesne forests of Woodstock, Cornbury and Wychwood, and the hunting was excellent, which accounted for it quickly becoming 'the favourite seat of his retirement and privacy'.[4] Henry dated many charters in the house, which had a spacious hall with two aisles of white pillars. He built a stone wall surrounding the deer park in 1111. Yet no charters were signed or witnessed at Woodstock by Matilda, who probably never went there, and other evidence suggests that this was where Henry resorted with his mistresses.[5]

At Winchester in 1110, when they kept great state together, they personally assisted at the exhumation of the bodies of King Alfred and his Queen, Ealhswith, which were borne in state through the city from the ruinous abbey church of Newminster and reinterred before the high altar of the newly built Hyde Abbey, which the King and Queen had founded and endowed as a suitable shrine for one of England's greatest kings – and Matilda's direct ancestor. The bones of Alfred's son, King Edward the Elder, were moved at the same time.

Christmas was kept in great state at Windsor Castle. There Henry gave the earldom of Northamptonshire to Matilda's brother David.[6] David, then twenty-five, was four years younger than Matilda and like her in many ways, being a pious, 'just, chaste and humble' prince, 'loved for his gentleness, admired for his purity, and approachable by everyone through his humility'.[7] Clearly he was fond and proud of his sister, for he styled himself 'brother of the Queen of the English', and called his heir after Henry I.[8] He was to succeed Alexander I in 1124, and would become one of Scotland's greatest kings, and a champion of Matilda's daughter in her time of need.

At the Great Council that met at Westminster at Whitsun 1111, 'Matilda, the good Queen' did her best to persuade Henry 'to love all his folk and leave all his disputing, and bear with his barons' and 'the lords of towns and burgesses of cities'.[9] She visited Waltham Abbey on 8 August, and issued a charter to the city of Bath.[10]

Soon afterwards Henry went to Normandy, leaving her as regent. At Michaelmas she was in Winchester, where she presided over 'her court and that of her husband' – probably the court of the Exchequer, part of the King's Council – in the treasury there, referring to it in documents as 'my justiciary', and to 'the peace of the King and me', arrogating to herself an authority that no English regent had hitherto exercised.[11] She took decisions in her own right, and affixed her own seal to official documents, another break with tradition.[12]

She was present when the relics of St Ethelwold were translated from the crypt to the choir of Winchester Cathedral.[13] It was probably early in 1112 that she travelled to Gloucester to witness Robert Gernon granting two churches to St Peter's Abbey.[14] Here she may have stayed to the north of the city at the royal hall at Kingsholm, built of timber by Edward the Confessor before 1051; it was here that the Norman kings held court when visiting Gloucester, and here, in 1085, that the Conqueror had given the order for the compiling of Domesday Book.[15]

Early in 1113, Matilda's nine-year-old son, William Atheling, was betrothed to Mahaut, daughter of Fulk V, Count of Anjou, sealing a peace with Anjou. That year the Queen kept great state at Winchester until, in July, the King returned to England. He may have come because she was unwell, for around this time she suffered an unspecified illness of some duration. In Bishop Hildebert's last surviving letter to her, written possibly in 1114, he asked after her condition, adding:

> Holy love ignores the discomforts of time or place. Affection rules it, which is always its own law, prejudiced by no alien force. It is always permitted to love, even if it is not permitted to see the one you love. So, though I am separated from you by land and sea, I love you in Christ, and mention you there where honourable thought is promised reward and illicit thought, punishment. To the altar of the Lord, indeed, your memory accompanies me, fearing lest it bring down judgment on me if I defraud you of that intervention which you, O Queen, bought with your gifts.[16]

Herbert de Losinga composed a special prayer to be offered up to St John the Evangelist for her 'long-awaited recovery',[17] which was complete by the following year.

15

'All the Dignity of a Queen'

O n 7 January 1114, Maud, now nearly twelve, was married to the Emperor Heinrich, who was twenty-seven. They celebrated their nuptials at Worms Cathedral 'with great magnificence', the bride 'bearing herself with all the dignity of a queen, despite her youth'. The congregation included five archbishops, thirty bishops, five dukes and so many nobles, abbots, provosts and clergy that 'no one present could tell their numbers. So numerous were the wedding gifts that various kings and primates had sent to the Emperor, and the gifts that the Emperor gave from his own store to the throngs of jesters and jongleurs [minstrels] and people of all kinds, that not one of his chamberlains who received or distributed them could count them.'[1]

A drawing of the wedding feast survives in a manuscript in the library of Corpus Christi College, Cambridge, and in the accompanying description Maud's beauty, dignity and lineage are effusively lauded.[2] Heinrich 'endowed' her with eleven hundred knights,[3] ladies and chaplains. She did not have her own chancellor, for her household was run by the Imperial chancellor. Following her marriage, England and the Empire grew closer.

'All hoped that Queen Maud might be the mother of an heir to the Roman Empire',[4] but she was to bear Heinrich just one child, who died soon after birth.[5] Herman of Tournai, who believed that Maud's mother had been a professed nun when she married, saw in the loss of this child divine retribution. Other chroniclers saw the Emperor's lack of a legitimate heir as God's punishment for his conflict with the Church. Heinrich had at least one bastard, and Maud was later to prove fruitful with her second husband, so it is hard to determine why they had no other children.

The chroniclers were unanimous in praising Maud. She was 'held to bring glory and honour to both the Roman Empire and the English realm'.[6] 'The Emperor loved his noble wife deeply',[7] while her 'prudent and gracious behaviour to her Imperial spouse won the esteem of the German princes'.[8] She played an active supporting and ceremonial role from the start of her marriage and 'carried out the duties of imperial rule virtuously and piously',[9] witnessing royal *acta*, carrying petitions to her husband, interceding for others and keeping her father informed of events.[10] Like her mother and grand-mother, she shared in the rule of her husband's vast territories, supported by his advisers and clergy.[11] She was loved by the Imperial nobles as their lady, while the poor came to regard her as a pious mother figure,[12] and in Germany she became known as 'the good Maud'.[13] This was in marked contrast to the way in which she would later be viewed by English chroniclers.

In 1115, the Benedictine chronicler Hugh, Abbot of Fleury, having obtained her permission, dedicated his book, *Modernorum regum francorum actus* (*The Modern Acts of the Frankish Kings*):

> To Matilda, glorious Empress, Hugh, unworthy monk of the monastery of Father Benedict at Fleury, to rejoice equally in temporal and eternal felicity. I decided to collect this little book for you, my lady, so that the loftiness of your family might be known to posterity and the nobility of your ancestors published to future centuries. So I shall take pains to put forth briefly to you in the book of the modern kings of the Franks the acts of those who ruled after Emperor Louis the Pious in France, for the raising of your spirits. In this prologue, moreover, I shall take pains to recount to you the splendid genealogy of your ancestors and I shall briefly narrate their actions equally among the deeds of the aforesaid kings, and I shall declare clearly to those who do not know it, the nobility of your lineage.

He wrote of the rulers of Normandy all the way back to Rollo, and of Maud's grandfather, the Conqueror, who 'appeared glorious to the ends of the earth beyond all the kings and princes of our time. Few later kings will, I think, imitate him and enjoy the afflu-ence and elegance of his customs with which God and happy fortune endowed him in this life. His son and heir was Henry, magnificent king of the English, your father. I ask you, receive favourably this gift offered to you and strengthen it with the sign of your authority. Omnipotent God bless you with his grace and make you fertile with progeny and happy always with prosperity. Amen.'

The see of Canterbury had remained vacant since the death of Anselm in 1109, until, in April 1114, the King consented to the election of a new archbishop. He and the monks of Canterbury wanted Abbot Faricius, but Bishop Roger and Robert Bloet, Bishop of Lincoln, were opposed to Faricius on the grounds that he had been the Queen's physician and that 'smelling women's urine' did not qualify him for the primacy. Henry did not press the point, and Ralph d'Escures, Bishop of Rochester, was elected instead.[14]

In September 1114, Henry visited Normandy again, once more leaving Matilda ruling England as regent. At Christmas he had his Norman barons swear fealty to William Atheling as his heir.[15] William was now eleven, and in the charge of a tutor, Othuer FitzEarl, a bastard son of Hugh d'Avranches, Earl of Chester.

Matilda spent Easter 1115 at Odiham Castle, Hampshire.[16] Weeks later she was mourning the passing of her sister, Mary, Countess of Boulogne. While visiting England, Mary (according to her epitaph) had been taken ill suddenly and died in great pain on 31 May[17] at the Cluniac priory at Bermondsey. Here she was buried in a beautiful marble tomb on which her august royal connections were carved in gold letters,[18] probably at the command of her sister the Queen.

Mary's only child, Matilda, was about two years old at the time of her death. According to Agnes Strickland, her grieving father placed her in Bermondsey Priory to be raised and educated there, but there is no contemporary evidence for this. As her father's sole heiress, the young Matilda of Boulogne was one of the most desirable brides in Europe, not only on account of the great inheritance that would come to her on her father's death – the counties of Boulogne and Lens on the Continent and the honour of Boulogne in England – but also because, like Matilda of Flanders and Adeliza of Louvain, she was impeccably descended from Charlemagne, and was also the great-niece of Edward the Confessor, and the niece of the beloved Matilda of Scotland.

Unsurprisingly, Henry I had already arranged a royal match for this valuable prize in the marriage market, betrothing her to her first cousin, the King's dearest nephew,[19] Stephen of Blois, the son of William the Conqueror's daughter Adela by Stephen, Count of Blois. Two years earlier, Adela had sent her son to Henry's court, for the King had promised him great prospects. True to his word, he had knighted him, given him estates in England and the county of Mortain in Normandy, and betrothed him to this wealthy heiress. On marriage, Stephen would acquire the great honour of Boulogne. In return, he would fight for Henry in Normandy when Robert of Normandy's son, William Clito, began inciting disaffection in the duchy. The betrothal had taken place before June 1115.[20]

16

'Blessed Throughout the Ages'

Henry returned to England in July 1115. Since the time of William the Conqueror, the Normans had been pushing westward into Wales, but by the reign of Henry I, both the Welsh and the Normans were focused on achieving a peaceful accord. On 19 September 1115, Matilda's chancellor, Bernard, a royal chaplain from Hereford, was consecrated the first Bishop of the Welsh see of St David's. There had been some debate as to where the ceremony was to take place, but in the end it was held in Westminster Abbey, as Matilda wanted to be present.[1]

By now, 'the multitude of brethren praising God day and night' in Matilda's foundation, Holy Trinity, Aldgate, had so increased 'that all the City was delighted in the beholding of them, insomuch that, in the year 1115, certain burgesses of London' came together in the chapter house with Prior Norman, and gave to the church substantial lands in London, their grant being afterwards confirmed by charter of the King. Thanks to such benefactions, 'the priory, in process of time, became a very fair and large church, rich in lands and ornaments, and surpassed all the priories in the City of London'.[2] It had also acquired many daughter houses.

On 28 December 1115, Matilda, Henry and their twelve-year-old son William attended the consecration of the rebuilt abbey church at St Albans, where they and their court were spending the Christmas season as guests of Abbot Richard d'Albini. Matilda's brother, David, now Prince of the Cumbrians, was with them. Geoffrey Brito, Archbishop of Rouen, officiated, and the ceremony was performed with great magnificence.[3] Matilda was one of the benefactresses of the abbey. The fourteenth-century Golden Book of St Albans[4] records that she gave it two manors, and has a fine illumination of her wearing fourteenth-century dress.[5] The royal couple stayed until 6 January.

Henry and Matilda sometimes made use of the royal manor at Brampton, near Huntingdon. There was good hunting to be had there, and in King John's reign it was recorded that the King and Queen had worn their crowns on three occasions in the wooden chapel of the royal manor.[6]

Matilda took an interest in Merton Priory, Surrey, founded in 1114 by Gilbert the Norman, Sheriff of Surrey, for whom she had a special affection. Once, in the days before his ordination, when he had been at court, she had seen him looking melancholy, and learned from others that his mother had died. She gently asked him why he had not told her, and he replied that he feared his excessive grief might disturb her royal dignity, whereupon she took his hand and offered to adopt him as her own son and treat him with maternal affection for as long as she lived.[7] Gilbert came to regard her as a second mother, for she had furthered his career and protected his interests.[8]

Soon after Merton's foundation, Matilda visited the Augustinian community to see how the building works were progressing and give gifts. She brought her son William, whom she allowed to play in the grounds, hoping that his happy memories of the occasion would lead him in time to extend his patronage to Merton. He was with her when she returned in 1117, when the priory moved to a new site, which it would occupy until the Dissolution.[9]

In April 1116, having had the Witan pay homage to William as the heir to England, Henry went back to Normandy, leaving Matilda as co-regent with her son, just as Matilda of Flanders had ruled in association with her eldest son. We find the Queen presiding over a lawsuit and commanding Ansfrid, Lord of Allington Castle, 'that you should justly take action to return to Hugh de Floriac, the Abbot of St Augustine, his ship and all his things which were captured. And all those men who took them should be put under pledge that they should be at the King's justice when he should wish to have them. And I order that all his things should be at peace just as they were on the day the King crossed the sea, until he himself should return to England.' Three writs related to this matter were issued jointly by the Queen and William.[10]

That spring, Matilda received the excited guards of a prisoner, a former pawnbroker called Bricstan of Chatteris. Having desired to become a monk and been accepted as a novice at Ely Abbey, this 'honest man' had been falsely accused of usury and imprisoned in chains in London for five months. His guards told the Queen how, one night, they had heard his chains being flung forcefully against the wall of his prison, and had gone to see what was happening. They found Bricstan unfettered, and he told them he had dreamed that the Saxon royal saint Etheldreda, the first Abbess of Ely, had appeared to him along with St Benedict and struck off his chains.

Matilda sent the Justiciar, Ralph Bassett, the man who had falsely accused Bricstan, to investigate. Bassett had to concede that the prisoner was sincere and telling the truth; he and the Queen were convinced that a miracle had taken place. Matilda, 'being a good Christian', pardoned Bricstan and had him paraded through London, ordering that the bells of the City be rung, and Masses said, in celebration of his miraculous deliverance. She also had the unfortunate Ralph Bassett consigned to prison. She asked Bricstan if she might keep his chains, but he chose to take them back to his abbey. Matilda is said to have gone to Ely with him and witnessed his offering them up at the high altar.[11]

At the end of August 1116, Matilda headed a council of bishops set up to discuss the terms on which Papal legates might be allowed to visit England. The King was informed that the council was in favour of upholding the ancient liberties of the realm, and that the Queen and the bishops were ready to 'annihilate' the Pope's demand that legates be allowed to visit England without royal permission.[12] Hearing this, Henry made a lightning visit to England to prevent the Papal legate from entering the realm.

By Christmas 1117, Matilda's health was failing. We do not know what ailed her, but it was serious enough for Henry to return briefly from Normandy and spend Christmas with her.[13] She must have rallied, for he evidently felt able to leave her to go back to the duchy.

Matilda spent most of her last months at Westminster.[14] It was probably in 1118 that she founded the leper hospital of St James and St Mary Magdalene just outside the east gate of Chichester, for eight men.[15] In Oxford she performed her last public act in favour of a chapter of eremitical monks, who had established a hermitage in the royal forest at Luffield, Northamptonshire, but been driven out by the foresters of Roger de Beaumont's son Robert, now earl of Leicester. Once they had shown that they were living there with the King's permission, Matilda issued a writ ensuring their protection from all injury.[16]

Her brother David apparently visited her in 1118, for she appears as a witness, with her son William, to two charters he issued to Durham Cathedral, one of which was witnessed by John, Archbishop of Glasgow, who had been consecrated in January 1118.[17] Possibly David was concerned about a deterioration in his sister's health.

Henry was still in Normandy when Matilda, aged only thirty-seven, was 'snatched away from her country, to the great loss of her people'.[18] She was at Westminster when 'the first day of May' 1118, the feast of St Philip, 'at night time, took her away, to enter into endless day'.[19] 'Cut off from the light of day', she 'entered into rest. She died willingly, leaving the throne after a reign of seventeen years and six months, experiencing the fate of her family, who almost all departed in the flower of their age.'[20] It was recorded that, that year, 'nothing happened to trouble the King save the death of his Queen'.[21] Most chroniclers testify to Henry's suffering great 'heaviness' at Matilda's passing. His grief was manifested in the numerous gifts he gave to churches in her memory and the 47,000 Masses he funded for the salvation of her soul.[22] But he did not immediately return to England, being much preoccupied with affairs in Normandy.[23]

On the day she died, Matilda's body was laid on a bier and carried to Westminster Abbey. There was a reason for the hasty burial. When the King returned to England in 1120, the monks of Holy Trinity, Aldgate, formally complained that they had not been permitted to bury the Queen in their priory, as had been her wish, because the monks of Westminster had immediately claimed her body. Henry would not sanction a reburial, but he confirmed all Matilda's grants to Holy Trinity, and gave them holy relics he had been given by Alexius I Comnenus, Emperor of Byzantium.[24]

Matilda's funeral was 'splendidly celebrated at Westminster'.[25] On that day, nearly 68,000 poor people were fed at the King's expense to mark her obsequies, and alms were distributed in abundance.[26] Bishop Roger of Salisbury officiated at the service, and gave a sermon praising the late Queen's virtues. The leading clergy, 'whom she had loved greatly while living', kept vigil for thirty days by her resting place,[27] among them her friend Herbert de Losinga, Bishop of Norwich, who himself would die the following year.

'Fittingly', the Queen's body 'was buried at Westminster, and is now at peace'.[28] She was laid to rest 'in the revestry' (the sacristry) of the Confessor's church;[29] excavations have shown that Henry III's sacristy, which probably stood on the same site, was beyond the north door of the nave.[30]

In 1562, Matilda's resting place was located to the south of the shrine of St Edward the Confessor, not far from where his Queen, Edith of Wessex, was buried before the high altar. (Possibly her remains had been moved to this position when the abbey was rebuilt in the thirteenth century, or they had been buried here in the first place.) Her grave was opened and her skeleton was found to be wearing robes of estate and a royal ring on one finger.

There is no record of a monument ever being raised above the Queen's remains, although an inscription was placed on the grave: 'Here lies the renowned Queen Matilda, the second, excelling both young and old of her day, she was for everyone the benchmark of morals and the ornament of life.'[31] A Latin epitaph written by the chronicler Henry of Huntingdon and placed above Matilda's resting place in the reign of her grandson Henry II read: 'Here lies Matilda II, the good Queen of the English, formerly the wife of King Henry I, mother of the Empress Maud, and daughter to Lord Malcolm, the former King of Scots, and his consort, Saint Margaret. If we wished to speak of her goodness and probity of character, the day would be too short. May her spirit be greatly soothed. Amen.'[32]

In 1631, John Weever recorded that Matilda lay in Westminster Abbey 'without any tomb', and that only four verses (couplets) remained of the epitaph. He translated the surviving lines thus:

> No prosperous state did make her glad,
> Nor adverse chances made her sad.
> If Fortune frowned, she then did smile,
> If Fortune smiled, she feared the while.
> If beauty tempted, she said nay,
> No pride she took in sceptre's sway.
> She only high her self debased,
> A lady only fair and chaste.

Today, Matilda's resting place is unmarked and the epitaph has disappeared.[33]

Matilda was widely mourned. The counsel of this 'kind woman and true', 'Matilda of blessed memory', had been immeasurably beneficial to England. 'The goodness that King Henry and Queen Matilda did to this land cannot all be written, and may never be told, nor by any man understood.'[34] Her death, wrote William of Malmesbury, was 'to her own advantage, for she entered into rest and her spirit manifested, by no trivial implications, that she was a resident in Heaven'.[35] It was not to Henry's advantage, certainly: his future misfortunes were attributed to Matilda not being alive to pray for the weal of his realm.[36]

Matilda's brother David granted Westminster Abbey 30s. annually for candles to be lit on her tomb, two by day and two by night, on the anniversary of her death, with provision for food and wine for the monks celebrating her obits.[37] He also gave money for Mass to be celebrated annually in the abbey in her memory. From 1120, Henry I paid a halfpenny every day for a lamp of remembrance to be kept burning perpetually above the high altar,[38] where one for Queen Edith was already hanging. In 1130, the sheriffs of London were ordered to ensure that its flame was never extinguished.[39]

Neither of Matilda's children was with their mother when she died. William was in Normandy, and the Empress Maud in Italy. In 1115, Matilda of Canossa, Countess of Tuscany, had died, leaving her considerable landed property to Heinrich V, after having promised it to the Papacy, whose ally she had been in the investiture controversy. This led to another quarrel with the Pope, and the Emperor's excommunication, whereupon, in February 1116, after keeping Christmas with Maud at Speyer, Heinrich marched from Augsburg, invaded Italy and seized his inheritance. He took Maud with him on this campaign, crossing the Brenner Pass in March in the snow. On the way to Tuscany they stayed at Treviso, and then for the nights of 11 and 12 March in the Doge's Palace in Venice, before journeying south to Padua, Mantua and Governolo, finally taking up residence in the impregnable castle of Canossa,[40] which stood on a rocky summit overlooking Reggio Emilia. Here, in the place where Heinrich IV had stood bare-headed in the snow for three days, waiting for the Pope to lift his excommunication, they received a warm welcome from a reception committee of vassals, and laudatory verses were composed 'On the coming of the Emperor and Queen', which hailed the fourteen-year-old Empress as a fitting replacement for Matilda of Tuscany.

They stayed at Canossa for a year, while the Emperor consolidated his position with the Tuscan people and Maud supported him. By Easter 1117, he had driven the Pope out of Rome and seized control of the Eternal City. There, possibly on Easter Sunday, 25 March, and certainly at Pentecost (13 May), Maud was ceremonially crowned with Heinrich in the chapel of St Gregory the Great in St Peter's Basilica by Maurice Bourdin, Archbishop of Braga, in defiance of the Pope.[41] These were ceremonial crown-wearings, not coronations.

Late in May, Heinrich took Maud back to Canossa, where he continued the task of consolidating his rule. Needing to suppress an insurrection in Germany, he returned there the following year, having left Maud to act as regent in northern Italy, under the protection of his army,[42] and with the support of the Imperial chancellor of

Italy, Filippo, Bishop of Ravenna (from 1118), and her chaplains, Altmann and Burchard. Young as she was, she presided over courts, dispensing justice and gathering experience that would serve her well in the future. On 11 September 1117, at Rocca Carpineto, she adjudicated in favour of Hugh, provost of the church at Reggio Emilia; and on 14 November 1118, at Castrocaro near Forli, she and her chancellor gave judgement in a dispute between a bishop and the convent of Santa Maria at Faenza. With Burchard the chaplain keeping a record, Maud decided in favour of the latter, and threatened an Imperial prohibition on anyone who challenged her judgement.[43]

It would have taken about a month to six weeks for her to receive the sad news from England that the mother she had not seen for over eight years was dead. It was a grief she had to bear alone, for not until the autumn of 1119 would she rejoin her husband in Lotharingia (Lorraine), where, in November, she witnessed his charter to a church.[44] Later that month they travelled on to Liège and Goslar.[45]

Robert of Torigni refers to a lost 'Life of Queen Matilda', and historians have speculated that it may have been commissioned by her daughter Maud.[46]

Memories of Queen Matilda's oppressive taxation, her extravagance and her lust for glory soon receded. She was remembered as 'the good Queen',[47] with great affection and reverence. 'From the time England first became subject to kings, out of all the queens, none was found to be comparable to her, and none will be found in time to come, whose memory will be praised and name will be blessed throughout the ages.'[48]

Her reputation for holiness long outlived her. There were reports of miracles taking place at her tomb, and soon it had become an object of veneration.[49] In the ten years after her death, as many pilgrims received Papal indulgences for visiting it on St Peter's Day as did those who did reverence at the shrine of Edward the Confessor,[50] who would be canonised in 1161. King David may have tried to promote the late Queen's cult of sanctity. But Matilda never officially achieved sainthood. The movement for her canonisation foundered for several reasons: rivalry between Westminster Abbey and St Paul's Cathedral, Henry I's failure to promote his wife's cult after her male line died out, and the future King Stephen's aversion to supporting the canonisation of the mother of his rival for the throne, the Empress Maud, for he believed that Matilda had been a professed nun and that her daughter was therefore a bastard.

Centuries after her death, however, Matilda's goodness was still being spoken of far and wide.[51] The fourteenth-century chronicler Langtoft wrote: 'Whoever desires to know fully all her acts of goodness, let him go to Westminster; there they are registered.'

Part Three

Adeliza of Louvain
Second Queen of Henry I

1

'Without Warning'

After Matilda's funeral, a grief-stricken Henry took himself off to Normandy and embraced a life of celibacy[1] – but not for long. An affair with a married noblewoman, Robert de Beaumont's daughter Isabella, produced a daughter, another Isabella, around 1120, and in the 1140s Henry's bastard son Gilbert was young and unwed,[2] so was probably conceived around this time.

Still hopeful of begetting more legitimate sons and securing a male succession,[3] the King was contemplating marrying again when he was approached by a vassal of his son-in-law, the Emperor Heinrich V. 'The warlord of Louvain',[4] Godfrey (or Geoffrey) VII 'the Great' or 'Barbatus' ('the Bearded'), was a powerful ruler whose lands encompassed part of what is now Belgium and eastern France: he was duke of Lower Lotharingia (Lorraine), landgrave of Brabant, marquess of Antwerp and count of Brussels and Louvain (or Leuven), and he was offering his eldest daughter, Adeliza, the 'fair maid of Brabant', as a bride for the King. Henry expressed interest.

The duchy of Brabant and all Godfrey's other territories were part of the Roman Empire. Brabant was then divided into four parts, and Godfrey's landgraviate comprised Lower Brabant, the capital of which was Louvain. Godfrey's wife, Ida, Countess of Namur, daughter of Otto II, Count of Chiny, had died in 1117; through her, Adeliza of Louvain – like Matilda of Flanders – was descended from Charlemagne.

The city of Louvain had been established in the late ninth century on the site of a Roman settlement, and was becoming an important mercantile centre with a population of two thousand. Its name means 'the marsh in the forest', for forests then surrounded the marshy valley of the River Dijle. It had come into the possession of Godfrey's forebears at the end of the tenth century. The castle of the dukes of Brabant, where Adeliza spent much of her childhood, had been built soon after the founding of Louvain, and stood on an island on the Dijle. It was abandoned by the fourteenth century, and nothing survives today. Nearby stood the ancient, possibly eighth-century, church of St Peter, which was later rebuilt in the Gothic style.

Adeliza probably also spent time at the hilltop castle of Coudeneberg in Brussels,[5] or at Antwerp, which was still essentially a Roman city. The castle there, the Antwerpen Burcht (later renamed Het Steen), had been built in stone by the Emperor Otto II in 980, less than a mile from the old Roman settlement at Viersel. It incorporated an ancient wharf and a new church dedicated to St Walpurgis, patron saint of Antwerp.[6]

Duke Godfrey had been at violent odds with the Emperor Heinrich until 1118, but since then they had been allies, and in 1119 the Emperor had helped Godfrey to regain Lotharingia. At this time Adeliza had perhaps stayed at the Imperial court at Aachen and become acquainted with the Empress Maud. Possibly her marriage to Henry I was already being discussed by her father and his ally.

For Duke Godfrey, an alliance with the Emperor's father-in-law would have been highly prestigious. A defensive treaty with England against their mutual enemy, Flanders, would also have been advantageous, since Godfrey's border was under threat.

Henry was said to have chosen Adeliza 'because of her beauty',[7] but there were political advantages for him too. The union would reinforce his friendship with the Roman Empire, which had been fostered by the marriage of his daughter Maud; it would also establish bonds with Brabant and so strengthen his position in the northern marches of France. He may have put out feelers for an alliance in 1119, and Maud was perhaps instrumental in furthering negotiations.[8]

On 6 January 1120, in London, on the advice of Ralph d'Escures, Archbishop of Canterbury, and some of his nobles, Henry informed his Council of his need to take a second wife, and revealed to them his choice.[9] The chroniclers struggled with the young lady's name, giving it variously as Adeliza, Adelid(a), Adelicia, Adela, Adala, Adelaide, Adelheite, Adeline, Adelina, Aeliz, Aethelice, Aleyda, Alice, Alicia, Aaliz and Adelidis. To Flemish and Provençal poets, she was Alise, Adelais or 'Alix la Belle'.

Envoys from Duke Godfrey came to London to negotiate the terms of the alliance with Henry. Willingly the King 'renounced the celibacy he had cherished since Matilda's death, anxious for future heirs by a new consort'[10] and desirous of keeping himself from 'disgraceful conduct'. The betrothal contract was signed on 16 April 1120, with the King waiving a dowry but promising a lavish dower, and Adeliza was proclaimed Lady of the English.[11] She would not be styled queen until she was crowned.

Adeliza did not come to England immediately. Possibly she was not old enough to cohabit with her future husband, who was now fifty-two. Her date of birth is not recorded, but she was described as a young girl or maiden (*puella*) at the time of her betrothal. Possibly she was under twelve, and therefore below the permitted canonical age for cohabitation, which might account for the delay in the marriage taking place, and place Adeliza's date of birth around 1109.

In 1119, Henry had celebrated the marriage of his heir, William, to Mahaut of Anjou, and in 1120 he created him duke of Normandy. The young Duke was no unifier of peoples like his father; he was heard to boast, 'When I am king, I will yoke the English like oxen to the plough.' His future subjects were spared such a fate. On 25 November 1120, the King and his court were preparing to return from Normandy to England. Two ships awaited them at Barfleur. Henry boarded one, with his daughter-in-law and many courtiers; his seventeen-year-old son embarked on the other, which was called the *Blanche-Nef* – the *White Ship* – with 'almost all the young nobility flocking around him'. The *White Ship*'s master was the son of the man who had captained the *Mora*. Also with William were his tutor, two of the King's bastard children – Richard of Lincoln and Matilda, Countess of Perche – and Stephen of Blois. Seeing that the crew were 'immoderately filled with wine'[12] lavishly provided by the young Duke, and that the ship was 'overloaded with foolish, headstrong young people', Stephen – pleading an attack of diarrhoea – and several others disembarked and boarded the King's ship, which sailed away just before twilight with about three hundred on board.

When it was 'dark night',[13] the *White Ship* shot out of the harbour, urged on by its inebriated company to overtake the King's vessel, but in the attempt she 'struck violently against a huge rock' and 'capsized without warning. Everyone cried out at once in their great peril, but the water pouring into the boat soon drowned their cries and all alike perished.'[14]

William had managed to clamber into a small boat, but as it was pulling away, he heard his half-sister Matilda crying for help. Being especially fond of her, he ordered the boat to be turned around, but desperate survivors swamped it, and it sank, dragging him down to his death. Three hundred people had drowned; only one man, a butcher of Rouen, survived the wreck. The *Anglo-Saxon Chronicle* states that Queen Matilda's son Richard was also lost, but the chronicler was almost certainly referring to Richard of Lincoln, who drowned with Matilda of Perche.

'No ship was ever productive of so much misery. None was ever so notorious in the history of the world.'[15]

Henry reached England safely, and for two days was unaware of the disaster. When the news came, no one had the courage to break it to the King, so a young boy was sent to throw himself, weeping, at Henry's feet and tell him that his son was dead. 'Immediately Henry fell to the ground, overcome with anguish, and after being helped to his feet by friends and led into a private room, gave way to bitter laments.'[16] It was said that he never smiled again. He had not only lost two sons and a daughter, but he now had no male heir to succeed him. His only surviving heir was his daughter by the late Queen, the Empress Maud.

2

'A Fortunate Beauty'

In the depths of his grief, Henry spent a miserable Christmas at Brampton,[1] then, knowing that his most urgent priority now was to father more sons, he crossed the Channel to bring his young bride to England.[2] What Adeliza made of her bridegroom is unrecorded, but Henry roused himself and chivalrously expressed the view that he 'knew of no woman as fair as she was seen on Earth'.[3]

The chroniclers lauded Adeliza's 'good morals and modest countenance'.[4] She must have been remarkably beautiful, given their ecstatic praise. One called her 'a lovely woman', another 'a young woman of great beauty and modesty'.[5] Henry of Huntingdon was moved to write 'in elegaics' of Adeliza's beauty: 'O Queen of the English, Adeliza, the very muse who prepares to call to mind your graces is frozen in wonder. What, to you, most beautiful one, is a crown? What, to you, are jewels? A jewel grows pale on you and a crown does not shine. Put adornment aside, for Nature provides your adornment, and a fortunate beauty cannot be improved. Beware ornaments, for you take no light from them; they shine brightly only through your light. I was not ashamed to give my modest praise to great qualities, so be not ashamed, I pray, to be my lady.'

Adeliza's native language was Flemish, but she understood, and perhaps could read, French, which suggests that she had received some formal education.[6] She was also skilled with the needle. She had embroidered a beautiful standard in silk and gold for her father to bear in his campaigns to recover all his patrimony in Lower Lotharingia. It became famous throughout Christendom, but in 1129 it was captured by his enemies in a battle near Duras, which became known as the Field of the Standard, and placed as a trophy in the cathedral of St Lambert at Liège. For centuries, it was carried through the streets on Rogation days, until the church was destroyed in the French Revolution.[7]

In January 1121,[8] Henry arrived in England with Adeliza, disembarking at Dover. He took her to Windsor, and there they were married, probably on 24 January 1121, in the castle chapel.[9] William of Malmesbury and the chronicler John of Worcester claim that the ailing Ralph d'Escures, Archbishop of Canterbury, deputed William Giffard, Bishop of Winchester, to marry them, but in fact there was a row between the Archbishop and Bishop Roger of Salisbury over who should officiate. Bishop Roger claimed that it was his right, since Windsor fell in his diocese, but the Archbishop disagreed, insisting that it was his right as primate of England. An ecclesiastical council was promptly convened, which decreed that, wherever they might be in England, the King and Queen were parishioners of the Archbishop of Canterbury, whereupon Ralph d'Escures performed the marriage ceremony.

On marriage, Henry dowered Adeliza with Queenhithe and lands in the counties of Oxford, Essex (including Waltham Abbey), Hertford, Buckingham, Bedford, Lincoln, Berkshire, Gloucester, London, Surrey, Middlesex and Devon.[10] He also exempted her from paying land tax on untenanted properties. Later he granted her part of his estate at Berkeley, Gloucestershire.[11]

It was arranged that Adeliza would be crowned at Westminster Abbey on Sunday 30 January.[12] All the members of the Great Council were present. To compensate Bishop Roger, the King had invited him to perform the ceremony, and the wily Bishop began the service early in the morning, hoping to pre-empt the Archbishop. But the avenging Primate tottered in halfway through the proceedings, just as the Queen had been crowned and Bishop Roger had placed the King's crown on Henry's head. The Archbishop promptly snatched it off, and put it on again with his own hands before re-crowning Adeliza, but then collapsed with exhaustion and had to ask Bishop Roger to complete the service after all.[13] Adeliza maintained her dignity, her 'beauty dazzling her diadem'.

From Windsor, Henry took Adeliza to Winchester, and thence to Westminster, where he left her while he led what proved to be a lacklustre military expedition to Wales. He was back at Westminster by Whitsun (29 May), when he and his new Queen wore their crowns together.[14] On 23 June, Adeliza witnessed the foundation charter of the Cluniac abbey of Reading, which the King had established for the salvation of the souls of himself, his parents, his brother Rufus, and his late wife and son. The earliest known English carving of the coronation of the Virgin Mary was found at Reading Abbey, suggesting that the King and his family were devotees of the spreading cult of Mary.[15] Adeliza became a benefactress of Reading Abbey, and in 1125 witnessed a further charter granting lands to the community.[16] In December, she witnessed a grant Henry made to Merton Priory. Christmas was spent at Norwich.[17]

Adeliza would be remembered as 'the May withouten vice'.[18] She was young and untried, and was to play virtually no public role in politics. She witnessed few charters in England and Normandy, and issued only one short writ in her own name.[19] She attended some meetings of the Great Council, the first in May 1121. In 1129, she received the first recorded payment of queengold, twenty marks out of the forty-five paid by the elderly widowed Lucy of Bolingbroke, Countess of Chester, to the King, in return for his allowing her to remain unmarried for five years;[20] this was a higher percentage than the share granted to Matilda of Flanders.

Initially Adeliza's lack of political activity may have been down to her youth, but there would be little opportunity as she grew older for her to gain experience or exercise as regent any political acumen she might have had, for in the first decade of their marriage, Henry kept her with him whenever he travelled to Normandy. Moreover, the late Queen Matilda's political role had been capably filled by Bishop Roger of Salisbury,[21] and the increasing centralisation of the royal administration now left little room for a queen to exercise power. Yet in private this 'good and beauteous' girl may have come to exercise a gentle influence on the King.

Henry was amenable to the promotion of the Lotharingians whom Adeliza had brought in her train. Among them were Godfrey of Louvain, who was to serve as her chancellor until 1123, when he was made bishop of Bath; Rothardus, who became chamberlain to Bishop Godfrey that year; and her chaplains, Herman, Franco of Brussels, and Simon,²² who succeeded Godfrey as her chancellor and was consecrated bishop of Worcester in May 1125 in Canterbury Cathedral.²³ He remained close to Adeliza until his death in 1150, and witnessed some of her charters.²⁴

Adeliza also brought with her several ladies, including her second cousin, Melisende (or Millicent) de Rethel,²⁵ who would marry twice in England. Her first husband was Robert, Lord Marmion of Tamworth, 'a warlike man, hardly equalled in his time for his ferocity, cleverness and boldness'.²⁶ Before 1141, Adeliza gave Melisende land worth £40 from the manors of Stanton Harcourt and South Leigh in Oxfordshire, which King Henry granted her before 1130. Marmion died violently in 1144 in Coventry, whereupon Melisende married Richard de Camville, to whom her lands passed.²⁷ She shared Adeliza's devotion to Reading Abbey, to which, at her behest, Richard de Camville gave the chapel of South Leigh.²⁸

Another countrywoman was Juliana, daughter of Godeschalch, a 'wise and beautiful girl who had come to England with Queen Adeliza from the region of Louvain'.²⁹ Juliana became the wife of a young Norman courtier, Jordan d'Auffay, to whom the King gave the manor of Norton Ferris at Kilmington, Somerset.³⁰

In her years as queen, Adeliza failed to emulate the example of her predecessors in her patronage of religious houses. Examples of her pious deeds are few. The annalist of Waltham Abbey owed his appointment as a canon to her influence in placing him in the abbey in 1124, when he was a boy, and she also gave gifts to the abbey.³¹ Like her predecessor, she corresponded with Hildebert of Lavardin, Bishop of Le Mans, and gained his permission to become a lay daughter of the ancient royal abbey of Saint-Vincent at Le Mans. She won his praise for her dedication to 'sacred studies' and her devotion to the brothers there, whom she visited whenever she could. In one of his letters he urged her to favour the poor,³² possibly because he felt that she was not doing enough to succour them.

There is no doubt that she was pious, though, and she did forge friendships with other churchmen. William de Vere, Bishop of Hereford from 1186 to 1198, would one day donate land in memory of Henry I and Adeliza, recalling how she had 'nurtured' him when he had been brought up in their court.³³ She granted a charter to

Bishop Roger's nephew, Alexander, Bishop of Lincoln, calling him her 'dearest friend'.[34]

Among the thirteen charters she did witness, the first was to the monks of the abbey of Tiron,[35] near Chartres, in September 1121, the abbey being the mother house of the eremitical Tironensian Order founded in 1106. She witnessed other charters to the abbeys of Bec-Hellouin and Savigny in Normandy, St Mary of Kemeys, Newport, and her predecessor's foundation, Holy Trinity, Aldgate.[36] The first charter she granted in her own name, in 1126, at Woodstock, was to Holy Trinity.[37] Her seal survives in the British Library; it was based on the same matrix that had been used for the seal of Matilda of Scotland.

Like Matilda of Scotland before her, Adeliza was a patron of poets and men of letters. She commissioned a troubadour or trouvère called David the Scot to write an account in French of the King's deeds, and set it to music as a metrical *chanson*. It was the first history written in a language other than Latin. Adeliza herself provided David the Scot with material for it. The Anglo-Norman chronicler and philosopher Geoffrey Gaimar was laughing up his sleeve at how dull the *chanson* was, and at Adeliza's ignorance: 'If I had chosen to have written of King Henry, I had a thousand things to say, which the troubadour knew nought about; neither had he written, nor was the Louvain Queen herself in possession of them.' Nevertheless he was willing to oblige his patroness, Constance FitzGilbert, to whom Adeliza had given a manuscript of David the Scot's work, and who wanted a copy made of it. Sadly, neither Constance's text nor Gaimar's copy survives.

It is often stated that it was Adeliza, rather than Matilda of Scotland, who commissioned 'The Voyage of St Brendan', but while it is true that three of the four surviving manuscript texts call the Queen in question 'Aaliz' (Adeliza), the other calls her Mahaut (another version of Matilda); and in his dedication, Benedeit clearly refers to the charter that Matilda persuaded Henry to grant his subjects in 1100, whereas no such charters are associated with Adeliza. Therefore the Queen who commissioned the translation was probably Matilda, and possibly it was re-dedicated to Adeliza in due course.[38]

Around 1125, Philippe de Thaon wrote *Li Bestiare* (*Bestiary*), or *Physiologus*, 'an elementary book of animals, in plain French' – the first of its kind – for Adeliza. Its dedication reads: 'He, Philippe de Thaon, into the French language has translated the Bestiary, a book of science, for the honour of a jewel, who is a very handsome woman. Aliz is she named, a queen she is crowned, Queen she is of England, may her soul never have trouble! In Hebrew, in truth, Aliz means praise of God. I will compose a book, may God be with its commencement.'[39] Henry I had an interest in exotic animals, and by 1120 had made Woodstock 'the celebrated place for the habitation of man and beasts'[40] by establishing a menagerie there – the first zoo in England, which he stocked with wild beasts from other lands, among them lions, leopards, lynxes, camels and a porcupine.[41] This may well have inspired Adeliza's interest in animals.

Her chief role, however, was to bear the King a son, and she must have felt under tremendous pressure to do so. To achieve this end, Henry kept her at his side as much as possible, and this is probably the reason why he took her with him when he visited Normandy, as he had rarely taken his first wife. Thus Adeliza was never appointed regent of England. When Henry took her abroad, he left his trusted chancellor, Bishop Roger of Salisbury, in charge, at least until 1128, when he lost confidence in the Bishop's management of the administration.

Henry probably took Adeliza with him when he travelled around his realm in 1122, visiting Northampton at Easter (26 March), then Hertford, Waltham, Oxford and Windsor, where, on 14 May, he kept his Whitsun court.[42] That month, the Empress Maud was planning to visit him in England, possibly to discuss the worsening situation in Normandy, where William Clito was doing his best to draw baronial support away from the King. Henry travelled down from London to Kent to receive her, but he waited in vain at Canterbury, for Charles I 'the Good', Count of Flanders (cousin of Baldwin VII), had refused Maud permission to travel through his domains.[43] Charles was at war with Henry's son-in-law, Heinrich V, whose ally was Godfrey of Louvain, the father of Queen Adeliza, which accounts for Charles's hostility.

On 23 September that year, Maud was probably present at the Concordat of Worms, where the Emperor and the Pope finally agreed a solution to the investiture controversy, on much the same terms as Henry I had made with the Church years earlier. Heinrich and Maud spent Christmas at Strasbourg, before visiting Mainz, Liège, Duisberg and Utrecht.

Meanwhile, Henry had continued his progress through England, spending time at Westminster before taking Adeliza north to York, Durham and Carlisle, then returning to York on 6 December to

celebrate St Nicholas's Day, before coming south via Nottingham to
Dunstable, where they kept Christmas at Kingsbury, a stone palace
that Henry had built some years earlier, which stood in nine acres
of land.[44]

After Christmas, the court moved on to Berkhamsted and
Woodstock,[45] where, on 25 March 1123, Henry gave the bishopric
of Bath to Adeliza's chancellor and countryman, Godfrey of Louvain.[46]
The King and Queen spent Easter (15 April) at Winchester, where
Adeliza attended a meeting of the Great Council, and witnessed a
charter to Exeter Cathedral. Around this time, she made the acquaint-
ance of Wulfric of Haselbury, a Somerset priest who was falsely
accused by Drogo de Munci, one of Henry's courtiers, of secreting
away some of the King's treasure. When Drogo suggested that Wulfric's
possessions be searched, he was struck down with fits, which only
abated when the King and Queen begged Wulfric to heal him.[47]

On 11 June 1123, Henry went alone to Normandy, where a revolt
had broken out, but in March 1124, having successfully quelled it
and defeated the rebels at the Battle of Bourgtheroulde, he sent for
Adeliza to join him at Rouen. Together they viewed the relics of
St Romanus, which were displayed that year in Rouen Cathedral, in
the presence of the Papal legate. The royal couple may have stayed
in the new palace Henry was building at Quevilly, adjacent to the
priory of Notre-Dame de Pré. This complex was built in a similar
arrangement to the palace and abbey at Westminster.[48]

In Rouen, Adeliza witnessed just how savage Henry could be.
She may not have heard of what had happened when, in 1119, his
bastard daughter Juliana's husband, Eustace de Pacy, had rebelled
against him and unlawfully occupied the chateau of Ivry. To ensure
his submission, the King demanded that hostages be exchanged,
himself taking into custody the two daughters of Eustace and Juliana,
with Eustace holding as pledge the son of the constable of Ivry. But
Eustace, on malevolent advice, put out the boy's eyes and sent him,
blinded, back to his father, who demanded vengeance of the horrified King. Much moved by the constable's distress, Henry turned his
granddaughters over to him and allowed him to put out their eyes
and cut off the tips of their noses. 'Thus innocent childhood, alas,
suffered for the sins of the fathers.'[49] An incandescent Juliana took
her husband's part, which led Henry to lay siege to her castle at
Breteuil. She asked to meet with him, but attempted to shoot a
crossbow bolt into his heart. In the end she had to surrender and
seek forgiveness, before disappearing into the abbey of Fontevrault.

Now, in April 1124, Adeliza was present when Henry summoned three prisoners to appear before him. All were his vassals, and one, Luc de la Barre, had been his friend, but had circulated satirical songs against him. Henry sentenced them all to have their eyes burned out and to perpetual imprisonment. Even when Charles the Good, Count of Flanders, interceded on behalf of the condemned knights, the King remained obdurate. 'They broke their faith, violated their oath of allegiance: and therefore they deserve death, or at least to be punished by the loss of a limb,' he insisted. But when, on the public scaffold, the executioners seized Luc de la Barré to put his eyes out, he wrenched himself away and crashed his head against the wall, splitting it open and dying soon afterwards. Adeliza was seeing another side to the man she had married.

3
'His Only Heir'

On 23 May 1125, 'in the very flower of his age and victories',[1] the Emperor Heinrich died of cancer at Utrecht, his wife at his side.[2] He was thirty-eight. The last years of their marriage had been less turbulent, after Heinrich was reconciled to the Pope in 1122 at Worms. As he neared his end, he entrusted the Imperial regalia to Maud for safe keeping in Trifels Castle until his successor was elected; and, by placing his sceptre in her hands, signified his will that she rule the Empire in the period immediately following his death, for 'her prudent and gracious behaviour to her Imperial spouse was one of the causes which won the esteem of the German princes'.[3] Heinrich was buried with his forebears in Speyer Cathedral. After the obsequies, Adalbert of Saarbrucken, Archbishop of Mainz, persuaded Maud to resign the Emperor's regalia into his keeping. He was one of the electors who would choose Heinrich's successor,[4] Lothar II, who was no friend to Maud.

At twenty-two, Maud was a widow; her fate was now in the hands of her father. Henry I was then in Normandy, and as soon as he learned of the Emperor's death, 'he recalled his daughter by honourable messengers'[5] and sent an escort to bring her to Normandy. Her late husband's subjects were dismayed at the prospect of her departure. She was greatly loved,[6] and the German princes 'were urgent in their entreaties to her royal father for her restoration', but there was nothing for her now in Germany, and Henry was insisting that 'she was his only heir and must dwell among her own people'.[7]

Maud had 'become habituated to the country which was her dowry and had large possessions there' – and she had thrilled to the prospect of remaining as empress.[8] Having enjoyed certain freedoms in Germany – where she was known as 'the good Matilda'[9] – and still mourning her husband, she did not want to live in subjection to her father, who might arrange an unwelcome second marriage in pursuance of his policy of empire-building. Henry was unlikely to let her remain a widow for other reasons too. He wanted grandsons to assure the succession.

Thus Maud had no choice but to renounce her lands in Germany and say farewell to those who had peopled her world for the past fifteen years. In December 1125, she 'returned with reluctance'[10] to Normandy, 'not through any desperate need or feminine levity, but in response to a summons from her father. And though she had attained such high rank, she was in no way puffed up with pride, but meekly submitted in all things to her father's will.'[11] She arrived in time to join the King for Christmas, bringing with her jewels, precious relics, and several years' experience in the troubled world of Imperial politics. Although she had not been crowned empress, but had signed herself 'Queen of the Romans' when witnessing her husband's charters, she would never forget that she had been a Roman empress, and was to use the title until she died, styling herself '*imperatrix augusta*', and being widely known and addressed as 'the Empress'.[12]

In 1125, Count Eustace of Boulogne retired from the world to become a Cluniac monk, probably at Rumilly Priory near Boulogne, and ceded the county of Boulogne and all his rich estates in England to his daughter Matilda, making her one of the most desirable heiresses in Europe – not only on account of her great inheritance, but also because, like Matilda of Flanders and Adeliza of Louvain, she was impeccably descended from Charlemagne, and was also the great-granddaughter of King Cnut, the great-niece of Edward the Confessor, and the niece of the beloved Matilda of Scotland. Royal Saxon, Scottish and Imperial blood ran in her veins. This heritage, together with her courage and determination, would in time make her one of the Empress Maud's great adversaries.

The young Countess's seal is affixed to her father's abdication charters.[13] In one that he granted that year, Eustace described himself as 'once count of Boulogne, but now, at the dispensation of God, monk of Cluny', and confirmed that the charter had been 'confirmed and upheld by Stephen, count of Boulogne, to whom I gave my patrimony with Matilda, my daughter, who also upheld and confirmed this gift, in the presence of many people'.[14]

Count Eustace died soon afterwards, probably that same year, and 'when she became marriageable, after the death of her father', Henry I arranged for Matilda of Boulogne's marriage to Stephen of Blois, Count of Mortain, to take place. This suggests that Matilda turned twelve – marriageable age for girls – after Count Eustace died, so she must have been born around 1113. Her husband-to-be was at least twenty-eight. On their wedding, which probably took place in 1125, perhaps at Westminster, Stephen became the wealthiest magnate in England, by virtue of acquiring the rich honour of Boulogne. He took the title of count of Boulogne in right of his wife, and by acquiring her port of Wissant, advantageously gained control of the shortest Channel crossing to England and thereby trade in the Channel, so crucial for the English wool trade, which was probably Henry I's primary reason for arranging the match.[15] It was a highly successful marriage and there is much evidence in charters for Stephen's affection for Matilda and the children she bore him. In later years he would come to rely on her heavily.

Stephen was ambitious, as time would prove. Should Henry I leave no legitimate son to succeed him, his next male heirs were the sons of his sister Adela by the Count of Blois; thus Stephen stood near, but not next, in line to the English throne, which in the years to come would have serious implications for the royal succession. He had two older brothers. The eldest, William the Simple, was mentally unbalanced and never considered for the throne, but the second brother, Theobald, was an able man.

Tall, with a good physique, Stephen was 'a man of activity, but imprudent', as time would show, 'a mild man, soft and good'[16] – 'a fine knight, but in other respects a fool'.[17] His love of convivial feasting and hunting, and his 'readiness to joke and sit and regale, even with low people', won him many friends.[18] He was attractive to women and had had three bastard sons with a Norman mistress called Dameta, and possibly a daughter, all born before his marriage. He was dashing, charming and courteous to all classes, genial, candid, generous, tolerant, brave and well liked, yet he was also unreliable and vacillating, with poor judgement and little capacity for leadership, and was to manifest a fatal inability to sustain any enterprise or action. He was bold and brave, but a bad general in war, while the courage that both friends and foes praised was marred by recklessness.

He proved a good husband to Matilda, having the loving example of his parents before him, which is evident in a letter that his father wrote to his mother: 'Count Stephen sends to Adela, his sweetheart and spouse, the best and the tenderest love that his spirit may tender. I have travelled to Rome, my dear, surrounded in honours ...'[19] Stephen had also grown up seeing his outstandingly able, well-educated widowed mother capably ruling his father's domains, and his admiration and respect for the abilities of the female sex underpinned his attitude towards his wife, who was no less capable.

When in London, the young Count and Countess of Boulogne resided at the Tower Royal, a fortified tower house built by Henry I, who had presented it to them as a wedding gift. Located near Cheapside, in the parish of St Michael Paternoster, it was also known as La Riole, Le Riall or La Ryole. It was rebuilt in the reign of Henry III, and became the Queen's Wardrobe.

Matilda's first child was a daughter called Marie (or Mary) after her grandmother; Marie became abbess of Romsey in 1155–6. The minimum age for election as an abbess was then thirty, so she must have been born in 1125–6. (Her date of birth is often given as 1136, although there is no contemporary evidence for that.) Eustace, the second child and eldest son, was born between 1126 and August 1131, when he is mentioned in a charter issued by his parents.[20] He was named for his maternal grandfather. A second son, called Baldwin after Matilda's uncle, the King of Jerusalem, arrived between 1127 and 1135.[21] Around 1133–4, Matilda bore a second daughter, who was called after her. The child's year of birth is estimated from the fact that she was betrothed, aged two, to Waleran de Beaumont, Count of Meulan, in 1136.

On 1 July 1127, Stephen and Matilda founded Furness Abbey in Cumberland, and endowed it with land, for the salvation of their souls. It was a religious house of the eremitical Order of Savigny, which was much favoured by Stephen and Henry I, but would be incorporated into the Cistercian Order in the middle of the twelfth century. Furness Abbey was destroyed by the Scots and rebuilt in 1141. It is now a ruin, but still boasts contemporary crowned busts of Stephen and Matilda on either side of the chancel window. Matilda is shown with loose hair and a gown with a brooch at the throat.

Matilda had been brought up to emulate the pious example of her grandmother, Ida of Lorraine, wife of Eustace II. Ida had founded several religious houses and gained a reputation for sancity. In 1130, seventeen years after her death, her tomb at the abbey of St Vaast, near Arras, was opened and her body found to be incorrupt. This was regarded as a sign of holiness, and soon afterwards Ida was beatified by the Church; in time she would be venerated as a saint. Within about five years of her exhumation, Matilda may have commissioned the Latin life of her that was written by Hugo, a monk of St Vaast.[22] He mentions that 'love of her kin, for which she living had been distinguished, did not desert Ida after death', and relates how, after 1130, her intercession was believed to have saved the life of her granddaughter when she was 'bitterly assailed' by 'a relentless and grievous feverish illness'. The young Countess, 'not a little worn down through a time of too much pain, at last presented herself to be cured with many others at the venerated tomb, confiding and anticipating in the sanctity of the most blessed Ida, as well as her own blood which descended from Ida, with devoted and multitudinous prayers'; and, by 'the merits of the most blessed lady, after a very short delay withdrew healthy and unharmed'.[23]

4
'Royal English Blood'

Henry and Adeliza were in Normandy from the autumn of 1125 until 11 September 1126, when they returned to England with the widowed Empress and Stephen of Blois.[1] In Maud's travelling chests were the treasures she had owned during her marriage, among them her jewels, and two crowns: her heavy gold Imperial crown adorned with golden flowers, and Heinrich's coronation crown of solid gold decorated with gems, an enormous jewel and a cross. This crown was so weighty that two silver rods were needed to support it while being worn. Maud also brought to England the incorrupt hand of the Apostle James, which had been among the treasures of the Imperial chapel, and an anonymous chronicle of the life of Heinrich V, which is now in Corpus Christi College, Cambridge.

Between 1126 and 1133, she gave the hand of St James to Reading Abbey, which her father had founded.[2]

Maud was now twenty-three, and of striking appearance. She had German manners and probably spoke Norman French with a German accent, in a deep, masculine voice.[3] By all accounts, the prudent and gracious young girl beloved by the Emperor's subjects had matured into a formidable character, confident, unbending and independent-minded – 'a young woman of clear understanding and masculine firmness'.[4] The sympathetic William of Malmesbury, to whom Maud was patron, referred to her as a 'virago', which then meant a female warrior or courageous heroine, and had not yet acquired its modern sense of being domineering, scolding or shrewish. Other chroniclers mentioned Maud's masculine stridency. She 'had the nature of a man in the frame of a woman'. Her enemy Arnulf, Bishop of Lisieux, wrote that she was an 'intrepid spirit' but 'had nothing of the woman in her'. The virulently hostile anonymous author of the *Gesta Stephani*, the chronicle history of the deeds of King Stephen, stated that she was 'always superior to feminine softness'. Indefatigable, brave, tenacious and resourceful, she was in many respects her father's daughter. William of Malmesbury wrote admiringly that she resembled him in her energy, her iron will and her fortitude, 'and her mother in sanctity. Piety and assiduity vied with each other in her character, nor was it easy to discern which of her good qualities was most commendable.'

By 1126, William of Malmesbury's *Gesta Regum Anglorum*, commissioned by the late Queen Matilda, was completed, and he and his brother monks were hopeful that Matilda's daughter would become their patron. Through the good offices of David, King of Scots, who was then visiting the English court, the Empress received from their messenger William's book and a letter expressing their desire, in which they wrote of her royal lineage, the renowned virtues of her mother, and the interest the Queen had shown in her ancestors, an interest they trusted her daughter shared. Thus it came about that the book was dedicated to Maud.[5]

One of the works of the Neoplatonist philosopher Bernard of Chartres was dedicated to Maud by a pupil of his, who clearly thought that she would appreciate Bernard's teaching that reality is composed of three invisible, immutable principles: God, ideas, and matter. It was he who coined the saying, 'We are dwarfs astride the shoulders of giants.'

★

Soon after the royal party arrived in England, Maud witnessed a charter issued by her father at Portsmouth. Another signatory was a friend of her half-brother Robert, 'a certain Brian FitzCount, a man of distinguished birth and splendid position',[6] who was a bastard son of Alan IV, Duke of Brittany (who had married Constance, daughter of William the Conqueror). Brian had been brought up and well educated at the court of the man he would always think of as 'good King Henry'.[7] Henry had knighted him and married him to an heiress, Matilda of Wallingford, a widow several years his senior.[8] Brian was to become a faithful lifelong friend of Maud's – and more, it would be hinted. A thoughtful man, he had 'a great love of truth', as he once wrote to Henry of Blois, Bishop of Winchester. 'I know, to the best of my power and knowledge, that I do not deserve to be ranked among the unfaithful.'[9]

It was on Maud's advice, and that of King David of Scots, that Henry transferred his captive brother Robert from the custody of Bishop Roger at Devizes Castle to Bristol Castle, where he was placed under the guardianship of the King's bastard son Robert, Earl of Gloucester.[10] Possibly they feared that Robert might incite the distrusted Bishop Roger to support the claims of his son, William Clito.

After nearly six years of marriage, Henry was 'in grief' that Adeliza had not conceived a child.[11] In a queen, barrenness was abject failure and often interpreted as a sign of divine displeasure, but possibly Henry knew that the problem lay with him. Certainly he does not seem to have blamed his wife for failing to bear him a son, although it worried her, as she confided in a letter (now lost) to Hildebert of Lavardin, now archbishop of Tours, in which she sought his advice on the matter. He responded consolingly, exhorting her to channel her maternal instincts into charitable works for the poor: 'If it has not been granted to you from Heaven that you should bear a child to the King of the English, in these you will bring forth for the King of the Angels, with no damage to your modesty. Perhaps the Lord has closed up your womb, so that you might adopt immortal offspring. It is more blessed to be fertile in the spirit than the flesh.'[12]

That would have been small consolation to the King, who saw a succession crisis looming. 'Fearing that his Queen should be perpetually childless, with well-founded anxiety, he turned his thoughts on a successor to the kingdom.'[13] It was unthinkable that his troublesome nephew, William Clito – the obvious candidate under the rule of primogeniture – should succeed, especially after Henry had done so much to crush the dynastic claims of his older brother Robert's line. The Norman kings had not hitherto favoured primogeniture, but Henry himself subscribed to the contemporary view that being born in the purple (porphyrogeniture) – that is, to a reigning monarch, as he himself had been – conferred a stronger title to the succession. This ruled out the sons of his sister Adela by Stephen, Count of Blois. That left Maud, who, although a woman, yet had many of the qualities admired in men, and had been born the daughter of a reigning king.

Shortly before he rode to Windsor for Christmas, Henry convened a great number of the clergy and nobility at a council in London, at which he assigned the revenues of the counties of Shropshire and Rutland to Queen Adeliza, who was present.[14] The assembled lords swore to her that they would always regard as hers the lands that the King had given her.[15] They may have been compensation for her public humiliation at having failed in her foremost duty when Henry openly broached the subject of the succession.

Maud stayed with the King and Queen at Windsor for the festive season. Henry summoned another large gathering of lords to a meeting of the Great Council at Windsor, engaged in much 'long-continued deliberation' with them[16] and took counsel from his chief advisers.[17] Few details of their discussions survive. 'After deliberating long and deeply', the King spoke to his lords of the Empress and her doubly royal descent from the Norman and Saxon kings, and demanded that, 'if he should die without male issue, they would, without delay or hesitation, accept his daughter as their sovereign'.[18] They were reminded that, 'through her, who was now his only heir, they should come to be governed again by the royal English blood',[19] inherited from her mother.

There can be little doubt that Henry intended that Maud herself should rule after him, although historians have speculated that he was hoping that her title to the throne would be transmitted to her male heirs, if she had any, and that one would succeed him. But she was unmarried and childless, and he was fifty-six, only four years younger than his father had been when he died, so it is unlikely that he anticipated living until a son of his daughter was of an age to rule.

It was commonplace for feudal estates to descend to female heirs, but most of those heiresses married husbands who took over their lands. Maud had no husband, and her choice of one – or Henry's – would have a crucial bearing on the future of the Anglo-Norman realms.

Naturally the assumption was that she would marry, and that the throne would ultimately pass to a son of hers; but, in naming Maud his heir, Henry was taking a huge risk in regard to the succession, since in eleven years of marriage she had produced only one short-lived child, and might never bear any more. Furthermore, he might be sowing the seeds of civil war, as there were four men who might challenge her title: her uncle Robert (although he was now seventy-five and still a prisoner), Robert's son, William Clito, and Theobald and Stephen of Blois.[20]

After Christmas, the Great Council adjourned to Westminster, where, on New Year's Day 1127, Henry compelled 'all the nobility of England, as well as the bishops and abbots, to make oath that they would accept his daughter Maud as their sovereign', for it was to her alone that 'the legitimate succession belonged, from her grandfather, uncle and father, as well as from her maternal descent for many ages back'.[21] John of Worcester states the oath provided that, if Henry died without a male heir, and Maud had a son, she was to receive the English kingdom under Christ's protection with 'her lawful husband, should she have one'. The barons swore to defend her loyally against all others; but, fearing foreign interference, they insisted on their oath being conditional upon Maud not marrying outside England without their consent.[22]

They all came forward, in order, to swear the oath: William de Corbeil, Archbishop of Canterbury; the bishops; David I, King of Scots; Queen Adeliza; Stephen, Count of Boulogne and Mortain; then the other barons, headed by the King's eldest bastard, Robert of Caen, Earl of Gloucester, now aged about thirty-six and one of the greatest magnates in the land – 'a man of proved talent and admirable wisdom'.[23] But for his illegitimate status, Robert might have been a contender for the succession, for he had the qualities requisite for kingship; but attitudes to bastards inheriting had hardened since William the Conqueror had succeeded his father as Duke of Normandy in 1135.

There was 'a singular dispute' between Stephen and Robert, who contended, 'with laudable emulation', which of them should take the oath first, at which the abbots entered the affray. The King barked that they should all stop talking and swear the oath.[24] Most barons gave their allegiance reluctantly, and many historians have assumed that they were dismayed at the prospect of being ruled by a woman. But not one actually voiced this opinion.

Although there was no legal bar to a woman succeeding, there was no tradition of female rule in England or Normandy, and Norman

England was a military society. Leadership in battle was one of the chief obligations of a feudal ruler, which was why men usually ruled, or ruled in their wives' names. Yet there was no debate at the time, or later, about Maud's suitability, as a woman, to be queen. In fact, not one chronicler mentions her sex as a drawback to her succeeding, which strongly suggests that it was not in itself seen as an issue.

Maud had been highly respected as empress, had ruled effectively in her husband's name and dispensed justice. But clearly there was concern among the barons, and many doubted that she would ever become queen.[25] Chiefly they were preoccupied with the probability that she would remarry, in which case her husband would undertake her military duties. He might also use her resources to pursue his own interests, or subsume England within his own domains.

There was one immediate, tangible effect of the oath, for it prompted Louis VI immediately to renew his support for Willam Clito, anticipating that the Anglo-Norman barons might prefer him to Maud. That very month, Louis arranged William Clito's marriage to Jeanne of Montferrat, half-sister of his own Queen, Adelaide of Maurienne. Clito thereupon laid claim to Normandy.

At this time Maud 'was abiding continually in the chamber of Adeliza'.[26] They shared a European, Imperial perspective that may have forged a bond between them. Philippe de Thaon, who had enjoyed Adeliza's patronage, dedicated his last work, *Le Livre de Sibile*, to Maud. It appears that the two women were close, and that Adeliza was sympathetic to Maud. She may have been genuinely fond of the stepdaughter who was probably older than her; but she must also have been aware of the necessity for cultivating the favour of the woman who might one day be her Queen.

5
'The Offence of the Daughter'

During Lent, the court moved to London, and on to Woodstock for Easter (3 April), then back to London before 8 May. By then Henry had determined upon a second marriage for his daughter – but his choice of bridegroom was to prove a contentious one.

In the months after Maud's arrival in England, 'several princes of Lorraine and Lombardy came to ask her in marriage and to demand her as their sovereign, but they lost the fruit of their labours', because their aims did not fit with Henry's political strategy.[1] His nephew William Clito was vigorously asserting his claims to England and Normandy, and, to Henry's consternation, Louis VI had installed William as count of Flanders, following the murder of Charles the Good at the end of March. Fulk V, Count of Anjou, was also supporting him.

Anjou had long 'flourished under high-spirited and warlike rulers' descended from Charlemagne, who had 'dominated the peoples surrounding them with terror. They wrought all the destruction within their power upon their neighbours and subjugated the lands around.'[2] With France and Flanders hostile, Henry wanted Anjou on his side, protecting his southern border. 'Minded to make peace by his daughter's marriage',[3] he successfully weaned Count Fulk away from his allies by forging an alliance with him to secure assistance against William Clito.[4] Under its terms, Maud was to marry Geoffrey of Anjou, Fulk's heir by Aremburga of Maine, a thirteen-year-old boy[5] 'of high nobility and noted courage',[6] 'blooming in the first flower of youth'. Henry was aware that this 'talented' prodigy, although not yet a knight, was celebrated far and wide, and promptly dispatched heralds to Count Fulk 'to inform him of the royal will' in regard to the performance of the espousals.[7]

Maud was outraged. She refused the marriage. She had been an empress, and evidently considered it beneath her to marry the mere son of a count, that rank being 'lower than that of Roman emperor'.[8] At twenty-five, she did not want a husband who was eleven years her junior. Furthermore, it was widely believed that the Angevin rulers were descended from Satan, through the beautiful witch Melusine, who was said to have married an early count of Anjou, but – the story went – flew out of a window when he forced her to attend Mass, and was never seen again. The two children she left behind were Geoffrey's ancestors, and through him the ancestors of the Plantagenet line of kings who ruled England for three hundred years. Even the great Bernard of Clairvaux credited the tale; he said of the Angevin family, 'From the Devil they came, and to the Devil they will return.'

One tale had Henry locking Maud up until she agreed to the marriage. A tradition that may have had its origins in her protests links her to Mortemer Abbey at Lyons-la-Forêt, which was built on land gifted to the Cistercians by Henry I, and later re-founded by Maud for the soul of her father. In its day, it was the largest Cistercian monastery in Christendom. Local legend has it that Henry had his daughter shut up in a room there for five years, and that her ghost, a white wraith, haunts the ruins.

The truth is less prosaic. Maud wrote, hinting at her distress and her father's anger, to her mother's old correspondent, Hildebert, Bishop of Tours. He replied asking her to unburden herself more fully:

> I say what is known and proved by frequent experience. It is more satisfying to the thirsty to extinguish the ardour of thirst from a fountain than a stream. Wines taken from the first cask retain their native savour. Transferred from one to another, they degenerate. So your page fulfils my desire to know about you more richly than other's accounts. For whatever I get from you about yourself will be more certain to me than what common rumour might bring to my ears. Therefore when I learned that winds blew in your service favourable to sending a message across the channel, I immediately sent letters to you about what had been conveyed from England revealing the will of the King and what the father's breast was feeling about the offence of the daughter. I claim from you what I deserve to know through you. I claim, indeed, but as your friend in the Lord, as your servant in Christ, as one who puts your honour at the forefront of my happiness. What you know, therefore, about the King and yourself that should be told to a friend, I ask you to tell me.[9]

In Maud's response, she evidently lamented her situation at length, whereupon the Bishop wrote expressing sorrow at her intransigence and asked for her reassurance that she would cease causing distress to her father by persisting in her disobedience to his wishes.[10] His letter may have prompted her capitulation before the King's insistence that the marriage take place, for 'on his advice, she took a second husband'.[11]

It appears that the King envisaged Maud and Geoffrey ruling England jointly,[12] but none of the nobility of England had 'advised the match, or indeed knew of it'.[13] Bishop Roger of Salisbury would later complain that only Earl Robert, Brian FitzCount and John, Bishop of Lisieux, had been privy to the King's plans.[14] Henry deliberately kept the treaty a secret because it contravened his promise to the barons not to marry his daughter outside England without their consent, and because of the intense rivalry between Normans and Angevins, arising from the latter coveting Maine. Both factors made it unlikely that the barons would accept Geoffrey as Maud's future consort. Henry's priority was to unite the rival peoples of Normandy and Anjou.

At Whitsun (22 May) 1127, Henry sent Maud ahead to Normandy, escorted by Robert, Earl of Gloucester, and Brian FitzCount. Robert instructed Geoffrey Brito, Archbishop of Rouen, secretly to negotiate the terms of her betrothal. 'Pledges were given, and a pact, supported by oaths', sealed the negotiations in Anjou. At Henry's behest, Fulk agreed to send his son in style to Rouen to be knighted by the King.[15]

Geoffrey set out with a train of barons and knights, while Henry 'rejoiced' at the prospect of his arrival.[16] He himself arrived in Normandy on 26 August,[17] and sent several distinguished nobles to conduct his future son-in-law to Rouen. When Geoffrey entered the hall of the royal palace, 'the King, who was accustomed to stand for nobody, rose and went to meet him and, clasping him in an affectionate embrace, gave him a little kiss as though he were his son'. Taking him by the hand, he bade him sit next to him, and laid several problems before him, to determine how wise Geoffrey's responses were. His 'profound admiration grew at every moment', and he was so 'delighted by the youth's sense and his replies' that the whole day was 'spent in rejoicing and exultation'.[18]

The next day, Henry knighted Geoffrey, who appeared at the ceremony wearing a cuirass of chain mail, iron boots, gold spurs and a helmet encrusted with precious stones, and carrying a shield on which were emblazoned golden lions. The ceremony took place 'amid regal festivities' that lasted seven days.[19]

Maud was present, and the couple were introduced. She would have seen that Geoffrey was not nicknamed 'le Bel' ('the Fair') without cause: he was a sharp-eyed 'youth of high nobility and noted courage',[20] 'tall in stature, handsome and red-headed', and 'exceptionally well educated'.[21] But Maud was distinctly underwhelmed, and the antipathy seems to have been mutual.[22] Despite her reluctance,[23] the betrothal took place before the Archbishop of Rouen,[24] with Henry promising Geoffrey a string of castles along Normandy's southern border as a dowry.[25] It was agreed that the marriage would be celebrated the following spring.

Henry and Maud returned from Normandy soon afterwards. He and Adeliza celebrated Christmas in London. They stayed in Normandy for much of the following year.

In the spring of 1128, Henry sent messengers to Fulk of Anjou informing him that he should go to Le Mans eight days after Whitsun to celebrate his son's marriage. The Count arrived 'in great splendour', while the King travelled from Rouen with Maud and Geoffrey, and they all 'assembled for the nuptial sacrament' at Whitsun (17 June) at Le Mans Cathedral, where the marriage was solemnised by Turgis, Bishop of Avranches, assisted by 'archbishops, bishops, abbots and priests'. The bishops were careful to ensure that it took place by mutual consent of the couple, and 'both consented and each promised their faith to the other'.[26]

We do not know what Maud wore to her second wedding, but by 1130 the 'corse' (or 'body'), an early form of corset, had made an appearance, satisfying the growing fashion for tiny waists. It was a bodice made of leather stiffened with wood or metal, and laced in front. At the same time, the pleated or gauffered bliaut, a light, shaped gown of Eastern origin, became popular with women of rank in western Europe. Elaborately stitched at the shoulders and elsewhere, it fell in soft folds to the floor. Over it was worn a sleeveless fitted bodice called a corsage, which covered the stomach and was often banded with embroidery or fancy stitchwork. A wide belt stretching from bust to hips was frequently tied over it. The girdle was worn on top, high on the waist and crossed at the back, so that its ends could be tied low over the stomach in front. If Maud had dressed in these fashions, she would have made an impressive bride.

'There was rejoicing amidst the clergy, dancing by the people, and the shouting of praise by all and sundry.' An abundance of dishes was served at the wedding feast, 'both sexes reclining to eat a varied meal'. Three weeks of celebrations followed, then Henry departed, having given his daughter and son-in-law the kiss of peace. Count Fulk was with the couple when they made their triumphal entry into Angers, the capital city of Anjou. When they were still some way off, 'the whole city hurried to prepare for them; the walls of the churches were decorated with hangings and covers' and all the clergy went in procession to meet them, 'singing hymns and praises. The new lord and lady were received by priests and people with solemn dances',[27] the joyful pealing of bells and the cheers of the people packing the streets.[28]

Maud found herself conducted to a great house that dominated the south-east of the city, being situated by the River Maine and enjoying views overlooking vine-clad hills. It was 'worthy to be called a palace', for not long before, luxurious chambers fit for a king had been constructed.[29] For Maud, it may have felt like a gilded prison.

The marriage displeased not only the Empress, but also the King's subjects, for the bridegroom was not regarded as worthy of her, and it was a blatant violation of the terms of the oath they had sworn to Maud earlier that year. 'All the French and English thought ill of it', the French being even more offended,[30] having lost a valuable ally. Those who had sworn to recognise Maud as Henry's successor 'all declared prophetically that, after his death, they would break their plighted oath'.[31] Bishop Roger of Salisbury angrily kept repeating that he was freed from the oath, for he had sworn it on condition that the King should not marry his daughter to 'anyone outside the kingdom without consulting himself and the other chief men'; that none of them advised the match or indeed even knew of it.[32] Maud was prevailed upon to release the Bishop from his oath,[33] but it made little difference. The ageing King had been determined on the alliance with Anjou, and continued to be so, even after William Clito, trying to quell his rebellious Flemish subjects, suffered a fatal wound just over a month after Maud's wedding; and of course Henry was thinking of the succession. He told Geoffrey that, unless he himself had a son by Adeliza, the crown of England would be his.[34] Nevertheless, the marriage significantly undermined Maud's support among the barons.

Soon after his wedding, Geoffrey became count of Anjou, for his father, Fulk, abdicated and departed for the Holy Land to marry Melisende, heiress to the kingdom of Jerusalem. They wed in 1129 and became joint king and queen of Jerusalem two years later. Fulk never returned to Europe; he died in 1143, when a fall from his horse crushed his skull 'and his brains gushed forth from both ears and nostrils'.[35]

Before he left Anjou, Fulk visited his daughter Mahaut, the widow of William Atheling, at Fontevrault Abbey, where she had taken the veil. With him went his sons Geoffrey and Helias, and probably Maud too. It may have been on this occasion that Maud's reverence for Fontevrault was born.[36]

Fontevrault was a fashionable double monastery in Anjou, where monks and nuns followed the Benedictine Rule. Founded in 1100 by an itinerant preacher called Robert d'Arbrissel, it had quickly attracted the attention of royalty and people of rank. The Empress was an early patroness. Fontevrault was dedicated to the Virgin Mary, for whom Maud clearly felt a special veneration, since many of the monasteries she patronised, and all the Cistercian ones, were dedicated to the Virgin.[37] In May 1129, she confirmed a generous charter granted by her father to Fontevrault.[38] In 1141, she would give the community a perpetual annuity of fifty marks of silver and confirm all Henry I's charters to Fontevrault.

She also gave a golden flower from one of her crowns to Abbot Suger for the abbey of Saint-Denis, near Paris,[39] and (in 1131) a charter and many gifts to the abbey of Cluny, among them a fragment of the True Cross, a great bell, a set of 'Anglican' bells with unique chimes, gold crucifixes, vestments of gold damask encrusted with gems, and a gold candelabrum to stand before the high altar. The latter stood on a pedestal seven feet tall, was adorned with precious stones and metals, and had seven branches, like the Menorah that Moses set up in the wilderness.[40] Maud had long been a friend to the Order of Cluny; in Germany, she had witnessed the grant of privileges to its priory of Rüeggisberg. Before he died in 1156, Abbot Peter the Venerable called her the living image of her father in her generosity to Cluny, declaring that she loved it as much as he had done.[41]

Geoffrey's marriage to Maud proved an unhappy one. She apparently despised him, preferring to style herself 'empress and daughter of the King of the English' rather than countess of Anjou. Immediately after King Henry and Queen Adeliza had returned to England on 15 July 1129, Geoffrey repudiated Maud and sent her, with all her goods and chattels, and just a few attendants, to her father's city of Rouen,[42] where she remained for over two years. His reason for putting her away is not recorded. It has been suggested that, having married her in the expectancy of ruling England and Normandy in her name after Henry's death, he had been angered to discover that that was not the King's intention after all,[43] but in fact Geoffrey showed no interest in England after Henry died; his preoccupation was solely with Normandy. However, there does appear to have been a falling-out between Henry and Geoffrey over Maud.[44] Certainly Geoffrey's repudiation of her was a blow to Henry's plans for the succession.

6

'The Peril of Death'

Henry and Adeliza kept the Christmas of 1129 at Worcester. At Easter (30 March) 1130 they stayed at Woodstock,[1] then it was on to Clarendon, where the Sheriff of Oxford submitted an account for the conveying of their provisions from one royal hunting lodge to the other.[2] On 4 May, the royal couple were at Canterbury for the consecration of the newly rebuilt cathedral. They returned to Normandy at Michaelmas (29 September),[3] and were at Rouen in May 1131, when the Empress Maud witnessed her father's charter to the abbey of Cluny. The King and Queen returned to England in June 1131, with Maud in their train,[4] almost being shipwrecked on the way. So violent were the seas that Henry vowed that, if God spared him, he would remit all Danegeld for seven years and make a pilgrimage to the shrine of St Edmund at Bury, a vow he kept.[5] Adeliza appears for the last time as a witness to a royal grant of Henry I in July 1131.[6]

In 1130–1, the King apparently suffered some crisis of conscience, attested to by the numerous gifts he gave at this time to religious houses, especially convents. It has been speculated that this was spurred by guilt for his years of fornication;[7] more likely it was part of one final attempt to persuade the Almighty to make his marriage fruitful.

Disencumbered of his wife, Count Geoffrey had been planning to go on pilgrimage to the shrine of St James at Compostela, but when King Henry heard, he was most displeased. His views were conveyed to Geoffrey by Hildebert of Lavardin in a letter sent probably in 1131, in which Hildebert reminded the Count that his duty lay in ruling his lands.[8] Geoffrey abandoned the idea of the pilgrimage, and soon afterwards asked for Maud to be returned to him, saying he would receive her with all the honour due to her station[9] – from which it might be inferred that he had not treated her with appropriate honour in the past. Possibly he was concerned that, if he died childless, Anjou would pass to his young half-brothers in Jerusalem.[10]

Henry sought the advice of his barons at a packed meeting of the Great Council at Northampton, and on 8 September 1131, they consented that Maud be restored to her husband.[11] It was politically desirable that she do so, in order to bear the heirs that would safeguard the succession. Soon afterwards, Hildebert of Lavardin wrote to the King to say how pleased he was that Henry was reconciled with his son-in-law, 'who had now fallen in with his wishes in everything concerning him and his daughter'.[12]

That same day, Henry made the barons renew their oath to Maud as his heir, and those who had not sworn before were obliged to do so.[13] This was of course a tactical move, given that, in marrying her to Geoffrey, Henry had ignored the barons' proviso to the first oath, but their resentment still simmered. The fact that Henry did not once demand the allegiance of the barons for Geoffrey reveals his awareness of how contentious the marriage was. Afterwards, Maud was 'sent to her husband, and was received with the pomp that befitted such a great heroine'.[14] Thereafter she and Geoffrey tried to make their marriage work, both politically and personally, and Maud spent time in Rouen learning how her father's administration functioned.[15]

Geoffrey was developing into an astute politician and strategist, 'intelligent and of strong character', 'brave and resolute'.[16] According to the laudatory Chronicle of the Counts of Anjou, he was 'an outstanding soldier and a man of admirable worth, outstandingly just, dedicated to military deeds, most eloquent amidst the clergy and the laity'. He 'spent his time riding around the country, performing illustrious feats'. Thanks to good fortune and hard work, he was to become 'great in the eyes of the world at large'. Dedicated to defending his own, and to 'the liberal arts, he strove to be loved and was honourable to his friends'. He not only 'had the kindest soul', but was 'shrewd in his upright dealings', gentle, gracious, energetic, trustworthy, good-humoured, admirable, affable, jovial, generous, patient, likeable, 'graced with all good habits' and well informed, with 'a thorough knowledge of antiquity'. 'With outstanding competence he returned the principality to peace and his people to a quiet life.'[17] Apart from the assertion that Geoffrey excelled at arguing, Maud might not have agreed with all aspects of this paean of praise; she probably shared the Norman prejudice against the Angevins. But Geoffrey could be cold, calculating and cruel, and he was also a philanderer who fathered several bastards.

In charters Geoffrey acknowledged his wife's superior rank, signing himself 'the husband of Matilda, daughter of the King of the English and former wife to Henry, Roman Emperor'.[18] Preoccupied with his own ambitions, he made no attempt to rule Maud, and let her pursue her affairs autonomously.[19]

Henry might have recognised Maud as his heir, but in his final years he refused to allow her any power. Nor, clearly, did he intend that Geoffrey should share in her queenship when the time came; he had not even handed over the castles he had promised as Maud's dowry. These factors inevitably led to bad feeling and strife between father and daughter, which lost Maud considerable support among the barons; for in supporting the King, they had to oppose the woman who might soon be their sovereign. It did not augur well for her succession.

In 1131, Adeliza gave lands for the foundation of a leper hospital dedicated to St Giles at Fugglestone St Peter near Wilton, Wiltshire, for poor brethren and sisters. There was once an inscription describing her as the foundress above the door of its chapel.[20] That year she and Henry kept Christmas at Dunstable.[21]

The King and Queen were at Oxford at Easter (26 March) 1132, where they stayed at Beaumont Palace, the King's 'new hall' outside the North Gate. It boasted an aisled hall, a chapel and cloisters.[22] They had taken up residence at Winchester by 30 April, for a meeting of the Great Council early in May.[23] They spent Christmas 1132 at Windsor, but Henry was unwell and had to take to his bed. When he left the castle, restored to health, it would be for the last time.

On 25 March 1133, at Le Mans, Maud bore a healthy red-haired son and named him Henry after her father, although he would be known as Henry FitzEmpress. The birth of a male heir strengthened his mother's position immeasurably, with its promise of a masculine succession. She wept with joy when Bishop Guy de Ploermel baptised the child on Easter Eve in Le Mans Cathedral, after which she donated a rich pallium to the shrine of St Julian. Henry I was delighted at the news, foreseeing that his grandson would one day rule over England, Normandy, Maine and Anjou, and he made a gift of an annual rent to Le Mans Cathedral.[24]

On 2 August 1133, Henry departed for Rouen, having left Adeliza in England. By now, he had apparently given up hope of her conceiving a child, and had ceased taking her with him on his travels. During the voyage across the English Channel there was an eclipse of the sun, followed by the appearance of Halley's Comet. As before, when it had been seen prior to the Norman Conquest, people took it for an omen.[25]

In the last quarter of the twelfth century, the chronicler Roger of Hoveden stated that, in 1133, King Henry had the lords and barons of all his dominions swear fealty to Maud and her infant son as his successors. There is no mention of this in contemporary sources, and if an oath was administered, it could only have been sworn by those magnates who were present in Normandy.

On 10 February 1134, Henry's old antagonist, his brother Robert, died in prison at Cardiff Castle, aged about seventy-eight. He was buried in St Peter's Abbey in Gloucester, now the cathedral, where his painted tomb, bearing the effigy of a knight, can still be seen.

That spring, a heavily pregnant Maud took her year-old son to Argentan to see his grandfather the King. As Henry I looked proudly upon the child, he may have prayed that he would live long enough for the boy to succeed him. Whatever his hopes, he could not have foreseen that Henry FitzEmpress would become one of the greatest rulers of the age.

On 1 June 1134, at Rouen, Maud came close to death giving birth to her second son, who was called Geoffrey after his father.[26] The King was at her bedside afterwards as she lay critically ill and made her will, in which 'the prudent matron distributed her treasures to widows, orphans and the poor'. She also made bequests to various churches, hospitals and religious houses, 'lavishing more of her bounty on Bec than on any other monastery'[27] in gold, silver and precious stones. In addition, she left money for the completion of the Pont de Pierre (later known as the Pont Mathilde), the large stone bridge she was building across the Seine at the Île de la Roquette in Rouen.[28] She expressed her wish to be buried at Bec-Hellouin, but Henry opposed it. 'He said it was not worthy that his daughter, an empress who had twice been crowned in Rome by the hands of the Supreme Pontiff [sic], should be buried in any monastery, even one of the very purest religious observance; she should be taken into the city of Rouen, the metropolis of Normandy, and buried in the cathedral church beside her ancestors.' But Maud 'knew it was salutary for the souls of the departed if their bodies might lie in the place where prayers for them were offered most frequently and devoutly to God'. Henry capitulated, and soon afterwards Maud 'escaped the peril of death', thanks, it was believed, to divine approval of her charitable bequests.[29]

Henry remained in Normandy 'to rejoice in his grandsons',[30] and that year, as '*Matilde imperatrice*', Maud witnessed a charter he granted to Coutances Cathedral, and herself issued one settling a dispute between the cathedral and the canons of Cherbourg. This was the last of only three charters she issued in her own right during her father's lifetime, proof that he did not involve her in the government of his realms,[31] probably because of the tensions between Anjou and Normandy. In fact, apart from the few months she spent in England between 1126 and 1131, Maud never went there, which meant that she was virtually a stranger to her future subjects.[32]

7

'Cast Down in Darkness'

In the spring of 1135, Henry and Maud quarrelled, because 'Geoffrey of Anjou aspired to the great riches of his father-in-law and demanded castles in Normandy'.[1] The castles had in fact comprised Maud's dowry, but they had never been given to Geoffrey, so he had a legitimate grievance. 'The proud-spirited monarch, however, was not prepared to set anyone above himself as long as he lived, or even to suffer any equal in his house or in his kingdom, for he never forgot the maxim of divine wisdom that no man can serve two masters.'[2] Maud supported Geoffrey's demand, and when he asked that the Norman barons submit to him as their overlord, she was as angered as her husband when Henry refused. An incandescent Geoffrey 'vexed the King by not a few threats and insults'.[3]

William Talvas, Count of Ponthieu, was the son of Robert of Bellême, Earl of Shrewsbury, a 'grasping and cruel'[4] rebel baron who had been imprisoned by Henry I since 1112. Talvas had also opposed Henry, and in 1135 the King confiscated his estates, whereupon Talvas fled to Anjou, where he sought Geoffrey's aid. Maud pleaded with Henry to reinstate Talvas, but in vain. In the summer of 1135, Geoffrey supported – or perhaps instigated – a minor revolt in Normandy against the King.[5]

Maud and Geoffrey demanded that Henry 'do fealty to his daughter and her husband for all the fortresses in Normandy and England, which they required of him out of regard for their sons, who were King Henry's lawful heirs'.[6] Such a gesture would have gone a long way towards ensuring a peaceful transition of power in England to Maud when the time came, but Henry was not about to pay homage to Geoffrey, and refused out of hand. But he did put Robert, Earl of Gloucester, in command of Dover, so that, when the time came, Maud could land in England unopposed.

Maud was blamed for the discord between her and her father, and even for hastening his death. Henry had planned on several occasions to return to England,[7] but each time he was 'detained by his daughter on account of various disputes, which arose on a number of issues between the King and the Count of Anjou, due to the machinations of the King's daughter. The King was provoked by these irritations to anger and bitter ill feeling, which were said by some to have been the origin of the chill in his bowels, and later the cause of his death.'[8] Instead of going to England, he marched to protect his southern border with Anjou, wishing he could take Maud from her aggravating husband by force.[9]

Maud's first loyalty was to her husband and sons. She had sent the children to Angers, and in the autumn, she herself joined them, little realising that she would never see Henry again. Her decision to go to Angers was to have a fatal bearing on her future.

On 25 November 1135, the King was staying at his hunting lodge at Saint-Denis-le-Ferment, which lay between Gisors and Lyons-la-Forêt in Normandy. 'He had been hunting, and when he came back to Saint-Denis, he ate the flesh of lampreys, which always made him ill, though he always loved them. When his physician forbade him to eat the dish, the King did not take this salutary advice.'[10] Lampreys were much enjoyed by the higher ranks of society in the Middle Ages, but some species were poisonous and needed thorough washing before being cooked. It was the opinion of the King's contemporaries that his cook's failure to do this 'violently excited' an attack of food poisoning. 'The meal brought on a most destructive humour, and violently stimulated similar symptoms, producing a deadly chill in his aged body, and a sudden and extreme convulsion.' He suffered 'an acute fever with very heavy sweating'.[11] Food poisoning such as salmonella can take time to develop, so it is more likely that Henry suffered an acute gastrointestinal episode, such as a peptic or duodenal perforation, which rapidly led to peritonitis.[12] Soon it was clear that all his powers of resistance were failing.[13]

As Henry lay dying, 'much weakened by strenuous labours and family anxieties',[14] his bastard son Robert came to be with him. 'His malady increasing', the King summoned Hugh of Amiens, Archbishop of Rouen, while reports of his sickness prompted four nobles, all connections of his natural family, to hasten to his side. William of Malmesbury, a partisan of Maud's, wrote that, 'being interrogated by these persons as to his successor, he awarded all his territories on either side of the sea to his daughter in legitimate and perpetual succession, being somewhat displeased with her husband, as he had irritated him both by threats and by certain injuries'.[15] The hostile anonymous chronicle known as the *Gesta Stephani* states that, as Henry lay dying, he repented of 'the forcible imposition of the oath on his barons'.

Henry I passed away just before midnight on 1 December 1135, with Earl Robert and the four other lords beside him. Queen Adeliza was in England at the time. The next day his inexpertly embalmed body was carried to Rouen, where his entrails, brain and eyes were buried[16] in Notre-Dame de Pré, 'which he had honoured with no mean presents, as it had been begun by his mother'.[17] After being coffined and lying in state for four weeks in the Conqueror's abbey in Caen, the remains were transported to England, stinking to high heaven.

'King Henry is dead, once the pride, now the sorrow of the world,' mourned Henry of Huntingdon. 'England, which shone on high with the cradle and sceptre of this divine being, is now cast down in darkness – she along with her King, Normandy with her Duke. The former nourished the boy, the latter has lost the man.'

'What a terrible night was the first of December,' wrote William of Malmesbury, 'that all England and Normandy now mourn! For you are dead, Henry. Throughout your life these two nations knew peace; and now they know tears.'

Henry had been a successful monarch, 'certainly, in an extraordinary degree, the greatest of all kings',[18] but a feared one; yet after he was gone, men who had grumbled about his harsh rule had cause to regret his loss. 'A good man he was, and there was great dread of him. No man durst do wrong to another in his time. Peace he made for man and beast. Whoso bare his burden of gold and silver, durst no man say aught to him but good.'[19] He had indeed brought peace, but it was soon to be shattered.

Many nobles had remained in Normandy for the King's funeral, but Hugh Bigod, the royal steward and constable of Norwich Castle, hastened to Count Stephen in Boulogne to inform him that King Henry, on his deathbed, 'had disinherited the Empress Maud and adopted his most dear nephew, Stephen, for his heir', on account of 'certain things that she had done against him'.[20] He had also, Bigod stated, released his barons from their oaths to her.[21] Bigod swore to this on oath before William de Corbeil, Archbishop of Canterbury, 'openly perjuring himself',[22] for although he said he had heard it from Henry's own lips, he had not even been present at the deathbed. The Archbishop, believing him, declared that all the oaths sworn to the Empress 'were null and void and contrary to the laws and customs of the English, who had never permitted a woman to reign over them'.[23]

Hugh of Amiens, Archbishop of Rouen, had been with Henry when he died, and had sent an account of his last days to the Pope, in which he made no mention of the King changing his mind and leaving the crown to Stephen. Audoen of Bayeux, Bishop of Evreux, was also present. Yet both they and the four barons who had attended the King all supported Stephen's claim. Only Robert of Gloucester would declare for Maud. This does not necessarily mean that Henry did nominate Stephen as his heir; it suggests, rather, that these lords were unhappy at the prospect of a woman ruling over them, at Matilda's recent unfilial behaviour, and at her marriage to an Angevin.

Part Four

Matilda of Boulogne, Queen of King Stephen, and the Empress Maud, Lady of the English

1

'In Violation of His Oath'

In the twelfth-century church of St Peter at Tickencote, Rutland, a pair of stone crowned Janus heads on the Norman chancel arch turn disdainfully away from each other. They are said to represent Stephen and Maud, and as such encapsulate the conflict to come. For Henry I's death left England open to civil war.

Stephen, probably believing what Bigod had told him, and perhaps having sounded out various barons in recent years,[1] acted with unusual decisiveness and impressive speed. Disregarding the oath of fealty he had sworn to the Empress, and taking advantage of the absence of the barons mourning the late King, he left his pregnant wife Matilda in Boulogne and raced across the English Channel, resolved to seize the crown. Dover, guarded by Earl Robert's soldiers, would not admit him, but he managed to land elsewhere in Kent. The exact date is not recorded, but on that very morning, there was 'a terrible peal of thunder, with most dreadful lightning, so that the world seemed well-nigh about to be dissolved',[2] which some saw as ill-omened.

Stephen rode like the wind for the capital, Winchester. He may well have laid contingency plans for his accession with his younger brother, Henry of Blois,[3] an ambitious man whose rise had been meteoric thanks to Henry I's patronage. Henry of Blois had been twenty-eight when his uncle summoned him from Cluny in Burgundy to become abbot of Glastonbury; he had been appointed bishop of Winchester at thirty-one, and was now the richest clergyman in the kingdom. He was a strong-minded, energetic and ambitious man, 'crafty and inordinately fond of money',[4] in a very different mould from his brother, but staunch in his support of Stephen from the first, and he readily opened up the royal treasury at Winchester, giving him the wherewithal to bribe those who had not yet declared for him.

Thus enriched, Stephen hastened on to London, at this time a city of between 15,000 and 30,000 inhabitants. Here he won enthusiastic support by declaring it a self-governing commune with the power to raise the taxes it needed. The London merchants were also pleased that Channel trade would be protected and tariffs kept low, thanks to Stephen's control of shipping from Boulogne.

Stephen's promise to uphold the liberties of the Church secured for him the support of the Justiciar, Bishop Roger of Salisbury. Archbishop William de Corbeil, who had initially declared that the oath to Maud could not be broken, was also won over, especially by Hugh Bigod's testimony. The Archbishop had been the first to swear fealty to the Empress, which moved Henry of Huntingdon – who had been firmly in Bishop Roger's camp and therefore hostile to Maud[5] – to comment that there was 'nothing to praise' in him. The Archbishop's acceptance more or less guaranteed that the rest of the clergy would follow his example. Thus bolstered, Stephen 'snatched the crown in violation of his oath', 'shamelessly tempting God'[6] – and unopposed by Maud or her adherents.

Modern historians might not wholly agree with Henry of Huntingdon's view of Stephen as 'a man of great resolution and audacity', yet he did display these traits on this and other occasions, and certainly he was a man who 'trusted in his own strength'.[7] He had several advantages. He was much favoured by the barons and the officers of the royal household as Henry I's successor. His territorial power lay in the east and the Midlands, and his wife's estates were strategically located in and around London. He was the late King's nephew and was married to a descendant of the House of Wessex. He was rich, he was popular, and he had spent much of his life at the English court. Maud, by contrast, having spent much of her life in Germany, must have seemed like a foreigner – and she was married to a hated Angevin. There seemed to be no contest.

Striving for legitimacy, Stephen wrote to the Pope insisting that Maud was illegitimate because her mother had been a professed nun. The Pope, waiting upon events, held back from pronouncing her a bastard, while tacitly acknowledging Stephen as king. His sanction had arrived in England by Easter.

Stephen was crowned by William de Corbeil on 22 December 1135 in a poorly attended ceremony at Westminster. 'Shamelessly he received the crown.' As for the Archbishop who had broken his oath, 'God visited him with the same judgement which He had inflicted on him who had stricken Jeremiah, the great priest, namely that he should not live out the year.'[8] William de Corbeil would indeed die in 1136.

For a time, confusion reigned among the barons,[9] but the substantial majority of those who had sided with Henry I in his recent conflicts with the Empress welcomed the news that he had left the crown to his nephew, and were happy to abjure their oaths to Maud and acknowledge Stephen as king. Most readily acquitted him of perjury in breaking his oath, which he himself was now claiming had been exacted under duress. Of course, they too had broken their oaths.

Few wanted Geoffrey of Anjou ruling over them. Bishop Roger of Salisbury spoke for many when he declared that Maud's betrothal to Geoffrey, which had breached the terms of their original oath to her, absolved them of their allegiance to her. Although many barons recognised that she had the better claim, and 'everyone knew' that Stephen was a usurper,[10] the fact that Stephen had been elected, crowned and anointed, and that many lords and clergy had sworn allegiance to him as king, seriously undermined Maud's right to the throne. Even Stephen's enemies would refer to him as king, for all that they upheld Maud's claim. Nevertheless, some barons continued to support her right, and inevitably that led to friction between them and the new King.

Late in 1135, as soon as he heard that Stephen had been crowned, David I sent his armies into northern England to enforce his wife's claim to Northumberland, asserting that he was acting on behalf of his niece Maud.[11] Of course, he was also uncle to Matilda of Boulogne, which must have led to some ill feeling, but David had benefited from Henry I's bounty. He soon withdrew his forces when faced by a host of the King's mercenaries, but in February 1136 he informed Stephen that he would never forswear his oath to Maud. Subsequently he received from northern magnates 'vows and pledges of fidelity to his niece'.[12] Stephen pacified David by giving him Cumbria for his son, in return for all the castles he had seized, save for Carlisle.[13]

2

'Ravening Wolves'

The Empress merited hardly a mention by chroniclers who recorded the events of that winter.[1] News of her father's death reached her in Anjou, where Geoffrey was temporarily laid low by illness, and 'for certain causes', she delayed going to England.[2] She was expecting another child, and may have been experiencing the debilitating nausea and exhaustion of early pregnancy, which might explain why she lost her advantage by staying with her family.[3] Being at a distance from her father when he died, failing to attend his obsequies and not hastening to England, as Stephen had, and play her part at the centre of events – in short, doing nothing to claim the kingdom that was rightfully hers – would have fatal consequences. Yet how could she have secured England at that time? She was barely known in the kingdom, and had no base or lands there;[4] most of the magnates and clergy had declared for Stephen, her husband was not in a position to back her with military might, and her half-brother Robert, who could have given her valuable support, was wrestling with divided loyalties.

She was outraged when, early in 1136, she was informed of Stephen's usurpation and perjury. She must have been aware that her quarrel with her father had left her isolated in Anjou, critically distanced from what was happening in England. Immediately both she and Geoffrey claimed the crown, on account of the oaths sworn to Maud by the barons.[5]

England may have seemed out of reach, but Normandy was on her doorstep, and it was Normandy on which Geoffrey had his sights. He was not interested in England, probably because he knew that he was never likely to be acceptable there as Maud's consort. Early in December, he made what turned out to be the mistake of sending Maud across the southern border into the duchy to claim her dower castles,[6] following with his own forces. It was his right as her husband to conquer her inheritance and preserve it for their son,[7] but his aims encompassed more than that. He and Maud apparently foresaw that, in the circumstances, taking Normandy was the most effective strategy for taking England, for England had been conquered from Normandy once before, and the duchy could again be used as a springboard from which to launch an invasion. But Geoffrey miscalculated, for Normandy would not willingly bow the knee to an Angevin, and while Maud was there and he was fighting to subdue it, Stephen was able to establish himself unopposed on the English throne.

'Stubborn Normandy' was descending into turmoil, 'an unhappy mother country suffering wretchedly from her viper brood', for the moment King Henry died, his Norman subjects had 'rushed out hungrily like ravening wolves to plunder and ravage mercilessly'.[8] At Argentan, Maud was admitted by the steward,

Guigan Algason, who gave her the keys to the border strongholds of Domfront and Exmes,[9] while those of Alençon and Sées, which were among the castles that Henry I had confiscated from William Talvas, fell quickly to Geoffrey,[10] affording Maud a strong foothold in Normandy. But Geoffrey's troops 'made themselves hated forever by their brutalities',[11] laying waste the land, burning and pillaging, and he had to retreat into Anjou. Maud's cause was further weakened by public outrage at her husband's depredations, which undermined much of her support in the duchy. Geoffrey was so loathed by the Normans that only one baron declared for her, as the rest resolved to elect Stephen's older brother, Theobald IV, Count of Blois, as their Duke; but they recognised Stephen as soon as they heard that he had been crowned, and five Norman bishops crossed to England to assure him of their loyalty.

Maud's bastard half-brother Robert, Earl of Gloucester, had remained in Normandy. He was the greatest magnate in England, a proud and powerful man 'of proved talent and admirable wisdom' and a patron of letters. William of Malmesbury's *Historia Novella* and his revised version of his *Gesta Regum* were dedicated to him, as was Geoffrey of Monmouth's *History of the Kings of Britain*.

Some advised Robert to claim the throne himself, but he was 'deterred by sounder advice', and 'by no means assented, saying it was fairer to yield it to his sister's son, than presumptuously to arrogate it to himself'. At Lisieux, in December, he had met with some Norman barons and discussed the possibility of putting forward Theobald of Blois as king of England. But Theobald declined the honour.[12]

Stephen was later to brand Robert as an opportunist 'with the mouth of a lion and the heart of a rabbit',[13] but the admiring William of Malmesbury states that Robert was counting on Stephen losing the barons' support when they saw what sort of king he made, which would give the Earl the advantage when urging them to acknowledge Maud. But clearly Robert did not initially expect that Maud herself would press her claim.

Despite her advancing pregnancy, Maud evidently did not rest idle. She pressed on as far as she could into Normandy, accompanied probably only by an entourage and a military escort, but it was hostile terrain and she could not get near the coast, still less to any ships, and it would have been foolhardy anyway to cross to England, where she had no support. All she could do was wait for Geoffrey to assist her in her laborious advance across the duchy. But Geoffrey had his hands full, quelling a rebellion in Anjou.

Another severe blow was dealt to her cause when, around March 1136, Earl Robert crossed to England and acknowledged Stephen as king at Oxford. Later, he would explain that he had felt it expedient to do so as an interim measure. Given his vast landholdings in England, he dared not remain too long in Normandy. His motto, after all, was 'to do what he could, when he could not do what he would'. But at the time he was torn: 'if he became subject to Stephen, it seemed contrary to the oath he had sworn to his sister; if he opposed him, he saw that such conduct could nothing benefit her or his nephews, but would certainly most grievously injure himself'.[14]

3

'A Manly Heart in a Woman's Body'

Matilda of Boulogne had not been crowned with her husband, for whom haste had been imperative; moreover, she had just given birth.[1] It was probably in December 1135, when she was already queen, that she met the renowned Bernard, Abbot of Clairvaux, in Boulogne. Bernard already had a towering reputation for sanctity, and Matilda 'revered the holy man of the Lord with incredible intensity, so much so that she ran outside the town to him as he approached Boulogne, when she was pregnant'.

A few days later her labour began, and went badly wrong. 'She was so gravely afflicted that both she and all her household despaired of her life; and then, having consigned all her chattels to paupers and churches, the Queen even prepared the clothes in which she was to be buried, just as if she would die on the spot. The hour of delivery was most gravely fraught with danger, so much that she expected only death, and prepared for the funeral exequies.'

Suddenly, she remembered Bernard, 'the man of God', and 'invoked his name with full faith', begging for his help. Seemingly miraculously, 'in the same moment, she gave birth without the desperate danger', which she attributed to his spiritual aid – for even though he had not yet received her message, he must have known of her ordeal, being in Boulogne at the time, probably lodging in the castle, and had doubtless been praying for her.

The Queen sent a monk to render very devoted thanks to her liberator. Nor did she delay distributing the pledged bequests, by which she gave thanks to her celebrated rescuer, calling the newborn himself, not unmeritedly, his son. Possibly Bernard consented to be the child's godfather. Whenever people mentioned his divine intervention in the prince's birth, Bernard would say, 'not a little humbly, refuting it jokingly, "That certainly is to be imputed to me, as I was entirely unconscious of him."'[2]

Having been born in the purple, the child was given the Anglo-Norman royal name of William; he was probably named after William the Conqueror. In a letter that Abbot Bernard wrote to Matilda soon afterwards, he enjoined her, 'Preserve my son for me, to whom you just gave birth, since I also — if it does not displease the King — lay claim to a portion in him.'[3]

Matilda arrived in England in January 1136.[4] Her coronation, at which William de Corbeil officiated, was lavishly performed at Westminster Abbey on Easter Sunday, 22 March 1136, when an Easter court was being held with great splendour at the palace opposite,[5] a court that was 'more splendid for its throng and size, for gold, silver, jewels, robes and every kind of sumptuousness, than any that had ever been held in England'.[6] It was attended by all the leading churchmen and nearly thirty peers, including Robert, Earl of Gloucester, and at the King's right hand sat Henry, heir to David, King of Scots. With his father's sanction, Henry had sworn fealty to Stephen for Cumbria,[7] David having decided to wait and 'see to what end the enterprise [between Stephen and Maud] would come, pondering the ultimate result'.[8] The King and Queen wore their crowns, and their son and heir, Eustace, was present; on his father's accession, Eustace, who was ten years old at most, had became count of Boulogne in right of his mother.[9] Like William the Conqueror, who had also been crowned in haste, Stephen used his wife's coronation to underline his royal estate.

There was a twofold cause for celebration, since Stephen had just received a letter from the Pope endorsing his coronation and absolving him from his oath to Maud.[10] During the festivities, Matilda, the eldest daughter of the King and Queen, was married, aged two, to thirty-two-year-old Waleran de Beaumont, Count of Meulan,[11] son and heir of Robert de Beaumont, Earl of Leicester, and the owner of vast lands in Normandy.[12] The princess's hand was a reward for Waleran's offering his allegiance to the King, and with it he received the earldom of Worcester. The marriage was never consummated, for young Matilda died in the Tower of London before the winter of 1141–2, when Waleran married Agnes de Montfort.[13] Clearly Stephen and his family were using the royal apartments in the Tower.

Matilda's brother Baldwin also died in the Tower on an unspecified date. The fact that the two children died in the same place suggests that they succumbed to the same illness around the same time. Both were buried by the high altar of the priory of Holy Trinity, Aldgate,[14] founded by their great-aunt, Matilda of Scotland, where their parents would raise monuments to their memory. The priory's cartulary records: 'King Stephen and the Queen so much loved Prior Ralph and that church that their son Baldwin and their daughter Matilda should be buried honourably in that church: that is, Baldwin at the northern part of the altar and Matilda at the southern.'[15]

Matilda of Boulogne proved a strong, resourceful queen, feisty, energetic and indefatigable in her support of her ineffective husband, whom she far exceeded in vigour and capabilities. She was 'a woman of subtlety with a man's resolution'.[16] She demonstrated sound judgement and an ability to deal with men effectively. In the years to come, she would win praise for her unwavering loyalty to her husband, her courage, her honour and her conciliatory diplomacy, and for having 'a manly heart in a woman's body'.[17] She enjoyed great popularity with Stephen's subjects.

Matilda wielded considerable power. She spent most of her time in and around London, for her honour of Boulogne encompassed an area that included London and Colchester, which gave her a strong territorial advantage. Evidence in charters shows that she was closely involved in the affairs of Stephen's court and with his chief advisers.[18] She sought the friendship of the pious crusader Thierry of Alsace, who had replaced William Clito as count of Flanders, and was thus able to hire Flemish mercenaries, who would prove useful in the years to come.

Stephen trusted Matilda's political judgement. Following the example of his predecessors, he relied on her support in government, and she enjoyed great influence. One of her first acts as queen was to subscribe a charter to Reading Abbey.[19] Styling herself 'Queen of the English and Countess of Boulogne', she granted forty-six charters and writs in her own right, thirty-five of them to religious institutions, and witnessed fifty-two royal charters.[20]

She adjudicated in disputes. Around 1143–7, she issued a stiffly worded charter to Baldwin of Wissant, constable of the honour of Boulogne, complaining that Henry of Blois, Bishop of Winchester, had objected 'at the home of the King and me that you harass his land and his canons of Good Easter, Essex, and surround their men. Therefore I command to you and order that you keep peace for them. May I hear no more complaint from there.' Matilda gave lands to St John's Church in Colchester, and ordered 'Malcolm de St Liz, his son Walter and her own tenants, who had dispossessed the church and the monks of that same place of their tenement of Tey, to return the land to the monks' control'.[21]

Matilda became the patron of Holy Trinity, Aldgate, founded by her aunt, Matilda of Scotland. At Christmas 1136, she acted as advocate for Prior Norman in a dispute against Aschill, keeper of the Tower of London, who was determined to retain possession of lands his predecessor had appropriated from the priory.[22] Norman's successor, Ralph, was licensed as the Queen's chaplain by Theobald, Archbishop of Canterbury, in 1147.[23] Ralph was a venerable and amiable man of mature years, 'very well educated in divine and humane letters'. Born and raised in London, he was devoted to all its citizens, and greatly loved by Stephen and Matilda and their courtiers.[24]

Another Ralph served as the Queen's chancellor, at least between 1137 and 1141. He witnessed her charters and supervised the clerks of her chapel, who issued documents and letters in her name. Her household was headed by her chamberlain, Hubert, who was responsible for her treasury and assisted with the education of her children.[25]

According to her epitaph, Matilda was 'a true worshipper of God and a real patroness of the poor. She lived submissive to God, that she might afterwards enjoy His presence.'[26] Shared religious interests strengthened the close bond between her and Stephen. Like William the Conqueror and Matilda of Flanders, they gave their daughter Marie to God, placing her, while she was still a child, in the abbey of Saint-Sulpice La Forêt at Rennes, Brittany.[27] Like her great-aunt Cecilia at Caen, she would have been an oblate. The date of her admission is not recorded.[28]

The pious Queen made several benefactions; the land she gave
to religious houses came from her wealthy honour of Boulogne.
In 1147–8, she granted the canons of Holy Trinity lands in
Braughing, Hertfordshire. She and Stephen jointly gave Holy
Trinity lands in Clayhurst, Kent, and Hertfordshire[29] in exchange
for 'their mill and those parts of their land which they conceded
to me next to the Tower of London where I made a paupers'
hospital'; this land was in the parish of St Botolph, in which
Matilda established what she described in the foundation charter
as 'my hospital next to the Tower of London', which became
known as the Royal Hospital of St Katharine's by the Tower and
stood to the east of the fortress.[30] It was founded, the Queen
stated, so that prayers might be said 'in perpetual alms for the
repose of the souls of Baldwin my son and Matilda my daughter,
who rest buried in that same church' of Holy Trinity.[31] In associating herself with Holy Trinity in this way, Matilda was identifying
herself with the pious and popular Matilda of Scotland[32] – as she
consciously did in several other ways, an affinity that was reinforced
by Stephen in charters that linked his wife to 'the time of her
aunt'.[33]

The Queen's intention was 'to maintain in the said Hospital in
perpetuity thirteen poor persons for the salvation of the soul of my
lord, King Stephen and of mine, and also for the salvation of our
sons, Eustace and William and of all our children'.[34] Granting £20
a year from her income from Queenhithe,[35] Matilda provided for a
master, three brethren, three sisters, chaplains, ten poor almswomen
and six poor clerks, reserving for herself the right to choose the
master.[36]

In 1145–7, again for the safety and peace of her children's souls,
Matilda gave the church of Witham, Essex, to the canons of St Martin
le Grand in London, a house that enjoyed the special patronage of
her and the King.[37] This monastery received more charters from
Stephen and Matilda than any other, demonstrating their particular
devotion to it, while Matilda's patronage was of great benefit to the
canons in their legal disputes.[38]

Stephen granted Matilda the great Saxon abbey at Barking, Essex,
'just as Queen Matilda her aunt once held it'.[39] Around 1139, he
also granted her Waltham Abbey, which had been the property of
Matilda of Scotland and Adeliza of Louvain. Matilda of Boulogne
held her own court at Waltham, in which, Stephen decreed, 'if any
of the men of the aforesaid vill is accused of any offence, he shall

go before the court of the Queen, and there canons shall plead in accordance with their rule and laymen in accordance with secular law'. She was also a benefactress of the abbeys of Godstow and Bec-Hellouin.[40]

Matilda, like Stephen, supported the new eremitical monastic orders to which the early twelfth century had given birth. She lived in an age of monastic revival, when many felt that the oldest-established Order, the Benedictines (called black monks, after the colour of their habits) – and even the Cluniacs, who had been founded in the tenth century in the interests of monastic renewal – had grown too worldly and lax in their observance of the Rule laid down by St Benedict in the sixth century. In this climate, new orders flourished. The first Cistercian abbey had been established in 1098, and this austere Order of white-clad monks, with their strict observance of the Rule and return to the primitive ideals of monasticism, was spreading rapidly; by 1200, they would have five hundred houses. The even more austere Carthusians lived silent, solitary existences within their communities. The Augustinian and Premonstratensian white canons and the eremitical orders of Savigny and Arrouaise (Calais) had been founded in recent years by groups of hermits who followed a simple, ascetic mode of life. The founder of Savigny came from Fontevrault Abbey, which had also been founded by a hermit, Robert d'Arbrissel; Matilda witnessed a charter granted to it by Stephen in 1137.

Stephen had founded the first Savigniac house in England[41] in 1124 at Tulketh, near Preston. Three years later, he moved the community to Furness Abbey, his own foundation. Another Savigniac abbey, Longvilliers in Boulogne, was founded by him and Matilda in 1135. Around 1139–41, the royal couple and their son Eustace established another at Coggeshall, Essex, which was part of the Queen's honour of Boulogne; in the foundation charter she granted to the monks the manor of Coggeshall.[42] The abbey church was not completed until 1167, although today nothing remains from Matilda's time. In 1147 the Order of Savigny was incorporated into the more powerful Cistercian Order.[43]

In 1141 and 1142, Matilda issued charters granting lands jointly with her son Eustace to the Augustinian abbey of the Holy Trinity and Saint-Nicholas at Arrouaise in Calais.[44] The Order of Arrouaise, like that of Savigny, was eremitical; it had been founded in 1105 and gained momentum in the 1130s.

4
'The First Anniversary of My Lord'

The widowed Queen Adeliza had been present with King Stephen when, on 4 January 1136, Henry I was buried before the high altar in Reading Abbey. A tomb was raised to his memory, and on it was placed the earliest recorded royal effigy in English history.[1]

After the funeral, Adeliza retired from public life. She may have taken up residence at Arundel Castle, which had been bequeathed to her, with its wealthy honour, by the late King, who also gave her in dower, in perpetuity, the city of Chichester and the Isle of Wight.[2] In 1067, William the Conqueror had granted Arundel to his kinsman Roger of Montgomery, who in return was to build a castle, one of a defensive chain of strongholds along the south coast. Roger raised a mighty fortress. Located four miles from the English Channel, near a Saxon earthwork, Arundel Castle was constructed on a very similar plan to Windsor Castle, with a motte crowned by a timber keep, having two baileys on either side, a gatehouse tower of stone – the oldest surviving part of the castle, dating from *c.*1070 – and a massive curtain wall, which substantially survives.[3]

A long-standing local tradition asserts that Adeliza lived close to her leper hospital at Fugglestone St Peter near Wilton for at least the first year of her widowhood, in a house that was still standing, and called after her, in the nineteenth century. In widowhood she held the great abbeys of Wilton, Romsey and Waltham, traditionally part of the dower of queens,[4] so it is more likely that she spent some of that year in seclusion at Wilton Abbey. Late in 1136, a 'Master Serlo' witnessed a charter issued by Adeliza to Reading Abbey on the anniversary of her husband's death (see below). He was probably the poet Serlo of Wilton, who apparently returned home that year after completing his studies in the schools of France. In 1139, in a charter of her second husband, Serlo appears as the Queen Dowager's clerk, and she may have been his patron.[5] Several documents attest to his being in her service, and in one he refers to her as '*domine mee Aalide regine*'. He may have remained with her until her death, or until she left England.[6]

Widowhood, and the desire to ensure the safe passage of her late husband's soul to Heaven, spurred Adeliza to exercise the kind of monastic patronage she had omitted to bestow when Henry was alive. Between 1136 and 1141 she gave donations for his salvation to Winchester Cathedral, Eynsham Abbey and Osney Priory in Oxfordshire, the Cistercian foundations of Tintern and Waverley, Surrey, and the abbey of Saint-Sauver, a cell of Jumièges in the Norman Cotentin. She also gave churches in Salisbury, Stanton Harcourt and Berkeley Hernesse, Gloucestershire, to Reading Abbey.[7] She was an early patron of the Knights Templar.[8]

In the years of her widowhood, Adeliza may have commissioned the Shaftesbury Psalter, the earliest surviving example of a book commissioned by a woman, which was perhaps written at Arundel under the supervision of her chaplains. It is the prominence given to St Lambert, Bishop of Maastricht, a popular saint in northern Europe, that has led scholars to suggest that the psalter was made at Adeliza's behest. It contains coloured illustrations of a noblewoman kneeling before Christ and standing in adoration before the Virgin and Child; she is probably Adeliza.[9]

Adeliza's younger brother Joscelin of Louvain came to England to seek his fortune at this time. He was more likely to have been her father's bastard son by an unknown mistress than the son of Godfrey's second wife, Clementia of Flanders, and he was perhaps about fifteen years old. Joscelin was with Adeliza on the first anniversary of King Henry's death, in December 1136, when she visited Reading Abbey, attended by her almoner, her chaplains and her entire household. Having been received by a large company of abbots, priors and priests, she was conducted up the nave by the bishops of Salisbury and Worcester, and placed a rich pall on the altar.

On that day she granted two charters, one bestowing on the abbey funds for a solemn annual service for the repose of the soul of her late husband. The other read: 'Be it known to all the faithful of Holy Church of all England and Normandy that I, Adelidis, wife of the most noble King Henry, have granted and given for ever to God and to the church of St Mary of Reading, for the health and redemption of the soul of my lord, and of mine own, and also for the health of my lord Stephen, by the grace of God, King of the English, and of Queen Matilda his wife, and all the offspring of King Henry, my manor and church of Aston [Hertfordshire], which my lord the King gave to me as his Queen and wife.' She also gave 100s. annually for members of the convent attending the anniversary, and afterwards granted land at Stanton Harcourt, Oxfordshire, and 110s. annually, out of her Queenhithe profits, to keep a lamp burning perpetually before the King's tomb. 'And this gift I have made on the first anniversary of my lord, the most noble King Henry, in the same church, by the offering of a pall, which I placed on the altar.'[10] Her charter was witnessed by Roger, Bishop of Salisbury, several other prominent members of the clergy, Master Serlo, the Queen Dowager's clerk, Gozo, her constable, Reginald of Windsor, her steward, and Joscelin, her brother.[11]

Joscelin of Louvain grew up to be 'of handsome presence and great skill in tourney',[12] although he could not have taken part in tournaments in England because Henry I had banned them.[13] Adeliza's tolerance towards her late husband's bastards, whose souls she had included as beneficiaries of her charter to Reading Abbey, was of a piece with the patronage she extended to her bastard half-brother.[14] She granted him the manor and honour of Petworth, Sussex, which had been bequeathed to her by Henry I. In tenure, he gave her knight's service as 'castellan' (the Lotharingian title for a constable) of Arundel Castle,[15] which – if it were ever besieged – he was to help defend for forty days.[16]

In placing King Stephen and his Queen immediately after her late husband in her charter, Adeliza, despite her oath to her stepdaughter, was effectively declaring her loyalty to him as her father's successor. The Empress is not mentioned, save indirectly as one of Henry I's offspring.

5
'Unable to Break Through'

At the great Easter court in 1136, Stephen declared himself in favour of reforming the Church and restricting royal interference in its affairs, and made lavish promises, which bolstered his support among the clergy. But then he was taken so ill that reports of his death were circulated. Hearing that the King was dead, Hugh Bigod – he who had claimed that Henry I had left the crown to Stephen – seized Norwich Castle, probably anticipating that the Empress would make a bid for the throne. But Stephen rallied, marched on the city and laid siege to the castle, forcing Hugh to surrender it.

Stephen's illness alerted him to the need to have his son recognised as the heir to Normandy by Louis VI, to pre-empt any possibility of Louis offering his support to Maud. As soon as he was well, he hastened with Eustace to Paris, leaving Matilda in England, and prevailed on Louis to recognise his son as duke of Normandy.

At Whitsun 1136, another great court – probably a crown-wearing – was held at Winchester and attended by many nobles. The King and Queen had their son Eustace with them, and Matilda and Eustace witnessed a charter granted by Stephen to the abbey of Cluny.[1]

Queen Matilda spent part of the hot summer of 1136 at Corfe Castle, while Stephen and Robert, Earl of Gloucester, had Exeter under siege from June to August,[2] its castle having been seized by Baldwin de Redvers, who was extorting onerous dues from the citizens. Matilda planned to join Stephen there. On the way, she visited the renowned holy man and seer Wulfric of Haselbury, who was now an anchorite at the church of St Michael and All Angels at Haselbury Plucknett, Somerset, to which his cell was attached. Wulfric had correctly predicted the death of Henry I and the accession of Stephen, and foretold disasters for the latter. Now he castigated Matilda for snubbing Gwladus ferch Rhiwallon, the Welsh wife of his neighbour and patron, Sir William FitzWalter, Constable of Windsor Castle, when Gwladus had attended her at Corfe. He warned her that she would find herself desperate for friends in the future.[3]

The Queen apparently arrived while Exeter was still under siege. She appears as a witness to charters granted to Exeter churches.[4] When it became clear that the rebels could no longer hold out against his besieging forces, Earl Robert urged the King to show mercy, upon which Stephen's brother, Bishop Henry, counselled that justice be meted out to Baldwin without further ado. Possibly Henry suspected that Robert was covertly doing his best to undermine the King's authority. If so, he succeeded, for Stephen set all the rebels free, unpunished, sending out the unmistakable message that traitors would be dealt with softly.[5]

Baldwin fled to Normandy and the protection of Count Geoffrey and the Empress.[6] There, he and all the others Maud had induced to obey her were urged 'by continual treaties and reminders' to resort to raiding, plundering and committing arson in her husband's cause.[7]

Maud had held her position at Argentan, which Geoffrey used as a springboard for campaigns in the rest of Normandy. There, on 22 July 1136, she bore her third son, William,[8] said to have been her favourite child. This birth also seems to have been a difficult one, for it was said to have given rise to an illness that would eventually incapacitate Maud, and might have been one reason why she never bore another child.

Soon afterwards, Maud sought divine help against Stephen. 'In order to obtain a happy enterprise against the usurper, and at the same time to fulfil her good intentions in times past', and out of affection for the late Norbert of Xanten, the saintly founder of the Premonstratensian Order, whom she had known in Germany, she resolved to found an abbey dedicated to the Virgin Mary. She sent Drogo, her knight, to Premontré to consult Norbert's successor, Abbot Hugh, who offered to send canons to help establish a community, the abbey of Notre-Dame de Silly-en-Gouffern.[9]

In September 1136, Geoffrey again invaded Normandy, determined to secure it for Maud and their heir, Henry. On 1 October, Maud brought a company of two hundred men to reinforce her husband, who was then besieging the castle of Le Sap, which was holding out on behalf of King Stephen.[10] Although she never engaged personally in warfare, throughout her struggle with her rival she rode on horseback at the head of her troops as a figurehead, and may have worn armour. She had her own armourer, called Robert, who is known from a charter issued to him by Maud, that may belong to this period.[11] The fact that Maud had an armourer suggests that he fashioned for her some kind of protective mail, of which she had need, residing in the midst of a theatre of war.

Disaster struck on the very evening she arrived with her men. Geoffrey was wounded in the foot by a javelin, which prevented him from maintaining his position and obliged him to retreat. In March 1137, he was still battling to establish Maud firmly in Normandy, and being resisted by lords who hated the Angevins, when, in the third week of that month, accompanied by 'a large retinue'[12] that included Queen Matilda, her son Eustace and Robert of Gloucester, Stephen landed at La Hougue, determined to oust his rival.

Matilda went to Evreux, where, in March or April, she issued the first of her own charters that survive. She took a special interest in the crusading orders of knighthood, which was to be expected, since her father had distinguished himself in the First Crusade, and his brothers, her uncles Godfrey de Bouillon and Baldwin, had become the first two crusader rulers of Jerusalem, Baldwin taking the title of king. Her father had been the first to grant land in England to the Knights Templar, who were also indebted to Matilda, as well as to Stephen, for helping them to establish themselves there, for Matilda had endowed them with lands from her honour of Boulogne. In the charter given that spring at Evreux, she granted them the manor and church of Cressing and the manor of Witham, both in Essex.[13]

Cressing was the second property to be owned by a crusading Order in England, and its income was boosted in 1147–8 by a further grant by Stephen, Matilda and their son Eustace of lands in Witham.[14] In 1138–9, the Queen gave four hides of land for the foundation of another preceptory, at Cowley, near Oxford, for the souls of her father and all her children, and before 1140, she granted the Templars lands at Uphall, Essex. Otto of Boulogne, Grand Master of the Order, witnessed two of her charters.[15]

Stephen's attempt to rout Geoffrey proved abortive. He got within twenty-five miles of Argentan before his army of mercenaries quarrelled amongst themselves and succeeded in arousing the hostility of the Norman barons and people. In July, he was forced to conclude a three-year truce with Geoffrey, promising him a substantial annuity that he would struggle to pay. For Geoffrey, this was fortuitous, since his army was stricken with dysentery and he knew that, 'for the present, he was unable to break through the royal forces'.[16]

Matilda was with Stephen at Rouen that July, where she witnessed a charter to the abbey of Fontevrault.[17] At some point the couple stayed at the hunting lodge in Lyons-la-Forêt, where Henry I had died, and here Matilda was a signatory to a charter to Mortemer Abbey.[18] She also gave funds for the building of a magnificent new church[19] and four guest houses for pilgrims.[20]

At a tournament at Bourges, held in the summer of 1137 to celebrate the marriage of Louis VII, the new King of France, to Eleanor, Duchess of Aquitaine, William d'Albini (or d'Aubigny), Lord of Buckenham, Norfolk, won the prize.[21] A colourful legend claimed that Adelaide of Maurienne, the forty-six-year-old widowed Queen of Louis VI of France, was much taken with Albini's prowess and wanted to marry him herself, but he declined, telling her 'that his troth was pledged to Adeliza, the Queen of England'. The story goes that Adelaide suggested he take a walk in her gardens, where – astonishingly – a famished lion had its lair in a cave. It pounced on William, as the Queen had intended, but he managed to wrap his arm in his cloak and tear out the beast's tongue, which he handed to one of the Queen's ladies to give to her mistress.[22] The tale is obviously apocryphal, as is a similar one asserting that the Queen of France in question was Adelaide's newly married daughter-in-law, Eleanor of Aquitaine.

That Albini had recently become betrothed to Adeliza is true, though. By then, she had been a widow for over eighteen months. She may have known him for some time, since his father of the same name had been Chief Butler of England under Henry I, with the right to serve the monarch at the coronation banquet;[23] and his grandfather, another William d'Albini, had been cupbearer to the Conqueror. Adeliza's William d'Albini was a pious man and a generous benefactor of religious houses. He was a patron of Wymondham Priory, Norfolk, founded by his father (where he himself would one day be buried), and he established a leper hospital near his stronghold, Castle Rising, Norfolk, which he built around 1140. His betrothal to the Queen Dowager was a brilliant coup.

6
'Ties of Kinship'

Bishop Henry may well have persuaded his brother the King that Earl Robert was not to be trusted, for while he was in Normandy, Stephen prepared an ambush for the Earl, intending to intercept and seize him. Robert was warned in time. When he accused the King of plotting his murder, Stephen admitted it and apologised, but the rivalry and distrust between the two men could now no longer be hidden.[1]

On 20 November, having received reports of disturbances in England,[2] the King left Normandy, never to return, carrying with him the knowledge that he had lost the hearts of his subjects there.

Matilda was already back in England, acting as regent in concert with Bishop Roger of Salisbury.[3] The King and Queen travelled to Kingsbury Palace, Dunstable, for Christmas;[4] at Marlborough, on the way, Matilda witnessed a charter granted by Stephen.[5] After Christmas, Stephen rode off to besiege a rebel castle at Bedford.

In January 1138, he reneged on a promise and refused to confirm King David's right to Cumbria or give the earldom of Northumberland to David's son, Henry, Earl of Huntingdon. David responded by raiding across the border, plundering and laying waste the northern shires. Stephen marched north on 2 February, taking Matilda with him. At Eye Priory, she witnessed a charter.[6] It is unlikely that she travelled all the way to the north, where Stephen routed the Scots.[7]

Maud's supporters, meanwhile, had taken Ralph d'Esson, a Norman lord who had resisted her rule; she imprisoned him, chained, until he agreed to surrender his castles to her.[8] She remained determined to fight for her right to the crown of England, and was working hard to win support in the kingdom.

Earl Robert had stayed at Caen and offered his support to Geoffrey. He spent the winter wrestling with his conscience, asking many churchmen if, having sworn allegiance to the King, he could renounce his oath.[9] After all, had he not sworn a prior oath to the Empress?

In May 1138, Robert decided that he could no longer support Stephen. Possibly the deciding factor had been Stephen's failure to stem a Welsh threat to Robert's lands in south Wales, but his change of heart may also have been influenced by Scripture, in particular a passage in the Book of Numbers: 'It seemed to some that, by the weakness of their sex, women should not be allowed to enter into the inheritance of their father. But the Lord, when asked, promulgated a law that everything their father possessed should pass to the daughters.'[10]

Robert 'sent representatives and abandoned friendship and faith with the King in the traditional way, also renouncing homage, giving as the reason that his action was just, because the King had both unlawfully claimed the throne and disregarded, not to say betrayed, all the faith he had sworn to him'.[11] Robert now offered his allegiance to Maud, promising to help her take the English throne.[12] It was a great breakthrough for her, and gave her the advantage she had long needed, for Robert had great territorial power in England and could raise an army there for her.

Robert's action was effectively a declaration of war.[13] He was to stand staunchly by his sister for the rest of his life, and was determined to see Stephen overthrown and Maud set up in his place. 'He alone, or almost alone, was never swayed from his loyalty by the hope of gain or the fear of loss.'[14]

After hearing of Robert's defection, Stephen promptly sequestered his lands, but the Earl's supporters rose on his behalf and seized the castles of Hereford, Bristol, Leeds in Kent, Castle Cary, Dudley,

Dunster, Wareham, Malton, Dover and Shrewsbury.[15] Robert himself ceded his strongholds of Caen and Bayeux to Count Geoffrey, and started arming for the war he knew was now inevitable.

In June 1138, Maud and her sons, Henry and William, were at the recently captured chateau of Carrouges,[16] near Argentan, when Geoffrey arrived. He had wasted no time. Being in possession of Caen and Bayeux placed him in a much stronger position, and when he arrived at Carrouges he had with him a large army that he had marched into Normandy for the purpose of pressing on with the conquest of the duchy.[17]

He asked his wife and sons to witness a charter he had granted at Le Mans to the people of Saumur, Anjou, who in return had given him three silver cups for his children. Having given two to Henry and William, he rode on to Saumur, where his second son Geoffrey, now four, was being raised in the house of his vassal, Goscelin Rotonard, so that the little boy could witness the charter too and receive his cup.[18] It was customary for boys to be raised away from their mothers after the first few years, yet Henry, the eldest, was still with Maud. Possibly Geoffrey had kept the boy with him in Anjou, and sent him to join Maud in Normandy after Earl Robert declared for her,[19] to underline the fact that Henry was her heir and that the royal blood of Henry I flowed in his veins.

Stephen fought on, trying to break Earl Robert's power in the west, but soon, thanks to his own lack of forethought, he would be fighting a war on another front. In the summer of 1138, Maud sought the aid of her uncle, King David, writing that 'she had been disinherited and deprived of the kingdom promised to her on oath, that the laws had been made of no account, justice trampled underfoot, the fealty of her barons of England and the compact to which they had sworn broken and utterly disregarded, and therefore she humbly and mournfully besought him to aid her as a relation, since she was abandoned, and assist her as one bound to her by oath, since she was in distress'. Her request fell on receptive ears. 'The King groaned deeply. Inflamed by zeal for justice, on account of the ties of kinship, and because he owed the woman the fealty he had promised, he disposed himself to set the kingdom of England in confusion, that when rebellion had been raised up everywhere against its King, he might be compelled, with God's help, to leave one juster than himself what he had seized.'[20] He was, of course, referring to Maud.

Supporting Maud gave David a convenient pretext for invading England, sending his soldiers once more on raids across the English border. 'Under cover of piety, on account of the oath he had sworn to King Henry's daughter, he commanded his men in barbarous deeds. For they ripped open pregnant women and tore out the unborn foetuses. They tossed children on the points of their lances. They dismembered priests on their altars. They put onto the bodies of the slain the heads cut off crucifixes, and put back on the crucifixes the heads of the dead. Everywhere that the Scots attacked would be filled with horror and barbarity.'[21]

David took Carlisle and Newcastle. He exacted 'from the chiefs and nobles of that locality pledges of fidelity to his niece, the Empress'.[22] But an English army led by the elderly Thurstan, Archbishop of York, soundly vanquished the Scots on 22 August at the bloody Battle of the Standard near Northallerton, Yorkshire. David's invasion did Maud's cause no good at all, for the English naturally came to associate her with the barbaric behaviour of the Scots.

7
'Feminine Shrewdness'

Earl Robert's garrison already controlled the port of Dover, and in August he sent his vassal Walchelin Maminot across from Normandy with an invading army, intending to land it there.

Queen Matilda was, literally, up in arms. With his presence desperately needed to quell the rebels in the west, and with every confidence in his wife's ability, Stephen deputed her to retake Dover. She faced a huge challenge, for Dover Castle, on its massive cliff commanding the sea, was a formidable bridgehead into England and well-nigh impregnable; but she had considerable resources at her command. 'The Queen besieged Dover with a strong force on the land side, and sent word to her friends and kinsmen and dependants in Boulogne to blockade the foe by sea. The people of Boulogne proved obedient, gladly carried out their lady's commands and, with a great fleet of ships, closed the narrow strait to prevent the garrison receiving any supplies.' Thanks to the strategy Matilda deployed, in concert with her commander and close kinsman Pharamus of Boulogne,[1] Dover was surrounded by land and sea, with Matilda herself commanding the men who laid siege to the castle. At the end of August, or early in September, Maminot was forced to 'surrender it to the Queen',[2] which he did willingly, having learned that Stephen was hanging his captives.[3] With Pharamus of Boulogne firmly in control of Dover Castle, Matilda rejoined Stephen.

Matters were not going well for Maud's cause in Normandy either. On 1 October, Count Geoffrey besieged Falaise, the birthplace of the Conqueror, but he could not force its surrender and had no choice but to withdraw his troops the following month.[4] But he was only retrenching.

King David had retreated north, yet, undeterred, his forces continued to ravage Northumberland and hold sway over the north, and in September 1138, understanding the urgent need for a cessation of hostilities on the northern front, Queen Matilda opened peace negotiations with him, supported by the Papal legate, Alberic, Cardinal of Ostia. Alberic had been 'engaged most discreetly and earnestly in treating with several persons, and especially with the Queen of England, respecting the renewal of peace between the two kings. Finding that the Queen's mind was much set on the accomplishment of this object, with her mediation, and backed by her feminine shrewdness and address, he frequently appealed to the King himself about this matter', and sought Matilda's help in bringing about a truce.[5] She 'lent her aid to his wishes by her private entreaties, being by no means indifferent to the preservation of peace between her husband and the King of Scotland, her uncle'.[6]

'They found King Stephen at first stern and apparently opposed to a reconciliation', for his barons were firmly against it, having suffered severe losses in the fighting, 'but, notwithstanding this, the zeal of a woman's heart, ignoring defeat, persisted night and day in every species of importunity till it succeeded in bending the King's mind to its purpose. For she was warmly attached to her uncle, David, King of Scots, and his son Henry, her cousin, and on that account took the greatest pains to reconcile them to her husband.' This was all very encouraging to Cardinal Alberic.[7]

Finally, in December, a treaty was agreed, whereby Stephen was to grant to Henry of Scots the earldom of Northumberland (excepting the towns of Newcastle and Bamburgh). In return, David and Henry, 'with all their dependants, were bound therefore to remain for life amiable and faithful to Stephen. They were bound also to observe unalterably the laws, customs, and statutes which his uncle, King Henry, had established in the county of Northumberland.'[8]

Stephen and Matilda spent Christmas at Westminster,[9] but during the festive season, Stephen committed another fatal error of judgement. He managed to alienate his brother, Bishop Henry, who had been one of his mainstays, having won him the crucial support of the Church. Henry's great ambition was to become archbishop of Canterbury, that episcopal see having been vacant since the death of William de Corbeil in December 1136. But Stephen, probably fearing that Henry would become too powerful as archbishop, and perhaps indulging a degree of sibling rivalry, was not willing. Moreover, he doubtless wanted to please Matilda, for Theobald, Abbot of Bec-Hellouin, was the candidate of the Queen, and of two of Stephen's favourites, the unpopular aristocratic twins, that 'expert in deceit' Waleran de Beaumont, Count of Meulan,[10] and Robert de Beaumont, 2nd Earl of Leicester. Matilda was instrumental in securing the primacy for Theobald, and in this she may have been influenced by the twins, who probably foresaw Stephen becoming his brother's puppet, and by Bishop Roger of Salisbury, who doubtless feared that Henry would rival his political ascendancy.[11]

On 24 December, in an election timed to take place while Henry was away, the King appointed Theobald archbishop of Canterbury, with Matilda looking on.[12] That same day, she may have played a part in the appointment of Walter de Lucy as abbot of Battle.[13] On 8 January 1139, Cardinal Alberic consecrated Theobald in the presence of the King and Queen.

Henry was 'violently indignant' at being 'cheated of the much-desired honour by the King as well as the Queen',[14] and relations between him and Stephen were never the same afterwards. Theobald's appointment also led to a power struggle between him and Henry, with Henry ascendant because his authority as Papal legate – an office he secured in 1139 – was greater than that of Theobald as archbishop.

Immediately after Theobald was installed in Canterbury, Stephen, Matilda, Eustace and their court were present at the consecration of Godstow Abbey, near Oxford, by the new Archbishop, and all gave generous gifts.[15]

After Cardinal Alberic left England on 13 January,[16] Matilda continued to build on the foundations he and she had laid. In the spring, she travelled to Durham, where she probably stayed in the castle built by the Conqueror on a cliff south of the mighty Romanesque cathedral. Here she put pressure on David's son, Henry, to confirm the treaty with Stephen. Her 'shrewdness and eloquence triumphed',[17] for on 9 April, 'at the instance of the Queen of the English',[18] Henry ratified it, 'in the presence of Matilda and many earls and barons of the south of England'.[19] Under the terms dictated by the Queen, David was to keep Carlisle Castle. This agreement achieved peace in the north, but it infuriated Earl Robert's son-in-law, Ranulf de Gernon, Earl of Chester, one of the most powerful magnates in the kingdom. His father had held Carlisle Castle, and although Henry I had confiscated it, Ranulf had had hopes that it would be restored to him.

Afterwards the Queen invited Henry to court as a gesture of good faith and friendship, probably hoping to win over his father to Stephen's cause. He rode south with her to Nottingham, where he was formally invested with his earldom and paid homage to Stephen as earl of Northumberland,[20] thereby ensuring the future protection of the troubled border county.

8

'Touch Not Mine Anointed'

In April 1139, Maud appealed to Pope Innocent II to uphold her cause. That month her representative, the 'venerable' Ulger, Bishop of Angers, travelled to Rome to attend the Lateran Council, to which the Pope had summoned five hundred bishops and abbots to deal with numerous ecclesiastical matters. Maud must have seen the Council as the most effective platform on which to make her appeal; the more prelates who supported her, the better. Stephen was aware of what she intended, and sent his own representatives. In 1167, the great scholar John of Salisbury, later Bishop of Chartres, wrote an account of the proceedings to explain why the Pope had persistently refused to sanction the crowning of Stephen's son Eustace in the King's lifetime,[1] following the French custom. John himself supported Maud's claim in his *Historia Pontificalis*, even though he felt that women in general were too weak to wield power.

In the ancient basilica of St John Lateran, Bishop Ulger declared that Maud was the rightful ruler of England by hereditary right and by virtue of the oaths sworn to her, and put forward her complaint that Stephen had sworn fealty to her and undertaken to 'aid her against all men to obtain and hold England and Normandy after her father's death'. He 'argued that the King was perjured and had unlawfully seized the kingdom'.

As leading counsel for King Stephen, Arnulf, Archdeacon of Sées (later bishop of Lisieux), 'publicly alleged that the Empress was not a fit person to succeed her father because she was born of an incestuous union, and was the daughter of a nun whom Henry had dragged away from Romsey Abbey and deprived of the veil'. This was untrue, as John of Salisbury scathingly noted, but Ulger did not leap to Maud's defence. In 1143, in a letter to Brian FitzCount, Gilbert Foliot, Abbot of Gloucester (later bishop of London), who supported Stephen but was sympathetic to Maud's claim, and who was present, would give an account of the hearing, and claim that at this juncture Ulger had stayed silent.[2]

Arnulf 'admitted the oath' that the barons had made to Maud, 'but maintained that it was forcibly exacted, and that it was conditional, namely that King Stephen would support the succession of the Empress with all his might, unless her father should change his mind and name another heir, for it was possible that he might have a son by his wife'. He submitted that Henry *had* changed his mind on his deathbed and designated Stephen as his heir, as Hugh Bigod had sworn.

Ulger countered that: 'As for your statement that the King changed his mind, it is proved false by those who were present at the King's death. Neither you nor Hugh could possibly know his last requests, since neither was there.'[3]

His protest fell on deaf ears. 'Pope Innocent would not hear their arguments further, nor would he pronounce sentence or adjourn the case to a later date.' Probably he felt that it would be more harmful to dismiss or reverse Stephen's coronation, and his own earlier recognition of Stephen's title, than to uphold Maud's claim, and certainly he was bribed. On 22 May, 'acting against the advice of certain cardinals, he accepted Stephen's gifts and, in letters to the King, confirmed his occupation of the kingdom of England and the duchy of Normandy'.[4]

When the outcome became known in England, and word got around that some of the cardinals had disagreed with the Pope,[5] opinion among the clergy was divided. The damning arguments used in St John Lateran put paid to any hopes of the canonisation of Maud's mother, whose saintly memory had been smeared by the allegation of incest.[6] That gave further injury to the Empress, whose cause had been dealt a bad blow.

John of Salisbury expressed what Maud must have thought when she heard the news: that Stephen, by invading the kingdom, had wrongfully disinherited not only her, but her son, the Lord Henry, 'the child who was still crying in his cradle', 'for whom, if there was loyalty in the man, he was sworn to die'.

But, having got the Pope on his side, Stephen now proceeded to alienate the Church, and with it many of his supporters.

Roger, Bishop of Salisbury, had enjoyed a resurgence of power under Stephen. His nephews, Alexander and Nigel, were bishops of Lincoln and Ely, and his son, Roger le Poer, served the King as Treasurer. The wealthy Roger had built 'the most splendid castle in Europe' at Devizes, Wiltshire,[7] and he was highly influential at court. Stephen had even declared expansively that 'if Roger demanded half of the kingdom he should have it', but since then he had been informed by the malicious and jealous Beaumont twins that the Bishop and his adherents had begun fortifying their strongholds in support of the Empress and Earl Robert.[8] Stephen chose to believe them.[9]

In June 1139, while the Great Council was meeting at Oxford, the Beaumonts' men picked a fight with the bishops' men, and a knight was killed. This gave Stephen a pretext for suddenly demanding that the three bishops surrender all their castles. When they refused, he had them arrested, and sequestered their property, including Devizes Castle.

The clergy were outraged, for Scripture enjoined: 'Touch not mine anointed.' Henry of Blois, already in no good mood with his brother, thundered that the King had infringed the Church's authority. As newly appointed Papal legate, he summoned him to appear before a legatine council at Winchester, and demanded that Bishop Roger be set at liberty – and that the King do penance for his actions. On their knees, Archbishop Theobald and Bishop Henry begged the King 'not to allow a divorce to be made between the monarchy and the clergy', but Stephen would not listen. The matter would be settled by Bishop Roger's death later that year, and by the Pope upholding the King's justice, but with one rash, unjustified act, Stephen had wantonly undermined the valuable support of the

English clergy – and of disgusted members of his household, many of whom would soon defect to Maud.[10]

Stephen had already alienated his brother by not making him archbishop of Canterbury, and Henry saw this latest outrage as insupportable. Secretly he began sending frequent letters to the Empress and Earl Robert, urging them to invade England.[11] Maud herself would later state that Henry had invited her.[12]

Stephen was beset on all sides. 'It was like the fabled Hydra of Hercules: when one head was cut off, two or more grew in its place.'[13] By the summer of 1139, Geoffrey of Anjou was master of much of Normandy, and with his strong foothold established there, 'rumours were prevalent in England that Earl Robert was on the very eve of coming from Normandy with his sister. Under such an expectation, many persons revolted from the King, for as soon as the Empress should arrive, they would immediately greet their sovereign with the surrender of their fortresses.'[14]

9

'His Extraordinary Queen'

Queen Adeliza and William d'Albini were married before September 1139.[1] They resided mainly at Arundel Castle, and probably at Albini's new castles at Castle Rising and Buckenham, Norfolk,[2] or his hunting lodge at Stansted, Sussex.[3] Castle Rising, which still stands today, an impressive ruin, was modelled on Norwich Castle and contained prestigious apartments – a hall (in which there was apparently a niche for Adeliza's throne), a great chamber, a chapel and a kitchen. Rich arcading decorates the forebuilding housing the steep staircase to the grand entrance doorway.[4]

In charters, Adeliza continued to style herself as queen.[5] Before the couple wed, Stephen created Albini earl of Lincoln. It was as earl of Lincoln that he granted charters to Lewes Priory and Reading Abbey and confirmed one of Adeliza's granting lands in Sussex to the Benedictine abbey of Affligem in Brabant. In another charter, Adeliza gave Affligem three English villages. Affligem Abbey, which lay twelve miles north-west of Brussels, had been founded in 1062, and was later re-founded by Adeliza's father and her uncle, Henry of Louvain. Thanks to a charter granted by Henry I, prayers were already being said at Affligem for Adeliza, her parents and her sister Ida, Countess of Cleves. Adeliza's charter was granted after the death of her father, Count Godfrey, who passed away, aged about seventy-nine, on 25 January 1139, in the abbey where he had spent his last years, and was buried there.

These charters were all issued before Christmas 1141, when Albini resigned the earldom of Lincoln for that of Arundel, which he held in right of Adeliza's lands in Sussex, making him a very wealthy man. He is sometimes referred to in contemporary sources as earl of Chichester, and in 1154 he would come into possession of Chichester Castle. The annalist of Waltham Abbey states that, after his marriage, Albini became 'so puffed up that he looked down on every man except the King, and became arrogant and inordinately conceited, so that he could not bear anyone being his equal, and anything that our world possessed that was special, apart from the King, was worthless in his eyes'.[6]

The marriage appears to have been happy. To Albini, Adeliza was his 'inestimable Queen'. He and Adeliza founded and endowed an Augustinian priory dedicated to St Mary and St James at his manor of Buckenham, Norfolk, for the safety of their souls and those of King Stephen and his wife. In 1146, he gave his castle at Buckenham, with eighty acres of land, as well as woods and meadows, to the canons, so that they could use its stones to build a priory on the site. Albini provided for prayers to be said there for himself, Queen Adeliza, King Stephen, the Empress and the souls of their ancestors. He built a new castle two miles away.

Adeliza had made no monastic foundations as queen, but during her marriage to Albini she founded a small Augustinian priory dedicated to St Bartholomew at Lyminster near Arundel, which was known as Pynham Priory, or the Priory *de Calceto* ('of the Causeway').[7] It had a practical purpose, for the two monks provided for by Adeliza were to maintain the causeway, a wooden bridge over the River Arun, and a hospital for poor travellers.

Adeliza was also a benefactress of Chichester Cathedral and Boxgrove Priory, Sussex, where carved heads flanking the central light of the east window of *c.*1220 are said to represent her, wearing her crown, and William d'Albini. Possibly she also patronised the leper hospital at Arundel. She commanded the monks of Reading not to alienate any of her gifts, and ensured that her men at Waltham paid their tithes to the abbey.[8] In a charter that she granted to Reading Abbey, she gifted the church of Berkeley Hernesse, Gloucestershire, with endowments and 100s. a year from the profits of her wharf at Queenhithe,[9] in return for prayers for the souls of King Henry and her father, 'and also for the health of her present lord, William, Earl of Chichester, and for her own health and the health of her children'. Her husband confirmed all her gifts and charters.[10]

Surprisingly, after fourteen years of barren marriage with Henry, Adeliza proved fruitful, which suggests that Henry I's sexual powers had been on the wane in his later years. She bore Albini seven children. Robert of Torigni initially stated that there were three, William, Godfrey and a daughter, Adeliza, who married in turn John, Count of Eu, and Alvred de Saint-Martin, and died in 1188; but later he wrote that Albini left four sons: William (the 2nd Earl of Arundel), Reyner, who is mentioned in the cartulary of Wymondham Priory,[11] Henry and Godfrey. There were two other daughters besides Adeliza. Albini granted undated charters giving gifts to Boxgrove Priory for the souls of his sister Olivia, his daughters Olivia and Agatha, and his wife,[12] which gave rise to the incorrect assumption that Queen Adeliza too was buried there. Olivia and Agatha died unwed, probably in infancy or childhood. From Albini and Adeliza were descended the earls of Arundel and dukes of Norfolk, and two Tudor queens, Anne Boleyn and Katherine Howard.

10

'A Desert Full of Wild Beasts'

The Empress was at last coming to England, determined to capitalise on the recent impasse between Stephen and the Church. She and Robert of Gloucester were intent on overthrowing Stephen and establishing her as queen. It was an opportune moment, for discontent with Stephen's feeble rule was mounting and law and order were breaking down. 'Though by sex a woman, yet with manly strength did she plan to attack the English, maintaining that the inheritance which was hers by right she would obtain by arms.'[1]

She also came 'for the purpose of subduing the kingdom for Henry, her son'.[2]

Geoffrey was not coming with Maud. They both evidently realised the necessity for him to secure Normandy while she focused on gaining the English throne. Their three young sons would remain with him, under the tutelage of the scholar and poet Peter of Saintes, who taught them Latin.

For the next two years, Maud would refer to herself in documents as a *'femme sole'*. It was not usual for a woman to act autonomously of her husband, and there is no evidence that Geoffrey objected to Maud taking the initiative alone, or of what his plans were should she be successful. It is quite possible that, knowing how unpopular he was likely to prove in England, they had come to an arrangement that she would rule in England and he in Normandy.

Earl Robert had already been successful in raising support for his sister in the West Country, where the lands of his earldom lay and he had a strong following, although the King had seized many of his castles. Maud herself had secured the support of several disinherited barons, men who nurtured grievances because they had not received the lands once held by their fathers. Among them were Geoffrey Talbot, Gilbert de Lacy, William Peverell of Dover and Baldwin de Redvers. Some who declared for her were motivated purely by self-interest.

In August 1139, Maud fired the first salvo in what was soon to be an open war with Stephen for the throne, sending Baldwin de Redvers to capture Wareham, Dorset, in the hope of distracting the King – which he did successfully, although he was soon driven back to Corfe Castle by the royal forces.

Stephen had ordered that the ports be barred, and that careful watch be kept night and day on all the harbours. Robert, having surmounted 'every cause of delay', was 'relying on the protection of God and his lawful oath', anticipating that he would be venturing 'into a desert full of wild beasts'.[3]

Adeliza had often sent messages to Maud in Normandy, pledging her faith to her stepdaughter's cause.[4] Robert of Torigni states that it was William d'Albini who invited Maud and Earl Robert to Arundel. Albini was outwardly a loyal adherent of Stephen, and relations between the monarch and Adeliza had been cordial.[5] Therefore many historians have thought it unlikely that Maud's adherents had been able to bring pressure to bear on him, for Stephen had only recently created Albini earl of Lincoln, and in 1138 he had been a guest at Arundel, where he had confirmed Adeliza's grants to Reading Abbey.[6] But Albini had good cause secretly to support the Empress. His family's lands in Normandy lay in an area where her half-brother, Henry I's bastard Reginald de Dunstanville, Earl of Cornwall, and Baldwin de Redvers were active in her cause. Maud's commander in Normandy, Alexander de Bohun, was the uncle of Ralph FitzSavaric, a close associate of Albini in Sussex.[7] Critically, Stephen had recently deprived Adeliza of some of her dower lands, notably the wealthy abbey of Waltham, which he had given to Queen Matilda.[8] Albini was angered at the loss of Waltham, and was doing his best to secure its restoration. So he may well have joined Adeliza in inviting Maud to Arundel.

On 30 September 1139, Maud, accompanied by Earl Robert, 140 Angevin knights and 3,000 troops, landed at Littlehampton, Sussex, and sailed five miles up the River Arun to Arundel Castle, where Robert 'for a time delivered his sister and his wife, Mabel FitzHamon, into the safe-keeping, as he supposed', of her stepmother, while he took twelve knights and 'boldly' hurried off in the night through hostile country to secure Bristol,[9] which, alone of his former strongholds, had held out against the King. His army was to follow.

On the way, he met Bishop Henry, making for Arundel with 'a large body of cavalry'. Henry, still outwardly loyal to his brother, had 'had all the byroads blocked by guards' as soon as he heard Maud had landed, but he made no attempt to apprehend Robert. Robert would have known that Henry had secretly been urging the Empress to come to England, and at their meeting they agreed a firm 'compact of peace and friendship'.[10] Robert charged the Bishop and Waleran de Beaumont, Count of Meulan, with escorting Maud to Bristol, where he himself would place her 'in safe quarters'.[11] Henry gave him the kiss of peace and went on his way,[12] leaving Robert to go on his, unharmed.[13]

One of those who hastened to join Robert and offer his allegiance to Maud was Brian FitzCount, who was 'delighted' at her arrival in England.[14] As he later revealed in a letter later sent to the Bishop, it was 'you yourself, who ordered me to join the daughter of King Henry, your uncle, and help her to acquire her right, which was taken from her by force',[15] which is further evidence of Henry's duplicity.

Around 1138–9, Brian FitzCount sent his friend Gilbert Foliot, Abbot of Gloucester, a treatise (now lost) asserting Maud's right to her royal inheritance as Henry I's lawfully begotten heir. Foliot wrote back, commending him for his devotion and loyalty, and bolstering the argument with quotations proving that her claim was supported by all laws natural, human and divine; they included the passage from the Book of Numbers that – Foliot said – Earl Robert was always citing. 'In all this,' he declared, 'you will not find any cause why she should have been disinherited.'[16]

As lord of Wallingford in right of his wife, Matilda d'Oilli, Brian FitzCount would hold its strategically important castle for Maud for thirteen years, in the face of repeated attacks by the King's forces. It had been built in 1067–71 as part of the Conqueror's chain of defences circling London. He proved to be one of the Empress's staunchest supporters – and possibly more than that. According to the *Gesta Stephani*, Maud and Brian 'gained a title to boundless fame, since as their affection for each other had before been unbroken, so even in adversity, great though the obstacle that danger might be, they were in no wise divided'. The implication perhaps was that they were closer than they should have been. The speed with which Brian had raced to Maud on hearing of her arrival in England might suggest that there was already something between them. But, had their relationship been adulterous, rather than a close bond of platonic devotion, her enemies would surely have made greater political capital out of it.

11

'Treacherous Advice'

The arrival of the Empress placed Adeliza and Albini in a compromising position. Adeliza may have been pregnant at this time, or had the safety of her first baby to consider. Earl Robert and his party turned up at Arundel 'as though he were merely to be a guest there, but he was admitted with a strong body of troops'.[1]

The Queen Dowager and her husband nevertheless welcomed Maud to the keep, escorting her through its Norman doorway decorated with zigzagged and scrolled mouldings. It used to be claimed that she was accommodated in the Gatehouse Tower, where 'Queen Matilda's Room' has only been so named since the eighteenth century,[2] but she was almost certainly offered hospitality in the imposing new oval shell keep of Caen stone built by Albini, in which he and Adeliza had their hall and private apartments in wooden penthouses built against the walls. Their windows looked out on the inner courtyard; there was no external views. The royal chambers would have been luxuriously appointed by the standards of their day, but the present fireplaces date only from the fourteenth century.

On the top floor of the entrance tower was St Martin's Chapel, where the family worshipped. Their two chaplains came from the priory of St Nicholas at Arundel, and Adeliza entrusted to the safe keeping of the Bishop of Chichester lands in Arundel to fund salaries for them. On the ground floor of the castle was a well fed by fresh clean water, and within the open spaces of the bailey were stables, barracks and service buildings, and a garden in which herbs, vegetables and flowers were cultivated.[3]

Possibly Adeliza was hoping to exercise her queenly power of intercession and bring about some accord between Maud and Stephen. Albini too may have thought he could negotiate a peace. Probably both were hoping that the grateful parties would reward them with the restoration of Waltham Abbey. No doubt its seizure was discussed, and ways of recovering it.

When news of the coming of Maud and Earl Robert spread, 'England at once was shaken and quivered with intense fear, because all who favoured the Earl were keener than usual to trouble the King'.[4] Stephen was besieging Baldwin de Redvers at Corfe Castle when he heard the news. He also received a message from Adeliza. Fearful of losing her queenly rank, she swore she had not invited Maud, and assured the King that 'none of his enemies had reached England by her means'.[5] William of Malmesbury accuses her of reneging on her pledges 'with a woman's fickleness'.

She explained that she had admitted Maud not as his enemy, but as her stepdaughter and long-standing friend, who had claimed her hospitality, 'which respect for the memory of her late royal lord, King Henry, forbade her to refuse; and these considerations would compel her to protect her Imperial guest while she remained beneath the shelter of her roof. If he came in hostile array against her castle of Arundel, with intent to make Maud his prisoner, she must frankly say she was resolved to defend her to the last extremity, not only because she was the daughter of her late dear lord, King Henry, but as the widow of the Emperor Henry, and her guest.' She begged Stephen, 'by all the laws of courtesy and the ties of kindred, not to place her in such a painful strait as to compel her to do anything against her conscience'. She asked only 'that Maud might be allowed to leave the castle and retire to her brother'.[6]

Abandoning his assault on Corfe, Stephen 'made a very bold forced march and appeared unexpectedly' before Arundel Castle, where he learned 'from trusty scouts that Earl Robert had stolen away with his men and made for Bristol in the silence of night, and that his sister, with the Angevins she had brought with her, had remained lurking in the castle'. Leaving his men blockading her inside, Stephen raced off in pursuit of Robert, but the Earl could not be found, having travelled 'by a hidden byway'. So Stephen turned back and laid siege to Arundel.[7] Maud sent a letter out to him, urging him to promise her safe conduct to Bristol,[8] which Albini and Adeliza now evidently regarded as the best solution, doubtless feeling that they had no choice but to surrender Arundel to the King, to whom, thereafter, they would remain loyal. But Stephen was reluctant to let Maud go, which shows that Adeliza did not enjoy any special influence or status as queen dowager.

When Bishop Henry arrived with his forces, he told the King that 'the plan was useless, for if he were preparing to besiege the Empress in one part of England, her brother would immediately rise up to disturb the kingdom in another'.[9] Arundel was a mighty fortress and well provisioned, so it would be some time before it fell anyway. Henry thought it 'wiser for the King himself, and more beneficial to the kingdom, to let her go to her brother unharmed, so that when both their forces had been brought into one place, he might more easily devote himself to shattering their enterprise'.[10] It was 'treacherous advice',[11] for by capturing the Empress, Stephen could have put an end to the conflict. But the Bishop had his own agenda, and was doubtless anticipating that Maud might soon be his sovereign lady and would be grateful to the man who had saved her from capture.

Henry now appealed to his brother's chivalry, whereupon Stephen reluctantly conceded that 'it was not the custom of honourable knights to refuse even their bitterest enemy' a noble escort.[12] 'Either because he trusted treacherous advice, or because he thought the castle impregnable, he agreed to a sworn truce and allowed the Empress to go to Bristol',[13] under safe conduct with the Countess Mabel, escorted by Bishop Henry and Waleran, Count of Meulan. The King also ordered that Maud 'be led with honour, since she was his cousin'.[14]

Waleran accompanied them as far as Calne, Wiltshire, while Henry rode on with Maud to the agreed meeting point, where her brother was waiting with his troops to receive her 'from the very midst of her enemies'.[15] She was handed over without acrimony. Indeed, she and Henry may have had much to talk about on their thirty-five-mile journey together.

Maud saw Adeliza's actions as a betrayal. She believed her step-mother, 'through female inconstancy, had broken the faith she had repeatedly pledged by messengers sent into Normandy'.[16] In fact Adeliza delivered Maud into Stephen's hands only on condition that she be given safe conduct to Earl Robert at Bristol.[17] This helped Maud to gain the freedom to fight on, and in so doing, Adeliza had risked offending the King. Nevertheless, it would be some time before Maud had any further dealings with her stepmother.

In agreeing to free Maud and let her go to Robert in Bristol, instead of responding repressively 'after the fashion of his ancestors', Stephen had again displayed a fateful lack of judgement that one chronicler thought 'incredible'. He had been 'very foolish' and in so doing bore the responsibility for the violence that followed.[18]

12
'May Your Imperial Dignity Thrive'

Bristol was then 'almost the richest city in the country, receiving merchandise by sailing ships from lands near and far'. It was, 'by its very situation, the most strongly fortified of cities'.[1] The motte-and-bailey castle, which stood on a narrow strip of land between the Avon and Frome rivers, had stout defences. Maud herself strength-ened them by ordering the building of a great keep that would be acknowledged as the flower of all the keeps in England.[2] There were towers at each of its four corners, and the walls were twenty-five feet thick at ground level.[3] She would be safe there.

Once installed in her rival court, Maud and Robert 'announced their coming to all the barons of the kingdom, pitifully and tear-fully imploring their most zealous aid, promising gifts to some and enlargement of their estates to others; they met the wishes of all with every advantage in their power'. As their letters were received across England, 'all their supporters who formerly served the King, but insincerely and with treacherous intent, broke the compact of oath and homage that they had pledged to him, and turned to them; and all together, with one mind and a common purpose to resist the King, assailed him most furiously on every side'.[4]

Thanks to Robert's help, and his loyal following, Maud quickly built a strong power base in the west of the kingdom. She spent 'more than two months at Bristol, receiving homage from all men and disposing freely of the royal rights'.[5] Earl Robert 'advanced her in all things to the utmost of his power, ever busied on her account, and neglecting his own interest to secure hers, while some persons, taking advantage of his actions, plundered his possessions on every side'.[6]

All the bishops, apart from Henry of Blois, declared for Maud. The disaffected and dispossessed were ready to offer their allegiance. Gradually her cause gathered momentum. Having lost control of the north of England, Stephen had effectively lost the west too,[7] though he was still firmly entrenched in the south-east, thanks to Queen Matilda's loyal honour of Boulogne.

On 7 November, Earl Robert took Gloucester, and soon afterwards Maud moved her court to Gloucester Castle. She was received by the sheriff, Miles FitzWalter, a military genius and one of Robert's landed vassals, who paid homage to her as his liege lady and was entrusted with the safe keeping of her person.[8] Gloucester Castle was Miles's stronghold as hereditary sheriff of Gloucester. It had been built in stone by his father around 1112, a massive keep resembling the Tower of London with walls twelve feet thick, and stood west of Barbican Hill, with commanding views of the River Severn.[9]

Miles was 'unquestioning in his loyalty to King Henry's children',[10] and he soon conceived a strong personal loyalty to Maud. In return for his protection, she put him in charge of St Briavel's Castle and the royal Forest of Dean,[11] where only the King was permitted to hunt. All the chroniclers bear witness to Miles's vigour as a commander and his devotion to Maud. 'He broke the faith he had pledged to the King and rose against him with the utmost determination; receiving all the King's opponents who flocked around him, he exercised every kind of depredation in the regions around Gloucestershire.' Yet he 'always behaved to the Empress like a father in deed and counsel',[12] and later he would reveal to the chronicler John of Worcester that she had lived at his expense throughout her time in England, having 'received nothing except by his own munificence and forethought'.[13]

'The whole country then, around Gloucester to the extremity of Wales, partly by force and partly by favour, in the course of the remaining months of that year, gradually espoused the party of their sovereign, the Empress.'[14] That Maud 'received the homage of the citizens and neighbouring lords'[15] was largely thanks to the efforts of two men, Earl Robert and Miles of Gloucester. When Stephen, riding west in fruitless pursuit of Maud, besieged Brian FitzCount in Wallingford Castle, it was Miles who came to his relief and seized the fortress for the Empress. Stephen, anticipating that Miles might try to take London for her, marched off to secure it. But Miles galloped off in the opposite direction and captured Waleran of Meulan's stronghold at Worcester. Soon afterwards, long-drawn-out hostilities broke out in the Cotswolds and the upper Thames Valley, with both sides striving for supremacy.

The monks of Malmesbury Abbey were among those who welcomed Maud's arrival in the West Country. The history that Matilda of Scotland had asked William of Malmesbury to write had not been finished in her lifetime, but had been completed in 1125 and revised in 1127, the latter version being dedicated to Robert, Earl of Gloucester. Now, around 1139–40, the monks presented a copy to the Empress, with this laudatory letter:

> To the most glorious Empress and their lady, Matilda, the convent of the brothers of Malmesbury, greetings and loyal prayers of those serving God and St Mary and St Aldhelm. The royal piety and holy religion of true piety of your most revered mother, Queen Matilda, gave us cause long after her death to expect no less from your goodness than from hers. And just now that truth satisfied our hope in this, because you are the trunk of all rectitude, the origin of all clemency, the state of all mercy with the King, we thank God with all our prayers. And justly so! For when she was alive, she helped in almost all our affairs. But infamous Fortune, envying the successes of our church, struck us all the more sharply with pain and sorrow at her end, the more that the place had thrived in glory and honour in that government. And the consolation of hope

scarcely gave breath to our desolation with your happy arrival in England, most excellent lady, for it is quite fitting that you, Empress, rule where your mother, rightly to be revered, ruled as distinguished queen. Particularly since nothing can be reproached in her life except that she left that church without a rector,[16] most justly to be corrected by the wisdom of such a daughter, where the ignorance of the most blessed mother could heretofore be reproached.

The monks told Maud that they seized on her rule

as much as we can in our spirits and with this book, which we had written at the command of our lady about the deeds of the kings of the English, we submit ourselves and our possessions to your royal intercession. This kind of book used to be written in antiquity for kings and queens to instruct them in life by example, to follow the triumphs of some and avoid the misfortunes of others, to imitate the wisdom of some and scorn the folly of others. Which was not unknown to your mother when she, that most holy spirit, commissioned the writings. But we had scarcely begun when Fortune, envying the success of England, suddenly dedicated her, as we hope, to the seats of immortality. Distressed by sorrow, we decided to abjure the zeal of the pen, when we saw that the exhorter of our studies had left us. Then both the request of friends to break the silence of the earlier time, and the usefulness of the thing made it seem, as it was, unworthy that the memory of such men be buried, that their deeds die away.

Now this book can be sent to no mortal more justly than to you, since it is all about your ancestors and how powerfully the Imperial Artificer brought your race up to you. In it you will be able to discern that none of those memorialised in this book, not king or queen, awaited more royally or splendidly than you the rights of the hereditary kingdom of the English.

Let your Imperial mercy, therefore, receive this little gift and with our gift, dominion over us. We also charge you, through the bearer of the book, that you imperially hear and take pains to show your mercy to us, for the soul of your mother and all your ancestors. May your Imperial dignity thrive.[17]

13
'Christ and His Saints Slept'

Maud was lucky that her arrival in England coincided with an upsurge of baronial and clerical discontent with Stephen's ineffectual rule, which drew supporters to her cause. Stephen had much with which to contend, for Maud had strong allies in Normandy, Anjou and Scotland, and he was virtually surrounded, with his chief enemy now in his own kingdom. But he had not capitalised on his advantage, the best opportunity he would ever have to capture his rival. Had he kept custody of Maud at Arundel, or taken the offensive and attacked her in Gloucester and Wales, he might have won the conflict before it escalated, but he lacked the decisiveness, sound judgement and ruthlessness that had characterised his predecessors, and what it took to inspire loyalty. He was 'a man of less judgement than energy, an active soldier, of remarkable spirit in different undertakings, lenient to his enemies and easily placated, courteous to all. Though you admired his kindness in making promises, you doubted the truth of his words and the reliability of what he promised.'[1] He had 'such a kindly disposition that he commonly forgot a king's exalted rank'.[2] One chronicler gave a damning judgement: 'It was the King's custom to start many endeavours with vigour, but to bring few to a praiseworthy end.'[3]

Notwithstanding, Maud was still in a precarious position. Even though Stephen's authority as king had been undermined, she did not have sufficient power to overthrow him. The realm was divided and fatally weakened, and it was this that led to anarchy in the kingdom, as feudal lords exploited the situation and looked to their own interests and protection. Neither side had the decisiveness or the ability to strike a telling blow. Stephen was no Henry I, who had ruled by brute force, and Maud was no politician or diplomat. In the absence of a strong ruler and effective central government, chaos began to reign.

'In the days of this king there was nothing but strife, evil and robbery.'[4] Modern received wisdom is that the horrors of the civil war have been much exaggerated, but every chronicler gives such detailed, anguished and corroborative descriptions of them – too many to quote from here – that it is clear that they were all too real, and that there was little redress or relief. Because of Stephen's 'undue softness, public discipline had no force',[5] for he 'did no justice'.[6]

By Christmas 1139, 'the ceremonies of the court and the custom of royal crown-wearings had completely died out. The huge store of treasure had by now disappeared. There was no peace in the realm, but through murder, burning and pillage, everything was being destroyed. Everywhere, the sound of war, with lamentation and terror.'[7] 'It was distressing to see England, once the cherisher of peace and home of tranquillity, reduced to such a pitch of misery.'[8]

Law and order broke down, to be replaced with the arbitrary rule of unscrupulous, opportunist barons, who were quick to take advantage of the fact that the King was 'a mild man and soft and good, and did no justice'. Lacking the authority of his ruthless forebears, he inflicted few punishments 'and did not exact the full penalties of the law' for wrongdoing. With impunity, these miscreant lords 'committed all manner of horrible crimes' and 'perpetrated every enormity. They had done the King homage and sworn oaths of fealty, but not one of their oaths was kept. For every great man built his castles and held them against the King; and they filled the whole land with these castles.'[9]

Over a thousand castles were constructed in this period, many of them unlicensed, but with the King and the Empress effectively engaged in a civil war, it was easier than ever to flout the law. 'There were many castles throughout England, each defending its own neighbourhood, or, to be more truthful, plundering it. Some of the castellans wavered in their allegiance, hesitating as to which side to support, and sometimes working entirely for their own profit.'[10] Grasping barons imposed crippling taxes, often exacted at swordpoint, and 'sorely burdened the unhappy people of the country with forced labour on the castles; and when the castles were made, they filled them with devils and evil men'.[11]

A witness in a Norwich court complained that, 'because of the stress of the war, justice has fled and laws are silenced, while the liberties of churches had, in many places, perished'.[12] There was 'a shadow of peace' in the west and east, where Maud and Stephen held sway respectively, but 'the north was harried and pillaged by the Scots, the rich corn-lands of the south were spoiled by foreign mercenaries, which both sides employed, and the whole country was given over to rapine, torture and arson'. Local communities were terrorised by the 'devils' who commanded the castles, pursued private feuds and acted rapaciously outside the law.

Trade and commerce went into a decline as these 'devils' despoiled and robbed prosperous people and subjected them to wanton cruelties.

> By night and day, they seized those whom they believed to have any wealth, whether they were men or women, and, in order to extort their gold and silver, they put them in prison and tortured them with indescribable tortures. They hung them up by the feet and smoked them with foul smoke. They strung them up by the thumbs, or by the head, and hung coats of mail on their feet. Knotted ropes were put round their heads and twisted till they penetrated to the brains. They put them in prisons where there were adders and snakes and toads, and killed them like that. Some they put in an instrument of torture: a chest which was short and narrow, but not deep, and they put sharp stones in it and pressed the man so that he had all his limbs broken. Many thousands they starved to death. I neither can nor may tell all the wounds or all the tortures which they inflicted on wretched men in this land; and that lasted the nineteen long winters while Stephen was king, and it always grew worse and worse. Never did a country endure greater misery, and never did the heathen act more vilely than they did.[13]

'When the wretched people had no more to give', the robber barons 'plundered and burnt all the villages, so that you could easily go a day's journey without ever finding a village inhabited or a field cultivated. To till the ground was to plough the sea; the earth bare no corn, for the land was all laid waste by such deeds. The corn was dear, and butter and cheese, because there was none in the country. Wretched people died of starvation.' The oppressors 'respected neither church nor churchyard, but took all that was inside and burned the church. The bishops were constantly excommunicating them, but they thought nothing of it because they were all utterly accursed. And so it lasted till the land was all undone and darkened with such deeds; and men said openly that Christ and His saints slept.'[14] 'It was a dreadful thing that England, once the noblest purse of peace, the habitation of tranquillity, had sunk to such wretchedness.'[15] Not for nothing would Stephen's reign come to be known as 'the Anarchy'.

Among the offenders were Hugh Bigod, John the Marshal,[16] William de Say and Robert FitzHubert, a Flemish mercenary who captured Devizes Castle in 1140. 'He was the cruellest of all men, and a blasphemer against God, for he used to boast gratuitously that he had been present when eighty monks were burnt together with their church, and said he would do the same thing again and again in England. He used to smear prisoners with honey and expose them naked in the open air in the full blaze of the sun, stirring up flies and similar insects to sting them.'[17]

In 1140, Maud's adherent Geoffrey Talbot entered Hereford Cathedral and, 'impiously driving out the ministrants at God's table, recklessly brought in a throng of armed men. The townspeople were disturbed because the graves of the newly dead were dug up to provide earth for ramparts, and catapults were put up on the Tower from which they had heard the sweet and pacific admonition of the bells.'[18]

Brian FitzCount also drew bitter criticism for pillaging the land around Wallingford, but, as he excused himself to Bishop Henry, he had lost most of his lands and was 'in the greatest distress', for he was 'not harvesting one acre of corn' from the estates granted him by Henry I.[19] He told the Bishop: 'I am sorry for the poor and their plight, when the Church provides scarcely any refuge for them, for they will die if peace be longer delayed.'[20]

14
'Hunger-Starved Wolves'

The energetic Queen Matilda proved a formidable political opponent to the Empress. The two women had much in common: both were strong characters, heiresses with royal Saxon blood and nieces of King David of Scots. Both were married to forceful, acquisitive men, and ambitious for their sons.[1] Matilda was well placed strategically to help fight her husband's cause. She was a skilled negotiator, as brave and determined as the Empress, but never as arrogant or dictatorial, despite operating effectively as a female warlord, and thus she avoided alienating those who disapproved of women breaking through the boundaries imposed on them by a male-dominated society.

From her honour in London and Colchester, thanks to her loyal tenantry, she could control much of Essex, where her lands neighboured those of William de Say's brother-in-law, Geoffrey de Mandeville, hereditary Constable of the Tower of London and Earl of Essex from 1140. He was the King's man, 'remarkable for the ability of his shrewd mind, and admired for the firmness of his unbending courage in adversity and his excellence in the art of war. In the extent of his wealth and the splendour of his position, he surpassed all the chief men of the kingdom', and was a valuable ally for the Queen. 'He controlled not only the Tower, but also other strongholds around London.'[2]

Matilda's neighbour in Kent was the sympathetic William of Ypres, a cousin of King Stephen[3] who held the county of Kent even though he was never created its earl. From 1125, he had claimed to be count of Flanders, and Stephen had backed that claim, but William had been passed over by Louis VI in favour of William Clito and banished. He had come to England in 1133. William of Malmesbury, a supporter of the Empress, called him 'an abandoned character', and Earl Robert said of him, 'Words have not been invented which can properly describe the extent and ramification of his treacheries, the filth and horror of his obscenities.'[4] Yet these two men were hostile to Stephen's cause, while William of Ypres proved unfailingly loyal to the King and Queen.

After spending Christmas of 1139 at Salisbury with her husband, Matilda crossed to France with her eldest son, Eustace. It had been agreed, after the magnates of England and France had been consulted, that Stephen's son should marry the French king's sister, Constance.[5] Stephen's aim in urging this alliance was 'to strengthen the son who was to succeed him against the count of Anjou and his sons'.[6] He was even willing to take the princess without a dowry. Matilda had been instrumental in arranging the betrothal of her son, another instance of an English queen involving herself in the marriages of her children; and she took with her the large sum of money needed to secure the support of Louis VII.

Constance was about fifteen, Eustace perhaps five years younger. Their betrothal and marriage took place in February 1140 amid lavish splendour, 'in the presence of the Queen of England and of many of the highest nobility of both kingdoms'.[7] Matilda persuaded Louis to invest Eustace as duke of Normandy and to give aid to maintain him as nominal ruler of the duchy under her direction. This was in one respect a godsend, for she could now afford to send troops of mercenaries to England to aid Stephen in his troubles, but it also drew bitter criticism, for the English were soon protesting that 'these hunger-starved wolves' stole food, adding to their misery, and 'completed the destruction of the land's felicity'.[8] After the celebrations, Matilda brought the young couple to England.

At Michaelmas 1140, Matilda learned, to her dismay, that Earl Robert's son-in-law, Ranulf de Gernon, Earl of Chester, was planning to waylay Henry of Scots as the prince rode north, and hold him hostage until he agreed to return Carlisle Castle. Immediately she prevailed on Stephen to have Henry escorted safely all the way to Scotland.[9]

At Lent there was an eclipse of the sun 'so remarkable' that it was said by many that the King 'would not continue a year in the government'.[10]

The whole of the year 1140 'was embittered by the horrors of war'.[11] The Empress was still insisting that she was the rightful Queen of England and that Stephen was a usurper. Henry of Blois, worried about the escalating lawlessness, went to France to discuss the deadlock with his brother Theobald and Louis VII, and came up with a compromise. In August 1140, he arranged a conference near Bath, 'that, if possible, by God's help, peace might be restored'. The Queen, Henry of Blois as Papal legate, and Archbishop Theobald represented the King, and Robert of Gloucester 'and other of her friends' represented the Empress.[12] The latter were willing to accept the compromise, which suggests that it may have involved the succession devolving on Maud's son Henry, overlooking Stephen's heirs.[13] Naturally the Queen was opposed. Earl Robert demanded that the dispute be referred to the judgement of the clergy, and when this was put to her, 'the Empress, more inclined to justice, declared that she was not averse to the decision of the Church'; but the Queen and her party 'most cautiously avoided this' because 'the King put off a decision from day to day', and therefore 'vainly they wasted both words and time to no purpose, and parted without making peace'. Bishop Henry 'withdrew within himself, watching, like the others, to see how things would turn out'.[14]

In February 1140, Thurstan, Archbishop of York, had died, and Stephen had put forward his kinsman William FitzHerbert as his successor. The Cistercians vigorously opposed his election because they wanted one of their Order appointed to the see; moreover, they suspected FitzHerbert of bribery and simony. Nevertheless, the King brought pressure to bear, and in January 1141, FitzHerbert received the temporalities of York.

The news prompted an angry Bernard of Clairvaux to write to Queen Matilda, enlisting her help in overthrowing the election. (Of note in his letter is his employment of the style 'your Majesty', which was not in use in England in the twelfth century, but was an accepted form of address in European courts.) He urged her:

> Do everything to prevent that man from occupying the church of York any longer, about whose life and entry into the epis-copacy religious men in whom one must trust give such testi-mony. We commit this, God's cause, to you – act so that it be brought to worthy conclusion, and protect all those who have worked for this side, that they not suffer offence from the King or any harm on its account. They have done good work. Further, if you get the lord King to renounce this sacrilege of intrusion into the election before his bishops and princes, which he only should have assent to, know that it would bring great honour to God, great safety and security to the King and to what is his, and great utility to the whole kingdom.[15]

Bernard's letter made little difference. More momentous events intervened, and the Queen was unable to prevent FitzHerbert's consecration in September 1143. Not until 1147 was he deposed in favour of the Cistercian Henry Murdac.[16]

15
'Shaken with Amazement'

The civil war of the 1140s was essentially a series of sieges, light-ning strikes and skirmishes, rather than pitched battles, and a tense, prolonged period of shifting loyalties. But there was one crucial, decisive engagement.

Furious at the loss of Carlisle Castle, Ranulf de Gernon, Earl of Chester, had declared for the Empress and seized the royal castle at Lincoln. In February 1141, Stephen laid siege to the castle. Ranulf had already departed, leaving his wife behind. On 2 February, Stephen was suddenly confronted by a great army of Normans and Welsh, which had been raised by Ranulf and his father-in-law, Earl Robert, on the Empress's behalf. Weary of the country being 'harassed with rapine and slaughter for the sake of two persons', Robert wanted to bring the conflict 'to an issue at once'.[1]

Stephen was urged to escape, but he made the rash decision to fight, and met the earls in battle the next day. In the face of this great host, most of the royalist magnates fled, leaving Stephen and just his personal bodyguard to face the enemy. The King fought bravely until the handle of his battleaxe broke and he was knocked out by a blow to the head.[2] He came to his senses to find himself a prisoner in Lincoln Castle. It was a humiliating defeat, but Earl Robert was a chivalrous knight and treated him courteously, commanding that no man harm the King further or insult him.

When Maud learned of the victory, a week later, she was 'ecstatic at this turn of events, having now, as she thought, gained possession of the kingdom that had been promised to her by oath'.[3] Stephen was brought to her at Gloucester by Earl Robert.[4] Capturing the King would prove to be the pinnacle of her success, but there is no account of this momentous meeting. We know only that, four days later, by agreement between Maud and Robert, Stephen was 'put under guard in the tower of Bristol, to be kept there until the last breath of his life'.[5] Bishop Henry appears to have been instrumental in advising Maud, for she later revealed 'that her taking the King and holding him in captivity had been done principally by his connivance'.[6] It is not known what role, if any, Henry played behind the scenes prior to the siege of Lincoln, but he may well have pressed for Stephen to be kept in perpetual imprisonment, doubtless fearing his retribution.

We might wonder why Maud did not deal with Stephen as a traitor who had stolen her throne. For such a serious offence the penalty was usually mutilation in the form of castration or blinding, but she probably felt that was a step too far for one who had been crowned and hallowed, and she may have feared the reaction if she put the King to death. She probably followed the precedent set by her father when he kept his brother Robert a prisoner for life. This is corroborated by the *Anglo-Saxon Chronicle*: 'When the King was in prison, the earls and the powerful men expected that he would never get out.'

When it became known that Stephen was a captive, 'the whole of England was shaken with amazement, and to some it was an occasion of festival and seemed the dawning of a new day, as they hoped that thereby an end might be put to strife and war; to others, it seemed that the wrong they had done their King could not be atoned for without very great prejudice to the kingdom, nor yet could the turbulent strife be so easily ended. But still the greater part of the kingdom at once submitted to the Empress and her adherents, and some of the King's men were either captured or forcibly expelled from their possessions. Others, very quickly forswearing the faith they owed to the King, were voluntarily surrendering themselves and what was theirs to the Empress.'[7] In fact, there was a near stampede of men rushing to demonstrate their loyalty to Maud – 'effeminates', the *Gesta Stephani* sneeringly called them.

This hostile chronicler asserted that, in her triumph, Maud 'unsexed' herself. 'She at once put on an extremely arrogant demeanour, instead of the modest gait and bearing proper to a woman; and she began to walk and speak and do things more stiffly and more haughtily than she had been wont.' There was probably a good reason for the anonymous chronicler's vitriol, for it has been credibly argued that he was Robert of Lewes, Bishop of Bath,[8] who must have endured a traumatic time as the King's sole supporter in a region controlled by Earl Robert, and who was at one time captured by Maud's supporters in Bristol and threatened with hanging. Yet criticism of her hauteur came not only from antagonistic sources, but also from those who were pro-Angevin,[9] which argues that it was well founded.

Queen Matilda was in London when she received the dread news of her husband's capture. Her presence there on 9 February 1141 is attested by a charter, which she granted 'for the health of our lord, King Stephen'.[10] Determined to have him set free, she was quickly to become the focus for resistance to Maud.

For a short while, security around Stephen seems to have been lax. 'At first he was kept with every mark of honour, except the liberty of going at large.' He had no trouble in cajoling or bribing his guards into letting him out of his apartments to wander the castle at night, but 'he had been found, more than once, beyond the appointed limits'.[11] When Maud heard, 'provoked by this into a womanly rage, she ordered the King, the Lord's Anointed, to be put in irons',[12] and Earl Robert gave the order[13] for Stephen to be chained to the wall of his prison. 'At this very moment, Stephen, King of England languishes wretchedly in a dungeon,' lamented the dying Orderic. 'The princes of the world are overwhelmed by misfortunes and disastrous setbacks.'

The fettering of the King drew much comment from the chroniclers, and undoubtedly undermined Maud's cause. It also galvanised
the Queen to herculean efforts to free her husband.

16

'Dragged by Different Hooks'

In the King's absence, Geoffrey de Mandeville made a pragmatic
decision and switched sides. Stephen had left Matilda and Constance
of France in Mandeville's safe keeping in the Tower of London. 'It
chanced that the Queen sought to go elsewhere with this daughter-
in-law, but Geoffrey opposed her.' An outrageous struggle ensued
when 'he seized the daughter-in-law from the hands of her mother-
in-law, who resisted as best she could, and detained her, allowing
the Queen herself to depart in humiliation. The King later demanded
Constance back, hiding for the moment his just anger; and Geoffrey
reluctantly surrendered his outstanding prize to the King her father-
in-law.'[1] The insult to his womenfolk stung; Stephen probably never
forgot it.

'Then was England much divided; some supported the King and
some the Empress. For, when the King was in prison, the earls and the
great men came to terms with the Empress.'[2] Among them was
Mandeville's brother-in-law, Hugh Bigod, who was still angry at
Stephen's seizure of Norwich Castle. He had fought for the King
at Lincoln, but then changed sides, for which Maud bestowed on
him the earldom of Norfolk, as either an incentive or a reward.
Waleran of Meulan, William de Warenne, Earl of Surrey, William
Martel, steward of the royal household, 'and many others remained
loyal to the Queen, and vowed to fight manfully for the King and
his heirs'.[3] Ranulph de Gernon, Earl of Chester, had offered his
support, but Matilda rebuffed him, knowing him to be untrustworthy,
and the cause of Stephen being captured, whereupon Ranulf offered
his sword to the Empress.

Already some who had declared for Maud had been alienated by
the hauteur and tactlessness she had displayed after her victory at
Lincoln. Apart from in the West Country, she was not well liked:

the paucity of signatories to her charters testifies to this. In all, she issued 88 (of which 22 survive in their original form), compared to 720 by Stephen, illustrating that the King, generally, held a stronger position.

Matilda had taken her son Eustace and sought refuge in Kent, where they made a stand against the Empress. While Maud had Robert of Gloucester to support her, Matilda had William of Ypres, who helped her to raise troops of Flemish mercenaries and organise resistance to Maud. Charter evidence shows that he was close to her in interests, connections and location.[4] In Kent, 'the Queen and William of Ypres opposed her with all their might'.[5] Matilda was in a strong position for she held control over Kent and Essex and could command substantial military strength as well as the English Channel. William of Ypres and Pharamus of Boulogne now assumed command of the King's household and troops,[6] and Matilda herself would ride with them at the head of her forces, although she did not take part in the fighting. She would also take upon herself something of the royal authority and some of the executive and bureaucratic functions of the Crown in the King's absence.[7] It was probably during Stephen's imprisonment that she issued an undated writ to a justice, John the Sheriff of London, and the barons of the city, which began, 'I order and command you on the King's part, and on my own …'

Meanwhile, Maud had marched, with her ever-growing following of bishops, barons, knights and supporters, from Gloucester to Cirencester.[8] She had been advised 'to win the attachment of Henry, Bishop of Winchester, because he was reckoned to surpass all the great men of England in judgement and wisdom, and to be their superior in virtue and wealth; for, she was told, if he were willing to favour her party, he must be honoured and made her first counsellor; but if he showed himself in any way hostile and rebellious, the whole armed force of England must be sent against him'.[9] Winning over Bishop Henry, the Papal legate in England, was also the best means of securing the full backing of the Church – and the path to the throne, as Henry I and Stephen had demonstrated, lay via Winchester and London.[10]

Henry had already given Maud cause to hope for a rapprochement. From 16 February, as she moved eastwards, she made several attempts to set up a meeting with him. She and Earl Robert 'dealt by messengers' with the Bishop, 'that he should receive her immediately in the cathedral as queen, since she was King Henry's daughter, to whom all England and Normandy had sworn allegiance'.[11]

Maud's demands placed Bishop Henry 'in a quandary'. 'On the one hand, it was most difficult to support the King's cause; on the other, it appeared to him a dreadful thing, and unseemly in the sight of men, to yield so suddenly to his brother's foes while that brother was still alive. So he was in bewilderment, dragged this way and that by different hooks until, strengthened by advice, he resolved to make a pact of peace and friendship with his enemies for a time, that with peace thus assured to him and his, he might quietly watch the inclinations of the kingdom, and might rise more briskly and with less hindrance to assist his brother if a chance were offered.'[12] At the time, however, he may well have had other motives. He was an ambitious man. What he was clearly trying to avoid was looking like a traitor to Stephen and an opportunist who was serving his own best interests. Brian FitzCount would later assert that the Bishop 'had a remarkable gift of discovering that duty pointed in the same direction as expediency'.[13]

A joint 'pact of peace and concord' was duly made between Maud and Henry,[14] and 'by means of negotiators, they agreed to meet in conference'. This took place on Sunday 2 March 1141, 'a dark and rainy day', on an open plain[15] near Wherwell Abbey, Hampshire. Henry greeted Maud 'in cordial fashion',[16] but because Stephen had reneged on his promises, he was determined to get guarantees from Maud, who was so keen to secure his support that she obligingly 'swore and pledged her faith to the Bishop, that all matters of importance in England, and especially the bestowing of bishoprics and abbeys, should be under his control, if he, with the Holy Church, would receive her as sovereign and observe perpetual fidelity towards her. Her brother swore as she did, and pledged his faith for her', as did Miles FitzWalter, Brian FitzCount and others.[17]

When Maud agreed to appoint Henry chancellor, so that his power would be second only to hers,[18] he did not hesitate to acknowledge her as the rightful ruler of England, and pledged his faith that, 'so long as she did not infringe the covenant, he would keep faith with her' and receive her formally into his church as his sovereign lady.[19]

The next day, 3 March, Maud rode to the capital, Winchester. When she neared the city, 'the nobles of England met her, and many abbots with barons and many knights, two convents of monks and a third of nuns, with the clergy and populace, among praises and processional songs'.[20] Bishop Henry received her and admitted her to the city, escorting her in 'splendid procession' to the cathedral, walking at her right hand, with Bernard, Bishop of St David's (former chancellor to Queen Adeliza), at her left.[21]

Five other bishops assisted in the reception ceremony, during which Henry formally handed over 'the rule of the city'[22] and Winchester Castle to Maud, along with the crown and regalia, 'which she had always most eagerly desired', and the 'scanty' treasure the King had left in the treasury, which effectively amounted to little more than his crown. Then, at a public meeting in the marketplace, he bade the people 'salute her as their lady and their Queen',[23] and, 'standing on high, cursed all who would curse the Empress or oppose her, and blessed all those who would bless and consent to her. And when this formality was finished, she departed from Winchester',[24] but not before granting a charter to Glastonbury Abbey, where Bishop Henry had been abbot.[25]

Maud wasted no time in having a great seal in the German style struck for her in Winchester, on which she was styled '*Romanorum Regina Mathildis*';[26] it was round, as was appropriate for an empress, the seals of queens being oval.

Securing Bishop Henry's support had paved the way for her acceptance by many others. But Maud, 'being raised with such splendour and distinction to this pre-eminent position, began to be arbitrary, or rather headstrong, in all that she did. Some former adherents of the King, who had agreed to submit themselves and what was theirs to her, she received ungraciously and, at times, with unconcealed annoyance; others she drove from her presence in fury after insulting and threatening them. By reckless innovations, she lessened or took away the possessions and lands of some, held on a grant from the King, while the fees and honours of the very few who still adhered to the King she confiscated altogether and granted to others.'[27] This was not unreasonable, given that Maud believed she was the rightful monarch, but being ungracious to those who had belatedly changed sides showed a woeful lack of judgement and forethought.

Yet she treated even her chief supporters with what looked like contempt.

Displaying extreme haughtiness and insolence when the King of Scots, the Bishop of Winchester and her brother, the Earl of Gloucester, the chief men of the whole kingdom, whom she was then taking around with her as a permanent retinue, came before her with bended knee to make some request, she did not rise respectfully, as she should have, when they bowed before her, or agree to what they asked, but repeatedly sent them away with insolence, rebuffing them by an arrogant answer, and refusing to hearken to their words; and by this time she no longer relied on their advice, as she should have, and had promised them, but ordained everything as she herself thought fit, by her own arbitrary will.[28]

She repeatedly failed to follow the advice of King David and, 'elated by woman's levity, assumed a majestic haughtiness of demeanour, and so she provoked the nobles by arrogant denunciations'.[29]

These were not the only blunders she made. 'She arbitrarily annulled any grant fixed by the King's royal decree. She hastily snatched away and conferred on her own followers anything he had given in unshakable perpetuity to churches or to his comrades in arms', a measure guaranteed to upset the clergy. Her tactlessness fuelled the flaring of discontent and unrest that pervaded the realm. 'All England was disturbed more than it had been before, and there was every evil in the country.'[30] The land was 'filled with plundering and burning and massacres'.[31] What it needed was a strong ruler who could put an end to the lawlessness.

17
'Sovereign Lady of England'

The Empress rode on in triumph to Oxford, which opened its gates on the orders of Robert d'Oilli, the hereditary royal constable of the castle, where Maud now took up residence. Almost encircled by two rivers, the Thames and the Isis, it had been built in 1071 and stood at the western end of the city, with walls sixty feet high. Within its precincts was a collegiate chapel dedicated to St George. Its Romanesque crypt survives today, as does St George's Tower, which was 'of great height'[1] and probably the bell tower of the chapel.[2]

On 30 March, Maud kept Easter royally at Oxford,[3] and issued a charter granting pasture and easement of the forest laws to the Knights Templar of Cowley, the preceptory founded by her rival, Queen Matilda; in it she instructed: 'All their things shall be firm in my peace. Let no one do them harm.'[4] Her uncle, King David, hastened south from Scotland to pay homage to her for his lands in England. He joined her in Oxford, appearing as a witness to charters dated there.[5]

Maud was still in Oxford on 7 April, when a legatine council of the English Church was convened by Bishop Henry at Winchester. William of Malmesbury, who was present, wrote a detailed account of the proceedings. Although Archbishop Theobald was also present, attendance was poor, but 'what was to be done engrossed the minds and conversations of all'.

Henry began by taking soundings in private of the clergy.[6] The next day he made a long speech to the assembly, in which he declared that, 'by the condescension of the Pope, he acted as vice-regent in England', and that it was on his authority that they had come to 'deliberate the peace of the country, which was exposed to immediate danger'. He reminded his listeners that the late King Henry had caused the whole realm to acknowledge the Empress as his heir, by sworn oaths. To excuse his and others' initial support for Stephen, he put his own tactful spin on the events that had followed the King's death, asserting that, 'because it seemed tedious to wait for the lady, who made delays in coming to England, since her residence was in Normandy, thought was made for the peace of the country, and my brother allowed to reign'.

He reminded everyone that Stephen had sworn to 'honour and advance Holy Church, uphold good and abrogate evil laws, yet it grieves me to recall, it shames me to say, how far justice failed and prosperity ended almost within the year. Then were the bishops captured, their possessions seized, abbeys sold, churches robbed, the counsels of the wicked taken, and of the virtuous despised. I should love my brother in the flesh, but as the greatest duty I must sustain the cause of my immortal Father. And as God, without my help, has executed His judgement on my brother in allowing him to fall into the power of the strong, I invite you to deliberate lest, for lack of a ruler, the realm should decay. Having first, as is fit, invoked the aid of Almighty God, I have invited you all here to elect the daughter of that most peaceful, that glorious, that rich, that good and incomparable King as sovereign of England and Normandy, and to her we promise fealty and support.'

There was no great acclamation, but no dissenting voices. The clergy 'either becomingly applauded his sentiments, or by their silence assented thereto',[7] and the Bishop proclaimed 'that the Empress Maud was lawfully elected as the sovereign lady of England'.[8] Bishop Henry threatened the excommunication of anyone who supported Stephen, whose deposition was now proclaimed.

'The Empress was received as Lady by all the English nation except for the men of Kent, where the Queen and William of Ypres opposed her with all their might',[9] with the Queen enlisting support for Stephen and raising troops in Kent and Surrey in her son's name.

Acting again as a *femme sole*, with no nod to her married status, Maud would from now on normally style herself '*Anglorum Domina*' (Lady of the English),[10] Empress or Queen of the Romans, and 'daughter of King Henry', to emphasise the legitimacy of her title. It was not the custom of the Norman rulers of England to style themselves king until they had been crowned, for their sovereignty was only conferred by that sacred act and sanctified by the anointing with holy oil. A drawing of a lost seal attached to a charter Maud gave Geoffrey de Mandeville in 1141 shows her as 'Queen of the English'; if an authentic copy, it may have been a seal made in anticipation of her coronation.[11] Nevertheless the word '*Domina*' made it clear that Maud exercised dominion and power over the people,[12] and we are told that 'she gloried in being so called'.[13]

Bishop Henry was well aware that London strongly supported Stephen, and that the Queen was there, trying to secure the City,[14] making 'supplication to all, and importuning with prayer, promises and fair words for the deliverance of her husband'.[15] He had diplomatically sent for a deputation of its citizens, 'who, from the importance of their city in England, are nobles, as it were'. On 9 April, they arrived at the legatine council in a dour mood and, to Henry's consternation, 'urged that their lord the King might be liberated from captivity'. To their plea was added that of Queen Matilda's clerk, Christian of London, who produced a letter from his mistress.

Bishop Henry protested, raising his voice to 'the highest pitch', but Christian, 'with notable confidence', insisted on reading the letter out loud to the assembly. In it, 'the Queen earnestly entreated all the clergy assembled, and especially the Bishop of Winchester, the brother of her lord', to restore Stephen to his kingdom, whom 'abandoned persons and even such as were under homage to him, had cast into chains'.[16] She 'made supplications to all, and importuned all with prayers, promises, and fair words for the deliverance of her husband'.[17] They fell on deaf ears.

'It was now a work of great difficulty to soothe the minds of the Londoners', who went home in a fury after the meeting came to a fraught end on 10 April. Bishop Henry closed its final session after excommunicating many of Stephen's supporters and absolving all who had supported Maud.[18]

Soon afterwards, Maud rode to Wilton, where she was received by Archbishop Theobald,[19] who had come at Bishop Henry's invitation, and large crowds 'flocking together, so that the town gates were hardly wide enough for the mass which entered'.[20] The Empress and the Archbishop met privately in Wilton Abbey. Despite Maud's affection for Bec-Hellouin, of which Theobald had been abbot, and the likelihood that they had met several times, there is no evidence of any great rapport between them.[21] The Archbishop 'deferred swearing fidelity to Maud, deeming it beneath his reputation and character to change sides, till he had consulted the King. In consequence, he and many other prelates were allowed to visit Stephen and converse with him; and, graciously obtaining leave to submit to the exigency of the times, they embraced the sentiments of the legate',[22] Stephen having released them from their allegiance.

England, it seemed, was Maud's. Coins showing her crowned profile were issued by the mints of Bristol, Cardiff, Oxford and Wareham,[23] but of a weight below the usual standard. To underline her dynastic credentials, she began associating her son Henry with herself in charters.[24] Earl Robert used every means in his power to win support for her, 'kindly addressing the nobility, making many promises and intimidating the adverse party', deploying the generosity, tact, charm and wisdom that were sometimes lacking in his sister. He and his adherents had 'almost half of England, from sea to sea, under their own laws and ordinances',[25] and he was doing his best to restore justice and the law of the land 'throughout every district that favoured the Empress'.[26]

Maud herself wooed the barons. Reginald de Dunstanville, Earl of Cornwall, had enthusiastically supported her and held Cornwall for her, but in February 1140 Stephen had deprived him of his earldom and given it to Alan of Brittany, one of his own adherents. Around April, assuming regal powers as the fount of honour, Maud restored Cornwall to her half-brother. Over the next months, with a view to ensuring the support of great men who could command military strength (while ignoring lesser mortals who could not), she created five earldoms (thirty-seven were established during the Anarchy) to buy support:[27] Kent, which was awarded to William of Ypres (although he was never formally made earl); Somerset, given to William de Mohun between April and June; Devon, bestowed on Baldwin de Redvers before midsummer; Hereford, given to Miles FitzWalter on 25 July; and Oxford, given in 1142 to Mandeville's brother-in-law, Aubrey de Vere, who was also promised the earldom of Cambridge, but never received it.

The men who received these earldoms were given charge of various areas of the country, but of course not all the people in those parts were ready to declare for the Empress. Maud made the mistake of taking the lands of those who opposed her, far more lands than Stephen had ever confiscated, which undermined her cause. When barons who had supported Stephen came to offer their allegiance, she received them with ill grace.[28] Predictably, she never won the love of the English as she had that of the Emperor's subjects.

On 7 May, Maud pressed on to Reading, where the people came out in multitudes to greet her. Here she issued a charter granting land to her father's abbey,[29] and received Robert d'Oilli, who came with the keys to Oxford Castle.[30] Her onward progress was briefly impeded by a hostile royalist garrison at Windsor, obliging her to go north to St Albans and another warm reception. Here she issued a charter granting land to Llanthony Priory.[31]

It was at St Albans that, ignoring her promise to consult Bishop Henry in Church matters, Maud flouted her father's accord with Archbishop Anselm in regard to the investiture of bishops. King David had put forward his chancellor, William Cumin, for the bishopric of Durham, much against the wishes of the cathedral chapter, who were horrified that David had refused to allow the burial of their late Bishop until Cumin had been elected. They sent their representatives to Maud and Bishop Henry, pleading with them to confirm their right to make a free election. Henry supported them, but Maud was having none of it, and around 11 May secretly agreed with David to bestow the bishopric on William Cumin, promising to invest him herself with the ring and staff as soon as she was crowned.[32]

18

'Insufferable Arrogance'

It was essential that Maud win over London to her cause, but she must have known that it would not be easy. Its citizens had supported Stephen because he had granted them privileges and liberties; thanks to him and Matilda, they also enjoyed safe and easy trading access via Boulogne to their important markets on the Continent. The King had been generous to them, and he and the Queen were great patrons of religious houses in the City, where they were well liked, and where, the evidence suggests, they had both built up a network of mutually advantageous relationships.[1] Maud would have to work hard to win the Londoners' favour.

At a conference at St Albans, in June, she made a poor beginning by buying the continuing support of Geoffrey de Mandeville, confirming him in the earldom of Essex, which Stephen had conferred on him, and making him sheriff of London and Essex and justiciar of Middlesex.[2] The Londoners hated him (as noted in Maud's charter granting him the sheriffdom), but she was hoping that, from his strategically placed landholdings in Essex, he would assist her in the expulsion of the Queen's loyal tenants from the honour of Boulogne. In fact she could not have entered London without securing his allegiance, for he was all-powerful there. At this time, she gave a house at Westminster to Miles FitzWalter, of whom it was said, 'he made her queen of all England'.[3]

That summer, in defiance of Stephen and Matilda, she confirmed Waltham Abbey as part of Queen Adeliza's dower, with all the customs the community had enjoyed in the time of her mother, Queen Matilda,[4] and also the gift of the church in Stanton Harcourt that Adeliza had made to Reading Abbey.[5] This was perhaps an olive branch extended in hope of a reconciliation with her stepmother – or perhaps there already had been a reconciliation. Maud maintained her patronage of her father's foundation at Reading, granting several charters in the 1140s, one 'for the peace and stability of the realm'.[6]

England was all but hers. Her chief aim now was to be crowned, and a deputation from London met with her in St Albans, but they were openly hostile towards her, and it took some time and negotiating to persuade them to admit her, for they were jealous of, and fearful for, their liberties, and probably resentful of her appointment of Geoffrey de Mandeville as their sheriff.[7] But her army was camped just north of the City, so they conceded her claim and agreed terms.

When, at last, Maud had received homage from the chief citizens, and taken hostages to ensure that they stayed loyal, 'she had brought the greater part of the kingdom under her sway, and on this account was mightily puffed up and exalted in spirit. Finally she came to London with a vast army, at the request of the inhabitants, who met her with entreaties.'[8] A few days before the Nativity of St John, 24 June, she entered the City,[9] riding in procession to Westminster[10] in the company of Earl Robert, King David and Bishop Henry, and being 'received with honour'[11] by the citizens. Here 'bishops and belted knights assembled with overweening display for the enthronement of their lady'.[12]

London was a great city. In the description of it he wrote thirty years later, William FitzStephen mentions the 'royal citadel' of the Tower to the east, the great fortresses of Baynard and Montfichet to the west, 'the wall, tall and wide', that encircled London, with its seven gates, and the Thames 'well stocked with fish, with tidal flow and ebb. Everywhere, without the houses, the citizens' gardens side by side, yet spacious and splendid and set about with trees. To the north lie arable fields, pasture lands and lush, level meadows with brooks flowing amid them, which turn the wheels of watermills with a happy sound. Close by is a mighty forest with well-timbered copses, lairs of wild beasts, stags and does, wild boars and bulls.' Most of the houses in the crowded streets were built of timber, but some wealthy merchants had erected substantial ones of stone. Within the city walls there were 126 churches and many religious houses. Outside the walls lay the palace of Westminster, which Maud had chosen for her residence; it was now 'a building of the greatest splendour with outwork and bastions'.[13]

The Empress's reception in the City was strained, but the citizens had little choice but to swim with the tide, for by then 'great parts of England had readily submitted' to her government. The see of London had been vacant for three years, but she now nominated a new bishop, Robert de Sigello, a monk of Reading who had been keeper of the King's Seal under Henry I, and who was probably promoted on the recommendation of Bishop Henry, a fellow Cluniac.[14] It was on Bishop Henry's advice that Maud made a grant to St Martin le Grand, the church that had been much favoured by Stephen and Matilda; it was a gesture intended to pacify the citizens. She also granted a charter to her mother's foundation, Holy Trinity, Aldgate, conferring pasture rights.[15]

Maud could have done much more to win over the Londoners, but she disdained to woo them. Instead, she took a high-handed, punitive approach and succeeded in arousing their hostility even further. When, soon after her arrival, 'the citizens thought they had attained to joyous days of peace and quietness, and that the calamities of the kingdom had taken a turn for the better',[16] they appealed to her to restore the laws of King Edward the Confessor because those her father had passed since were so severe. But, refusing to accept good advice, and 'swelling from too much bitterness',[17] Maud 'very harshly rejected their petition, in consequence of which there was a great tumult in the City'.[18]

Then 'she sent for the richest men and demanded from them a huge sum of money, not with unassuming gentleness, but with a voice of authority'[19] – as any king might have been expected to use to recalcitrant subjects. The money was for a tallage – an arbitrary feudal tax – that was to be their punishment for supporting Stephen.

The burghers were appalled. They 'complained that they had lost their accustomed wealth owing to the strife in the kingdom, that they had spent a great deal to relieve the acute famine that threatened them, and that they had always obeyed the King until they were brought to the extremity of want'. Their obedience to Stephen was unlikely to have impressed Maud, and may have angered her. But they humbly petitioned her 'that she might take pity on their misfortune, set a limit to the exaction of money from them and spare the harassed citizens, even for a little while, the burden of any extraordinary payment. Later, when, after the lulling of the disturbances of war throughout the kingdom, peace returned with more security, they would aid her the more eagerly as their own wealth expanded.'

Maud heard them out 'with a grim look, her forehead wrinkled into a frown, with every trace of a woman's gentleness removed from her face'. She 'blazed into insufferable fury, saying that many times the people of London had made very large contributions to the King, that they had lavished their wealth on strengthening him and weakening her, that they had long conspired with her enemies for her hurt, and therefore it was not just to spare them in any respect, or make the smallest deduction from the money demanded.

On hearing this, the citizens went away gloomily to their homes without gaining what they had asked.'[20]

Maud also had good reason to feel aggrieved. The Londoners had supported the usurper Stephen, to her detriment. They had no cause to expect leniency from their rightful sovereign. Immediately, she announced her intention of reversing Stephen's decrees granting the City self-government and privileges, plainly intending to open the door to wider monarchical interference in its affairs. As if this was not enough to incite outrage, she made the further blunder of showing herself 'lifted up to an insufferable arrogance because the hazard of war had favoured her supporters, and she alienated the hearts of almost everyone'.[21]

Meanwhile, Queen Matilda was skilfully exploiting the unrest in London, never letting anyone forget that their anointed King languished in chains, and championing the rights of her son.

'About this time, the Queen sent envoys to the Empress and made earnest entreaty for her husband's release from his filthy dungeon and the granting of his son's inheritance, though only that to which he was entitled by her father's will'[22] – namely the counties of Boulogne and Mortain. The Queen offered herself and Eustace as hostages, as well as castles and great riches, in exchange for Stephen's release.[23] She promised that, if her husband was released, she would personally ensure that he relinquished his claim to the throne. All that mattered to her was that he was safe and free.

Her plea was backed by 'the chief men and greatest nobles of England, who offered to give the Empress many hostages, castles and great riches if the King were to be set free and allowed to recover his liberty, if not the crown. They promised to persuade him to give up the crown, and thereafter live devoted to God alone as a monk or pilgrim.'[24]

The Empress was in no position to seize the Queen's lands, for to do so she would have had to contend with Matilda's loyal tenantry; nevertheless, she refused the request in no uncertain terms. Several romantic paintings and engravings portray her haughtily turning down the supplicant Queen, although it is clear that they did not meet personally at this time, but communicated through Matilda's envoys.

Still Maud remained obdurate. She had good reason, for Stephen had already shown himself capable of breaking a sacred oath, and therefore it was unlikely that he would keep any promises made by the Queen and the lords in his name. 'She would not listen to them, nor would she listen to the Bishop of Winchester's plea that the earldom which belonged to his brother [i.e. the county of Boulogne] should be given to his nephew, the King's son.'[25]

The Queen, facing the fact that bargaining was futile, was now determined to ensure that the Empress was never crowned queen. 'When she was abused in harsh and insulting language, and both she and those who had come to ask on her behalf completely failed to gain their request', Matilda resolved 'to obtain by arms what she could not by supplication'. In Kent, she and William of Ypres had been busily raising a 'magnificent' army of Flemish mercenaries and, in company with him and other lords, she marched on London at the head of her troops and camped on the southern shore of the River Thames, thereby impressing upon the citizens that their support of the Empress could lead to dire consequences. To demonstrate that Maud lacked the resources to protect them, the Queen ordered her forces to 'rage most furiously around the City with plunder and arson, violence and the sword, in sight of the Empress and her men'.[26]

'The people of London were then in grievous trouble.' They watched in impotent terror as the outlying suburbs were 'stripped before their eyes and reduced by the enemy's ravages as a habitation for the hedgehog, and there was no one ready to help them. That new lady of theirs was going beyond the bounds of moderation and sorely oppressing them. They had no hope that in time to come she would have bowels of mercy for them, seeing that, at the very beginning of her reign, she had no pity on her subjects, and demanded what they could not bear.'[27]

But if aggravating the Londoners was one blunder too many on Maud's part, provoking Bishop Henry was a fatal mistake.

William Cumin had come south with King David, ostensibly to persuade Henry to support the right of the canons of Durham freely to elect their bishop. But Henry found out that Maud had already promised the see to Cumin. He and the clergy were outraged. It was clear that, despite her promises, Maud was determined to assert her rights as queen above the liberties of the Church, and did not care that she had reignited the investiture controversy. And this when she had undertaken to defer to Bishop Henry in ecclesiastical matters. Without hesitation, Henry declared Cumin's election irregular (he never did become bishop) and wrote to the Pope seeking his advice.[28]

It was madness on Maud's part to alienate the one man whose support could make or break her. 'The Bishop, seeing these things done without his approval, and a good many others without his advice, was sufficiently vexed and irritated, yet he disguised his feelings with caution and craft, and watched silently to see what end such a beginning would have.'[29]

The Londoners were bitterly regretting abandoning the King who had brought them such advantages. They had exchanged a bountiful ruler for 'the tyranny of usurpers'. Fearful for their property, they were fast concluding that the best course was to ally themselves with Queen Matilda and 'join together with one mind to rescue their King from his chains'.[30] When Matilda's troops laid siege to the Tower, the Londoners sent covert messengers to treat with her.

The wheel of Fortune that so excited the medieval imagination had turned against the Empress. 'If Robert's party had trusted to his moderation and wisdom, it would not afterwards have experienced so melancholy a reverse.' Bishop Henry still 'appeared of laudable fidelity in furthering the interests of the Empress. But behold! At the very moment when she imagined she should get possession of all England, everything was changed. The Londoners, who had always been suspicious and in a state of secret indignation, now burst out into open expressions of hatred',[31] and decided 'to seize upon her dishonourably'.[32] The glaring omission and implication in this passage is that it was Maud who wrecked her own cause, which was why some of her supporters hurriedly abandoned her. According to Henry of Huntingdon and the hostile *Gesta Stephani*, she had only her arrogant mishandling of the Londoners to blame.

On 24 June, when Maud, 'confident of gaining her will, was waiting for the citizens' answer to her demand' for money, all the bells of London were set clanging as a signal for battle, and the 'whole city flew to arms, with the common purpose of making a most savage attack' on the Empress and her forces. The Londoners unbarred Ludgate and surged in an angry body along the Strand towards Westminster, 'like a swarm of bees from a hive'. It was the dinner hour, and Maud, 'with too much boldness and confidence, was just bent on reclining at a well-cooked feast; but on hearing the frightful noise from the City, and getting secret warning from someone about the betrayal on foot against her, she, with all her retinue, immediately sought safety in flight'.[33] The Empress, Earl Robert, Bishop Henry and the King of Scots mounted swift horses, and, 'in short, all her partisans, to a man, escaped in safety'.[34]

'Their flight had hardly taken them further than the suburbs when behold, a mob of citizens, great beyond expression or calculation, entered their abandoned lodgings and found and plundered all that had been left behind in the speed of the unpremeditated departure.'[35] The Empress 'suffered there great loss', but far worse than that, having effectively been driven from London by force,[36] her hopes of being formally acknowledged as queen and crowned had suffered a shattering setback.

19
'Terrified and Troubled'

'When they had thus been frightened away from London, all who favoured the King and were in deep depression from his capture, joyously congratulated each other, as though bathed in the light of a new dawn; and, taking up arms with spirit, attacked the Empress's adherents on every side.' Early in July, Queen Matilda 'was admitted to the City by the Londoners', attended by William of Ypres, and received a warm reception. 'Forgetting the weakness of her sex and a woman's softness, she bore herself with the valour of a man. Everywhere, by prayer or price, she won over invincible allies. She urged the King's lieges, wherever they were scattered throughout England, to demand their lord back to her.'[1]

In every way Matilda was an agreeable contrast to the Empress. To raise funds for the rescue of the King, she negotiated a loan from Gervase of Cornhill, the Justiciar of London, pledging her village of Gamlingay, Cambridgeshire (part of the honour of Boulogne), as security, and granting London greater privileges in return. Thus she bought the support of Geoffrey de Mandeville and secured the Tower. Mandeville had done very well financially from switching his loyalty to the Empress and the Queen in turn, but Matilda allowed him to return to his allegiance because she needed his support. When he tried to excuse his treachery to her, she listened with good grace; soon she would be grateful for his backing.

★

William of Malmesbury asserts that Maud's party had left London 'without tumult, and in a certain military order', but the *Gesta Stephani* relates how they fled in terror and disarray to Oxford with their depleted forces, with many soldiers deserting on the way. 'Though a number of barons had fled with the Empress under the stress of fear, she did not keep them as permanent companions in this disorderly flight. They were so wonderfully shaken by the sudden panic that they quite forgot about their lady, and thought rather of saving themselves by making their own escape and taking different turnings, the first that met them as they fled. They set off for their own lands by a multitude of byroads, as though the Londoners were hot on their heels.'[2]

During their flight, Bishop Henry 'spoke with Earl Robert and the Empress, and swore them oaths that never more would he side with the King. He promised that he would deliver up Winchester' to Maud, and invited her and Robert to join him there.[3]

But then there arose 'a misunderstanding' between Bishop Henry and Maud, one that William of Malmesbury believed could be 'justly considered as the melancholy cause of every subsequent evil in England'. Echoing Queen Matilda's plea, Henry again urged Maud to agree that, for as long as Stephen remained in captivity, the counties of Boulogne and Mortain should be bestowed on Eustace, his heir and the Bishop's nephew. 'This the Empress altogether opposed', possibly because she had promised these lands to others.[4]

This was the end for Henry, who was 'offended by the repulse'.[5] There was a parting of the ways. He cantered off to Winchester, while Maud and Robert 'came at full speed to the city of Oxford'.[6]

Already it was being said that Bishop Henry was 'privy to' the Londoners' plot, and was a secret ally of the Queen, and that he had incited and won over 'the minds and strength of the citizens' to put an end to Maud's pretensions.[7]

'He kept from the Empress's court many days and, though repeatedly sent for, persisted in refusing to go thither.' Furious and disillusioned – he may well have been considering his position since St Albans – he absolved, without consulting any other bishops, all those supporters of Stephen whom he had excommunicated, and ensured that 'his complaints against the Empress were disseminated through England: that she wished to seize his person, that she observed nothing which she had sworn to him, that all the barons of England had performed their engagements to her, but that she had violated hers, as she knew not how to use her prosperity with moderation'.[8]

In the last week of July, desperately trying to establish an accord with the Londoners, Maud ceded her right to intervene in any matters between them and Geoffrey de Mandeville, and granted him even wider powers and more lands in East Anglia. In return, he demanded that her husband, her son Henry and even the King of France should swear to her maintaining faith in this matter.[9] Of course, he knew that was unlikely, and that London was irrevocably lost to her.

Earl Robert realised that Maud could not afford to alienate the Church as well as the Londoners, and hastened to limit the damage she had caused. He rode to Winchester, but could get nowhere with the Bishop. Returning to Oxford, he warned Maud that Henry 'had no friendly dispositions towards her', whereupon, 'with such forces as she could muster',[10] hurriedly raised, she left Oxford on 31 July with Earl Robert and King David, and marched on Winchester 'to catch the Bishop if she could'. Arriving 'before the citizens knew anything of her coming',[11] she was 'immediately admitted into the royal castle'.[12]

Alarmed at intelligence that Maud was planning to bestow Mortain and Boulogne on one of her supporters, the Queen had ridden to Guildford for a 'friendly conference' with Bishop Henry.[13] There she stayed in the round shell keep of Guildford Castle, which she had visited with Stephen in 1136 in happier days. Now she had her son Eustace with her, and he joined in her pleas to Henry to abandon the Empress and help her restore Stephen to the throne. The Queen 'humbly besought the Bishop to take pity on his imprisoned brother and exert himself for his freedom, that, uniting all his efforts with hers, he might gain her a husband, the people a king, the kingdom a champion'.[14]

She so 'wrought upon'[15] Henry that, 'moved by the woman's tearful supplications, which she pressed on him with great earnestness, and by the dutiful compassion for his brother' and the concessions she offered, he 'turned over in his own mind how he could rescue his brother from the ignominy of bondage and most skilfully restore him to his kingdom'.[16] Finally he capitulated, himself weeping, and returned to his allegiance to Stephen, having, he said, been offended by the Empress's intransigence towards the Queen. He vowed to forsake Maud's cause and 'bend his mind to the liberation of Stephen'.[17]

Henry hurried off to Winchester to look to its fortifications, arriving on 31 July to find that Maud had arrived earlier that day and was in residence in the royal castle, 'surrounded by a very large retinue', and that she had with her a large, 'highly equipped'[18] force commanded by King David, Earl Robert and Reginald de Dunstanville. Maud had 'sent out a summons on every side and gathered into a vast army the whole array of those who obeyed her throughout England',[19] much of it probably recruited on the fifty-six-mile journey south from Oxford.

The Bishop took refuge in Wolvesey Castle, 'which he had built in very elegant style in the middle of the town',[20] but hard on his heels came a message from the Empress 'requesting that, as she was upon the spot, he would come to her without delay. Not thinking it safe to go',[21] and correctly suspecting that she was 'cunningly anticipating his craft',[22] he sent back the messenger, saying, 'I will prepare myself', and immediately summoned 'all as he knew were well-disposed towards the King', including the Queen, William of Ypres and those lords 'who were irritated by the disdainful tyranny of the woman', begging them to march on Winchester to relieve him.[23] 'In consequence, almost all the earls of England came, for they were full of youth and levity, and preferred military enterprise to peace. Few, however, attended the Empress.'[24]

The Queen, accompanied by Eustace, William of Ypres and Geoffrey de Mandeville, led 'all her strength' to Winchester,[25] riding at the head of her Kentish troops and 'an invincible band' of a thousand angry Londoners, magnificently equipped with 'helmets and coats of mail'. She arrived before the city late on 31 July, to find that Bishop Henry had already fled, having 'mounted a swift horse and made off to his castles at full speed'.[26]

Maud now gave orders 'for a most rigorous investment of the Bishop's castle'. On 2 August, Earl Robert, Brian FitzCount and Miles FitzWalter besieged the garrison in Wolvesey Castle 'with concentrated strength',[27] and all Maud's supporters, 'with wonderful concentrations of large forces from every quarter, devoted themselves alike to the siege with one mind and the same unflagging zeal'.[28]

It was a rash move on Maud's part, for the Queen, in turn, block-aded Winchester, 'besieging the inner ring of besiegers from outside with the greatest energy and spirit'. In this venture, 'she obtained the aid of the legate Henry, and the Londoners, and a great number of the nobles of the kingdom, who assembled from day to day, with whom also was Ranulf, Earl of Chester'.[29] Matilda had all roads leading into the city watched, lest supplies be smuggled in to the Empress. Anyone found attempting to do that was killed or maimed.[30] London kept the Queen and her army well supplied; the citizens 'were making the greatest efforts, and not letting slip a single thing that lay in their power whereby they might distress the Empress'.[31] 'This was a remarkable siege: nothing like it was ever heard of in our times. The whole of England, together with an extraordinary number of foreigners, was there in arms.'[32]

Bishop Henry, having sent 'all over England for the barons who had obeyed the King', and also hired 'ordinary knights at very great expense, devoted all his efforts to harassing the Empress's forces outside the town'. He had received Papal endorsement of his actions, for Pope Innocent II had written urging him to use every means in his power to restore King Stephen.[33] Nevertheless, he was castigated by Henry of Huntingdon – and no doubt others – as 'a new kind of monster, compounded of purity and corruption'.

On 2 August, Henry's besieged garrison 'flung out firebrands' from Wolvesey Castle, which started a conflagration 'and completely reduced to ashes the greater part of the town'.[34] The royal abbeys of Hyde and Nunnaminster, founded by King Alfred and his wife, were destroyed, along with twenty churches, with much loss of life, as was the greater part of the royal castle built by the Conqueror.[35] The blaze also seriously depleted food supplies stored in the city. Some accused Bishop Henry of personally starting the fire.[36]

The siege lasted for nearly two months. 'The people of Winchester were – though secretly – inclined to the Empress's side, and rather wished success to her than to the Bishop.'[37] Maud sent three hundred knights to take Wherwell Abbey, which lay ten miles from Winchester, hoping to establish a base from which they could overcome the Queen's forces, but William of Ypres, learning that they were there, burned the church and took the Empress's men captive.[38]

In the end, rampant disease and a scarcity of food and drink settled the deadlock. 'The people were suffering very severely from wasting hunger and lack of food.'[39] Even Maud 'suffered the gravest ills of a long-lasting siege'.[40] When she and her courtiers could endure it no longer, Earl Robert 'despaired entirely of continuing the siege, and thought of seeking safety in flight as soon as they could. So they assembled their baggage', and on Sunday 14 September, he 'deemed it expedient to yield to necessity' and ordered his forces to leave the beleaguered city.[41] By now, Maud was desperate 'to change location and rest her troubled mind more comfortably somewhere else'.[42] John of Worcester claims that Bishop Henry sent orders that the gates of Winchester be opened to her. Possibly Henry was hoping for an opportunity to capture her and Robert.

The Empress and her party 'were emerging from the gates together, when the King's army, in numbers beyond expression, surrounded them on every side, charged them heavily and unflinchingly, and scattered them in different directions'.[43] Maud escaped unscathed, Robert having placed her 'in the vanguard, that she might proceed without interruption. Thus they departed from Winchester',[44] as Robert, commanding the rearguard, kept the royal forces at bay, suffering heavy losses in the process, so that Maud could make good her escape. She, 'always superior to feminine softness, with a mind steeled and unbroken in adversity, was the first to fly', noted the hostile author of the Gesta Stephani.

Bishop Henry 'ordered his men to assemble to arms, rigorously pursue the enemy, seize them and kill them. And so the followers of the Bishop, leaping up, with great force and uproar attacked those departing, killed them, clove them, and bound quite a few captives in chains. Terrified, the Empress flew most swiftly.'[45]

'The retreat became a flight, the flight a rout.' Archbishop Theobald, who had joined Maud in Winchester, 'could scarcely escape to safe hiding places'.[46] In the melee, Maud was separated from all her escort apart from Brian FitzCount, but they managed to link up with Reginald de Dunstanville. Together with 'servants and many friends',[47] they fled the city, their flight becoming known as 'the Rout of Winchester'.[48] Even Maud, who was 'always breathing a spirit of unbending haughtiness, was greatly shaken.[49] She was riding side-saddle, 'as women do', but it hindered progress, so she was persuaded to ride astride.[50]

That night, she sought refuge at John the Marshal's castle at Ludgershall, twenty-four miles from Winchester. John had enthusi-astically supported her since joining her at Reading, and had been partially blinded when the church of Wherwell was burned.[51] Maud arrived 'very much terrified and troubled',[52] appearing 'sorrowful and breathless'.[53] She found Ludgershall 'no safe resting place because of her fear of the Bishop'.[54] 'Whereupon, all her friends urging, she was placed upon a horse with manly skill and carried all the way to Devizes.'[55]

Just twenty-four miles behind her, the Londoners were sacking Winchester without mercy.[56]

20

'Rejoicing and Exultation'

Maud's remaining forces were routed by the Queen's. King David was captured three times, but managed to bribe his captors and, at length, escaped and fled north. He would have realised that, with London, Winchester and the Church lost to her, Maud's cause was irretrievably defeated.

Earl Robert had fought his way northwards, making for Gloucester, and tried to mount another diversionary attack at Stockbridge, to give Maud time to get away safely.[1] But, while attempting to cross the River Test, he was captured by William de Warenne, 3rd Earl of Surrey, and some Flemish mercenaries,[2] and brought to Winchester, where he was presented to the Queen by Bishop Henry.[3]

The taking of Robert cost Maud any advantage she had. Without her chief commander and mainstay, she could do nothing.

'Even at the moment of his capture, no one perceived the Earl either dispirited or humbled. He seemed so far to tower above fortune that he compelled his persecutors to respect him. Wherefore the Queen, though she might have remembered that her husband had been fettered by his command, never suffered any fetters to be put on him, nor presumed on her dignity to treat him dishonourably.' She placed him in the custody of William of Ypres, and herself accompanied them to Rochester Castle, where Robert was to be held. Within its walls, she allowed him to move freely wherever he pleased, to attend 'the churches below the castle, and to converse with anyone he chose', insisting only that she herself was present at any discussions. After her departure, he was held 'in free custody' in the keep, and was even allowed to buy horses.[4]

There was no question of Robert being executed. He was far too valuable a captive, who could be used as a bargaining counter or ransomed for a fortune. At Rochester, the earls loyal to the Queen tried in vain to win him over to her cause, offering to liberate him in exchange for the King. His wife, the Countess Mabel, 'would have embraced those terms the moment she heard them, yet he, in wiser policy, refused'.[5]

'Twenty earls would not be of sufficient importance to ransom a king,' he told her. 'How then, my lady, can you expect that I should so far forget the interest of the Empress, my sister, as to propose that she should exchange him for only one?' He would consent, he said, only on condition that all who had been taken with him were freed. The barons would not agree to this; 'they were anxious for the King's liberty, but not their own pecuniary loss', for they intended to ransom their noble captives.

Instead, 'they anxiously endeavoured to seduce the Earl with magnificent promises'. If he would abandon his sister, and allow Stephen to be reinstated as titular king, he could rule England in his name. He refused. They offered him the office of justiciar if he would work for a peace settlement whereby Stephen would have England and the Empress Normandy.[6]

'I am not my own master,' he told them, 'but I am in another's power.' He insisted he could not agree to any proposal without the Empress's agreement, and said he doubted she would ever sanction such terms. Seeing they could not persuade him by fair means, the earls threatened to send him across the sea to Boulogne and 'keep him in perpetual bondage till death'. Still wearing 'a serene coun-tenance', Robert protested that 'he feared nothing less', and warned that, if they carried out their threat, his partisans would send the King to Ireland.[7]

Matilda's attitude hardened. Robert had broken his oath of alle-giance to Stephen, she reminded him, and his life was forfeit. Robert countered that his first oath of allegiance had been to Maud; in regard to that which he had sworn to Stephen, he had come to see the error of his ways, even if Stephen had not. For Stephen had also sworn an oath to Maud. It was he who was the oath-breaker.[8]

Matilda knew it was the truth. She saw that she would get nowhere with Robert. Throughout his captivity and beyond, 'numberless and magnificent promises' were made to entice him to abandon his sister, 'yet he always deemed his fraternal affection of greater importance'.[9]

By now, Maud's host had dispersed far and wide, pursued by the royal forces. 'Plunder of incalculable value was scattered everywhere for the taking. You could have seen fine chargers straying about after throwing their riders, fainting from weariness and at their last gasp; sometimes shields and coats of mail and arms of every kind lying everywhere strewn on the ground; sometimes tempting cloaks and vessels of precious metal, with other valuables, flung in heaps.'[10]

In 1140, Earl Robert had secured Devizes Castle for his sister, hanged the sadistic Robert FitzHubert, and returned the magnificent, impregnable stronghold built by Bishop Roger to the diocese of Salisbury. On 15 September, Maud reached the safety of Devizes, accompanied by Brian FitzCount and 'a few others'. She was 'worn out, almost to the point of utter collapse'.[11]

While Maud and her party were recovering from their ordeal, Miles FitzWalter arrived, alone, half-naked and dropping with fatigue, his armour and weapons cast away in his flight,[12] and informed them that Robert had been taken. It was crushing news, with the gravest implications. They all knew that without Robert, Maud's cause was lost.

But she herself had more immediate concerns. She was still suffering from extreme fatigue, and 'terrified that she would not be safe' at Devizes. It was decided that they would press on to Gloucester Castle, but she was 'now nearly dead' and too exhausted to sit on a horse, so 'she was carried on a bier and, like a corpse, tied with ropes to horses bearing her'.[13] When they arrived in Gloucester, she was faint from fasting for so long, and still in great fear. Miles FitzWalter urged her to go to Oxford, which was strategically situated and the scene of her former triumph, but she would not – not yet.

Reduced in circumstances as she was, she proved as obstinate as her brother when it came to negotiating a settlement, and refused to agree to an exchange of the prisoners, King Stephen and Earl Robert. Instead she offered Queen Matilda twelve earls she was holding captive and a substantial sum in gold in return for the release of Robert.

Matilda had worked ceaselessly for the release of her husband, putting pressure on those who had influence with Maud. In the end, she chose to deal with the Countess Mabel, who was chatelaine of Earl Robert's castle at Bristol, where Stephen was being held. 'The Queen worked hard on the King's behalf, and the Countess of Gloucester on the Earl's, many messengers and reliable friends going to and fro.' Matilda warned Mabel that, if her wishes were not speedily heeded, she would send Robert to Boulogne and have him straitly held in one of her castles there. After some tough negotiations, 'it was finally agreed on both sides that the King should be restored to the royal dignity, and the Earl should be raised to the government of England under the King, and that both should be just rulers and restorers of peace just as they had been instigators and authors of dissension and upheaval'.[14]

Maud, who was escorted in safety to Bristol in October by Robert de Beaumont, would not agree to this, but was finally persuaded to sanction a solution to the impasse. In the end, an unconditional exchange was agreed upon, 'at the insistence' of the Queen.[15] It deprived Maud of any real chance of becoming queen – and indeed, as soon as he was at liberty, Stephen would declare her deposed.

Matilda and her sons hastened to Bristol, arriving on All Saints Day, 1 November. On that day, after nine months in captivity, Stephen was entirely restored to his liberty, 'to great rejoicings'.[16] It was a brief reunion. Under the terms of the agreement, he had to leave his wife and boys at Bristol in the charge of 'two men of high rank', as hostages for the liberation of Earl Robert. Stephen sped to Winchester. Apprised of the King's arrival there, Robert's gaolers freed him, and he left Rochester 'with quick despatch' for Bristol, leaving his heir, William, with Stephen at Winchester as surety for the Queen's release. As soon as he arrived, on 4 November, he liberated Queen Matilda and the two princes, and on their return to Winchester, William was set at liberty. Earl Robert exchanged brief courtesies with Stephen, telling him that he had opposed him only on a matter of principle,[17] then the King was welcomed by a throng of supporters with 'cries of rejoicing and exultation that he was restored to them unharmed'.[18]

The Empress, who had now 'recovered her health', retreated to Oxford with 'a strong body of soldiers',[19] and there she 'fixed her residence and held her court'. Robert joined her. 'Leaving his property and his castles, he continued unceasingly near her.'[20] By entrenching herself at Oxford, where she had once been victorious, Maud was proclaiming to the world that she had not abandoned hopes of a revival of her cause and was determined to fight on.

In November, Stephen and Matilda entered London in triumph. She had been tireless in his cause, and he had much for which to be thankful to her. Now, he rewarded her by bestowing that which she wanted more than anything. 'In the presence of the magnates, he ceremonially girded with the belt of knighthood his son Eustace, a young man of noble nature, and after most bountifully endowing him with lands and possessions, and giving him the special distinction of a most splendid retinue of knights, advanced him in rank to the dignity of count of Boulogne.'[21]

Many of the clergy had willingly reverted to their allegiance to the King, although Bishop Henry now had some explaining to do.

On 7 December, as Papal legate, he assembled a council at Westminster, which hastily concluded that Stephen was the rightful King after all, and that anyone who had sworn fealty to Maud was not bound by his oath.[22]

Maud sent one layman to the council, who openly forbade the Bishop, 'by the faith he had pledged to her, to ordain anything in that council repugnant to her honour'. He pointed out that Henry had sworn not to assist her against his brother; that her coming to England had been effected by the Bishop's frequent letters; and that her taking the King and holding him in captivity had been done 'principally by his connivance'. Maud's advocate stressed this 'with great harshness of language, by no means sparing the legate', but the Bishop 'could not be prevailed upon, by any forces of argument, to lay aside his animosity'.[23]

Henry protested that he had supported 'the Countess of Anjou' against his will. 'In truth he had received her, not from inclination, but compulsion, for that she had surrendered Winchester with her party, that she had obstinately persevered in breaking every promise she had made pertaining to the right of the Church, and that he had it from unquestionable authority that she and her partisans not only had designed on his dignity, but even on his life.' Thankfully, 'God, in His mercy, had caused matters to fall out contrary to her hopes, so that he might avoid destruction himself and rescue his brother from bondage'.[24] He was exaggerating, of course, for he had been in league with Maud before she invaded England, and there is no evidence for a plot on his life. But he had much at stake, and was determined to protect his interests at all costs. Not for nothing did Bernard of Clairvaux, one of the towering religious figures of the twelfth century, call Henry 'the man who walks behind Satan, the son of perdition, the man who disrupts all rights and laws'.

The Bishop called on everyone present to swear fealty to Stephen, and warned that Maud and those who had 'disturbed the peace' in her favour should be excommunicated, since they were in breach of the Pope's judgements. Thus Maud, 'conceiving that she might now perhaps experience some little respite, became again involved in calamity'.[25]

At Christmas, as his subjects 'rejoiced on recovering their King', Stephen, 'gratefully coming at the Nativity of the Lord together with the Queen and the chief nobles, was crowned on that same holy solemnity in Christ Church [Canterbury Cathedral] by the venerable Theobald; the Queen herself wore a gold crown on her head with him in that place'.[26] This makes it clear that this was not just a crown-wearing, but that Stephen had chosen to reassert and reaffirm his authority and sanctity as king by a second coronation. He had a coin struck to mark his restoration; it depicted full-length figures of the King and Queen, in acknowledgement that he owed his crown to Matilda.

21

'The Lawful Heir'

There followed a long period of stasis, possibly because Stephen's health had been undermined by his long imprisonment. 'The respective parties of the Empress and the King conducted themselves with quiet forbearance from Christmas to Lent, anxious rather to preserve their own than to ravage the possessions of others. Lent gave all a respite from war.'[1] At Canterbury, the Queen issued a charter to Geoffrey de Mandeville, granting that he could retain all that the Empress had bestowed on him as long as he remained loyal to Stephen.[2] From Oxford Maud issued a charter to St Benet's Abbey at Holme, Norfolk.

In the new year of 1142, further attempts were made to wean Earl Robert from the Empress's cause, but he remained loyal to her, affirming 'that it was neither reasonable nor natural that he should desert his sister, whose cause he had justly espoused'; moreover, he had been 'enjoined by the Pope to respect the oath he had taken to her in the presence of his father'.[3]

In the middle of Lent, a truce was agreed, and Maud and her train moved to Devizes Castle. Some of Stephen's supporters came seeking her there, offering their alleigiance. At Devizes, she lived on the revenues of the lands that were loyal to her, thanks to the assist-ance of supportive sheriffs, some of whom she appointed within her western power base. She had coins minted at Bristol and Cardiff. She made grants of royal estates. She granted a charter giving the collegiate chapel of St George in Oxford Castle to Osney Priory, to which she had already made benefactions in a charter of March 1141.[4] She also granted five charters to Godstow Abbey, which she took under her protection. King Stephen and Queen Matilda were also among its benefactors.[5]

At Devizes, Maud convened a council of war at which 'her secret designs were debated'. Soon it was known that 'all her partisans had agreed to send for the Count of Anjou, who was most interested in the defence of the inheritance of his wife and children in England'.[6]

Up until now, Geoffrey of Anjou had played no part in English politics, having been busy in Normandy taking advantage of Stephen's captivity, after which many Norman castles had surrendered to him. He had taken all of Normandy south of the Seine, and breached many of its northern defences in his inexorable march to conquer it. As Stephen had been in no position to fight back, most of the many English barons who held lands in Normandy had felt it expedient to safeguard their estates by offering allegiance to Geoffrey. Among them was Waleran de Beaumont.[7] This augured well for Maud's cause.

Taking her supporters' advice, she dispatched 'men of respectability' to Anjou to ask Geoffrey to come to her aid.[8]

Although the kingdom was unsettled and there were sporadic skirmishes, after Easter the King and Queen departed on a progress to York,[9] where Ranulf, Earl of Chester, made a superficial peace with the King. Stephen was making efforts to re-establish his regal authority, but during the Easter holidays he was 'detained by an acute disease at Northampton'. It was 'so severe that he was reported, almost throughout England, as being at the point of death'.[10] He had summoned a great army to attend him at York, but lacked the strength or will to deploy it, and it had to be stood down.

Had Stephen died then, the crown would almost certainly have been Maud's, and she would have been prepared for it, for she had been 'strengthening and encouraging her garrison to resist the King'. Sending 'a great many troops of cavalry to plunder in every direction, she earnestly besought, by letter and message, those who were bound to her by faith and homage to lend their best support to her enterprise'. She 'fortified castles in various places, wherever she most conveniently could, some to keep the King's men more effectively in check, some to give her own more careful protection'. Among them were Woodstock, Radcot, Cirencester and Bampton. 'A good many others in different parts of England she allowed her adherents to fortify, the result being a most grievous oppression of the people, a general depopulation of the kingdom, and the sprouting everywhere of seeds of war and strife.'[11]

But any rejoicing on the part of Maud and her supporters was premature. Stephen was well on the way to recovery by 7 June,[12] and on 23 June the Queen felt able to cross the Channel with Eustace and hold court in her town of Lens, where she had perhaps gone to raise a force of mercenaries. 'By the concession and command of my lord, King Stephen, for the good of our souls and our relatives', she granted a charter 'to God and the church of Saint-Nicholas of Arrouaise, which is in the hand of Dom Gervase the Abbot, a religious man and our dear friend, for the use of the abbot and canons fighting for God there'.[13]

The 'men of respectability' duly returned from Anjou and, on 14 June, saw the Empress in council at Oxford,[14] whither she had returned. They told her that her husband 'in some measure favoured the mission of the nobility, but that, among them all, he was only well acquainted with the Earl of Gloucester'. If Robert would make a voyage to see him, 'he would, as far as he were able, accede to his wishes'. It sounded lukewarm, but Geoffrey had his hands full trying to conquer Normandy for Maud.[15]

'The hopes of the assembly thus excited, they entreated that the Earl would condescend to undertake this task on account of the inheritance of his sister and nephews. At first he excused himself.' He was worried that Maud would be endangered by his absence, as those who had nearly deserted her during his captivity could not be relied upon to defend her − and maybe he did not hold out much hope of Geoffrey coming to her aid. But at length he yielded, demanding that hostages accompany him to Normandy, and insisting 'that all continuing at Oxford should unite in defending the Empress from injury to the utmost while he was absent. His propositions were eagerly approved, and hostages given to him to be conducted into Normandy.'[16]

That June, Maud tried to win back Geoffrey de Mandeville to her cause. She saw him in Oxford, where he obtained from her charters in favour of himself and his brother-in-law, Aubrey de Vere. She promised him Stortford Castle if Robert de Sigello, Bishop of London, could be persuaded to exchange it for another castle, while Aubrey was to have Colchester Castle, Maud declared, 'as soon as I am able to grab hold of it'.[17] These charters proved worthless. The castles of Stortford and Colchester were strategically placed for another descent on London, but Maud's power did not extend to Essex, where they were situated. It was at this time that she bestowed the earldom of Oxford on Aubrey de Vere. Mandeville was merely keeping his options open, while remaining – outwardly at least – on Stephen's side.

Later in June, Earl Robert bade farewell to his sister at Oxford Castle and marched to Wareham, Dorset, whence he sailed for Normandy, arriving on 24 June and making for Caen.[18] Stephen immediately raised another army to burn and blockade Wareham to prevent Robert's return, then, having heard of Maud's mustering of her supporters and their depredations, 'vigorously and boldly he shook himself out of sluggish inaction' and with a large force took back the castles of Cirencester, Bampton and Radcot.[19] That accomplished, taking advantage of Robert's absence, he marched on Oxford.

At Caen, Robert met up with Count Geoffrey, who came to the meeting 'without reluctance, but stated his difficulties, and those not a few', chiefly that he would be prevented from coming to England 'by the rebellion of many castles in Normandy'. This rebellion was to delay Robert's return longer than he had intended, 'for, that he might deprive the Count of Anjou of every excuse, he assisted him in subduing ten castles in Normandy. Yet, even by this activity, he furthered the end of his mission but little.' Geoffrey 'stated fresh causes, as the former were done away with', to excuse his coming into England. However, he did furnish Robert with a company of 'knights ready for action' and, 'as a very singular favour, he permitted his eldest son by the Empress to accompany his uncle to England, by whose presence the chiefs might be encouraged to defend the cause of the lawful heir'.[20] The timely appearance of young Henry FitzEmpress would remind people in England that the right line of Henry I would be continued in Maud's son.

Already it is clear that Geoffrey had come to regard the fight for the English crown as his son's rather than his wife's. This, still, was not how Maud saw it. Her cause was effectively lost, but she could not accept it. All her acts hitherto had been those of a queen regnant, while a charter she issued that year to Bordesley Abbey, Worcestershire, was headed: 'Maud, Empress, daughter of King Henry and Lady of the English, to the archbishops, bishops, abbots, earls, barons, justices, sheriffs and all the faithful of England ...'[21]

Geoffrey's inability to come to her aid was another factor that undermined Maud's cause. Had the barons seen her husband at the head of her forces, a man with whom they could deal on men's terms, her campaign might have been immeasurably boosted, especially since her opponents regarded and disparaged her followers as effeminate lightweights whose chief aim was 'wanton delights rather than resolution of mind'.[22] Maud may have alienated many barons because she acted independently of her husband, although she had little choice in the matter. In the eyes of male contemporaries, she had behaved in an imperious, unwomanly fashion, while at the same time manifesting the weaknesses of her sex. Queen Matilda, on the other hand, had shown herself as tough and thrusting as Maud, and men had praised her 'manly courage',[23] yet she had retained support because she had acted in Stephen's name, and won sympathy because she had had to act alone while he was imprisoned.[24]

22

'One of God's Manifest Miracles'

The Empress had spent the summer entrenched at Oxford with her diminished court,[1] attended by the faithful Brian FitzCount, Miles FitzWalter, John the Marshal and his brother William, who was serving as her chancellor. Oxford was 'a city very securely protected, inaccessible because of the very deep water that washes it all around, most carefully encircled by the palisade of an outwork on one side, and on another finely and very strongly fortified by an impregnable castle and a tower of great height'. But on 16 September, 'behold, the King approached with a large and well-trained army, and appeared suddenly on the other side of the river [Thames]'.[2] The shock of seeing him there must have been great.

Yet Maud had with her 'a magnificent body of troops' and 'felt excessive confidence in herself and her men because the castle and all the country around were under her authority; and also because of the impregnable fortifications of the place'.[3]

Stephen camped before the castle for ten days, 'seeking the Empress's surrender rather than that of the town'.[4] Maud's soldiers jeered at him and the royal army, using 'insulting language, and some were doing grievous harm to his men from the other side of the river by vigorous archery'. But on 26 September, being shown a deep ford across Castle Mill Stream, Stephen swam across, 'plunging in the foremost' and compelling his men to follow. Dripping wet, he and his forces 'charged the enemy'. Pushing them back to the city gates, he attacked, prompting them to flee into Oxford, leaving the gates wide open. The King's men surged in 'without resistance', threw torches into the houses and fired the town,[5] blocking any chance of escape and forcing Maud to shut herself up in the castle 'with all her domestic goods' and her household troops.[6]

'With determined resolution',[7] Stephen now laid the castle under siege, 'thinking he could easily put an end to the strife in the kingdom if he forcibly overcame her through whom it began to be at strife'. He posted vigilant guards in strategic vantage points, to watch the approaches closely 'night and day'.[8] He made it known that 'no hope of advantage or fear of loss should induce him to depart till the castle was delivered up and the Empress surrendered to his power'.[9] He would not let her go free as he had at Arundel.

Meanwhile, Brian FitzCount and all the other nobles of Maud's party, 'ashamed at being absent from their sovereign in violation of their compact' with Earl Robert, 'assembled in large bodies at Wallingford with the determination of attacking the King, if he would risk a battle in the open plain; but they had no intention of assailing him within the city, as the Earl of Gloucester had so fortified it with ditches that it appeared impregnable, unless by fire'.[10] What they were hoping to do was rescue Maud.

Queen Matilda had remained in Boulogne and its environs. It was probably in the autumn of 1142 that she was reunited with Abbot Bernard of Clairvaux at the Cistercian abbey of Clairmarais, near Saint-Omer, which she had Stephen had perhaps co-founded with Thierry of Alsace, Count of Flanders, and his wife, Sybilla of Anjou, after Thierry returned from a pilgrimage to Jerusalem in 1139.[11] Matilda had insisted that this abbey was to be as much her foundation as the King's, and Stephen confirmed that.[12]

As soon as Matilda arrived back in England, in the autumn of 1142, she was plunged again into the turmoil of the civil war. Stephen needed reinforcements at Oxford, and it was her task to raise them from her own tenantry. Having risen to the occasion with her usual efficiency, she arrived in Oxford 'with all her forces' to assist the King. But blockading the castle was proving no easy enterprise. Maud and her small garrison were holding out. The siege lasted just over two months, from Michaelmas to Advent. By then, since 'food and every means of sustaining life were almost exhausted in the castle, and the King was toiling with spirit to reduce it by force and siege engines', Maud was very hard pressed and 'altogether hopeless that help would come'.[13]

Hearing of Maud's plight, Robert had hastened his return from Normandy, accompanied by Henry FitzEmpress and between 3,000 and 4,000 men assigned to him by Geoffrey. He had stormed into Wareham and seized it, and on 29 November, at the beginning of Advent, he 'summoned the whole of Maud's partisans to Cirencester, where all resolved to afford their sovereign every possible assistance'. It was decided that they should march on Oxford to 'give the King battle, unless he retreated'. But on the way, at the beginning of December, they received 'pleasing' news.[14]

Maud had escaped, pulling off what Henry of Huntingdon disparagingly described as 'a woman's trick'; but, as William of Malmesbury observed, 'necessity discovers means and ministers courage'. 'Very hard-pressed as she was, and altogether hopeless that help would come, she left the castle by night', with only three or four 'knights of ripe judgement to accompany her'.[15] William of Malmesbury thought her escape 'one of God's manifest miracles'.[16] 'Deceiving the eyes of the besiegers' by 'wearing white garments'[17] to camouflage themselves against the blizzard, she and her escort were let down from St George's Tower by ropes.[18] It was an 'evident sign of a miracle'[19] that she had managed to 'trick the besiegers' eyes in the dazzle of the snow'.[20]

'Unhindered and unharmed', Maud walked out of the castle through a small postern and 'crossed, dry-footed, without wetting her clothes at all, the very waters that had risen above the heads of the King and his men', which had frozen over. She and her companions got past the King's pickets,[21] who were everywhere, and 'breaking the silence of the night with the blaring of trumpeters or the cries of men shouting loudly';[22] 'but no one was any the wiser except for one man on the King's side who knew of her escape and was the only person to betray it'.[23] She may have bribed him to keep quiet until she had got away, following the course of Castle Mill Stream south to the Thames.

By the time the alarm was raised, Maud was stealthily proceeding on foot across the 'very thick crust of ice' on the River Thames.[24] Even the disapproving author of the *Gesta*

Stephani was impressed: 'I do not know whether it was to heighten the greatness of her fame in time to come, or by God's judgement to increase more vehemently the disturbance of the kingdom, but never have I read of another woman so luckily rescued from so many mortal foes and from the threat of dangers so great.'

Stephen, fortunately, was not a vindictive man. When he learned of Maud's escape, he let the castle garrison leave unmolested. Oxford was his, and he now 'exercised absolute authority over a very wide tract of country in that region'.[25]

In the bitter cold, Maud walked the nine miles to Abingdon,[26] 'by very great exertions on the part of herself and her companions, through the snow and ice, for all the ground was white with an extremely heavy fall of snow'. At Abingdon she acquired horses and rode for Wallingford,[27] and 'by very great effort reached the town during the night', unharmed.[28] The author of the *Gesta Stephani* was amazed by Maud's luck. 'She went from the castle of Arundel uninjured through the midst of her enemies, and escaped without scathe from the midst of the Londoners when they were assailing her in mighty wrath, then stole away alone in wondrous fashion from the rout of Winchester, when almost all her men were cut off; and then, when she left besieged Oxford, came away safe and sound.'

At Wallingford Castle Brian FitzCount readily gave her shelter, and Earl Robert joined her there with her nine-year-old son, Henry FitzEmpress, from whom she had been parted for three years. At the sight of him, 'she was so greatly comforted that she could forget all her troubles and mortifications for the joy she had of his presence'.[29] But their time together was brief. For Henry's safety, she felt it necessary to send him to Robert's city of Bristol, where he would be secure in his uncle's household and continue his military training and education under Robert's captains and a new tutor, Master Matthew, who may have been Maud's chancellor. Under his auspices, and possibly at St Augustine's Abbey in the city,[30] Henry learned Latin and gained a working knowledge of 'all the tongues used from the French sea to the Jordan'.[31] The boy also met Adelard of Bath, who dedicated his work *On the Astrolabe* to him around this time.[32] In Henry rested all Maud's hopes for the future. If she could not win the crown for herself, she would continue her fight to ensure that it passed to him, so that the line of King Henry might be restored.

23
'Wretchedness and Oppression'

Soon afterwards, the Empress moved to Devizes Castle, and made it her headquarters.[1] Here she established her court, presided over by her chamberlain, Drogo of Polwhele.[2] Occasionally, her son Henry visited her there and witnessed her charters, at least one of which was addressed to her faithful subjects,[3] showing that she was still aiming for the throne, even though she had her supporters pay homage to Henry as her heir.

There was some cause for optimism. At this time, many fortresses were still held for her: Chester, Stafford, Tamworth, Dudley, Worcester, Hereford, Abergavenny, Monmouth, Cardiff, Bristol, Gloucester, Cirencester, Marlborough, Trowbridge, Ludgershall, Salisbury, Wallingford, Lincoln, Framlingham, Orford, Bungay, Ramsey and Ely. The castles that were forcibly surrendered to her in 1142–3 were Bath, Wells, Glastonbury, Castle Cary, Taunton, Sherborne, Barnstaple, Dunster, Wilton, Lulworth and Wareham, which provided her with a base for good connections with Normandy and blocked Stephen's links with the West Country.

Maud's power base, therefore, still lay mainly in the west, with a few strongholds elsewhere. With this strength behind her, she saw no reason to give up, and neither did the barons, who had been emboldened and empowered by the civil war, and had a vested interest in prolonging it. The conflict dragged on as a war of attrition, with no end in sight.

In the next few years, 'England began to be troubled in many different ways: on the one hand to be very hard-pressed by the King and his supporters, and on the other to be most violently afflicted by the Earl of Gloucester – but always and everywhere to be in a turmoil and reduced to a desert.' Those that could fled overseas. Others 'lived in fear and suffering', enduring the effects of widespread famine. Villages stood abandoned, harvests went ungathered. Lawless mercenaries whose employers could no longer afford to pay them, and foreign freebooters, committed outrages on the poor, robbing, pillaging and murdering at will. The author of the *Gesta Stephani* deplored the fact that this 'utterly shameful tragedy of woe' was being openly performed all over England. Even the bishops did not dare to 'set themselves up as a wall before the House of Israel'. He meant, of course, the chosen of God, or the House of Blois. Many of the predators shut themselves up in their castles with provisions and stocks of arms; others joined the destroyers. 'All England was wearing a look of sorrow and misfortune, an aspect of wretchedness and oppression.'⁴

Queen Matilda's charters show that, for the five years after her return to England in 1142, she was based chiefly in and around London, keeping a watchful finger on the pulse of affairs, and dealing with state business while Stephen was occupied elsewhere.⁵ She may even have controlled revenues from the Exchequer,⁶ which at this time was not yet established at Westminster.

From 1143, Maud was based mainly at Devizes, Gloucester or Bristol. Her chief mainstay was her brother. Brian FitzCount remained loyal too, and in 1143, in retaliation for Bishop Henry accusing him of looking only to his own interests, he wrote a sharp letter haranguing the Bishop on his own inconsistent loyalties: 'Even you yourself, who are a prelate of Holy Church, have ordered me to adhere to the daughter of King Henry, your uncle, and to help her acquire that which is hers by right, but has been taken from her by force, and to retain what she already has,' he reminded him. 'Be assured that neither I nor my men have done this for money or fee, but only because of your command and for my honour and that of my men.' Bishop Henry had enjoined him to remember the fate of Lot's wife and not look back to the oath he had made to Maud, but he retorted, 'As for Lot and his wife, I never saw them nor knew them, nor their city, nor were they alive at the same time.'⁷

Stephen was now doing his best to regain control of Wiltshire and Dorset, but on 1 July 1143, he and Bishop Henry were routed by Earl Robert's forces near Wilton, which fell to the Empress, leaving the King vulnerable. Yet while Robert still controlled the territory west of Winchester, Maud lacked the power to make decisive inroads on the King's supremacy in the east of the kingdom, where he ruled effectively; her support base was too widely scattered, and she had too few men at her command. It was a bitter blow when Miles FitzWalter was killed in a hunting accident on 24 December 1143. Her cause was irrevocably lost, but still she would not give up.

Her lack of resources became evident when a quarrel erupted between Bishop Henry and William de Pont de l'Arche, who had held Winchester Castle and the royal treasury for the King, but deserted to Maud in 1141. William appealed to Maud for aid, but she could send only a small troop led by a mercenary, Robert FitzHildebrand, who took the castle, put William in chains and seduced his wife, then promptly went over to Bishop Henry and the King.

By 1143, Geoffrey de Mandeville's power had become insupportable, and a threat to the King. He had those regions that were loyal to Stephen so firmly under his control 'that everywhere in the kingdom he took the King's place, and was listened to more eagerly than the King, and received more obedience when he gave orders'. Many resented this, complaining that Mandeville 'had cunningly appropriated all the royal prerogatives', and it was 'commonly reported that he had determined to bestow the kingdom' on the Empress. His detractors urged the King to proceed against him as a traitor. Their persuasions took root, for Stephen had come to fear Mandeville, and how his ambition threatened the Queen's honour of Boulogne, and he had probably not forgotten the unlawful imprisonment of his daughter-in-law Constance in 1141. Yet it was some time before he was stirred to action.[8] Finally, at Michaelmas 1143, he had Mandeville arrested.

Charged with treason, Mandeville was forced to surrender the Tower and his other castles to the Crown in exchange for being spared the noose and set at liberty. He stalked out of the court 'like a vicious and riderless horse, kicking and biting'. Then, 'savage and turbulent as he was, he set the whole kingdom more at variance', and took up arms against the King. With his followers, he resorted to terrorising and plundering Cambridge and the fenland around Ely, 'raging everywhere with fire and sword', seizing Ramsey Abbey and ejecting the monks, so that he could fortify it and use it as his head-quarters. Despite modern attempts to overturn his sinister reputation, the chronicle evidence is clear. He spared no one. 'Fevered with a thirst for brutality that could not be slaked', he committed everywhere acts of 'refined cruelty'.[9] Soon tales of his atrocities spread. They may have been the basis of the descriptions of the tortures inflicted during the Anarchy written by the Anglo-Saxon chronicler at Peterborough, who was well placed to testify to the Earl's reign of terror.

The King declared Mandeville an outlaw and laid siege to Ramsey, but to little effect. Mandeville's depredations were only halted when he received a fatal arrow wound while besieging Burwell, Cambridgeshire. He died excommunicate on 16 September 1144, and was initially refused Christian burial. It was not until twenty years later that the Knights Templar permitted the interment of his remains in their round church in London, where his effigy, clad in a forbidding helm and chain mail and placed there by his son, still survives today. That son, also Geoffrey, remained faithful to Maud, who recognised him as earl of Essex after his father's death.

24
'A New Light had Dawned'

Rouen fell to Geoffrey in January 1144. He had now conquered the duchy in its entirety, and from 19 January he was styled duke of Normandy in right of his wife. Louis VII recognised his title, and on 23 April, Geoffrey was invested as duke in Rouen Cathedral. He was suddenly 'popular with all for accomplishing the acquisition of Normandy',[1] but he was to rule it chiefly as a caretaker for his son, to whom Normandy would descend when the Empress died. In March, young Henry returned to his father's household at Angers, where he would complete his education under the French humanist scholar William of Conches, who praised Geoffrey for encouraging his sons, from their infancy, in the study of letters rather than dice, and for instilling in Henry an enduring love of learning.[2] It was Geoffrey's intention that Henry would 'succeed me in the governance of my land of Normandy',[3] and to that end he began to involve his son in the practical administration of the duchy.[4]

Geoffrey's conquest of Normandy was beneficial to Maud and gave a boost to her cause, for the many English barons who held lands in Normandy were now bound to her as their feudal overlord. If they abandoned her, they risked losing their fiefs. But in 1145, Fortune's wheel turned again, when Stephen scored a victory over the Empress at the Battle of Faringdon, Gloucestershire, which enabled him to cut off communications between her at Wallingford and Earl Robert at Gloucester. Yet still the land remained irrevocably divided, with neither side having the strength to overcome the other. And thus, it seemed, the civil war and all its attendant miseries would go on and on until one of the protagonists died.

By now

there was universal turmoil and desolation. Some, for whom their country had lost its charms, chose rather to make their abode in foreign lands. Others drew to the churches for protection and, constructing mean hovels in their precincts, passed their days in fear and trouble. Food being scarce, there was a dreadful famine throughout England. Some of the people disgustingly devoured the flesh of dogs and horses; others appeased their insatiable hunger with the garbage of uncooked herbs and roots.

There were seen famous cities deserted and depopulated by the death of the inhabitants of every age and sex, and fields ripe for the harvest, but none to gather it, all having been struck down by the famine. Thus the whole aspect of England presented a scene of calamity and sorrow, misery and oppression. These unhappy spectacles, these lamentable tragedies, were common throughout England. The kingdom, which was once the abode of joy, tranquillity and peace, was everywhere changed into a seat of war and slaughter, devastation and woe.[5]

Maud seemed impervious to the havoc that civil war had wrought. She was resolved to fight to the bitter end. That year, hostilities were largely confined to the west, as she made increasingly desperate attempts to retake Malmesbury with forces commanded by William Peverell of Dover and Earl Robert's fourth son, Philip. William Peverell was a follower of Earl Robert and 'a man crafty and bold in warfare'. In subduing the lands of the Thames Valley, and at Malmesbury, he and his mercenaries had 'committed the cruellest excesses on the King's adherents'.

It was William Peverell who, during a skirmish, captured Walter de Pinkney, the royalist constable of Malmesbury, and delivered him up to the Empress. Apparently a war of attrition had been waged between Maud and Walter, for Maud, 'having got possession of the man whom she hated more unrelentingly than any of her opponents, sometimes cajoled him, mingling endearments with her words, and sometimes uttered threats of torture and death if he did not deliver up to her the castle of Malmesbury; but he, most resolutely resisting all she said, could neither be weakened in any degree by the woman's coaxing allurements, nor induced to hand over the castle, though repeatedly assailed with threats. Indeed, he could not have handed it over because his comrades in the King's service, who had withdrawn into the castle when he was taken, would certainly not have agreed, and the King arrived at once, on hearing of Walter's capture, put in reinforcements and a large supply of food, then went away to other tasks.'

Thwarted, Maud 'burnt with one emotion' towards Walter, 'that of cruelty, and after fettering him very tightly, delivered him to torment in a filthy dungeon'.[6] She could not execute him, for he was a friend of Miles FitzWalter's son Roger FitzMiles, who had succeeded him as earl of Hereford; so she contented herself with imprisoning him for a year. In December 1145, overcome with remorse for his part in Walter's fate, William Peverell answered the Pope's call for a second crusade, to expiate his sin.[7] He died in the Holy Land in 1147–8, just one of a number of Maud's supporters who abandoned her to go on crusade.

Before he left, William Peverell had taken Cricklade Castle, and Maud installed Philip of Gloucester there with a strong body of troops. Philip, unlike his father, was 'a man of strife, supreme in savagery, daring in what should not be dared, in fact a perfect master of every kind of wickedness'. He 'raged most furiously' against the King's men in the region, fought battles, pillaged and burned, and plundered Church property. This 'burdensome and unendurable' man frequently had the advantage, for he got aid from his father and Maud's supporters. But, seeing that the King had the upper hand in the war, Philip went over to Stephen, and was rewarded with lands and castles.[8] His desertion was a crushing blow to Maud and his father, as was the defection of Ranulf de Gernon, Earl of Chester, through the possible mediation of Philip, in 1145–6.

Late in 1145, another attempt was made to resolve the conflict. Maud sent Reginald de Dunstanville as an emissary to Stephen, hoping to woo back Philip of Gloucester, but he was taken prisoner by Philip, who was then obliged to set him free when a truce was called. A conference was set up, but 'when the King with his supporters and the Empress with hers met together to establish peace, since an overweening spirit prevailed on each side and both parties courted strife, they accomplished nothing'. Maud's adherents insisted that the throne was hers by hereditary right, while Stephen was adamant that it was his, and 'firmly stated that he would not make them any concession at all'. Negotiations broke down and they 'went back again to their former condition of hostility'.[9]

At Christmas 1146, Stephen held a ceremonial crown-wearing in Lincoln, the scene of his first defeat.[10] He and the Queen stayed in the castle for a few days.[11]

The previous August, showing poor judgement as so often, he had had Ranulf, Earl of Chester, arrested on a trumped-up charge of treason and imprisoned in chains, which drove Ranulf promptly to re-embrace Maud's cause and deterred other would-be defectors from abandoning her. But her support base was decreasing. In 1142–3, thirty-five castles had been held for her. In 1146–7, that number had dwindled to twenty, most of them in the west.[12] Her adherents were falling away too, among them the earls of Pembroke and Hertford, and Nigel, Bishop of Ely.

Late in 1146, Maud sent another plea for aid to her husband. Geoffrey had heard about Earl Ranulf's arrest, and early in 1147 he sent Henry FitzEmpress, now fourteen, to England with a small force. Even the partisan author of the *Gesta Stephani* was now referring to Henry as 'the lawful heir and claimant to the kingdom of England'. Stephen's heir, Eustace, had not yet been knighted. Already he was showing signs of a vicious character, which may not have endeared him to the King's supporters, and may have contributed to the growing consensus that Henry FitzEmpress, the grandson of Henry I, had a better claim to succeed Stephen.

Henry came with a small force of mercenaries, intending to go to the support of his mother, who was then in Wiltshire. 'At his arrival the kingdom was straightway shaken and set in a turmoil, because report stated falsely that he was at the head of many thousand troops, soon to be very many thousand.' His adherents 'joyfully pricked up their ears; it seemed to them a new light had dawned', while the King's supporters, 'as though cowering beneath a dreadful thunderclap', were disheartened. But Henry's mission was not a success. After being trounced twice by adherents of Stephen, running out of funds, and feeling overwhelmed and ashamed, 'he appealed to his mother, but she herself was in want of money and powerless to relieve his great need'. So Henry appealed to Earl Robert, but he, 'brooding like a miser over his moneybags, preferred to meet his own needs only'.[13]

'As all in whom he trusted were failing him', Henry, wanting to get back to Normandy, sent a secret appeal, 'in friendly and imploring terms', to the man he had come to overthrow, his cousin the King. The chivalrous Stephen, 'being ever full of pity and compassion', paid for the boy to go home, but he too had been shaken into turmoil by inaccurate reports that Henry had come at the head of 'many thousand troops' and was plundering and ravaging as he marched, and it was doubtless those rumours that moved him to pay the youth to go away. Many blamed him for acting unwisely and 'childishly' towards 'one to whom he should have been implacably hostile',[14] but maybe, weary of war, Stephen was trying to extend an olive branch to his enemies. Henry left England in May 1147.[15]

Around 1147, Maud gave land to a small community of anchorites established by Stephen at Radmore, Staffordshire, and persuaded them to establish a Cistercian abbey.[16] That year, when Earl Robert founded a Cistercian abbey at Margam in Wales, the devout Nivard, youngest brother of Bernard of Clairvaux, came to England for the dedication ceremony. There is no evidence that Maud attended, but she was in contact with Nivard during his visit.[17]

Stephen had never approved of Maud's appointment of Robert de Sigello as bishop of London, chiefly because Sigello, having sworn allegiance to her, had repeatedly refused to swear an oath of fealty to him. That had led to the Bishop feeling persecuted, and driven him to appeal to Pope Eugenius III. On 6 July 1147, Eugenius wrote to the King pleading Sigello's case, and to Queen Matilda in the hope that she could persuade Stephen to accept a promise of loyalty instead.

On Solomon's testimony, we learn that a wise woman edifies the home, but a foolish one destroys the construction with her hands. We rejoice for you and praise your zeal of devotion in the Lord; we have heard from some religious that you have the fear of God before your eyes, and are intent on works of piety and love, and honour ecclesiastical persons. That you may therefore progress from good to better, with God's inspiration, we ask your nobility in the Lord and asking we instruct and exhort in the Lord, that you join better results to good beginnings, and more attentively love and honour our venerable brother, Bishop Robert of London, out of reverence for him who had been rich in the past, but wanted to become poor for us. With your husband, our beloved son Stephen, the distinguished King of the English, strive to bring about, with instructions, urging, and counsel, that he receive him with benignity and love, and hold him commended out of reverence for St Peter and us. And since, as truth testifies, he cannot bind our aforementioned son without danger to his salvation and position, we wish and counsel you, with paternal affection for him and you, that it be sufficient for you to accept his promise with true and simple words, that he will not bring hurt or harm to him or his land.[18]

Matilda was evidently successful, for Robert de Sigello remained in post until his death in 1150.

25

'An Example of Fortitude and Patience'

The Empress lost her greatest champion and commander when Earl Robert died of a fever on 31 October 1147, at Bristol. William of Malmesbury felt that, 'for his steadfast loyalty and distinguished merit', his patron the Earl 'pre-eminently deserved that the recollection of him shall live for all time'.

Her brother's death was a terrible blow to Maud. Even though she was 'an example of fortitude and patience',[1] she now had to face up to the fact that the crown would never be hers. For all her efforts, she had never borne or received the title of queen.[2] She could not maintain herself in England without Robert's help. Joscelin de Bohun, the new Bishop of Salisbury, had demanded the return of her chief place of refuge, Devizes Castle, and late in 1146 Pope Eugenius III had backed him, threatening anathema to anyone unjustly depriving him of his castle.[3]

With her other supporters falling away and wearily giving up the fight, Maud came to the decision to leave England for good. She hung on at Devizes until February 1148, when she travelled south to Arundel – which must have evoked bitter memories of the hopes she had cherished when she first came there in 1139 – and there took ship for Normandy, leaving behind the faithful and now ageing Brian FitzCount, who was himself soon to die, and may have taken monastic vows in his last months.[4] Around 1145–50 Maud granted the manor of Blewbury to Reading Abbey for the souls of her ancestors and the love and loyal service of Brian FitzCount.[5]

The ruthless Geoffrey Plantagenet,
Count of Anjou.

ROBERT CONSUL, EARL OF GLOUCESTER,
in St James's Church, Bristol.

Robert, Earl of Gloucester, loyal mainstay
of the Empress Maud.

Norman keep of
[A]ndel Castle, where
[E]mpress Maud sought
[shelt]er with Queen Adeliza
[in 11]39.

Stone heads, probabl[y] Adeliza and her sec[ond] husband, Wil[liam] d'Albini, on either [side] of the east wind[ow,] Boxgrove Priory, Sus[sex.]

Head said to represent Matilda of Boulogne, from Furness Abbey.

Victorian engraving of Matilda o[f] Boulogne, based on the stone head[.]

King Stephen's brother, the wily Henry of Blois, Bishop of Winchester.

Above: The Empress
Maud: modern
illustration showing the
kind of dress she would
have worn.

Left: The great Norman
cathedral at Winchester,
where Maud was
received as 'Lady of the
English' in 1141.

Seal of the Empress Maud.

Artist's impression of the Empress Ma[...]
based on her seal.

Coin showing Stephen and Matilda of Boulogne,
struck to mark the King's restoration in 1141.

t George's Tower, Oxford Castle, from which Maud descended by ropes in 1142.

One of many popular images of Maud, camouflaged in white, making her miraculous escape from Oxford.

t: Wallingford Castle, *re* Maud sought refuge the devoted Brian Count.

t: The wall *rc*ling the mound the gatehouse are *at* remain of the *ty* Devizes Castle, *d's* headquarters *everal* years.

Hedingham Castle, Essex,
where Matilda of Boulogne died.

Golden, jewel-studded reliquary cross fr
the abbey of Valasse, of German work, sai
have been the gift of the Empress Mau

Interior of the keep, showing the largest surviving Romanesque arch in Britain.

Henry II and Eleanor of Aquitaine: contemporary stained glass in Poitiers Cathedral commemorating their marriage in 1152.

The marriage of Maud's granddaughter Matilda to Henry the Lion, Duke of Saxony, in 1168. this manuscript illustration, Maud appears posthumously, standing beside her son Henry II on the right, and taking precedence as empress over Queen Eleanor, who is behind her.

Henry II quarrelling w[...]
Archbishop Thomas Bec[...]
Maud tried to brok[...]
peace between th[...]

Right: The chapel of Saint-Julien at Petit-Quevilly, founded by Henry II in 1160, and adorned with frescoes that may have been commissioned by Maud.

Left: Rouen Cathed[...]
where Maud's rem[...]
were reinterred in 1[...]

Few noticed Maud's departure; it was recorded by just one chronicler, who observed that this humbled wife had returned 'to the
haven of her husband's protection'.[6] Never again would she style
herself 'Lady of the English'.[7] After her departure, the civil war,
lacking focus, dragged on for a time in a desultory fashion.

Crossing to Normandy that February, the Empress was caught in
such a violent storm that her ship was in danger of sinking. Believing
that she was in imminent danger, she made a vow to found an abbey
to the Virgin on the very spot where her ship safely made land. She
came ashore west of Cherbourg, at the mouth of a brook that would
afterwards be called Chantereine, because, during the worst part of
the storm, she had promised to sing a hymn as soon as she could
see land. The pilot of the vessel, sighting the shore, called out to her:
'*Chante reine, voici terre!*'

Maud's grandfather, William I, had founded the abbey of Saint-
Marie nearby, and in fulfilment of her promise, she re-founded it,
dedicated it to Saint-Marie *de Voto* – Our Lady of the Vow – and
built a new chapel.[8] After 1151, Richard, Bishop of Coutances, wrote
to 'his worshipful lady, the Empress Matilda, daughter of King Henry',
that 'she may make the abbey [of St Mary] *de Voto* at Cherbourg
free for whatever order it may please her Highness, saving the rights
of the church of Coutances. May God grant her perseverance in
well-doing and, to the house she has founded, increase.' The twelfth-
century abbey church of Saint-Marie *de Voto* still survives today,
much restored.

Spurned in England, Maud must have been heartened to find
that, on her arrival, 'all the people in Normandy turned from the
King and gave fealty to the Count of Anjou, for he had besieged
them in their castles until they surrendered them'.[9]

Maud rode to Rouen, where, by the autumn, she had been reunited
with her husband and sons.[10] After being apart for nine years, she
and Geoffrey did not resume married life, although they remained
allies, resolved to press Henry FitzEmpress's claim to England.

Maud took up residence in the palace built by Henry I at Quevilly,
which lay to the south of the city in his hunting park on the left
bank of the Seine. Here she set up her court, with her own household knights, administrative clerks and chaplains.[11] She came to rely
on the monks of nearby Notre-Dame de Pré for spiritual support
and intellectual conversation,[12] and often retreated to the lodgings
they kept for her in their guest house, living among them as if she

was a member of their community,[13] and growing increasingly pious as she aged.[14]

Her Norman charters were all dated at Quevilly or de Pré.[15] She was lavish with her gifts to Bec-Hellouin in her later years,[16] and the monks of the mother house and the priory were staunch in their support of her son's claim to the English throne. She probably visited Bec-Hellouin itself, as she dated a charter there.[17] In March 1149, probably at her instigation, and as provision for her, Geoffrey made the abbey a substantial gift of three prebends.[18]

Henceforth, Maud resided chiefly at Rouen, where her court offered a refuge for those of her party who had chosen exile, and for the poor and the wretched, who benefited from her extensive good works.[19] She remained a threat to Stephen, as she did not, for some time, give up hope of launching another invasion of England; for with Geoffrey supreme in Normandy, many barons preferring to give their allegiance to him, and Stephen in weakening health, the tide might have turned. In the meantime, she led a peaceful existence that gave her leisure to pursue pious and charitable works and impart her experiences, and the wisdom she had learned from them, to her son, over whom she would always exert considerable influence.

On 10 June 1148, she rode to Falaise and personally apologised to Bishop Joscelin for keeping his castle of Devizes from him. Then she wrote to her son, explaining that she had decided to restore it to the Church, and asking him if he would take care of the formalities.[20]

That year Geoffrey sent Milon, Bishop of Therouanne, to Rome to press the Pope to recognise Henry's claim to England.

26

'For the Good of my Soul'

Stephen and Matilda had kept the Christmas of 1147 in London, where they also held the Easter court of 1148.[1]

Relations between King Stephen and Archbishop Theobald had long been antagonistic, not least because Theobald had faced constant challenges from Henry of Blois, and Stephen had fallen out with the Pope. In March 1148, Stephen forbade Theobald to attend a Papal council at Rheims, but Theobald, 'being more afraid of God than the King', went anyway.[2] A furious Stephen exiled the Archbishop.

In the interests of making peace, the Queen and William of Ypres summoned Theobald to Saint-Omer, urging him to remain there, at the abbey of Saint-Bertin, where royal messengers could easily find him, and hold himself in readiness to negotiate,[3] while Matilda interceded for him. It was probably during this trip that Matilda was at Steenvorde, issuing a charter to Coggeshall Abbey.[4] Steenvorde is only thirty-two miles from Saint-Omer.

An angry Pope Eugenius III placed England under an interdict as punishment for the King's treatment of the Archbishop, but while it was in force, Mass was nevertheless celebrated for the Queen at Canterbury.[5] In response to her pleas, Theobald returned to England soon afterwards, in defiance of the King, and sought refuge at Framlingham Castle, Suffolk, which was held by Hugh Bigod for the Empress. Stephen quickly capitulated and made a fragile peace with the Archbishop, but it was soon to be shattered. Aware that Henry FitzEmpress was determined to wrest his throne from him, Stephen resolved to follow the French tradition and have his heir Eustace crowned in his lifetime; but on the advice of the Papal Curia, Theobald refused to comply. The message was clear: Stephen might be an anointed king, but his was not the right line.

Around 1148, Stephen and Matilda transferred their daughter Marie and some other nuns from Saint-Sulpice in Brittany to the Benedictine priory of St Leonard at Stratford-le-Bow, which had been founded before 1122, and lay near the Queen's estates in Essex. It was in this convent school that Geoffrey Chaucer's fourteenth-century Prioress, in his *Canterbury Tales*, learned to speak the anglicised version of Norman French 'after the school of Stratford-atte-Bowe, for French of Paris was to her unknowe'. Matilda gave her daughter the manor of Lillechurch, near Rochester, Kent, as dowry.[6]

But disputes arose between the English and Breton nuns, for the Prioress of St Leonard's imposed a sterner rule on the latter, and 'the nuns could not take it on account of the stringency of the order and the conflict with its customs'. It seems that the Queen offered to found a cell of Saint-Sulpice for Marie and her companions at Lillechurch. In her presence, Hilary, Bishop of Chichester, Clarembald, Abbot of Faversham, and Theobald, Archbishop of

Canterbury, agreed to this. The community at Stratford returned
the manor of Lillechurch, 'on condition that the nuns of Saint-
Sulpice who received it with Marie should now leave them and
entirely quit the church of Stratford'. These sisters even had to
reclaim 'all their buried dead'. Once the transaction had been made,
and Marie and her fellow sisters had 'collected their belongings and
gathered up everything of theirs', they 'left entirely the church of
Stratford' for Queen Matilda's new foundation, Lillechurch, or
Higham (as it became known), Priory.[7]

The transfer of Marie to Lillechurch coincided fortuitously – or
intentionally – with the foundation of Faversham Abbey by the King,
who, 'for the good of my soul and Queen Matilda my wife's, and
Eustace my son's, and all my other children's and those of my predecessors the kings of England', gave his manor of Faversham to found
an abbey of the Cluniac Order dedicated to St Saviour. 'My wife,
Queen Matilda, and I give to William of Ypres, in exchange for his
manor of Faversham, Lillechurch with its appurtenances from the
Queen's inheritance, and the surplus from my manor of Milton.'[8]

Matilda was closely associated with Faversham Abbey, which
Stephen intended to be the mausoleum of the House of Blois. From
March to August 1148, 'the Queen was accustomed to frequent the
court' of St Augustine's Abbey, Canterbury, 'because she wanted to
complete the work at Faversham, which she herself with her husband
King Stephen began from the foundations; and, because silence had
been imposed on the Augustinians, she used to summon the monks
of Christ Church, so that they could celebrate mass for her at St
Augustine's'.[9] Some historians have interpreted this to mean that
Matilda stayed continuously in Canterbury from March to August,
but the word 'frequent', then as now, meant to visit regularly.

St Augustine's Abbey was the oldest religious house in England,
dating from 598. It had been founded as a mausoleum for the Saxon
kings of Kent, and was situated not far from Canterbury Cathedral,
just outside the city walls. The church, which almost rivalled the
cathedral in size, had recently been rebuilt in the Romanesque style,
and the Great Court, in which Matilda stayed on her visits, lay just
inside the main gateway. From here she could ride the ten miles to
Faversham to oversee the building of the new monastery and watch
its mighty church rise from the foundations – it was to be 360 feet
long, larger than Rochester Cathedral. She probably also visited
Lillechurch Priory to see her daughter. The Rule of St Benedict
provided for a nun to receive guests with the Abbess's permission.

Monks from Bermondsey were brought in to establish the conventual rule at Faversham under the ruler of Abbot Clarembald, former prior of Bermondsey,[10] and the Queen gave her new abbey many gifts, including her manor of Tring and a precious relic, a fragment of the True Cross, which had been sent to her by her uncle, Godfrey de Bouillon, ruler, or 'Advocate', of Jerusalem.[11] Soon after the abbey's foundation, Archbishop Theobald, 'favourably disposed by the requests of our lady Matilda, Queen of the English', consecrated a burial place for the monks.[12]

Matilda also gave an acre of land for an anchorhold to house a holy nun, Helmid, near Faversham Abbey. After Helmid's death, the land was to pass to the abbey to support perpetual alms for the souls of Matilda, Stephen and their children.[13]

At Christmas that year, Stephen and Matilda held a splendid court at Lincoln.

In 1149, Henry FitzEmpress returned again to England, visited Bishop Joscelin and obtained his permission to hold on to Devizes Castle until God had brought victory to his cause.[14] Henry was now sixteen, 'taller than the tallest men of middle height, and blessed with soundness of limb and comeliness of face – one, in fact, whom men flocked to gaze upon. In agility of limb he was second to none; with no polite accomplishment was he unacquainted.'[15] This was unmistakably a king in the making. On 22 May, Henry was knighted by his great-uncle, David I, at Carlisle. During his stay he founded, in Maud's name, Stanley Abbey, at Loxwell, Wiltshire, the first of four Cistercian houses he established in association with his mother, at her behest.[16] He was back in Normandy by January 1150.

That year Stephen sent his brother, Bishop Henry, as ambassador to Louis VII in Paris, to seek an alliance against Henry. Queen Matilda accompanied the Bishop as far as the Flemish border, before returning home. In the spring of 1151, Louis invaded Normandy, but he fell ill and had to abandon the campaign and agree to a truce. In the summer, Maud and Geoffrey visited the French court, where they negotiated a peace with Louis and he ratified their secession of Normandy to Henry, who now took the title Duke of Normandy. By now Geoffrey had earned the nickname 'Plantagenet' after the broom flower (*planta genista*) he customarily wore in his hat. The dynasty he founded was to be known by that name.

It was during that visit to Paris that Henry, now eighteen, began lusting after Louis' Queen, the beautiful and spirited Eleanor of

Aquitaine, the greatest heiress in European history. While he was in Paris they became lovers, and after Henry left, Eleanor demanded an annulment of her marriage. She had borne Louis no son, only two daughters, and had complained that she had married a monk, not a king. For Louis, it was a choice between losing her, and her great domains, and marrying another woman who might give him the heir that France needed, for the Salic Law of the Franks forbade the succession of women to the throne. All that Eleanor wanted was to be free of her unwanted husband and marry Henry. At twenty-nine, she was eleven years his senior, but to him that was of no consequence. She was desirable, and she would bring with her half of what is now France.

It is often claimed that Queen Adeliza left England in 1148 and travelled to Aalst in her native Brabant to became a Benedictine nun at Affligem Abbey. But there is no record of her leaving England in 1148, or abandoning her husband and her children, who were all under ten, for the cloister. Moreover, Affligem was a house of monks. In 1150, in her last recorded charter, she granted the prebend of West Dean to Chichester Cathedral,[17] which probably places her in Sussex at that time. It is more likely that she chose to visit Affligem Abbey in the wake of her brother Henry becoming a monk there in 1149.

The foremost abbey in the province, Affligem had been under the protection of the counts of Brabant since 1085. It was also their mausoleum; Adeliza's father, Duke Godfrey, had been buried here in 1139. The Abbot, Fulgentius, had visited Adeliza at Henry I's court, 'where he was received with special honours'.[18] In 1146, Bernard of Clairvaux had come to Affligem, where God had vouchsafed him a vision of the Virgin Mary, in gratitude for which he gave the abbey his staff and chalice. Adeliza would have no doubt been shown them during her visit, and they can still be seen today.

She never returned to England. She became ill and died – she may even have died in childbirth – at Affligem[19] on 24, 25 or 26 March 1151, largely forgotten in England, her death recorded by only one chronicler.[20]

The Annals of Margam state that Adeliza was interred at Affligem near her father on 9 April 1151,[21] but probably it was her heart and viscera that were initially interred there,[22] while her body was taken back to England. A charter issued by her brother Joscelin states that he gave land in Petworth to Reading Abbey in her memory when he was there for her burial. Her effigy, crowned and veiled, was placed beside that of Henry I on his tomb. Nothing remains of either effigy. However, a note in the margin of a manuscript of Reading Abbey[23] confirms that Adeliza's body was buried in the presbytery between two piers on the north side of the choir, and not in the same sepulchre as her first husband, because she had remarried.[24]

William d'Albini survived his 'extraordinary Queen' for twenty-five years. He granted land to Reading Abbey for the repose of her soul.[25] When he died in 1176, he was buried in the priory he had founded at Wymondham, Norfolk. Their four sons outlived him,[26] and their Albini descendants were earls of Arundel until the middle of the thirteenth century.

The *Continuatio Chronici Afflegemiensis* records that Adeliza's body was exhumed from its resting place at Reading and reburied in a tomb 'next to the clockwork' at Affligem after Albini's death in 1176. An eighteenth-century plan of the abbey shows that her tomb was in the nave.[27] We do not know what it looked like, and it has long disappeared. In 1796, during the French Revolution, the abbey was almost completely destroyed and the remains of Adeliza and Duke Godfrey were dug up and reburied in a churchyard. After the abbey was re-established in 1869, they were discovered in the vaults of the ruined church. A modern ledger stone now marks their resting place in the cloister.[28]

27
'Carried by the Hands of Angels'

Maud was not with her husband Geoffrey when, on 7 September 1151, he went swimming in the Loire and caught a chill. He died a week later, aged thirty-eight, at Château-du-Loir. Much mourned in Anjou as 'the father of his country and the scourge of pride',[1] he was buried in Le Mans Cathedral, where an enamel plaque marks his resting place. Henry, Duke of Normandy, was now count of Anjou and Maine. For the first two years of his rule, he would rely on his mother to assist him in the government of Normandy, especially when he was absent in

England. Jointly they issued charters relating to their interests in both Normandy and England.[2]

Queen Matilda was back in London by 1151, when she attended a council held there. Her dearest wish was to see Eustace crowned, and thereby secure his succession, and in the face of Theobald's repeated refusals she was happy to intervene, at the instigation of Abbot Bernard of Clairvaux, to resolve a quarrel between Stephen and Henry Murdac, who had been appointed archbishop of York in 1147 by the Pope, without the King's consent. Abbot Bernard had urged her to enhance 'the glory of your kingdom', and she knew that it was to her advantage to persuade her husband to acknowledge Murdac, who was willing to urge the Holy Father to agree to the coronation of Eustace. In 1151, he raised some support in Rome for it, but not enough for the Queen to achieve her ambition.[3]

At the end of March 1152, Stephen and Matilda presided over a meeting of the Great Council in London, where Matilda did her best to enlist support for the crowning of Eustace. On 6 April, Stephen induced a few barons to pay homage to his son, but there seems to have been little enthusiasm at the prospect of this unpleasant young man succeeding his father. Probably Eustace's reputation was increasingly undermining the King's cause. He was 'a good soldier, but an ungodly man. Wherever he was, he did more evil than good. He spoiled the lands and laid thereon heavy taxes.'[4] He was dissolute too, and fond of low company. His wife, Constance, 'was a good woman, but she had little happiness with him'.[5] That was hardly surprising, as he kept her shut up in Canterbury Castle for much of their married life.

There was still tension between Archbishop Theobald and Stephen, and at a synod attended by the King and Queen that April, Theobald again refused to crown Eustace, once more sending out the message that the Church did not smile on Stephen's dynasty. Bishop Henry was unable to help – Pope Eugenius III had revoked his office of Papal legate after he failed to attend a Papal council. The real reason for his demotion was probably that he had made himself unpopular by his ambitious scheming to turn Winchester into an archiepiscopal see to rival Canterbury.

These matters would have been troubling Matilda when she visited a lady who had once served her as damsel, Euphemia de Cantilupe, Countess of Oxford, at Hedingham Castle, Essex, late in April 1152.

Euphemia had married the wealthy Aubrey de Vere, Earl of Oxford, a year or so earlier, and the King and Queen had given her the manor of Ickleton, Cambridgeshire, as her dowry. The massive keep built by Aubrey at Hedingham twelve years earlier, which stands 110 feet high today, boasted a soaring great hall that still occupies the second and third floors and has the largest Romanesque arch in Britain (and perhaps in Europe), arched windows in deep embrasures, and an ornamented gallery embedded in the walls. Two of the castle's corner turrets survive. The remains of a chapel have been uncovered in the inner bailey.

While at Hedingham, Matilda fell sick with a fever. Feeling her strength failing, she sent for her confessor, Ralph, Prior of Holy Trinity, Aldgate. He 'was at the deathbed of the venerable Queen Matilda, having been called especially to it three days before her death. Prior Ralph ministered to the Queen all the sacraments which are needful for that journey, and by his advice that same Queen made many alms.'[6]

Stephen was summoned too. His presence is attested to by a grant confirming one he had drawn up at Hedingham, on Matilda's behalf, to Holy Trinity, Aldgate.[7] He was with her when she died on 3 May,[8] as was their son Eustace.[9]

The Queen's body was brought in procession to London, then carried to Faversham Abbey, where she was buried with great pomp in the choir.[10] In the seventeenth century, Weever recorded her lost epitaph: 'In the year one thousand, one hundred and fifty one [*sic*], not to her own, but to our great loss, the happy Matilda, the wife of King Stephen, died, ennobled by her virtues as by her titles. A true lover of God and patroness of the poor, she lived submissive to God that she might afterwards enjoy His presence. If ever woman deserved to be carried by the hands of angels to Heaven, it was this holy Queen.'[11]

Part Five

The Empress Maud
'Greatest by Motherhood'

1

'Joy and Honour'

Matilda did not live to see the end of the long conflict in which she had stoutly supported her husband. Henry FitzEmpress came again to England early in 1153. He was now twenty, and very much the son of his parents, being 'a man of reddish, freckled complexion with a large round head, grey eyes which glowed fiercely and grew blood-shot in anger, a fiery countenance and a harsh, cracked voice. His neck was somewhat thrust forward from his shoulders, his chest broad and square, his arms strong and powerful. His frame was stocky, with a pronounced tendency to corpulence. He was a prince of great eloquence and, what is remarkable in these days, polished in letters.'[1]

Henry was now in an unassailable position, for he had the support of the Pope. Louis VII had been persuaded by his advisers to agree to an annulment, and on 18 May 1152, at Poitiers, Henry had married Eleanor of Aquitaine, and was now master of a vast domain extending almost from the Loire to the Pyrenees, and from the Atlantic Ocean to the Massif Central. In a stroke, Henry had created a Plantagenet empire, the greatest feudal domain of the age.

In January 1153, Maud met her new daughter-in-law when Henry brought Eleanor to Rouen and left her with his mother before sailing to England,[2] enriched with funds Maud had given him. Sadly there is no record of what transpired at the meeting of these two feisty, independent ladies, and indeed little is known of Maud's relationship with Eleanor. Maud was twenty years older, and we can only speculate what she made of this notorious beauty who had captivated her son. Both were strong, tempestuous women, yet there is no evidence of a power struggle between them. The scanty evidence we have suggests that they co-operated. For example, Joscelin de Balliol, who had served Maud, became a clerk in Eleanor's household,[3] possibly at Maud's recommendation.

Maud remained entrenched at Rouen, supporting Henry with her advice and her mediation. Eleanor, who, like her mother-in-law, was eleven years older than her husband, appears not to have encroached on the older woman's territory. Whether she resented Maud's influence on Henry is not known, but she had had experience of an interfering mother-in-law in Adelaide of Maurienne, whose dominance over Louis VII she had much resented, and she was older and wiser now, so she may have decided not to ruffle the Empress's feathers[4] – and perhaps with good cause, for Maud may have heard gossip that Eleanor 'was secretly reputed to have shared Louis' couch' with her late husband, Geoffrey. It was the courtier Walter Map who first reported this, so the rumours must have been current at Henry II's court. By the early thirteenth century, the tale had been embroidered: Giraldus Cambrensis asserted that Geoffrey had raped Eleanor and warned Henry not to touch her 'because she had been known by his own father'.

If Maud knew, or suspected, that Geoffrey had betrayed her with Eleanor, she was perhaps hostile – or maybe her unloved husband's extramarital forays were of no interest to her. What would surely have concerned her more was that such an affair would have rendered her son's marriage to Eleanor incestuous, which had appalling implications for the legitimacy of their children and the succession.

It may be that Maud and Eleanor were together for too short a time for hostilities to develop between them. Eleanor was pregnant, a blessing of which Maud cannot but have approved, and may have taken her court off to Angers to await Henry's return.[5] In August, she bore the first of their eight children, and named him William. He was Maud's first grandchild. The children who followed were Henry (1155), Matilda (1156), the future Richard I (1157), Geoffrey (1158), Eleanor (1162), Joan (1165) and the future King John (1166).

Henry's absence in England left Maud vulnerable to a threatened attack on Normandy by King Louis, who was angered at his ex-wife having married his vassal without his permission. Maud could not count on the loyalty of all the Norman barons, some of whom were causing unrest and even ravaging religious houses. In a charter to the community of Mortemer, one of the monasteries that had suffered such depredations, she admitted that she was powerless to prevent the present disorder.[6] But her son could not come to her aid at this critical time.

In the face of Henry's supremacy, demoralised by the death of his beloved wife and mainstay, and in poor health, Stephen had no choice but to come to terms – terms to which Matilda might never have agreed. In 1153, Henry's men and Stephen's refused to engage in battle, which says much for the general desire to end the war.[7] That August, with the two sides shouting terms across the River Thames, a treaty was agreed at Wallingford, which provided that, on Stephen's death, Henry would succeed to the throne of England, restoring the succession to the descendants of Henry I. Henry, for his part, was to pay homage to Stephen and keep the peace for the rest of the King's life. This brought an end to the civil war.

The two former enemies then rode together to London, where they were received with great demonstrations of joy, yet we might wonder how Stephen felt, having been forced into agreeing to a treaty that disinherited his heir, Eustace, and his younger son, William, who had become earl of Surrey on his marriage to the heiress Isabella de Warenne in 1149 – a marriage that had been arranged by Queen Matilda to secure the Warenne estates for the King.

Eustace, who was violently jealous of Henry, naturally opposed the treaty, but on 17 August 1153, after ransacking church estates near Bury St Edmunds, Suffolk, he was staying at Cambridge Castle, where he took one mouthful of food that had been stolen from the abbey of Bury, and died suddenly of what was described as a fit of madness; probably he choked to death, or had a seizure. Contemporaries believed he had been struck down 'by the wrath of God' for the sacrilege he had committed.[8] Only then would Maud endorse the agreement at Wallingford being enshrined in the new Treaty of Westminster, which was signed in November, and in which she merited a mention only as 'the mother of the Duke'.[9] She had lost her battles, but her son had won the war, and the crown was to return to the rightful royal line.

The threat from France receded when Henry 'returned triumphantly' to Normandy in March 1154, and at Easter, in Rouen, 'was duly received with joy and honour by his mother, Maud, his brothers, and all the people of Normandy, Anjou, Maine and Poitou'.[10] Eleanor and the baby William also joined him and Maud for the festival. Afterwards, Henry and Eleanor rode off to visit Aquitaine, but in June they were back with Maud in Rouen, where, on the 24th, they celebrated the feast of John the Baptist. In the meantime, on 27 May, alongside Hugh of Amiens, Archbishop of Rouen, Maud had confirmed the election of the chronicler Robert of Torigni as abbot of Mont Saint-Michel.[11] Eleanor stayed on her own with Maud in Rouen in the autumn, while Henry was quelling

a rebellion in the Vexin, and the two women were together on 26
October when Archbishop Theobald's messenger arrived from
England.

2

'The Light of Morning'

On 25 October 1154, King Stephen died at Dover Priory of a
bloody flux that was perhaps symptomatic of acute appendi-
citis.[1] Having survived his beloved wife for over two years, he was
buried with her and Eustace in Faversham Abbey, Kent.[2] In 1216, a
Flemish clerk visited the abbey and recorded that Stephen and
Matilda lay side by side before the high altar, their resting places
marked by two ledger stones.[3] The fame of their abbey did not long
outlive their dynasty.[4]

None of their tombs survive today; all that remains of the abbey
is the outer gateway and fragments of the fabric that survive in local
buildings. In 1964, the site of the church was excavated and a pair
of empty subterranean vaults, each measuring 2.2 metres square, were
found in the middle of the choir. They contained fragments of carved
stone painted red, white, gold and purple, which may once have
been part of the monuments that stood above them.[5]

According to John Stow, the Elizabethan antiquarian, when the
abbey was dissolved and mostly demolished in 1538, the three royal
tombs were raided for jewellery and the lead of the coffins, and the
remains of Stephen, Matilda and Eustace were thrown into the River
Creek; but they were soon retrieved and reburied in the parish
church of St Mary of Charity in Faversham, where a canopy tomb
with no contemporary inscription,[6] but a carved face of a king
among the sculpted decorations of the canopy, is said to be theirs.

By right of their mother, Eustace's brother William had succeeded
him as count of Boulogne, but when he died in 1159, Boulogne
passed to their sister Marie. Around 1156–8, Marie had transferred
from Lillechurch Priory to Romsey Abbey to be its abbess. But the
following year, Matthew of Alsace, second son of Thierry, Count of
Flanders, abducted her from her convent and forced her to marry

him, so that he could get his hands on her inheritance, assuming the title of count of Boulogne and making a triumphal entry with Marie into Boulogne. She bore him two daughters, Ida and Matilda; Ida would succeed her as countess of Boulogne. Marie's marriage to Matthew was annulled around 1169–70, and she returned to the religious life, probably at the Benedictine nunnery of Saint-Austreberthe near Montreuil, where she died and was buried in 1182, the last surviving child of King Stephen and Matilda of Boulogne.

Henry FitzEmpress was now King Henry II of England. After suffering years of war, anarchy and misrule, his new subjects welcomed his accession joyfully, hailing him as the 'son to the most glorious Empress Maud'.[7] The chronicler Aelred of Rievaulx acclaimed him as the descendant of the two monarchies, Norman and Saxon, which had been united by the marriage of Henry I and Matilda of Scotland: 'Rising as the light of morning, he is like a cornerstone joining the two peoples. Now, certainly, England has a king of the English race.'

In a manuscript dedicated to the new King, Robert of Cricklade wrote of Maud's triumph: 'In our age there is one woman, daughter and wife of a king, who has seen her son become a most powerful king, and – what is even more wonderful – each of them has the name of Henry.' This was the way in which Maud would now be remembered and celebrated – not for her deeds, or her failings, but as the woman who had transmitted the legitimate right to rule to her descendants.

Before Henry left for his new kingdom, he went to Rouen and took counsel of his mother, now the respected and vindicated matriarch of the new dynasty, and his brothers. Walter Map, a witty observer of the period, did not like Maud, calling her partly good, but mostly evil.[8] He asserted that his master's unpleasant character traits were the fault of his mother's teachings. She had urged him to 'spin out all the affairs of everyone, hold long in his own hand all posts that fell in, take the revenues of them, and keep the aspirants to them hanging on in hope. She supported this advice by an unkind analogy: an unruly hawk, if meat is offered to it and then snatched away or hid, becomes keener and more inclinably obedient and attentive.' She had also enjoined that Henry 'ought to be much in his chamber and little in public. He should never confer anything on anyone at the recommendation of any person, unless he had seen and learnt about it.' To this advice, Map groused, she added 'much more of the worst kind',[9] including the injunction to be 'free in bed, infrequent in business'.[10] In fact, Maud gave Henry wise counsel, and he took good heed of it. From now on, though, he would increasingly act independently of his mother, although he still relied on her, and delegated to her, when the occasion required.[11]

He was crowned, with the heavy gold crown Maud had brought from Germany,[12] at Westminster Abbey with his Queen, Eleanor of Aquitaine, on 19 December 1154.

Maud had remained in Normandy; she was to visit England only once more. She had made too many enemies there, and she and Henry may have felt that, in the interests of peace and harmony, it was better that she stayed where she was, although Henry did confirm some charters and grants she had made in England.[13] She was mellowing with age, and remained greatly influential with her son, especially in regard to his dealings with foreign rulers; she was apparently his chief adviser on the affairs of Christendom. Clearly he trusted her implicitly. He always deferred to her, and let her take precedence before him, as an empress should before a king. In their joint charters, her name came first.[14]

In Normandy, Maud continued to rule in Henry's name, effectively as regent. She heard legal cases and administered justice during his frequent absences, issuing writs, confirming ecclesiastical appointments and winning praise for the beneficial guidance she gave him. She made land transactions, and issued or witnessed royal charters as '*Domina Imperatrix*'. One, dated 1155, was addressed to 'all her lieges of Normandy', and confirmed a gift of alms that had been bestowed on Foucarmont Abbey in her presence.[15] Her authority is apparent in Henry's order to his lords, justices and bailiffs to ensure that certain lands were given to the abbey of Fécamp, which he concluded: 'Let my lady and mother the Empress see that it is done.'[16]

It was Maud who kept pressing Henry to make an alliance with the Roman Empire. In 1164, even the King of France was among the great and the good who sought her mediation from time to time, himself acknowledging her authority in Rouen when he wrote to her on behalf of one of his subjects who was facing a legal action in Normandy. Maud instructed Lawrence, her clerk, to inform King Louis that she would see that his subject received justice as if he were one of the most important burgesses of the city.[17]

Although Queen Eleanor sometimes acted on Henry's behalf in England,[18] Maud served him as absentee regent there, as well as in Normandy, on at least one occasion. In 1159, when he was away trying to conquer Toulouse, the Justiciar, Robert de Beaumont, Earl of Leicester, sought her advice more than once.[19] Although her influence over Henry was regarded with suspicion in England,[20] the counsel she gave him in these years was laced with a wisdom that had not manifested itself while she was at war with Stephen. It was on her advice that, in March 1155, at Wallingford, he swore to confirm the laws of King Alfred and Edward the Confessor, as set forth in a charter granted by Henry I.

In Normandy, Maud was a munificent benefactor of the Church, and gave alms, lands and property to various religious houses, often for the souls of her father and mother, her late husband and her son Henry. After 1154, most of her charters were to religious establishments.[21] She had long been a great patron of the abbey of Bec-Hellouin, even during her years in England, and remained so all her life.[22]

On 10 June 1157, a delegation of monks from Mortemer Abbey was dispatched by Stephen, their Abbot, to meet with Maud near Rouen. They were escorted to Valasse, near Bolbec and Lillebonne, where they found Maud and her half-sister Matilda, Abbess of Montvillers (a bastard daughter of Henry I), waiting for them in a meadow by the Seine. The Abbess urged the Empress to aid and protect the monks, and five days later, on the advice of her friend Hugh of Amiens, Archbishop of Rouen, Maud re-founded the Cistercian abbey of Notre-Dame du Voeu at Valasse. It had originally been founded in 1149–50 by Waleran de Beaumont, as a gesture of gratitude after being shipwrecked on his way home from the Second Crusade.[23] Now, after years of fraught negotiations, Maud took over his foundation, in fulfilment of a vow that she herself had made while under siege in Oxford – that, if she was spared, she would found an abbey. She managed to offend Waleran by replacing his monks with the monks of Mortemer, but by the following year he had forgiven her and sought her protection for the abbey's endowments.[24]

A reliquary in the shape of a jewel-studded golden filigree cross from the abbey of Valasse, dating from the tenth or eleventh century and now in the Musée Departmentale des Antiquités in Rouen, is of German work and associated with the Empress Maud. She had it set within a larger cross, and possibly gave it as a gift to Valasse. It is the only treasure she owned to survive.[25]

In 1153, Henry FitzEmpress had become a benefactor of Radmore Abbey, founded by his mother, and on his coronation day, at her instigation, the monks came to him to ask if they might exchange Radmore, which was suffering the depredations of local foresters, for the royal manor of Stoneleigh, Warwickshire. Henry agreed.[26]

Maud retained a special affection for her father's foundation at Reading, and issued a writ, dated at Rouen, commanding the Sheriff of Hereford to take the abbey's lands under his protection.[27] When the Emperor Frederick Barbarossa demanded the return of the hand of St James in 1157, Henry ensured that it stayed at Reading Abbey, and pacified the Emperor with lavish gifts, among them a rich ceremonial tent so heavy that it required a crane to lift it. Maud, with her understanding of Imperial diplomacy, may have had a hand in negotiations and the choice of gift.[28]

Between 1156 and 1161, Henry granted his mother 'the chapelry of Valognes' for her abbey at Cherbourg, and in 1160, the Empress herself ordered Osbert de Hosa, Constable of Cherbourg, to give the Abbot of Cherbourg possession of land at Beaumont 'at once'.

3
'A Woman of the Stock of Tyrants'

At Michaelmas 1155, Maud returned to England after an absence of seven years, to attend a meeting of the Great Council at Winchester. According to the account of her friend Stephen of Rouen, a monk at Bec-Hellouin, she had learned that Henry had dreamed up an ill-advised scheme to invade Ireland and make his youngest brother William its king, and when he laid the plan before his barons at the meeting, she opposed it. Ireland, she said, was a land of barbarians, which would not be worth the trouble it would bring the King; moreover, the Irish were likely to resist his scheme.[1]

Maud warned Henry that his priority should be to deal with his other brother, the landless, untrustworthy and treacherous Geoffrey, who had tried unsuccessfully to kidnap and marry Eleanor of Aquitaine when she was on her way to Poitiers after her divorce from King Louis. When Louis had turned on Henry, his vassal, for

marrying Eleanor without his permission, Geoffrey had sided with
him.[2] Since then, Geoffrey had been taken prisoner by Theobald V,
Count of Blois, and it had been Maud who persuaded a reluctant
Henry to secure his release, and urged the slighting of Theobald's
castle at Chaumont-sur-Loire.[3]

Geoffrey, who had been left only three castles, was now claiming
that their late father had promised that, once Henry had succeeded
to the English throne, he, Geoffrey, would be count of Anjou and
Maine. That, and Maud's opposition, persuaded the King to abandon
the Irish plan and compensate William with large estates.[4] Given the
problems Henry II would later face in trying to conquer Ireland
after her death, his mother's advice was wise and prescient. Her
mission accomplished, Maud returned to Rouen.

When Henry made it clear that on no account would he allow
Geoffrey's claims to Anjou and Maine, Geoffrey stormed off into
Anjou and took up arms against him. On 2 February 1156, Maud
was present at a fraught family gathering in Rouen, at which Geoffrey
accused Henry of failing to keep their father's promise.[5] It was
possibly at her insistence that Henry pardoned his brother, forcing
him to abandon his claim and two of his castles in exchange for an
annuity,[6] but Geoffrey went away unsatisfied, and only ceased plaguing
the King when, at Henry's behest, the people of Nantes rebelled
against their overlord and invited Geoffrey to be their count later
that year.[7] Maud's role in keeping the peace between her sons was
pivotal, but her primary aim was to protect Henry's interests, which
she had fought for and upheld all his life.[8]

Both Geoffrey and William, Maud's younger sons, would prede-
cease her, 'nipped in the bud despite the great hopes held of them'.[9]
Geoffrey died on 26 July 1158, aged just twenty-four. Maud herself
suffered a dangerous illness in 1160, and in gratitude for her recovery
she donated her silk mattress to the leper hospital of Saint-Jacques
in Rouen.[10] Many of the charters she issued in the 1160s were
witnessed by one 'Hugh', who may have been her physician. In her
last years she is said to have endured an increasingly incapacitating
illness caused by the difficult birth of her last child in 1136. If left
untreated, severe bleeding, infection, obstructed or prolonged labour,
birth injuries or pregnancy-induced hypertension can leave a woman
with gynaecological problems for months, years or a lifetime afterwards. Without more specific evidence we cannot diagnose Maud's
illness, which she seems to have endured in silence for decades, not
allowing it to interfere with her life, yet it might account for her

flares of aggression and occasional exhaustion, and over time her symptoms would have worsened.

As her health weakened, Maud's influence with Henry began to diminish. In 1162, she opposed his plan to make his Chancellor, Thomas Becket, archbishop of Canterbury, for she had seen at first hand in Germany, between 1112 and 1122, how the two roles could clash, recalling the bitter conflict that had followed when the Imperial Chancellor, Adalbert of Saarbrucken, Archbishop of Mainz, had put the needs of the Church before those of the Emperor, and had turned on his earthly master.[11] She and Gilbert Foliot, Bishop of Herford, argued that Becket was too worldly for high ecclesiastical office, having been chancellor of England and enjoyed a life of great state and luxury.[12] For the first time, Henry disregarded his mother's advice.

Yet he shared her anger when, a year later, Becket forbade the match the King had arranged for his surviving brother, William, Count of Poitiers, with Isabella de Warenne, the widow of Stephen's son, William, Count of Boulogne, on the grounds that they were too closely related. In 1159, on the death of the Count of Boulogne, Henry had settled upon his brother a substantial part of his estates, thus making him one of the richest magnates in England, with lands in fifteen counties. William was devastated at Becket's ban, and crossed the sea to Rouen, seeking succour from his mother. When he died, aged twenty-seven, in January 1164, with Maud beside him, it was said that the cause was a broken heart. He was buried in Notre-Dame de Pré, among the monks of Bec-Hellouin, who, like his mother, he accounted amongst his friends.[13] In his memory, Maud bought land for the abbey of Valasse.[14]

Maud took Henry's part in his bitter dispute with Becket about ecclesiastical jurisdiction over 'criminous clerks' – offenders in holy orders. Henry wanted them punished by the King's courts and to receive the same penalties as everyone else, and his aims were enshrined in sixteen articles of law called 'the Constitutions of Clarendon', which were drawn up in 1164. But Becket stood up for the traditional right of the clergy to be tried in the more lenient ecclesiastical courts. Early in 1165, Henry sent his clerk, John of Oxford, to Maud in Rouen, to express the opinion that the Archbishop was fighting for ecclesiastical privileges for the sake of personal ambition and worldly gold, and that his defence of the liberty of the Church was aimed at preserving its right to practise extortion. Evidently Maud wrote to Henry approving of his stand.[15]

Three days later, Nicholas, Prior of Mont-Saint-Jacques in Rouen, who was hopeful of finding a solution to the conflict, sought an audience with the Empress to plead for his friend Becket, then an exile on the Continent, and took with him letters for her from the Archbishop. She refused to see Nicholas, or read the letters. He kept asking, and on the third attempt she relented, receiving him privately in her chamber, and having the letters read out to her, by him, not by her clerks, whom she did not trust and feared might misrepresent what Becket had written. Nicholas described their interviews in a letter to Becket. After hearing his arguments, Maud expressed regret for what she had written to Henry, stating her belief that he had concealed the full extent of his poor relations with the Church from her because he knew she valued its freedom more than she did his will.[16]

When Prior Nicholas had gone, Maud wrote another letter to Henry, asking him to inform her of his intentions towards the Church and his Archbishop. 'And if, when I know his wishes, I consider that any efforts of mine can accomplish anything, I will do all in my power to bring about a peace between him and the Church,' she stated.

Soon afterwards, Prior Nicholas visited her again and brought her a copy of the Constitutions of Clarendon. She asked him to read them out to her in Latin, which she understood, then explain them in French. Nicholas gave his opinion that some were contrary to the Christian faith, and almost all to the liberty of the Church, and warned that she and her son ought to fear for their spiritual as well as their temporal welfare.[17]

Maud's response dismayed the Prior, who had been expecting her to react more favourably. He wrote to Becket: 'She is a woman of the stock of tyrants', but went on to relate how reasonably she had approached the matter:

> She approved some, such as the one about not excommunicating the justices and ministers of the King without his consent. Others she condemned. Above all, she thought it wrong that they had been reduced to writing, and the bishops forced to promise to observe them; such a thing had never been done by their predecessors. After much discussion, when I urgently pressed her to suggest what might be a basis for peace, I made the proposal, and she agreed, that an attempt should be made to induce the King to submit to the advice of his mother and other reasonable persons, who might find a compromise, so that, setting aside the written document and the promises, the

ancient customs of the realm might be observed, with the proviso that the liberty of the Church should neither be diminished by the secular justices nor abused by the bishops.

You must know that the Lady Empress was ingenious in defence of her son, excusing him now by his love of justice, and now on account of the malice of some of the bishops. She was acute and discreet in comprehending the origin of the church disturbances. She said some things in which we greatly praise and admire her sense, and made many acute remarks on the plurality of benefices and the idleness and luxury of some of the clergy, who have no fear of being called to account, do what they will. And these statements she illustrated by recent examples. Bishops ordain clerks irresponsibly without a title to any church, and large numbers of ordained clerks turn to crime through poverty and idleness. They do not fear either losing their benefice, because they have none, or suffering any penalty, because the Church defends them. They do not fear the prison of the bishop, who would rather allow them to go unpunished than have the trouble of feeding and guarding them. Yet one clerk might hold anything from four to seven churches or prebends, though the canons of the Church everywhere forbade clerks to hold even two.[18]

In giving these examples, Maud showed herself to be well informed and cogent about the dispute and its causes. Nicholas gave Becket wise advice: 'If you love the freedom of the Church, show by your words and deeds that you disapprove of these things. If you send letters to the Lady Empress, make your disapproval clear. I could not possibly have sent word to you more quickly, for I prepared these letters when I was reading the Constitutions with the Empress.'[19] By this, Becket was given to understand that she had dictated them.[20]

Becket himself asked Maud to act as mediator between him and the King. He wrote her an impassioned, peremptory letter that contained a hint of reproof:

We thank God, who illumined your nobility with signs of virtue greater than of birth, for your name is great, and the churches of the saints recount your alms. Although the subsidy of temporal things which you extend to Him in His members pleases God greatly, we believe He is no less pleased by your solicitude for ecclesiastical peace and liberty which, as it is rumoured, you strive for with such feeling. Wherefore we, who by reason of your humanity and beneficence, speak very confidently in your ear about the peace of the Church, asking and praying assiduously to the Lord for your salvation and the temporal as well as eternal glory of your son, that you charge him diligently to procure peace for the Church.

Let him remember, we beg, by your prayers and exhortations, how God lifted him beyond the titles of his noble fathers and extended his boundaries beyond the boundaries of his elders. What good will it do a ruler if he transmits sins to his heirs and makes them enemies of God and the Church in his testament? What good to his ancestors if, having seized the occasion of their crimes, he offends God as if by hereditary right?

If he came to his senses, the Father of mercies is prompt to forgiveness, but beyond doubt He will render judgment without mercy to those who exercise no mercy. He is powerful and the powerful punish powerfully; he is terrible and destroys princes.

You ought, if you please, to employ the diligence of a mother and the authority of a lady to recall him to duty, you who acquired the kingdom and duchy for him with much effort, and transmitted hereditary rights to him in succession, by the use of which the Church is now oppressed and trampled, innocents punished, and the poor intolerably afflicted. We willingly do what we can for your salvation and his soul, imploring the mercy of God by our prayers as best we can continuously. We will pray more confidently if, with peace restored to the churches, he returns to God, his author and benefactor, with prompt devotion. Let him not be ashamed to humble himself before God in penitence.[21]

Maud tactfully refused to become further involved, telling Prior Nicholas that Henry never discussed such matters with her these days. But at Pope Alexander III's instigation, she did try to negotiate a peaceful agreement between the two protagonists. In 1165, she wrote in admonitory vein to Becket:

To Thomas, Archbishop of Canterbury, Matilda the Empress.
My lord Pope sent to me enjoining me, for the remission of my sins, to interfere to renew peace and concord between you and the King, my son, and to try to reconcile you to him. You, as you well know, have asked the same thing from me, wherefore, with the more good will, for the honour of God and the Holy

Church, I have begun and carefully treated of that affair. But it seems a very hard thing to the King, as well as to his barons and Council, seeing he so loved and honoured you, and appointed you lord of his whole kingdom and of all his lands, and raised you to the highest honours in the land, believing he might trust you rather than any other; and especially so because he declares that you have, as far as you could, roused his whole kingdom against him; nor was it your fault that you did not disinherit him by main force. Therefore I send you my faithful servant, Archdeacon Lawrence, that by him I may know your will in these affairs, and what sort of disposition you entertain towards my son, and how you intend to conduct yourself, if it should happen that he fully grants my petition and prayer on your behalf. One thing I plainly tell you, that you cannot recover the King's favour except by great humility and most evident moderation. However, what you intend to do in this matter signify to me by my messenger and your letters.[22]

Just two of Maud's letters relating to the conflict survive: the one quoted above, and another, undated but probably sent in 1165, to Louis VII, begging him to cease hostilities against Henry II. But Louis was sympathetic to Becket, for pious reasons and because, while Henry was wrangling with Becket, he was not threatening Louis territorially.

Her plea having failed, Maud wrote to Pope Alexander III — then himself an exile in France — seeking his help in avoiding a war between Henry and Louis, begging him to meet with her to mediate between them. The Pope sent the Abbot of Valasse to ask her to arrange a meeting, which she set up in April that year at Gisors, Normandy, herself presiding with Rotrou, Archbishop of Rouen. John of Canterbury, Bishop of Poitiers, a close supporter of Becket, made him attend, assuring him that he had the support of the Empress. Maud even joined forces with Eleanor to resolve the conflict. Late in the summer, John of Salisbury informed Becket that, 'at the request of the Empress and the Queen', Thierry of Alsace, Count of Flanders, was working for a settlement.[23]

It is clear that Maud saw the chief issues as Becket's pride, and his lack of appropriate loyalty and gratitude, but she had tried to be just. When Henry imprisoned and tortured one of Becket's messengers to make him reveal who had sent him, Maud wrote to him insisting that the wretched man be freed.[24]

4
'A Star Fell'

M aud had long worked for an alliance between Henry II and
the Roman Empire, but in April 1165, she opposed Emperor
Frederick Barbarossa's proposal of a marriage between Henry's
daughter Matilda, the granddaughter born in 1156 and named after
her, and Henry the Lion, Duke of Saxony and Bavaria. England and
the Empire were then supporting rival popes, a conflict that caused
much bitterness. When the Imperial envoys arrived at Rouen to
discuss the marriage and other matters, Maud would not receive
them.[1] Rotrou, Archbishop of Rouen, warned the Papal legate,
Cardinal Henry of Pisa, 'Do not imagine for a moment that she will
vacillate in any way.'[2]

But in 1168, after Maud's death, when the marriage eventually
took place, it brought to fruition her hopes of a new alliance between
England and the Empire. In a manuscript illustration showing
the hands of God placing the ducal crowns on the couple's heads, the
Empress is shown standing beside Henry II, with Eleanor of Aquitaine
behind her, demonstrating that Maud's memory was still prominent
in Germany, and that she was strongly identified with her granddaughter and namesake.[3]

In 1165–7, Maud witnessed a charter granted by Henry II to
Rotrou, Archbishop of Rouen. In 1166, she founded the Cistercian
abbey of La Noe near Evreux.[4] It was her last religious foundation.
Before August that year, she was devoting her energies to averting
a war between Henry II and Louis VII over the allocation of funds
collected in Henry's domains for the relief of the Holy Land.[5]
Henry wanted to send them directly, but Louis wanted to act as a
middleman. In the interests of peace, Maud wrote to the King of
France:

> To Louis, by the grace of God excellent King of the Franks
> and her natural lord, Maud, Empress and daughter of a king,
> sends greetings and loyal service with love. May your Excellency
> recall that I have often asked you about the quarrel between
> you and my son, the King of England, but you have made no
> response which satisfies or informs me. Therefore I am sending

Rainald of Saint-Valéry [Justiciar of Normandy] to implore your Highness: do not delay, if it please you, to send me the details about the quarrel. For unless you do so, such may happen between you that I will not be able to amend; especially for the people you ought to rule and for the people of Jerusalem who are now desolate and terrified. It is useful and will be an honour to you to take pains so they have peace. Witnessed by Alduin, chaplain of Pratum.[6]

In a show of strength, Henry raided Louis' arsenal. To avert further conflict, Maud counselled him to satisfy the French King's honour by letting him take Les Andelys, one of Henry's towns.[7] In August, as a result of her intervention, Henry and Louis agreed a truce of sorts.

In 1166, Becket sent Maud a letter informing her that he had excommunicated several bishops for supporting Henry in their escalating quarrel, yet she merely observed to Prior Nicholas that those bishops were already excommunicate. But she would not speak to a messenger from one of them, Richard of Toclyve, Bishop of Ilchester, because he was under divine anathema.[8] She did not live to see the violent and tragic culmination of Henry's quarrel with Becket. In 1170, four of the King's knights blazed into Canterbury Cathedral with drawn swords and murdered the Archbishop, an atrocity that shocked Christendom. Henry had not intended for it to happen, and did penance for it, but he had blamed Becket for the death of his brother William. It had not been forgotten. Striking a blow, one of the knights had cried, 'Take this, for the love of my Lord William, the King's brother!'[9]

Around 1167, Maud was present with Henry in Rouen when he settled a dispute between his chamberlain, Ralph FitzStephen, and the monks of Saint-Georges-de-Boscherville.[10] That summer, she wrote to King Louis urging him to help resolve the impasse between Henry and Becket. In August, a truce between the protagonists was agreed, and Henry galloped off to conquer Brittany.

Maud had for a long time suffered a debilitating fever, but now, at the age of sixty-five, she was in a mortal decline. According to the chronicler Geoffrey of Vigeois, as she lay dying at Notre-Dame de Pré, she asked to be veiled as a nun of Fontevrault;[11] it was not an unusual request on the part of a pious woman, but neither Stephen of Rouen nor any other source mentions it.

Maud died at one o'clock on the morning of 10 September 1167, surrounded by the monks who had become her friends in the years she had lived at Quevilly. They had come to look upon her as their spiritual mother, and she had loved them as if they were her own children. Stephen of Rouen wrote that, when she passed away, the flower of the meadow withered and a star fell. 'Great as was her distinction as empress, daughter and mother of kings, it was a greater thing that she was wise and pious, merciful to the poor, generous to monks, the refuge of the wretched and a lover of peace. She excelled in good works; she, who lived well, died well.'[12] This is in vivid contrast to how Maud was seen in England, but Stephen of Rouen loved her for her piety.

Thirty-three years earlier, in 1134, and again in 1160, Maud had made her will, in which she asked to be buried at Bec-Hellouin. Henry I had opposed this, arguing that the only fitting resting place for her was Rouen Cathedral. But now her wish was honoured, and her body, sewn into an ox hide, was interred before the high altar of the Virgin Mary at Bec-Hellouin, with Rotrou, Archbishop of Rouen, presiding over her obsequies, which were attended by Arnulf, Bishop of Lisieux.[13]

Stephen of Rouen described them in detail, relating how, in the dimness of the Romanesque church, her grave was illuminated by a massive seven-branched candelabrum and a crown of lighted lamps. Around 1155, Peter the Venerable, the brilliant and saintly Abbot of Cluny, had visited Maud, at her request, to advise her on how those obsequies should be celebrated. It was usual to have thirty Masses said over as many days, but he recommended that twice that number be celebrated at Cluny and in all its daughter houses, and that alms be distributed to the poor in Maud's name. Masses and alms were offered for her in all the Cluniac monasteries, just as Peter the Venerable had advised.[14]

Stephen of Rouen was probably the monk who carried the news of her death to Henry in Brittany,[15] prompting the King's immediate return to Rouen.[16] As testimony to his love for his mother, Henry donated generous sums of money in her memory to churches, religious houses, leper hospitals and the poor; he executed every provision of her will, and gave money for a marble tomb to be raised to her memory. On it was placed the famous epitaph that has come to define her life: 'Here lies Henry's daughter, wife and mother: great by birth, greater by marriage, but greatest by motherhood.'[17]

Maud had given her two Imperial crowns to the monks of Bec–Hellouin. Her many other gifts to the abbey included two golden chalices, a gold cross encrusted with precious stones, two Gospels bound in gold and studded with jewels, two silver censers decorated with gold, a silver box for incense with a spoon, a gold dish, a gold pyx for the Eucharist, three silver flasks, a ewer for holy water, a silver basin, an ebony chest filled with relics, two portable altars of marble mounted in silver, plate, chasubles, dalmatics, copes and her Imperial cloak of gold.[18]

She bequeathed £1,500 to the austere order of Grandmont, another of the religious orders that had come into being in the previous century, and a favourite of her son's, who matched the gift.[19] She left Bec–Hellouin the contents of her chapel, among them liturgical books, a gold chalice and spoon, two silver censers, two silver basins, four chasubles, two tunics, two dalmatics, six copes, two woven in silver, and two egg-shaped boxes of silver resting on griffins' talons. For centuries, the monks celebrated her obit annually on her anniversary, 10 September. The treasures she gave the abbey remained at Bec–Hellouin until war and revolution caused them to be destroyed or dispersed in the fifteenth and eighteenth centuries.[20]

In 1263, the abbey church of Bec–Hellouin burned down and Maud's tomb was lost. When the church was rebuilt in 1282, her remains were discovered in a coffin, still wrapped in ox hide. A new sepulchre was raised in the chancel, where they were reburied before the high altar with great solemnity. That tomb was destroyed in 1421 by English soldiers at the time of Henry V's conquest of Normandy, but during renovations in 1684 by the Congregation of Saint-Maur, some of Maud's bones were found with rags of silk fabric and an inscription. They were wrapped in green silk embroidered with gold and reburied in a new double coffin of wood and lead, with an inscribed brass plate marking the site of the grave. This was lost in 1793, when Bec–Hellouin was destroyed and left in ruins.

The remains of the church were finally demolished in 1841. In January 1847, Maud's leaden coffin was rediscovered; it was identified by an inscription recording that it contained the bones of 'the illustrious Maud', and was found to contain bone fragments and a lace of silver. In 1847, the Empress was reinterred in Rouen Cathedral, just as her father had wished.[21]

It is easier in today's cultural climate than it was in the twelfth century to applaud Maud's dogged strength of character and her fearless pursuit of her rights, but such a view does not take into account her appalling lack of political judgement, her vindictiveness and her lack of mercy. But would those shortcomings have been so evident had she succeeded her father unopposed in 1135? And how do we reconcile the good Maud whom the Germans had revered and the wise, measured and respected elder stateswoman of later years with the woman who so offended the Londoners in 1141? Can she have changed so much in two decades? Before 1134, there is no recorded blemish on her character. She was popular, even loved, in Germany. The differences between her and Geoffrey could have been due to incompatibility, and his fault as much as hers. Her quarrels with her father arose because she had impossibly divided loyalties.

The chroniclers who wrote about her had their own partisan agendas, and possibly they exaggerated, but the fact remains that the citizens of London did drive Maud out. They had all along made it clear that they preferred Stephen, and Maud, for her part, had probably been on the defensive, seeing them as her enemies. Stress, frustration, fear and anger at the injustice of her situation could have made her the termagant she appeared to them. But diplomatic handling of the citizens could have saved the day.

Several modern historians have made the valid point that decisive, aggressive behaviour that would have been seen as a sign of strength in a king was regarded as unacceptable in a female ruler, and that Maud was in an impossible position because of contemporary expectations of her sex. They have also argued that Matilda of Boulogne did much the same things as Maud, but preserved her good reputation because her efforts were on her husband's behalf; indeed there was an enduring literary tradition that assigned masculine virtues to heroic women who were said to have transcended the limitations of their sex, much as the *Gesta Stephani* praised Queen Matilda.[22] The same might have been said of Maud, had she not alienated those she should have courted. But it is inappropriate to take a feminist approach to the twelfth century, which did not question double standards in what we now call gender issues.

Undoubtedly Maud shocked her contemporaries with her unwomanly behaviour, but it was her lack of sound political judgement, above all else, that had been her downfall. She acted arbitrarily, without tact, and refused to take advice. Matilda of Boulogne did not alienate the Londoners or the Church, nor did she treat her chief supporters dismissively. Had she done any of those things, she would surely have earned the same measure of disapprobation. What she did was act in support of legitimate royal authority, which is why she escaped censure.

A long-standing medical condition arising from the birth of her last child may have accounted for Maud's mood swings, inappropriate emotional reactions, aggression and intolerance. The Earl of Onslow, her biographer, suggested in 1939 that she was menopausal at the time of her invasion of England and its aftermath. In 1139, she was thirty-seven years old. Most medieval sources give fifty as the most common age for the change of life,[23] but then, as now, there could be variations of ten years or more. Menopausal women can suffer extreme and intense mood swings, with immoderate emotional responses. These may have a negative impact on life and relationships. For some of these women, rage, aggression, irritability and impatience can be responses to stress and trauma,[24] and there can be no doubt that Maud experienced more than her fair share of that. It is a plausible theory, bolstered by the fact that character traits inherited from her father predisposed Maud to aggression and sudden rages that might have been exacerbated by her fluctuating hormones.

As she aged, she remained an autocrat, and still appeared to some to be 'of the stock of tyrants',[25] and yet her admirer Robert of Torigni asserted that she 'was a woman of excellent disposition, kind to all, bountiful in her alms-giving, a friend of religion, of honest life, one who loved the Church, by the abundance of whose gifts the church of Bec has achieved no small degree of splendour'. In the late twelfth century, the chronicler Ralph of Diceto recalled how Maud had set a sterling example to Matilda, Eleanor and Joan, the daughters of Henry II and Eleanor of Aquitaine: 'the nobility of their grandmother, the Empress, and her masculine courage in a female body showed her granddaughters an example of fortitude and patience'. At Valasse, the Cistercian monks would celebrate her as an intelligent and sensible woman who had given generously in many causes and had a heart devoted to God.[26]

Yet Maud has gone down in history much as her old opponents saw her, as a harsh virago with little judgement but great tenacity – and as a failure: the woman who should have been England's first queen regnant but who scuppered her chances because of her 'intolerable feminine arrogance'.[27] She is infamous, rather than famous – the woman whose example so put the English off being ruled by a queen that it was centuries before they accepted one. It has been said that she established a model for female political power,[28] but it did not survive her; nor is there any evidence that the Tudor queens regnant used her as their model. Rather her reputation – which rested largely on her behaviour during those short weeks she spent in London in 1141 – had ensured that hers was not an example of queenship to be followed.

Not for another four hundred years would the English accept a female monarch, and it was left to Elizabeth I to prove that a queen could be as successful as a king in governing the realm.

Appendix I
A Guide to the Principal Chronicle Sources

Aelred of Rievaulx (1110–67)

Educated at the court of Scotland, he served there as master of the household, but hated life at court. In 1134, he became a Cistercian monk at Rievaulx Abbey, Yorkshire, and in 1147 he was elected its abbot. He became one of the most influential Cistercians of the age. His works include *Eulogium Davidis Regis Scotorum*, a life of David I, King of Scots (1153); *Genealogia regum Anglorum*, a genealogy of the kings of England (1153–4), dedicated to the future Henry II; and *Relatio de Standardo*, an account of the Battle of the Standard (1153–4). The most famous is *The Mirror of Charity*, written at the request of St Bernard of Clairvaux. His writings made him famous and respected throughout England. He was popularly reputed a saint, but never canonised.

The Anglo-Saxon Chronicle

This English chronicle was begun around 890 at the behest of Alfred the Great, King of Wessex, and recounted events in England, year by year, from the beginning of the Christian era until 1154. Its authors remain unknown. Despite its occasional inaccuracies and bias, it is one of the most important English sources for the Saxon and Norman periods. It exists today in nine related versions, compiled at Winchester, Abingdon, Worcester, Peterborough and Canterbury. Much of it is written in a dry, concise style, but it is of huge value for studying the history of the period from an English viewpoint.

Arnulf of Lisieux (d.1184)

Bishop of Lisieux, Normandy, from 1141, he had studied canon law in Rome. He supported Henry FitzEmpress's claim to the throne of England, and later sided with Henry in his quarrel with Archbishop Thomas Becket.

Baudri de Bourgeuil (c.1046–1130)

A Benedictine monk at the abbey of Bourgeuil in the Loire Valley, he became its abbot in 1079. He was elected bishop of Dol, Brittany, in 1107. As abbot, he wrote a number of Latin poems. One, in praise of Adela, daughter of William the Conqueror, runs to 1,368 lines. He also wrote an epitaph for William the Conqueror.

Eadmer (c.1064–1123/6)

A monk of Christchurch Priory, Canterbury, and archbishop of St Andrews in Scotland from 1120, Eadmer was the close friend and spiritual director of Archbishop Anselm from 1093 to the latter's death in 1109. Later he wrote a hagiographic life of Anselm. He also wrote *Historia Novorum in Anglia*, a Latin history of England from 1066 to 1122. The great chronicler William of Malmesbury admired his work, which is refreshingly free of the sensationalist and credulous style of some chronicles of the period.

Gervase of Canterbury (c.1141–c.1210)

Gervase was a monk of St Augustine's Abbey, Canterbury. Around 1180, he chronicled the reigns of Stephen, Henry II and Richard I, and wrote a history of the archbishops of Canterbury in the twelfth century. He is most famous for his account of the murder of Archbishop Thomas Becket.

Gesta Stephani

Chronicle dating from the middle of the twelfth century, recounting the deeds of King Stephen, probably written by Robert of Lewes, Bishop of Bath. Accurate and detailed, it is the most important source for Stephen's reign, but heavily biased in his favour and hostile to the Empress Maud.

Henry of Huntingdon (*c.*1084/8–1155/7)

Archdeacon of Huntingdon from 1109, his history of England, *Historia Anglorum*, written at the request of Alexander, Bishop of Lincoln, covers the period up to 1154, and was the most extensive work composed in King Stephen's reign. Henry modelled his works on those of the Venerable Bede and the *Anglo-Saxon Chronicle*. It was popular and widely used as a source for the next two centuries. He had an accomplished narrative style, and gave colourful accounts of battles and other events, while striving scrupulously for accuracy. A partisan of King Stephen, he was hostile to the Empress Maud.

Herman of Tournai (1095–1147)

He was the Abbot of Saint-Martin, Tournai, but was expelled for laxness in 1136, when he went to Laon, France, and thence to Spain. Around 1140, he wrote a chronicle, *The Restoration of the Monastery of Saint Martin of Tournai*. He was a great storyteller with an eye for detail, and his work encompasses far more than the history of his abbey.

Histoire de Guillaume le Maréchale

A Norman-French history in verse form of William the Marshal, written around 1220–9 by 'John the Troubadour' for the Marshal's son, William, 2nd Earl of Pembroke. It runs to 19,214 lines, and was written to laud and glorify the great Marshal as 'the flower of chivalry'.

John of Hexham (*fl. c.*1160–1209)

Prior of Hexham, Northumberland, from *c.*1160, he wrote a continuation of the chronicle of Simeon of Durham, covering events from 1130 to 1154, focusing largely on the ecclesiastical history of the north. He relied on other sources, and his dating is faulty, usually a year out.

John of Worcester (d. *c.*1140)

A monk and scribe at Worcester Cathedral, who was instructed by Bishop Wulfstan to write a Latin chronicle. It covers the period from the Creation to 1140. A fellow monk, Florence of Worcester, assisted with the work, and his skill and industry are acknowledged under the year 1118; the account of the period prior to that used to be attributed to Florence, but there is no change in style after 1118, and Orderic Vitalis records that John was writing the chronicle when he visited Worcester in 1124. Other scholars may have collaborated, but John was the primary author.

Marbodius (or Marbod), Bishop of Rennes (*c.*1035–1123)

A native of Anjou, he was educated at its capital, Angers, and had family connections at the court of the counts of Anjou. Around 1068, after a youth of excess, he became a canon of the cathedral of Saint-Maurice at Angers. In 1096, Pope Urban II consecrated him bishop of Tours. He was celebrated for his Latin poetry and prose works, which covered sacred and secular subjects.

Orderic Vitalis (*c.*1075–*c.*1143)

Born at Atcham, near Shrewsbury, Shropshire, Orderic was the son of a French priest and an Englishwoman. He was sent to the abbey of Saint-Evroul in Normandy to be educated, and remained there as a monk. He visited England while he was researching his *Historia Ecclesiastica*, which he wrote between 1114 and 1141. It runs to thirteen books, and his original holograph version survives in the Bibliothèque Nationale, Paris. The *Historia* recounts the history of Normandy and England from the dawn of Christianity to 1141, and is one of the chief authorities for the Norman period. In his accounts of the Conquest of 1066 and other events, Orderic betrays a lively sympathy with his countrymen, the English, yet he was fair: he saw the English Church as degenerate and welcomed the Conquest because it brought ecclesiastical reform. He wrote from a moral, Christian point of view, hoping that men might benefit from the example of history. He used extensive oral and written sources, and was careful to establish their provenance; some of his evidence came at first hand, as in the case of what happened to the *White Ship*, which was recounted to Orderic by someone who had been on board.

Matthew Paris (*c.*1200–59)

A Benedictine monk at St Albans Abbey, Hertfordshire, from 1217, he succeeded Roger of Wendover as the abbey's chronicler in 1236.

He wrote several works, including the substantial *Chronica Majora*, and is recognised as the greatest chronicler of the thirteenth century.

Richard of Hexham (d. 1155/67)

An Augustinian canon, and, later, prior of Hexham, Northumberland, from about 1141, he wrote careful histories of the church in Hexham from 674 to 1138, and of the deeds of King Stephen and the Battle of the Standard, which is useful for northern history in the period 1135–9.

Robert of Gloucester (*fl. c.*1260–1300)

Reputed to be the author of a metrical, or rhyming, chronicle in Middle English, recounting events from the legendary founding of England by Brutus to 1135.

Robert of Torigni (*c.*1110–86)

Norman chronicler and bibliophile whose work is important for the study of Anglo-Norman history in the twelfth century. Of noble family, he became a deacon at Bec-Hellouin, Normandy, in 1131, and prior in 1149. In 1154, he was elected abbot of Mont Saint-Michel, Normandy. He visited England in 1157 and 1175, played host to Henry II of England and Louis VII of France at Mont Saint-Michel in 1158, and had an international perspective on affairs. He knew the Empress Maud personally, and admired her. Her son, Henry II, chose him as godfather for his daughter Eleanor. Robert's chronicle was held in high esteem by his contemporaries for its erudition and literary style; however, his chronology is unreliable and there are errors in his work.

Robert Wace (*c.*1115–*c.*1183)

An Anglo-Norman poet and chronicler, born in Jersey and educated in Paris, he was appointed a canon at Bayeux Cathedral, Normandy, by Henry II, and served there from 1160 to 1170. He wrote several lives of the saints, but his chief work was the *Roman de Brut* (1155), a Norman-French version, in 15,000 couplets, of Geoffrey of Monmouth's *History of the Kings of Britain*. It was finished in 1155 and dedicated to Eleanor of Aquitaine, queen of Henry II. Wace also wrote the *Roman de Rou* (Rollo), a history of the dukes of Normandy. His works are well written and logical.

Simeon of Durham (d. after 1141)

He was a Benedictine monk at Jarrow, County Durham, from *c.*1181, becoming precentor at Durham Cathedral. He wrote a history of the church at Durham, as well as *Historia Regum Anglorum* (*History of the Kings of England*), which covers the period from the seventh century to 1129. It is a compilation of annals, myths and material from other sources, some of them now lost.

Stephen of Rouen (d. *c.*1170)

A monk of Bec-Hellouin, Normandy, Stephen was a poet who wrote an unfinished Latin metrical chronicle, 'Draco Normannicus' ('The Standard of the Normans', named after the dragon-shaped banners of Normandy) (1169–70), which covers the period from the mythical origins of the duchy to 1169, and was composed in memory of the Empress Maud, whom he much admired and accounted his friend, and who was the focal point of his work.

Turgot, Prior of Durham (*c.*1050–1115)

He was a Saxon monk at Durham, where he became archdeacon and helped to found the cathedral. He became confessor to St Margaret, Queen of Scots, and wrote a biography of her at the request of her daughter, Matilda of Scotland, Queen of England. From 1109, he was archbishop of St Andrews.

William of Jumièges (*c.*1025–*c.*1090)

Norman Benedictine monk of the royal abbey of Jumièges, who compiled a history (in eight books) of the dukes of Normandy (*Gesta Normannorum Ducum*) from 851 to 1137, which gives a valu-able account of the Norman Conquest. The work was based on earlier histories and William's own research and observations, and its main thrust was to justify Duke William's conquest of England in 1066. William of Jumièges sent a copy to the Conqueror. It is one of the foremost authorities for the history of Normandy in this period.

William of Malmesbury (*c.*1090/5–*c.*1143)

Born near Malmesbury, Wiltshire, he became a monk there and was appointed librarian and precentor. He was one of the most distinguished of English chroniclers. His history of the Norman kings (*Gesta Regum Anglorum*) is a vivid account covering the period 1066–1126. Its sequel, the *Historia Novella*, covers the period to 1142. He also wrote the *Gesta Pontificum*, an ecclesiastical history of the bishops and chief monasteries of England until 1123; accounts of the church of Glastonbury; and lives of St Dunstan and St Wulfstan. He was the first full-scale English chronicler since the Venerable Bede (d.735), and a polymath who wrote vividly and enlivened his work with topographical descriptions, reminiscences, anecdotes and personal observations. His work is not always objective, and it displays a bias to the Empress Maud and to his patron, her half-brother Robert, Earl of Gloucester, to whom two of his works were dedicated.

William of Newburgh (*c.*1135–*c.*1198)

Perhaps from Bridlington, Yorkshire, he became a canon at Newburgh Priory, near Coxwold, Yorkshire. His *Historia rerum Anglicarum*, begun in 1196, is one of the chief historical sources for the period 1066–1198, but suddenly ceases in 1198, when William perhaps died. It is well written, critical and objective, and its author strove to achieve historical accuracy.

William of Poitiers (*c.*1020–90)

Born at Préaux, Normandy, he became one of the knights of Duke William of Normandy before studying at Poitiers. When he returned to Normandy, he became chaplain to the Duke and archdeacon of Lisieux, Normandy. He wrote his life of William the Conqueror, *Gesta Willelmi Ducis Normannorum et Regis Anglorum*, between 1071 and 1077, in the King's lifetime. It is a panegyric, but an extremely important source for the Conqueror's life, written by one who knew him well.

Appendix 2
Letters

1 Anselm, Abbot of Bec-Hellouin, to Adeliza, daughter of William I

To the venerable Adelaide [*sic*], a lady of royal nobility, but nobler in the character of a virtuous life: brother Anselm, wishing that your earthly nobility may be so adorned with the ornament of virtues that it may deserve to be united with the King of Kings in eternal felicity.

As to the *Flowers of the Psalms* that your Highness, dear to me in God, has deigned to require of me, our faithful humility could not carry it out for you more speedily or any better. For our obedience followed your command devotedly, to the degree that the command itself proceeded from holy devotion. I wish and I pray that Almighty God may so preserve and nourish this devotion in you that He may fill your mind with His sweetest affection on earth and in heaven with His blessed sight. I beg your wealthy nobility not to despise the small and worthless gift which our poor paltriness sends you. For although it is not encrusted with gold and gems, it is certainly made entirely of charitable fidelity and given with faithful charity.

I have added seven prayers, of which the first is less a prayer than a meditation. In it, the soul of the sinner briefly examines itself; despises what it finds, is humbled by what it despises; in humiliation is smitten with terror of the Last Judgement, and breaks into tears and lamentations. Among the prayers there are two to St Stephen and St Mary Magdalene, which, if received into the heart, will tend to an increase of love. There are seven in all, and I exhort you, as your servant and friend of your soul, to offer them as a sacrifice of humility, fear and love.

Farewell in God both now and in eternity; farewell, and take the little book sent as a pledge of our loyalty in God and of our prayers, for what they are worth. At the end of the letter, I utter what I wanted to instil throughout the letter: despise with an elevated mind everything that must be given up even while you have it. Strive with a humble mind towards that which alone can blessedly be kept for ever as long as you do not have it. This is what I want to convince you of and I pray the Holy Spirit may convince you of. With this in mind, I say for the third time, farewell.[1]

2 Pope Gregory VII to Matilda of Flanders

Gregory, bishop, servant of the servants of God, to Matilda, Queen of the English, greetings and apostolic blessing. Having heard the letters from your nobility, beloved daughter, we understood that your generosity is intent on love and humility, which we receive joyfully as indication and certain hope of your salvation. For we believe that her salvation is indeed not to be doubted, who is known to serve from the heart with humility and love, in which the law is completely contained. We expect, we deeply desire with all our mind to receive these and similar gifts from you, that, as you are noble by blood, you may live more nobly in the honourable custom of the saints. Urge your husband, do not cease to suggest useful things to his soul. For it is certain that, if the infidel husband is saved by a believing wife, as the Apostle says, a believing husband can be made better by a believing wife.[2]

3 Pope Gregory VII to Matilda of Flanders

Having read the letters of your noble-mindedness, we have understood with how faithful a mind you obey God, with how much love you cling to his faithful. We also perceive no less how your mind keeps us present in memory from the promises of your greatness by which you made clear that whatever we wished from you, if we made it known to you, we would receive without delay. You should know, dearest daughter, with what love we receive this and whatever gifts we may obtain from you. What more are gold or gems, the precious things of this world that I might expect from you, than a chaste life, the distribution of your things to the poor, the love of God and your fellows? We pray your nobility that we shall obtain these and similar gifts from you, that you love simply and wholly, that you obtain what you love and never lose what you have. With these and similar weapons arm your husband, when God gives you the opportunity, and do not cease to do so. The other things we sent [orally] charging our son, Hubert, faithful to both of us.[3]

4 Hildebert of Lavardin to Matilda of Scotland

The humble priest of Le Mans, Hildebert, to Matilda, venerable Queen of the English, most worthy in glory and honour, greetings and prayers. It is difficult to place benefits always discreetly and prudently. The highest powers do not know the prudence of what is lovely or improper to bestow. I who have experienced such munificence from you, respond to your blessing with thanks, amazed equally by the glory of the gift and the affection of the giver. Your gift must be commended for the magnificence of its material and the splendour of its carving. Its value is increased by the majesty of the sender; art and nature add less to it than that it comes from the Queen. Which if it did not please by the weight or skill in the craft, I would still embrace as those above did offerings of frankincense and fat sacrifices. They consider not the offering but the affection, giving thanks for their devotion not the cost. A pure and whole spirit bends them wherever it wishes, a penny mitigates heavenly indignation no less than a pound. So with me your spirit commends your gift, magnifies and illumines it. Though it shines indeed with its gold, it shines more with your spirit, a spirit pleased to bestow not by prompting but by innate desire to give; a spirit, I say, which wished from within, which offered swiftly, eager to be accepted, not importunate to be pressed.

It is manifest from this how devoted you are to the Lord's sacraments for which you provide the instruments since, as a woman, you cannot administer them, imitating as far as possible the holy women who first came to the Cross with tears and then to the tomb with spices. They were enflamed with great desire to suffer with the crucified and serve the entombed with zeal. You are also present when Christ is sacrificed, when He is buried; neither is celebrated without your service, since you prepared the lamps there where we believe in our hearts and confess with our mouths that the author of light is present. It does not matter that the service is different, which is celebrated with the same affection.

There are, however, two things which, unless I am mistaken, you determined to suggest to the Bishop: memory of you and a reminder of pastoral duty. I understand the candelabra sent to me as instruction placed before me that I remember to give the light of doctrine and to pray for you. Their presence stirs and excites my spirit, demanding with secret exhortations that while I use the gift, I should advance by the example. Indeed covertly but very sharply I am ordered to be attentive to what divine eloquence says about [my role as] the bearer of light: 'You are the light of the world' and 'They do not light a lantern nor place it under a bushel, but over a candelabrum so that it may give light to all who are in the house.'

I embrace your exhortation, daughter of Christ, which even if it were not your intention, if you simply gave, yet as I accept the service of the gift, I shall not scorn its lesson. For it is fitting to advance and be taught from any source, for virtually all things carry mystic meanings and it is easy to extract beauty of customs from anything. For nothing is created for itself, nothing is so simple that there is not something in it by which we can be taught either to avoid what is harmful or to provide what is helpful.

What shall I say about remembering you? That memory burst deeply into my breast, occupied it broadly, possesses it firmly and lives with it while it lives. It lives with me, lives, I say, and will even more frequently, whenever I stand at the altar of the Lord, a sinner, but a priest. There the candelabra and the Pontiff perform the services through you, venerable Queen, and your memorial. Fare well.[4]

5 Matilda of Scotland to Anselm, Archbishop of Canterbury

To the venerable father Anselm, Archbishop of the prime see of the English, Primate of the Irish and of all the northern islands which are called the Orkneys, from Matilda, by the grace of God Queen of the English, his most humble handmaid, wishing that after having happily passed through the course of this life he may reach the end, which is Christ.

Since scarcely anybody doubts that you are turning your daily fasting against nature; even I am not ignorant of it. I admire this greatly, but I have learned from frequent reports of many honourable men that, after a long fast you do not take the usual food according to the claims of nature, but only after having been persuaded by somebody of your household. I am not unaware that you take even this with such frugality that you seem rather to have inflicted violence in detracting from the inherent right of nature than in fulfilling its law. Therefore it is greatly to be feared by many people as well as by myself that the body of such a father may waste away.

I am under great obligation to your kindness. You are such a brave athlete of God, a vanquisher of human nature, a man by whose untiring vigour the peace of the kingdom and the dignity of the priesthood have been strengthened and defended; such a faithful and prudent steward of God, by whose blessing I was sanctified in legitimate matrimony, by whose consecration I was raised to the dignity of earthly royalty, and by whose prayers I shall be crowned, God granting, in heavenly glory. Moreover, it is also to be feared that the windows of your sight, your hearing and your other senses may become clouded, and your voice, the creator of things spiritual, may grow hoarse so that which was accustomed to dispense the Word of God melodiously and sweetly by peaceful and gentle discourse might become so much more gentle in the future as to deprive those who are removed from you for a while of hearing your voice and even leave them without fruit.

Therefore, good and holy father, do not let the strength of your body be so inopportunely undermined by fasting lest you cease to be a preacher, because, as Cicero says in the book he wrote *On Old Age*, 'the orator's gift resides not only in his intellect, but also in his lungs and strength'. To what end is that great quickness of your mind hastening to its ruin? Such a memory of things past and such foresight of things to come, so many accomplishments, so much learning, so many discoveries, so much knowledge of human matters and such experience of divinity accompanied by candour?

Consider the multitude of talents your rich Lord has given to you, what He has entrusted to you, and what He exacts of

you. Bring goodness to everybody, so that what has been brought
may shine more brightly and be carried back to the Lord with
manifold increase. And do not cheat yourself. Just as spiritual
food and drink are necessary for the soul, so bodily food and
drink are necessary for the body. Therefore you have to eat
and drink, since, by the will of God, a long journey still remains
to you in this life; a great crop is to be sown, tended and reaped,
and gathered into the Lord's barn where no thief will come
near. You see that the labourers in the great harvest are very
few. You have entered into the labours of many so that you
may carry back the profit of many.

Remember indeed to consider yourself like John, the Apostle
and Evangelist, dear to the Lord, whom the Lord wished to
survive Him, so that His virgin friend might take care of His
Virgin Mother. You have accepted to bear the responsibility for
Mother Church, for whose sake the brothers and sisters of
Christ will be daily endangered unless you come to their help
with your profound knowledge. Christ entrusted them to you,
having redeemed them by the price of His own blood. O shepherd of so great a Lord, feed His flock, lest lacking in food
they grow faint on the journey! Let the holy priest [St] Martin,
that ineffable man, be an example to you: when he foresaw the
heavenly repose prepared for him, nevertheless said that he
would not refuse the laborious task because of the destitution
of the people. Indeed I know that by the example of many
people and by many witnesses in Holy Scripture you are invited
and encouraged to fast. No doubt your continual reading often
brought to your mind how after a fast the raven fed Elijah, the
widow fed Elisha and the angel fed Daniel through Habakkuk;
how by a fast Moses merited to receive the tablets inscribed
by the finger of God, and after they had been broken, recovered
them by the same means. Also, many examples of the Gentiles
invite you to frugality. For there is no one who does not know
that you have read about the frugality of Pythagoras, Socrates,
Antisthenes and other philosophers, whom it would be tedious
to enumerate and not necessary in this little work. Therefore,
we must come to the grace of the new law. Jesus Christ, who
honoured fasting, also honoured eating by going to the marriage
feast where He changed water into wine, by going to Simon's
banquet, where, having cast seven demons out of Mary, He first
fed her with spiritual dishes, and by not refusing the meal of

Zacchaeus, whom He had drawn away from the power of secular service and called to celestial service.

Listen, Father, listen to Paul persuading Timothy to drink some wine to ease the pain in his stomach saying, 'Drink water no longer, but take a little wine.' See how the Apostle dissuades the holy Disciple from his intended fast. For when he tells him, 'Drink water no longer,' he openly criticises him for having drunk nothing but water before. I beseech you to imitate Gregory, who alleviated the weariness and weakness of his stomach with the help of food and drink and applied himself manfully and unfailingly to teaching and preaching. Therefore, do what he did so that you reach what he reached, that is Jesus Christ, the fountain of life and lofty mountain, with whom he then rejoiced in eternal glory, is now rejoicing and will continue to rejoice world without end.

May your Holiness thrive in the Lord, and with your prayers do not give up helping me, your faithful handmaiden, who loves you with all the affection of her heart. Deign to receive, read, listen to and take notice of this letter which I am sending to you not with feigned but with faithful and strong charity.⁵

6 Anselm, Archbishop of Canterbury, to Matilda of Scotland

To Matilda, glorious Queen of the English, reverend lady, dearest daughter, Archbishop Anselm, sending due honour, his service, his prayers and the blessing of God and his own, as far as he is able.

I give great thanks for your generosity, but even greater thanks for the holy love from which your gifts proceed. Your love urges me with pious solicitude to be kind to my body by taking a greater quantity of food lest my voice and my strength fail me for the duty laid upon me. Since you hear that I feel no hunger after a whole day's fast, even if it happens daily, you fear that hoarseness of my voice or bodily weakness may befall me. If only enough wisdom and vigour as I need would come to me – as much voice and strength as I have – sufficient for the work laid upon me. Even though I may be able to fast without pangs of hunger, I nevertheless can and intend, when I ought, to give my body as much nourishment as is expedient.

Your kind dignity recalled in your letter that through me your Highness was espoused in legitimate marriage, crowned and raised to the eminence of royalty with my blessing. Indeed, since you call this to mind so kindly and with such gratitude to me, who acted in this matter as a minister as faithfully as I could, one can fully appreciate what immeasurable thanks you must be rendering in your heart to Christ, who is the author and dispenser of this gift.

If you wish to render these thanks in a proper, good and efficacious manner by your deeds, consider that Queen whom it pleased the Lord to choose for Himself as His bride from this world. She is the one whom He calls beautiful, and His love and His dove in the Scriptures, and of whom it is said to Him, 'The Queen is standing at Your right hand.' She is the one to whom it is said about her bridegroom, Christ: 'Listen, my daughter, and see; incline your ear, forget your people and your father's house, and the King will desire your beauty.' Indeed, the more she forgets, despising the secular way of life and her father's dwelling place – that is to say, this world – the more beautiful and lovable she will be seen in the eyes of her Spouse. He proved how much He loved her when He did not hesitate to surrender Himself freely to death for love of her.

Now consider, I say, how this woman, an exile, a pilgrim, groans and sighs like a widow with her true children, waiting for her Husband until He returns from the distant region to which He went to receive for Himself a kingdom, and, taking her to His kingdom, repays everyone according to what they did to His beloved, whether good or evil. Those who honour her will be honoured in her and with her; those who maltreat her will be maltreated away from her. Those who exalt her will be exalted with the angels; those who degrade her will be degraded with the demons. Therefore, exalt, honour and defend this spouse so that with her and in her you may be pleasing to her Spouse, God, and live, reigning with her, in eternal beatitude. Amen. May it be so.[6]

7 Ivo, Bishop of Chartres, to Matilda of Scotland

To Matilda, revered Queen of the English, Ivo, humble minister of the church of Chartres, to hear the wisdom of Solomon to the ends of the earth.

Since we know from your reputation that you are one of the prudent women, though we are physically far apart, the odour of good opinion has made you present to us and excited us to loving the charity which the Bridegroom of chaste minds ordained in you. Wherefore we desire to deserve mutual love from your excellence which the queens of the Angles before your time showed in splendid memory of the Queen of the Angels, Mary, to the Church which we, though unworthy, serve by God's disposition. It is not unfitting to your religion and reputation if one whom you ought to love as a fellow man, you love with a certain privilege as a priest of Christ, more beloved in the manner of his Christian religion. Confident in this, we send to your Liberality two of our canons, who will tell you about the needs of our church and receive the favour God will inspire in your heart. I ask also that, in order to impress the memory of your excellence more sharply on my mind, you send a chausuble or some other priestly garment to my smallness which is fitting for a queen to give and a bishop to wear in celebration of the divine sacraments. Farewell.[7]

8 Ivo, Bishop of Chartres, to Matilda of Scotland

Ivo, humble minister of the church of Chartres, to Matilda, Queen of the Angles, to reign in heaven with the Queen of the Angels.

Since every gift is to be valued not so much by its quantity as by the affection of the giver, we have received the bells which you gave to the blessed and perpetual Virgin in the place of that perpetual Virgin, grateful as much for your devotion as for their lovely sound, and have had them placed in a special place to be heard by the people who come together there. Whenever they are sounded to announce the hours, they touch the minds of the hearers renewing your memory in the hearts of individuals. Such memory is not to be valued lightly which blossoms again when the peerless Host offered on the altar of the Cross for our redemption is consecrated daily at the Lord's table by ministers of the new priesthood, when with heavenly hymns like sacrifices of the lips God is honoured by the faithful, when an offended God is inclined to mercy by sinners beating their guilty breasts in the sacrifice of a contrite spirit. There is no doubt that they participate in these goods who offer the goods which they have in abundance to the ministers of God who lack them for His honour and love.

So what was lacking to our poverty, your abundance has already begun to administer benignly, and has promised to supply even more richly in completing or restoring the roof of our church. So the ancient people of God, at His command given through Moses, offered for the use of His tabernacle gold, silver, and bronze, flax and scarlet, purple and jacinth, women also their jewels and earrings, so that the vestment of the Pontiff and the tabernacle would be visibly adorned, signifying the holy customs of the ministers of the New Testament. Those who did not have these precious things offered the hair of goats to make hair-cloth to preserve the splendour of the inner ornaments so they would not be soiled by dust or spoiled by rain. Your Excellence will follow this form of piety when you supply the necessary tools or materials to repair the house of God, as you wish and as much as you wish. For all of these, expect without doubt reward from Him who, you have learned, ordered them.[8]

9 Hildebert of Lavardin to Matilda of Scotland

To Matilda, Queen of the English.

I rejoice in your honour and your good reputation, which is better known to me each day. I rejoice, I say, and give thanks to the Lord God for your goodness, since your goodness is nothing other than His gift. For what do you have that you did not receive? And we all, the Evangelist says, have received from His fullness. From that fullness from which you have what you are, you have that you are good, but you also have that you may be better. Be attentive therefore to what you have from your good Creator and understand that you owe Him for His great kindness. Be attentive, I say, to how your Artificer laboured over you, and labour so that His labour not deteriorate.

I speak of temporal and fallen things; but temporal and fallen things are also gifts of your Lord God. You did not deserve to be born noble, and you were born of royal blood; you did not labour, and you were made rich. You produced nothing of your own power, but you were placed over the heads of the sons of men. You implored no one for the glory of your form, and you were made beautiful to the delight of a king. The Lord God did these things. God is good, His works are good; the highest good. He made all things very good. Men are not good by these goods, but they may become good by using them well. That you may therefore become good before your Lord God, use His good favour well. If you use it well, it is His favour and your good; if badly, His favour is still good, but by using the good favour of God badly you make yours bad: for nothing is good for man unless he is good. But for the good and those loving God, all things work together for good.

Moreover the favours of God are harmful to idle possessors who do not turn them to gain, but to punishment. Understand what I say, for God gave you understanding. Our God is a great lender. I say this in His presence. This Creditor of ours importunately demands usury. This Creditor of ours is hard; He is a man who goes abroad and returns in the full moon. When He returns, He asks double from you, but when He receives it, He will reward you a hundredfold. O blessed commerce, in which asking usury is not criminal, paying it is not a burden. O happy trade, in which the Creditor is opportunely importunate and owes the debtor more than He is owed.

One should fear coming to judgment without mercy, if, let it not be so, you dream that negligence in this commerce will go unpunished and forgotten. Understand what I say: this Creditor of ours has a long memory. You are punishably forgetful if you think He will forget the debt. He forgets no time, no occupation. He collects equally what He lends today and what He lent yesterday because His today is also yesterday. Days and days, years and years pass, but a thousand days and a thousand years are before His eyes, like yesterday.

Will He not number how much He lent you, who alone reckons the sand of the sea and the drops of water and the days of the world? Will He not divide in detail your talents, who divides waters from waters in his wisdom? Perhaps you will take your Creditor to law when He asks for what He committed to you?

Understand what I say: He is a good advocate who will argue with you. He refers before the angels, He defers to truth, He proffers terrible things, He infers horrible things. But you say to me: if offended, He promises to be merciful, He puts by punishment, He admits the penitent, He remits threats, He dismisses debts, He commits more. That is so, I say. I confess it.

The earth is filled with the mercy of the Lord. Many strive for themselves who, though they have rejected any zeal for doing well, still hope for mercy from God when they deserve judgment, as if mercy were to be well-disposed to iniquity rather than to religion, as we believe. But it is not so. For the evil do not earn the mercy of God which even the good can not promise themselves except timidly. To hope for it is very salutary advice, but to depend on it completely is a dangerous refuge. For it is fitting that some good things mitigate judgment if we want many bad things to be judged mercifully. Partial guilt may cause mercy, not total. Virtue which accompanies the beloved to judgment intervenes. They experience a judgment of mercy who give themselves to justice. Who will act for you if He – let it not be so – pleads against you and adverse to you? It is a serious matter to fall into the hands of the living God.

Fare well, and use your delights for the Queen, not for yourself.[9]

10 Herbert de Losinga to Matilda of Scotland

As a nursing child desires the breast, a thirsty man water, a tired one quiet, an exile the fatherland, so my soul desires the restorative power of your presence. Your name is poured oil, to whose fragrance the lovers of truth in our fatherland hasten. Esther, who delighted more in piety than in the daintiness of the kingdom, the eastern Queen [of Sheba] who filled the earthly Jerusalem with gowns and stones, unguents and spices, whose excellence amazed Solomon, did not have a spirit beyond yours. So you, most blessed Queen, have so enriched our west with wealth of faith and virtues, customs and acts, that we do not wish to adhere with similar love to any beyond what we have.

The odour of your religion has penetrated to the ends of the world and the firmness of your integrity and chastity are known to the surrounding regions. The Queen (the Virgin Mary), the prophet says, is at the right hand of God in a golden gown, enveloped in various colours. You are next to this Queen, whom none but queens serve, so much the happier as they are more devoted to her service. You are, I say, beside this Queen whose sons, Christ and John, you serve with insatiable desire, whose power of giving is as great as yours of receiving will be. The Queen you serve can do all things, since she brought forth the most powerful One of all, that is Christ her Son, the Spouse of your soul, beautiful in form above the sons of men.[10]

11 Anselm, Archbishop of Canterbury, to Matilda of Scotland

I give great thanks for the generosity I received from you, but even greater thanks for your holy love for me which I have experienced. Since I am not able to accomplish this through the service of my body, I desire incessantly to pay through the affection of my heart. For however much I may feel your bodily absence, the presence of your faithful love can never be taken from my mind. Wherefore I fervently pray, and by praying I desire, that God Himself may repay you in my stead for what I am unable to do myself and that as far as He knows it to be expedient He may bring His love for you and yours for Him to perfection.

With as much affection as I can, and as far as I dare to presume on your Highness, I beg, beseech, entreat and faithfully advise that your piety should strive for the peace and tranquillity of the churches in England. May you particularly come to the help of their weakest sons and those least powerful in their tribulations and desolation, as orphans of Christ; and according to the parable of the hen in the Gospel, console and foster them under the wings of your protection.

May the anointing of the Holy Spirit teach you in all things and persuade you to do those things which are more pleasing to Him and expedient for you, and after the temporal kingdom may He lead you to the eternal one.[11]

12 Anselm, Archbishop of Canterbury, to Matilda of Scotland

To his dearest lady Matilda, Queen of the English, Anselm the Archbishop, sending her his faithful service and wishing her the continual protection of divine grace.

I am not unaware that it is pleasing to the benevolence of your dignity to know how matters are with me and how I am. Rejoicing therefore, and giving thanks about such good will of yours, I inform you that since I left England the mercy of God has kept me and everything that pertains to me in complete prosperity. Up to now I have been staying at Bec, waiting for a suitable time to resume my journey; but in the near future, before the Assumption of Saint Mary, I shall start out from here with the intention of completing, God willing, what I have begun.

I have recently learnt that God is pleased to exalt the dignity of the kingdom of my lord the King and yours, and to restore, according to your will, those things for your honour and use which were not to his liking or yours or that of your faithful servants. Therefore, as your faithful servant desiring your good in the present life and in the life to come, I rejoice and give thanks as I ought to the heavenly King from whom all these things come to you, and I pray and desire that, as you always keep undefiled the good things He has given you, He may lead you in His grace to greater and better things.

Since it is my duty to encourage you to desire the heavenly kingdom, I exhort, beg and advise with as much affection as I can that you do not have more pleasure in rejoicing exceedingly in the passing glory of an earthly kingdom than in yearning for the eternal bliss of the celestial one. You could do this more sincerely and efficaciously if you arranged the matters subject to your authority according to the design of God rather than to the design of men. 'For the wisdom of this world is folly with God,' as Holy Scripture says; and 'The wisdom of the flesh is at enmity with God, since it is not subject to the law of God.' Reflect on these things, tell them to our lord the King in private and in public and repeat them often, and as far as they concern you consider them carefully again. For the glory of the world passes by, as you are accustomed to say. Oh, may God make you both after this passing glory proceed to eternal glory. Amen.[12]

13 Matilda of Scotland to Pope Paschal II

To the highest Pontiff and universal Pope Paschal, Matilda, by God's grace, Queen of the English, trusting he will so dispense in this life the rights of the Apostolic dignity that he may deserve to be numbered among the Apostolic senate in the joys of perpetual peace with the companies of the just.

I give all the thanks and praise I can to your sublime Holiness, O Apostolic Man, for the things which your paternal charity, as though for admonition, has deigned to send to me and to my lord the King, both frequently by the words of your legates, and also by your own writings. I visit the threshold of the most holy Roman Apostolic seat, and as far as it is lawful and I am able, clasping your paternal knees with my whole heart, my whole soul, my whole mind, praying with importune and opportune petition, I cease not, nor will I cease, to entreat, till I know that my submissive humility, or rather the persevering importunity of my application, is heard by you. Yet let not your Excellency be angry, let not the prudent Roman clergy, people or senate be amazed at this my rashness, that thus I presume to speak. Once, once, I say, we and the English people – then how happy! – had, under your Apostolic dignity, Anselm, our Archbishop, a foster-child of the Holy Ghost, the most prudent counsellor and pious father of us and the aforesaid people. From the most opulent treasures of his Lord, whereof we knew him to hold the keys, he took abundantly, and bestowed them upon us more abundantly; for this same faithful minister and prudent dispenser of the Lord seasoned those things which he bestowed with the most excellent salt of wisdom, softened them with the sweetness of eloquence, and sweetened them by the wonderful conceits of rhetoric. And so it was that neither did the tender lambs lack the abundant milk of the Lord, nor the sheep the richest fatness of the pastures, nor the pastors the most opulent satiety of ailments.

But now, when all these things are otherwise, nothing remains but that the pastor, wanting food, the flock pasture, the young milk, utter forth the heaviest groans, since, by the absence of the chief pastor, Anselm, each is deprived of something, or rather, all of all things. In such lugubrious mourning, in such opprobrious grief, in such deformity and loss of our kingdom, nothing remains to me, stunned as I am, but, shaking off my stupor, to fly to the blessed Apostle Peter and his vicar, the Apostolic man. Therefore, my lord, I fly to your benignity, lest we and the people of the kingdom of England perish in such a defect and lapse. What good will our life do us when we go down to corruption?

Let your Paternity take good counsel concerning us, and deign, within the term which my lord the King asks of your goodness, to let your paternal bowels be moved towards us, that we may both rejoice at the return of our dearest father, Archbishop Anselm, and preserve uninjured our subjection to the Holy Apostolic See. I indeed, taught by your most sound and gracious advice, will, as far as women's strength may suffice, and with the help of worthy men, which I shall procure, endeavour with my whole power that my humility may, as far as possible, fulfil what your Highness advises. May your Paternity enjoy eternal happiness.[13]

14 Pope Paschal II to Matilda of Scotland

Paschal, the Bishop, servant of the servants of God, to his dearest daughter Matilda, Queen of the English, greeting and apostolic blessing.

We are greatly saddened about your husband because, although he started well at the beginning of his reign, he is now trying to spoil what follows. Now, having been placed in the fullness of power, he does not fear to provoke to fury the Almighty Lord, who was well-disposed to him in his need. We do not believe that you are unaware of what this husband of yours promised the Almighty Lord in faithful devotion when he first accepted the royal crown. Now he has taken over the churches through investitures, and he has expelled the holy man, Bishop Anselm, from the kingdom because he opposed his wicked deeds, and has taken on counsellors of perdition. Therefore we fear greatly for his salvation since we love him dearly for his previous good deeds.

Therefore, beloved daughter, we beg you to watch more carefully over his keeping and to turn his heart away from wrong counsel so that he will not continue provoking God's fury so greatly against himself. Remember what the Apostle says: 'The unbelieving husband will be saved by the believing wife.' Reprove, beseech, rebuke, so that he may reinstate the aforesaid Bishop in his See and permit him to act and preach as his office demands, and also return the churches to his God, lest God take from him what He has given. Otherwise we can no longer endure it without smiting him and his counsellors, and those who unrightfully take possession of churches through him, with perpetual anathema. But if he consents to obey, he will obtain the help of Almighty God and the Apostolic See against all his enemies, and by the freedom of those churches he will gain protection within his kingdom through the grace of God.[14]

15 Matilda of Scotland to Anselm, Archbishop of Canterbury

To her piously esteemed father and devoutly revered Lord, Archbishop Anselm, Matilda, by the grace of God, Queen of the English, lowliest handmaid of his Holiness, sending perpetual greeting in Christ.

I render countless thanks to your unceasing goodness which has not forgotten me but has deigned to show the presence of your present absence through a letter of yours. Indeed, after the clouds of sadness in which I was wrapped were driven away, the stream of your words broke through to me like a ray of new light. I embrace the parchment sent by you in place of a father, I press it to my breast, I move it as near to my heart as I can, I reread with my mouth the words flowing from the sweet fountain of your goodness, I go over them in my mind, I ponder them again in my heart and when I have pondered over them I place them in the sanctuary of my heart.

Where everything is worthy of praise, I only wonder at what the excellency of your judgement has added about your nephew.

For myself, I do not consider that I make any distinction between what is yours and what is mine; that means of course between what is mine and what is mine. Indeed what is yours by kinship is mine by adoption and love. Truly, the consolation of your writing strengthens my patience, gives me hope and maintains it, lifts me up as I fall, sustains me when I am slipping, gives me joy when I grieve, mitigates my anger and calms my weeping. Frequently and secretly it wisely assures me of the return of the father to his daughter, the lord to his handmaid, the shepherd to his sheep.

In the same way however, the confidence which I have in the prayers of good men and the benevolence which, after careful investigation, I consider comes from the heart of my lord, gives me assurance. For he is more kindly disposed towards you than most people might think. With God's help and my suggestions, as far as I am able, he may become more welcoming and compromising towards you. What he now permits to be done concerning your revenues, he will permit to be done better and more abundantly in future when you ask for it in the right way and at the right time. Although he considers himself more than a fair judge, nevertheless I beg the abundance of your loving-kindness that, having excluded the rancour of human bitterness which is not usually found in you, you may not turn away the sweetness of your love from him. May you rather show yourself before God as a devoted intercessor for

him and for me, as well as for our child and the state of our
kingdom. May your holiness always prosper.[15]

16 Anselm, Archbishop of Canterbury, to Matilda of Scotland

To his reverend lady, his dearest daughter Matilda, by the grace
of God Queen of the English, Anselm, Archbishop of
Canterbury, sending his faithful service, his prayers and the
blessing of God and his own, if it is worth anything.

I give boundless thanks to your Highness by loving and
praying for you for the magnitude of your holy love towards
my humble self which I perceived in your letter. In it you clearly
displayed with what affection you love me when you received
and treated my parchment in the way you describe. Your dignity
raised my spirits so much by declaring that what nature denies
me your grace bestows, that those who are mine by kinship are
yours by adoption and love.

By trying to soften the heart of my lord the King towards
me because of your desire for my return I perceive that you
are doing what is fitting for you and advantageous for him. For
if he has any bitterness of heart towards me, I am not aware
of ever having deserved it in any way at all, as far as I can see.
If at any time I served him he knows it, and I think he will
not consign it to oblivion. If, in some respects, he dislikes me
without cause, it would be advantageous for him to drive this
rancour away from him lest he sin before God.

You promise me that the King will in future grant me better
and more abundant access to our revenues, of which at present
he allows me a small amount. I should not be ungrateful to
your benevolence because you are doing this, as far as you are
able through your goodwill. But it should not be necessary to
make me such a promise because no confiscation or decrease
of them should take place against my will. Whoever advised
him to appropriate any of these revenues advised him to commit
a sin which is no slight one, nor one that should ever be tolerated. For whoever despoils a bishop of his goods can in no way
be reconciled to God unless he restores to him all his goods
intact. You should know that however small a part of these
goods I am deprived of, it is as if I were deprived of everything.
I do not say this for love of money but for the love of God's
justice.

Your kindness prays me not to take my love away from my lord the King, but to intercede for him, for yourself, for your offspring and for your realm. I have always done this up to now. But as to the future I commit myself to the providence of God, with whom the son does not bear the iniquity of the father nor the wife that of her husband. I hope in God that I may not harbour any rancour against anybody in my heart which could separate me from God.

May almighty God guard you and your offspring forever in His grace.[16]

17 Matilda of Scotland to Anselm, Archbishop of Canterbury

To her truly eminent lord and father Anselm, by the grace of God archbishop of Canterbury: Matilda, Queen of the English, his humble handmaid, with the assurance of deep devotion and service.

Turn, holy lord and merciful father, my mourning into joy and gird me with happiness. See, lord, your humble handmaid throws herself on her knees before your mercy and, stretching suppliant hands towards you, begs you for the fervour of your accustomed kindness. Come, lord, come and visit your servant. Come, I beg, Father, appease my groans, dry my tears, lessen my pains, put an end to my sorrow. Fulfil my desires, grant my request.

But you will say: 'I am prohibited by law and bound by the restraints of certain obligations and dare not transgress the decrees of the Fathers.' How is it, Father, that the Teacher of the gentiles, the chosen Vessel, put all His efforts into the annulling of the laws? Did He not offer sacrifice in the temple for fear of scandalising those of the circumcision [the Jews] who still believed? Did not He who condemned circumcision circumcise Timothy so that he became all things to all men? What indeed should a child of mercy do, a disciple of Him who gave Himself up to death in order to redeem slaves? You see, yes, you see your brothers, your fellow-servants, the people of your Lord, now undergoing shipwreck, now slipping into the deep, and you do not come to their aid, you do not extend your right hand to them, you do not expose yourself to danger! Did not the Apostle choose to be accursed by Christ for the sake of his brothers?

My good lord, tender father, bend this severity a little and soften — let me say it, with your leave — your heart of iron. Come and visit your people, and among them your handmaid who yearns for you from the depths of her heart. Find a way by which neither you, the shepherd who leads the way, may give offence, nor the rights of royal majesty be diminished. If these cannot be reconciled, at least let the father come to his daughter, the lord to his handmaid, and let him teach her what she should do. Let him come to her before she departs from this world. Indeed if I should die before being able to see you again — I speak shamelessly — I fear that, even in the land of the living, every joyful occasion of exulting would be cut off. You are my joy, my hope, my refuge. My soul [thirsts] for you like a land without water. Therefore I even stretch out my hands to you, so that you may drench its dryness with the oil of gladness and water it with the dew of your natural sweetness. If neither my weeping nor the wish of the people can move you, putting aside my royal dignity, giving up my insignia, putting off my honours, spurning my crown, I will trample the purple and the linen and will come to you, over-come with grief. I will embrace your knees and kiss your feet, and even if Giezi [a corrupt and avaricious servant of the prophet Elisha, who was punished by being made a leper] came, he would not move me until the greatest of my desires had been achieved.

May the peace of God which surpasses all understanding guard your heart and your mind and cause you to abound with tender mercy.[17]

18 Anselm, Archbishop of Canterbury, to Matilda of Scotland

My heart gives as much thanks as it can engender for the great generosity of your Highness, and what it cannot achieve it does not cease to desire. May He who inspires it Himself repay. Indeed, the pious and sweet affection you feel towards me through the inspiration of God you express most clearly when you write to me about the bitterness, sadness and solicitude which you feel on account of my absence. This absence of mine, as far as I and those who consider the case carefully understand it, has not been extended for so long through any fault of mine.

With devout affection, your excellency complains that my lack of moderation has disturbed the peace of mind of my lord the King and his nobles, and that this has prevented the good, begun by your efforts, from being brought to an end. Indeed, in our letter, which is said to contain that lack of moderation, nothing indiscriminate, nothing unreasonable (although this was imputed to me in the King's letter) can be found if what is written there, and the prohibition which I heard, and which everybody knows about, is examined with an unbiased judgement and a calm mind.

I uttered nothing against the King's father and Archbishop Lanfranc, men of great and religious renown, when I showed that I had not promised either in baptism or in my ordinations to obey their law and customs, and stated that I was not going to disobey the law of God. What is now required of me on the grounds that those men acted as they did I cannot do without committing a most serious offence because of what I heard with my own ears in Rome. If I were to scorn that, I should certainly be acting against the law of God.

Therefore, in order to show with what reasons I refused to do what was required of me according to their customs, I showed how I would much rather be under obligation to observe the Apostolic and ecclesiastical decree known to everybody. In this the law of God can be perceived without doubt, since it was promulgated to strengthen the Christian religion. I need not say here how dangerous it would be to despise this law, since Christians who have ears to hear may daily learn it from divine utterances.

That distorted interpretation of my utterances, according to which I am said to have spoken unreasonably, I do not ascribe to the King's mind or yours. The King received our letter kindly at first, according to what I heard, but later someone with a spiteful and insincere intention, I know not who, incited him against me by a distorted interpretation through no fault of mine. Who that may be I do not know; but I do not doubt that either he does not love, or does not know how to love, his lord.

May almighty God so favour you and your children with prosperity in this life that He may lead you to the happiness of the life to come.[18]

19 Anselm, Archbishop of Canterbury, to Matilda of Scotland

To Matilda, glorious Queen of the English, reverend lady, most beloved daughter, Anselm, Archbishop of Canterbury, sending the blessing of God and his faithful service with prayers.

Let me speak briefly, but from the heart, as to that person whom I desire to advance from an earthly kingdom to a heavenly one. When I hear anything about you which is not pleasing to God or advantageous for you, and if I then neglected to admonish you, I would neither fear God nor would I love you as I should.

After I left England I heard that you were dealing with the churches in your hands otherwise than is expedient for them or for your own soul. I do not wish to say here how you are acting – according to what I have been told – because to no one is it better known than to yourself. Therefore, I beseech you as my lady, advise you as my Queen and admonish you as my daughter – as I have done before – that the churches of God which are in your power should know you as mother, as nurse, as kind lady and queen. I do not say this concerning those churches alone but about all the churches in England to which your help can be extended. For He who says that each one will receive according to what he has done in his body whether good or evil does not exclude anyone.

Again I beg, advise and admonish you, my dearest lady and daughter, not to consider these things heedlessly in your mind, but, if your conscience testifies that you have anything to correct in this matter, hasten to correct it so that in future you will not offend God, as far as this is possible for you through His grace.

Concerning the past, if you see that you have failed in your duty, you should make Him favourable towards you. Surely, it is not enough for someone to desist from evil unless he takes care, if possible, to make amends for what he has done.

May almighty God always guide you so that He may repay you with eternal life.[19]

20 Anselm, Archbishop of Canterbury, to Matilda of Scotland

Your Highness gave me great joy with your letter, insofar as you have given me good hope about yourself. For the humble acceptance of disapproval and admonition is usually followed by hope of improvement. Therefore I give thanks to God who gives you the good will you indicated in your reply to me, and I give thanks to you that you maintain it with sweet affection. Wherefore I pray God that what He himself inspires in you in His mercy He may preserve and increase so that when your soul leaves your body it may be brought before His sight and receive from Him the reward of eternal felicity.

If your prudence needed to be taught how you ought to live in order to please God I would strive to demonstrate this according to my ability. But since I am fully aware that, by the grace of God, you can distinguish between good and evil through the understanding of your mind, this I ask, this I beseech, this I admonish: that the unfailing intention of your heart be that in all your actions, great and small, you rather choose what you consider pleases God more.

In that letter you demonstrated sufficiently with holy and sweet affection that you desire my return to England. But I do not see that he in whose power my return chiefly rests – as far as it depends on a man – agrees in this matter with the will of God, and it would not be good for my soul to disagree with God's will. I fear that he may realise too late that he has gone astray from the right path, having despised God's counsel and having followed the advice of princes, which the Lord brings to nothing. I am certain, however, that he will realise this one day.

May almighty God gladden your excellency and my lowliness one day by the sight of one another, according to His will, and may He multiply the gifts of His grace in you.[20]

21 Matilda of Scotland to Anselm, Archbishop of Canterbury

To her lord and father Anselm, Archbishop of Canterbury, equally to be revered and honoured: from Matilda the Queen, devout handmaid of his holiness, sending greeting with Christ.

As often as you grant me the protection of your Holiness, through the kindness of a letter, you brighten the nebulous gloom of my soul through the light of renewed happiness. Holding your letter and the pleasing, oft-repeated reading of it, is, as it were, like seeing you again, although you are absent. Indeed, my lord, what is there more wonderfully adorned in style and more replete with meaning than your writings? They do not lack the seriousness of Fronto, the fluency of Cicero or the wit of Quintilian; the doctrine of Paul, the precision of Jerome, the learning of Gregory and the interpretation of Augustine are indeed overflowing in them. And what is even greater than all this: from them pours the sweetness of evangelical eloquence. Through this grace pouring over me from your lips, my heart and my flesh thrill with joy at the affection of your love and the effect of your paternal admonition. Indeed, by the most frequent repetition of your exhortation and of your most kind entreaty memory causes the portal of my heart to resound and decide in favour of compliant obedience.

Relying on the favour of your Holiness I have committed the abbey of Malmesbury, in those things which are under my jurisdiction, to Dom Eadwulf, a monk and once sacristan of Winchester, who I believe is known to you. You retain completely whatever pertains to that monastery for your own donation and disposition, so that the bestowal of the crozier and pastoral care is delivered wholly to the judgement of your discretion. May the worthy gift of the grace of your good will, which never grows cold towards me, recompense him like the reward of heavenly grace. Moreover, may Christ, who blesses you on earth, redeem your dignity, and may He soon give me reason to rejoice over your return. Amen.[21]

22 Anselm, Archbishop of Canterbury, to Matilda of Scotland

Most beloved lady, your excellency should know that concerning the abbey of Malmesbury, and the brother about whom you wrote to me, I would gladly confirm your will if I could. For, in what pertains to you, you have acted well and according to the will of God, in what you did there; but he himself did something very foolish in this matter which he should not have done. For, by the same messengers who brought me the letters from you and from others about this case, he sent me a goblet. This goblet I did not wish to keep under any circumstances, but I was very sorry because I do not see how he can be excused from guilt in this matter.

May almighty God guide all your actions in His good pleasure and defend you from all evil.[22]

23 Ivo, Bishop of Chartres, to Matilda of Scotland

To Matilda, excellent Queen of the English, Ivo, humble minister of the church of Chartres, the service of devoted prayers.

The reputation of your pious devotion has inspired the minds of many religious and sweetened them with a certain delight of holy love. Wherefore for the grace divinely conferred on us we give thanks to the Bestower of all goods who placed a man's strength in a woman's breast, not only to avoid shame and crime but also to give necessary aid to those in need.

We who are mindful of common as well as private benefits, devoutly received the prayers of your excellence and we pour out devoted prayers to God for the soul of your brother, the religious King, which, given our sins, are of little value though we are confident that his soul reposes in Abraham's bosom, if his life was what it is said to have been. But since the state of souls after life is uncertain, it does not seem superfluous for us to intercede for those who already enjoy rest, that their rest be increased, and for those who are in purgatory, that they receive indulgence through the prayers of the faithful. These and other things which do not exceed our strength, your Excellence can place on our shoulders.[23]

24 Bernard, Abbot of Clairvaux, to Matilda of Boulogne

To the most illustrious ruling lady and most beloved daughter in Christ – which I say not with presumption but in affection – Matilda, by the grace of God, Queen of the English, Bernard.

If I presume on your Highness, it is no wonder. I do not feel it alone, but almost all know how you keep receiving us and with how much affection you love us. On that account, I am asked by a certain friend of yours, the venerable Abbot of Capelle, to ask you for a certain tithe, about which, if you remember well, I asked you at Boulogne, and you in your customary way heard me benignly. But since what we ask is not yet done, it is time that that request be filled. For the rest, preserve my son for me, to whom you just gave birth, since I also – if it does not displease the king – lay claim to a portion in him. Fare well.[24]

25 Bernard, Abbot of Clairvaux, to Matilda of Boulogne

To his most beloved daughter in Christ, Matilda, by the grace of God Queen of the English, Bernard, called Abbot of Clairvaux, to reign in perpetuity with the angels.

Since the occasion offers, we greet your Majesty in the Lord willingly and from affection of the heart, suggesting not only willingly but confidently what we know pertains to your salvation and the glory of your kingdom. Accordingly, if you fear God and if you wish to acquiesce to our counsel in anything, do everything to prevent that man from occupying the church of York any longer, about whose life and entry into the episcopacy religious men in whom one must trust give such testimony. We commit this, God's cause, to you — act so that it be brought to worthy conclusion, and protect all those who have worked for this side, that they not suffer offence from the King or any harm on its account. They have done good work. Further, if you get the lord King to renounce this sacrilege of intrusion into the election before his bishops and princes, which he should only have assent to, know that it would bring great honour to God, great safety and security to the king and to what is his, great utility to the whole kingdom. Fare well.[25]

26 Thomas Becket, Archbishop of Canterbury, to the Empress Maud

We thank God, who illumined your nobility with signs of virtue greater than of birth, and one whom He brought forth most brilliant by blood in the Roman orb, He did not fail to light with good works in the world. For your name is great in the Lord from east to west, and the churches of the saints recount your alms. Although the subsidy of temporal things which you extend to Him in His members pleases God greatly, we believe He is no less pleased by [your] solicitude for ecclesiastical peace and liberty which, as it is rumoured, you strive for with such feeling, so that you may say with the Apostle: 'Who is sick and I am not sick? Who is offended and I not burn?' Wherefore we, who by reason of your humanity and beneficence, consider it to be properly responsible if we speak very confidently in your ear about the peace of the Church, asking and praying assiduously to the Lord for your salvation and the temporal as well as eternal glory of your son, that you charge him diligently to procure peace for the Church with the assiduousness of devotion with which he desires to procure the peace of God for his heirs and his lands through the merits of the saints.

What particularly saddens us: it is spoken of from east to west that he afflicts the churches of his kingdom intolerably and requires unheard-of and unaccustomed things from them, which if ancient kings sought them, they should not have. It may be that, in his time, from one on whom God conferred such wisdom, such affliction can in some way be tolerated, but perhaps after his day, will rule those who wish to devour the church with their mouths, and who, hardened, will say with Pharaoh: 'I do not know the Lord and I shall not let Israel go.' Let him remember, we beg, by your prayers and exhortations, how [God] lifted him beyond the titles of his noble fathers and extended his boundaries beyond the boundaries of his elders. What good will it do a ruler if he transmits sins to his heirs and makes them enemies of God and the Church in his testament? What good to his ancestors if, having seized the occasion of their crimes, he offends God as if by hereditary right?

God was to be placated, most serene lady, by other services; it was fitting to offer other gifts for the salvation of elders and redemption of sins. Sacrifices from plunder do not please God, unless perhaps it may please the father that his son be sacrificed. If he came to his senses, the Father of mercies is prompt to forgiveness, but beyond doubt He will render judgment without mercy to those who exercise no mercy. He is powerful and the powerful punish powerfully; He is terrible and destroys princes, so the tortured may threaten the stronger more forcefully.

You ought, if you please, [to] employ the diligence of a mother and the authority of a lady to recall him to duty, you who acquired the kingdom and duchy for him with much effort, and transmitted hereditary rights to him in succession, by the use of which the Church is now oppressed and trampled, innocents punished, and the poor intolerably afflicted. We willingly do what we can for your salvation and his soul, imploring the mercy of God by our prayers as best we can continuously. We will pray more confidently if, with peace restored to the churches, he returns to God, his author and benefactor, with prompt devotion. Let him not be ashamed to humble himself before God in penitence, when to ancient kings who are blessed in memory, nothing was a source of greater glory than the title of penitent, the zeal for divine law, veneration of priests, and most faithful humility, guardian of virtues. For by such sacrifices, David, Hezekiah, Josiah, and Constantine pleased the Lord, and achieved glory among men from generation to generation.[26]

Select Bibiography

Primary Sources

The Rolls Series, referred to below, comprises a collection of original sources known as *Chronicles and Memorials of Great Britain and Ireland during the Middle Ages*, published by HM Stationery Office, London, under the direction of the Master of the Rolls.

'Les actes de Guillaume le Conquérant et de la reine Mathilde pour les abbayes caënnaises' (ed. L. Musset, *Mémoires de la Société des Antiquaires de Normandie*, vol. 37, 1967)

Actus pontificum in urbe degentium (ed. G. Busson and A. Ledru, Société des Archives historiques de Maine, 2, 1902)

Additional Charters (The British Library)

Additional MSS (The British Library)

Adelard of Bath: *Des Adelard von Bath Traktat De eodem et diverso zum ersten Male herausgegeben und historisch-kritisch untersucht* (ed. Hans Edouard Ernst Wilner, Munster, 1903)

Aelred of Rievaulx: 'Eulogium Davidis Regis Scotorum' (in *Vitae antiquae sanctorum qui habitaverunt in ea parte Britanniae nunc vocatia Scotia*)

————'Genealogia regum Anglorum' (in *Patrologia Latina*, vol. 195)

————*Relatio de Standardo* (in *Chronicles of the Reigns of Stephen, Henry II and Richard I*)

Ambrose (*fl. c.*1190): *L'Estoire de la Guerre Sainte* (ed. Gaston Paris, Paris, 1897)

Analectes pour server a l'Histoire Ecclesiastique de la Belgique (ed. E. de Marneffe, Louvain, 1864)

Ancient Charters, Royal and Private, prior to AD 1200 (ed. J. H. Round, Pipe Roll Society, 1888)

Ancient Lives of Scottish Saints (tr. W. M. Metcalfe, Paisley, 1895)

Andrew of Wyntoun: *The Orygynale Cronykil of Scotland by Androw of Wyntoun* (3 vols., ed. David Laing, Edinburgh, 1872)

Anglica, Hibernica, Normannica, Cambrica, a veteribus scripta: ex quibus Asser Meneuensis, Anonymus de vita Gulielmi Conquestoris, Thomas VValsingham, Thomas de la More, Gulielmus Gemeticiensis, Giraldus Cambrensis (ed. William Camden, Frankfurt, 1602)

The Anglo-Latin Satirical Poets and Epigrammatists of the Twelfth Century (2 vols., ed. Thomas Wright, Cambridge, 1872)

The Anglo-Saxon Chronicle (ed. and tr. G. N. Garmonsway, London, 1953)

The Anglo-Saxon Chronicles: The authentic voices of England from the time of Julius Caesar to the coronation of Henry II (tr. and ed. Anne Savage, London, 1982)

'Annales Abbatae de Bermondsey' (in *Annales Monastici*)

Annales Monastici (5 vols., ed. H. R. Luard, Rolls Series, 1864–9)

Annales Patherbrunnenses (ed. Paul Scheffer-Boichorst, Innsbruck, 1870)

'Annals of Margam, 1066–1232' (in *Annales Monastici*)

'Annals of Tewkesbury Abbey' (in *Annales Monastici*)

'Annals of Waverley Abbey' (in *Annales Monastici*)

The Anonimalle Chronicle, 1333 to 1381: From a MS. Written at St Mary's Abbey, York (ed. V. H. Galbraith, Manchester, 1970)

Anselm of Aosta: *The Letters of St Anselm of Canterbury* (3 vols., tr. Walter Frohlich, Kalamazoo, 1990–4)

————*S. Anselmi Cantuariensis archiepiscopi opera omnia* (6 vols., ed. F. S. Schmitt, Seckau, 1938–61; Edinburgh, 1946–63)

————*Sancti Anselmi Opera omnia* (2 vols., ed. J. Migne, Paris, 1854)

Archaeologia, or Miscellaneous Tracts relating to Antiquity (102 vols., various editors, The Society of Antiquaries of London, 1773–1969)

Archives départementales du Calvados

Asser, Bishop of Sherborne: *Alfred the Great: Asser's Life of Alfred and Other Contemporary Sources* (tr. Simon Keynes and Michael Lapidge, London, 1983)

Baldwin of Avesnes (1219–95): 'The Chronicle of Baldwin of Avesnes' (tr. Frank Jewett Mather Jr, *Record of the Museum of Historic Art, Princeton University*, vol. 5, 1, 1946)

Baudri de Bourgeuil: *Oeuvres poétiques* (ed. P. Abrahams, Paris, 1926)

Beati Lanfranci opera omnia, ed. L. d'Archery, Paris, 1648)

Benedeit: *The Anglo-Norman Voyage of St Brendan* (ed. Ian Short and Brian S. Merrilees, Manchester, 1979)

Benoît de Saint-Maure (d. *c.*1173): *Chronique des ducs de Normandie* (3 vols., ed. Carin Fahlin, Uppsala, 1951–4)

Bernard of Clairvaux: *Sancti Bernardi Opera* (8 vols., ed. J. LeClercq and H. Rochais, Rome, 1955–77)

Bibliotheca Rerum Germanicarum (6 vols., ed. Philipp Jaffé, Berlin, 1869)

Boece, Hector: *The Chronicles of Scotland, compiled by Hector Boece* (2 vols., Edinburgh, 1938)

The Brut, or the Chronicles of England (2 vols., ed. F. Brie, Early English Texts Society, London, 1906, 1908)

Calendar of Charter Rolls preserved in the Public Record Office (6 vols., London, 1903)

Calendar of Documents preserved in France illustrative of the History of Great Britain and Ireland, Vol. 1: 918–1206 (ed. J. H. Round, London, 1899)

Calendar of Documents relating to Scotland (5 vols., ed. Joseph Bain, Edinburgh, 1881–8)

Calendar of Entries in the Papal Registers relating to Great Britain and Ireland (ed. W. H. Bliss, 1893; London, 1960)

Calendar of Patent Rolls preserved in the Public Record Office (London, 1906)

Calendars of Charter Rolls (The National Archives)

Calendars of Close Rolls (The National Archives)

Calendars of Patent Rolls (The National Archives)

Camden, William: *Annales rerum Anglicarum et Hibernicarum regnante Elizabetha* (London, 1615)

Capgrave, John (1393–1464): *The Book of the Illustrious Henries* (ed. and tr. F. C. Hingeston, London, 1858)

———*The Chronicle of England* (ed. F. C. Hingeston, London, 1858)

Cartulaire de l'Abbaye d'Affligem (1432) (in *Analectes pour server a l'Histoire Ecclesiastique de la Belgique*)

'Cartulaire de l'abbaye de Sainte-Trinité du Mont de Rouen' (ed. Achille Deville, in *Collection des cartulaires de France*, Paris, 1840)

Le cartulaire de la chapitre cathedral de Coutances (ed. Julie Fontanel, Saint-Lo, 2003)

The Cartulary of Holy Trinity, Aldgate (ed. Gerald A. J. Hodgett, London Record Society, 1971)

Catalogue of Romances in the Department of Manuscripts in the British Museum (ed. J. A. Herbert, London, 1883–1910)

Charters of David I (ed. G. W. S. Barrow, Woodbridge, 1999)

Charters and Documents illustrating the History of the Cathedral Church and Diocese of Salisbury in the Twelfth and Thirteenth Centuries (ed. W. R. Jones and W. D. Macray, Rolls Series, 1891)

Charters and Records among the Archives of the Ancient Abbey of Cluni in the National Library of France, from 1077 to 1534 (2 vols., ed. G. F. Duckett, Lewes, 1888)

Chartes de Saint-Julien de Tours 1000–1300 (ed. J.-L. Denis, Le Mans, 1912–13)

The Chartulary of Boxgrove Priory (ed. L. Fleming, Sussex Record Society, 59, 1960)

'Chronicae Sancti Albini Andegauensis' (in *Chroniques des églises d'Anjou*)

The Chronicle of Battle Abbey (ed. E. Searle, Oxford, 1861)

'The Chronicle of Holy Trinity, Aldgate' (printed as an appendix to *The Cartulary of Holy Trinity, Aldgate*)

Chronicle of London, 1089–1483 (15th C) (ed. Sir Harris Nicolas, The Society of Antiquaries of London, 1827)

'The Chronicle of Melrose' (in *The Church Historians of England*)

The Chronicle of Tewkesbury Abbey, 1066–1262 (Bodleian Library MS. Lat. misc. b. 2 (R))

'The Chronicle of Tours' (*Chronicon Turonense*) (in *Recueil des historiens des Gaules et de la France*)

Chronicles of the Reigns of Stephen, Henry II and Richard I (ed. R. Howlett, Rolls Series, 1885)

Chronicon Monasterii de Abingdon (2 vols., ed. Joseph Stevenson, Cambridge, 1858)

Chronicon Valassense (ed. F. Sommenil, Rouen, 1868)

Chronique du Bec (ed. A. A. Porée, Rouen, 1883)

La Chronique de Marigney (ed. Leon Mirot, Paris, 1912)

Chroniques Anglo-Normandes (3 vols., ed. Francisque Michel, Rouen, 1836)

Chroniques des comtes d'Anjou (1100–60) (ed. L. Halphen and R. Poupardin, Paris, 1913)

Chroniques des comtes d'Anjou et des seigneurs d'Amboise (ed. P. Marchegay and A. Salmon, Paris, 1856–71)

Chroniques des églises d'Anjou (ed. Paul Marchegay and Emile Mabille, Paris, 1869)

Chroniques de Normandie (1350–70) (ed. Francisque Michel, Rouen, 1839)

The Church Historians of England (5 vols., ed. J. Stevenson, London, 1856)

Clare, Osbert de: *The Letters of Osbert de Clare, Prior of Westminster* (ed. E. W. Williamson, Oxford, 1929, reprinted 1998)

A Collection of Wills of the Kings and Queens of England from William the Conqueror to Henry VII (ed. J. Nichols, Society of Antiquaries of London, 1780)

'Constitutio Domus Regis' (1136) (in *Dialogus de Scaccario, and Constitutio Domus Regis*)

Contemporary Chronicles of the Middle Ages (tr. Joseph Stephenson, Felinfach, 1988)

Continuatio Chronici Afflegemiensis (in *Veterum Aliquot Scriptorum Qui in Galliae Bibliothecis, maxime Benedictinorum latuerant, Spicilegium*, Vol. 10, Paris, 1671)

Corpus Christi College MS. 373

Cotton MSS (The British Library)

Crispin, Milo (d.1149): 'Vita Lanfranci' (in *Beati Lanfranci opera omnia*)

The Culture of Christendom: Essays in Medieval History in Commemoration of Denis L. T. Bethell (ed. Marc A. Meyer, New York, 1993)

Curia Regis Rolls (National Archives)

Dialogus de Scaccario, and Constitutio Domus Regis/The Dialogue of the Exchequer, and The Establishment of the Royal Household (ed. Emilie Amt and Stephen Church, Oxford, 2007)

Domesday Book (Ordnance Survey, 1861–4)

Dugdale, William: *Monasticon Anglicanum: a History of the Abbies and other Monasteries, Hospitals, Frieries, and Cathedral and Collegiate Churches, with their Dependencies, in England and Wales* (6 vols., London, 1817–30)

The Durham *Liber Vitae* (British Library Cotton MS. Domitian VII)

Eadmer: *Historia Novorum in Anglia* (ed. M. Rule, London, 1884; tr. G. Bosanquet, London, 1964)

————*Vita Sancti Anselmi* (ed. M. Rule, London, 1884)

The Early Charters of the Augustinian Canons of Waltham Abbey, Essex 1062–1230 (Studies in the History of Medieval Religion) (ed. Rosalind Ransford, Woodbridge, 1989)

Early Sources of Scottish History, AD 500–1286 (2 vols., ed. Alan Orr Anderson, Edinburgh, 1922)

Early Yorkshire Charters (13 vols., ed. William Farrer and Charles Travis Clay, Cambridge, 1914–65)

Encomium Emmae Reginae (1041–2) (ed. Alistair Campbell, London, 1949; reprinted Cambridge, 1998)

English Coronation Records (ed. Leopold George Wickham Legg, London, 1901)

English Episcopal Acta 28: Canterbury 1070–1136 (ed. Martin Brett and David Michael Smith, Oxford, 2004)

English Lawsuits from William I to Richard I (2 vols., ed. R. C. Van Caenegem, London, 1990)

Epistolae: Medieval Women's Latin Letters (www.epistolae.ccnmtl.columbia.edu)

Epistolae Selectae, Das Register Gregors VII (2 vols., ed. Erich Caspar, Monumenta Germaniae Historica, Berlin, 1920–3)

Epistolari Herberti de Losinga, primi Episcopi Norwicensis, nunc primum (8 vols., ed. Robert Anstruther, Brussels and London, 1846)

Excerpta Historica (ed. S. Bentley and Sir Harris Nicolas, London, 1831)

The First Register of Norwich Cathedral Priory (ed. H. W. Saunders, Norfolk Record Society, 1939)

FitzStephen, William (d.1190): *Vita Sancti Thomae (Life of St Thomas)* (ed. Leo T. Gourde and Mary Ailred Sinclair, as *An Annotated Translation of the Life of St Thomas Becket by William Fitzstephen*, 3 vols., Chicago, 1943. FitzStephen's 'Descriptio nobilissimae civitatis Londoniae' is the preface to this work.)

Flete, John (*c.*1398–1456): *The History of Westminster Abbey* (ed. J. Armitage Robinson, Cambridge, 1909)

Fleury, Hugh de: 'Modernorum regum francorum actus' (ed. D. G. Waitz, Monumenta Germaniae Historica, SS ix, Hanover, 1851)

Foliot, Gilbert: *The Letters and Charters of Gilbert Foliot* (ed. Z. N. Brooke, A. Morey and C. N. L. Brooke, Cambridge, 1967)

Gaimar, Geoffrey (*fl.*1136–7): *L'Estoire des Engles* (ed. T. D. Hardy, tr. C. T. Martin, Rolls Series, 1888–9)

Geoffrey of Auxerre: 'Fragmenta ex tertia vita Sancti Bernardi' (in *Patrologia Latina*, Vol. 185)

————'S. Bernardi Vita Prima' (in *Patrologia Latina*, Vol. 185)

Geoffrey of Vigeois (*c.*1140–after 1184): 'Chronica Gaufredi coenobitae monasterii D. Martialis Lemovicensis, ac prioris Vosiensis coenobii' (in *Novae bibliothecae manuscriptorum librorum tomus secundus: rerum aquitanicarum*, ed. Philippe Labbe, Paris, 1657)

Gervase of Canterbury: *Historical Works* (ed. W. Stubbs, Rolls Series, 1879–80)

Gervase of Tilbury (*c.*1150–1228): Dialogue concerning the Exchequer (Ripon Cathedral Library VI.F.13)

Gesta Stephani (*The Deeds of Stephen*) (ed. K. R. Potter, London, 1955; also in *Chronicles of the Reigns of Stephen, Henry II and Richard I*)

Giraldus Cambrensis (*c.*1146–*c.*1223): *Opera*, incorporating *De Principis Instructione*, *Gemma Ecclesiastica* and *Speculum Ecclesia* (ed. J. S. Brewer and G. F. Warner, London, 1861)

Guibert of Nogent-sous-Coucy: *The Autobiography of Guibert, Abbot of Nogent-sous-Coucy* (ed. and tr. G. G. Coulton and C. C. Swinton, London, 1925)

Hardying, John (1378–1465): *The Chronicle of John Hardying* (ed. H. Ellis, London, 1812)

Harleian MSS (The British Library)

Hastings MSS (Historical Manuscripts Commission)

Helgald (mid-12th C): *Vita Roberti regis* (in *Recueil des historiens des croisades*)

Henry of Huntingdon: *Historia Anglorum* (ed. T. Arnold, Rolls Series, 1879; published as *The History of the English People, 1000–1154*, ed. and tr. Diana Greenway, Oxford, 1996)

Herbert de Losinga: *Epistolae Herberti de Losinga, Primi Episcopi Norwicensis* (ed. A. Robert Anstruther, New York, 1846, 1969)

Herman the Archdeacon and Goscelin of Saint-Bertin: *Miracles of St Edmund* (ed. Tom Licence, Oxford, 2014)

Herman of Tournai (*c.*1140): *The Restoration of the Monastery of Saint Martin of Tournai* (ed. and tr. Lynn Harry Nelson, Medieval Texts in Translation, Washington, 1996)

Hildebert of Lavardin: *Carmina Minora* (ed. A. B. Scott, Leipzig, 1969)
————'Letters' (ed. J.-P. Migne, in *Patrologia Latina*, Vol. 171)

Histoire de la congregation de Savigny (3 vols., ed. R. C. Auvry and A. P. Laveille, Rouen, 1896–8)

Histoire des ducs de Normandie et des rois d'Angleterre (13th C) (ed. Francisque Michel, Société de l'Histoire de France, Paris, 1840)

Histoire de Guillaume le Maréchale (ed. Paul Meyer, Société de l'Histoire de France, Paris, 1891–1901; published as *The History of William Marshal*, 3 vols., ed. and tr. A. J. Holden, S. Gregory and David Crouch, London, 2002–6)

Historia et cartularium monasterii Sancti Petri Gloucestriae (3 vols., ed. William Henry Hart, Rolls Series, 1863–7)

The Historians of the Church of York and its Archbishops (3 vols., ed. J. Raine, Rolls Series, 1879–94)

Hugh the Chanter: *The History of the Church of York, 1066–1127* (ed. Charles Johnson, M. Brett, C. N. L. Brooke and M. Winterbottom, Oxford, 1990)

Hugh of Fleury: *Hugonis Liber qui Modernorum Regum Francorum Continet Actus* (ed. D. G. Waitz and G. H. Pertz, Monumenta Germaniae Historica, Hanover, 1851)

Hugo of St Vaast: 'Beatae Idae Vita Auctore Monacho Wastensi Coaeva' (in *Patrologia Latina* Vol. 348A)

Illustrations of Ancient State and Chivalry from Manuscripts Preserved in the Ashmolean Museum (ed. W. H. Black, Roxburgh Club, London, 1840)

Ingulph: *The Chronicle of the Abbey of Croyland* (ed. H. T. Riley, London, 1854)

Intimate Letters of England's Queens (ed. M. Sanders, London, 1957)

Ivo of Chartres: 'Epistolae' (ed. J.-P. Migne, in Vol. 139 of *Patrologia Latina*)

Jocelin of Brakelond: *Chronicle* (1173–1202) (ed. G. Rokewoode, Camden Society, 1840; ed. H. E. Butler, London, 1949)

John of Forde: *The Life of Wulfric of Haselbury* (ed. E. M. Bell, Somerset Record Society, 1933)

John of Fordun: *Chronica Gentis Scotorum* (ed. William F. Skene, Edinburgh, 1871)

John of Hexham: *Historia Regum* (ed. T. Arnold, Rolls Series, 1882–5)

John of Salisbury: *Historia Pontificalis* (*c.*1163) (ed. R. L. Poole, Oxford, 1927; ed. M. Chibnall, Oxford, 1986)

————*The Letters of John of Salisbury* (ed. W. J. Miller and C. N. L. Brooke, 2 vols., Oxford, 1979, 1986)

John of Worcester: *The Chronicle of John of Worcester, 1118–1140* (ed. J. R. H. Weaver, Oxford, 1908)

Keepe, Henry: *Monumenta Westmonasteriensia* (London, 1683)

Kings' Letters: From the Days of Alfred to the Accession of the Tudors (ed. Robert Steele, London, 1903)

Lambeth Palace MS. 371 (Lambeth Palace, London)

Lanfranc: *The Letters of Lanfranc, Archbishop of Canterbury* (ed. Helen Clover and Margaret Gibson, Oxford, 1979)

Lansdowne MSS (The British Library)

Leland, John: *The Itinerary of John Leland in or about the years 1535–1543* (5 vols., ed. Lucy Toulin Smith, London, 1906–10)

Letters of the Kings of England (ed. J. O. Halliwell, London, 1846)

Letters of the Queens of England, 1100–1546 (ed. Anne Crawford, Stroud, 1994)

Letters of Royal and Illustrious Ladies of Great Britain (3 vols., ed. Mary Anne Everett Wood, London, 1846)

Lettres de Rois, Reines et Autres Personnages de Cours de France et d'Angleterre (2 vols., ed. J. J. Champollion-Figeac, Paris, 1839–47)

Liber Eliensis (The Book of Ely) (ed. and tr. Janet Fairweather, Woodbridge, 2005)

Liber Feodorum: The Book of Fees, commonly called 'Testa de Nevill', reformed from the earliest MSS (3 vols., HMSO, London, 1920–31)

Liber Monasterii de Hyde (ed. E. Edwards, Rolls Series, 1866)

Liberate Rolls (The National Archives)

The Life of Gundulf, Bishop of Rochester (ed. R. Thomson, Toronto, 1977)

The Life of King Edward who rests at Westminster (ed. Frank Barlow, London, 1962)

'The Life of Lanfranc' (in *The Abbey of Bec and the Anglo-Norman State*)

Lisiard of Crépy, Bishop of Soissons, and Hariulf, Abbot of Oldenburg: *The Life of Saint Arnulf, Bishop of Soissons* (1081–7) (tr. John S. Ott, 2012, http://www.web.pdx.edu/%7Eott/vitaarnulfi/index.html)

Le Livere de Reis de Brittanie e le Livere de Reis de Engleterre (Anglo-Norman, *c.*1300) (ed. John Glover, London, 1865)

Luffield Priory Charters, Part 2 (ed. G. R. Elvey, Buckinghamshire and Northamptonshire Record Societies, 1975)

Magni Rotuli Scaccarii Normanniae sub Regibus Angliae (2 vols., ed. Thomas Stapleton, London, 1840)

Map, Walter (1140–*c*.1208): *De Nugis Curialium* (ed. T. Wright, Camden Society, 1850)

Marbodius, Bishop of Rennes: 'Letters' (ed. J.-P. Migne, in Vol. 171 of *Patrologia Latina*)

Materials for the History of Thomas Becket (7 vols., ed. J. C. Robertson, Rolls Series, London, 1875–85)

Medieval Age: Specimens of European Poetry from the 9th to the 15th Century (ed. Angel Flores, 1963)

Memoranda Rolls (The National Archives)

Memorials of St Edmund's Abbey (3 vols., ed. T. Arnold, Rolls Series, 1890–6)

Merton College MS. 249 (University of Oxford)

Miscellanea Genealogica et Heraldica (ed. W. Bruce Bannerman, London, 1912)

Mouskes, Philippe, Bishop of Tournai: M. de Reu, 'Philippe Mousket, Chronique rimée; Historia regum francorum' (in *The Narrative Sources from the Medieval Low Countries*)

Munimenta Gildhallae Londoniensis (4 vols., ed. H. T. Riley, Rolls Series, 1859–62)

The Narrative Sources from the Medieval Low Countries. De verhalende bronnen uit de Zuidelijke Nederlanden (ed. M. de Reu, Brussels, 2009)

Niger, Ralph (c. 1140–*c*.1217): *Chronica* (ed. R. Anstruther, Caxton Society, 1851)

The Northamptonshire Geld Roll (2 vols., tr. Abraham Farley, London, 1783)

Oorkondenbock van het Sticht Utrecht tot 1302 (ed. S. Muller and A. C. Bouman, Utrecht, 1920)

Orderic Vitalis: *Historia Ecclesiastica* (5 vols., ed. A. L. Le Prevost, Société de l'Histoire de France, Paris, 1838–55; ed. M. Guizot, and tr. as *The Ecclesiastical History of England and Normandy* by Thomas Forester, London, 1854)

Original Letters illustrative of English History (11 vols., ed. H. Ellis, London, 1824–46)

Paris, Matthew: *Flores Historiarum* (3 vols., ed. H. R. Luard, Rolls Series, 1890)

———*Historia Anglorum* (3 vols., ed. Sir F. H. Madden, Rolls Series, 1866–9)

———*Matthaei Parisiensis monachi Sancti Albani Chronica Majora* (7 vols., ed. H. R. Luard, Rolls Series, 1872–83)

Patrologia Latina (221 vols., Paris, 1844–64)

Peter of Blois: *Petri Blensis Archidiaconi Opera Omnia* (4 vols., ed. J. A. Giles, Oxford, 1846–7)

Piers of Langtoft (d. *c.*1305): *The Chronicle of Pierre de Langtoft* (2 vols., ed. T. Wright, Rolls Series, 1866–8)

Pipe Roll 31 Henry I (ed. J. Hunter, London, 1833)

The Pipe Rolls (The National Archives)

The Plantagenet Chronicles (ed. Elizabeth Hallam, London, 1986)

Ralph of Diceto (d. *c.*1202): *Imagines Historiarum* (ed. W. Stubbs, Rolls Series, 1876)

Reading Abbey Cartularies (2 vols., ed. Brian R. Kemp, London, 1986–7)

Recueil des actes des ducs de Normandie (911–1966) (ed. Marie Fauroux, Caen, 1961)

Recueil des actes de Henry II (4 vols., ed. Leopold Delisle and Elie Berger, Paris, 1909–17)

Recueil d'annales Angevines et Vendômoises (ed. L. Halphen, Paris, 1903)

Recueil des chartes de l'abbaye de Cluny (6 vols., ed. Alexandre Bruel, Paris, 1876–1903)

Recueil des chroniques de Touraine (ed. A. Salmon, Société archéologique de Touraine, Tours, 1854)

Recueil des historiens des croisades (17 vols., Paris, 1841–1906)

Recueil des historiens des Gaules et de la France (25 vols., ed. M. Bouquet and L. Delisle, Paris, 1840–1904)

Recueil de travaux d'érudition dédiés à la mémoire de Julien Havet (1853–1893) (ed. Julien Pierre Eugène Havet, Paris, 1895, and by M. L. Delisle, Geneva, 1972)

Regesta Regum Anglo-Normannorum, 1066–1154 (4 vols., ed. David Bates, H. W. C. Davis, Charles Johnson, H. A. Cronne and R. H. C. Davis, Oxford, 1913–98)

Regesta Regum Anglo-Normannorum: The Acta of William I (1066–1087) (ed. D. Bates, Oxford, 1998)

Regesta Stephani (ed. H. A. Cronne and R. H. C. Davis, Oxford, 1968–9)

The Register of Pope Gregory VII, 1073–1085 (ed. and tr. H. E. J. Cowdray, Oxford, 2002)

'La reine Mathilde et la fondation de la Trinité de Caen (Abbaye aux Dames)' (ed. L. Musset, *Mémoires de l'Académie Nationale des Sciences, Arts et Belles Lettres*, 21, 1984)

Relazioni degli Ambasciatori Veneti al Senato durante il Secolo Decimo Sesto (15 vols., ed. E. Alberi, Florence, 1839–63)

Richard of Devizes (*fl.* late 12th C): *Chronicon Richardi Divisensis de tempore Regis Richardi Primi* (ed. J. T. Appleby, London, 1963)

Richard of Hexham: *Historia de gestis regis Stephani ci de bello Standardii* (in *Chronicles of the Reigns of Stephen, Henry II and Richard I* and *Contemporary Chronicles of the Middle Ages*)

Robert of Cricklade: Defloratio historie naturalis Plinii (British Library, Royal MS. 15 C. XIV)

Robert of Gloucester: *The Metrical Chronicle of Robert of Gloucester* (2 vols., ed. W. A. Wright, Rolls Series, 1886–7)

Robert of Torigni: *Chronica* (after 1154) (in *Chronicles of the Reigns of Stephen, Henry II and Richard I*)

Roger of Hoveden (*fl.* 1174–1201): *Chronica* (4 vols., ed. W. Stubbs, Rolls Series, 1868–71)

The Roll of Battle Abbey (Auchinlek MS. ff. 105v–107r, National Library of Scotland; 14th C copy of the original roll of companions of the Conqueror, missing since the 16th C)

Rouleaux des morts du Ixe au Xve siècle (ed. Leopold Delisle, Paris, 1866)

Royal MSS (The British Library)

Rudborne, Thomas (mid 15th C): 'Historia Major' (in Wharton: *Anglia Sacra*)

Rymer, Thomas: *Foedera* (London, 1704–35; ed. T. Hardy and others, Records Commission, 1816–69)

Scriptores rerum Germanicarum, praecipue Saxonicarum (3 vols., ed. Johann Burkhard Mencken, Leipzig, 1728–30)

Scriptores rerum gestarum Willelmi Conquestoris (ed. J. A. Giles, London, 1845)

Simeon of Durham: *Historia Regum Anglorum* in *Symeonis monachi opera omnia* (2 vols., ed. T. Arnold, Rolls Series, 1882–5)

————'Opera et Collectanea' (ed. H. Hinde, *Proceedings of the Surtees Society*, 51, 1867)

Six Town Chronicles of England (ed. R. Flenley, Oxford, 1911)

Statutes of the Realm, 1101–1713 (11 vols., Records Commissioners, London, 1810–28)

Stephen of Rouen: 'Draco Normannicus' (in *Chronicles of the Reigns of Stephen, Henry II and Richard I*)

Stow, John: *The Annals of England* (London, 1580)

————*The Survey of London* (London, 1598; 2 vols., ed. C. L. Kingsford, Oxford, 1908; ed. H. B. Wheatley, London, 1987)

Sturluson, Snorri (1230): *The Saga of Harald Hardrada* (ed. Hermann Paulsson and Magnus Magnusson, London, 1976)

Suger, Abbot of Saint-Denis: *On the Abbey Church of St Denis and its Art Treasures* (ed. and tr. Erwin Panofsky, Princeton, 1946)

Thaon, Philippe de: *Bestiary* (*c.*1122) (in *Medieval Latin and French Bestiaries*)

————*Le Livre de Sibylle by Philippe de Thaon* (ed. Hugh Shields, Anglo-Norman Text Society, 37, 1979)

Turgot, Prior of Durham: 'Life of St Margaret' (in *Ancient Lives of Scottish Saints*)

'Vita Beati Simonis Comitis Crespeiensis Auctore Synchrono: Guiberti Opera Illustranda (Additamenta)' (in *Patrologia Latina*, Vol. 156)

Vitae antiquae sanctorum qui habitaverunt in ea parte Britanniae nunc vocatia Scotia (ed. John Pinkerton, London, 1789)

Vita Sanctae Margaretae Scotorum Reginae (in Simeon of Durham: 'Opera et Collectanea')

Wace, Robert: *Roman de Brut* (ed. and tr. Judith Weiss, Exeter, 2002)

———*Roman de Rou et des ducs de Normandie* (tr. Alexander Malet , London, 1860)

Walsingham, Thomas: *Gesta abbatum monasterii Sancti Albani* (ed. Henry Thomas Riley, London, 1867)

The Waltham Annals (1066–1447) (in *English Historical Literature of the Fifteenth Century*, ed. C. L. Kingsford, Oxford, 1913)

Wardrobe and Household Accounts (The National Archives)

Warrants for Issues (Exchequer Records, The National Archives)

Weever, John: *Ancient Funeral Monuments within the United Monarchies of Great Britain, Northern Ireland and the Islands Adjacent* (London, 1631)

Westminster Abbey Charters 1066–c.1214 (ed. E. Mason and J. Bray, London, 1988)

Wharton, Henry: *Anglia Sacra* (2 vols., London, 1691)

William of Jumièges: *Gesta Normannorum Ducum* (ed. J. Marx, Société de l'Histoire de Normandie, 1914)

William of Malmesbury: *A History of the Norman Kings (1066–1125)* [*Gesta Regum Anglorum*] *with the Historia Novella, or History of His Own Times (1126–1142)* [*The Contemporary History*] (tr. John Sharpe and ed. Joseph Stevenson, London, 1854; reprinted Llanerch, 2000)

William of Newburgh: *Historia rerum Anglicarum* (in *Chronicles of the Reigns of Stephen, Henry II and Richard I*)

William of Poitiers: *Gesta Willelmi Ducis Normannorum et Regis Anglorum* (ed. and tr. R. H. C. Davis and Marjorie Chibnall, Oxford, 1998; in *Scriptores rerum gestarum Willelmi Conquestoris*; in Thorpe: *The Bayeux Tapestry and the Norman Invasion*; and published as *Histoire de Guillaume le Conquérant*, ed. R. Foreville, Paris, 1952)

William of Saint-Thierry, Arnold of Bonneval and Geoffrey of Auxerre: *The First Life of Bernard of Clairvaux (The Vita Prima)* (Collegeville, 2015)

William of Tyre: *A History of Deeds Done Beyond the Sea* (tr. Emily A. Babcock and A. C. Krey, New York, 1943)

William of Worcester: *Itineraries of William Worcester; edited from the unique MS. Corpus Christi College, Cambridge, 210* (tr. John H. Harvey, Oxford, 1969)

Secondary Sources

The Abbey of Bec and the Anglo-Norman State (ed. Sally N. Vaughn, Woodbridge, 1981)

Abbott, Judith: 'Political Strategies at the Coronation of Queen Matilda I' (unpublished conference paper, 1990)

Abernethy, Susan: *Adeliza of Louvain, Queen of England* (www. thefreelancehistorywriter.com)

Adair, John: *The Royal Palaces of Britain* (London, 1981)

Adam, R. J.: *The Conquest of England: The Coming of the Normans* (London, 1965)

'Adeliza of Leuven' (in *World Heritage Encyclopaedia*, www.gutenberg.us)

Adeliza of Louvain (www.familysearch.org)

Aird, William M.: *Robert Curthose, Duke of Normandy (c.1050–1134)* (Woodbridge, 2008)

Alexander, Marc: *Britain's Royal Heritage* (Stroud, 2011)

Amundsen, Darrel W., and Diers, Carol Jean: 'The Age of Menopause in Medieval Europe' (*Human Biology*, Vol. 45, 4, December 1973)

Anglo-Norman Studies: Proceedings of the Battle Conference 3 (ed. R. Allen Brown, Woodbridge, 1981)

Anglo-Norman Studies: Proceedings of the Battle Conference 8 (ed. R. Allen Brown, Woodbridge, 1986)

Anglo-Norman Studies: Proceedings of the Battle Conference 10 (ed. R. Allen Brown, Woodbridge, 1988)

Anglo-Norman Studies: Proceedings of the Battle Conference 12 (ed. R. Allen Brown, Woodbridge, 1989)

Anglo-Norman Studies: Proceedings of the Battle Conference 13 (ed. Marjorie Chibnall, Woodbridge, 1991)

Anglo-Norman Studies: Proceedings of the Battle Conference 19 (ed. Christopher Harper-Bill, Woodbridge, 1997)

Appleby, John T.: *The Troubled Reign of King Stephen* (London, 1969)

Aristocratic Women in Medieval France (ed. Theodore Evergates, Philadelphia, 1999)

The Art of Needlework from the Earliest Ages (ed. the Countess of Wilton, London, 1841)

Asbridge, Thomas: *The Greatest Knight: The Remarkable Life of William Marshal, the Power behind Five English Thrones* (London, 2015)

Ashdown, Dulcie M.: *Royal Weddings* (London, 1981)

Ashley, Maurice: *The Life and Times of William I* (London, 1973)

Ashley, Mike: *British Monarchs* (London, 1998)

Atkyns, Robert: 'The History of Llanthony Prima' (in *The Ancient and Present State of Gloucestershire*, London, 1768)

Avril, François: 'The Cross from Valasse' (in *The Year 1200: A Symposium*, New York, 1975)

Bagley, J. J.: *Life in Medieval England* (1960)
Baker, T.: *The Normans* (London, 1966)
Banbury, John; Edwards, Robert; Poskitt, Elizabeth, and Nutt, Tim: *Woodstock and the Royal Park: Nine Hundred Years of History* (Oxford, 2010)
Barber, Richard: *The Devil's Crown: A History of Henry II and his Sons* (London, 1978)
————*Henry Plantagenet* (London, 1964)
Barlow, Frank: 'The Carmen de Hastingae Proelio' (in *Studies in International History*, ed. K. Bourne, K. Watt and D. C. Watt, London, 1967)
————*The Feudal Kingdom of England, 1042–1216* (London, 1961)
————*William I and the Norman Conquest* (London, 1965)
————*William Rufus* (Yale, 1983)
Barrow, G. W. S.: *The Kingdom of the Scots: Government, Church and Society from the Eleventh to the Fourteenth Century* (Edinburgh, 2003)
Barton, John, and Law, Joy: *The Hollow Crown* (London, 1971)
Bates, David: *The Normans and Empire* (Oxford, 2013)
————*William the Conqueror* (Stroud, 2001)
Baverstock, Keith: *Footsteps Through London's Past* (London, 1972)
Baxter, Ron: *The Royal Abbey of Reading* (Woodbridge, 2016)
The Bayeux Tapestry: Embroidering the Facts of History (ed. Pierre Bouet, Brian Levey and François Neveux, Caen, 2004)
Bayley, J.: *The History and Antiquities of the Tower of London* (London, 1830)
Beech, George T.: 'Could Duke Philip the Good of Burgundy have owned the Bayeux Tapestry in 1430?' (*Revue belge de philologie et d'histoire*, 83 fasc. 2, 2005)
————'Queen Mathilda of England (1066–83) and the Abbey of La Chaise-Dieu in the Auvergne' (*Frühmittelalterliche Studien*, 27, 1993)
Beem, Charles: 'Greater by Marriage: The Matrimonial Career of the Empress Matilda' (in *Queens and Queenship in Medieval Europe*)
————'"Greatest in Her Offspring": Motherhood and the Empress Matilda' (in *Virtuous or Villainess?*)
————'The Virtuous Virago: The Empress Matilda and the Politics of Womanhood in Twelfth-century England' (in *Scholars and Poets Talk About Queens*)
Bernstein, David J.: *The Mystery of the Bayeux Tapestry* (London, 1986)
Bertrand, Simone: *The Bayeux Tapestry* (Rennes, 1978)
Biddle, Martin: 'Seasonal festivals and residence: Winchester, Westminster and Gloucester in the tenth to twelfth centuries' (in *Anglo-Norman Studies: Proceedings of the Battle Conference 8*)

Black, Edward: *Royal Brides: Queens of England in the Middle Ages* (Lewes, 1987)

Borman, Tracy: *Matilda, Queen of the Conqueror* (London, 2011)

Boüard, Michel de: *Guillaume le Conquérant* (Paris, 1984)

Boutemy, André: 'Notice sur le recueil poétique du Manuscrit Cotton Vitellius A xii du British Museum' (*Latomus*, 1, 1937)

Bouvet, J.: 'Le récit de la fondation de Mortemer' (*Collectanea Ordinis Cisterciensium reformatorum*, 22, 1960)

Boyd, Douglas: *Eleanor, April Queen of Aquitaine* (Stroud, 2004)

Bradbury, Jim: *The Battle of Hastings* (Stroud, 1998)

————*Stephen and Matilda: The Civil War of 1139–53* (Stroud, 1996)

Brewer, Clifford: *The Death of Kings: A Medical History of the Kings and Queens of England* (London, 2000)

Brindle, Stephen, and Kerr, Brian: *Windsor Revealed: New Light on the History of the Castle* (London, 1997)

Britton, John, *et al.*: *The Beauties of England and Wales* (18 vols., London, 1801–15)

Brooke, Christopher: *From Alfred to Henry III, 871–1272* (1961)

————*The Saxon and Norman Kings* (London, 1963)

Brooke, Christopher, and Keir, Gillian: *London, 800–1216: The Shaping of a City* (London, 1975)

Brown, Geoff: *The Ends of Kings: An Illustrated Guide to the Death and Burial Places of English Monarchs* (Stroud, 2008)

Brown, Linda Dorothy: '*Elegit domum sibi placabilem:* Choice and the Twelfth-Century Religious Woman' (D.Phil. thesis, University of Missouri-Kansas City, 2015)

Brown, R. R.: *The Normans and the Norman Conquest* (1969)

Burges, Alfred: 'Account of the Old Bridge at Stratford-le-Bow, Essex' (*Archaeologia*, 27, 1893)

Burke, John, and Bernard, John: *The Royal Families of England, Scotland and Wales, with their Descendants etc.* (2 vols., London, 1848 and 1851)

Burke's Guide to the Royal Family (Burke's Peerage, 1973)

Cadell, D., and Davies, W.: *The Environs of London: Volume 1, County of Surrey* (London, 1792)

Cannon, John, and Griffiths, Ralph: *The Oxford Illustrated History of the British Monarchy* (Oxford, 1988)

Cannon, John, and Hargreaves, Anne: *The Kings and Queens of Britain* (Oxford, 2001)

Carlton, Charles: *Royal Childhoods* (London, 1986)

Cartwright, Charlotte: 'Before She Was Queen: Matilda of Flanders and the use of Comiitissa in the Norman Ducal Charters' (*Haskins Society Journal*, 22, 2010)

Castor, Helen: *She Wolves: The Women who ruled England before Elizabeth* (London, 2010)

Chadwick, Elizabeth: *Adeliza of Louvain. Lady of the English. The Forgotten Queen* (www.livingthehistoryelizabethchadwick.blogspot.co.uk)

————*Adeliza of Louvain: an Understated Heroine* (www.freshfiction.com)

————*Empress Matilda's Bling* (www.livingthehistoryelizabethchadwick. blogspot.co.uk)

————*The Enigmatic Brian FitzCount* (www.livingthehistoryelizabethchadwick. blogspot.co.uk)

————*Today's research snippet. Empress Matilda and the Hand of St James* (www.livingthehistoryelizabethchadwick.blogspot.co.uk)

Chambers, James: *The Norman Kings* (London, 1981)

Chandler, Victoria: 'Gundrada de Warenne and the Victorian Gentleman-Scholars' (*Southern History*, 12, 1990)

Chester Waters, R. E.: *Gundred de Warenne* (Exeter, 1884)

Chibnall, Marjorie: 'The Charters of the Empress Matilda' (in *Law and Government in Medieval England and Normandy*, ed. George Garnett and John Hudson, Cambridge, 1994)

————'The Empress Matilda and Bec-Hellouin' (in *Anglo-Norman Studies: Proceedings of the Battle Conference 10*)

————'The Empress Matilda and Church Reform' (*Transactions of the Royal Historical Society*, 38, 1988)

————*The Empress Matilda: Queen Consort, Queen Mother and Lady of the English* (Oxford, 1991)

————'The Empress Matilda and her Sons' (in *Medieval Mothering*)

————'Women in Orderic Vitalis' (*Haskins Society Journal*, 2, 1990)

Colbert, E. P.: 'St Adelelm of Burgos' (*New Catholic Encyclopaedia*, January, 2003)

Colker, M. L.: 'Latin Texts concerning Gilbert, founder of Merton Priory' (*Studia Monastica*, 12, 1970)

The Complete Peerage (13 vols., ed. V. Gibbs, H. A. Doubleday, D. Warrand, Thomas, Lord Howard de Walden, and G. H. White, 1910–59)

Cook, Petronelle: *Consorts of England: The Power Behind the Throne* (New York, 1993)

Cooke, Sir Robert: *The Palace of Westminster* (London, 1987)

Coss, Peter: *The Lady in Medieval England, 1000–1500* (Stroud, 1998)

Couppey, L.: 'Encore Héauville! Supplément aux notes historiques sur le prieur, conventuel d'Héauville la Hague' (*Revue catholique de Normandie*, 10, 1900–1)

Crofton, Ian: *The Kings and Queens of England* (London, 2006)

Cronne, H. A.: *The Reign of Stephen, 1135–1154: Anarchy in England* (London, 1970)

Crouch, David: *The Beaumont Twins: The Roots and Branches of Power in the Twelfth Century* (Cambridge, 1986)

———'Between Three Realms: The acts of Waleran II, Count of Meulan and Worcester' (in *Records, Administration and Aristocratic Society in the Anglo-Norman Realm*)

———*The Normans: The History of a Dynasty* (London, 2002)

———*The Reign of King Stephen* (London, 2014)

———'Robert of Gloucester's Mother and Sexual Politics in Norman Oxfordshire' (*Historical Research*, 72, 1999)

The Cultural Patronage of Medieval Women (ed. J. H. McCash, Georgia, 1996)

Cunnington, Phyllis, and Lucas, Catherine: *Costume for Births, Marriages and Deaths* (London, 1972)

Dark, Patricia A.: 'The Career of Matilda of Boulogne as Countess and Queen in England' (D.Phil. thesis, Oxford, 2005)

Dart, John: *The History and Antiquities of the Abbey Church of Westminster* (2 vols., 1723)

Davenport, Mila: *The Book of Costume* (New York, 1948)

Davey, Richard: *The Pageant of London* (2 vols., London, 1906)

David, Charles Wendell: *Robert Curthose, Duke of Normandy* (Cambridge, 1920)

Davis, H. W. C.: 'The Anarchy of Stephen's Reign' (*English Historical Review*, 18, 1903)

———*England under the Normans and Angevins, 1066–1272* (London, 1905)

———'Henry of Blois and Brian Fitz Count' (*English Historical Review*, 25, 1910)

Davis, Michael R.: *Henry of Blois, Prince Bishop of the Twelfth-Century Renaissance* (Baltimore, 2009)

Davis, R. H. C.: 'The Authorship of the *Gesta Stephani*' (*English Historical Review*, 77, 1962)

———*King Stephen* (London, 1967)

———'The College of St Martin-le-Grand and the Anarchy, 1135–1154' (in *The London Topographical Record*, 23, 1974)

———'What Happened in Stephen's Reign' (*History*, 49, 1964)

De-La-Noy, Michael: *Windsor Castle, Past and Present* (London, 1990)

Delderfield, E. R.: *Kings and Queens of England and Great Britain* (1966)

Dewhurst, John: 'A Historical Obstetric Enigma: How tall was Matilda?' (*Journal of Obstetrics and Gynaecology*, 1, 1981)

The Dictionary of National Biography (22 vols., ed. Sir Leslie Stephen and Sir Sidney Lee, 1885–1901; Oxford, 1998 edition)

Dodson, Aidan: *The Royal Tombs of Great Britain: An Illustrated History* (London, 2004)

Doran, J.: *The History and Antiquities of the Town of Reading in Berkshire* (London, 1836)

Douglas, D. C.: *William the Conqueror* (London, 1964)

Dowling, Janet: *Surrey Folk Tales* (Stroud, 2011)

Ducarel, A. C.: *Anglo-Norman Antiquities: Considered in a Tour Through Part of Normandy* (London, 1767)

Duffy, Mark: *Royal Tombs of Medieval England* (Stroud, 2003)

Dugdale, Thomas, and Burnett, William: *Curiosities of Great Britain, England and Wales Delineated* (9 vols., London, 1854–60)

Dugdale, William: *The Baronage of England* (London, 1675)

Duggan, Alfred: *The Devil's Brood: The Angevin Family* (London, 1957)

Earenfight, Christina: *Queenship in Medieval Europe* (London, 2013)

Eleanor of Aquitaine: Lord and Lady (ed. Bonnie Wheeler and John Carmi Parsons, New York, 2003)

England and Normandy in the Middle Ages (ed. D. Bates and A. Curry, London, 1994)

Erickson, Carolly: *Royal Panoply: Brief Lives of the English Monarchs* (New York, 2003)

Evans, Michael: *The Death of Kings: Royal Deaths in Medieval England* (London, 2003)

Eyton, R. W.: *Court, Household and Itinerary of Henry II* (London, 1878)

Family Trees and the Roots of Politics (ed. K. S. B. Keats-Rohan, Woodbridge, 1997)

Farrer, W.: 'Itinerary of Henry I' (*English Historical Review*, 34, 1919)

Fawcett, Richard: *The Abbey and Palace of Dunfermline* (Historic Scotland, 1990)

Fettu, Annie: *Queen Matilda* (Cully, 2005)

————*William the Conqueror* (Cully, 2007)

Fletcher, Benton: *Royal Homes near London* (London, 1930)

Fletcher, John M.: *Sutton Courtenay: The History of a Thameside Village* (Sutton Courtenay, 1990)

Ford, David Nash: *Sutton Courtenay: Home of Royals, Ecclesiastics and Politicians* (www.berkshirehistory.com)

Foulds, Trevor: *The Thurgarten Cartulary* (Stamford, Lincs., 1994)

Fraser, Antonia: *Boadicea's Chariot: The Warrior Queens* (London, 1988)

Freeman, E. A.: *History of the Norman Conquest* (6 vols., Oxford, 1867–79)

————'The Parentage of Gundrada, Wife of William of Warren' (*English Historical Review*, 3, 1888)

Freeman, Eric F.: 'The Identity of Aelfgyva in the Bayeux Tapestry' (*Annales de Normandie*, 41, 1991)

Friend, A. C.: *Serlo of Wilton: The Early Years* (Union Académique Internationale, Bruxelles, 1954)

Fry, Plantagenet Somerset: *Castles* (Newton Abbot, 2005)

Fuller, Thomas: *The Church History of Britain* (6 vols., Oxford, 1655)

Galbraith, V. H.: 'Royal Charters to Winchester' (*English Historical Review*, 35, 1920)

Gathagan, Laura L.: 'Embodying Power, Gender and Authority in the Queenship of Matilda of Flanders' (unpublished doctoral dissertation, City University of New York, 2001)

————'"Mother of Heroes, Most Beautiful of Mothers": Mathilda of Flanders and Royal Motherhood in the Eleventh Century' (in *Virtuous or Villainess?*)

————'The Trappings of Power: The Coronation of Mathilda of Flanders' (*Haskins Society Journal*, 13, 1999)

Gillingham, John: *Conquests, Catastrophe and Recovery: Britain and Ireland, 1066–1485* (London, 2014)

————'Love, Marriage and Politics in the Twelfth Century' (*Forum for Modern Language Studies*, 25, 1989)

Given-Wilson, C., and Curteis, A.: *The Royal Bastards of Medieval England* (London, 1984)

Goodall, John: *The English Castle* (Yale, 2011)

Grant, Lindy: 'The architecture of the early Savigniacs and Cistercians in Normandy' (in *Anglo-Norman Studies: Proceedings of the Battle Conference 10*)

Green, Judith A.: *The Government of England under Henry I* (Cambridge, 1989)

————*Henry I, King of England and Duke of Normandy* (Cambridge, 2009)

Green, Mary Anne Everett: *The Lives of the Princesses of England* (6 vols., London, 1849–55)

Grinnell-Milne, D.: *The Killing of William Rufus* (London, 1968)

The Handbook of British Chronology (ed. Sir F. Maurice Powicke and E. B. Fryde, Royal Historical Society, 1961)

Hassall, W. O.: *They Saw It Happen, 55 BC to 1485* (Oxford, 1957)

————*Who's Who in History, Vol. 1: British Isles, 55 BC to 1485* (Oxford, 1960)

Haswell, Jock: *The Ardent Queen* (1976)

Hausmann, Frierich: 'Reichskanzlei und Hofkapelle unter Heinrich V und Konrad III' (Monumenta Germaniae Historica, Stuttgart, 1956)

Haverkamp, Alfred: *Medieval Germany 1056–1273* (tr. Helga Braun and Richard Mortimer, Oxford, 1988)

Hedley, Olwen: *Royal Palaces* (London, 1972)

Heslop, T. A.: 'English Seals from the Mid-Ninth Century to 1100' (*Journal of the British Archaeological Association*, 133, 1980)

Hibbert, Christopher: *The Court at Windsor* (London, 1964)

———*The Tower of London* (London, 1971)

Hilliam, David: *Crown, Orb and Sceptre: The True Stories of English Coronations* (Stroud, 2001)

———*Kings, Queens, Bones and Bastards* (Stroud, 1998)

Hilton, Lisa: 'Medieval Queens' (in *Royal Women, BBC History* Magazine special, Bristol, 2015)

———*Queens Consort: England's Medieval Queens* (London, 2008)

Hinde, Thomas: *Hinde's Courtiers: 900 Years of English Court Life* (London, 1986)

The History of the City and County of Norwich (ed. R. Browne, Norwich, 1768)

The History of the King's Works, Volume II: The Middle Ages (ed. H. M. Colvin, London, 1963)

Hollister, C. Warren: *Henry I* (Yale, 2001)

Holmes, U. T.: *Daily Living in the Twelfth Century, based on the Observations of Alexander Neckham in London and Paris* (Madison, 1952)

Hourquet, Michel; Pivard, Gilles; and Sehier, Jean-François: *William the Conqueror* (Bayeux, 2015)

A House of Kings: The History of Westminster Abbey (ed. Edward Carpenter, London, 1966)

The Houses of Parliament: History, Art, Architecture (ed. Iain Ross, London, 2000)

Houts, Elisabeth van: 'Adelida (d. before 1113)' (*Oxford Dictionary of National Biography*, 2004)

———'The Echo of the Conquest in the Latin Sources: Duchess Matilda, her daughters and the enigma of the Golden Child' (in *The Bayeux Tapestry: Embroidering the Facts of History*)

———'The *Gesta Normannorum Ducum*: a history without an end' (in *Anglo-Norman Studies: Proceedings of the Battle Conference 3*)

———'Latin Poetry and the Anglo-Norman Court: The Carmen de Haestingae Proelio' (*Journal of Medieval History*, 15, 1989)

———*The Normans in Europe* (Manchester, 2000)

———'The Ship List of William the Conqueror' (in *Anglo-Norman Studies: Proceedings of the Battle Conference 10*)

Howard, Henry: *Indications of Memorials, Monuments, Paintings and Engravings of Persons of the Howard Family* (privately printed, Corby Castle, 1834)

Huneycutt, Lois L.: '"Another Esther in Our Times": Matilda II and the formation of a queenly ideal in Anglo-Norman England' (Ph.D. dissertation, University of California at Santa Barbara, 1992)

————'The idea of the perfect princess: The Life of St Margaret in the reign of Matilda II (1100–1118)' (in *Anglo-Norman Studies: Proceedings of the Battle Conference 12*)

————*Matilda of Scotland: A Study in Medieval Queenship* (Woodbridge, 2003)

————'"Proclaiming her dignity abroad": The Literary and Artistic Network of Matilda of Scotland, Queen of England, 1100–1118' (in *The Cultural Patronage of Medieval Women*)

————'The rise and fall of the cult of Queen Matilda II' (unpublished paper cited by Hollister)

————'Royal Mothers 1070–1204' (in *Medieval Mothering*)

Impey, Edward, and Parnell, Geoffrey: *The Tower of London: The Official Illustrated History* (London, 2000)

Januauschek, Leopold: *Originum Cisterciensium* (2 vols., Vienna, 1877)

Jenner, Heather: *Royal Wives* (London, 1967)

Joelson, A.: *Heirs to the Throne* (London, 1966)

Jones, Christopher: *The Great Palace: The Story of Parliament* (London, 1983)

Jones, Dan: *The Plantagenets: The Kings who Made England* (London, 2012)

Jones, Nigel: *Tower: An Epic History of the Tower of London* (London, 2011)

Kauffmann, C. M.: 'British Library, Lansdowne MS. 383: the Shaftesbury Psalter?' (in *New Offerings, Ancient Treasure*)

Kealey, Edward J.: *Medieval Medicus: A Social History of Anglo-Norman Medicine* (Baltimore, 1981)

Keats-Rohan, Katherine S. B.: *Domesday People: A Prosopography of Persons Occurring in English Documents: 1066–1166, Vol. I: Domesday Book* (Woodbridge, 1999)

Keen, Maurice: *Chivalry* (Yale, 2005)

Kelly, Amy: *Eleanor of Aquitaine and the Four Kings* (Cambridge, MA, 1950)

Kerr, Julie: *Life in the Medieval Cloister* (London, 2009)

Keynes, Simon: 'Giso, Bishop of Wells (1061–1088)' (in *Anglo-Norman Studies: Proceedings of the Battle Conference 19*)

King, Edmund: 'Eustace, Count of Boulogne' (*Oxford Dictionary of National Biography*, 2004)

————*Medieval England* (London, 1988)

————'The Memory of Brian FitzCount' (*The Haskins Society Journal*, 13, 1999)

Kings and Queens of England (ed. Antonia Fraser, London, 1975)

Knowles, David, and Hadcock, R. Neville: *Medieval Religious Houses: England and Wales* (London, 1971)

Könsgen, E.: 'Zwei unbekannte Briefe zu den *Gesta Regum Anglorum* des Wilhelm Von Malmesbury' (*Deutsches Archiv*, 31, 1975)

Labarge, Margaret Wade: *Women in Medieval Life* (London, 1986)

Lack, Katherine: *Conqueror's Son: Duke Robert Curthose, Thwarted King* (Stroud, 2007)

Lane, H. M.: *The Royal Daughters of England* (2 vols., London, 1910)

Langlois, P.: *Histoire du Prieure de Mont-aux-Malades-les-Rouen* (Rouen, 1851)

Laplane, Henri de: *L'abbaye de Clairmarais, d'après ses archives* (Saint-Omer, 1863)

Latzke, Therese: 'Der Topos Mantelgedicht' (*Mittelateinisches Jahrbuch*, 6, 1970)

Laver, James: *A Concise History of Costume* (London, 1969)

Lawson, M. K.: *The Battle of Hastings 1066* (Stroud, 2003)

Laynesmith, Joanna: 'A Canterbury Tale' (*History Today*, 62, 2012)

Leete, Michael: *The Bayeux Tapestry* (2005) (www.bayeuxtapestry.co.uk)

Leyser, Henrietta: *Medieval Women* (Oxford, 1988)

———*Medieval Women: A Social History of Women in England, 450–1500* (London, 1995)

Leyser, Karl: 'The Anglo-Norman Succession 1120–1125 (in *Anglo-Norman Studies: Proceedings of the Battle Conference 13*)

———*Medieval Germany and its Neighbours, 900–1250* (London, 1982)

Licence, Amy: *Royal Babies: A History, 1066–2013* (Stroud, 2013)

Lindsay, Philip: *Kings of Merry England* (London, 1936)

The Lives of the Kings and Queens of England (ed. Antonia Fraser, London, 1977)

Lloyd, Alan: *The Year of the Conqueror* (London, 1966)

Loades, David: *The Kings and Queens of England: The Biography* (Stroud, 2013)

Lofts, Norah: *Queens of Britain* (London, 1977)

LoPrete, Kimberly A.: 'Adela of Blois: Familial Alliances and Female Lordship' (in *Aristocratic Women in Medieval France*)

Lot, Ferdinand: *Études critiques sur l'abbaye de Saint-Wandrille* (Paris, 1913)

Louda, J., and MacLagan, M.: *Lines of Succession: Heraldry of the Royal Families of Europe* (London, 1981)

Mackley, Jude S.: *The Legend of St Brendan: A Comparative Study of the Latin and Anglo-Norman Versions* (Leiden, Boston, 2008)

Manning, Owen, and Bray, William: *The History and Antiquities of the County of Surrey* (3 vols., London, 1809)

Marcombe, David: *Leper Knights* (Woodbridge, 2003)

Marsden, Jonathan, and Winterbottom, Matthew: *Windsor Castle* (London, 2008)

Marshal, E.: *The Early History of Woodstock Manor* (Oxford, 1873)

Marshall, Christopher William Fairholm: 'The Origins and Foundation Charter of St Mary de Voto, Tintern, County Wexford, 1189–1211' (Dissertation, University of Wales, 2013)

Martindale, J.: 'The French Aristocracy in the Early Middle Ages: A Reappraisal' (*Past & Present*, 75, 1977)

Mason, Emma: *Westminster Abbey and its People, c.1050–c.1215* (Woodbridge, 1996)

———*William II: Rufus, the Red King* (Stroud, 2005)

Matthew, D. J. A.: *The Norman Conquest* (London, 1966)

McCulloch, Florence: *Medieval Latin and French Bestiaries* (North Carolina, 1962)

McLynn, Frank: *1066: The Year of the Three Battles* (London, 1998)

McNamara, JoAnn, and Wemple, Suzanne: 'The Power of Women through the Family in Medieval Europe, 500–1100' (in *Women and Power in the Middle Ages*)

Meade, Marion: *Eleanor of Aquitaine: A Biography* (New York, 1977)

Medieval Mothering (ed. John Carmi Parsons and B. Wheeler, New York, 1996)

Medieval Queenship (ed. John Carmi Parsons, Stroud, 1994)

Meyer von Knonau, Gerold: *Jahrbucher des deutschen Reiches unter Heinrich IV und Heinrich V* (7 vols., Leipzig, 1890–1909)

Montague-Smith, P.: *The Royal Line of Succession* (Andover, 1967)

Montfaucon, Bernard de: *Les monuments de la monarchie française* (5 vols., Paris, 1729–33)

Montgomery-Massingberd, H.: *Burke's Guide to the British Monarchy* (Burke's Peerage, 1977)

Morris, Marc: *The Norman Conquest* (London, 2012)

Neilson, M.: 'Matilda of Scotland' (*The Lady*, November 1968)

Neveux, François: *A Brief History of the Normans: The Conquests that Changed the Face of Europe* (Paris, 2006)

———*Guillaume le Conquérant: Le batard qui s'empara de l'Angleterre* (Rennes, 2013)

New Offerings, Ancient Treasure: Studies in Medieval Art for George Henderson (ed. P. Binski and W. Noel, Stroud, 2001)

Nicholas, David M.: *Medieval Flanders* (London, 1992)

Norgate, Kate: *England under the Angevin Kings* (2 vols., London, 1887)

Norris, Herbert: *Costume and Fashion, Volume Two: Senlac to Bosworth, 1066–1485* (London, 1927)

Norton, Elizabeth: *She Wolves: The Notorious Queens of England* (Stroud, 2008)
———*England's Queens: The Biography* (Stroud, 2011)

O'Brien O'Keeffe, Katherine: *Stealing Obedience: Narratives of Agency and Identity in Later Anglo-Saxon England* (Toronto, 2012)
Onslow, Richard W. A., 5th Earl of: *The Empress Maud* (London, 1939)
Ormrod, W. M.: *The Kings and Queens of England* (Stroud, 2001)
Owen, D. D. R.: *Eleanor of Aquitaine, Queen and Legend* (Oxford, 1993)
The Oxford Book of Royal Anecdotes (ed. Elizabeth Longford, Oxford, 1989)

Pain, Nesta: *Empress Matilda: Uncrowned Queen of England* (London, 1978)
Palmer, Alan and Veronica: *Royal England: A Historical Guide* (London, 1983)
Panton, Kenneth J.: *Historical Dictionary of the British Monarchy* (Plymouth, 2011)
Patterson, Benton Rain: *Harold and William: The Battle for England, AD 1064–1066* (New York, 2001)
Pernoud, Regine: *Eleanor of Aquitaine* (London, 1967)
Petit-Dutaillis, C.: *Feudal Monarchy in France and England from the Tenth to the Thirteenth Century* (London, 1936)
Pignot, J. Henri: *Histoire de l'ordre de Cluny (909–1157)* (3 vols., Paris, 1868)
Pine, L. G.: *Heirs of the Conqueror* (London, 1965)
Planché, J. R.: *The Conqueror and His Companions* (London, 1874)
Platt, Colin: *The Traveller's Guide to Medieval England* (London, 1985)
Poole, Austin Lane: *From Domesday Book to Magna Carta, 1087–1216* (Oxford, 1951)
———*Late Medieval England* (2 vols., Oxford, 1958)
Poole, R. L.: *Illustrations of the History of Medieval Thought* (London, 1884)
Porée, A. A.: *Histoire de l'abbaye du Bec* (2 vols., Evreux, 1901)
Poulle, B.: 'Savigny and England' (in *England and Normandy in the Middle Ages*)
A Prayerbook Fit for a Queen? (British Library Medieval Manuscripts Blog, www.britishlibrary.typepad.co.uk)
Pyne, W. H.: *The History of the Royal Residences* (3 vols., London, 1819)

Queens and Power in Medieval and Early Modern England (ed. C. Levin and R. Bucholz, Nebraska, 2009)
Queens and Queenship in Medieval Europe (ed. Anne Duggan, Woodbridge, 1997)

Ramsay, J. H.: *The Revenues of the Kings of England, 1066–1399* (1925)

Records, *Administration and Aristocratic Society in the Anglo-Norman Realm: Papers Commemorating the 800th Anniversary of King John's Loss of Normandy* (ed. Nicholas Vincent, Woodbridge, 2009)

Rex, Peter: *1066: A New History of the Norman Conquest* (Stroud, 2009)

———*William the Conqueror: The Bastard of Normandy* (Stroud, 2011)

Richard, A.: *Histoire des comtes de Poitou* (2 vols., 1903)

Richardson, H. G., and Sayles, G. O.: *The Governance of Medieval England from the Conquest to Magna Carta* (Edinburgh, 1963)

Rigg, A. C.: 'Serlo of Wilton: Biographical Notes' (*Medium Ævum*, 65, 1,1996)

Ritchie, R. I. G.: 'The Date of The Voyage of St Brendan' (*Medium Ævum*, 19, 1950)

Roberts, George: 'Llanthony Priory, Monmouthshire' (in *Archaeologia Cambrensis*, 1, 1846)

Roberts, Marilyn: *The Mowbray Legacy* (Scunthorpe, 2012)

Robinson, John Martin: *Arundel Castle: Ancient Stately Home and Gardens* (Arundel, undated)

———*Arundel Castle: The Seat of the Duke of Norfolk, E. M.* (Andover, 2011)

———*Royal Palaces: Windsor Castle: A Short History* (London, 1996)

Ronzani, Rinaldo: *Conversion and Reconciliation: The Rite of Penance* (Nairobi, 2007)

Rose, Alexander: *Kings in the North: The House of Percy in English History* (London, 2002)

Rose, Tessa: *The Coronation Ceremony of the Kings and Queens of England and the Crown Jewels* (London, 1992)

Rössler, Oskar: *Die Kaiserin Matilda* (Berlin, 1897)

———'Kaiserin Mathilde und das Zeitalter ger Anarchie in England' (*Historische Studien*, 7, 1897)

——— 'Kaiserin Mathilde, Mutter Heinrichs von Anjou, und das Zeitalter der Anarchie in England' (*Historische Studien*, 7, Appendix 1)

Routh, C. R. N.: *Who's Who in History, Vol. 2: England 1485–1603* (1964)

Rowell, Christopher: *Petworth House* (The National Trust, 1997)

Rowse, A. L.: *The Tower of London in the History of the Nation* (London, 1972)

———*Windsor Castle in the History of the Nation* (London, 1974)

Royal *Palaces of England* (ed. R. S. Rait, London, 1911)

Rozec, Jeanne, and Vochelet, Benoit: *À la table de Guillaume le Conquérant* (Louviers, 2015)

Saltman, Avrom: *Theobald, Archbishop of Canterbury* (London, 1956)

Sanderus, Antoine: *Chorographia Sacra Brabantiae* (2 vols., Brussels, 1659, 1663)

Sandford, Francis: *A Genealogical History of the Kings and Queens of England and Monarchs of Great Britain, 1066–1677* (1677; continued by Samuel Stebbings, Newcombe, 1707)

Saul, Nigel: *A Companion to Medieval England, 1066–1485* (Stroud, 1983, 2000)

Saunders, Hilary St George: *Westminster Hall* (London, 1951)

Scheffer-Boichorst, Paul: 'Urkunden und Forschungen zu der Regesten der staufischen Periode' (*Neues Archiv*, 27, 1902)

Scholars and Poets Talk About Queens (ed. C. Levin and C. Stewart-Nuñez, London, 2015)

Scott, A. F.: *Every One a Witness: The Plantagenet Age* (London, 1975)

Scott, Margaret: *Medieval Dress and Fashion* (The British Library, London, 2003)

Scott-Moncrieff, M. C.: *Kings and Queens of England* (London, 1966)

Seward, Desmond: *The Demon's Brood: The Plantagenet Dynasty that Forged the English Nation* (London, 2014)

Sharpe, Richard: 'King Harold's Daughter' (*Haskins Society Journal*, 19, 2007)

Sharpe, Richard, and Doherty, Hugh: *Godstow Abbey* (Charters of William II and Henry I Project, 2014)

'Simon Valois, called "Saint Simon"' (http://www.mouthe.fr/article_9)

Slocombe, George: *Sons of the Conqueror* (London, 1960)

Smith, Emily Tennyson (Bradley), and Micklethwaite, J. T.: *Annals of Westminster Abbey* (London, 1898)

Softly, Barbara: *The Queens of England* (London, 1976)

Souden, David: *The Royal Palaces of London* (London, 2008)

Southern, R. W.: *St Anselm and his Biographer: A Study of Monastic Life and Thought* (Cambridge, 1963)

————*Saint Anselm: A Portrait in a Landscape* (Cambridge, 1990)

Southouse, Thomas: *Monasticon Favershamiense* (London, 1671)

Stafford, Pauline: *Queens, Concubines and Dowagers: The King's Wife in the Early Middle Ages* (London, 1983)

————*Queen Emma and Queen Edith: Queenship and Women's Power in Eleventh-Century England* (Oxford, 1997)

Stapleton, Thomas: 'Observations in disproof of the pretended marriage of William de Warenne, Earl of Surrey, with a daughter begotten of Matildis, daughter of Baldwin, Comte of Flanders, by William the Conqueror, and illustrative of the origin and early history of the family in Normandy' (*The Archaeological Journal*, 3, 1846)

Starkey, David: *Crown and Country: A History of England through Monarchy* (London, 2010)

Steane, John: *The Archaeology of the Medieval English Monarchy* (London, 1993)

Stenton, F. M.: *Anglo-Saxon England* (Oxford, 1971)

————*The Bayeux Tapestry: A Comprehensive Survey* (London, 1957, 1965)

————*William the Conqueror and the Rule of the Normans* (London, 1908; revised 1957)

Stevenson, Katie: *Chivalry and Knighthood in Scotland* (Woodbridge, 2006)

Strickland, Agnes: *The Lives of the Queens of England* (8 vols., London, 1851; reprinted Bath, 1973)

Strong, Roy: *Coronation: A History of Kingship and the British Monarchy* (London, 2005)

————*Tudor and Jacobean Portraits* (2 vols., London, 1969)

Stubbs, W.: *The Foundation of Waltham Abbey: the tract 'De invencione Sanctae Crucis nostrae in Monte Acuto'* (Oxford, 1861)

Tanner, H. J.: 'Between Scylla and Charybdis: The Political Role of the Comital Family of Boulogne in Northern France and England (879–1159)' (D.Phil. thesis, University of California, Santa Barbara, 1993)

————'Queenship: Office, Custom, or Ad Hoc?: The Case of Queen Matilda III of England (1135–1152)' (in *Eleanor of Aquitaine: Lord and Lady*)

Taute, Anne; Brooke-Little, J.; and Pottinger, D.: *Kings and Queens of England: A Genealogical Chart showing their Descent, Relationships and Coats of Arms* (1970; revised edition 1986)

Thompson, Kathleen: 'Queen Adeliza and the Lotharingian Connection' (*Sussex Archaeological Collections*, 140, 2002)

Thompson, Pauline A., and Stevens, Elizabeth: 'Gregory of Ely's Verse Life and Miracles of St Aethelthryth' (*Analecta Bollandiana*, 106, 1988)

Thomson, Rodney M.: *William of Malmesbury* (Woodbridge, 1987)

Thornton-Cook, E.: *Her Majesty: The Romance of the Queens of England* (New York, 1926)

Thorpe, L.: *The Bayeux Tapestry and the Norman Invasion* (Folio Society, London, 1973)

Tierney, M. A.: *The History and Antiquities of the Castle and Town of Arundel* (2 vols., London, 1834)

Tomkeieff, O. G.: *Life in Norman England* (London, 1966)

Trease, Geoffrey: *Seven Queens of England* (London, 1953)

Truax, J. A.: 'Winning over the Londoners: King Stephen, the Empress Matilda, and the Politics of Personality' (*Haskins Society Journal*, 8, 1996)

Turgis, S.: *La très véridique histoire de la bonne Mathilde de Flandre, Duchesse de Normandie, Reyne d'Angleterre, Femme de Guillaume le Conquérant, auteur de la tapisserie-broderie de Bayeux* (Paris, 1912)

Turner, Ralph V.: *Eleanor of Aquitaine* (Yale, 2009)

Turton, T. E.: *The Dragon's Breed* (1969)

Tyerman, Christopher: *Who's Who in Early Medieval England* (London, 1996)

Vaughn, Sally N.: *Anselm of Bec and Robert of Meulan: The Innocence of the Dove and the Wisdom of the Serpent* (Berkeley, CA, 1987)

Verhulst, Adriaan: *The Rise of Cities in North-West Europe* (Cambridge, 1999)

The Victoria County Histories (www.british-history.ac.uk)

Virtuous or Villainess? The Image of the Royal Mother from the Early Medieval to the Early Modern Era (ed. C. Fleiner and E. Woodacre, London, 2016)

Walker, Ian: *Harold: The Last Anglo-Saxon King* (Stroud, 1997)

Walne, P.: 'A Double Charter of the Empress Matilda and Henry, Duke of Normandy, c.1152' (*English Historical Review*, 76, 1961)

Ward, Jennifer: *Women in England in the Middle Ages* (London, 2006)

Warren, W. L.: *Henry II* (London, 1973)

———*The Governance of Norman and Angevin England 1086–1272* (London, 1987)

———*Henry II* (London, 1973 or 1977)

———*King John* (London, 1961)

Weir, Alison: *Eleanor of Aquitaine: By the Wrath of God, Queen of England* (London, 1999)

Weldon Finn, R.: *An Introduction to Domesday Book* (London, 1963)

Wertheimer, L.: 'Adeliza of Louvain and Anglo-Norman Queenship' (*Haskins Society Journal*, 7, 1995)

Westminster Abbey: Official Guide (Norwich, 1953, 1966)

Wharton, Henry: *Anglia Sacra* (2 vols., London, 1691)

Who Made the Bayeux Tapestry? (www.bayeux-tapestry.org.uk)

William the Conqueror Trail (ed. Catherine Marie and Anne Forest, Hastings, undated)

Williams, Ann: *The English and the Norman Conquest* (Woodbridge, 1995)

——— 'A west-country magnate of the eleventh century: the family, estates and patronage of Beorhtric son of Aelfgar' (in *Family Trees and the Roots of Politics*)

Williams, Brenda and Brian: *Secrets of the Bayeux Tapestry* (Andover, 2008)

Williams, Brian: *Life in a Medieval Castle* (Andover, 2011)

Williams, John R.: 'Godfrey of Rheims, a Humanist of the Eleventh Century' (*Speculum*, 22, 1, 1947)

Williams, Watkin: *Saint Bernard of Clairvaux* (Manchester, 1935)

Williamson, David: *Brewer's British Royalty* (London, 1996)

———*The National Portrait Gallery History of the Kings and Queens of England* (London, 1998)

Wilson, Derek: *The Tower, 1078–1978* (1978)

Women and Power in the Middle Ages (ed. Mary Erler and Maryanne Kowaleski, London, 1988)

Women and Sovereignty (ed. Louise Olga Fradenburg, Edinburgh, 1992)

Wree, Oliver de: *Genealogia comitum Flandriae* (Bruges, 1642)

Yorke, Barbara: 'St Edith' (*Oxford Dictionary of National Biography*, 2004)

Notes and References

Introduction

1 Huneycutt: *Matilda of Scotland* **2** It was kept at the College of Navarre in Paris for hundreds of years, but has long been lost.

'We Are Come for Glory'

1 Wace; William of Malmesbury **2** *The Anglo-Saxon Chronicle*. The site of the battle has been disputed in recent years, but it is attested to early on, and the traditional location is almost certainly the correct one. The arguments and evidence are well laid out here: http://www.english-heritage. org.uk/learn/story-of-england/medieval-part-1/battle-of-hastings-location/.

Part One: Matilda of Flanders

1 'A Very Beautiful and Noble Girl'

1 William of Poitiers **2** Ibid. **3** Baudri de Bourgeuil **4** William of Malmesbury **5** Ibid. **6** Orderic Vitalis. Matilda was perhaps named for her ancestress, Matilda of Saxony-Billung (d.1008), wife of Count Baldwin III. **7** William of Poitiers **8** William of Jumièges **9** Orderic Vitalis **10** The church was demolished in 1799; its foundations were rediscovered in the 1950s and can be seen in the cellars of the Crowne Plaza Hotel. The castle has long since disappeared, but the remains of some of its walls have also been uncovered. **11** *Encomium Emmae Reginae*. Baldwin 'Iron Arm' married the French princess Judith, widow of King Ethelwulf of Wessex. **12** In the thirteenth century, the chapel was removed to Lille Cathedral, which is dedicated to Notre Dame de la Treille. The present cathedral dates from 1854. **13** Verhulst **14** Borman. The 'bourg' was destroyed in the eighteenth century. Nothing remains of the castle of Therouanne. **15** Lisiard of Crépy **16** *Encomium Emmae Reginae* **17** Hilton: *Queens Consort*. He was the son of King Cnut's first marriage or 'handfasting'. **18** *The Anglo-Saxon Chronicle* **19** Ibid. **20** Ibid. **21** Wace; Orderic Vitalis **22** Douglas. See Chapter 5 of this book for a discussion of these charters. **23** Wace **24** Williams: 'A west-country magnate of the eleventh century' **25** The Chronicle of Tewkesbury Abbey. The story also appears in Cotton MS. Cleopatra.

2 'Great Courage and High Daring'

1 William of Malmesbury; William of Poitiers **2** William of Jumièges **3** William of Malmesbury **4** Cited Hilton: *Queens Consort* **5** William of Poitiers **6** Ibid. **7** Ibid. **8** Ibid. **9** William of Jumièges; William of Poitiers **10** Wace says the courtship took place before William visited England, which, according to *The Anglo-Saxon Chronicle*, was in the latter part of 1051. **11** *Recueil des actes des ducs de Normandie* **12** William of Poitiers **13** 'The Chronicle of Tours' **14** William of Poitiers; Baldwin of Avesnes **15** William of Jumièges **16** 'The Chronicle of Inger, likewise called Ingerius', cited by Strickland **17** 'The Chronicle of Tours' **18** Baldwin of Avesnes; Mouskes **19** Baldwin of Avesnes **20** 'The Chronicle of Inger, likewise called Ingerius', cited by Strickland **21** Baldwin of Avesnes; Mouskes **22** 'The Chronicle of Inger, likewise called Ingerius', cited by Strickland; Baldwin of Avesnes **23** William of Malmesbury **24** 'The Chronicle of Tours'; Baldwin of Avesnes; 'The Chronicle of Inger, likewise called Ingerius', cited by Strickland **25** Baldwin of Avesnes **26** Ibid.

3 'William Bastard'

1 William of Malmesbury **2** Orderic Vitalis **3** *The Anglo-Saxon Chronicle* **4** In the later sixteenth century, Huguenots desecrated William's tomb in the abbey of Saint-Étienne, Caen, and during the French Revolution most of his remains were thrown in the River Orne. All that was spared was one thigh bone, which was authenticated and reburied in 1987, with some ceremony, under a simple ledger stone before the high altar. **5** Douglas. The portrait no longer survives, but in the eighteenth century paintings of William and Matilda were made for St Stephen's, where they hung in the galleries. William's survives. It dates from 1708 and now hangs in the sacristy. An inscription states that it is a copy of the authentic portrait painted on an ancient panel – probably the portrait painted in 1522, for the sitter wears sixteenth-century dress. **6** William of

Jumièges   **7** William of Malmesbury   **8** William of Jumièges   **9** William of Malmesbury   **10** Hilton: *Queens Consort*

4 'The Greatest Ceremony and Honour'

1 The Lateran Council of 1139 changed this to the fourth degree.   **2** William of Jumièges   **3** William of Poitiers   **4** Orderic Vitalis   **5** Ibid.   **6** William of Poitiers   **7** William of Malmesbury   **8** Orderic Vitalis   **9** Bates: *William the Conqueror*   **10** Stapleton   **11** 'Cartulaire de l'abbaye de Sainte-Trinité du Mont de Rouen', number 37   **12** *Chartes de Saint-Julien de Tours*   **13** *Recueil des actes des ducs de Normandie*, 124, 126; Lot, nos. 30, 31   **14** William of Malmesbury   **15** William of Poitiers   **16** Ibid. Herleva died soon afterwards, and was buried in the abbey of Saint-Grestain, which, in gratitude to the Virgin for having cured him of leprosy, Herluin and their son, Robert, Count of Mortain, founded around 1050 (Robert of Torigni), when the name of Herluin's second wife appears in a list of benefactors.   **17** Strickland calls it by its Latin name, Augi, which has led to some confusion. The chateau now standing on the site dates from the sixteenth to nineteenth centuries.   **18** Patterson   **19** William of Poitiers   **20** Ibid.   **21** Wace   **22** William of Jumièges   **23** Orderic Vitalis   **24** William of Jumièges   **25** Orderic Vitalis; Aird   **26** Gathagan: '"Mother of Heroes, Most Beautiful of Mothers"'. Matilda's chamberlains were William 'le Flamand' (the Fleming), who probably came to Normandy with her, and Fulchold.   **27** William of Jumièges   **28** William of Poitiers

5 'Illustrious Progeny'

1 William of Malmesbury   **2** Orderic Vitalis   **3** William of Jumièges   **4** Fulcoius of Beavais in *Recueil de travaux d'érudition dédiés à la mémoire de Julien Havet*   **5** Wace   **6** Orderic Vitalis   **7** William of Malmesbury   **8** His engravings of them are in his work *Les monuments de la monarchie française*, and in the Archives départementales du Calvados, Series F.   **9** Not 1961, as is often stated.   **10** Dewhurst   **11** Morris; Bates: *William the Conqueror*   **12** Dewhurst   **13** Hugo of St Vaast   **14** Orderic Vitalis   **15** Ibid.   **16** Aird   **17** *Recueil des actes des ducs de Normandie*   **18** Mason: *William II*   **19** See evidence for his age at death in Chapter 16.   **20** Barlow: *William Rufus*   **21** Bates: *William the Conqueror*   **22** *Regesta Regum Anglo-Normannorum, 1066–1154*   **23** Norton: *England's Queens*   **24** Domesday Book records that Geoffrey, 'the chamberlain of the King's daughter Matilda', held Hatch Warren, Hampshire, of the King, for the service he had performed for her.   **25** *Rouleaux des morts du Ixe au Xve siècle*. After Cecilia was professed as a nun in 1075, Baudri, Abbot of Bourgeuil, wrote to her, and sent greetings to a sister she had with her at Holy Trinity, whose name he had forgotten, although he knew 'she was of Bayeux and then of Anjou'. This unnamed sister cannot have been a nun in or near Bayeux, because there were no convents in the area, although she could have been a nun in Anjou, perhaps at Fontevrault or Ronceray (Barlow: *William Rufus*). She is perhaps to be identified with Matilda, or Adeliza, both of whom who are mentioned in the mortuary roll of 1112. **26** Foulds **27** Keats-Rohan **28** Planché; Foulds; Sharpe: 'King Harold's Daughter'; *Domesday Book*. A case has also been made for Matilda d'Aincourt having been the illegitimate daughter of Gunhilda of Wessex, daughter of Harold II of England, by Alan Rufus, Lord of Richmond. St Mary's Abbey was his property, and Matilda d'Aincourt's gifts to it came from his revenues. However, the register of the Honour of Richmond records that, early in 1069, Queen Matilda persuaded King William to grant many of the lands in North Yorkshire of the rebel Edwin, Earl of Mercia, to Alan Rufus. Furthermore, Walter d'Aincourt and Alan Rufus were partners in the lead trade; Walter owned lead mines, while Alan built the port of Boston, Lincolnshire, whence the lead was shipped. These links might also explain the connection between Matilda d'Aincourt and Lord Alan (Sharpe: 'King Harold's Daughter') **29** Orderic Vitalis **30** Houts: 'Adelida'; Thomas Forester, in his translation of Orderic Vitalis's *The Ecclesiastical History of England and Normandy* **31** *Rouleaux des morts du Ixe au Xve siècle* **32** Houts: 'Adelida' **33** Letter 1 in Appendix 2. **34** Orderic Vitalis **35** *Miscellanea Genealogica et Heraldica*; Burke: *The Royal Families*, vol.1: 'Descendants of William the Conqueror' and pedigree LXVIII; The Roll of Battle Abbey; Barlow: *The Feudal Kingdom of England* **36** Stapleton **37** Orderic Vitalis **38** *Liber Monasterii de Hyde* **39** Stapleton **40** *Early Yorkshire Charters* **41** Chester Waters; Freeman: 'The Parentage of Gundrada, Wife of William of Warren'; Chandler; *Early Yorkshire Charters* **42** Anselm of Aosta: *The Letters of St Anselm of Canterbury* **43** Orderic Vitalis **44** *Recueil de travaux d'érudition dédiés à la mémoire de Julien Havet* **45** Orderic Vitalis

6 'The Tenderest Regard'

1 William of Malmesbury **2** Cartwright **3** *Regesta Regum Anglo-Normannorum: The Acta of William I* **4** William of Malmesbury **5** William of Poitiers **6** Orderic Vitalis **7** *Le cartulaire de la chapitre cathedral de Coutances*; Bates: *The Normans and Empire* **8** *Calendar of Documents preserved in France*; Borman **9** William of Malmesbury **10** Sturluson **11** Many sources were consulted for the royal household, the court and royal life, but I am chiefly indebted to the 'Constitutio Domus Regis'; Brian Williams; Goodall; Steane; Tomkeieff and Norris. **12** The term 'ladies' bower' is a nineteenth-century invention. **13** Now in the Victoria and Albert

Museum.   **14** Holmes   **15** Baudri de Bourgeuil   **16** Hedley   **17** 'Constitutio Domus Regis'   **18** Map   **19** Holmes

7 'The Piety of Their Princes'

1 William of Malmesbury   **2** Ibid.   **3** Borman   **4** Orderic Vitalis   **5** William of Jumièges; Orderic Vitalis   **6** Orderic Vitalis   **7** William of Malmesbury   **8** According to Milo Crespin, Abbot of Bec-Hellouin, writing around 1130, and, later, Wace.   **9** William of Malmesbury   **10** William of Jumièges   **11** Freeman: *History of the Norman Conquest*   **12** William of Jumièges; Orderic Vitalis; Wace   **13** William of Jumièges   **14** Cited Fettu: *William the Conqueror*   **15** *The Cultural Patronage of Medieval Women*   **16** Borman   **17** *Regesta Regum Anglo-Normannorum: The Acta of William I*; 'Les actes de Guillaume le Conquérant et de la reine Mathilde pour les abbayes caënnaises'; Borman   **18** Gathagan: 'Embodying Power, Gender and Authority in the Queenship of Matilda of Flanders'   **19** Freeman: *History of the Norman Conquest*; Borman   **20** Orderic Vitalis   **21** After wartime bombing, only ruins remain today.   **22** Chibnall: 'The Empress Matilda and Bec-Hellouin'. It was later endowed in Matilda's memory by her children, notably Henry, who completed the church and whose bowels would later be buried there. It was destroyed and rebuilt many times, and any vestiges of the abbey Matilda knew were razed in 1418.   **23** *Regesta Regum Anglo-Normannorum: The Acta of William I*   **24** *The Cultural Patronage of Medieval Women*; 'La reine Mathilde et la fondation de la Trinité de Caen'   **25** Bates: *William the Conqueror*. The foundations of the palace were excavated in the 1960s, and may be seen next to the hall built by William and Matilda's son Henry.

8 'Without Honour'

1 William of Poitiers   **2** Eadmer   **3** William of Malmesbury   **4** Ibid.   **5** William of Poitiers   **6** Orderic Vitalis   **7** William of Malmesbury   **8** Sturluson   **9** Orderic Vitalis   **10** Sturluson   **11** William of Poitiers   **12** According to William of Poitiers, the Duke's chaplain, who was in a position to know. William of Jumièges, Orderic and Robert of Torigni all state that one princess was betrothed in turn to Harold and the Spanish prince.   **13** William of Poitiers; Orderic Vitalis; Robert of Torigni   **14** The Aelfgyva in the Bayeux Tapestry is a small figure who stands in a doorway while a tonsured man apparently draws away her veil from her face. Above is the unfinished sentence '… where a clerk and Aelfgyva …' Possibly the unfinished sentence is meant to be suggestive. This is unlikely to have been a betrothal, since the male party is absent. There have been many theories about Aelfgyva's identity. Recently it has been suggested that she was the subject of some otherwise unrecorded sexual scandal – in the border below her there is an image of a priapic nude man reaching up towards her, mimicking the stance of the priest above – and even that she might be Emma of Normandy, whom gossip credited with a shocking liaison with a bishop. (Laynesmith; Freeman: 'The Identity of Aelfgyva in the Bayeux Tapestry') Another theory is that she was Harold's sister, Aelfgyva Godwinsdottir, whose marriage to one of William's barons was under discussion (Eadmer), and that the intention was to show her as being unworthy. By October 1066 she had died, before any marriage took place. (Eadmer) William of Malmesbury perhaps confused her death with that of the princess who had been betrothed to Harold. (Borman) It is highly unlikely therefore that 'Aelfgyva' was one of the ducal princesses, and inconceivable that an embroiderer would have impugned one of them by placing her above such a blatantly sexual image (Borman). **15** Barlow: *William Rufus* **16** Orderic Vitalis **17** Sturluson **18** Eadmer **19** Orderic Vitalis. William of Malmesbury states that, in 1066, Harold repudiated his oath to William because the princess to whom he had been betrothed had died before she was old enough to marry. There is no record of any of the other daughters dying before 1066. **20** Eadmer **21** Orderic Vitalis

9 'A Prudent Wife'

1 William of Jumièges **2** The lower parts of the nave and towers, a section of the wall of the south aisle, much of the Romanesque arcading in the nave, and the basic structure of the upper storeys survive from the church Matilda knew. **3** Benoît de Saint-Maure **4** Borman **5** Houts: *The Normans in Europe*; Gathagan: '"Mother of Heroes, Most Beautiful of Mothers"' **6** Orderic Vitalis **7** Houts: 'The Echo of the Conquest in the Latin Sources' **8** Cartwright **9** Fettu: *Queen Matilda* **10** Orderic Vitalis **11** William of Malmesbury **12** Ibid. **13** Orderic Vitalis **14** Cited Fettu: *Queen Matilda* **15** William of Poitiers **16** Orderic Vitalis **17** Wace **18** Ibid. **19** Houts: 'The Echo of the Conquest in the Latin Sources'; Houts: 'The Ship List of William the Conqueror' **20** Wace **21** Norton: *England's Queens*; Borman **22** William of Poitiers; William of Jumièges **23** William of Poitiers

10 'The Splendour of the King'

1 Orderic Vitalis **2** William of Malmesbury **3** William of Poitiers **4** William of Jumièges **5** Bates: *William the Conqueror* **6** Aird **7** William of Malmesbury **8** Orderic Vitalis **9** William of Poitiers **10** Williams: 'Godfrey of Rheims'; Hilton: *Queens Consort*; Fettu: *Queen Matilda* **11** Houts: 'The Echo of the Conquest in the Latin Sources' **12** Extensive foundations of the Norman nave were found beneath the existing one in 1930, and the undercroft of the Confessor's church still survives. **13** Rose: *The Coronation Ceremony* **14** Barlow: 'The Carmen de Hastingae Proelio' **15** Rose: *The Coronation Ceremony* **16** William of Jumièges **17** A late-eleventh-century copy of the *Laudes Regiae* survives in the British Library, and is probably the text used for William's coronation (Cotton MS. Vitellius, E. xii. Fo. 160v) **18** Orderic Vitalis **19** William of Poitiers **20** Cited Fettu: *William the Conqueror* **21** William of Poitiers **22** Today it is an impressive ruin. **23** Orderic Vitalis **24** William of Poitiers **25** Orderic Vitalis **26** William of Poitiers **27** William of Jumièges **28** The *Cygne de Croix* – the Swan's Cross – stands on the site. **29** Fettu: *Queen Matilda*; Boüard; Turgis **30** Planché; Borman **31** Orderic Vitalis **32** William of Jumièges; Orderic Vitalis **33** William of Malmesbury **34** Strickland **35** Ibid.; Robert of Gloucester; Borman **36** Hilton: *Queens Consort*; Borman **37** Crouch: *The Normans*

11 'Power and Virtue'

1 Stafford: *Queen Emma and Queen Edith*; Hilton: 'Medieval Queens' **2** Hilton: *Queens Consort* **3** Huneycutt: *Matilda of Scotland* **4** Asser, Bishop of Sherborne **5** Hilton: *Queens Consort*; Huneycutt: *Matilda of Scotland* **6** Stafford: *Queen Emma and Queen Edith* **7** Orderic Vitalis **8** *The Anglo-Saxon Chronicle* **9** Borman **10** Orderic Vitalis **11** Ibid. **12** *The Anglo-Saxon Chronicle* **13** William of Malmesbury **14** *The Anglo-Saxon Chronicle* states that Matilda was crowned in the Old Minster at Winchester, soon to be demolished to make way for a new Romanesque cathedral. However, a charter of William I is dated the day of the coronation, 'when my wife Matilda was consecrated in the church of St Peter at Westminster' (*Regesta Regum Anglo-Normannorum: The Acta of William I*) **15** *The Life of King Edward who rests at Westminster* **16** Keynes **17** *The Anglo-Saxon Chronicle* **18** Crispin **19** Rose: *The Coronation Ceremony* **20** *Women and Sovereignty* **21** Stafford: *Queen Emma and Queen Edith* **22** Strong: *Coronation* **23** Ibid. **24** Hilton: *Queens Consort* **25** Borman **26** Lack; Gathagan: 'The Trappings of Power' **27** *The Anglo-Saxon Chronicle* **28** Cadell and Davies; Hilliam: *Crown, Orb and Sceptre*; Dowling; *Domesday Book* **29** Baudri de Bourgeuil

12 'In Queenly Purple'

1 Turgot, Prior of Durham **2** McNamara and Wemple **3** Hollister **4** Abbott **5** Orderic Vitalis. Godfrey of Winchester, Prior of St Swithun's, Winchester, having met Matilda, wrote a short laudatory poem about her in his '*Epigrammatica Historia*' (*The Anglo-Latin Satirical Poets*). **6** Ibid.

7 Keynes; *Regesta Regum Anglo-Normannorum: The Acta of William I*   **8** Crouch: *The Normans*   **9** Norton: *England's Queens*   **10** *Regesta Regum Anglo-Normannorum: The Acta of William I*   **11** Turgis   **12** *Domesday Book*   **13** *Recueil de travaux d'érudition dédiés à la mémoire de Julien Havet*   **14** Holmes   **15** Davey; Scott: *Medieval Dress and Fashion*

13 'Sword and Fire'

1 Orderic Vitalis; William of Poitiers   **2** Some websites state, incorrectly, that Sancho's wife, Alberta, was William and Matilda's daughter.   **3** William of Poitiers   **4** Orderic Vitalis; William of Poitiers   **5** *Rouleaux des morts du Ixe au Xve siecle*   **6** Additional MS. 50002, British Library   **7** Orderic Vitalis   **8** *The Anglo-Saxon Chronicle*   **9** William of Jumièges   **10** Fuller   **11** Dugdale: *Monasticon Anglicanum*   **12** The *Anglo-Saxon Chronicle* states that Henry's birth took place 'not many days' after Matilda's coronation, but William of Malmesbury says he was 'born in England the third year after his father's arrival', that is, after 28 September 1068, while Orderic states he was born 'before a year was ended', meaning within the year after Matilda's coronation, i.e. before Whitsun 1069. If he was conceived before his father left Normandy on 6 December, he could have been born any time up to early September 1068; but if he had been conceived late in March, after Matilda arrived in England, he would have arrived around 17 December. As king, in 1122, Henry is said to have celebrated his birthday in York; he was there en route to Carlisle that year, in November, and returned on 6 December. (*The Historians of the Church of York and its Archbishops*; *Early Yorkshire Charters*)   **13** Orderic Vitalis   **14** Borman   **15** Simeon of Durham   **16** Borman   **17** Orderic Vitalis; Henry of Huntingdon; Robert of Torigni; *The Anglo-Saxon Chronicle*   **18** William of Malmesbury   **19** *The Anglo-Saxon Chronicle*; Bates: *William the Conqueror*   **20** *Regesta Regum Anglo-Normannorum, 1066–1154*; Borman   **21** Stafford: *Queen Emma and Queen Edith*. They would not be assigned to Matilda on Edith's death in 1075 because by then Matilda was already provided for.   **22** Walker   **23** Orderic Vitalis   **24** Hilton: *Queens Consort*; Lofts   **25** 'Vita Beati Simonis'; Orderic Vitalis   **26** *Regesta Regum Anglo-Normannorum: The Acta of William I*; Williams: 'A west-country magnate of the eleventh century'; Borman. Matilda later bestowed Tewkesbury on Roger de Busci, and granted other lands formerly owned by Brihtric to the abbeys of Holy Trinity and Saint-Étienne, Caen, and Bec-Hellouin.   **27** The Chronicle of Tewkesbury Abbey; Wace; Cotton MS. Cleopatra, British Library; Ann Williams: 'A west-country magnate of the eleventh century'.   **28** *Domesday Book*   **29** Gathagan: '"Mother of Heroes, Most Beautiful of Mothers"'   **30** Strickland   **31** Borman   **32** *Letters of the Queens of England*   **33** *Domesday Book*   **34** Borman   **35** Saul   **36** William of Jumièges   **37** Bates: *William the*

Conqueror **38** Steane **39** *Domesday Book* **40** William of Jumièges **41** Orderic Vitalis **42** John of Worcester **43** Simeon of Durham **44** Orderic Vitalis

14 'Much Trouble'

1 *The Anglo-Saxon Chronicle* **2** Orderic Vitalis **3** Green: *Henry I, King of England and Duke of Normandy* **4** Orderic Vitalis **5** Ibid.; William of Malmesbury **6** *Regesta Regum Anglo-Normannorum: The Acta of William I* **7** Ibid.; Couppey **8** Substantial ivy-clad ruins of the chateau remain today. **9** *Regesta Regum Anglo-Normannorum: The Acta of William I*; Houts: *The Normans in Europe*. Trials by ordeal lost favour with the Church and the practice began to die out in the twelfth century. **10** Gathagan:"'Mother of Heroes, Most Beautiful of Mothers'" **11** Hilton: *Queens Consort*; Aird **12** Orderic Vitalis **13** Hilton: *Queens Consort* **14** Baudri de Bourgeuil **15** Orderic Vitalis **16** Ibid. **17** Ibid. **18** 'The Life of Lanfranc' **19** William of Malmesbury **20** *Chronicon Monasterii de Abingdon* **21** William of Malmesbury **22** Gathagan: "'Mother of Heroes, Most Beautiful of Mothers'" **23** William of Jumièges **24** Orderic Vitalis **25** Douglas **26** Orderic Vitalis **27** Ibid. Matilda would later be reconciled with her brother Robert. **28** William of Jumièges **29** *The Anglo-Saxon Chronicle* **30** Ingulph **31** Orderic Vitalis

15 'An Untimely Death'

1 William of Malmesbury **2** Herman the Archdeacon **3** Camden **4** The others were at Berkhamsted, Hertford, Ongar, Rayleigh, Rochester, Tonbridge, Reigate and Guildford. **5** Robinson: *Royal Palaces: Windsor Castle* **6** *Chronicon Monasterii de Abingdon*; *English Lawsuits from William I to Richard I* **7** Ingulph **8** Orderic Vitalis **9** Eadmer **10** Bates: *William the Conqueror* **11** William of Malmesbury **12** Ibid. **13** Henry of Huntingdon **14** William of Malmesbury **15** Godfrey of Cambrai, Prior of Winchester, recorded the date (*The Anglo-Latin Satirical Poets*); Robert of Torigni records the year as 1074. After 1073 Richard witnessed no more charters – Rufus was signing them instead. According to a seventeenth-century genealogist, Père Anselme de Guibours, cited by Lane, he died in 1081. Some modern historians suggest he could have died as early as 1069. **16** Later chroniclers claimed that Richard was gored to death by a stag about four years before his father's death. **17** Orderic Vitalis **18** Godfrey of Cambrai, in *The Anglo-Latin Satirical Poets*. Robert of Torigni also says that Richard 'died in his youth'. **19** William of Malmesbury; Orderic Vitalis **20** Barlow: *William Rufus*; William of Malmesbury; Orderic

Vitalis **21** Stevenson; Keen **22** Williams: *The English and the Norman Conquest*; Williams: 'A west-country magnate of the eleventh century'; Borman; Stafford: *Queen Emma and Queen Edith*. Matilda exempted a widow, Edgiva of Edmondsham, Dorset, from paying geld, a tax on each hide of land, which was used to raise armies; William gave the town of Tewin, Hertfordshire, to one Halfdane and his mother.

16 'The Praise and Agreement of Queen Matilda'

1 Orderic Vitalis **2** William of Malmesbury **3** Borman **4** Letter 2 in Appendix 2. **5** Orderic Vitalis. She would be elected abbess of Caen in 1112. **6** Kerr; Borman **7** *Regesta Regum Anglo-Normannorum: The Acta of William I.* She was also there when William gave a charter in 1077. **8** *Regesta Regum Anglo-Normannorum: The Acta of William I* **9** 'Vita Beati Simonis'. **10** Lack **11** *The Anglo-Saxon Chronicle* **12** William of Malmesbury

17 'Ties of Blood'

1 Orderic Vitalis; William of Malmesbury **2** Orderic Vitalis **3** William of Jumièges; Bates: *William the Conqueror* **4** Orderic Vitalis **5** *Who Made the Bayeux Tapestry?* **6** Leete **7** Wace **8** Montfaucon **9** Beech: 'Could Duke Philip the Good of Burgundy have owned the Bayeux Tapestry in 1430?' **10** Stenton: *The Bayeux Tapestry*; *Who Made the Bayeux Tapestry?* **11** Orderic Vitalis **12** William of Jumièges **13** 'Vita Beati Simonis'; *Guibert of Nogent-Sous-Coucy*. There were supposedly two rival suitors for Adela's hand: 'Anfursus, King of the Spains', and Robert Guiscard, Prince of Apulia, who was sixty-two and married. The only possible identification of 'Anfursus' can be with Alfonso VI of León, who in 1077 was designated 'Emperor of all Spain' and was a widower. There appears to have been some confusion with the earlier marriage of Adela's sister Agatha to Alfonso. **14** *The History of the King's Works*. The little castle has long since disappeared, all traces of it swept away by succeeding building works. **15** It was not called the White Tower until Henry III had it whitewashed in 1241. **16** The third floor was not added until the fifteenth century.

18 'A Mother's Tenderness'

1 Orderic Vitalis **2** *The Anglo-Saxon Chronicle* **3** William of Jumièges **4** John of Worcester **5** *The Anglo-Saxon Chronicle* **6** *The Anglo-Saxon Chronicle* says this happened in 1079, but John of Worcester is more likely to be correct, given the sequence of events. **7** Orderic Vitalis **8** John of

Worcester **9** William of Malmesbury **10** John of Worcester **11** Adela, who claimed to have seen a vision of the Virgin Mary, was later canonised as a saint. **12** Orderic Vitalis **13** Ibid. **14** Ibid. **15** William of Malmesbury **16** Strickland says it was Roger de Beaumont, William's most trusted counsellor and friend, but there is no contemporary evidence to support this. (Borman) **17** Orderic Vitalis **18** Ibid. **19** Ibid. **20** Ibid. **21** William of Malmesbury **22** Beech: 'Queen Mathilda of England'; Borman; Colbert **23** William of Malmesbury **24** Ibid. **25** Orderic Vitalis **26** Ibid. **27** Ibid. **28** *The Register of Pope Gregory VII* **29** Orderic Vitalis **30** Not to be confused with the Holy Shroud of Turin, it was lost in the French Revolution. **31** 'Vita Beati Simonis'; Lack; Simon Valois **32** Orderic Vitalis **33** *Regesta Regum Anglo-Normannorum: The Acta of William I* **34** Letter 3 in Appendix 2 **35** *Regesta Regum Anglo-Normannorum: The Acta of William I* **36** LoPrete 36 Baudri de Bourgeuil **37** William of Malmesbury

19 'The Noblest Gem of a Royal Race'

1 Turgot **2** Only foundations of the later stone walls of this rectangular building survive today. **3** Turgot. Margaret's abbey was rebuilt in the twelfth century, but some remains of her church were found beneath the nave in 1916. (Fawcett) **4** Orderic Vitalis; The Durham *Liber Vitae* **5** William of Malmesbury **6** Foliot, who had been told this by Edith herself. **7** Turgot **8** Hilton: *Queens Consort* **9** Turgot **10** Hildebert of Lavardin: 'Letters' **11** Turgot **12** Ibid.

20 'Twofold Light of November'

1 Borman **2** *Regesta Regum Anglo-Normannorum: The Acta of William I* **3** Lack **4** Borman **5** Orderic Vitalis **6** 'Vita Beati Simonis'; Simon Valois **7** *Regesta Regum Anglo-Normannorum: The Acta of William I* **8** Ibid. **9** *Domesday Book* **10** Crouch: *The Normans* **11** *Regesta Regum Anglo-Normannorum, 1066–1154* **12** *Regesta Regum Anglo-Normannorum: The Acta of William I* **13** Ibid. **14** Borman **15** Orderic Vitalis **16** Turgis **17** It was kept, with an inventory of her wardrobe, jewels and toilette, in the archives of Holy Trinity, Caen, and is now in the Bibliothèque Nationale, Paris (*Regesta Regum Anglo-Normannorum: The Acta of William I*; 'Les actes de Guillaume le Conquérant et de la reine Mathilde pour les abbayes caënnaises') **18** Orderic Vitalis **19** *The Anglo-Saxon Chronicle* **20** Orderic Vitalis **21** William of Malmesbury **22** Orderic Vitalis **23** William of Malmesbury **24** Orderic Vitalis **25** Ibid. **26** Another translation of Orderic's epitaph reads: 'The lofty structure of this splendid tomb hides great Matilda, sprung from royal stem; child of a Flemish duke [*sic*], her mother was Adela, daughter of a king of France, sister of Henry, Robert's royal son. Married to William joined, most illustrious King, she gave this site and raised this noble house, with many lands and many goods endowed, given by her, or her toil procured. It was here her holiest work was seen, this shrine, this house, where cloistered sisters dwell, and with their notes of praise the anthem swell, endowed and beautified by her earnest care. Comforter of the needy, duty's friend, her wealth enriched the poor, left her in need. At daybreak on November's second day, she won her share of everlasting joy.' Another modern translation by Michel de Boüard reads: 'This beautiful grave shelters with dignity Matilda, of royal blood and of remarkable moral value. Her father was duke [*sic*] of Flanders, and her mother, Adela, daughter of Robert, King of France, and sister of Henry, who took seat on the royal throne. United in marriage to the magnificent King William, she founded an abbey and built this church, of so many lands and precious goods, endowed and hallowed by her will. She was providence to the miserable full of goodness; dealing out her treasures, she was poor to herself and rich to the needy. Thus she gained her eternal dwelling, on the first [*sic*] day of November, following the hour of Prime.' Both the *Anglo-Saxon Chronicle* and Orderic Vitalis, transcribing the epitaph, give Matilda's date of death as 2 November.   **27** Gathagan: '"Mother of Heroes, Most Beautiful of Mothers"'   **28** *Recueil de travaux d'érudition dédiés à la mémoire de Julien Havet*   **29** Fettu: *Queen Matilda*; Ducarel; Strickland. I can find no record of what happened to Matilda's ring, which is presumably lost. The name 'Anne' was used in France for both men and women.   **30** Duffy   **31** Ducarel; Borman   **32** Orderic Vitalis; William of Malmesbury   **33** *Recueil de travaux d'érudition dédiés à la mémoire de Julien Havet*   **34** Orderic Vitalis   **35** Rudborne, who drew on many earlier sources.   **36** *The Anglo-Latin Satirical Poets*

Part Two: Matilda of Scotland

1 'Casting Off the Veil of Religion'

1 Orderic Vitalis   **2** William of Malmesbury   **3** Orderic Vitalis; Crouch: *The Normans*   **4** *The Anglo-Saxon Chronicle*   **5** Turgot   **6** William of Malmesbury   **7** Huneycutt: *Matilda of Scotland*   **8** Orderic Vitalis   **9** Ibid.   **10** Eadmer   **11** Ibid.   **12** Orderic Vitalis   **13** Hilton: *Queens Consort*   **14** Yorke   **15** There are theories that Christina also transferred to Wilton, but William of Malmesbury states that she grew old at Romsey.   **16** William of Malmesbury   **17** Eadmer   **18** Hollister   **19** Herman of Tournai   **20** Mason: *William II*   **21** Orderic Vitalis   **22** Sharpe; Huneycutt: *Matilda of Scotland*   **23** Mason: *William II*   **24** Herman of Tournai   **25** *The Anglo-Saxon Chronicle*; Simeon of Durham; John of Worcester   **26** Eadmer;

Herman of Tournai **27** The text continues: 'to Earl [*sic*] Alan, who stood by', but this is an error, as Alan was dead by then. **28** Eadmer **29** Huneycutt: *Matilda of Scotland* **30** Orderic Vitalis **31** Ibid.; Southern: *St Anselm and his Biographer* **32** *The Anglo-Saxon Chronicle* **33** Orderic Vitalis **34** Turgot **35** Ibid. **36** *Early Sources of Scottish History* **37** Orderic Vitalis, cited by Huneycutt: *Matilda of Scotland* **38** Anselm of Aosta: *The Letters of St Anselm of Canterbury*; O'Brien O'Keeffe **39** William of Malmesbury **40** Ibid. **41** Orderic Vitalis

2 'Her Whom He So Ardently Desired'

1 William of Malmesbury **2** Orderic Vitalis **3** *The Anglo-Saxon Chronicle*; William of Malmesbury **4** William of Malmesbury; Orderic Vitalis; Alexander, Archdeacon of Salisbury, in Tracts of the Exchequer, in Gervase of Tilbury **5** Henry of Huntingdon; Marbodius, Bishop of Rennes; Paris; William of Malmesbury **6** Orderic Vitalis **7** Eadmer **8** Hollister; Hilton: *Queens Consort* **9** William of Malmesbury **10** Barrow; Huneycutt: *Matilda of Scotland*; Hilton: *Queens Consort*. For example, Matilda gave the church of Carham-on-Tweed to Durham Cathedral. **11** *Liber Monasterii de Hyde* **12** Boutemy **13** Peter of Blois **14** William of Malmesbury **15** Ibid. **16** Ibid. **17** Henry of Huntingdon **18** William of Malmesbury **19** Henry of Huntingdon **20** Orderic Vitalis **21** Clare **22** Wace **23** Henry of Huntingdon **24** William of Malmesbury **25** Orderic Vitalis **26** William of Malmesbury

3 'A Matter of Controversy'

1 Eadmer **2** William of Malmesbury **3** Eadmer **4** Herman of Tournai **5** Eadmer **6** Ibid. **7** The archbishops of Canterbury did not adopt Lambeth as their London residence until *c.*1200; prior to that, it was a manor of St Andrew's cathedral priory in Rochester, and Rochester Cathedral was then the priory church. It may not have been a coincidence that Reynelm, a priest of Rochester, served as Edith's chancellor before being preferred to the see of Hereford in 1102 (Eadmer). **8** Eadmer **9** William of Malmesbury **10** Eadmer **11** Ibid.; Lanfranc **12** Eadmer **13** William of Malmesbury **14** Eadmer **15** Herman of Tournai

4 'Godric and Godgifu'

1 Eadmer **2** *The Anglo-Saxon Chronicle* **3** Westminster Abbey was not then established as the royal marriage church, as it is now. It was possibly the scene of two other medieval royal weddings, those of Richard III and Henry VII, although they may have taken place in St Stephen's Chapel in

Westminster Palace. The modern tradition was established only in 1919.
4 Eadmer **5** Huneycutt: *Matilda of Scotland* **6** Ibid.; Huneycutt:' "Another
Esther in Our Times" ' **7** Huneycutt: *Matilda of Scotland* **8** Eadmer
9 Huneycutt: *Matilda of Scotland* **10** Crouch: *The Normans* **11** *The Anglo-
Saxon Chronicle*; Eadmer. Orderic Vitalis states that Matilda was crowned
by Gerard, Archbishop of York, but he may only have assisted. **12** *English
Coronation Records*; Green: *Henry I* **13** *The Life of King Edward who rests at
Westminster* **14** Andrew of Wyntoun **15** Hildebert of Lavardin: *Carmina
Minora* **16** Hildebert of Lavardin: 'Letters' **17** Eadmer **18** William of
Malmesbury **19** Eadmer **20** Aird **21** Map **22** Orderic Vitalis **23** Cited
Rose: *Kings in the North* **24** William of Malmesbury **25** Letter 15 in
Appendix 2

5 'Another Esther in Our Own Time'

1 Hardying **2** By *The Anglo-Saxon Chronicle* and Robert of Gloucester, for
example. **3** Herbert de Losinga **4** Aelred of Rievaulx:'Genealogia regum
Anglorum' **5** Dark **6** Thompson and Stevens **7** *Regesta Regum Anglo-
Normannorum, 1066–1154;* Hilton: *Queens Consort*; Wertheimer; Huneycutt:
Matilda of Scotland. Only two of Matilda's original charters survive. **8** Crouch:
The Normans **9** William of Malmesbury **10** John of Worcester **11** Hardying
12 Letter 4 in Appendix 2 **13** Leland **14** *Regesta Regum Anglo-Normannorum,
1066–1154* **15** *Chroniques Anglo-Normandes* **16** Henry of Huntingdon
17 *The History of the King's Works* **18** The original roof was replaced by
the present hammerbeam roof at the end of the fourteenth century. **19** Steane
20 Hilton: *Queens Consort* **21** Stow: *The Survey of London* **22** *Regesta
Regum Anglo-Normannorum, 1066–1154* **23** Flete; Huneycutt:' "Proclaiming
her dignity abroad" ' **24** William of Malmesbury **25** *Regesta Regum Anglo-
Normannorum, 1066–1154* **26** William of Malmesbury **27** Könsgen
28 *Regesta Regum Anglo-Normannorum, 1066–1154*. Henry and Matilda also
conceived the idea of enlarging the small Cluniac priory at Montacute in
Somerset, founded between 1091 and 1102, but this plan came to
nothing. **29** Latzke **30** Hilton: *Queens Consort*; Huneycutt: *Matilda of
Scotland* **31** Heslop **32** Marbodius, Bishop of Rennes

6 'Lust for Glory'

1 'Constitutio Domus Regis'; Green: *The Government of England under Henry
I*; Warren: *The Governance of Norman and Angevin England*; Richardson and
Sayles **2** Hedley **3** *Regesta Regum Anglo-Normannorum, 1066–1154*
4 Hedley **5** Cotton MS. Vespasian B. X, f.11v, British Library **6** Huneycutt:
Matilda of Scotland **7** Capgrave: *The Book of the Illustrious Henries* **8** William

of Malmesbury **9** Lawson **10** Abbot of Malmesbury in the seventh century. **11** Könsgen **12** Hollister **13** Huneycutt: '"Proclaiming her dignity abroad"'

7 'The Common Mother of All England'

1 *Letters of Royal and Illustrious Ladies* **2** Letter 5 in Appendix 2 **3** Letter 6 in Appendix 2 **4** Turgot **5** Labarge **6** Houts: 'Latin Poetry and the Anglo-Norman Court' **7** Letter 7 in Appendix 2 **8** Letter 8 in Appendix 2 **9** Ivo of Chartres **10** Letter 9 in Appendix 2 **11** Hildebert of Lavardin: 'Letters' **12** *Chronicon Monasterii de Abingdon* **13** *The First Register of Norwich Cathedral Priory* **14** Letter 10 in Appendix 2 **15** Herbert de Losinga **16** *The Cartulary of Holy Trinity, Aldgate* **17** Hardying **18** Ronzani **19** Turgot **20** William of Malmesbury **21** Aelred of Rievaulx: 'Eulogium Davidis Regis Scotorum'; Huneycutt: *Matilda of Scotland*. William of Malmesbury, Robert of Gloucester and the annalist of Matilda's foundation of Holy Trinity, Aldgate, all recount the same episode.

8 'Most Noble and Royal on Both Sides'

1 Wace; Gervase of Canterbury **2** Wace; *Chroniques de Normandie* **3** Wace; *Chroniques de Normandie*; Orderic Vitalis; William of Malmesbury **4** William of Malmesbury **5** *Regesta Regum Anglo-Normannorum, 1066–1154* **6** John of Worcester **7** William of Malmesbury. It is sometimes asserted that Eustace and Mary married in 1096, but he was away at that time, acquitting himself heroically as one of the leaders of the First Crusade. **8** Tanner: 'Between Scylla and Charybdis' **9** *Gesta Stephani* **10** *The Early Charters of the Augustinian Canons of Waltham Abbey* **11** Bermondsey did not become an abbey until 1399. **12** Huneycutt: *Matilda of Scotland* **13** *Chronicon Monasterii de Abingdon* **14** *Victoria County History: Berkshire* **15** Eulogy by Peter Moraunt, monk of Malmesbury, 1140, in *Chronicon Monasterii de Abingdon* **16** John of Worcester **17** *Regesta Regum Anglo-Normannorum, 1066–1154*; Huneycutt: *Matilda of Scotland* **18** Cited Licence **19** *Chronicon Monasterii de Abingdon*; www.suttoncourtenay.co.uk; www.sclhs.org.uk; Fletcher: *Sutton Courtenay* **20** *The Anglo-Saxon Chronicle*, which records that her daughter was eight years and fifteen days old when she left England at the beginning of Lent 1110 to be married. **21** Gervase of Canterbury; Crouch: *The Normans*; Morris **22** Or Adelaide. John of Hexham calls her both Aaliz and Adela. **23** Corpus Christi College MS. 373 **24** Chibnall: *The Empress Matilda*

9 'Daughter of Archbishop Anselm'

1 Vaughn **2** Hugh the Chanter **3** Vaughn **4** Anselm of Aosta: *S. Anselmi Cantuariensis archiepiscopi opera omnia* **5** Hilton: *Queens Consort* **6** Letter

18 in Appendix 2   **7** Letter 11 in Appendix 2   **8** Letter 12 in Appendix 2
9 Schmitt, in Anselm of Aosta: *S. Anselmi Cantuariensis archiepiscopi opera omnia*

10 'Reprove, Beseech, Rebuke'

1 Henry of Huntingdon   **2** His approximate date of birth has been
estimated from the fact that, on 23 November, the Pope wrote to Henry
congratulating him on the birth of a son. William was not Maud's
younger twin, as was suggested by Rössler: William of Malmesbury states
that they were born at different times, and other evidence supports
that.   **3** William of Malmesbury   **4** *The Life of Gundulf, Bishop of
Rochester*   **5** William of Malmesbury   **6** Ibid.   **7** Letter 13 in Appendix
2   **8** Anselm of Aosta: *S. Anselmi Cantuariensis archiepiscopi opera omnia*;
Epistolae: Medieval Women's Latin Letters   **9** Letter 14 in Appendix 2
10 Anselm of Aosta: *The Letters of St Anselm of Canterbury*   **11** *Letters of
Royal and Illustrious Ladies*   **12** Letter 15 in Appendix 2   **13** Letter 16 in
Appendix 2   **14** Letter 17 in Appendix 2   **15** Letter 18 in Appendix 2

11 'Incessant Greetings'

1 Wertheimer   **2** Hilton: *Queens Consort*   **3** Robert of Gloucester   **4** Hildebert
of Lavardin: 'Letters'   **5** *Regesta Regum Anglo-Normannorum, 1066–1154*
6 Huneycutt: *Matilda of Scotland*   **7** *Chronicon Monasterii de Abingdon*; Keats-
Rohan; Huneycutt: *Matilda of Scotland*   **8** *Chronicon Monasterii de Abingdon*;
Regesta Regum Anglo-Normannorum, 1066–1154   **9** William of Malmesbury
10 Eadmer   **11** Ibid.   **12** Letter 19 in Appendix 2   **13** Huneycutt:
'"Proclaiming her dignity abroad"'   **14** Letter 20 in Appendix 2   **15** Eadmer
16 Huneycutt: *Matilda of Scotland*   **17** Farrer. Kingsbury Square is on the
site.   **18** Anselm of Aosta: *S. Anselmi Cantuariensis archiepiscopi opera
omnia*   **19** Ibid.   **20** Letter 21 in Appendix 2   **21** *Letters of Royal and
Illustrious Ladies*   **22** Letter 22 in Appendix 2   **23** Eadmer

12 'Pious Devotion'

1 This Latin title was the equivalent of the Saxon 'Atheling'.   **2** Orderic
Vitalis   **3** Anselm of Aosta: *S. Anselmi Cantuariensis archiepiscopi opera
omnia*   **4** Letter 23 in Appendix 2   **5** *Regesta Regum Anglo-Normannorum,
1066–1154*   **6** Adelard of Bath. It is also possible that the Queen he played
for was Adelaide of Maurienne, wife of Louis VI of France.   **7** *The Anglo-
Saxon Chronicle*   **8** *Regesta Regum Anglo-Normannorum, 1066–1154*   **9** *The
Anglo-Saxon Chronicle*   **10** *Regesta Regum Anglo-Normannorum, 1066–1154*
11 Around 1110, the monks of Tynemouth built a chapel dedicated to the
Holy Trinity at Old Bewick; a woman's effigy in that church was once

thought to be Matilda's, but in fact it dates from the fourteenth century. **12** *Regesta Regum Anglo-Normannorum, 1066–1154* **13** Tyerman **14** Herbert de Losinga **15** *Munimenta Gildhallae Londoniensis.* The dock was in use until the twentieth century, and survives today, but is heavily silted up. **16** Stow, in *A Survey of London*, says around 1117. **17** Hilton: *Queens Consort* **18** *Victoria County History: Middlesex* **19** Stow: *A Survey of London.* The church was rebuilt in 1628, and again in 1730. **20** Labarge **21** Weever **22** Stow: *A Survey of London* **23** Manning and Bray, who cite a lost document of 1239 relating to an inquiry into the maintenance of the bridge. **24** Hilton: *Queens Consort* **25** Green: *Henry I* **26** The first was at Colchester, founded in 1096. In the fourteenth century, the *Anonimalle Chronicle* of York claimed that 'Henry I, because of the industry and counsel of Queen Matilda, placed regular canons in the church of Carlisle.' In 1102, Henry had given land in Carlisle for the purpose of founding a religious house, which may have been at Matilda's behest, although there is no contemporary evidence for it – but the priory of Augustine canons that became Carlisle Cathedral in 1133 was not established until 1122. **27** *The Cartulary of Holy Trinity, Aldgate* **28** Green: *Henry I* **29** *The Cartulary of Holy Trinity, Aldgate.* These amounted to £25. **30** Stow: *A Survey of London* **31** *The Cartulary of Holy Trinity, Aldgate*; Huneycutt: *Matilda of Scotland* **32** Labarge **33** Green: *Henry I* **34** Brooke and Keir **35** Roberts: 'Llanthony Priory, Monmouthshire' **36** Atkyns; Norton: *England's Queens*; Huneycutt: *Matilda of Scotland*

13 'A Girl of Noble Character'

1 Henry of Huntingdon; Robert of Torigni **2** Heinrich IV had died in 1106. **3** Anselm of Aosta: *Sancti Anselmi Opera omnia* **4** *Bibliotheca Rerum Germanicarum*; Hollister; Leyser: *Medieval Germany and its Neighbours* **5** *The Cartulary of Holy Trinity, Aldgate* **6** Henry of Huntingdon **7** Ibid. **8** Ingulph **9** *The Anglo-Saxon Chronicle* **10** Ibid. **11** *Regesta Regum Anglo-Normannorum, 1066–1154* **12** Tyerman says she later recalled being beaten regularly by a terrifying aunt, but she has apparently been confused with her mother. **13** Corpus Christi College MS. 373 **14** Henry of Huntingdon **15** Robert of Torigni **16** Orderic Vitalis **17** He is sometimes confused with Henry I's nephew, Henry of Blois, who later became bishop of Winchester. **18** Orderic Vitalis **19** Foliot **20** Robert of Torigni **21** *Annales Patherbrunnenses* **22** *The Anglo-Saxon Chronicle* **23** Robert of Torigni **24** Leyser: *Medieval Germany and its Neighbours*; Hollister; *Oorkondenbock van het Sticht Utrecht tot 1302* **25** Robert of Torigni **26** Truax **27** Chibnall: *The Empress Matilda* **28** Robert of Torigni **29** Ibid.

14 'The Peace of the King and Me'

1 Henry of Huntingdon   **2** A stone wall encircling wooden buildings.
3 Hedley; Brindle and Kerr. Parts of the palace's foundations were uncovered
during excavations after the fire of 1992. At that time, traces of the
Conqueror's wooden palisade were also found.   **4** *Gesta Stephani*   **5** Crouch:
'Robert of Gloucester's Mother and Sexual Politics in Norman
Oxfordshire'   **6** *The Anglo-Saxon Chronicle*   **7** Aelred of Rievaulx: 'Eulogium
Davidis Regis Scotorum'   **8** Cannon and Griffiths   **9** Piers of Langtoft   **10** *The
Anglo-Saxon Chronicle*   **11** *Regesta Regum Anglo-Normannorum, 1066–1154*;
Huneycutt: *Matilda of Scotland*; Dark   **12** Huneycutt: *Matilda of Scotland*;
Heslop   **13** *The Anglo-Saxon Chronicle*   **14** *Historia et cartularium monasterii
Sancti Petri Gloucestriae*   **15** Some ruins of Kingsholm survived until the
late eighteenth century, but nothing remains today.   **16** Hildebert of
Lavardin: 'Letters'   **17** Herbert de Losinga

15 'All the Dignity of a Queen'

1 Corpus Christi College MS 373   **2** Ibid.   **3** *Le Livere de Reis de
Brittanie*   **4** Corpus Christi College MS. 373   **5** Herman of Tournai.
Doubts have been expressed as to whether Maud actually bore a child
at all, but there is no reason to doubt Herman's statement, and it is highly
unlikely that Henry I would have considered naming Maud his heir had
she been barren.   **6** Corpus Christi College MS. 373   **7** Orderic
Vitalis   **8** *Anglica, Hibernica, Normannica*   **9** Foliot   **10** Tyerman;
Rössler   **11** Leyser: 'The Anglo-Norman Succession'   **12** Stephen of
Rouen   **13** Chronicle of Repkav, in *Scriptores rerum Germanicarum, praecipue
Saxonicarum*   **14** Eadmer; Huneycutt: *Matilda of Scotland*   **15** *The Anglo-
Saxon Chronicle*   **16** Strickland says Henry and his family spent Easter
there, but he was abroad.   **17** The date is usually given as 1116, but the
Queen issued a charter for the soul of her sister to Durham Cathedral
before April 1116 (*The Early Charters of the Augustinian Canons of Waltham
Abbey, Essex 1062–1230*).   **18** John of Fordun   **19** *Gesta Stephani*
20 Stephen is referred to as the Countess Mary's son-in-law in a charter
of 1115 issued by Count Eustace in confirmation of one granted by her
to Bermondsey Abbey the year before. (Annales Abbatae de Bermondsey,
in *Annales Monastici*)

16 'Blessed Throughout the Ages'

1 Eadmer. Bernard would later serve as chancellor to Queen Adeliza.
2 Stow: *A Survey of London*   **3** Walsingham   **4** Cotton MS. Nero D.

VII, f.7, British Library   **5** It is often, incorrectly, assumed to be her daughter, the Empress Maud.   **6** Curia Regis Rolls for 1242. The dates of these crown-wearings are not recorded.   **7** Colker; Huneycutt: *Matilda of Scotland*   **8** Crouch: *The Normans*   **9** Colker; Huneycutt: *Matilda of Scotland*   **10** *Regesta Regum Anglo-Normannorum, 1066–1154*   **11** Orderic Vitalis; *Liber Eliensis*; Thompson and Stevens   **12** Eadmer   **13** Ibid.   **14** William of Malmesbury   **15** *Victoria County History: Sussex*. It burned down in 1781 and was the subject of a recent archaeological excavation. Labarge and Kealey both suggest that she may have had some connection with the leper hospital of St James at Westminster, but there is no record of its history before 1189.   **16** Hilton: *Queens Consort*; Huneycutt: *Matilda of Scotland*; *Luffield Priory Charters*   **17** *Charters of David I*   **18** William of Malmesbury   **19** Henry of Huntingdon; *The Anglo-Saxon Chronicle*; John of Worcester   **20** William of Malmesbury   **21** John of Worcester   **22** *Liber Monasterii de Hyde*; Erickson   **23** Green: *Henry I*   **24** *The Cartulary of Holy Trinity, Aldgate*. In the fourteenth century, Piers of Langtoft claimed that Matilda was 'entombed in St Paul's', while the monks of Reading later asserted, falsely, that she was buried in their abbey with Henry I. These claims may have arisen as a result of memorial tablets being erected to her memory in many churches. The *Anglo-Saxon Chronicle*, citing Winchester Cathedral's registers, incorrectly asserts that, in 1158, her bones were reburied with those of 'Queen' Frideswide in one of the mortuary chests in Winchester Cathedral. Frideswide was in fact a Saxon saint who was buried in Oxford.   **25** William of Malmesbury   **26** *Liber Monasterii de Hyde*   **27** Ibid.   **28** John of Worcester; Orderic Vitalis   **29** *The Anglo-Saxon Chronicle*   **30** Dodson mentions a false tradition that has her buried by the entrance to the Chapter House at Westminster.   **31** *Liber Monasterii de Hyde*   **32** *The Cartulary of Holy Trinity, Aldgate*. Queen Margaret had been canonised in 1250.   **33** Hardying; Stow: *A Survey of London*; *Westminster Abbey: Official Guide*   **34** Robert of Gloucester   **35** William of Malmesbury   **36** *Liber Monasterii de Hyde*. At least nine laudatory poems were written in her memory (Houts: 'Latin Poetry and the Anglo-Norman Court').   **37** *Charters of David I*   **38** *Westminster Abbey Charters*   **39** *Pipe Roll 31 Henry I*   **40** Meyer von Knonau   **41** Chibnall: *The Empress Matilda*; Biddle   **42** Meyer von Knonau   **43** Hausmann; Castor; Chibnall: *The Empress Matilda*   **44** Scheffer-Boichorst   **45** Chibnall: *The Empress Matilda*   **46** Robert of Torigni; Houts: 'The *Gesta Normannorum Ducum*: a history without an end'; Huneycutt: *Matilda of Scotland*   **47** *Liber Monasterii de Hyde*   **48** *The Anglo-Saxon Chronicle*   **49** William of Malmesbury; Mason: *Westminster Abbey and its People*   **50** Hilton: *Queens Consort*   **51** Hardying

Part Three: *Adeliza of Louvain*

1 'Without Warning'

1 William of Malmesbury **2** Given-Wilson and Curteis **3** Gervase of Canterbury **4** *The Anglo-Saxon Chronicle* **5** The castle burned down in 1731, and Royal Square now occupies the site, but there are extensive archaeological remains below the ground. **6** The castle was extensively rebuilt in the sixteenth century. **7** Henry of Huntingdon **8** Chibnall: *The Empress Matilda* **9** John of Worcester **10** William of Malmesbury **11** John of Worcester. It is clear that the betrothal was negotiated in 1120, not 1121, as is sometimes stated. **12** William of Malmesbury **13** Ibid. **14** Orderic Vitalis **15** William of Malmesbury **16** Orderic Vitalis

2 'A Fortunate Beauty'

1 *The Anglo-Saxon Chronicle* **2** Henry of Huntingdon **3** Robert of Gloucester **4** Eadmer; John of Worcester; Orderic Vitalis **5** John of Worcester **6** Abernethy **7** Strickland; *The Art of Needlework* **8** Some historians claim that Henry and Adeliza arrived in England at Michaelmas 1120 and were married at Ely soon afterwards, but Eadmer is quite clear that they were married in January 1121, and it is unlikely that Adeliza would have resided unmarried in England for three or four months before her marriage. **9** Eadmer. Other chroniclers give different dates: John of Worcester says the marriage took place on 29 January, the *Anglo-Saxon Chronicle* 'before Candlemas' (2 February). **10** Pipe Rolls for 1130; Wertheimer **11** Pipe Rolls for 1130; Hilton: *Queens Consort* **12** John of Worcester. *The Anglo-Saxon Chronicle* states that she was crowned on the same day she was married. **13** Eadmer **14** Henry of Huntingdon; John of Worcester **15** Chibnall: 'The Empress Matilda and Bec-Hellouin' **16** *Victoria County History: Berkshire*; Hilton: *Queens Consort*. Reading Abbey would not be completed until 1164, when its church was the largest in England, rivalling St Paul's in size. It became one of the richest and most powerful abbeys in the realm. After its dissolution under Henry VIII, it was largely demolished and the site turned into a quarry. The ruins that remain now stand in gardens; the inner gateway has been restored. **17** Henry of Huntingdon **18** Piers of Langtoft **19** Wertheimer **20** *Regesta Regum Anglo-Normannorum, 1066–1154* **21** Wertheimer **22** 'Annals of Waverley Abbey' **23** Henry of Huntingdon **24** Thompson **25** She was the great-granddaughter of Albert III, Count of Namur, and therefore the great-niece of his daughter, Ida, Adeliza's mother. **26** William of Newburgh **27** *Victoria County History: Oxfordshire* **28** Thompson

29 Orderic Vitalis. Godeschalch is probably to be identified with the Queen's clerk, Gozo. **30** *Victoria County History: Somerset* **31** *The Waltham Annals* **32** Wertheimer **33** *Reading Abbey Cartularies*; Norton: *England's Queens*; Wertheimer **34** *Reading Abbey Cartularies* **35** Hilton: *Queens Consort* **36** Stow: *A Survey of London* **37** Hilton: *Queens Consort*; Abernethy **38** Huneycutt: *Matilda of Scotland* **39** Merton College MS. 249, University of Oxford **40** Henry of Huntingdon **41** William of Malmesbury **42** Henry of Huntingdon **43** 'Annals of Waverley Abbey' **44** *The Anglo-Saxon Chronicle*; Henry of Huntingdon; Paris; Hedley **45** Henry of Huntingdon **46** *The Anglo-Saxon Chronicle*; Henry of Huntingdon **47** John of Forde **48** Chibnall: 'The Empress Matilda and Bec-Hellouin' **49** Orderic Vitalis

3 'His Only Heir'

1 William of Malmesbury **2** There is no substance to Giraldus Cambrensis's tale that he privately repudiated Maud, went into voluntary exile in England and led a holy, penitential life in the monastery of St Withburga, Chester. **3** *Anglica, Hibernica, Normannica* **4** Castor **5** William of Malmesbury **6** Orderic Vitalis **7** *Anglica, Hibernica, Normannica* **8** William of Malmesbury **9** Rössler: *Die Kaiserin Matilda* **10** William of Malmesbury **11** Foliot **12** Robert of Torigni; Chibnall: *The Empress Matilda* **13** Dark **14** *Recueil des chartes de l'abbaye de Cluny* **15** Hollister **16** *The Anglo-Saxon Chronicle* **17** Map **18** William of Malmesbury **19** *Recueil des historiens des croisades* **20** King: 'Eustace, Count of Boulogne' **21** Dark. It is unlikely, given his name, that Baldwin was born after Stephen became king of England in 1135, for the name Baldwin does not feature in the English royal line prior to that date. **22** Huneycutt: 'The idea of the perfect princess' **23** Hugo of St Vaast

4 'Royal English Blood'

1 *The Anglo-Saxon Chronicle*; Henry of Huntingdon **2** Chadwick: *Empress Matilda's Bling*; Earenfight; Corpus Christi College MS. 373. The hand of St James still survives today in St Peter's Church at Marlow. **3** Bradbury: *Stephen and Matilda* **4** Henry of Huntingdon **5** Könsgen; Thomson; Chibnall: *The Empress Matilda* **6** *Gesta Stephani* **7** Foliot **8** Chadwick: *The Enigmatic Brian FitzCount* **9** King: 'The Memory of Brian FitzCount' **10** *The Anglo-Saxon Chronicle* **11** William of Malmesbury **12** Hildebert of Lavardin: 'Letters' **13** William of Malmesbury **14** Ibid. **15** Simeon of Durham **16** William of Malmesbury **17** John of Worcester **18** William of Malmesbury **19** Henry of Huntingdon **20** Lack **21** William

of Malmesbury   **22** Ibid.   **23** *Gesta Stephani*   **24** William of Malmesbury;
John of Worcester   **25** *Gesta Stephani*   **26** Paris

5 'The Offence of the Daughter'

1 William of Malmesbury   **2** *Chroniques des comtes d'Anjou*   **3** William
of Malmesbury   **4** *The Anglo-Saxon Chronicle*   **5** Geoffrey had been born
on 24 August 1113.   **6** William of Malmesbury   **7** *Chroniques des comtes
d'Anjou*   **8** Robert of Torigni   **9** Hildebert of Lavardin: 'Letters'   **10** Ibid.
11 Foliot   **12** Henry of Huntingdon; *Chroniques des comtes d'Anjou*; Simeon
of Durham; William of Malmesbury   **13** William of Malmesbury
14 Ibid.   **15** *Chroniques des comtes d'Anjou*   **16** Ibid.   **17** Henry of
Huntingdon   **18** *Chroniques des comtes d'Anjou*   **19** Ibid.   **20** William of
Malmesbury   **21** *Chroniques des comtes d'Anjou*   **22** Gillingham: 'Love,
Marriage and Politics in the Twelfth Century'   **23** Robert of Torigni
24 William of Malmesbury   **25** Orderic Vitalis   **26** *Chroniques des comtes
d'Anjou*   **27** Ibid.   **28** Castor   **29** Ralph of Diceto   **30** *The Anglo-Saxon
Chronicle*   **31** William of Malmesbury   **32** Ibid.   **33** Ibid.   **34** Simeon of
Durham   **35** William of Tyre   **36** Green: *Henry I*   **37** Chibnall: *The
Empress Matilda*   **38** *Regesta Regum Anglo-Normannorum, 1066–1154*
39 Suger   **40** *Charters and Records among the Archives of the Ancient
Abbey of Cluni*   **41** *Recueil des chartes de l'abbaye de Cluny*   **42** Simeon
of Durham   **43** Green: *Henry I*   **44** Hildebert of Lavardin: 'Letters'

6 'The Peril of Death'

1 Henry of Huntingdon   **2** Pipe Rolls: Henry I   **3** Henry of Huntingdon
4 William of Malmesbury; Henry of Huntingdon   **5** John of Worcester
6 Hilton: *Queens Consort*   **7** Given-Wilson and Curteis   **8** Hildebert of
Lavardin: 'Letters'   **9** Henry of Huntingdon   **10** Tyerman   **11** Henry
of Huntingdon; Robert of Torigni   **12** Hildebert of Lavardin: 'Letters'
13 William of Malmesbury; Henry of Huntingdon. John of Worcester is
the only chronicler to state that the oath was renewed at the Easter court
of 1128. There is no other evidence for this.   **14** Henry of Huntingdon
15 Tyerman   **16** Foliot   **17** *Chroniques des comtes d'Anjou*   **18** *Chroniques
des comtes d'Anjou et des Seigneurs d'Amboise*   **19** Beem: 'Greater by
Marriage'   **20** Marcombe; Dugdale and Burnett. Strickland recorded that
Adeliza's deed, with part of her seal, was preserved in the corporation chest
at Wilton. The site of the hospital lies just within the north-eastern boundary
wall of Wilton Park.   **21** Henry of Huntingdon   **22** Hedley   **23** Henry
of Huntingdon   **24** Chibnall: 'The Empress Matilda and her Sons'; *Actus
pontificum in urbe degentium*; 'Chronicae Sancti Albini Andegauensis'.
According to the thirteenth-century chronicler Matthew Paris, the child

was not Geoffrey's, but the fruit of a love affair between Maud and her cousin, Stephen of Blois. Paris quotes Maud as saying that the two were 'acquainted' before she married Geoffrey, but in fact Henry was born five years after the wedding. Thus it is highly unlikely that he was Stephen's son. **25** William of Malmesbury **26** In the thirteenth century, Matthew Paris would claim that Geoffrey gave the child his name because he did not believe that the older boy Henry was his, but this is unlikely. **27** Robert of Torigni **28** The bridge was ruinous by 1603 and its remains were dismantled in 1661, the bases of the piers being retained in the hope that it would one day be rebuilt. In 1829 it was rebuilt as the Pont Circonflexe. It was renamed the Pont Corneille in 1848. The modern Pont Mathilde is in a different location. **29** Robert of Torigni **30** Henry of Huntingdon **31** Truax **32** Ibid.

7 'Cast Down in Darkness'

1 Orderic Vitalis **2** Ibid. **3** William of Malmesbury **4** Orderic Vitalis **5** William of Malmesbury **6** Robert of Torigni **7** Orderic Vitalis **8** Henry of Huntingdon; Robert of Torigni **9** King: *Medieval England* **10** Henry of Huntingdon **11** Ibid. **12** Brewer **13** Henry of Huntingdon **14** William of Malmesbury **15** Ibid. **16** Henry of Huntingdon **17** William of Malmesbury **18** Ibid. **19** *The Anglo-Saxon Chronicle* **20** William of Malmesbury; Henry of Huntingdon **21** John of Salisbury: *Historia Pontificalis* **22** Henry of Huntingdon **23** William of Malmesbury

Part Four: *Matilda of Boulogne and the Empress Matilda*

1 'In Violation of His Oath'

1 Starkey **2** William of Malmesbury **3** Goodall **4** William of Newburgh **5** Hollister **6** Henry of Huntingdon **7** Ibid. **8** Ibid. **9** Orderic Vitalis **10** John of Salisbury: *Historia Pontificalis* **11** Richard of Hexham, cited by Chibnall: *The Empress Matilda* **12** Richard of Hexham **13** Chibnall: *The Empress Matilda*

2 'Ravening Wolves'

1 Castor **2** William of Malmesbury **3** Robert of Torigni **4** King: *Medieval England* **5** Henry of Huntingdon **6** Orderic Vitalis **7** *Chroniques des comtes d'Anjou*; Beem: 'Greater by Marriage' **8** Orderic Vitalis **9** Ibid. **10** Robert of Torigni **11** Orderic Vitalis **12** Given-Wilson and Curteis **13** Henry of Huntingdon **14** William of Malmesbury

3 'A Manly Heart in a Woman's Body'

1 Tanner: 'Between Scylla and Charybdis' 2 Geoffrey of Auxerre: 'Fragmenta ex tertia vita Sancti Bernardi' and 'S. Bernardi Vita Prima' 3 Letter 24 in Appendix 2 4 Tanner: 'Between Scylla and Charybdis' 5 Gervase of Canterbury 6 Henry of Huntingdon 7 Hilton: *Queens Consort*; Chibnall: *The Empress Matilda* 8 *Gesta Stephani* 9 Some modern sources state that his brother, Baldwin, had therefore died before Stephen's accession (for example, *Burke's Guide to the Royal Family*), on the mistaken assumption that Baldwin was the eldest son. 10 Castor 11 Orderic Vitalis 12 Martindale 13 Crouch: 'Between Three Realms'. Some sources give 1137 as the date of Matilda's death, but it was probably nearer 1141. 14 Stow: *A Survey of London*; *The Cartulary of Holy Trinity, Aldgate* 15 *The Cartulary of Holy Trinity, Aldgate*. Ralph did not succeed Norman of Kent as prior until 1147, but he was sub-prior for some years before that (*Victoria County History: London*). 16 *Gesta Stephani* 17 Ibid. 18 Dark 19 *Regesta Regum Anglo-Normannorum, 1066–1154* 20 Dark 21 *Regesta Regum Anglo-Normannorum, 1066–1154* 22 *The Cartulary of Holy Trinity, Aldgate; Regesta Regum Anglo-Normannorum, 1066–1154*. The Queen, Bishop Roger and others successfully interceded with the King on behalf of some smiths and a butcher, who came seeking Henry's aid in favour of Holy Trinity, Aldgate, over disputed land (*The Cartulary of Holy Trinity, Aldgate*). 23 He replaced Thomas, her chaplain from around 1142 (Dark). 24 *The Cartulary of Holy Trinity, Aldgate* 25 *Regesta Regum Anglo-Normannorum, 1066–1154*; Dark; Warren: *The Governance of Norman and Angevin England*; Green: *The Government of England under Henry I*; Richardson and Sayles. One of Matilda's clerks was her countryman, Richard of Boulogne, a canon of St Martin le Grand. William Monk was her steward in Boulogne. 26 Weever 27 Wree 28 Brown: '*Elegit domum sibi placabilem*' 29 *The Cartulary of Holy Trinity, Aldgate*; Truax 30 *Regesta Regum Anglo-Normannorum, 1066–1154*; Stow: *A Survey of London* 31 *Regesta Regum Anglo-Normannorum, 1066–1154* 32 Dark 33 *Regesta Regum Anglo-Normannorum, 1066–1154*; Dark 34 *Regesta Regum Anglo-Normannorum, 1066–1154* 35 Ibid. 36 Stow: *A Survey of London*. The ancient buildings were demolished in 1825 to make way for the building of St Katharine's Dock, but the foundation was re-established at Regent's Park and still survives today at Limehouse in London's East End as a charitable retreat. 37 *Regesta Regum Anglo-Normannorum, 1066–1154* 38 Davis: 'The College of St Martin le Grand and the Anarchy, 1135–1154'. For details of Matilda's gifts, see Dark. 39 *Regesta Regum Anglo-Normannorum, 1066–1154* 40 Ibid. 41 Poulle; Dark 42 *Regesta Regum Anglo-Normannorum, 1066–1154* 43 *Histoire de la congregation de Savigny*; Poulle 44 *Regesta Regum Anglo-Normannorum, 1066–1154*

4 'The First Anniversary of My Lord'

1 *The Anglo-Saxon Chronicle*. Henry I's tomb and remains were lost when the abbey was dissolved during the Reformation. A cross now marks where the tomb stood before the high altar, and a stone plaque on a ruined wall states that Henry was buried nearby. **2** *Reading Abbey Cartularies*; Wertheimer **3** Robinson: *Arundel Castle*. While the keep still stands, the present Arundel Castle was built in the eighteenth century in the bailey, or quadrangle, below it, and extensively restored in 1890. **4** Wertheimer **5** Friend **6** Rigg **7** *Reading Abbey Cartularies* **8** Hilton: *Queens Consort*; Wertheimer. Osney Priory had been founded by Henry I's former mistress, Edith Forne, in 1129. Before 1145, Adeliza issued a charter to two knights who were her tenants at Crowcombe, Somerset, ordering them to attend Bishop Henry at Winchester Cathedral and perform military service for him and for his cathedral, as they had used to do for her. It was witnessed by her former chaplain, Simon, Bishop of Worcester, Seffrid, Bishop of Chichester, Herman and Franco of Brussels, her chaplains, and Rainald, her 'dapifer' (seneschal). (*Regesta Regum Anglo-Normannorum, 1066–1154*) **9** Lansdowne MS. 383, British Library; Kauffman; Thompson; *A Prayerbook Fit for a Queen?* **10** *Reading Abbey Cartularies* **11** Ibid.; Doran; Hilton: *Queens Consort*; Wertheimer **12** Cited Rowell **13** William of Newburgh **14** Thompson **15** Ibid. **16** After 1154, Joscelin married Agnes, co-heiress of William de Percy, a grandson of one of the companions of the Conqueror. There is no evidence that he adopted his wife's surname, as is often claimed, but their son Richard took the name Percy, and through him, Joscelin and Agnes became the ancestors of the Percy earls of Northumberland. The Percy emblem of a blue lion on a gold ground probably derives from the blue lion of Louvain.

5 'Unable to Break Through'

1 Dark; *Regesta Regum Anglo-Normannorum, 1066–1154* **2** Crouch: *The Reign of King Stephen* **3** John of Forde **4** *Regesta Regum Anglo-Normannorum, 1066–1154* **5** Castor **6** Richard of Hexham **7** *Gesta Stephani* **8** 'Chronicae Sancti Albini Andegauensis' **9** Robert of Torigni; *Magni Rotuli Scaccarii Normanniae sub Regibus Angliae*; *Regesta Regum Anglo-Normannorum, 1066–1154*. In later life, before 1158, Drogo took vows and joined this community. **10** Orderic Vitalis **11** *Regesta Regum Anglo-Normannorum, 1066–1154* **12** Ibid. **13** *Regesta Regum Anglo-Normannorum, 1066–1154* **14** Dark **15** *Regesta Regum Anglo-Normannorum, 1066–1154* **16** Henry of Huntingdon **17** *Regesta Regum Anglo-Normannorum, 1066–1154* **18** Orderic Vitalis **19** Bouvet **20** Chibnall: *The Empress Matilda* **21** Strickland

22 Dugdale; Roberts: *The Mowbray Legacy*   **23** The office was associated with the manor of Kenninghall, Norfolk, which was granted by Henry I to the elder Albini and later inherited by the dukes of Norfolk.

6 'Ties of Kinship'

1 William of Malmesbury   **2** Orderic Vitalis; William of Malmesbury; Robert of Torigni; Henry of Huntingdon   **3** Dark; *Regesta Regum Anglo-Normannorum, 1066–1154; English Episcopal Acta 28: Canterbury 1070–1136*   **4** John of Worcester   **5** *Regesta Regum Anglo-Normannorum, 1066–1154*   **6** Ibid.   **7** Richard of Hexham; John of Hexham; Orderic Vitalis; Henry of Huntingdon; *Gesta Stephani*   **8** Orderic Vitalis   **9** William of Malmesbury   **10** Foliot   **11** William of Malmesbury   **12** John of Worcester   **13** Bradbury: *Stephen and Matilda*   **14** William of Malmesbury   **15** Henry of Huntingdon; William of Newburgh; Orderic Vitalis; Robert of Torigni   **16** The original fortress was destroyed by the English during the Hundred Years War. The present building dates from the fourteenth century and later periods.   **17** Orderic Vitalis   **18** *Recueil des Actes de Henry II*; Chibnall: *The Empress Matilda*; Chibnall: 'The Empress Matilda and her Sons'   **19** Chibnall: 'The Empress Matilda and her Sons'   **20** *Gesta Stephani*   **21** Henry of Huntingdon   **22** Richard of Hexham

7 'Feminine Shrewdness'

1 He was the son of William, a bastard son of Eustace II, Count of Boulogne.   **2** Orderic Vitalis; Henry of Huntingdon; John of Worcester   **3** Henry of Huntingdon   **4** Orderic Vitalis   **5** Richard of Hexham   **6** John of Hexham   **7** Richard of Hexham   **8** Ibid.   **9** *Regesta Regum Anglo-Normannorum, 1066–1154*   **10** Henry of Huntingdon   **11** Davis: *Henry of Blois*   **12** Robert of Torigni; Henry of Huntingdon   **13** *The Chronicle of Battle Abbey*   **14** Gervase of Canterbury   **15** *Regesta Regum Anglo-Normannorum, 1066–1154; Victoria County History: Oxford; English Episcopal Acta 28: Canterbury 1070–1136*   **16** Richard of Hexham   **17** Cited Hilton: *Queens Consort*   **18** John of Hexham   **19** Richard of Hexham   **20** Ibid.

8 'Touch Not Mine Anointed'

1 Chibnall: *The Empress Matilda*   **2** Foliot   **3** John of Salisbury: *Historia Pontificalis*   **4** Ibid.; William of Malmesbury   **5** John of Salisbury: *Historia Pontificalis*   **6** Huneycutt: *Matilda of Scotland*   **7** Henry of Huntingdon. What little remains of it is on private land and not accessible to the public.   **8** *Gesta Stephani*   **9** William of Malmesbury

10 Henry of Huntingdon **11** Gervase of Canterbury; William of Malmesbury **12** William of Malmesbury **13** *Gesta Stephani* **14** William of Malmesbury

9 'His Extraordinary Queen'

1 According to Henry Howard's *Indications of Memorials*, they wed in 1138. **2** The only remains of Albini's original castle at Buckenham are a large rectangular earthwork and traces of the curtain wall. **3** Stansted Park now occupies the site. **4** Goodall **5** Norton: *England's Queens* **6** Cited Robinson: *Arundel Castle: The Seat of the Duke of Norfolk* **7** It was among the small, impoverished religious houses dissolved by Cardinal Wolsey in 1524–5, before the Reformation. Nothing survives of Adeliza's original foundation. Only part of a square thirteenth-century tower remains, incorporated into a farmhouse. **8** *Reading Abbey Cartularies*; *The Early Charters of the Augustinian Canons of Waltham Abbey* **9** Doran **10** Thompson. Some of her charters were witnessed by her countryman Rothardus, who appears to have left the service of Godfrey of Louvain, Bishop of Bath, after the Bishop's death in August 1135, and returned to Adeliza's service. **11** Cotton Titus MS. C viii, British Library **12** *The Chartulary of Boxgrove Priory*

10 'A Desert Full of Wild Beasts'

1 *Chroniques des comtes d'Anjou* **2** Wace **3** William of Malmesbury **4** Ibid. **5** Orderic Vitalis **6** Hilton: *Queens Consort* **7** Thompson **8** *Victoria County History: Essex* **9** William of Malmesbury **10** *Gesta Stephani* **11** William of Malmesbury **12** Given-Wilson and Curteis **13** *Gesta Stephani* **14** Ibid. **15** Davis: 'Henry of Blois and Brian Fitz Count' **16** Ibid.; Foliot; Chibnall: *The Empress Matilda*

11 'Treacherous Advice'

1 *Gesta Stephani* **2** In the nineteenth century, the bed she had purportedly slept in was shown to visitors. (Robinson: *Arundel Castle: The Seat of the Duke of Norfolk*) **3** Robinson: *Arundel Castle: The Seat of the Duke of Norfolk* **4** *Gesta Stephani* **5** John of Worcester **6** Gervase of Canterbury **7** *Gesta Stephani* **8** Gervase of Canterbury **9** *Gesta Stephani*. The hostile anonymous author of the *Gesta Stephani* always referred to Maud disparagingly as the Countess of Anjou, or King Henry's daughter, or even the Earl of Gloucester's sister; when quoting from his chronicle, I have substituted 'the Empress' for 'the Countess' to avoid confusion. **10** *Gesta*

Stephani **11** Henry of Huntingdon **12** William of Malmesbury **13** Henry of Huntingdon **14** John of Worcester **15** William of Malmesbury **16** Ibid. **17** John of Worcester **18** Orderic Vitalis

12 'May Your Imperial Dignity Thrive'

1 *Gesta Stephani* **2** Robert of Gloucester **3** William of Worcester **4** *Gesta Stephani* **5** John of Worcester **6** William of Malmesbury **7** Starkey **8** *Gesta Stephani*; *Regesta Regum Anglo-Normannorum, 1066–1154* **9** Gloucester became a royal castle in 1155, but in the late fifteenth century it was turned into the town gaol. The keep was demolished in 1787, and a new gaol built on the site. The castle site was the subject of an archaeological dig in 2015. **10** *Gesta Stephani* **11** *Regesta Regum Anglo-Normannorum, 1066–1154* **12** *Gesta Stephani* **13** John of Worcester **14** William of Malmesbury **15** John of Worcester **16** Shortly before Queen Matilda's death in 1118, Bishop Roger of Salisbury had expelled Abbot Eadwulf and himself taken over the jurisdiction of the abbey (*The Anglo-Saxon Chronicle*). In 1139, King Stephen had commanded the election of John of Malmesbury as abbot. **17** William of Malmesbury

13 'Christ and His Saints Slept'

1 William of Malmesbury **2** *Gesta Stephani* **3** Gervase of Canterbury **4** *The Anglo-Saxon Chronicle* **5** William of Newburgh **6** *The Anglo-Saxon Chronicle* **7** Henry of Huntingdon **8** William of Malmesbury **9** Ibid. **10** Ibid. **11** *The Anglo-Saxon Chronicle* **12** Cited Starkey **13** *The Anglo-Saxon Chronicle* **14** Ibid. This account is corroborated by others written by William of Malmesbury, Henry of Huntingdon and Aelred of Rievaulx. **15** William of Malmesbury **16** *Annales Monastici* **17** William of Malmesbury **18** *Gesta Stephani* **19** Cited Starkey **20** King: 'The Memory of Brian FitzCount'

14 'Hunger-Starved Wolves'

1 Hilton: *Queens Consort*; Crouch: *The Normans* **2** *Gesta Stephani* **3** He was the bastard son of Philip of Loo, grandson of Robert the Frisian, Count of Flanders. **4** Henry of Huntingdon **5** John of Worcester **6** William of Newburgh **7** John of Worcester **8** Gervase of Canterbury **9** John of Hexham **10** William of Malmesbury **11** Ibid. **12** Ibid. **13** King: *Medieval England* **14** William of Malmesbury **15** Letter 25 in Appendix 2 **16** William FitzHerbert was restored to the see of York in 1153, on Murdac's death, and retained it until he died in 1154.

15 'Shaken with Amazement'

1 William of Malmesbury **2** Henry of Huntingdon **3** John of Worcester **4** William of Malmesbury; *Gesta Stephani* **5** *Gesta Stephani* **6** William of Malmesbury **7** *Gesta Stephani* **8** Davis: 'The Authorship of the *Gesta Stephani*' **9** Crouch: *The Normans* **10** *Regesta Regum Anglo-Normannorum, 1066–1154* **11** William of Malmesbury **12** Henry of Huntingdon, who, like Robert of Torigni, gives her expulsion from London as the reason why she had Stephen chained, but there are several references to his being in chains before then. **13** William of Malmesbury

16 'Dragged by Different Hooks'

1 William of Newburgh **2** *The Anglo-Saxon Chronicle* **3** Orderic Vitalis **4** Dark **5** Henry of Huntingdon **6** John of Hexham **7** Dark **8** Gervase of Canterbury **9** *Gesta Stephani* **10** King: *Medieval England* **11** William of Malmesbury **12** *Gesta Stephani* **13** Davis: 'Henry of Blois and Brian Fitz Count' **14** *Gesta Stephani* **15** William of Malmesbury **16** *Gesta Stephani* **17** William of Malmesbury **18** *Gesta Stephani*; Davis: *Henry of Blois* **19** William of Malmesbury **20** Gervase of Canterbury **21** William of Malmesbury **22** Gervase of Canterbury **23** *Gesta Stephani* **24** Gervase of Canterbury **25** *Regesta Regum Anglo-Normannorum, 1066–1154* **26** Now in the archives of Durham Cathedral. **27** *Gesta Stephani* **28** Ibid. **29** John of Hexham **30** *The Anglo-Saxon Chronicle* **31** Orderic Vitalis

17 'Sovereign Lady of England'

1 *Gesta Stephani* **2** Oxford Castle was a ruin by the thirteenth century. While residing there, Maud issued charters granting lands to the prior and convent of St Frideswide. (*Regesta Regum Anglo-Normannorum, 1066–1154*) **3** William of Malmesbury **4** *Regesta Regum Anglo-Normannorum, 1066–1154* **5** Ibid. **6** William of Malmesbury **7** Ibid. **8** *Gesta Stephani* **9** Henry of Huntingdon **10** William of Malmesbury **11** *Regesta Regum Anglo-Normannorum, 1066–1154*; Chibnall: *The Empress Matilda* **12** Castor **13** *Gesta Stephani* **14** Hilton: *Queens Consort* **15** *Gesta Stephani* **16** William of Malmesbury **17** John of Hexham **18** William of Malmesbury **19** Gervase of Canterbury **20** John of Worcester **21** Chibnall: 'The Empress Matilda and Bec-Hellouin' **22** William of Malmesbury **23** Norton: *England's Queens* **24** Chibnall: 'The Charters of the Empress Matilda' **25** *Gesta Stephani* **26** William of Malmesbury **27** Goodall **28** *Gesta Stephani* **29** *Regesta Regum Anglo-Normannorum, 1066–1154* **30** Bradbury: *Stephen and Matilda* **31** *Regesta Regum Anglo-Normannorum, 1066–1154* **32** Simeon of Durham

18 'Insufferable Arrogance'

1 Truax   **2** Stow: *A Survey of London*   **3** *Gesta Stephani*   **4** *Victoria County History: Essex*; Stubbs; Chibnall: *The Empress Matilda*   **5** *Reading Abbey Cartularies*; Wertheimer   **6** *Reading Abbey Cartularies*; *Regesta Regum Anglo-Normannorum, 1066–1154*; Hollister   **7** Truax   **8** *Gesta Stephani*   **9** William of Malmesbury   **10** Bradbury: *Stephen and Matilda*   **11** Gervase of Canterbury   **12** *Gesta Stephani*   **13** FitzStephen   **14** Davis: *Henry of Blois*   **15** *Regesta Regum Anglo-Normannorum, 1066–1154*   **16** *Gesta Stephani*   **17** Gervase of Canterbury   **18** John of Worcester   **19** *Gesta Stephani*   **20** Ibid.   **21** Henry of Huntingdon   **22** *Gesta Stephani*   **23** Gervase of Canterbury   **24** John of Worcester   **25** Ibid.   **26** *Gesta Stephani*   **27** Ibid.   **28** Chibnall: 'The Empress Matilda and Church Reform'   **29** *Gesta Stephani*   **30** Ibid.   **31** William of Malmesbury   **32** Gervase of Canterbury   **33** *Gesta Stephani*   **34** William of Malmesbury   **35** *Gesta Stephani*; William of Malmesbury   **36** Henry of Huntingdon

19 'Terrified and Troubled'

1 *Gesta Stephani*   **2** Ibid.   **3** *The Anglo-Saxon Chronicle*   **4** William of Malmesbury   **5** Ibid.   **6** *Gesta Stephani*   **7** Ibid.; Gervase of Canterbury; 'Annals of Waverley Abbey'; John of Worcester   **8** William of Malmesbury   **9** King: *Medieval England*   **10** William of Malmesbury   **11** *Gesta Stephani*   **12** William of Malmesbury   **13** Ibid.   **14** *Gesta Stephani*   **15** William of Malmesbury   **16** *Gesta Stephani*   **17** William of Malmesbury   **18** *Gesta Stephani*   **19** Henry of Huntingdon   **20** *Gesta Stephani*   **21** William of Malmesbury   **22** *Gesta Stephani*   **23** William of Newburgh; Henry of Huntingdon; Robert of Torigni   **24** William of Malmesbury; Henry of Huntingdon   **25** *The Anglo-Saxon Chronicle*; 'The Chronicle of Melrose'; John of Hexham   **26** *Gesta Stephani*   **27** Henry of Huntingdon   **28** *Gesta Stephani*   **29** John of Hexham   **30** William of Malmesbury; John of Worcester   **31** William of Malmesbury   **32** *Gesta Stephani*   **33** Chibnall: *The Empress Matilda*   **34** *Gesta Stephani*; Gervase of Canterbury   **35** It would not be rebuilt until the reign of Henry II (1154–89).   **36** John of Worcester; Gervase of Canterbury   **37** William of Malmesbury   **38** *Gesta Stephani*; William of Malmesbury   **39** *Gesta Stephani*   **40** Gervase of Canterbury   **41** William of Malmesbury   **42** Gervase of Canterbury   **43** *Gesta Stephani*   **44** William of Malmesbury   **45** Gervase of Canterbury   **46** *Gesta Stephani*   **47** Gervase of Canterbury; *Histoire de Guillaume le Maréchale*   **48** A much later account of it, probably heavily embellished, is to be found in the *Histoire de Guillaume le Maréchale*.   **49** *Gesta Stephani*   **50** John of Worcester. In the *Histoire de Guillaume le Maréchale*, this was at the insistence of John the Marshal, but he did not accompany her on her journey. His role in her escape is highly inflated in this text, which states incorrectly that, to avoid their pursuers, her party paused to take shelter in the ruins of Wherwell Abbey. **51** *Histoire de Guillaume le Maréchale* **52** John of Worcester **53** Gervase of Canterbury **54** John of Worcester; Gervase of Canterbury **55** Gervase of Canterbury **56** *Gesta Stephani*

20 'Rejoicing and Exultation'

1 William of Malmesbury **2** Gervase of Canterbury **3** Ibid.; John of Worcester **4** William of Malmesbury **5** Ibid. **6** Ibid. **7** Ibid. **8** Given-Wilson and Curteis **9** William of Malmesbury **10** *Gesta Stephani* **11** Ibid. **12** Gervase of Canterbury **13** Ibid. **14** John of Worcester **15** William of Malmesbury; *Gesta Stephani*; 'The Chronicle of Melrose' **16** Henry of Huntingdon **17** William of Malmesbury **18** *Gesta Stephani* **19** Ibid. **20** William of Malmesbury **21** *Gesta Stephani* **22** William of Malmesbury **23** Ibid. **24** Ibid. **25** Ibid. **26** Gervase of Canterbury

21 'The Lawful Heir'

1 William of Malmesbury **2** *Regesta Regum Anglo-Normannorum, 1066–1154* **3** William of Malmesbury **4** Osney Priory became an abbey in *c.*1154. **5** *Regesta Regum Anglo-Normannorum, 1066–1154*; Sharpe and Doherty. It may have been while Maud was at Devizes that she donated land, pasture and a dwelling at nearby Tytherington, near Heytesbury, to support two chaplains for the chapel there dedicated to St James. (She did not forget her connection with the area. In 1165 she endowed the church of St Peter and St Paul at Heytesbury.) She also made benefactions to the abbeys of Haughmond, Shrewsbury and Lilleshall in Shropshire. (*Regesta Regum Anglo-Normannorum, 1066–1154*) The poet Siegfried Sassoon, who lived in Heytesbury House, commemorated her connection with the place in his poem 'A Remembered Queen'. **6** William of Malmesbury **7** Crouch: *The Beaumont Twins* **8** William of Malmesbury **9** John of Hexham **10** William of Malmesbury **11** *Gesta Stephani* **12** William of Malmesbury **13** *Regesta Regum Anglo-Normannorum, 1066–1154*; Norton: *England's Queens* **14** William of Malmesbury says this happened at Devizes, but in the next passage he refers to 'all continuing at Oxford', implying that they were already there. **15** William of Malmesbury **16** Ibid. **17** Cited King: *Medieval England* **18** William of Malmesbury **19** *Gesta Stephani* **20** William of Malmesbury **21** *Regesta Regum Anglo-Normannorum, 1066–1154*. Bordesley had been founded in 1138 by Waleran de Beaumont, but Maud had insisted on taking over its patronage as a condition of receiving his allegiance. (Chibnall: *The Empress Matilda*) **22** *Gesta Stephani* **23** Ibid. **24** Beem: 'The Virtuous Virago'

22 'One of God's Manifest Miracles'

1 William of Malmesbury **2** *Gesta Stephani* **3** Ibid. **4** John of Hexham **5** *Gesta Stephani* **6** William of Malmesbury **7** Ibid. **8** *Gesta Stephani* **9** William of Malmesbury **10** Ibid. **11** Laplane; Januauschek **12** Bernard himself had re-founded Clairmarais on 26 April 1140 (Williams: *Saint Bernard of Clairvaux*). He and three other abbots of the Order – among them Matilda's friend Thierry of La Capella - witnessed the Queen's charter granting land in the forest of Beaulo at Eperlecques to the abbey. (*Regesta Regum Anglo-Normannorum, 1066–1154*) Around 1142, at Matilda's request, King Stephen was to give more lands to the brethren of Clairmarais to help build their abbey; six years later, he, Matilda and Eustace would further endow this foundation (ibid.), doubtless hoping to retain the support of Count Thierry. (Laplane; Dark) **13** *Gesta Stephani* **14** William of Malmesbury **15** *Gesta Stephani*, who says there were three knights; William of Malmesbury says there were four. **16** William of Malmesbury **17** Henry of Huntingdon **18** *The Anglo-Saxon Chronicle* **19** William of Malmesbury; Henry of Huntingdon **20** Henry of Huntingdon **21** William of Malmesbury; *Gesta Stephani* **22** *Gesta Stephani* **23** William of Malmesbury; *Gesta Stephani* **24** *Gesta Stephani* **25** Ibid. **26** It was not six miles away, as the *Gesta Stephani* states. **27** William of Malmesbury; *The Anglo-Saxon Chronicle* **28** *Gesta Stephani* **29** Gervase of Canterbury **30** *Regesta Regum Anglo-Normannorum, 1066–1154* **31** Map **32** Barber: *Henry Plantagenet*

23 'Wretchedness and Oppression'

1 Chibnall: *The Empress Matilda* **2** *Regesta Regum Anglo-Normannorum, 1066–1154* **3** Ibid. **4** *Gesta Stephani* **5** *Regesta Regum Anglo-Normannorum, 1066–1154* **6** Hilton: *England's Queens* **7** Davis: 'Henry of Blois and Brian Fitz Count' **8** *Gesta Stephani* **9** Ibid.

24 'A New Light Had Dawned'

1 *Chroniques des Comtes d'Anjou* **2** Poole: *Illustrations of the History of Medieval Thought* **3** *Chartes de Saint-Julien de Tours* **4** Chibnall: *The Empress Matilda* **5** Henry of Huntingdon **6** *Gesta Stephani* **7** Ibid. **8** Ibid. **9** Ibid. **10** Henry of Huntingdon **11** William of Newburgh **12** Maud held the castles at Tamworth, Dudley, Worcester, Hereford, Gloucester, Cardiff, Bristol, Devizes, Trowbridge, Salisbury, Castle Cary, Sherborne,

Exeter, Wareham, Newbury, Marlborough, Wallingford, Bungay, Framlingham and Orford. **13** *Gesta Stephani* **14** Ibid. **15** Robert of Torigni **16** *Regesta Regum Anglo-Normannorum, 1066–1154* **17** Chibnall: 'The Empress Matilda and Church Reform'; Chibnall: *The Empress Matilda* **18** *Patrologia Latina*, Vol. 180

25 'An Example of Fortitude and Patience'

1 Ralph of Diceto **2** William of Malmesbury **3** *Charters and Documents illustrating the History of the Cathedral Church and Diocese of Salisbury* **4** *Liber Feodorum*. The date of his death is not recorded, but in 1151 his widow, Matilda of Wallingford, confirmed by charter the grants that she and Brian had made to Bec-Hellouin, with the consent of the Empress and Henry, Duke of Normandy. (*Regesta Regum Anglo-Normannorum, 1066–1154*) **5** Additional Charters 19577, 19579, 19581, British Library **6** Gervase of Canterbury; Hilton: *Queens Consort* **7** Chibnall: *The Empress Matilda* **8** Marshall **9** *The Anglo-Saxon Chronicle* **10** *Regesta Regum Anglo-Normannorum, 1066–1154* **11** Crouch: *The Normans* **12** Chibnall: 'The Empress Matilda and Bec-Hellouin' **13** Stephen of Rouen **14** The area has been engulfed by modern industrial development, and nothing remains of the palace or the priory apart from the chapel of Saint-Julien at Petit-Quevilly, founded by Henry FitzEmpress in 1160, which contains frescoes that Maud may have commissioned herself (Chibnall). In 'The Empress Matilda and Bec-Hellouin', Chibnall stated that they dated from after Maud's death, but she revised this view after reading Lindy Grant's article, 'The architecture of the early Savigniacs and Cistercians in Normandy'. **15** Chibnall: *The Empress Matilda* **16** Stephen of Rouen **17** *Regesta Regum Anglo-Normannorum, 1066–1154* **18** Ibid.; Chibnall: *The Empress Matilda* **19** Stephen of Rouen **20** *Charters and Documents illustrating the History of the Cathedral Church and Diocese of Salisbury; Regesta Regum Anglo-Normannorum, 1066–1154*; Castor; Chibnall: *The Empress Matilda*

26 'For the Good of My Soul'

1 *Regesta Regum Anglo-Normannorum, 1066–1154* **2** Saltman **3** Gervase of Canterbury **4** *Regesta Regum Anglo-Normannorum, 1066–1154* **5** Hilton: *Queens Consort* **6** For an excellent account of Marie's life, see Brown: '*Elegit domum sibi placabilem*' **7** Cited Dark; Saltman **8** *Regesta Regum Anglo-Normannorum, 1066–1154* **9** Gervase of Canterbury **10** Ibid. **11** Ibid. A sixteenth-century carved panel relief depicting Stephen and Matilda can be seen at the entrance to the Old Grammar School in Faversham. It is thought to have originally been in a room above the town gate. **12** Saltman **13** *Regesta Regum Anglo-Normannorum, 1066–1154* **14** Castor **15** Map

16 *Regesta Regum Anglo-Normannorum, 1066–1154* **17** Ibid.; Tierney
18 Sanderus **19** Ibid. **20** 'Annals of Margam, 1066-1232'. The Canterbury
Obituary Lists (published in *The Culture of Christendom*) give the date as
26 March. Adeliza is listed on Affligem Abbey's mortuary roll (Sanderus).
21 Sanderus **22** Baxter **23** Lambeth Palace MS. 371 **24** Baxter
25 Norton: *England's Queens* **26** Robert of Torigni **27** 'Adeliza of
Leuven' **28** St Giles's Hospital at Fugglestone St Peter long claimed that
Adeliza was buried in its chapel. (Britton; Dugdale and Burnett) It was the
only part of the foundation still standing in 1814, but has now disappeared.

27 'Carried by the Hands of Angels'

1 *Chroniques des comtes d'Anjou* **2** Chibnall: *The Empress Matilda* **3** Hilton:
Queens Consort **4** *The Anglo-Saxon Chronicle* **5** Ibid. **6** *The Cartulary of
Holy Trinity, Aldgate* **7** Hilton: *Queens Consort* **8** *The Anglo-Saxon
Chronicle* **9** Crouch: *The Normans* **10** *Le Livere de Reis* **11** Southouse
gives a different translation from the Latin, calling Matilda the 'happy wife
of King Stephen. She died outstanding in character and titles. She was a
true follower of God and a follower of poverty. Here she was elevated by
God in whom she rejoices. If any woman whatever deserves to rise up to
heaven, she does. Angels hold this godly Queen in their hands.'

Part Five: *The Empress Maud*

1 'Joy and Honour'

1 Giraldus Cambrensis **2** *Regesta Regum Anglo-Normannorum, 1066–1154*
3 Turner **4** Ibid. **5** Richard **6** *Chronicon Valassense*, cited by Chibnall:
The Empress Matilda **7** A spurious thirteenth-century tale related by
Matthew Paris had Maud present, pleading with Stephen and Henry to
desist from fighting, for they were father and son, and it did not become
them to kill each other. **8** Gervase of Canterbury; *The Anglo-Saxon
Chronicle* **9** Castor **10** Henry of Huntingdon **11** Robert of Torigni

2 'The Light of Morning'

1 Brewer **2** *The Anglo-Saxon Chronicle* **3** *Histoire des ducs de Normandie
et des rois d'Angleterre*; Crouch: *The Normans* **4** Dark **5** Dodson **6** Stow:
The Annals of England **7** Aelred of Rievaulx: 'Genealogia regum
Anglorum' **8** Seward **9** Map **10** Cited Meade **11** Chibnall: *The
Empress Matilda* **12** Chadwick: *Empress Matilda's Bling*; Castor **13** Chibnall:
The Empress Matilda **14** Chibnall: 'The Charters of the Empress Matilda'
15 *Regesta Regum Anglo-Normannorum, 1066–1154* **16** *Recueil des Actes de*

Henry II **17** Robert of Torigni; *Recueil des Actes de Henry II* **18** Chibnall: *The Empress Matilda* **19** Crouch: *The Beaumont Twins* **20** Map **21** Norton: *England's Queens* **22** Other religious houses that received her bounty included the priory of Saint-Marie at Bondeville and the abbeys of Lannoy and Saint-André-en-Gouffern. **23** Marshall **24** *Chronicon Valassense*; Chibnall: *The Empress Matilda* **25** *Chronicon Valassense*; *The Plantagenet Chronicles*; Avril; Chadwick: *Empress Matilda's Bling*; Chibnall: *The Empress Matilda*; Chibnall: 'The Empress Matilda and Bec-Hellouin' **26** Knowles and Hadcock **27** Crouch: *The Normans* **28** Leyser: *Medieval Germany and its Neighbours*

3 'A Woman of the Stock of Tyrants'

1 Stephen of Rouen **2** Chibnall: *The Empress Matilda* **3** *Chroniques des comtes d'Anjou et des seigneurs d'Amboise* **4** Robert of Torigni **5** *Calendar of Documents preserved in France* **6** Chibnall: 'The Empress Matilda and her Sons' **7** Jones: *The Plantagenets* **8** Chibnall: 'The Empress Matilda and her Sons' **9** Giraldus Cambrensis **10** Langlois; Chibnall: *The Empress Matilda* **11** Kelly; Boyd **12** *Materials for the History of Thomas Becket* **13** Stephen of Rouen **14** *Regesta Regum Anglo-Normannorum, 1066–1154* **15** *Materials for the History of Thomas Becket*; Chibnall: *The Empress Matilda* **16** *Materials for the History of Thomas Becket* **17** *Materials for the History of Thomas Becket*, cited Chibnall: *The Empress Matilda* **18** *Letters of Royal and Illustrious Ladies*; *Materials for the History of Thomas Becket*; Chibnall: 'The Empress Matilda and her Sons' **19** *Materials for the History of Thomas Becket* **20** Chibnall: *The Empress Matilda* **21** Letter 26 in Appendix 2 **22** *Letters of Royal and Illustrious Ladies* **23** John of Salisbury: *The Letters of John of Salisbury* **24** Eyton

4 'A Star Fell'

1 Eyton; Robert of Torigni **2** *Materials for the History of Thomas Becket* **3** Haverkamp **4** *Regesta Regum Anglo-Normannorum, 1066–1154* **5** Chibnall: *The Empress Matilda* **6** *Epistolae: Medieval Women's Latin Letters* **7** Stephen of Rouen **8** *Materials for the History of Thomas Becket* **9** Ibid. **10** *Recueil des Actes de Henry II*; Chibnall: *The Empress Matilda* **11** *Recueil des historiens des Gaules et de la France* **12** Stephen of Rouen **13** *Chronique du Bec.* Some say incorrectly that she was buried first in Notre-Dame de Pré, near Rouen, the convent of Bonnes Nouvelles, and later moved to Bec-Hellouin. **14** Pignot; Chibnall: *The Empress Matilda* **15** Chibnall: 'The Empress Matilda and Bec-Hellouin' **16** Stephen of Rouen **17** Porée. The original epitaph was badly damaged when the tomb was destroyed in 1421, but these words were incorporated into the inscription placed on the new tomb by Jean Mabillon in 1684. **18** Chibnall: 'The Empress Matilda and Bec-Hellouin'; Porée; Chadwick: *Empress Matilda's Bling*. This cloak was not the dalmatic of gold silk and linen preserved in the church of Ambazac in France, which a late tradition associates with Geoffrey of Anjou, and modern popular opinion with Maud herself. In 1960, it was established that the dalmatic dates from no earlier than the thirteenth century, and that it bears the heraldic emblems of the counts of Vienne. (http://www.hubert-herald.nl/FraVienne.htm) **19** Chadwick: *Empress Matilda's Bling*; *Recueil des historiens des Gaules et de la France*; Castor **20** Chibnall: 'The Empress Matilda and Bec-Hellouin' **21** Porée; Chibnall: *The Empress Matilda* **22** Truax **23** Amundsen and Diers **24** See, for example: http://www.34-menopause-symptoms.com/mood-swings/articles/violent-mood-swings.htm; https://www.myvmc.com/symptoms/mood-swings-inmenopause/; http://www.healthguidance.org/entry/2462/1/Menopause-andAnger.html; http://www.webmd.com/menopause/guide/emotional-roller-coaster; http://www.menopausecentre.com.au/informationcentre/symptoms/moodswings/; http://menopause-aid.blogspot.co.uk/2012/07/why-menopausal-woman-gets-angry.html; https://www.ncbi.nlm.nih.gov/pubmed/16857659 **25** *Materials for the History of Thomas Becket* **26** *Chronicon Valassense* **27** William of Newburgh **28** Beem: 'The Virtuous Virago'

Appendix 2: Letters

1 Anselm of Aosta: *The Letters of St Anselm of Canterbury*; Anselm of Aosta: *S. Anselmi Cantuariensis archiepiscopi opera omnia*; Southern: *St Anselm and his Biographer* **2** Archives départementales du Calvados, 2H25/2, Trinity **3** *Epistolae Selectae, Das Register Gregors VII* **4** Hildebert of Lavardin: 'Letters' **5** Anselm of Aosta: *S. Anselmi Cantuariensis archiepiscopi opera omnia* **6** Ibid. **7** Ivo of Chartres **8** Ibid. **9** Hildebert of Lavardin: 'Letters' **10** Herbert de Losinga **11** Anselm of Aosta: *S. Anselmi Cantuariensis archiepiscopi opera omnia* **12** Ibid. **13** *Letters of Royal and Illustrious Ladies* **14** Anselm of Aosta: *S. Anselmi Cantuariensis archiepiscopi opera omnia* **15** Ibid. **16** Ibid. **17** Ibid. **18** Ibid. **19** Ibid. **20** Ibid. **21** Ibid. **22** Ibid. **23** Ivo of Chartres **24** Bernard of Clairvaux; William of Saint-Thierry, Arnold of Bonneval and Geoffrey of Auxerre. The abbey of La Capelle, near Les Attaques, had been founded by Matilda's grandmother, the sainted Ida of Lorraine. (Dark) **25** Bernard of Clairvaux **26** *Patrologia Latina*, Vol. 190

Index